BEST
of the
INTERNET

2003 Edition

Joe Kraynak

201 West 103rd Street, Indianapolis, Indiana 46290

BEST OF THE INTERNET, 2003 EDITION

International Standard Book Number: 0-7897-2860-5

Printed in the United States of America

First Printing: September 2002

05   04   03   02   4   3   2   1

WARNING AND DISCLAIMER

TRADEMARKS

Associate Publisher
Greg Wiegand

Acquisitions Editor
Stephanie J. McComb

Development Editor
Mark Cierzniak

Managing Editor
Thomas F. Hayes

Project Editor
Natalie Harris

Production Editor
Maribeth Echard

Proofreader
Leslie Joseph

Indexer
Chris Barrick

Technical Editors
Joe Kraynak
Mark Cierzniak

Design
Anne Jones
Sandra Schroeder

Layout Technicians
Rebecca Harmon
Ayanna Lacey

TABLE OF CONTENTS

A 1

B 19

C 33

D 51

E 60

F 71

G 82

H 94

I 107

J 113

K 117

L 122

M 132

N 179

O 203

P 208

Q 250

R 256

S 293

T 332

U 385

V 392

W 404

Y 437

Z 441

Index 447

Tell Us What You Think!

As the reader of this book, you are our most important critic and commentator. We value your opinion and want to know what we're doing right, what we could do better, what areas you'd like to see us publish in, and any other words of wisdom you're willing to pass our way.

As an associate publisher for Que, I welcome your comments. You can fax, email, or write me directly to let me know what you did or didn't like about this book—as well as what we can do to make our books stronger.

Please note that I cannot help you with technical problems related to the topic of this book, and that due to the high volume of mail I receive, I might not be able to reply to every message.

When you write, please be sure to include this book's title and author as well as your name and phone or fax number. I will carefully review your comments and share them with the author and editors who worked on the book.

Fax: 317-581-4666

Email: `feedback@quepublishing.com`

Mail: Greg Wiegand
        Que
        201 West 103rd Street
        Indianapolis, IN 46290
        USA

Here's a quick look at a few structural features designed to help you get the most out of the book. You'll find:

⟦Best⟧ This icon identifies THE best Web site in any given category. If you have time to visit only one site in a category, look for the Best of the Best!

$ The e-commerce icon identifies sites that process online transactions. If you're looking to purchase something from the Internet, be sure to look for listings with this icon.

ABORTION

Abortion Clinics On-Line

http://gynpages.com/ACOL/
choice.html

Abortion Clinics On-Line (ACOL) is a directory service comprised of providers of abortion and other reproductive healthcare. On this site, you'll find abortion rights articles, feedback on clinics, and a vehicle for listing a clinic in ACOL.

ACLU Reproductive Rights

http://www.aclu.org/issues/
reproduct/hmrr.html

Plenty of information about the ACLU's position on reproductive freedom, including regularly updated news on abortion, court cases, legislation, recommended book list, ACLU materials on abortion, and links to other sites.

Ethics Updates

http://ethics.acusd.edu/
abortion.html

A comprehensive resource of information regarding current legislation on abortion, public opinion poll results and statistics, and links to other Web sites about abortion.

Fast Track Index

http://www.mariestopes.org.uk/
fast_track_index.html

This site covers abortion from A to Z, including countries offering this service; obtaining an abortion in the United Kingdom, Ireland, or overseas; and an abortion FAQ. Additional information covers breast healthcare, contraception, infectious diseases, and more.

National Abortion Federation

http://www.prochoice.org/

This site is divided into the following categories: Abortion Fact Sheets, If You're Pregnant, Voices of Choice, Clinic Violence, Media Center, Legal Issues, Get Involved, Take Action, Contributions, and Join NAF.

Planned Parenthood Federation of America, Inc.

http://www.plannedparenthood.org/

A source for sexual health information for women. Topics covered include abortion, birth control, brochures and products, parenting and pregnancy, pro-choice advocacy, women's health and more. You'll also find links, fact sheets, FAQs, a guide for parents, job listings, and a nurse practitioner program. The online store offers books and pamphlets about Planned Parenthood as well as branded items such as T-shirts and coffee cups. Spanish translations are also available. Excellent content combined with an easily navigable format make this a hands-down choice for best of the best.

Planned Parenthood Golden Gate

http://www.ppgg.org

Home of the largest not-for-profit birth-control and reproductive health care organizations in the world. This site is devoted to helping educate women, men, and teenagers to make responsible decisions about their own sexuality and reproductive choices. Learn more about Planned Parenthood's medical services and education programs, shop its secure online store, donate online, or learn how to become a Planned Parenthood activist.

A
B
C
D
E
F
G
H
I
J
K
L
M
N
O
P
Q
R
S
T
U
V
W
X
Y
Z

ACTIVISM

CorpWatch.org

http://www.corpwatch.org

Home of the CorpWatch.org corporation watchdog group, dedicated to ensuring that large corporations follow ethical business, political, and environmental practices. Visit this site to learn more about CorpWatch.org's campaigns, activities, issues, and research.

Idealist.org

http://www.idealist.org

Home of Action Without Borders, a worldwide network of individuals and organizations devoted to promoting freedom and human dignity throughout the world. Features an excellent directory of activist organizations, lists of jobs and volunteer opportunities, available services and resources, and much more. If you're looking for ways to make the world a better place to live, check out this site.

tolerance.org

http://www.tolerance.org

Dedicated to promoting greater understanding and tolerance of diverse groups of people, this site provides information on how to combat hate and intolerance in our daily lives. Includes articles on hate and hate crimes, studies on hate and racial bias, information on gay rights, and advice on how to track hate groups.

ADD/ADHD

 National Attention Deficit Disorder Association

http://www.add.org/

This is an extremely comprehensive site on the topic of ADD, including the following categories: ADD Information, ABC's of ADD, ADD Research, ADD Treatment, ADD Coaching, Books on ADD, Family Issues, Kid's Area, Legal Issues, School & ADD, Support Groups, Teen's Area, Web Sites, Women & ADD, Work & Career, ADD Interviews, Creative Corner, Myth of the Week, Personal Stories, and ADD Book Store. If you or a loved one suffers from ADD or ADHD, bookmark this best of the best site now.

ADDICTIONS

EATING DISORDERS

 Anorexic Web

http://www.anorexicweb.com

Designed and written by a recovering anorexic, the site aims to provide understanding to those fighting eating disorders through information, photos, and reflective poems. Unlike more medically oriented sites, this one speaks directly to those afflicted with eating disorders. Because this site has been developed by a recovering anorexic, it provides a nonjudgmental forum that is highly empathetic. Top site for anyone who suffers from an eating disorder.

Center for Eating Disorders

http://www.eatingdisorder.org/whatyou.htm

A resource for gathering information on eating disorders. Includes FAQs and discussion groups for the eating disorder sufferer. Questions asked here are answered.

Eating Disorder Site

http://closetoyou.org/eatingdisorders/

This site provides information to help recognize if you or someone you know has a problem with eating. At the end of each brief article is a list of local organizations available to help individuals cope and treat their illness.

A
B
C
D
E
F
G
H
I
J
K
L
M
N
O
P
Q
R
S
T
U
V
W
X
Y
Z

Mental Health Net

http://
eatingdisorders.mentalhelp.net/

Learn about symptoms, treatments, online resources, organizations, and research materials related to eating disorders.

SUBSTANCE ABUSE AND RECOVERY

Alcoholics Anonymous

http://
www.alcoholics-anonymous.org/

From the home page, choose the English, Spanish, or French version of the text, and continue. You'll find 12 questions you can answer to help determine whether AA might be helpful. You'll also find local contact information and a special section for professionals.

Get It Straight: The Facts About Drugs

http://www.usdoj.gov/dea/pubs/
straight/cover.htm

A drug-prevention book targeted at kids, put out by the Drug Enforcement Administration. Provides serious resources and information about the laws related to drugs and drug abuse.

National Institute on Drug Abuse

http://www.nida.nih.gov/

The National Institute on Drug Abuse, established in 1974, works on research and programs to prevent and treat drug addiction. The site features information on the organization including its programs and publications on drug abuse.

Prevention Online

http://www.health.org/

Provides information for those people battling substance abuse, or who know someone battling substance abuse. Contains press releases, publications, forums, and calendars of upcoming events.

[Best] Adoption Benefits: Employers As Partners in Family Building

http://www.adopting.org/employer.html

Provides information about company-sponsored adoption benefit plans, including who is eligible for benefits, how company-sponsored benefit plans actually work, covered expenses and when they are paid, the types of adoption benefit plans cover, adoption leaves of absence from the workplace, and a list of companies that offer adoption benefits, as well as other adoption-assistance programs. If you are considering adopting a child, this is the place to go to learn about company-sponsored benefits.

International Adoption Resource

http://www.iaradopt.com

International Adoption Resource (IAR) is an international adoption agency with programs in Russia, Guatemala, and India, with plans to expand into Romania shortly. Visitors can find information on the international adoption process and search the photo database of available international children.

[Best] All Experts

http://www.allexperts.com

Ask a question of a volunteer expert on virtually any topic, from arts and entertainment to relationships to business, and more for free. Site is organized by category, so you can quickly browse for the desired topic and submit your question. Site covers virtually every topic from automobiles to television shows. If you can't find your answer here, you may not be able to find it anywhere.

drDrew

http://www.drdrew.com/

Learn more about sex, health, and relationships, from the co-host of MTV's Loveline, Dr. Drew. Submit questions, and participate in online communities with concerns about a wide range of personal health issues.

eHow
http://www.ehow.com

Use eHow to find out how to do anything, from asking someone out on a date to boiling an egg—two of the recent top 10 eHow questions.

AGRICULTURE

Best Agriculture Online
http://www.agriculture.com/

Read legislative news, market news, news from around the world, technology news, weather forecasts, and more. Clearly organized and visually attractive, this site is packed with all the most current information available for farmers and others who are devoted to agriculture and agribusiness. If you're a farmer or in the farming industry, be sure to bookmark this best of the best site, and visit it daily.

DirectAg.com
http://www.directag.com

Farmers looking for information on ag news, up-to-date ag prices, and weather should stop by DirectAg. In addition to purchasing agricultural products online at this site, farmers also can arrange immediate financing.

Economic Research Service (USDA)
http://www.ers.usda.gov/

Provides economic and social science information and analysis for public and private decisions on agriculture, food, natural resources, and rural America. It features reports, catalogs, publications, USDA data statistics, and employment opportunities. Also offers other agriculture-related links. This site is updated every weekday.

Gempler's
http://www.gemplers.com/

At Gemplers.com, you can search the secure online store for 9,000 hard-to-find products for agriculture, horticulture, and grounds maintenance.

John Deere–Agricultural Equipment

http://www.deere.com/

Offers product information on the entire John Deere farm machinery line, as well as other Deere products. Includes lists of dealers in the U.S. and Canada.

National Agricultural Library (NAL)

http://www.nalusda.gov/

Part of the USDA, this site is a resource for ag research, education, and applied agriculture. It contains a huge collection of downloadable agricultural images, as well as government documents, access to assistance from special research sites, and links to other Internet agriculture sites. In addition, its AGRICOLA database provides millions of agriculture-related citations from publications.

[Best] Allergy Info

http://www.allergy-info.com

Sponsored by the manufacturers of Zyrtec, this site promises to provide helpful tips for managing indoor and outdoor allergy suffering. Learn how to manage your allergies with a combination of allergy medication, environmental changes, and other treatments. Site provides excellent general information about allergies, as well. This site's excellent collection of information and easily accessible design make it well deserving as the best of the best.

HealthSquare.com: Asthma and Allergies

http://www.healthsquare.com/ftana.htm

With dozens of links to asthma and allergy information, this site is a great place for asthma and allergy sufferers to learn more about their condition and treatment options. This site provides information on everything from general issues to specific treatments and tips that can help relieve suffering immediately.

A
B
C
D
E
F
G
H
I
J
K
L
M
N
O
P
Q
R
S
T
U
V
W
X
Y
Z

ALTERNATIVE MEDICINE

ACUPUNCTURE

 Acupuncture.com

http://www.acupuncture.com/

This site features information for the practitioner, student, and the patient in different areas of traditional Chinese medicine. Also provides current events and news concerning laws that affect the practice of traditional Chinese medicine. Here you can research various Chinese medical practices, including acupuncture, Chinese herbal medicine, Qi Gong, Tui Na, dietetics, and more. Excellent sources for research and a comprehensive FAQ.

MedWebPlus: Acupuncture

http://www.medwebplus.com/
subject/Acupuncture.html

Search the enormous healthcare databases free to learn more about acupuncture and other alternative therapies.

AROMATHERAPY

 Aromatherapy Recipes–Using Pure Essential Oils of Aromatherapy

http://www.galaxymall.com/
aromatherapy/health/index.html

A great site for understanding which types of oils impact ailments and to help prepare healing mixtures. Check out the Aromatherapy Essential Oil Recipes link. Recipes

are divided into a number of categories, from medicinal to facial care, foot care, massage, and cosmetic, to name just a few. Although this site is not the most attractive of the bunch, it's packed with excellent resources for beginner and expert alike and is laid out in an easily navigable format.

CHIROPRACTIC

 MyBackStore.com

http://www.backworld.ca/mbs.asp

Back World specializes in selling products specifically for people suffering from back or neck pain. This includes home seating solutions and office seating solutions as well as all those products to help deal with back problems. This site offers sales in Canadian dollars as well as American dollars. If you're looking for products to help your back— at home, in the office, or on the road—this is your one-stop shop.

HOMEOPATHY

Homeopathy Online

http://www.lyghtforce.com/
HomeopathyOnline/

An international journal of homeopathic medicine for lay persons, students, and practitioners alike.

MASSAGE

Illustrated Guide to Muscle and Clinical Massage Therapy
http://danke.com/Orthodoc/

Presented by the Pain and Posture Clinic, this site offers animated guides to massage. A unique and informative site.

ALZHEIMER'S

Ageless Design, Inc.
http://www.agelessdesign.com

An education, information, and consultation service company founded to help seniors have what they really want—a home that is easy to live in and that accommodates the difficulties associated with growing older. Using Ageless Design's site, you can learn how to modify a home to care for a loved one with Alzheimer's, and access unique ideas and products that embrace the special needs of people as they age.

Alzheimer's Association
http://www.alz.org/

Superb site. Attractive, well laid-out, and very comprehensive, including FAQs, resources on medical issues relating to Alzheimer's (such as steps for proper diagnosis and current/future treatment options), updates on advances and legislation, and information about finding a local chapter.

Healthy Aging, Geriatrics, and Elderly Care
http://www.healthandage.com/

The Novartis Foundation for Gerontological Research supports education and innovation in healthy aging, geriatrics, and the care of elderly people. This site includes a Reuters Health Information newsfeed, which provides both healthcare professionals and patients with late-breaking health news. When you don't know where to turn for the latest information on aging and healthcare for the elderly, this is the place to start.

A
B
C
D
E
F
G
H
I
J
K
L
M
N
O
P
Q
R
S
T
U
V
W
X
Y
Z

AMUSEMENT AND THEME PARKS

A
B
C
D
E
F
G
H
I
J
K
L
M
N
O
P
Q
R
S
T
U
V
W
X
Y
Z

Disney.com—The Web Site for Families

http://disney.go.com/

Contains links to all things Disney, which by now is more than just a cute little mouse. Includes information about its theme parks as well as movies, the TV channel, videos, books, its cruise line, and much more. If you're looking for the best theme parks in the world and are leaning toward taking your family on a Disney adventure, introduce your entire family to this site. You can plan your trip and figure out the best places to go, and your kids can find plenty to keep them busily entertained.

Paramount's Great America

http://www.pgathrills.com/

This official site provides a virtual tour of the park and its attractions. Also contains employment and season ticket information, as well as a section about what's new.

Paramount's Kings Island

http://www.pki.com/

Visit the amusement park choice of the Brady Bunch! (Remember the infamous tube mix-up?) Take an online tour of the park and discover the latest live stage shows.

Sea World

http://www.seaworld.com

Get park information for one of several Sea World locations, order tickets online, and investigate new attractions.

Six Flags Theme Parks

http://www.sixflags.com/

The largest regional theme park company in the world, with 29 parks in the U.S., one in Mexico, and nine in Europe. According to the site, 85% of all Americans live within just a day's drive from a Six Flags Theme Park. Click pick a park and then click any of the dots on the globe to view detailed information about that particular Six Flags park or property.

Universal Studios

http://
themeparks.universalstudios.com/

Click the link for one of four Universal Studio Theme Parks: Orlando, Hollywood, Japan, or Spain. Check out park hours and new rides and attractions, buy merchandise, and order tickets online.

Walt Disney World

http://disneyworld.disney.go.com/
waltdisneyworld/index

Everything you need to plan your
magical Walt Disney World Resort
vacation is right here. Click the
Parks & More link to review a list
of Disney Theme Parks and then
click the park you want to tour. Use
the navigation bar that runs down
the left side of the screen to find
what you want. Order admission
tickets online, check out FAQs and
special events, review resort and spa
options, and lots, lots more!

Wild Adventures

http://www.wild-adventure.com/

Wild Adventures is a low-cost,
animal-oriented family theme park
that's open year-round and located
in Valdosta, Georgia. There are
hundreds of wild animals to see,
25 family thrill rides, and reasonably priced lodging within 10 to
15 minutes from the park.

Antiques Roadshow

http://www.pbs.org/wgbh/pages/
roadshow/

Even if you're an inexperienced
antiquer, PBS's Antiques Roadshow
is a great show and Web site to visit
to learn from the experts. The show
comes to cities around the country
to meet with the locals and appraise
their items. The show's experts not
only spot the real antiques but
make a point to appraise fake items
so you, the viewer, will learn what to
look for in your antiquing jaunts.
Check out the appraisal contest. You
can buy books and videos about
antiques through the online store.

⟦Best⟧ Circline

http://www.circline.com

Billing itself as "the marketplace of
the world's finest art, antiques, and
dealers," Circline enables users to
search an extensive database of
dealers and available inventory to
find just the right piece of art or
antique. A section on learning
about antiques is helpful for the
neophite collector. Excellent site for
beginners and experts alike.

A
B
C
D
E
F
G
H
I
J
K
L
M
N
O
P
Q
R
S
T
U
V
W
X
Y
Z

Maine Antique Digest

`http://www.maineantiquedigest.com`

The Web supplement to the print publication, the site offers articles, news, a hidden picture contest, dealer directory, price database, directory of appraisers, and antique discussion forum. Auction and show ads on the site will alert you to upcoming events.

Newel

`http://www.newel.com/`

Search the entire inventory of Newel antiques or study along with the tutorial to get started.

ARCHITECTURE

Architecture Magazine

`http://www.architecturemag.com`

Review back issues of this monthly magazine for the architecture industry, subscribe to the magazine, enroll for online courses, search for job openings or building services, or read one of several current articles on design and culture issues.

 Design Basics Home Online Planbook

`http://www.designbasics.com`

Design Basics, Inc. provides single-family home plans with available technical support and custom design options. Build your dream home with plans that are also marketed through catalogs, newsstand magazines, and home building industry trade publications. Decorative home accessories are available in the Web Store, making this a one-stop, comprehensive site for anyone seeking to build and decorate their own home.

Frank Lloyd Wright: Official Web Site

`http://www.cmgww.com/historic/flw/bio.html`

Check out the life and works of the most famous architect in the world. Here you can read a brief biography of Frank Lloyd Wright, scan a brief list of his major accomplishments, view photographs of his most beautiful buildings, and read some of his intriguing quotes. To order books or videos about Frank Lloyd Wright, click the Library link and click the item you want to order; this kicks you out to Amazon.com, where you can place your order.

A
B
C
D
E
F
G
H
I
J
K
L
M
N
O
P
Q
R
S
T
U
V
W
X
Y
Z

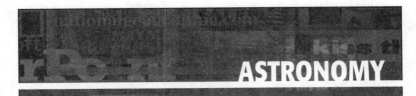

ASSOCIATIONS

⟦Best⟧ Rotary International
http://www.rotary.org/

Are you a business leader searching for something more to life? Do you want to give back to your community and make the world a better place? Then consider becoming a Rotarian. Rotary International is a worldwide organization of business and professional leaders who provide humanitarian services and uphold high ethical standards in their profession. Their well-designed Web site is packed with information about the organization and how you can become a member. Find a Rotary chapter in your area, learn about Rotary initiatives, download forms and information, and become a member.

ASTRONOMY

Amazing Space
http://amazing-space.stsci.edu/

Designed for classroom use, Amazing Space provides a collection of interactive Web-based activities to teach students various topics, such as understanding light and how black holes function. Some cool features, such as Planet Impact, where you can smash a comet into the planet Jupiter, make this site well worth a visit.

American Astronomical Society
http://www.aas.org/

Provides general astronomy information of interest to professionals and amateur enthusiasts. Maintains links to other astronomy resources on the Net.

⟦Best⟧ Astro!nfo
http://www.astroinfo.org/english.php

Check out the most recent astronomical events compliments of the Swiss Astronomical Society. When you reach the site, click the Planetarium tab to view the English version. At the top of the resulting page, click the Calendar link to view descriptions of celestial events on a given date, or click the desired heavenly body (Sun, Moon, Planets, Comets, and so on) to view dates on which you can witness events.

A
B
C
D
E
F
G
H
I
J
K
L
M
N
O
P
Q
R
S
T
U
V
W
X
Y
Z

Astronomy Magazine

http://www.astronomy.com/home.asp

This site contains an almanac of current sky happenings, a calendar of star parties, directories of planetariums and clubs, a well-stocked photo library, as well as product reviews on telescopes and binoculars. Well designed, this site is a pleasure to explore.

Constellation X

http://
constellation.gsfc.nasa.gov

This site offers information on studies of black holes and the life cycles of matter throughout the universe using an X-ray observatory. A very cool welcome screen, excellent graphics and video clips, and clear descriptions of various astronomical phenomena combine to make this one of the most intriguing astronomy sites in the group.

Earth & Sky

http://www.earthsky.com/

Read in-depth articles on astronomy and earth science here, where teachers can share information on the study of space and kids can enter astronomy contests. There are also Kid Science Quizzes worth checking out.

NASA Earth Observatory

http://earthobservatory.nasa.gov

This public access site is designed to provide visitors with current satellite images and information about the earth—mainly its environment and how environmental changes are affecting the landscape.

NASA HumanSpaceflight

http://spaceflight.nasa.gov/

Study the history of NASA's space missions from Mercury to the present, get real-time data on sighting opportunities, track the orbit of NASA spacecraft, obtain detailed information about the space station and space shuttle programs, check out NASA's photo gallery, and much more.

Amazon Auctions

http://s1.amazon.com/

Visit Amazon's newest addition— an auction area, where you can scout for deals on everything from antiques to jewelry to clothing, even automotive parts and accessories. For those users looking to simplify their life, Amazon Auctions also accepts items for sale. For an additional fee, Amazon will cross-sell your item on the Amazon Web site, which puts your products in front of millions of potential buyers.

CNet Auctions

http://auctions.cnet.com

This is a great place to find computers and peripheral devices for sale by auction. The auction interface is excellent and easy to use.

[Best] eBay

http://www.ebay.com

It's the world's largest trading online community. Bid on millions of items from books, to computer products, to antiques. Join more than 42,000,000 registered users who frequent this site. By some counts, eBay is the busiest site on the Internet. By some counts, eBay is the busiest site on the Internet, possibly the largest free market in the world. Because of its incredible popularity and its ease of use, this is truly the best of the best.

Priceline

http://www.priceline.com

Name your price for airline tickets, hotel rooms, cars, and mortgage rates on this site. Priceline then approaches potential sellers who might be willing to fulfill your request. Many users have reported saving hundreds of dollars on plane tickets using this site.

Sotheby's

http://www.sothebys.com

This, as you might expect, is a classy Web page. Read about upcoming auctions, order catalogs, learn how to begin a collection, but best of all, check out the Collector's Eye, which provides helpful explanations regarding collecting, such as "What is the significance of a maker's mark?"

uBid

http://www.ubid.com/

A huge auction site featuring every imaginable product. Opening page displays thumbnail photos of products, and the navigation bar on the left side of the page makes it easy to browse available items.

ZDNet Auctions

http://auctions.zdnet.com/

An auction site with a full range of services. You can buy, sell, search for items, create watchlists, and more at this site. Check out the computers and computer accessories.

AUTO RACING

A
B
C
D
E
F
G
H
I
J
K
L
M
N
O
P
Q
R
S
T
U
V
W
X
Y
Z

Motorsports Hall of Fame

http://www.mshf.com/

Dedicated to preserving the legacy of the "Heroes of Horsepower," the Motorsports Hall of Fame of America houses more than 40 racing and high-performance vehicles, including various types of cars, trucks, boats, motorcycles, air racers, and even racing snowmobiles. Click the Museum link to explore a small selection of the museum's offerings. Check out the list of Hall of Fame Inductees to read biographies of your favorite drivers.

⟦Best⟧ Winston Cup

http://www.nascar.com/series/wc/index.html

Packed with the latest articles and information about NASCAR's Winston Cup Series, this site serves up a feast of information about drivers, teams, statistics, sponsors, and history. If you're a NASCAR novice, click the Know Your NASCAR link to get up to speed. Seasoned fans will find plenty of features to keep them interested, as well.

FORMULA ONE

Shell-Ferrari

http://www.shell-ferrari.com/

If you want a history of Formula 1, pre- and post-race reports, and car statistics, come to this site sponsored by Shell-Ferrari. Very cool, well-designed site.

AUTOMOBILE CLUBS AND ORGANIZATIONS

⟦Best⟧ AAA Online

http://www.aaa.com/

Go directly to your state's "Triple A" office by entering your ZIP or Postal code in the AAA Web site. In addition to information about their famous Triptiks and the 24/365 road service that offers car lockout help, jump starts, and fixed flats, find out about their travel reservations and discounts, domestic and international tours, and $1,000 arrest bonds. If there is one auto club site you should visit, this is it.

AUTOMOBILES

BUYING ONLINE

Carprice.com

http://www.carprice.com/

Carprice.com is a search engine designed specifically to find vehicles (new and used) over the Internet. You simply specify the car you want and the desired options and enter your ZIP Code. For new cars, the search turns up the manufacturer's suggested retail price and the invoice price; you can then fill out a form to have a local dealer contact you. For used cars, the search displays the asking price and a link for contacting the seller.

Microsoft Carpoint

http://carpoint.msn.com/
homepage/default.asp

Yep, Bill Gates is selling cars, too. Microsoft's Carpoint offers new and used car information, interactive classifieds, 360-degree views of cars and trucks (inside and out), Kelley Blue Book pricing reports, reliability ratings, side-by-side comparisons, and news and advice on car-related issues.

CLASSIC CARS

Classic Car Source

http://www.classicar.com/

For car lovers interested in bonding with fellow classic car buffs, this site has a community spirit combined with articles, chat, auctions, message boards, and restoration help.

INFORMATION

Carfax Lemon Check

http://www.carfax.com/

An essential resource for anyone thinking of buying a used car. Enter the car's Vehicle Identification Number at the site and find out whether the car has been labeled a lemon, or one with repeated problems, free.

MANUFACTURERS

 Porsche

http://www.porsche.com

In addition to scoping out luscious models of Porsche engineering, you can also learn about the company's involvement with international motorsports. Catch up on race news and plan for upcoming events with the help of the Race Dates calendar. Current Porsche owners will want to check out the local Porsche clubs and visit the online shopping pages. Beautiful photography throughout the site.

Volvo

http://new.volvocars.com/

Visit the official Volvo site to browse the online showroom, build a custom Volvo, check out preowned Volvos, and find a dealer near you. Volvo owners can visit the site to obtain additional information about caring for and servicing their vehicles.

REPAIR

Car Talk

http://cartalk.cars.com/

The funniest show on radio. This is not a dead-serious "Whom do I call when the fan belt breaks in the middle of Death Valley?" site, but you'll find helpful material between the gags. Listen to the show for more information.

AVIATION

[Best] Air Combat USA

http://www.aircombatusa.com/

Find out how you can fly actual air-to-air combat in a real, state-of-the-art military aircraft! You don't even need a pilot's license. license. If you've been a student of aerial warfare for years and have only dreamed of taking a seat behind the wheel of a real warplane, check out this site!

Air Safe

http://www.airsafe.com

A treasure trove of information, for fearful flyers, about flying safely—whether that means identifying the safest airline, aircraft, or airport—and tips for having a safe, comfortable flight.

NASA Home Page

http://www.nasa.gov/

Acts as the starting point for all of NASA's Web-based information. Offers links to resources, including space shuttle information, home pages for the NASA centers around the country, space images, and educational resources.

National Air and Space Museum

http://www.nasm.edu/

This site features a robust collection of online versions of the museum's most popular exhibits. There's no replacement for visiting the museum in person, but this is pretty close. An excellent tool for parents and teachers to introduce kids to the wonderful world of flight.

⌐Best⌐ Babies Today Online

http://babiestoday.com

A community for new and new again parents full of information to guide parents through the formative years of their child's life. Site is organized by development stages, starting out with preconception topics and going all the way up to the teenage years. Print out a babysitter information sheet to ensure a safe night out, or meet other parents interested in making online connections. New parents will soon realize why we picked this site as the best of the best.

BALLOONING

⌐Best⌐ The Balloon Federation of America

http://www.bfa.net/

It's the American ballooning organization's recently renovated site. Includes membership information, events, competition standings, and products for sale—all geared to the experienced balloonist and junior balloonists. Basic site layout places all resources right at your fingertips.

A
B
C
D
E
F
G
H
I
J
K
L
M
N
O
P
Q
R
S
T
U
V
W
X
Y
Z

BARGAINS

⸢Best⸥ Overstock.com

http://www.overstock.com

Save as much as 70% by buying manufacturers' overstock and discontinued items at this site. Products in inventory change daily so visitors are encouraged to check back often, or to sign up for the overstock newsletter. With its huge collection of overstock items updated daily and its easy-to-use format, this site is the hands-down winner as the best of the best.

COUPONS

⸢Best⸥ CouponSurfer

http://www.couponsurfer.com

Visit this site for personalized coupons at national stores or for major brands. Browse categories such as baby items, books, health and beauty, or sports, and then take a look at coupons available toward a purchase.

FREEBIES

⸢Best⸥ Freaky Freddies Free Funhouse

http://www.freakyfreddies.com/

With the motto "If it ain't free, it's not for me," Freaky Freddy greets you with a stack of freebies, coupons, and special offers from hundreds of leading manufacturers and dealers. Free stuff for everyone, including free chocolate! This site is updated daily and features more than 70 categories of freebies. Sign up for Freaky Freddy's daily or weekly newsletter to keep up on the latest deals. Its excellent collection of freebies and devotion to keeping visitors informed about the latest deals combine to make this the best of the best.

BASEBALL

A
B
C
D
E
F
G
H
I
J
K
L
M
N
O
P
Q
R
S
T
U
V
W
X
Y
Z

American League Web Sites

Anaheim Angels
http://anaheim.angels.mlb.com/

Baltimore Orioles
http://baltimore.orioles.mlb.
com/

Boston Red Sox
http://boston.redsox.mlb.com/

Chicago White Sox
http://chicago.whitesox.mlb.com/

Cleveland Indians
http://cleveland.indians.mlb.
com/

Detroit Tigers
http://detroit.tigers.
mlb.com/

Kansas City Royals
http://kansascity.royals.mlb.
com/

Minnesota Twins
http://minnesota.twins.mlb.com/

New York Yankees
http://newyork.yankees.mlb.com/

Oakland Athletics
http://oakland.athletics.mlb.
com/

Seattle Mariners
http://seattle.mariners.mlb.
com/

Tampa Bay Devil Rays
http://tampabay.devilrays.mlb.
com/

Texas Rangers
http://texas.rangers.mlb.com/

Toronto Blue Jays
http://toronto.bluejays.mlb.
com/

National League Web Sites
(\$)

Arizona Diamondbacks
http://arizona.diamondbacks.
mlb.com/

Atlanta Braves
http://atlanta.braves.mlb.com/

Chicago Cubs
http://chicago.cubs.mlb.com/

Cincinnati Reds
http://cincinnati.reds.mlb.com/

Colorado Rockies
http://colorado.rockies.mlb.
com/

Florida Marlins
http://florida.marlins.mlb.
com/

Houston Astros
http://houston.astros.mlb.com/

Los Angeles Dodgers
http://losangeles.dodgers.mlb.
com/

Milwaukee Brewers
http://milwaukee.brewers.mlb.
com/

Montreal Expos
http://montreal.expos.mlb.com/

New York Mets
http://newyork.mets.mlb.com/

Philadelphia Phillies
http://philadelphia.phillies.
mlb.com/

San Francisco Giants
http://sanfrancisco.giants.mlb.
com/

St. Louis Cardinals
http://stlouis.cardinals.mlb.
com/

A
B
C
D
E
F
G
H
I
J
K
L
M
N
O
P
Q
R
S
T
U
V
W
X
Y
Z

 Best **Baseball Links**

http://www.baseball-links.com/

Skilton's Baseball Links is a comprehensive collection of links to baseball-related resources, containing more than 5,000 unique links. Check out baseball equipment, read daily analyses of player performance, participate in reader polls, and much more on this site for baseball fanatics.

Harlem Globetrotters Online

http://www.harlemglobetrotters.com/

The Globetrotters have been beating the Washington Generals (and entertaining us along the way) for decades, and now you can find them on the Web. The site covers the history, the current schedule, the players, and all things Globetrotter.

NBA Eastern Conference Web Sites

Atlanta Hawks
http://www.nba.com/hawks/

Boston Celtics
http://www.nba.com/celtics/

Charlotte Hornets
http://www.nba.com/hornets/

Chicago Bulls
http://www.nba.com/bulls/

Cleveland Cavaliers
http://www.nba.com/cavs/

Detroit Pistons
http://www.nba.com/pistons/

Indiana Pacers
http://www.nba.com/pacers/

New Jersey Nets
http://www.nba.com/nets/

New York Knicks
http://www.nba.com/knicks/

Miami Heat
http://www.nba.com/heat/

Milwaukee Bucks
http://www.nba.com/bucks/

Orlando Magic
http://www.nba.com/magic/

Philadelphia 76ers
http://www.nba.com/sixers/

Toronto Raptors
http://www.nba.com/raptors/

Washington Wizards
http://www.nba.com/wizards/

NBA Western Conference Web Sites

Dallas Mavericks
http://www.nba.com/mavericks/

Denver Nuggets
http://www.nba.com/nuggets/

Golden State Warriors
http://www.nba.com/warriors/

Houston Rockets
http://www.nba.com/rockets/

Los Angeles Clippers
http://www.nba.com/clippers/

Los Angeles Lakers
http://www.nba.com/lakers/

Memphis Grizzlies
http://www.nba.com/grizzlies/

Minnesota Timberwolves
http://www.nba.com/
timberwolves/

Phoenix Suns
http://www.nba.com/suns/

Portland Trail Blazers
http://www.nba.com/blazers/

Sacramento Kings
http://www.nba.com/kings/

San Antonio Spurs
http://www.nba.com/spurs/

Seattle SuperSonics
http://www.nba.com/sonics/

Utah Jazz
http://www.nba.com/jazz/

[Best] USA Basketball

http://www.usabasketball.com/

USA Basketball is the governing body of men's and women's basketball in the United States and is recognized by the International Basketball Federation and the U.S. Olympic Committee. The organization selects and trains U.S.A. teams for national and international play. Its Web site offers a FAQ, news releases, photos, links, schedules, athlete bios, and much more. If you like to keep abreast of the top up-and-coming basketball players in the nation, bookmark this site and visit it often.

[Best] RealBeer.com: The Beer Portal

http://www.realbeer.com

The quintessential site for home brewers and microbreweries alike.

Host to three beer-of-the-month clubs, plus more than 150,000 pages about beer, this site appeals to the most enthusiastic beer lovers on the Web. With a huge cache of links to other related Web sites, this site is truly the best of the best when it comes to breweries.

A
B
C
D
E
F
G
H
I
J
K
L
M
N
O
P
Q
R
S
T
U
V
W
X
Y
Z

A
B
C
D
E
F
G
H
I
J
K
L
M
N
O
P
Q
R
S
T
U
V
W
X
Y
Z

BICYCLES

⌐Best⌐ Bike Ride Online

http://www.bikeride.com

An exceptional bicycling Web directory that features links to hundreds of resources, including regional clubs, manufacturers, retailers, racing events, mountain biking, training, coaching, and more. And if you run out of links to click, you can check out the newsgroups to find messages posted by other bicycling enthusiasts.

Shimano

http://www.shimano.com

Learn more about the ins and outs of Shimano racing technology at this site, where you'll learn why so many professional racers choose to ride Shimano bicycles. This site also helps you locate a local dealer and contact customer support. Very well-designed site.

MAINTENANCE AND REPAIR

Bicycle Tune-Up and Repair

http://members.aol.com/biketune/

This is a free Internet tutorial on how to do everything from fixing flat tires to adjusting gears. A nice glossary of terms is available.

BILLIARDS

⌐Best⌐ Brunswick

http://
www.brunswick-billiards.com

Product information and dealer locations can be found at this manufacturer site, as well as information

about what makes a Brunswick table different. Great place to learn the basic rules controlling the most common games, including 8-ball, 9-ball, and straight pool. For the best information about billiards presented in the most easily accessible format, visit this site.

BINGO

Bingo Gala

http://www.bingogala.com/

With more than 29,000 registered players, Bingo Gala is one of the premier bingo sites on the Web. New games start every three to five minutes. Just register online, deposit at least ten bucks into your account (via credit card), pick your card, and join in the next game. Play at your own risk.

[Best] Bingo Heaven

http://www.bingo-vegas.com/

Play bingo and other games on the Internet at the Net's premier online casino—Casino Vega. Well-designed for navigation, this site makes losing money almost too easy.

BIRDS

[Best] Bird Watchers Digest

http://www.birdwatchersdigest.com

For bird watchers everywhere, this site provides advice on bird watching from the experts, whether you're watching birds from exotic locations or just out your back window. You can also learn about bird gardening, identification, and new birding products. Purchase binoculars, paintings, CDs, books, and other items online. Packed with useful information about bird watching in an easy-to-access format, this site is an easy pick as the best of the best.

Wild Birds Unlimited

http://www.wbu.com

Wild Birds Unlimited is the first and largest franchise system of retail stores catering to the backyard birdfeeding hobbyist. Find all kinds of seed, bird feeders, birdhouses, nesting boxes, books, and more at this one-stop shopping site. Email questions directly to the experts.

BOATS AND SAILING

⟦Best⟧ Internet Boats
http://www.internetboats.com/

Find over $100 million worth of boats, yachts, cabin cruisers, specialty boats, classic wood boats, sailboats, anything that travels on water and all for sale on Internet Boats! This is your source for buying, selling, and locating any type of new or used watercraft!

BOOKS

⟦Best⟧ City Lights Bookstore
http://www.citylights.com/

Creative and innovative site representing the historic City Lights Bookstore in San Francisco's North Beach area. Founded by poet Lawrence Ferlinghetti, this site offers cutting-edge literature and books on compelling social and political issues. Whether you're interested in the Beat Generation or the latest cutting-edge literary works, this is the place to track down copies of your favorite books.

AUDIO BOOKS

AudioUniverse
http://www.audiouniverse.com

Organized similar to Amazon.com, AudioUniverse advertises more than 15,000 audio books available at their site, at up to 60% off the retail price.

⟦Best⟧ Books on Tape
http://www.booksontape.com/

One of the very few audiobook sites that lets you rent, rather than buy tapes. You can also listen to audio clips of certain selections at the site. With its huge collection of audio samples, audio books for purchase, and easy navigation, this site is an easy pick for best of the best.

Best Book Buys

http://www.bestwebbuys.com/books/

Find the lowest prices for any book imaginable. Search for the book you want. Best Book Buys locates the book at several online bookstores and displays a list, showing which bookstore offers the best deal. Search includes new and used copies.

Books A Million

http://www.booksamillion.com/ncom/books?redirect=1

This online bookstore advertises discounts of 20% to 55% off retail book prices, which can be found at their brick-and-mortar locations as well. Search the database to find the title you're looking for.

BOOKSTORES

Barnes & Noble.com

http://www.bn.com

Visit the online version of the popular Barnes & Noble bookstore and search their inventory for new and out-of-print titles. Order online and have the book you want delivered right to your door. Barnes & Noble also carries audio CDs, VHS and DVD videos, and software.

Borders.com

http://www.borders.com/

Connects you to the Amazon/Borders team site, where you can search the largest collection of books and magazines and order them online. Also provides a list of Borders bookstore locations and events.

WordsWorth Books

http://www.wordsworth.com/

Besides offering a wonderful selection of books at a discounted price, WordsWorth Books is a book lover's dream, with its book selection of the day; interviews with authors; great selection of children's books; contests for adults and children; autographed copies of books; the independent bestseller list; and all literary award winners, for fiction, nonfiction, and children's literature.

PUBLISHERS

Pearson Technology Group

http://www.pearsonptg.com/

Free, unlimited access to Pearson Technology Group's vast collection of professional, technology, and computer books. Searchable collections of reference content, books and software for sale, links to valuable third-party sites, and related resources covering the topics business and technology professionals are looking for. Here you can find books on business, computers, engineering, science, vocational skills, and humanities and social sciences. The top imprints in the business call this site home, including Addison-Wesley Professional, Adobe Press, Alpha Books (publishers of the Idiot's Guides), PeachPit Press, Que, New Riders, and more.

A
B
C
D
E
F
G
H
I
J
K
L
M
N
O
P
Q
R
S
T
U
V
W
X
Y
Z

A
B
C
D
E
F
G
H
I
J
K
L
M
N
O
P
Q
R
S
T
U
V
W
X
Y
Z

BOWLING

AMF Bowling Worldwide

http://www.amf.com/

AMF is the largest company in the world that is focused solely on bowling. Check out AMF's site for more information on the company, its bowling centers, and its products; tips from the pros; fun and games; product reviews; and more.

Bowling Zone

http://www.bowlingzone.com/

With more than 1,300 linked sites, you can find directions to lanes, scores and stats, PBA players' home pages, clinics and instruction, and international organizations and associations.

⌐Best⌐ Brunswick Online

http://www.brunswickbowling.com/

Whether you're interested in building a bowling alley or just building your average, this site points the way. Find out about the Brunswick products that can help. There is also a Blockbuster Bowling online game you can play (if your browser supports Shockwave).

LeagueSecretary.com

http://www.leaguesecretary.com/

LeagueSecretary.com is the only site that can generate Interactive Standing sheets and provide your bowlers with a graphical image of the bowler's historical records. This is the only site that provides total integration between a leading software product, CDE Software BLS, and the Internet.

BOXING

⌐Best⌐ Cyber Boxing Zone

http://cyberboxingzone.com/
boxing/cyber.htm

The Cyber Boxing Zone offers late-breaking boxing news, bout previews, and a lineage of past to present champions in classes ranging from the straw-weights to heavyweights. You will also find the CBZ Boxing Encyclopedia, a book and video store, and Cyber Boxing Journal.

ESPN.com Boxing

http://espn.go.com/box/

The latest boxing news stories from ESPN. Updated daily, this is your best source for up-to-the-minute coverage. Home of Friday Night Fights with Max Kellerman.

Oscar De La Hoya

http://www.oscardelahoya.com/

The official online channel for this world champion boxer. The site includes fan club information, news, a calendar listing upcoming fights, photos, and much more.

Bigfoot

http://bigfoot.com/

Fast telephone, address, email, and home page finder. Accepts queries in several languages.

CorporateInformation

http://www.corporateinformation.com/

An online directory of corporate information resources organized by country. Searches over 350,000 company profiles.

Fast Company

http://www.fastcompany.com

Online magazine focusing on business innovation, creativity, and productive practices in the workplace.

〖Best〗 Forbes Digital Tool

http://www.forbes.com/

Technology, investing, media, and politics are all covered in this site from Forbes publications. There are also articles on companies, entrepreneurs, the economy, and the world's wealthiest people. Site features easy navigation, the latest financial news, and a good collection of personal finance tools, making it the best of the best business sites on the Web.

Switchboard: The Internet Directory

http://www.switchboard.com/

Offers all kinds of lookup features. You can find a person, a business listing, an email address, maps and directions, or you can search the Web.

A
B
C
D
E
F
G
H
I
J
K
L
M
N
O
P
Q
R
S
T
U
V
W
X
Y
Z

A
B
C
D
E
F
G
H
I
J
K
L
M
N
O
P
Q
R
S
T
U
V
W
X
Y
Z

CORPORATE HOME PAGES

American International
http://www.aig.com_Group, Inc.

Ameritech
http://www.ameritech.com

AT&T Corporation
http://www.att.com/

Bank of America Corporation
http://
www.bankamerica.com

Bell Atlantic Corporation
http://www.bellatlantic.com

Boeing http://www.boeing.com

Chase Manhattan Corporation
http://www.chase.com

Citigroup
http://www.citi.com

Coca-Cola Company
http://www.cocacola.com

DuPont
http://www.dupont.com

Federal Express Corporation
http://www.federalexpress.com

Ford Motor Company
http://www.ford.com/

General Electric Company
http://www.ge.com

General Motors
http://www.gm.com

Goodyear Tire and Rubber
Company
http://www.goodyear.com

Hewlett-Packard Company
http://www.hp.com

IBM Corporation
http://www.ibm.com

Intel Corporation
http://www.intel.com

Kmart Corporation
http://www.kmart.com

Lucent Technologies
http://www.lucent.com

Merck & Co.
http://www.merck.com

MCI WorldCom, Inc.
http://www.mciworldcom.com

Merrill Lynch
http://www.ml.com

Microsoft Corporation
http://www.microsoft.com

Mobil
http://www.mobil.com

Motorola
http://www.mot.com

The Procter & Gamble Company
http://www.pg.com

Prudential Insurance Company
of America
http://www.prudential.com

Sears, Roebuck & Company
http://www.sears.com

State Farm Insurance Companies
http://www.statefarm.com

SBC Communications
http://www.sbc.com

Texaco
http://www.texaco.com

TIAA-CREF
http://www.tiaa-cref.org

United Parcel Service of
America, Inc. (UPS)
http://www.ups.com

Wal-Mart Stores, Inc.
http://www.wal-mart.com

The Walt Disney Company
http://www.disney.com

FRANCHISING

Franchise Doctor

http://www.franchisedoc.com

Take the free FranchiseFit Entrepreneurial Survey before you invest in a franchise to see whether you're really meant to be a franchisee. The franchise reviews are very helpful, as are the newsletter and the articles related to franchise opportunities.

Best Franchise Zone by Entrepreneur.com

http://www.entrepreneur.com/ Franchise_Zone/

Dedicated to linking enthusiastic entrepreneurs with the top franchises, this site provides all the information you need to find the best franchises and become a successful franchisee. How-to articles, advice from experts, and lists of the top franchises in various categories make this the first site to turn for those considering the purchase of a franchise. Don't miss Entrepreneur's Guide To Franchising.

HOME-BASED BUSINESS

Best Bizy Moms

http://www.bizymoms.com/

Business ideas, recommended books and resources, and work-at-home scams and how to avoid them. Be sure to sign up for the free newsletter that's sent once a week. And don't forget to check out the message board for more ideas on a variety of topics! If you weren't busy before you visited this site, this place can keep you busy for days.

INTERNATIONAL BUSINESS

Infonation

http://www.un.org/Pubs/ CyberSchoolBus/infonation/ e_infonation.htm

Interested in statistics? This is the site for you. Compare data within the countries of the United Nations, including urban growth, top exports, and threatened species. A great resource for adults and kids.

Best The Internationalist

http://www.internationalist.com/

The source for books, directories, publications, reports, maps on international business, import/ export, and more. Very nice site— colorful, easy to navigate, and loaded with choices. Provides links to Amazon.com and other retailers.

NEWSWEEK International Business Resource

http://www.newsweek-int.com/

Newsweek's International news site, where you can read the latest news from around the world.

PATENT INFORMATION

Patent Act

http://www4.law.cornell.edu/ uscode/35/

Text of the Patent Act, covering patentability of inventions, grants of patents, protection, and rights.

A
B
C
D
E
F
G
H
I
J
K
L
M
N
O
P
Q
R
S
T
U
V
W
X
Y
Z

A
B
C
D
E
F
G
H
I
J
K
L
M
N
O
P
Q
R
S
T
U
V
W
X
Y
Z

SMALL BUSINESS— PRODUCTS AND SERVICES

American Express Small Business Central

http://www.americanexpress.com/smallbusiness/

One of the best features of American Express' small business section is the interactive tools section, where you can create a business plan with guidance from AMEX experts free. And there are expert columnists, too, providing helpful tips and ideas to make you more successful.

CenterBeam

http://www.centerbeam.com

Small businesses in need of sophisticated computing systems might want to check out CenterBeam for subscription computing services. Rather than invest in equipment, companies can pay a monthly fee to CenterBeam to provide what is needed.

Microsoft bCentral

http://www.bcentral.com/

The focus of bCentral is helping companies set up and run a business Web site, which Microsoft makes very attractive by offering a $29.95-per-month deal. But there's more than just Web site development information here; business owners can get advice on just about every aspect of running a business.

United States Post Office

http://www.usps.com

Use the post office's online ordering system and have postage stamps delivered to your door. No more waiting in line at the post office for all of your stamp and postal needs.

SMALL BUSINESS— WEBSTOREFRONT SUPPORT

EarthLink Business

http://www.earthlink.net/business/

Rely on EarthLink for a variety of business/e-commerce services, such as setting up an intranet, providing Web hosting, or holding an online meeting. You can also stay abreast of Internet news with regular online updates at the site. Plenty of services, but it's hard to know where to start.

[Best] Altrec.com

http://www.altrec.com/

Shop here for gear for hiking, camping, climbing, cycling, paddling, fly fishing, snow skiing, and running. Huge collection of the best outdoor gear and clothing available, excellent customer service, plus some great online deals make this the best of the best sites to go for all your camping and outdoor adventure needs.

Benz Campground Directory

http://www.bisdirectory.com/camping/

An extensive campgrounds and camping directory for the United States, Canada, and Mexico. Links to other pertinent sites.

Camp Channel

http://www.campchannel.com

Looking for a summer camp for your child? Then tune in to the Camp Channel. Here, you can search through a huge database of summer camps by theme and geographical location. Covers camps in the United States and all over the world. Visit the Camp Store for links to other sites that sell camping gear. Very attractive site, easy to navigate.

Campground Directory

http://www.gocampingamerica.com

Find a campground or RV park quickly and easily using the searchable directory or pull-down menus.

The Camping Source

http://thecampingsource.com/

The place on the Internet to find anything that has to do with camping: clothes, recipes, links, weather, trailers, RV shows, RV dealers, tents, backpacks, equipment for sale, RV classifieds, and more!

Coleman.com

http://www.coleman.com/

Besides descriptions of their products that you can buy online, you'll find advice on how to prepare for a camping trip, how to set up camp, cooking tips, where to go, and more.

HIKING

America's Roof

http://www.americasroof.com

View the map of the United States or the world to identify the highest points in the world that you might want to hike. In addition to help in finding places to hike, you can also catch up on hiking news and register online for upcoming events.

A
B

C
D
E
F
G
H
I
J
K
L
M
N
O
P
Q
R
S
T
U
V
W
X
Y
Z

Best GORP–Great Outdoor Recreation Page

http://www.gorp.com/gorp/
activity/hiking.htm

So, what do people actually do when they camp? Learn about all the great outdoor activities here: fishing, hiking, canoeing, bicycling, and more. Learn about little-known and uncrowded camping places in national (and some state) parks and forests. Ever wonder how those campground hosts got their jobs? Click on "Jobs in the Outdoors" for links to dream jobs. You can purchase books, maps, and outdoor gear, and even plan your trips or purchase packaged outings through the online store.

CANADA

Best Canada.com

http://www.canada.com/home/

$

The premier site for Canada and everything Canadian, this provides information about all of Canada's major cities, including Calgary, Edmonton, Winnipeg, Toronto, Montreal, and Ottawa. Here, you can find the latest local, national, and international news; obtain weather reports; check out the latest sports scores; and keep abreast of the latest news in business and finance. Whether you live in Canada or just plan a visit to this great country, bookmark this best of the best site and visit it daily!

CANCER

American Cancer Society

http://www.cancer.org

$

Online support resources include information on a wide variety of programs such as the Great American Smokeout, the Breast Cancer Network, and Man to Man prostate cancer information. You can buy books about cancer and coping with it through the online bookstore.

Avon: The Crusade

http://www.avoncompany.com/women/avoncrusade/

Avon touts itself as the largest corporate supporter of breast health programs in America. This site gives information about Avon's Breast Cancer Awareness Crusade, which is targeted at providing women—particularly low-income, minority, and older women—direct access to breast cancer education and early-detection screening services, at little or no cost. Find out how much has been raised to date and what grants have been awarded as a result.

Breast Cancer Action

http://www.bcaction.org

Home of one of the most popular and powerful breast cancer action groups, this site is designed to inform and empower breast cancer patients and others concerned about breast cancer. Learn about the latest preventions and treatments as well as political issues that should concern all citizens.

⟦Best⟧ Cancer411.com

http://www.cancer411.com/

The Mission of the Rory and Joyce Foundations is to "increase public awareness of and access to alternative and conventional choices available for the treatment of cancer." Take advantage of this site's tremendous library of cancer information and resources. Learn about the latest treatment options, even if they're not promoted by the mainstream medical community. This is the site to go for the latest information on cancer research and treatments.

Faces of Hope

http://www.facesofhope.org

First of its kind site in that it offers private one-on-one Internet mentoring and support to newly diagnosed breast cancer patients through its mentor-matching program. Visitors can read the stories of breast cancer survivors and access a message board offering breast cancer information resources.

National Cancer Institute

http://newscenter.cancer.gov/

The National Cancer Institute (NCI) coordinates the government's cancer research program. NCI is the largest of the 17 biomedical research institutes and centers at the National Institutes of Health (NIH). It is located just outside Washington, D.C., in Bethesda, Maryland. NCI's Web site is for cancer patients, the public, and the mass media; on it, you will find news and information on many of its programs and resources.

OncoLink: University of Pennsylvania Cancer Center Resources

http://oncolink.upenn.edu/

A comprehensive site for cancer patients and professionals that provides information on many types of cancer, treatments, the social and emotional aspects of coping with the disease, new drug treatments, clinical trials, and FAQs.

A
B
C
D
E
F
G
H
I
J
K
L
M
N
O
P
Q
R
S
T
U
V
W
X
Y
Z

A
B
C
D
E
F
G
H
I
J
K
L
M
N
O
P
Q
R
S
T
U
V
W
X
Y
Z

CANDY

 Best ### Godiva Chocolatier

http://www.godiva.com/godiva/

Offering some of the best chocolate in the world, this site enables you to order online or to locate the Godiva retailer nearest you. Even the graphics make your mouth water. Definitely a stop for chocoholics with discriminating taste.

Hershey Chocolate North America

http://www.hersheys.com/

Includes information on Hershey's chocolate, as well as pasta, Hershey's grocery, and an online cookbook.

LifeSavers

http://www.candystand.com

Enjoy lots of great games and visit the virtual theme park, all of which are designed to get you hungry for Lifesavers products. Targeted at children, but fun for adults, too.

CASINOS

  Best ### Casino Center

http://www.casinocenter.com/

The gaming enthusiast needs to bookmark this comprehensive site. Brush up on your gaming strategies with the online gaming magazine, find out information on hundreds of casinos across the country from an extensive database, and learn the rules of all the casino games from Keno to blackjack. Also, you can check out current stock prices and company news from the industry's publicly owned companies. You can buy merchandise from the online gift store or indulge in a magazine subscription.

CHEERLEADING

A
B
C
D
E
F
G
H
I
J
K
L
M
N
O
P
Q
R
S
T
U
V
W
X
Y
Z

[Best] Team Cheer Online

http://www.teamcheer.com/

Whether you want poms, jackets, team bags, or cheer shoes, Team Cheer Online offers competitive pricing based on volume (the more you buy, the better price you get). Browse the online catalog and call (toll free), fax, or mail in your order. The only drawback is that you can't place your order online, but otherwise, this site is a well-deserving best of the best candidate.

CHILD ABUSE AND MISSING CHILDREN

SOC-UM: Safeguarding Our Children-United Mothers Organization

http://www.soc-um.org/

Dedicated to safeguarding children both online and off, this site is an excellent resource for the prevention of child sexual abuse and violence. Provides links for education, prevention, pedophile information, and a collection of links to state sex-offender registries. Every parent with young children should check out this best of the best site.

38

A
B
C
D
E
F
G
H
I
J
K
L
M
N
O
P
Q
R
S
T
U
V
W
X
Y
Z

CHILDCARE

AFDS, Inc.

http://www.afds.com/

The American Federation of Daycare Services, Inc., provides insurance for in-home daycare providers. You can research insurance plans and get an online price quote on this site.

drSpock.com

http://www.drspock.com

Staying in the spirit of world-renowned pediatrician Dr. Benjamin Spock, this site is dedicated to providing parents with the expert information they need to raise healthy, happy children. Search this site for medical information, product alerts, and parenting advice from some of the world's top experts in childcare.

 Best **Individual States' Childcare Licensure Regulations**

http://nrc.uchsc.edu/states.html

Just what the title suggests. Click on your state to access the childcare licensure regulations that apply. The site lists each regulation and provides a full-text document so you can read the actual regulation. As indicated, the information is specific to each state. Use this site to prepare to set up your own childcare facility or to see what your state does to ensure the safety and well-being of your child. Whether you plan on opening your own daycare or are shopping for a daycare center for your children, you should check out this best of the best site.

CIGARS

 Best **Uptown Cigar Company**

http://www.uptowncigar.com/

Cigar store run by cigar aficionados for cigar aficionados, features a wide selection of brand-name cigars, a sampler of the month, smoking accessories, and links to lounges and clubs. The Cigar Info page provides a glossary of cigar terms and facts for the novice and enthusiast. Definitely a top choice site!

CIVIL RIGHTS

[Best] The American Civil Liberties Union

http://www.aclu.org/

Lots of information about this powerful organization, which champions the rights of individuals. Read about the issues that threaten our freedoms and rights and get on an alert list that warns you of events that threaten our liberties so you can participate. Learn about the latest legal cases in areas ranging from racial preferences to the separation of church and state. You can buy "liberty" items such as tote bags and T-shirts through the online store. For information on current civil rights issues and cases, no site is better than this!

CLASSIFIEDS

Classifieds2000

http://www.classifieds2000.com/

Formerly Excite Classifieds, Classifieds2000 is a directory of classifieds from millions of publications and online resources. You can search by entering the item you are looking for or clicking on a product category. You can also sign up for email notification when a new listing is added that matches your interests.

[Best] Trader Online

http://www.traderonline.com/

TraderOnline.com is a collection of more than 20 high-traffic Web sites receiving millions of visitors each month, and is a division of Trader Publishing Company, publisher of classifieds and editorial magazines with an emphasis on bringing buyers and sellers together efficiently. The publications cover a diverse mix of categories such as automobiles, trucks, heavy equipment, boats, motorcycles, aircraft and general merchandise, jobs, homes, and apartments. TraderOnline.com collects fresh data from each of Trader's more than 650 weekly and 14 monthly classifieds publications and posts this data to the Internet every day.

A
B
C
D
E
F
G
H
I
J
K
L
M
N
O
P
Q
R
S
T
U
V
W
X
Y
Z

CollectiblesNet.com

http://www.collectiblesnet.com

Place a free ad to sell a collectible, or search through many categories to find a new collectible to cherish. You'll find Barbie Dolls, Beanie Babies, Antiques, as well as Precious Moments, Star Trek, and more.

 COINS

 Best ### American Numismatic Association

http://www.money.org/

The ANA, a nonprofit, educational organization chartered by Congress, is dedicated to the collection and study of coins, paper money, tokens, and medals, and was created for the benefit of its members and the numismatic community. The association provides a comprehensive site with links, articles, online exhibits, educational programs, and much more. Excellent information and graphics presented in an easy-to-use format makes this an easy choice for best of the best.

CoinLink Numismatic and Rare Coins Index

http://www.coinlink.com/

Large rare coin index with links to more than 800 numismatic sites. Piles of links to sites dealing with currency exchange, gold prices, ancient coins, statehood quarters, and exonumia (coin-like objects, such as tokens and medals). Sites are rated, providing links to only the best resources.

Forum Ancient Coins

http://
www.ancient-coin-forum.com/

This site does not just sell coins, but also provides coin collectors, history buffs, and students a fun and informative place to explore and learn about ancient history, as well as coin collecting. All sales are guaranteed.

Heritage Rare Coin Gallery

http://www.heritagecoin.com/

World's largest numismatic dealer and auctioneer. Go online to view their $20 million inventory, but that's just the beginning—this site is chock-full of information and neat coin stuff to see and learn about. Participate in online auctions and maintain a list of coins you want. The site will notify you when items you have on your want list become available.

Best iQVC.com Shopping Home Page

http://www.qvc.com/scripts/
departments.pl?dept=coll

For those who love collector dolls, enjoy iQVC's corner of doll heaven. Here, you can browse through handcrafted dolls of fine porcelain, cloth, vinyl, and more. You'll find dolls by some of the world's most respected doll artists—Goebel, Madame Alexander, Lloyd Middleton, Precious Moments, and more. With so many enchanting choices, iQVC is a treasure trove for novices and experienced collectors alike. Definitely check them before you buy elsewhere—their prices are excellent!

STAMPS

Best American Philatelic Society

http://www.stamps.org/

This well-designed site features the American Philatelic Society's journal, a dealer locator, a searchable library catalog, a printable membership application, extensive information on the basics of stamp collecting, and details on their expertizing service. If you're interested in stamp collecting, whether you are a novice or an expert, bookmark this site and visit it often. This site is packed with the most useful information you'll find on the subject of stamp collecting, making it a sure winner of the best of the best designation.

COLLEGES AND UNIVERSITIES

COLLEGE ADMISSIONS

Best Mapping Your Future

http://
www.mapping-your-future.org

Having trouble narrowing down your choice of potential colleges? Mapping Your Future might be able to help, with their 10 Steps to Selecting a College. You can also receive counseling on financial aid packages and what you can afford here. Great place for parents and students to start planning for the college years.

Princeton Review Rankings

http://www.review.com/college/

This complete ranking of colleges provides feedback on various colleges' overall educational program. You enter the college name and receive a ranking report.

A
B
C
D
E
F
G
H
I
J
K
L
M
N
O
P
Q
R
S
T
U
V
W
X
Y
Z

A
B
C
D
E
F
G
H
I
J
K
L
M
N
O
P
Q
R
S
T
U
V
W
X
Y
Z

GRADUATE SCHOOLS

Gradschools.com

http://www.gradschools.com/

With 53,574 program listings as of March 2002, this site claims it is "the most comprehensive online source of graduate school information." Click on the Search function, select a program category, and see a list of not only U.S. programs, but international programs, too. One major drawback is that after you get to the program that interests you, there is only an email option—not a direct linkage.

COMICS, CARTOONS, AND ANIMATION

Chuck Jones Web Site

www.chuckjones.com

Check out the official site of Chuck Jones, the famous Warner Brothers/ Looney Tunes animator and animation director. At this site, you can read about Mr. Jones and his many famous cartoon characters. This is an exceptionally well-constructed site, both visually and contentwise.

Comic Sites Alliance

http://www.digitalwebbing.com/sites/

Links to the best comics sites on the Web broken down into categories including Creators, Publishers, TV and Film, Fandom, Files (games, screensavers, and so on), and Interaction (forums and chat rooms).

Dark Horse Comics Home Page

http://www.dhorse.com/

Provides news, information, art-work, and upcoming release information for Dark Horse Comics, publisher of Star Wars, Aliens, and many more titles. Includes many different articles about Dark Horse titles and artists.

Digital Webbing

http://www.digitalwebbing.com/

Great source for finding comic book–related Web sites and information. Includes an extensive database of comic book Web sites, news, interviews, previews, and talent search area.

Disney.com

http://disney.go.com/

A great Web site for families to explore together! Has links to some of Disney's best known cartoons, along with activities for kids and families. Also has a Disney shop online.

Iguana's Comic Book Café

http://www.go2iguanas.com/

This café is a gaming and comic book mail ordering service. Also specializes in toys, Beanie Babies, and manga videos.

 Best Marvel Comics

http://www.marvel.com/

The home of Spider-Man, the Hulk, Captain America, and other famous heroes, this site is marvelous! Here, you can learn about your favorite Marvel comic books, preview upcoming issues, shop online, and register to win free comic books. Some excellent free downloads and brilliant graphics. Bravo, Marvel!

The Simpsons

http://www.thesimpsons.com/

Explore Springfield using the virtual map and view the latest antics of Homer and Bart. Meet the voice actors, guest stars, and show's creator. Get character bios, view episode descriptions, and share your enthusiasm for the show with other fans. Excellent site!

Spider-Man: The Amazing Spider-Man Page

http://www.msu.edu/user/haleysco/spiderman/

Provides an unofficial fan page dedicated to Marvel Comics' Spider-Man. Includes artwork, news, and an interview with Marvel Comics' guru Stan Lee.

Super Marketing: Ads from the Comic Books

http://www.steveconley.com/supermarketing.htm

This site is dedicated to the classic ads that appeared in golden and silver age comics. Ads for such things as the Hypno-coin, six tapes for $1.49, and much more are quite humorous.

Wolverine's REALM

http://www.thevine.net/~falcon/comics/wolverine.html

Provides an unofficial fan page for Marvel Comics' character Wolverine. Includes facts, origin information, artwork, fan pictures, and much more.

A
B
C
D
E
F
G
H
I
J
K
L
M
N
O
P
Q
R
S
T
U
V
W
X
Y
Z

COMPUTERS

BUYING/ INFORMATION RESOURCES

egghead

http://www.egghead.com

At Amazon.com-powered egghead.com, check out a wide selection of Egghead products. Browse by category, check out some great deals, or view the list of 100 top electronics devices.

Gadget Boy Gazette

http://www.gadgetboy.com

Read reviews of consumer electronic and personal computing products as tested by syndicated columnist Stephen Jacobs, aka Gadget Boy.

COMPUTER COMPANIES: HARDWARE AND SOFTWARE

Apple Computer Home Page

http://www.apple.com/

Apple now provides an online storefront where you can purchase customized hardware configurations of your favorite Macintosh models. Provides information on Apple's latest products and also supplies software updates. Check out this site for the latest on Apple technology.

Best Dell.com

http://www.dell.com/

This site provides secure online shopping for Dell personal computer products. You can custom-configure a system and buy it online. The site also lets you search for information by type of user, as well as provides the standard corporate information. If you own a Dell computer, this site features excellent online technical support that can help you solve most of the problems you might encounter with your computer. Excellent site design and comprehensive information make this an easy best of the best selection.

Gateway

http://www.gateway.com/

This is a cool, interactive site providing two ways to access information about Gateway personal computers. You can select a link from a list of types of users, or go directly to information about a specific system. The site also provides access to technical support and corporate information. You can also configure and purchase a computer online from this site.

IBM Corporation

http://www.ibm.com

Here you can reach all of IBM's myriad divisions from the home page. You can also read about IBM systems solutions via articles. Take online training courses, attend real-time seminars, or chat with people with similar interests. An extensive search engine is also provided for navigating this very large corporate site. Take advantage of their Buy Today, Ship Today purchase program.

Intel

http://www.intel.com/

This site provides all the information you ever wanted to know about Intel's integrated circuits, and especially the Pentium II chip. The site showcases software running on Intel-based hardware, hardware implementations, and offers business opportunities as well as the standard technical support and news briefs.

MACINTOSH

Mac Design Online

http://www.macdesignonline.com/

Involved in the graphics industry? Mac Design is devoted to covering Macintosh graphics, multimedia, and Web issues specifically for Macintosh computers.

Ultimate Mac

http://www.ultimatemac.com

Named to several "Best of..." reports because of the comprehensive approach to Macintosh information. For beginners and programmers alike, the Ultimate Macintosh provides answers to user questions, downloadable software, product and software reviews, and just about anything else you need to know about the Mac.

PCS

GoToMyPC

http://www.gotomypc.com

Online service that enables you to connect to and use your desktop computer from any Internet-connected computer in the world via a secure connection. If you frequently find yourself on the road without access to the programs and documents you need to survive, connect to this site to sign up for a free trial.

[Best] WinPlanet

http://www.winplanet.com/

Premium site for all topics related to Microsoft Windows and Windows applications. Take an online tutorial to learn a new skill, pick up some tips and tricks, and learn how to customize Windows with some tech-savvy tweaks. Excellent collection of downloadable shareware and updated drivers. When you want to learn more about your computer's operating system, this is the place to go.

A
B
C
D
E
F
G
H
I
J
K
L
M
N
O
P
Q
R
S
T
U
V
W
X
Y
Z

PROGRAMMING LANGUAGES

MSDN Online

http://msdn.microsoft.com/

Resources, downloads, magazines, and more are available at this comprehensive site. Microsoft Developers Network (MSDN) is a resource site for programmers and developers. Links to additional information about .Net technology.

Perl: CPAN Comprehensive Perl Archive Network

http://www.cpan.org/

Comprehensive collection of links to the best Perl resources on the Web. Locate Perl source code, modules, and scripts; research documentation; and find answers to the most common questions.

Tutorials: Need Help with C/C++ and Other Languages?

http://www.andrews.edu/~maier/tutor.html

An online library that provides a number of FAQs and entire books online that you can download to teach yourself C++, ANSI C, Unix, HTML, vi, and email. All the documents at this site are public domain or freeware. An excellent site for novice programmers in any of these languages.

SOFTWARE— ANTIVIRUS

Dr. Solomon

http://www.drsolomon.com

Learn more about Dr. Solomon's Virex product and then order it online.

McAfee.com

http://www.mcafee.com

Get new virus alerts at McAfee, as well as help buying, installing, and running their VirusScan software, as well as instruction in eliminating existing viruses on your system.

Symantec

http://www.norton.com

Buy Norton AntiVirus here, learn about protecting your system from viruses and other threats, and download virus definition updates (if you own the program).

SOFTWARE— DOWNLOADS

Download Warehouse

http://www.downloadwarehouse.com

Find a great selection of software to order and download. From business applications to fun and games, this site has a huge selection.

Software Unboxed

http://www.unboxed.com/

Download popular locked commercial software directly from the publishers, and then purchase an unlocking password online. All types of software are available from business to personal finance to programmers' tools. A great way to save money if the box doesn't matter to you and you need a program in a hurry.

SOFTWARE— MISCELLANEOUS

Family Tree Maker Online

http://www.familytreemaker.com/

An online genealogy library, genealogy lessons, columns featuring researching techniques, and tips on how to trace immigrant origins. Buy genealogy software and family archive CDs online.

International Data Corporation

http://www.idg.com/

Publishers of magazines such as ComputerWorld/InfoWorld, PC World, Network World, MacWorld, Channel World, and Specialty. Find links to each of these publications. Many feature software previews, reviews, and recommendations.

Laurie McCanna's Photoshop, Corel, Painter, and Paintshop Pro Tips

http://www.mccannas.com/pshop/menu.htm

This site features tips and tutorials for Photoshop, Corel, Painter, and Paintshop Pro users. A multitude of examples for the applications that are offered.

SlaughterHouse

http://www.slaughterhouse.com/

Whatever your software vice (games, Internet, media, or utilities), SlaughterHouse (the parent site for Andover.net) has something for you.

SHAREWARE/ FREEWARE

Network ICE Corporation

http://www.networkice.com/downloads/blackice_defender.html

Protect your computer and files from potential hack attacks by downloading Black Ice Defender, a personal firewall. Tech support and customer service are also available on this site.

TROUBLESHOOTING

PC Pitstop

http://www.pcpitstop.com/

Have an automated technician check your PC for problems and help you optimize your system. PC Pitstop checks to see whether your computer is vulnerable to attacks from viruses or hackers, determines whether the hard drive has enough space and is fast enough, checks the memory, reports on the speed of your Internet connection, and much more. Very cool tool for tuning up a PC.

A
B
C
D
E
F
G
H
I
J
K
L
M
N
O
P
Q
R
S
T
U
V
W
X
Y
Z

48

A
B

D
E
F
G
H
I
J
K
L
M
N
O
P
Q
R
S
T
U
V
W
X
Y
Z

CONSUMER ISSUES

Consumer World

http://www.consumerworld.org/

Find 2,000 Internet consumer resources from reporting fraud to looking for the best airfare. Search the database for your specific consumer issue. Read the latest consumer news.

[Best] Federal Consumer Information Center

http://www.pueblo.gsa.gov/

Access 200 federal publications regarding consumer issues. Their catalog offers information on a wide range of areas, such as cars, healthcare, food, travel, and children. You can also order the entire catalog of publications. Because this site features an easy way to obtain some of the most useful government publications for the average citizen, we've chosen to award it the best of the best award for this category.

The National Fraud Information Center

http://www.fraud.org/

Originally formed in 1992 to battle telemarketing fraud, the NFIC now has a toll-free hotline for reporting telemarketing fraud, asking for advice about telemarketing calls, and investigating Internet fraud. The Web site also offers a section on fraud targeting the elderly.

COOKING AND RECIPES

Art of Eating

http://www.artofeating.com

You'll consider subscribing to this quarterly print publication after reading the description on the Web site. The Art of Eating is about the best food and wine—what they are, how they are produced, where to find them (the farms, markets, shops, restaurants).

CheeseNet 95

http://cheesenet.wgx.com/

The graphics-rich cheese bible of the Web—how to make it, its history, the different variations, a picture gallery, cheese literature, and cheese language. Features a cheese-making demonstration and free consultation with Dr. Emory K. Cheese.

Christiane's Collection of Cooking Recipes of Chemists and Physicists

http://chris_fra.tripod.com/recipes/

Contains easy-to-make and inexpensive recipes collected by German chemists and physicists. Recipes are available in both English and German. Includes a metric conversion chart.

Cookbooks Online Recipe Database

http://www.cook-books.com/reg.htm

Cookbooks Online recipe database is the largest recipe database on the Web. If you are looking for any recipes, this is the place to start!

Cooking.com

http://www.cooking.com

The weekly menu planner and menu of the day are two of the most helpful items on this site, which also offers every conceivable cooking utensil and piece of equipment for sale to help you cook up those meals.

Cooks Online

http://www.cooksillustrated.com

Calling itself the "Consumer Reports of Cooking," the site does a good job of evaluating cookware and testing recipes for its members, who can also find cookbook reviews and helpful cooking tips.

Fabulous Foods

http://www.fabulousfoods.com

Looking for some low-carb recipes to help you lose some weight? This site has several sets of recipes for people watching what they eat.

There are also primers on types of food, including how to prepare it and providing recipes to follow. Meet celebrity chefs and pick up some special-occasion menus.

Food TV Network

http://www.foodtv.com/

Incredible collection of cooking information and resources, including the Cooking 101 tutorial, recipe and menu search, links to celebrity chefs (including Emeril), live chats, video clips, and much more.

[Best] Good Cooking

http://www.goodcooking.com

Good Cooking features food, wine, and cooking with professional recipes, submitted recipes, recipe links, good cooking information, nutritional links, consumer information, fish/shellfish recipes, culinary schools links, food facts, wine links, wine information, free recipe submission, travel information, food definitions, culinary information, fun facts, and brain food. Advertise food, wine, cooking, and travel products. Shop via links to Amazon.com. If that's not enough, the site's design will almost make your mouth water!

Official French Fries Page

http://www.tx7.com/fries/

Fun-filled information about the world's most popular side dish. Besides the normal uses for french fries (eating), find out the legal specifications of french fries, how to make them, learn about their history, and find out about alternative condiments and applications of the world's greatest snack food.

A
B
C
D
E
F
G
H
I
J
K
L
M
N
O
P
Q
R
S
T
U
V
W
X
Y
Z

A
B
C
D
E
F
G
H
I
J
K
L
M
N
O
P
Q
R
S
T
U
V
W
X
Y
Z

Williams-Sonoma

http://www.williams-sonoma.com

Well-stocked online store for serious chefs and gourmets features cookware, dinnerware, cutlery, electronic appliances, and much more. Site also features gift ideas, recipes, and wedding gift registries.

CRAFTS AND HOBBIES

Do-It-Yourself Network

http://www.diynet.com

Huge collection of projects complete with step-by-step instructions for the do-it-yourselfer. Projects include everything from creating your own party favors to weatherproofing your home. If you're handy around the house or you just enjoy doing creative projects on your own, you'll find plenty to keep you busy.

HOBBY SHOPS AND CRAFT STORES

Fabri-Centers

http://www.joann.com/

Site for Jo-Ann, ClothWorld, and New York Fabrics and Crafts stores. Find your local store, enter a drawing, subscribe to the store newsletter, visit the investor relations page, find out about in-store specials, or post a message in Message Central to ask questions or share tips. Best of all, visit the creative center for

loads of crafts and sewing ideas and information. This one-stop kiosk for everything related to fabrics and crafts is an easy choice for the best of the best award.

HOBBYLINC

http://www.hobbylinc.com/

A full resource of hobby supplies—more than 10,000 items available. View an extensive graphical catalog, and take advantage of links, hints for hobbyists, biweekly specials, and educational information about various hobbies. Place or check the status of your order. Online gift certificates available for gift-giving.

Scentmasters

http://www.scentmasters.com

Offers an online catalog of all types of candle-making supplies for beginners through experts. Sells starter kits for novices. You can also pose candle-making questions or discuss problems via email, or you can order copies of the Wax House Newsletter.

Voice of Dance

http://www.voiceofdance.org

Providing the latest on news, events, and just plain fun stuff, this site has it all. From learning a new dance step to finding out about upcoming performances of virtually any major dance organization, staying current with dance news, reading reviews and commentary, and purchasing dance products, you'll find it here.

BALLET

New York City Ballet

http://www.nycballet.com

You'll find a fun take on ballet through trivia questions and games at the NYC Ballet site, which also features the standard information on getting tickets, planning trips to performances, and buying NYC Ballet merchandise. You can also read about the history of the organization and catch up on troupe members.

⌈ Best ⌉ Darts Directory

http://dartplayer.net/

This is a great site for everything darts. Here, you'll find information and links to everything you ever wanted to know about the game of darts. You can also play an online dart game. Meet other dart players from around the world and participate in online discussions and chats. Find places that are dart-friendly near you. An easily accessible layout combined with comprehensive links make this an easy choice for best of the best.

Smilie Darts

http://www.smiliegames.com/darts/

Pick a single or multiplayer game and enjoy an online game of darts. You can get help on how to play and see who are the best players.

A
B
C
D
E
F
G
H
I
J
K
L
M
N
O
P
Q
R
S
T
U
V
W
X
Y
Z

DATING

⟦Best⟧ Fantasy Generator

http://www.geocities.com/Paris/
2312/fantasy.html

Create your own torrid romance
novel scenarios! Intended solely to
solicit laughter and smiles and to
bring the experience of untold happiness and romance to people
everywhere. It is brought to you
through the diligent research of a
group of girlfriends who read
many, many romance novels while
imbibing alcoholic beverages during girls' night. This novel idea
makes the site well-deserving of its
best of the best designation.

Match.com

http://www.match.com/

Millions of singles have used the
services of Match.com worldwide.
Match.Com strives to provide a safe
and easy way for members to meet
other quality singles on the Web.
After you create your own unique
profile, their superior matching
technology provides you with
instantaneous matches based upon
your preselected dating criteria. It's
fast, convenient, and simple to use.
Whether you're looking for an activity partner, a casual date, or a lifelong companion, Match.com just
might have the person for you. You
can search for free, but if you want
to contact members, you must register and pay about $25 per month.

DEAFNESS

Animated ASL Dictionary

http://www.bconnex.net/~randys/
index1.html

This site offers an animated dictionary for American Sign
Language. To see how to sign a
word, click the Sign links. These
will take you to a table with both
the English and the manual alphabet. Click on the letter of your

choice, then scroll down the list in
the frame on the left for the desired
word. After the sign loads, it will
begin to animate, slowly repeating
the sequence four times. Click
Links to find other sites related to
ASL and deaf culture. You'll find
links to WWW resources, articles of
interest, businesses, educational
resources, nonprofit agencies,
search engines, and more.

⟦Best⟧ DeafZONE

http://www.deafzone.com/

Chat rooms, links, current events, and information on a wide variety of topics ranging from ADA laws to a workshop calendar. Find relay services and interpreters on this site. It even has a page with some hilarious jokes contributed by members. If you're deaf and you feel all alone, visit this site to tap the vast resources for the deaf and to make some friends along the way.

GG Wiz's FingerSpeller

http://www.iwaynet.net/~ggwiz/asl/

This is a must-see site. Type a phrase and see it finger spelled, and test your reading skills with hidden phrases.

National Institute on Deafness and Other Communication Disorders

http://www.nidcd.nih.gov/

Robust collection of information and resources for those suffering from hearing loss and for physicians and other health professionals. Includes links for information directed toward parents, children, and teachers. Plus Spanish translations of much of the material.

A
B
C
D
E
F
G
H
I
J
K
L
M
N
O
P
Q
R
S
T
U
V
W
X
Y
Z

DEATH AND DYING

Hospice Foundation of America

http://www.hospicefoundation.org/

Learn all about hospice and how it works, as well as read articles on grieving and loss. News archives contain information on death and events such as teleconferences enable individuals to deal with the prospect of someone close to them dying.

⟦Best⟧ Hospice Net

http://www.hospicenet.org/

Find a hospice location near you and learn more about the hospice concept at Hospice Net, as well as learn more about the role of caregiver, the bereavement process, and what patients can do to control how they die. A comprehensive site with information for just about everyone who faces losing a loved one.

A
B
C
D
E
F
G
H
I
J
K
L
M
N
O
P
Q
R
S
T
U
V
W
X
Y
Z

DEBT MANAGEMENT

[Best] The Center for Debt Management

http://center4debtmanagement.com/

Free debt counseling through a nonprofit agency. Reduce your payments, lower your interest, and stop late fees. This well-organized and user-friendly site provides 500 pages of information about debt consolidation, lending sources, credit repair, legal resources, and lots more! Its focus is primarily consumer debt and money management. If you owe money and are having panic attacks trying to figure out how you're going to pay off your debts, this is the best of the best site to learn about your options.

CREDIT COUNSELING

Consumer Credit Counseling by Springboard

http://www.credit.org/

A helpful resource for people struggling to stay afloat financially. Individuals can get budget counseling and debt management assistance online, as well as access several tools for analyzing their mortgage, car loan, and credit card debt.

iVillage Money: Personal Finance for Women

http://www.ivillage.com/money/

Free tax advice, three-step plan for eliminating debt, budgeting tutorial, divorce survival guide, investment basics, plus plenty of money-saving tips. Includes quizzes for testing your knowledge of personal finance topics, financial calculators, and Q&A sessions with financial experts. Supposedly directed toward women, but very useful for anyone who needs to take control of their personal finances.

DEPRESSION

Depression Alliance

http://
www.depressionalliance.org/

A Web site run by people who suffer from depression featuring the latest news and information about depression and its treatment. Be sure to sign up for the newsletter.

 ### National Depressive and Manic-Depressive Association

http://www.ndmda.org/

Find information about clinical depression, dysthymic disorder, major depression, bipolar disorder, treatments, as well as self-help resources online. Read general articles about depression and other mood disorders, find a local support group, or research a specific topic. You can buy books from the online store. Whether you're suffering from clinical depression or have a loved one who suffers from a serious psychiatric disorder, this is the best place to start your research.

Pendulum Resources: The Bipolar Disorder Port

http://www.pendulum.org/

A departure point for learning everything you need to know about bipolar disorder (manic-depression). Find out about the diagnostic criteria for bipolar disorder, the latest medications and treatments, and ongoing studies. Includes links to other sites, books, articles, and even some jokes.

SUICIDE PREVENTION

Suicide: Read This First

http://www.metanoia.org/suicide/

Addresses the causes behind suicidal thoughts and offers suggestions on how to overcome them. Links to sites from suicide prevention organizations are included.

Suicide Links

http://
enchantedwings.freeservers.com/
suicide.html

Huge list of links. The topic of suicide might appear within a category. For example, some sites under the topic Sexual Abuse might also have information on suicide and self-harm. Keep this in mind while browsing the information pages.

Yellow Ribbon Suicide Prevention Program

http://www.yellowribbon.org/

This site is for both parents and teens, but the program is designed for young people by teaching teens how to recognize the symptoms of depression in their friends. Teens are then given ideas what they can do to help their friends get the help they need.

A
B
C
D
E
F
G
H
I
J
K
L
M
N
O
P
Q
R
S
T
U
V
W
X
Y
Z

[Best] ADA

http://www.diabetes.org/

The American Diabetes Association Web site offers the latest information on diabetes and living with the disease. The American Diabetes Association is the nation's leading voluntary health organization supporting diabetes research, information, and advocacy. The association supports an affiliated office in every region of the country, providing services to more than 800 communities. If you or a loved one suffers from diabetes, make this best of the best site your first stop to learning more about the disease and available treatments.

Joslin Diabetes Center

http://www.joslin.harvard.edu/

Joslin is the only U.S. medical center dedicated solely to diabetes treatment, research, cure, and education. On its site, you'll find news, lifestyle and nutrition information, discussion groups, a directory of nationwide affiliates, and more.

American Heart Association

http://www.americanheart.org/

Better food habits can help you reduce your risk of heart attack. This comprehensive site offers a healthful eating plan by choosing the right foods to eat and preparing foods in a healthy way. One of the better sites for nutrition information. After opening the home page, click the Healthy Lifestyle link to access the nutrition page.

Center for Science in the Public Interest

http://www.cspinet.org/

The CSPI Web site features health-related newsletters, nutrition quizzes, updates on health news, and an archive of its reports and press releases. The page also includes links to other health-related sites.

Mayo Clinic Nutrition Center

http://www.mayohealth.org/home

Everything from quick breakfasts to elegant dinners, soups, sauces, and baked goods. Mayo Clinic registered dietitians take your recipes and make them healthier by reducing the calories, fat, and salt—but not the taste.

Meals for You

http://www.mealsforyou.com/

Fabulous recipe site. Calculator enables you to customize recipes based on the number of servings. Nutrition-conscious visitors will especially like the fact that each recipe is accompanied by complete nutritional information. There are also special sections devoted to dietary exchange information and recipes grouped by nutrition content and popularity.

Nutrition Explorations

http://
www.nutritionexplorations.org/

Maintained by the National Dairy Council, this fun site helps kids, teachers, parents, and families learn more about nutrition. Family Food Guide presents the food guide pyramid, recipes for families on the go, kids' recipes, an ask-the-expert feature, and much more. Some excellent teaching tools for educators.

⟦Best⟧ Nutrition.gov

http://www.nutrition.gov/

A new federal resource, provides easy access to all online federal government information on nutrition. Obtain government information on nutrition, healthy eating, physical activity, and food safety, as well as accurate scientific information on nutrition and dietary guidance. When you're ready to start eating a more nutritional diet, this best of the best site is the first place you should visit.

Prevention's Healthy Ideas

http://www.healthyideas.com/

Contains news and information about nutrition, natural healing, weight loss, fitness techniques, tips on healthy cooking, and lifestyle-related articles from Prevention magazine.

Virtual Nutrition Center

http://www-sci.lib.uci.edu/HSG/Nutrition.html

An extensive collection of resources on nutrition, this site includes sections on metabolism, anatomy, nutrition, calorie calculators, and more.

A
B
C
D
E
F
G
H
I
J
K
L
M
N
O
P
Q
R
S
T
U
V
W
X
Y
Z

A
B
C
D
E
F
G
H
I
J
K
L
M
N
O
P
Q
R
S
T
U
V
W
X
Y
Z

DINOSAURS

[Best] Discovering Dinosaurs

http://dinosaurs.eb.com/
dinosaurs/index2.html

Discovering Dinosaurs explores our evolving conceptions of these extra-ordinary creatures. Trace the great dinosaur debate through time by traveling down through each color-coded theme. The historical exploration of not only the scientific discoveries and the dinosaurs themselves but also the interpretation of those discoveries put in chronological order teaches us about the evolution of the current scientific theories as well as the steps in the evolution of life on earth. Excellent graphics combined with comprehensive information make this an easy best of the best pick.

Dr. Internet on Dinosaurs

http://www.ipl.org/youth/
DrInternet/Dinosaurs.html

Tour the dinosaurs in the Hawaii exhibit and see a baby Hypselosaurus hatch. Then skip over to the Field Museum of Natural History in Chicago and view the ancient birds and dinosaurs featured in the Life Over Time exhibit.

NMNH Dinosaur Home Page

http://www.nmnh.si.edu/paleo/
dino/

National Museum of Natural History dinosaurs. Learn about a dinosaur bone injury, view some mummified dinosaur skin impressions, learn about herbivore versus carnivore teeth, examine the brain cavity of a Triceratops, and much more.

Sue at the Field Museum

http://www.fmnh.org/sue/

Sue has her own Web site. Learn about the largest, most complete Tyrannosaurus rex, view an online image gallery, check out Sue's timeline, and find the answers to the most frequently asked questions.

DIVORCE AND CUSTODY

Children's Rights Council

http://www.gocrc.com/

Site of Children's Rights Council (CRC), a national, nonprofit, tax-exempt children's rights organization based in Washington, D.C. Provides information about children's rights, legislation regarding children's rights, and data on the state and national levels.

〖Best〗 DivorceNet

http://www.divorcenet.com/

Contains FAQs with the most common questions pertaining to divorce and family law, an online newsletter and index, a state-by-state resource center, an interactive bulletin board, international and national laws pertaining to child abduction along with a link to the U.S. State Department, and more. Also contains helpful information regarding child custody and child support. Whether you're divorced, going through divorce proceedings, or are considering divorce, this site has the information you need in an easy-to-find format.

DOMESTIC VIOLENCE

National Clearinghouse on Marital and Date Rape

http://members.aol.com/ncmdr/

An organization that conducts research, offers public education, provides technical assistance, and acts as litigation advocates for victims of rape.

〖Best〗 Victim Services Domestic Violence Shelter Tour and Information Site

http://www.dvsheltertour.org/

An outstanding resource for referrals to local help for victims of domestic violence from all over the world. This site also includes information and a children's art gallery. If you or someone you know is a victim of domestic violence, and you don't know where to turn, turn here.

A B C D E F G H I J K L M N O P Q R S T U V W X Y Z

A
B
C
D
E
F
G
H
I
J
K
L
M
N
O
P
Q
R
S
T
U
V
W
X
Y
Z

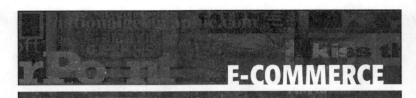

▌Best▐ E-Commerce Times

http://www.ecommercetimes.com

Lots of e-commerce news and discussions, as well as a free newsletter offered either on a daily or weekly basis, to keep you updated. The information is categorized into current events or news, marketing, opinions, special reports, industry reports, and emerging technology, to name a few. Even includes a cartoon. You can readily access stock quotes and watch the tech market from this site. For the latest in e-commerce, you can find no better site.

CONTINUING EDUCATION

DenTrek: Global Online Dental Education Network

http://www.dentrek.com/

Extensive catalogue of education programs and courses in dentistry. Some free tutorials and demos.

MarcoPolo

http://marcopolo.worldcom.com

Created and maintained by Worldcom, MarcoPolo is an excellent resource for K–12 teachers. This program provides teachers with lesson plans, classroom activities and materials, links to valuable content, and powerful search tools. Worldcom even provides professional trainers who can come to your school to instruct teachers on how to incorporate MarcoPolo into their curriculum. Visit this site for more information.

K–12

▌Best▐ ArtsEdge Network

http://
artsedge.kennedy-center.org/

The National Arts and Education Information Network focuses on using technology to increase access to arts resources and increase arts education in the K–12 school environment. Features an online newsletter, an information gallery, curriculum guides, and links to other arts-related online information. Teachers will find this best of the best site an invaluable resource.

Discovery Channel School

http://www.school.discovery.com/

From the Discovery Channel, resources for teachers of science, humanities, and social studies. Includes lesson plans, email lists, and a schedule of upcoming science specials. You can buy educational and stimulating toys and gifts for children including telescopes, dinosaurs, videos, and books through the online store.

Education Index

http://www.educationindex.com/

Huge collection of links to the best education-based Web sites. Browse by subject or life stage, hang out in the Coffee Shop with your pals, or play around with Web Weasel.

Microsoft Education

http://www.microsoft.com/education/

The Microsoft Education Web site is an online resource for school technology coordinators and educators. Offers articles, solutions, ideas, and resources for schools building connected learning communities and integrating technology in the classroom.

Scholastic.com

http://www.scholastic.com/

The home of the largest publisher of children's books in the world, including the Harry Potter series, Scholastic.com provides an excellent learning kiosk for parents, teachers, and children. Scholastic's goal is to instill the love of reading

and learning for lifelong pleasure in all children. This site is well designed and packed with high-quality content.

The Science Source

http://thesciencesource.com/

Manufactures and sells more than 300 items for teaching physics, physical science, chemistry, biology, environmental science, and design technology. High-quality innovative science and technology teaching materials.

K–12– EDUCATIONAL TELEVISION

The Discovery Channel

http://www.discovery.com

Cable channel covering history, technology, nature, exploration, and science-related issues. The site has special feature sections and "did you know" facts that make it a unique experience. Includes the standard programming schedules and sections on kid-related programming.

The Learning Channel

http://tlc.com/

Cable channel devoted to programming about history, science, and world culture, as well as commercial-free programs for preschoolers. Site includes programming schedules and information about upcoming shows. Shopping links take you to the Discovery Store.

A B C D E F G H I J K L M N O P Q R S T U V W X Y Z

Schoolhouse Rock

http://disney.go.com/
disneyvideos/animatedfilms/
schoolhouserock/

Remember these campy '70s edu-cartoons? Well, so does Disney. Soon you will be able to purchase a DVD with all your favorite Schoolhouse Rock cartoons. For now, however, you can cast a vote for your favorite tune here at Disney's Schoolhouse Rock site.

Stephen Hawking's Universe

http://www.pbs.org/wnet/hawking/

The show, on PBS, addresses the big bang theories, why the universe is the way it is, where we come from, and other cosmic questions in an entertaining way accessible to all adult audiences. The site includes a schedule of programs, teacher's guide, and a Strange Stuff Explained section, which discusses black holes and antimatter, among other topics.

K–12—HOMEWORK HELP

About Homework/Study Tips

http://homeworkhelp.about.com/

General information to help students develop productive homework attitudes and study habits, plus specific help for various subjects. Links to reference materials, study tools, and information about tutors.

Algebra Online

http://www.algebra-online.com

This interactive algebra forum, maintained by Samuel D. Glick and contributors, is a boon for anyone interested in solving the value of x.

California State Science Fair

http://www.usc.edu/CSSF/
Resources/GettingStarted.html

A great supporting resource for any student considering entering a science fair, and for any parent who's been requested to help. There are ideas for getting started, information about judging, and plenty of other science links to look through.

Dictionary.com

http://www.dictionary.com/

A complete resource library on the Web, this site features a searchable dictionary, thesaurus, medical dictionary, translator, grammar and style guide, and foreign language dictionaries. Toss those tomes in a tomb, and look stuff up online!

Homework Helper Page

http://www.geocities.com/Athens/
Parthenon/7726/

This page was created for all students on the Web by a Collingwood, West Vancouver parent. This site is a great place to research K–12 materials. Also be sure to investigate the "enrichment" Web sites, which are continually updated.

Researchpaper.com

http://www.researchpaper.com

Educators, students, and anyone engaged in basic research will want to give an apple to the folks at Researchpaper.com. Here, students can find a plethora of assistance in finding a research topic and developing essays and reports on a wide variety of topics.

K–12–PRIVATE EDUCATION

Peterson's Education Center

http://iiswinprd01.petersons.com/pschools/

Find day and boarding schools by name, location, or type of program. Or identify schools to meet your child's special needs. A rich database of information, including help on financing a private education. You can purchase books about colleges and how to apply as well as information to help you prepare for college through the online store.

PRESCHOOL

Education World

http://www.education-world.com/

Education World's stated goal is "to make it easy for educators to integrate the Internet into the classroom." The site offers articles, lesson plans, school information, employment listings, links, and other resources for educators of preschoolers through older children. Offers a search engine that searches 500,000 education-specific sites.

Family Education Network

http://www.familyeducation.com

A resource for families to learn more about encouraging children to learn. There are child development Q&As, links to other educational sites, ideas to get your child to read, and many other useful ideas for helping your child get ready for and succeed at school. You can buy books, videos, software, toys, and games through various vendors who advertise at this site.

SuperKids Software Review

http://www.superkids.com/aweb/pages/reviews/early/_3/elmopre/merge.shtml

Provides full reviews of educational software for early learners and older students. The reviews are written by teams of parents, teachers, and kids. Summary ratings of the titles include educational value, kid appeal, and ease of use.

RESOURCES

Infonation

http://www.un.org/Pubs/CyberSchoolBus/infonation/e_infonation.htm

The next time you or your child needs to do a report on a specific country, this is the first site you should visit. Compare data within the countries of the United Nations, including urban growth, top exports, and threatened species. A great resource for adults and kids.

infoplease.com

http://www.infoplease.com/

A huge library of reference material, including biographies, history, government facts, atlases, almanacs, encyclopedias, dictionaries, current events, and more.

Peterson's Education Center

http://www.petersons.com

Seeks to catalog all United States K–12 schools, colleges, and universities, both public and private, as well as community and technical colleges. Links to study guides for passing standardized tests, plus some free tips, strategies, and sample questions. Some excellent information on career and college planning.

A B C D E F G H I J K L M N O P Q R S T U V W X Y Z

A
B
C
D
E
F
G
H
I
J
K
L
M
N
O
P
Q
R
S
T
U
V
W
X
Y
Z

Web 66

http://web66.coled.umn.edu

Seeks to be a catalyst that integrates the Internet into K–12 school curricula. Facilitates the introduction of Internet technology into K–12 schools by helping them set up servers, design home pages, and find other online schools.

Web66: K–12 Schools Registry

http://web66.coled.umn.edu/schools.html

Consists of a clickable map of the United States, Canada, and Mexico; and each click takes you to a different region's online schools. Provides the same information in a text format. Also offers school listings by country. Helps find keypals or partners for an online project.

Web of On-Line Dictionaries

http://www.yourdictionary.com/

This Web site lists free and subscription online dictionaries and thesauri containing words and phrases to help students locate the best word to use.

ELECTRONICS

Best Buy

http://www.bestbuy.com

The number one specialty retailer of consumer electronics, personal computers, entertainment software, and appliances in the United States. Compare products, get coupons and rebate forms, shop, and rent DVDs online.

Circuit City

http://www.circuitcity.com/

This consumer electronics retailer offers products in a number of categories, including home video and audio, car audio, digital cameras, phone, games, computers, and movie and music titles. Before buying, however, you'll want to read purchasing tips, check out product comparisons, and scan online reviews.

Best **Electronics.cnet.com**

http://electronics.cnet.com

Get gift ideas, review product reviews, find out which are editors' choices, and select from a long list of product categories—from TVs to DVD players to MP3 players, digital cameras, handheld devices, and much more. Very current information presented in an easily accessible format makes this an easy pick for the best of the best award.

Radio Shack

http://www.radioshack.com/

Radio Shack is still one of the leaders in consumer electronics. Find out about its many products, including minisatellite TVs, toys, cellular services, and home security. Also get the details on the international franchise program and employment opportunities.

ShopNow

http://www.internetmall.com/

Huge online mall where you can shop for just about anything at hundreds of stores. When you reach the mall, click the Electronics link to view links for various electronics shops in the mall.

Tek Discount Warehouse

http://tekgallery.com/

Tek offers an enormous supply of appliances and electronics and promises a substantial savings from the manufacturer's suggested retail price. Products include stereo (home, car, and personal), microwaves, electric razors, camcorders, fax machines, telephones, copiers, digital cameras, vacuum cleaners, and much more. Order online or use the toll-free telephone number. The company promises quick ship times and a variety of payment methods.

EMERGENCY SERVICES

Best **American Red Cross**

http://www.redcross.org/

The jewel in the emergency services crown, the Red Cross exists to aid disaster victims and help people prevent and prepare for emergencies. Find out about the organization's current interests, locations in which it is currently helping disaster victims, and how to volunteer. Whether you're a victim of a terrible tragedy, or are looking for a way to contribute to your community and lessen someone else's suffering, you must visit this site.

A
B
C
D
E
F
G
H
I
J
K
L
M
N
O
P
Q
R
S
T
U
V
W
X
Y
Z

ENVIRONMENTAL AND GLOBAL ISSUES

CONSERVATION

 Arbor Day Foundation

http://www.arborday.com

Learn how you can help the environment by planting a tree in your community. Learn about the many Arbor Day programs for supplying trees to communities and educating the population about the importance of trees. You can find out what kinds of trees will do well in your area just by entering your ZIP Code. You can order a wide variety of trees from this site at discount prices with proceeds going to the foundation. Make a difference in your community by checking out this best of the best site.

National Audubon Society

http://www.audubon.org/

Get background information on the society, its namesake John James Audubon, and his natural art. Find your local chapter and get membership information. You can even join online.

National Oceanic and Atmospheric Administration

http://www.noaa.gov

Get the full story, complete with pictures, of some of the nation's natural disasters, from tornadoes in the Midwest to forest fires burning out of control on the West Coast. The NOAA has pictures and information on what's going on. An educational site with great pictures.

National Wildlife Federation

http://www.nwf.org/

Remember Ranger Rick magazine? Well, it's still being published by the NWF, which works to protect and teach people about nature and wildlife. At the site, you can learn about the work of this organization and how to support it, as well as order publications such as Ranger Rick, and introduce kids to the KidZone, where they'll learn more about the wild.

ECOLOGY

Greenpeace

http://www.greenpeace.org/

Promoter of biodiversity and enemy of ecological and environmental pollution, Greenpeace and its links are accessible through this site. Links include the biodiversity campaign, the North Sea oil rig tour, a hot page, and more.

Sierra Club

http://www.sierraclub.org/

Home page for the nonprofit public interest conservation organization. Site focuses on activist news, current critical "ecoregions," and the Sierra Club National Outings Program, as well as an internal Sierra Club search engine.

PRESERVATION

The Whale Museum's Orca Adoption Program

http://whale-museum.org

What better way to "save the whales" than to adopt one? By adopting Ralph, Saratoga, Missy, Princess Angeline, Deadhead, Raven, or any of the number of orcas that swim the waters of Puget Sound and southern British Columbia, you'll be supporting orca research and education.

ETIQUETTE

[Best] Good Housekeeping Advice

http://magazines.ivillage.com/goodhousekeeping

This is the index site for several Good Housekeeping advice columns, including Peggy Post's "Etiquette for Today." Search the list by topic, or just scroll through all the questions. If you have a question of your own, send it to Peggy via email. When you're ready to learn more about etiquette, there's no better site to start.

The Original Tipping Page

http://www.tipping.org/TopPage.shtml

How much do you tip a skycap at the airport? This site gives recommended tipping standards for 10 different service categories, covering dozens of different service workers and situations. Includes ushers at sports arenas, manicurists, cruise ship cabin boys, and much more. New software for Palm computers is equipped with a tip calculator.

A
B
C
D
E
F
G
H
I
J
K
L
M
N
O
P
Q
R
S
T
U
V
W
X
Y
Z

A
B
C
D
E
F
G
H
I
J
K
L
M
N
O
P
Q
R
S
T
U
V
W
X
Y
Z

EXERCISE AND FITNESS

FITNESS

 Fitness Online

http://www.fitnessonline.com/

The online home of Weider Productions, Inc., publisher of Flex, Men's Fitness, Natural Health, and other magazines, this site features an incredible wealth of information organized in an easy-to-navigate format. Links to exercise, nutrition, and health lead to articles on each subject. An online trainer, fitness calculators, and forums make this the best fitness site on the Web.

RUNNING

New York City Marathon

http://www.nyrrc.org/nyrrc/mar01/index.html

New York Road Runners Club maintains this site with information on the New York City Marathon. It includes application information, a course description, advice on how to train for a marathon, and more.

Running on Full

http://www.lifematters.com/rofintro.html

Running on Full is a reference to running while pregnant. This site's focus is to support women runners who are pregnant or contemplating it. Visitors will find lots of general pregnancy exercise and nutrition information. Special sections are devoted to running and pregnancy and also running and breastfeeding.

Terry Fox Foundation

http://www.terryfoxrun.org/

The Terry Fox Foundation offers pledge and participation information for this annual Canadian cancer research benefit. Also includes a brief biography of Terry Fox and information about the foundation.

WEIGHTLIFTING AND BODYBUILDING

 International Powerlifting Federation

http://www.powerlifting-ipf.com/

Everything a powerlifter needs to know about training, competition, and classification. A great site with tons of links! This site includes a link to the technical rulebook in PDF format as well as information on refereeing. There is information on the federation including the constitution and the bylaws.

EXTREME SPORTS

[Best] Boardz

http://www.boardz.com

Boardz is an online board sports magazine providing entertainment and information for board riders of all kinds, including snowboarders, skateboarders, surfers, skiers, and wakeboarders. In addition to chat and sports-specific information, you can also find surf forecasts and snow reports. Boarders visiting this site will soon realize why it's the best of the best.

HANG GLIDING

All About Hang Gliding

http://
www.all-about-hang-gliding.com/

Comprehensive resource for learning everything you need to know to begin hang gliding and improve your technique and enjoyment of hang gliding. Great collection of books, CDs, and videos you can purchase right online. Includes a Getting Started FAQ, photo and video galleries, a list of places to fly organized by state, lists of clubs and organizations, and much more.

SKYDIVING

[Best] DropZone

http://www.dropzone.com/

When looking for skydiving information on the Web, this is the first site you should drop in on. Here, you'll find an incredible collection of articles and interviews on skydiving, profiles of skydivers, a list of drop zones, photo and video galleries, discussion forums, calendar of events and upcoming competitions, and even an auction site where you can buy and sell equipment.

Skydive!

http://www.afn.org/skydive/

This excellent resource for skydiving enthusiasts is full of photos, FAQs, recommended places to skydive, skydiving humor, the sport's history and culture, the latest safety and equipment, training, links to other skydivers, and more. Also includes specific skydiving disciplines such as BASE jumping, paraskiing, relative work and canopy relative work, freestyle, VRW, and sit-flying. It is one of the most extensive Web sites available on skydiving and definitely a "don't miss" for any serious skydiver.

EYE CARE

〔Best〕 **American Academy of Ophthalmology**

http://www.aao.org/

This site provides all the information you would need in the field of eye care—from finding an ophthalmologist near you to keeping up with recent news stories pertaining to your eyesight, to career options for students interested in the field. You can also purchase educational modules for ophthalmologists as well as other doctors and allied healthcare workers on CD-ROM or in print through the online store. Other items available for purchase include kits to start your own practice.

FASHION

ELLE.com

http://www.elle.com/

Self-described as a "complement and counterpart to the magazine," this French fashion site provides a more intellectual, sophisticated approach to fashion, beauty, and style. In addition to being packed with beauty and fashion tips, ELLE.com goes behind the scenes in the fashion industry to provide readers with hands-on techniques and the best fashion secrets. The Shop link provides links to other sites where you can purchase items online.

STYLE.com

http://www.style.com

Home of Vogue magazine's online fashion forum, this site features fashion advice for the chic. Includes information on the latest styles, model and celebrity profiles, and fashion tips. Visit this site to keep up on the latest fashion and lifestyle trends.

 Best

ZOOZOOM.com Magazine

http://www.zoozoom.com

Intriguing, refreshing online fashion magazine goes beyond fashion to explore the interconnectedness of art, culture, society, and other human factors in the evolution of fashion. Very cutting edge, this site presents various fashion concepts and designs in slide-show format. Also features profiles of some of the top fashion designers. Easy pick for the best of the best award.

FINANCE AND INVESTMENT

About Credit

http://credit.about.com/

Learn how high-interest loans can torpedo your personal finances. Reduce and eliminate your personal debt by budgeting and consolidation.

Huge collection of articles dealing not only with credit management but also with personal and family finances, living a frugal lifestyle, investing, and planning for retirement.

A
B
C
D
E
F
G
H
I
J
K
L
M
N
O
P
Q
R
S
T
U
V
W
X
Y
Z

Money Magazine's Money 101 Tutorial

http://money.cnn.com/pf/101/

Money magazine's step-by-step tutorial on how to take control of your personal finances consists of 25 lessons covering everything from drawing up a budget to investing in stocks. Learn how to plan for retirement, save for a child's education, finance a new home, reduce your tax burden, and much more. When you decide to start taking control of your finances, be sure to bookmark this site, and return to it often for advice and ideas.

BONDS

 Bond Market Association

http://www.investinginbonds.com

Read about what percentage of your portfolio should be in bonds, run through the investors' checklist to determine whether you should invest in bonds, learn about the different types of bonds, and stay updated on current bond prices at this site. If the stock market frightens you, or you're just looking for investments that are a little less risky, this is the site for you.

INVESTMENT CLUBS

Motley Fool's Guide to Investment Clubs

http://www.fool.com/
InvestmentClub/
InvestmentClubIntroduction.htm

Excellent tutorial on investment clubs by two savvy, but motley fools. Explains what an investment

club is, why they're useful, how to join an existing club or create your own, and much more. Even discusses potential pitfalls. A must read for anyone considering joining an investment club.

INVESTMENT INFORMATION

10K Wizard

http://www.10kwizard.com

Online financial toolbox packed with tools designed to gather data concerning various companies whose stock is traded publicly. 10K Wizard, originally designed to help users search the SEC database, provides additional search tools for grabbing data from a multitude of online databases. Other products include the Portfolio Wizard, for helping you track your stocks, and a free trial of Hoover's Online, for gaining additional insights from professional analysts.

Hoover's Online

http://www.hoovers.com

A great research tool for investors. Hoover's provides company profiles plus free access to records on public and private companies. Here you can find out how well a company has done in the past.

Investor's Business Daily

http://www.investors.com/

Investor's Business Daily is a magazine focusing on issues important to today's investor. On this site you can read today's Investor's Business Daily. IBD also offers access to a free online IBD investment education course.

Kiplinger

http://kiplinger.com/

Kiplinger puts financial events in perspective on a daily basis. Stock quotes, mutual fund rankings, financial FAQs, financial calculators, and interactive resources are available.

[Best] Motley Fool

http://www.fool.com/

The Motley Fool is a well-known online financial forum originating on America Online. This is the Motley Fool's home on the Web. The Fool provides individual investors with investment tips and advice. The Motley Fool Web site offers The Fool's School, an online investment guide that is subtitled "13 Steps to Investing Foolishly." When you're ready to start investing "foolishly," visit this best of the best site.

Silicon Investor

http://www.siliconinvestor.com/index.gsp

Consists of five innovative areas for technology investors: Stocktalk, Market Tools, Market Insight, Customize, and Portfolio. These areas enable you to participate in discussion forums, create individual charts and comparison charts, view company profiles, get quotes and other financial information, and track your portfolio.

Wall Street City

http://www.wallstreetcity.com

Telescan's Wall Street City is a next-generation financial Web site, where you can get the answers to your investment questions. Custom design your own stock and mutual fund searches with the most powerful search engine in the world,

covering more than 700 different criteria. You can access real-time and delayed quotes on more than 300,000 domestic and international securities, and run full technical analysis on stock graphs from 1 day to 23 years.

MUTUAL FUNDS

Brill's Mutual Funds Interactive

http://www.brill.com/features.html

Features articles on what's happening in the mutual fund industry, including topics such as "Investing for Retirement" and "The Best Choices in Variable Annuities."

Dreyfus Corporation

http://www.dreyfus.com

The Dreyfus Online Information Center provides listings and descriptions of some of the mutual funds offered by Dreyfus, along with the Dreyfus services. The site provides information that can help investors get a clearer sense of the direction to take to meet their investment objectives. In addition to general information on investing, you will also find current economic commentaries on the financial markets updated weekly by Dreyfus portfolio managers.

Janus Funds

http://ww4.janus.com/

Janus Funds provides access to information on the funds they manage. You can check your funds' latest share price and account value 24 hours a day, seven days a week. You can also find projected year-end dividends for each fund. All account information is accessed through security-enhanced Web pages utilizing SSL (Secure Sockets Layer).

A
B
C
D
E
F
G
H
I
J
K
L
M
N
O
P
Q
R
S
T
U
V
W
X
Y
Z

A
B
C
D
E
F
G
H
I
J
K
L
M
N
O
P
Q
R
S
T
U
V
W
X
Y
Z

Putnam Investments

http://www.putnaminvestments.com

Get the latest news on new Putnam funds, decide whether a Roth IRA is for you, and find out how well your Putnam investment is doing.

ONLINE TRADING

American Express Financial Direct

http:// finance.americanexpress.com/

Trade online using the brokerage services of American Express. The fee is $19.95 on most trades, but fees vary depending on your account balance and the number of shares traded. At the site, you can also conduct research and stay updated on market moves.

⟦Best⟧ Ameritrade

http://www.ameritrade.com

Ameritrade provides quotes, account access, and online trading for independent investors. Ameritrade also provides discount brokering services. Their $8-per-trade rate is one of the best available on the Internet. Although Ameritrade lacks some of the in-depth research tools you might find from some of the more professional investment services, such as Schwab, Ameritrade makes online stock transactions easy and inexpensive. (Datek and Ameritrade merged early in the year 2002, so don't be surprised if your Web browser redirects you to another site when you enter the preceding address.)

Datek Online

http://www.datek.com

Sign up for free real-time quotes and trades of up to 5,000 shares for $9.99. The site also provides news, a learning center that can teach you the basics of online investing, and access to a help desk for questions. (Datek and Ameritrade merged early in the year 2002, so don't be surprised if your Web browser redirects you to another site when you enter the preceding address.)

E*Trade

http://www.etrade.com/

E*Trade is another online trading service geared toward the individual investor. With E*Trade, you can buy and sell securities online for NYSE, AMEX, and NASDAQ. Stock performance information and company information is available. $14.95 per trade.

HARRISdirect

http://www.harrisdirect.com/

HARRISdirect (formerly CSFB Direct, which was formerly DLJ Direct) is one of the most popular financial sites on the Net. HARRISdirect offers online trading, real-time quotes and news, research, and portfolio tracking. At $20 per trade, commissions using HARRISdirect are higher than some services, but HARRISdirect features more information and research tools than other services.

Morgan Stanley Dean Witter

http://
www.morganstanleyindividual.com/

A nice all-around solid site, with online trading available, as well as educational tools, mutual fund research, IPO information, market news, and the option to open a free, no-fee IRA. On this site, you can also track your checking and savings accounts as well as your credit cards.

FINANCIAL AID AND SCHOLARSHIPS

Embark

http://www.embark.com

One-stop information and resource center for helping students research institutes of higher education, prepare for entrance, explore financing options, and apply for admission and financial aid. Also provides services for colleges and universities to help in recruiting top students and services for businesses to locate qualified college graduates. High school college counselors will want to check out this site, as well.

⟦Best⟧ eStudentLoan.com

http://www.estudentloan.com

Compare student loans online to find the best deal for you. After completing the online application, you will be provided with 12 loan programs that meet your criteria. After you've selected one, you can complete the loan application

online, too. This one-stop approach to student loans makes this site an easy choice for the best of the best designation.

FinAid!

http://www.finaid.org

A huge site with information about applying to college and financing it. You can locate scholarships, calculate what you'll need to attend, learn about other ways to finance your studies, such as military service, and download financial aid application forms.

United Negro College Fund

http://www.uncf.org

Download program and scholarship information to learn more about money available through the United Negro College Fund. There is information about qualifying for a scholarship, as well as background facts about the organization itself.

A
B
C
D
E
F
G
H
I
J
K
L
M
N
O
P
Q
R
S
T
U
V
W
X
Y
Z

FISHING

eders.com

http://www.eders.com/

Choose to learn more about salt- or freshwater fishing through forums and tips at this site, which also has an extensive online catalog of fishing and hunting gear. Check out the huge online shopping area! Categories including Archery, Clothing, Camping, and Marine make it easy to browse the aisles and find what you need.

United States Fish and Wildlife Service

http://www.fws.gov/

The FWS, a division of the Department of the Interior, created this site to tell you a little about itself. Find out what the group does to protect endangered species, and learn what the government—and you—can do to keep your old fishing hole clean and healthy.

FOOD AND DRINK

Coca-Cola

http://www.coca-cola.com

Provides information about the most renowned soft drink company. Buy, sell, and trade Coca-Cola paraphernalia online. Check out Coca-Cola–sponsored sporting events. See how Coca-Cola is doing in the business world before you decide to buy some stock in soft drinks.

Fulton Street Lobster & Seafood Co.

http://www.fultonstreet.com/

Fulton Street means gourmet lobster, shrimp, crab legs, steak, seafood, and more! Order online; 24-hour delivery guaranteed.

Live Lobsters and Clambakes

http://www.lobster-clambake.com/

Live lobsters and clambakes shipped overnight via Federal Express.

Pickles, Peppers, Pots & Pans

http://www.p4online.com/

Cooking and specialty foods superstore. Featuring Calphalon, ScanPan, AllClad, Wusthof, Essence of Emeril, and much more.

⌐Best⌐ **Wet Planet Beverages**

http://www.wetplanet.com/

One of the best wet sites on the Web now. With the advantage of having a computer-oriented core audience of jacked up geeks, Global Beverage presents a Java-powered site featuring information on its carbonated beverages: Jolt, Pirate's Keg, DNA, and more. Its excellent product line, excellent site design, and incredible graphics combine to make this the best food and drink site on the Web.

ALCOHOL

MixedDrink.com

http://www.mixed-drink.com/

Don't know how to mix up your favorite drink? This site offers a comprehensive guide to making and serving mixed drinks.

The Pierre Smirnoff Company

http://www.smirnoff.com/

Try one of the Smirnoff cocktail recipes. Learn about the history of Smirnoff, the distillation process, and the ingredients. Read about the relationship of James Bond with Smirnoff by viewing downloadable files. Submit stories about the hippest place you've found to sample Smirnoff, your favorite Smirnoff combinations, or where in the world you have enjoyed your Smirnoff and what you were doing at the time.

COFFEES AND TEAS

Cafe Maison Coffee Roasters

http://gourmetcoffeeroaster.com/

What makes Cafe Maison gourmet coffees different from all other coffee roasters? They adhere to the 21 Day Rule, telling you the exact date of the roast and reminding you that coffee is fresh for only 21 days after roasting. Plus, Cafe Maison uses only authentic extracts and essences to flavor their coffee--never sugar syrups! Select the Coffee Roastery option, and you'll be guided through the process of ordering your own custom-roasted coffee.

Peet's Coffee & Tea

http://www.peets.com/

Order online for home delivery. Visitors to this site can browse through journal entries from travel writers as they search for fine coffees and teas. Also includes a page called Coffee Wisdom for tips on how to brew the best cup of java possible.

ORGANIC FOODS

GAIAM.com Lifestyle Company

http://www.gaiam.com/

This site sells natural and organic foods and beverages, as well as healthcare products, while offering information on the benefit of such purchases. There is also a database to research organic products and issues. A nicely designed site.

A
B
C
D
E
F
G
H
I
J
K
L
M
N
O
P
Q
R
S
T
U
V
W
X
Y
Z

A
B
C
D
E
F
G
H
I
J
K
L
M
N
O
P
Q
R
S
T
U
V
W
X
Y
Z

WINES

Food & Wine Magazine

http://www.foodandwine.com/

You can find wines, foods, recipes, and more at this colorful, comprehensive site. Be sure to check out the store where you can purchase everything from mustard to cookbooks.

Gruppo Italiano Vini

http://www.gruppoitalianovini.com/

This company not only produces and distributes Italian wine, it also manages historic wine cellars. See where the cellars are located on a map of Italy, and read about company news and information.

Into Wine

http://www.intowine.com

Explore the world of wine with the M2 Communications Wine Education Center.

K&L Wine Merchants

http://www.klwines.com

Named as the best wine shop on the Internet by Money magazine and one of the top 10 wine retailers in the nation by the publishers of the Wine Spectator.

[Best] Robin Garr's Wine Lovers Page

http://www.wine-lovers-page.com/

Frequently updated notes and advice on wines of good value are backed by an online wine-tasting tutorial, wine FAQs, vintage charts, interactive discussions, and more. Click the Wine Chat link to learn about upcoming chat sessions with respected wine connoisseurs. Wine questionnaire, wine lexicon, wine-grape glossary, and other resources, make this the most comprehensive wine site on the Web.

Wine Searcher

http://www.wine-searcher.com/

Wine-searcher is designed to help wine enthusiasts find reputable Web-based dealers that carry their favorite wines. Merchants place their lists on Wine-searcher so the wines can be more easily found via this site than with traditional Internet searches. Each offer is dated and is either updated or removed at regular intervals.

Wine Spectator

http://www.winespectator.com

Find answers to nearly every question you can think up about wine and wine tasting. There's a searchable database of wine information, wine ratings, news, a library, and forums. Links to retail sites that specialize in wine and wine-related products.

Wine.com

http://www.wine.com/

Home to the largest wine retailer in the United States, Wine.com features a huge wine cellar with a selection of over 5,000 wines. Here, you can find wine reviews, a FAQ list, accessories, gift certificates, special deals, and more.

Wines on the Internet

http://www.wines.com/

An excellent resource for wine-related topics. Provides links to online wineries and vineyards, features a virtual tasting room, and other notes of interest for the connoisseur and novice wine drinker alike. Also details upcoming events for wine enthusiasts and links to reputable online wine sellers.

 National Football League

http://www.nfl.com3

Get the latest information on every team, every player, and every game from the official NFL site. You can find statistics and scores, play fantasy football online, and even sign up for the official NFL email newsletter. Ticket information is also available, although tickets to games are not available from this site. You can even get information about international NFL. Links to other football-related sites. For the best that football has to offer, this is the site for you.

AFC Web Sites

Baltimore Ravens:
http://www.ravenszone.net/

Buffalo Bills:
http://www.buffalobills.com/

Cincinnati Bengals:
http://www.bengals.com/

Cleveland Browns:
http://www.clevelandbrowns.com/

Denver Broncos:
http://www.denverbroncos.com/

Houston Texans:
http://www.houstontexans.com/

Indianapolis Colts:
http://www.colts.com/

Jacksonville Jaguars:
http://www.jaguars.com/

Kansas City Chiefs:
http://www.kcchiefs.com/

Miami Dolphins:
http://www.miamidolphins.com/

New England Patriots:
http://www.patriots.com/

New York Jets:
http://www.newyorkjets.com/

Oakland Raiders:
http://www.raiders.com/

Pittsburgh Steelers:
http://www.steelers.com/

San Diego Chargers:
http://www.chargers.com/

Tennessee Titans:
http://www.titansonline.com/

A B C D E F G H I J K L M N O P Q R S T U V W X Y Z

NFC Web Sites

Arizona Cardinals:
http://www.azcardinals.com/

Atlanta Falcons:
http://www.atlantafalcons.com/

Carolina Panthers:
http://www.panthers.com/

Chicago Bears:
http://www.chicagobears.com/

Dallas Cowboys:
http://www.dallascowboys.com/

Detroit Lions:
http://www.detroitlions.com/

Green Bay Packers:
http://www.packers.com/

Minnesota Vikings:
http://www.vikings.com/

New Orleans Saints:
http://www.neworleanssaints.com/

New York Giants:
http://www.giants.com/

Philadelphia Eagles:
http://www.philadelphiaeagles.com/

San Francisco 49ers:
http://www.sf49ers.com/

St. Louis Rams:
http://www.stlouisrams.com/

Seattle Seahawks:
http://www.seahawks.com/

Tampa Bay Buccaneers:
http://www.buccaneers.com/

Washington Redskins:
http://www.redskins.com/

FOREIGN POLICY

 Carnegie Council on Ethics and International Affairs

http://www.cceia.org

Carnegie Council is an independent, nonpartisan, nonprofit organization dedicated to increasing the understanding of ethics and international affairs. Obtain edited transcripts and articles from the Council's "Ethics of the New War" forum, access interviews and book reviews, check out the online forums, and much more. You can order past issues and other publications online. This site's excellent design and top-notch information make it an easy choice as best of the best.

The United Nations

http://www.un.org/

Home page of the United Nations. Six languages to choose from and five categories of information to select from: Peace and Security, International Law, Humanitarian Affairs, Human Rights, and Economic and Social Development. Find out more about every facet of the UN.

FRUGAL SPENDING

[Best] Cheapskate Monthly

http://www.cheapskatemonthly.com/

Get your daily tip for debt-free living at this site, which also features a radio interview with author Mary Hunt, the site's creator. By joining the site and buying a subscription to her debt-free living newsletter, you'll also gain access to discussion boards and get even more information about saving money. You can purchase books written by Hunt and other money experts that offer more creative ways to live a frugal life. When you're ready to cut your expenses and live a simpler life, there's no better site for you.

eSmarts Newsletter

http://www.esmarts.com/

Each week, eSmarts publishes a newsletter full of great Internet deals, including new online shopping secrets, Internet coupons, and general shopping tips. By reading this newsletter every week, you can save hundreds, even thousands of dollars a year.

FUN SITES

Burning Man

http://www.burningman.com

Home of Burning Man, the famous and infamous annual personal-expression-art-fair-and-mayhem ritual, where more than 25,000 participants gather in the desert every summer to form an interactive community, in which participants do some pretty weird stuff. Visit this site to learn more about Burning Man and what it means to its various participants. The unique Burning Man concept combined with some excellent graphics and interesting articles make this best of the best site not only fun but also intriguing.

Shibumi

http://www.shibumi.org/eoti.htm

This is the site that every Web surfer has been looking for.

GAMES AND PUZZLES

Apple Corps

http://apple-corps.westnet.com/apple_corps.2.html

The game you lost all the pieces to as a child is back. Mr. Potato Head is here, under an online, noncopyrighted form, except now he's an apple. You are able to place eyes, nose, teeth, mouth, whatever, onto the apple. A new twist is also available—change the vegetable if you like.

Banja

http://www.banja.com

In this intriguing online, role-playing game, you take on the identity of Banja the Rasta, a hip islander who makes his way around a semi-inhabited island looking for hidden passages, useful tools, and other things that might make his adventure more rewarding. Check out this site and join in the fun!

Boxerjam.com

http://www.boxerjam.com/

Online game site where you can play against the computer or against other people at the site. Compete on virtual game shows, play solitaire, or try your hand at some puzzles.

Chinook

http://www.cs.ualberta.ca/~chinook/

If checkers is your game, Chinook is your Web site. Beat Chinook and you will have outmaneuvered the world man-machine checkers champion.

EA.com

http://www.ea.com

Home of Electronic Arts, producers of some of the most popular video games, this site provides information about EA's product line plus gobs of free games divided into categories that include everything from board games and bingo to online video games and trivia contests.

The Fruit Game

http://www.2020tech.com/fruit/

Offers the challenging fruit game. Players remove fruit from the screen; the last player to remove fruit wins. Try this mathematical adventure.

Gamasutra

http://www.gamasutra.com

Catering to the game developer, this site is designed for serious video game players and creators. Here, you can learn about the latest trends in video games, find out more about what game players want, pick up some new design techniques, learn about the latest programs and technologies, and much more.

Best Games Domain

http://www.gamesdomain.com

Download demos, read news and interviews with leading game programmers as well as game reviews, and chat with fellow gamers here. You can also find cheats to a number of games, as well as find links to official game pages. Many online games are available here, too. Overall, this is a jam-packed site for the avid gamer, an easy best of the best pick!

GameSpy

http://www.gamespy.com

This site plays host to a huge collection of multiplayer arcade games and a popular gaming community. Join more than 4.4 million members worldwide playing nearly 300 of today's hottest games!

Gamesville

http://www.gamesville.lycos.com/

Gamesville is a huge online gaming site, where visitors can play games against the computer or against each other. Play for cash prizes or play for fun. Plenty of links to online casinos, too.

IGN

http://www.ign.com

News, codes, reviews, previews, features, releases, hardware, contests, a game store, affiliates, links to subscribing to magazines, and more. This site is geared for serious gamers.

Kids Domain Online Games

http://www.kidsdomain.com/games/

Wide selection of games designed for fun and for educational purposes. Most games are for elementary-school kids. Plenty of trivia games that not only ask questions but present interesting facts in an engaging format. Excellent site for parents to introduce to their children.

Monopoly

http://www.monopoly.com

Pick up tips on winning at Monopoly, find out about upcoming Monopoly tournaments, learn about game news—such as a new token—and see the latest Monopoly merchandise at this site devoted to the famed board game.

MSN Game Zone

http://zone.msn.com/

Microsoft's gift to the gaming community, this high-tech site serves up a huge collection of free games broken down into categories which include Puzzle & Trivia, Card & Board, Zone Casino, Action & Strategy, and Sims & Sports. Free downloads and chat area populated by a very active community of gamers make this one of the best sites to play games on the Web.

Multiplayer Online Games Directory

http://www.mpogd.com/

A guide to the best multiplayer games. Game titles are broken down into categories ranging from action to sports. Game of the month poll helps you quickly identify the most popular games, and news headlines keep you abreast of the latest information in the online gaming world. Game reviews and other resources are also available.

The Ultimate Oracle: Pray Before the Head of Bob

http://www.resort.com/~banshee/Misc/8ball/

The online version of the legendary Magic Eight Ball. Ask Bob any question, and you are sure to get a response. You can even ask in several different languages.

A
B
C
D
E
F
G
H
I
J
K
L
M
N
O
P
Q
R
S
T
U
V
W
X
Y
Z

Who Wants to Be a Millionaire?

http://abc.abcnews.go.com/primetime/millionaire/millionaire_home.html

Play the online version of this popular TV game show and find out how to earn a spot as a contestant.

Yahoo! Games

http://games.yahoo.com

Excellent collection of multiplayer games. A very populous and active group of online gamers make this one of the best places to hang out and play checkers, chess, blackjack, poker, fantasy sports, and dozens of other games.

CHEAT CODES

GameWinners.com

http://www.gamewinners.com/

One of the most informative video game help sites on the Web, tips for more than 16,000 games played on nearly 50 different game systems. Features cheats, hints, FAQs, strategy guides, and gameshark codes. Links to game books and game stores for online shopping.

GARDENING AND LANDSCAPING

 Burpee Seeds Home Page

http://www.garden.com/

More than 12,000 products—plants, flowers, gardening supplies, accessories, and gifts. Gardening tips, an online magazine, and a 24-hour chat are also available. Membership and monthly newsletter are free. Whether you're a novice or expert gardener, you will find plenty to satisfy you at this best of the best site.

Cortesia Sanctuary and Center

http://www.cortesia.org/

This site is divided into five sections: The Cortesia Sanctuary Project (everything you need to know about creating a sanctuary), The Sanctuary Garden (gardening, garden products/books, garden inspiration, flower essences, composting, and so on), Music, Inspiration, and Publications & Products.

A
B
C
D
E
F
G
H
I
J
K
L
M
N
O
P
Q
R
S
T
U
V
W
X
Y
Z

Earthly Goods Online

http://www.earthlygoods.com/

Earthly Goods is a supplier of wild-flower seeds, wildflower seed mixtures, and grass seeds. Advice on growing from seeds, garden planning, and online ordering are a few of its features. Earthly Goods offers custom seed packets for advertising, fundraising, and special promotions.

Gardener's Supply Company

http://www.gardeners.com/

Huge mail-order gardening store now has a Web site where you can place your order online. Carries a wide variety of gardening tools and accessories designed to simplify your gardening experience, make it more enjoyable, and beautify your garden.

Gardenscape

http://www.gardenscape.on.ca/

Fine innovative garden products and accessories, including tools from companies such as Felco, Fiskars, Haws, and Dramm, and a unique line of gifts for gardeners.

National Gardening Association

http://www.garden.org

Gardeners will find the FAQs, tips, and reminders a great help, although the NGA was originally established to help foster gardening as a pastime. At the site, you'll find information on gardening programs in schools, available gardening grants, and other ways that the organization can help. Online shopping available through Red Barn Gardens.

New Jersey Weed Gallery

http://www.rce.rutgers.edu/weeds/

From Barnyardgrass to Yellow Rocket, an award-winning weed identification site from Rutgers University.

The Potting Shed

http://www.etera.com/

A free online gardening magazine containing information for the novice and the advanced gardener alike, including tips and how-to illustrations. You can buy everything from herbs to perennials here. This site is owned and operated by plant retailer, Etera.

Weekend Gardener

http://www.chestnut-sw.com/
weekend.htm

This site bills itself as the "Practical Horticulture for Busy People" site and contains everything from weather links to garden calendars and seed starting. The Weekend Gardener area has sections on starting your vegetable, flower, and herb seeds, plus a valuable calendar for when to do what. Participate in some interesting gardening forums on a wide variety of topics. Designed for the busy gardener.

A
B
C
D
E
F
G
H
I
J
K
L
M
N
O
P
Q
R
S
T
U
V
W
X
Y
Z

A
B
C
D
E
F
G
H
I
J
K
L
M
N
O
P
Q
R
S
T
U
V
W
X
Y
Z

GAY/LESBIAN/ BISEXUAL/TRANS

GayWired.com

http://www.gaywired.com/

One of the best sites focusing on the gay lifestyle, this site is packed with news, articles, profiles, travel information, business and financial information, and more. Read the latest on fitting into the gay culture or shop online.

PlanetOut

http://www.planetout.com/

Premier gay and lesbian Web site, features articles, photos, video clips, and products for the gay and lesbian community. By joining PlanetOut, you can post messages in numerous forums, chat online, create a member profile (with or without a photo of yourself), and subscribe to free newsletters.

COUNSELING

The Gay and Lesbian National Hotline

http://www.glnh.org/

A nonprofit organization dedicated to meeting the needs of the gay and lesbian community by offering free and totally anonymous information, referrals, and peer counseling. Offers a toll-free phone number that anyone can call for gay/lesbian support and information, and you can also submit email from their Web site and get a confidential reply.

GENERAL INFORMATION AND LINKS

Gay Men's Health Crisis

http://www.gmhc.org/

Find out more about the nation's oldest and largest not-for-profit AIDS organization: Gay Men's Health Crisis (GMHC), founded in 1981. Learn how you can get involved, get resources for support, access their AIDS Library, read about GMHC's latest efforts, and more.

GayScape

http://www.gayscape.com/

Specialized search tool for gay, lesbian, bisexual, and transgender sites on the Web. This search index lists more than 68,000 sites.

Queer Resources Directory (QRD)

http://www.qrd.org/qrd/

Widely thought to be the biggest and best gay and lesbian information source on the Internet, the Queer Resources Directory breaks down all kinds of resource information into easy-to-understand categories. You can surf the categories, or jump directly to the Resource Tree (http://www.qrd.org/qrd/www/tree.html).

HOME AND FAMILY

 Best **Parents, Families, and Friends of Gays and Lesbians (PFLAG)**

http://www.pflag.org/

PFLAG promotes the health and well-being of gay, lesbian, and bisexual persons, as well as their families and friends, through support, education, and advocacy. They provide counseling to help straight family and friends accept and support their gay and lesbian loved ones, and organize grassroots efforts to end discriminatory practices toward gays and lesbians. This site's excellent design and content combine to make it an easy best of the best pick.

MEDIA AND CULTURE

Women in the Arts

http://wiaonline.org/

WIA is the organization that produces the National Women's Music Festival, the oldest and largest all-indoor festival of women's music and culture (primarily lesbian) each June. Find out what they have in store for this year's festival, and learn more about this nonprofit organization.

POLITICAL AND LEGAL ISSUES

American Civil Liberties Union—Lesbian and Gay Rights

http://www.aclu.org/issues/gay/hmgl.html

A whole branch of the ACLU is devoted to lesbian and gay rights, and their section of the ACLU Web site provides updates on recent court rulings and bills coming up in Congress. You'll also find information about joining the ACLU here.

Gay and Lesbian Alliance Against Defamation (GLAAD)

http://www.glaad.org/org/index.html

GLAAD bills itself as "your online resource for promoting fair, accurate, and inclusive representation as a means of challenging discrimination based on sexual orientation or identity." If you or a gay or lesbian person you know has been the victim of discrimination or abuse, this is the group to contact to find out what you can do.

Human Rights Campaign

http://www.hrc.org/

The Human Rights Campaign is the United States's largest lesbian and gay political organization. They work to end discrimination, secure equal rights, and protect the health and safety of all Americans. This good-looking site contains a lot of political news for anyone interested in gay and lesbian issues.

A
B
C
D
E
F
G
H
I
J
K
L
M
N
O
P
Q
R
S
T
U
V
W
X
Y
Z

A
B
C
D
E
F
G
H
I
J
K
L
M
N
O
P
Q
R
S
T
U
V
W
X
Y
Z

PUBLICATIONS

The Advocate

http://www.advocate.com/

One of the oldest and most respected gay magazines. You can browse article summaries for the current issue here (but you have to buy the print edition for the full text), and participate in The Advocate's latest poll.

RELIGION

Unitarian Universalist Association

http://www.uua.org/main.html

The Unitarian Universalist Church is a "big tent" group that welcomes a wide variety of believers, including gay and lesbian people of all beliefs. Find out more about their organization at this page.

GENEALOGY

Ellis Island

http://www.ellisisland.org

If one of your ancestors passed through Ellis Island or the Port of New York on his or her way to becoming a United States citizen, chances are that this Web site can turn up a record of that person's arrival. At this site, you can search for and (optionally) purchase passenger documents that record a relative's arrival in the States. You can even build a family scrapbook online to share with other visitors or check out some family scrapbooks that other people have already constructed.

 Everton's Genealogical Helper

http://www.everton.com/

Search the genealogical database, buy products to help you in your research efforts, check out thousands of links listed here, and get help from others who've been at their search longer than you have. This site is packed with information and resources for novice and expert genealogists alike, making it our choice as the best genealogy site in the group.

FamilyTreeMaker.com

http://
familytreemaker.genealogy.com/

In addition to searchable databases and family-finder information, you can also access how-to information to help in your search, and buy genealogical products and reference material. FamilyTreeMaker is one of the most popular programs around for researching family history and constructing family trees.

Genealogy Pages

http://www.genealogypages.com/

The World's Premier Genealogy Portal is a search engine full of genealogy sites on the Internet. This site should be your first stop if you are doing genealogy research.

Geography World

http://members.aol.com/
bowermanb/101.html

Plenty of information for students studying geography—from homework help to background information on cultures and history of countries around the world. There is also climate, conservation, and calendar information, as well as geography games to enjoy.

[Best] National Geographic

http://
www.nationalgeographic.com/

Learn geography from the experts. Home of *National Geographic,* the magazine that has traveled the world and taught children and adults to appreciate geography,

nature, and various cultures for decades. Here, you will find online versions of *National Geographic's* award-winning photographs, plus the latest articles from around the globe. Special areas for kids, parents, and teachers. Easy to navigate and packed with great information, National Geographic is an obvious best of the best selection.

WorldAtlas.com

http://www.worldatlas.com/
aatlas/world.htm

Cool interactive globe. Click a continent and then a country to get a quick overview of its borders and geographical features plus a wealth of information about the country's economy, language, climate, currency, and more. Great resource for kids.

A
B
C
D
E
F
G
H
I
J
K
L
M
N
O
P
Q
R
S
T
U
V
W
X
Y
Z

A
B
C
D
E
F

H
I
J
K
L
M
N
O
P
Q
R
S
T
U
V
W
X
Y
Z

MAPS

David Rumsey Historical Map Collection

http://www.davidrumsey.com

With a focus on rare 18th and 19th century North and South American cartographic historical materials, this online collection features more than 6,400 maps which you can view using your Web browser, via Java, or by using a special GIS viewer which features map overlays. Collection also features historical maps of the world, Europe, Asia, and Africa. A great place for geography teachers to introduce students to cartography.

MapBlast

http://www.mapblast.com/mblast/

Vincinity Corporation's site that helps you create maps of your own. You can also get maps of popular destinations, such as major U.S. cities, national parks, state capitals, attractions, and U.S. regions.

Best MapQuest

http://www.mapquest.com/

$

Excellent and resourceful guide for those who are planning to travel in North America. Has travel guides, trip information, clickable maps, directions, and so much more. Share plans and tips with fellow vacationers, get relocation information, or order a road atlas on CD-ROM. When you're planning your next trip across town or across the country, don't forget to check out this site.

TIGER Mapping Service

http://tiger.census.gov/

Allows you to generate a high-quality, detailed map of anywhere in the United States using public geographic data. Maintained by the U.S. Census Department.

GIFTS

Best Gifts.com

http://www.gifts.com

$

Find great gifts and great gift ideas here. Seasonal gifts and ideas for special holidays are featured. You can find a large number of special gift ideas for him, for her, even for pet owners, for any occasion. Gifts range from plants to jewelry to gift baskets filled with food, wine, bath items, golf-related items, and more. Just about anything a gift giver could want can be found on this best of the best site!

giftsplash.com

http://www.giftsplash.com/

Huge collection of online gifts plus an innovative gift finder that provides you with a list of gift ideas based on the person's age, your relationship to the person, the desired price range, the occasion, and the person's hobbies or interests.

Hammacher Schlemmer

http://
www.hammacherschlemmer.com

Search for unusual gifts for business and personal gift-giving here.

MarthaStewart.com

http://www.marthastewart.com

Shop Martha By Mail for special gift ideas, as well as flowers, all from this site. She specializes in entertaining and keepsakes, so that's a lot of what you'll find here.

MuseumShop.com

http://www.museumshop.com/

Buy goods from a variety of well-known museums—and find out where to buy calendars for the new year. Store is well stocked with a variety of items, including jewelry, home and garden decor, sculpture, art prints and posters, books, stationery, clothing, and more. Excellent place to shop for the person who has everything.

Sharper Image

http://www.sharperimage.com

Select gifts from this catalog site, known for its unusual, harder-to-find personal and home items.

Spencer Gifts

http://www.spencergifts.com/home.asp

Looking for a gift that's out of the ordinary? Then check out Spencer Gifts's huge line of odd and irreverent gifts. Living dead dolls, bobble-head Spider-Man figurines, dorm room accessories (such as black lights and lava lamps), gag gifts, light-hearted birthday party accessories, erotic gifts, and more. Shop online, so you won't have to face the embarrassment of visiting the store in person.

A
B
C
D
E
F
G
H
I
J
K
L
M
N
O
P
Q
R
S
T
U
V
W
X
Y
Z

A
B
C
D
E
F
G
H
I
J
K
L
M
N
O
P
Q
R
S
T
U
V
W
X
Y
Z

GOLF

BadGolfMonthly.com

http://www.badgolfmonthly.com/

The golf site "for the golfer who really sucks," this site is more of a serious vacationer's guide to golf courses from TravelGolf.com. Some humorous articles provide a little levity for an otherwise frustrating sport.

Golfsmith

http://www.golfsmith.com/

Golfsmith International began more than 30 years ago and is now the largest direct marketer and superstore retailer of golf equipment in the world. They make and fit clubs and sell more than 20,000 different golf-related products. They even run their own golf academy.

⟦Best⟧ GolfWeb

http://www.golfweb.com/

Here you can access the regular golf stuff: tournament results, online pro shops, and so on. But you can also link to the Lesson Tee for golfing tips, go to a link for women in golf, and write a personal message to the winner of a current tournament. This site has an easily accessible design and is packed with useful information and golf tips, making it an easy selection as best golf site.

LPGA.com

http://www.Lpga.com

Get complete LPGA tournament coverage at the site, as well as an animated online lesson. You'll find schedules, player bios, headline golf news, and lots more about the LPGA at this official site.

PGA.com

http://www.pga.com/

PGA.com is the Official Web site of the PGA. PGA works with IBM as an alliance partner for the Web site. In addition, through IBM's role as official scoring and information system of the PGA, PGA.com continues to provide the world's best real-time golf event scoring system. PGA.com is one of the most highly trafficked golf sites on the Web, delivering millions of page views surrounding PGA major championships including the PGA Championship, Ryder Cup, PGA Seniors' Championship, and the MasterCard PGA Grand Slam of Golf.

GROCERIES

At Your Service

http://www.internetgroceries.com/default.asp

Buy your groceries, plus find recipes and nutritional guides at this site. Links to Internet florists and online electronic retailers.

Marsh Supermarket

http://www.marsh.net/

One of Indiana's largest grocery store chains, Marsh has always featured high-quality products and service, and now it even offers online grocery shopping. Just register with Marsh and pick the items you want to purchase. Marsh assembles your order, and you can either pick it up or have it delivered to your door. You can also visit this site to learn about weekly specials, obtain coupons, find recipes, and check out community events.

Best NetGrocer

http://www.netgrocer.com/

Thousands of food and general merchandise products to choose from. A great way to make sure your mother, grandmother, or child in college gets the food they need, no matter where you live. Just shop for food at NetGrocer and enter their shipping information at the checkout page. You can even set up a recurring order that sends your shipment to their house at an interval you choose. With this best of the best site, you may never need to go grocery shopping again!

Your Grocer.com

http://www.yourgrocer.com/

Bulk online groceries for Manhattan and Connecticut.

GYMNASTICS

Best GymWorld.com

http://www.gymworld.com/

Find a coach or a camp, read gymnastics news, or join technical discussion groups. Online ordering for gymnastics merchandise is available. Use gymnastics animations to learn about common mistakes, read tips on training, vote in monthly polls, and participate in discussions. Whether you're a gymnast, parent of a budding gymnast, or a fan of gymnastics, this site is a must-visit.

A
B
C
D
E
F
G
H
I
J
K
L
M
N
O
P
Q
R
S
T
U
V
W
X
Y
Z

AIDS/HIV TREATMENT AND PREVENTION

drSpock.com

http://www.drspock.com

Staying in the spirit of world-renowned pediatrician Dr. Benjamin Spock, this site is dedicated to providing parents with the expert information they need to raise healthy, happy children. Search this site for medical information, product alerts, and parenting advice from some of the world's top experts in childcare.

Marty Howard's AIDS Page

http://www.smartlink.net/~martinjh/

Marty Howard is a man living with AIDS. This page is designed and updated by him to help you find as much HIV/AIDS-related information as possible from one starting place. The links will take you all over the United States and the world to many additional links where information in English can be found. Marty also invites site visitors to chat with him via the AOL IM'er. This excellent site gives a name and face to AIDS, making it our selection as best of the best in this category.

DISEASES AND CONDITIONS

Down Syndrome WWW Page

http://www.nas.com/downsyn/

Information on Down Syndrome, including articles, healthcare guidelines, a worldwide list of organizations, and education resources. The site also features a brag book containing photos of a number of children with the syndrome.

GENERAL RESOURCES

WebMD

http://www.webmd.com

You'll find articles, news, and tips for improving your health and well-being. Searchable database packed with information, including definitions of diseases, prescription information, and treatments. An encyclopedia of health and medicine.

HEALTH CARE

Society for Medical Decision Making

http://www.smdm.org/

Focuses on promoting rational and systematic approaches to decisions about health policy and the clinical care of patients. Includes decision analysis, applications of quantitative methods in clinical settings and medical research, studies of human cognition and the psychology of clinical reasoning, medical ethics, medical informatics and decision making, artificial intelligence, evaluation of medical practices, and cost-effectiveness or cost-benefit assessments.

INSTITUTES

KidsHealth

http://www.kidshealth.org

Created by the medical experts at the Nemours Foundation, KidsHealth has trainloads of information on infections, behavior and emotions, food and fitness, and growing up healthy, as well as cool games and animations!

TRAVEL RESOURCES

Gimponthego.com

http://www.gimponthego.com

Pick up travel tips for disabled individuals on the go, as well as hearing hotel/motel and restaurant feedback from people who've visited. Find out which chains are the best in terms of wheelchair accessibility.

Herbal Encyclopedia

http://www.wic.net/waltzark/herbenc.htm

Search for information on a particular type of medicinal herb by clicking on the appropriate letter, or start by reading short articles on how to use herbs, how to collect and store them, and more. A complete herb site with an appropriate cautionary warning up front about the proper use of herbs.

A
B
C
D
E
F
G
H
I
J
K
L
M
N
O
P
Q
R
S
T
U
V
W
X
Y
Z

HISTORY

Biography

http://www.biography.com

Learn more about the backgrounds of your favorite historical figures or celebrities--they're all profiled here on the Biography site, which also includes information on the TV show and magazine of the same name. Many of the Biography television shows are available on videotape and are for sale at this site.

History Channel

http://www.historychannel.com

Select a decade back to 1800 and search for information on events during that time period at this site. Read articles about historical events, find out about upcoming TV reports on the History Channel, and chat with other history buffs. Don't miss the History Channel store and see what books and videotapes are available for purchase.

History Matters

http://historymatters.gmu.edu/

Developed by American Social History Project/Center for Media and Learning, City University of New York, and the Center for History and New Media, George Mason University, this site provides resources for high school and college-level history teachers. Provides sample syllabi, reference texts, teaching materials, and links to dozens of other resources on the Web. Whether you teach history for a living or just enjoy studying it, this is a fantastic site.

History Net

http://history.about.com/

A huge site full of information on ancient history, U.S. history, historical personalities, events, eyewitness accounts, and more. Hefty collection of links to other sites, as well.

History of Photography

http://www.rleggat.com/photohistory/

Information on some of the most significant processes used during the early days of photography, in addition to pen-portraits of many of the most important photographers of the period.

History On-Line

http://www.history.ac.uk/

Developed by the Institute of Historical Research (IHR), this site is devoted to "promoting high-quality resources for the teaching and learning of history in the U.K." Here you can learn about the Institute for Historical Research, search History On-Line, or check out a useful collection of links to resources on researching and teaching specific topics.

Best HyperHistory

http://www.hyperhistory.com/online_n2/History_n2/a.html

Comprehensive guide to the last 3,000 years of world history, this ever-growing tome attempts to provide a balanced view of history, covering not only wars and political events, but also scientific, cultural, and religious facets. A 116-chapter book on world history, by Frank A.

Smitha, provides a more cohesive view of world history. Innovative navigational tools make it easy to move through this best of the best site.

Smithsonian National Museum of American History

http://americanhistory.si.edu/

The National Museum of American History is part of the Smithsonian Institution in Washington, D.C. Here, you can check out many of the museum's most popular exhibits online, including the history of the presidency and the Star Spangled Banner; visit the music room, to learn about musical performances at the museum; and check out the time line of United States history.

Smithsonian Natural History Museum

http://www.mnh.si.edu/

The National Museum of Natural History is part of the Smithsonian Institution in Washington, D.C.,

and is dedicated to understanding the natural world and our place in it. This site provides an abundance of online resources about the natural sciences. Be sure to spend a few minutes browsing the online store!

HISTORICAL DOCUMENTS AND LANDMARKS

Guggenheim Museum

http://www.guggenheim.org

Read about the New York museum's history and architecture; its numerous programs, including tours; upcoming exhibitions; becoming a member and all the benefits of membership; and the museum store, where you can buy art books, gifts, jewelry, children's books and toys, and signature Guggenheim products. Also available is information on the other four international museum locations.

A B C D E F G H I J K L M N O P Q R S T U V W X Y Z

HOCKEY

American Hockey League Eastern Conference Team Sites
Albany River Rats http://www.albanyriverrats.com/
Bridgeport Sound Tigers http://www.soundtigers.com/

Hamilton Bulldogs
http://www.hamiltonbulldogs.com/

Hartford Wolf Pack
http://www.hartfordwolfpack.com/

Lowell Lock Monsters
http://www.lockmonsters.com/

Manchester Monarchs
http://www.monarchshockey.com/

Manitoba Moose
http://www.moosehockey.com/

Portland Pirates
http://www.portlandpirates.com/

Providence Bruins
http://
www.providencebruins.com/

Quebec Citadelles
http://
www.citadellesdequebec.com/

Saint John Flames
http://www.sjflames.com/

Springfield Falcons
http://www.falconsahl.com/

St. John's Maple Leafs
http://www.sjmapleleafs.ca/

Worcester Ice Cats
http://
www.worcestericecats.com/

American Hockey League Western Conference Team Sites

Chicago Wolves
http://www.chicagowolves.com/

Cincinnati Mighty Ducks
http://
www.cincinnatimightyducks.com/

Cleveland Barons
http://www.clevelandbarons.net/

Grand Rapids Griffins
http://www.griffinshockey.com/

Hershey Bears
http://www.hersheypa.com/
pro_sports/bears/
bears_info_frame.html

Houston Aeros
http://www.aeros.com/

Milwaukee Admirals
http://
www.milwaukeeadmirals.com/

Norfolk Admirals
http://www.norfolkadmirals.com/

Philadelphia Phantoms
http://www.phantomshockey.com/

Rochester Americans
http://www.amerks.com/

Syracuse Crunch
http://www.syracusecrunch.com/

Utah Grizzlies
http://www.utahgrizzlies.com/

Wilkes Barre/Scranton Penguins
http://www.wbspenguins.com/

Hockey Hall of Fame

http://www.hhof.com/index.htm

Play the Hockey Hall of Fame trivia game, track down statistics and rankings, and learn more about the best hockey players in history. Links to stores for online shopping.

 NHL: Official National Hockey League Web Site

http://www.nhl.com/

This is the official NHL Web site where you can get all the news about NHL hockey you could want. Check out individual teams and NHL schedules, and take the most recent poll. The gift shop is also worth a look for items ranging from hats to official NHL jerseys of your favorite player. This is a total and comprehensive site that delivers a lot of hockey information, a no-brainer choice as best of the best in the Hockey category.

National Hockey League Eastern Conference Team Sites
Atlantic Division

New Jersey Devils
http://www.newjerseydevils.com/

New York Islanders
http://
www.newyorkislanders.com/

New York Rangers
http://www.newyorkrangers.com/

Philadelphia Flyers
http://
www.philadelphiaflyers. com/

Pittsburgh Penguins
http://
www.pittsburghpenguins.com/

Northeast Division

Boston Bruins
http://www.bostonbruins.com/

Buffalo Sabres
http://www.sabres.com/

Montreal Canadiens
http://www.canadiens.com/

Ottawa Senators
http://www.ottawasenators.com/

Toronto Maple Leafs
http://www.mapleleafs.com/

Southeast Division

Atlanta Thrashers
http://
www.atlantathrashers.com/

Carolina Hurricanes
http://carolinahurricanes.com/

Florida Panthers
http://www.floridapanthers.com/

Tampa Bay Lightning
http://
www.tampabaylightning.com/

Washington Capitals
http://www.washingtoncaps.com/

National Hockey League Western Conference Team Sites
Central Division

Chicago Blackhawks
http://
www.chicagoblackhawks.com/

Columbus Blue Jackets
http://www.bluejackets.com/

Detroit Red Wings
http://www.detroitredwings.com/

Nashville Predators
http://
www.nashvillepredators.com/

St. Louis Blues
http://www.stlouisblues.com/

Northwest Division

Calgary Flames
http://www.calgaryflames.com/

Colorado Avalanche
http://
www.coloradoavalanche.com/

Edmonton Oilers
http://www.edmontonoilers.com/

Minnesota Wild
http://www.wild.com/

Vancouver Canucks
http://www.canucks.com/

Pacific Division

Mighty Ducks of Anaheim
http://www.mightyducks.com/

Dallas Stars
http://www.dallasstars.com/

Los Angeles Kings
http://www.lakings.com/

Phoenix Coyotes
http://www.phoenixcoyotes.com/

San Jose Sharks
http://www.sj-sharks.com/

A
B
C
D
E
F
G
H
I
J
K
L
M
N
O
P
Q
R
S
T
U
V
W
X
Y
Z

A
B
C
D
E
F
G
H
I
J
K
L
M
N
O
P
Q
R
S
T
U
V
W
X
Y
Z

HOLIDAYS AND CELEBRATIONS

[Best] Passover on the Net

http://www.holidays.net/passover/

This beautifully illustrated and easy-to-navigate site offers the story of Passover, information about the Seder meal (plus recipes), and a collection of downloadable Passover songs in MIDI format.

HOME

HOME BUILDING

[Best] Ask the Builder

http://www.askbuild.com/

Search the archives of this syndicated columnist (Tim Carter) to learn the best way to tackle a problem around the house. Project archives will tell and show you (using streaming video) how to clean a deck, for example. Straightforward advice. You can also purchase books, CDs, and other related merchandise here. This site's personal touch, excellent design, and comprehensive information make it our choice as best of the best in the Home Building category.

Building Industry Exchange

http://www.building.org/

Extensive directory of contractors, subcontractors, and suppliers for the building industry. Includes listings for architects, concrete workers, electricians, plumbers, and just about any other service required in the building industry. Also features discussion forums and job leads for construction professionals.

HOME DECORATING/ PAINTING

Ballard Design

http://www.ballarddesigns.com/home.jsp

Mail-order source for fine home furnishings and accents. You can find everything here from beds and bedding to office furniture.

Baranzelli Home

http://www.baranzelli.com/

Designer-quality home furnishings including fabrics, trims, furniture, and decorative accessories are now available directly to you through the Net; this site also serves as an information source for your decorating needs as well as a compendium of events and activities in the world of home décor.

Home and Garden Television (HGTV)

http://www.hgtv.com/

Home and Garden Television's Web site is arranged in "villages," letting participants home in on information on decorating, gardening, remodeling, crafts, and entertainment.

Longaberger Baskets

http://www.longaberger.com/

Introduces you to the Longaberger company and all the Longaberger products, including baskets, pottery, fabrics, home décor, and home accessories. The site does not allow you to purchase products directly, but it does help you locate an independent sales consultant. Jump to the kitchen, dining room, library, and living room areas to see the goods available and get valuable information.

Steptoe & Wife Antiques, Ltd.

http://www.steptoewife.com/

Architectural restoration products from iron staircases to drapery hardware are offered by this Canadian company whose motto is "100 years behind the times." Listings of products and distributors are provided.

HOME AUTOMATION

SmartHome.com

http://www.smarthome.com/

Take the guided tour of home automation products before viewing the catalog and considering products. You can also learn about the latest technology and why you need it. Incredible selection of home automation products.

HOME IMPROVEMENT AND RESTORATION

Ace Hardware

http://www.acehardware.com/

Find a hardware store close to you, get answers to frequently asked questions, and learn hardware hints and tips at this site. You can also participate in seasonal contests and find out about store specials.

A
B
C
D
E
F
G
H
I
J
K
L
M
N
O
P
Q
R
S
T
U
V
W
X
Y
Z

A
B
C
D
E
F
G
H
I
J
K
L
M
N
O
P
Q
R
S
T
U
V
W
X
Y
Z

Lowe's Home Improvement Warehouse

http://www.lowes.com/

Lowe's Companies, Inc., is one of America's top 30 retailers serving home improvement, home décor, home electronics, and home construction markets. Lowe's Web site offers step-by-step guides for home improvement projects, featured products, and tips from Lowe's Home Safety Council. There's also a store locator, recent corporate financial data, and a list of employment opportunities. You can also order merchandise from this site through a secure server.

MORTGAGES AND FINANCING

The Appraisal Institute

http://
www.appraisalinstitute.org/

This highly regarded group represents real estate appraisers and produces the professionally oriented Appraisal Journal. The site provides a number of services to its members and the public, such as the yearly curriculum of courses and seminars, a section on industry news, a bulletin board service, and an online library featuring real-estate papers, articles, and publications.

LendingTree.com

http://www.lendingtree.com/

LendingTree.com can fix you up with a great deal on a loan, whether you need money to finance a mortgage, purchase a car, pay tuition, consolidate your debt, or start a business. Just fill out a brief application online, and LendingTree.com will provide you with offers from four lenders. LendingTree.com can also help you find homeowner's insurance, an automobile warranty, or a real estate agent. Features some resources that can help make you a more well-informed borrower.

PlanetMortgage

http://www.planetloan.com/

Search tool for finding local mortgage lenders. You simply select your state of residence and specify the type of loan desired (for example, Purchase, Refinance, or Auto). Planet Mortgage displays a list of local lenders. Select a lender and enter the requested information to have the lender contact you with more information. Some excellent articles and tools to help you make well-informed financial decisions.

PLUMBING

Toiletology 101

http://www.toiletology.com/index.shtml

Everything you ever needed to know about fixing and maintaining your toilet. Helpful guidance and instruction.

HOMESCHOOLING

A to Z Home's Cool Homeschooling Web Site

http://www.gomilpitas.com/
homeschooling/

Created and maintained by Ann Zeise, an enthusiastic homeschooling advocate, this site is a huge directory to articles and resources on homeschooling. This site offers something for everyone, from those considering the homeschooling option to those in the trenches. Learn the basics, the laws, where to find study materials and lessons, how to homeschool gifted children, and much much more.

[Best] Home School World

http://www.home-school.com/

This award-winning site features a Home Life catalog, a listing of homeschool support groups, directories of courses and lesson plans, and a mammoth homeschool mall where shoppers can find hundreds of items. This site also offers online book purchases from their secured server. If you're a parent who's homeschooling your children or considering homeschooling, bookmark this best of the best site and return to it whenever you need assistance.

HORSES

[Best] The American Saddlebred Horse

http://
www.american-saddlebred.com/

Anyone interested in horses—and show horses in particular—will enjoy viewing the video clips of the various gaits displayed during competitions. Detailed descriptions and diagrams of the horses' structure and history of the breed are also featured. The site includes a small photo gallery and links to saddlebred horse museums and national organizations. Be sure to submit your favorite saddlebred picture for consideration in the annual calendar. Anyone interested in horses and horseback riding should visit this best of the best site and return to it often.

A
B
C
D
E
F
G
H
I
J
K
L
M
N
O
P
Q
R
S
T
U
V
W
X
Y
Z

The Art of Classical Riding

http://www.geocities.com/
gerrypony/

Maintained by "Egyptian Webmistress," Duaa Anwar, this site provides some excellent tutorials on the art of classical riding. Fully illustrated tutorials address the classical seat, posture, and positions of the hands and legs.

HUMOR

Centre for the Easily Amused

http://www.amused.com/

A phenomenal site where you can waste huge amounts of time browsing. The site's links are organized by category, such as Sites That Do Stuff and Random Silliness, to make up one of the best lists of odd humor on the WWW. You'll also find trivia games, daily jokes, and chat rooms.

Cursing in Swedish

http://www.santesson.com/
curshome.htm

Study sharp, succinct swearing in Swedish. According to the introduction, the Swedish language is remarkably limited when it comes to using four-letter words. If you're Swedish and short-tempered, or just interested in expanding your repertoire, let this page help you take out your aggressions. WAV files are supplied so you can learn to pronounce your curses properly.

 Despair.com

http://www.despair.com

Ever get tired of seeing those posters and note cards with soaring eagles and sappy motivational sayings? Despair.com has an answer to these annoying props. Check out the posters, calendars, and coffee mugs, and sign up for the newsletter. This is one of the most clever sites to come along in a long time.

HumorSearch

http://www.humorsearch.com/

Internet search engine for humorous sites and resources on the Web. Includes a gallery of Osama bin Laden cartoons, tax jokes, Clinton jokes, games, and more.

Jokes.com

http://www.jokes.com

Search the free jokes database to find just the right one, or read the daily headlines to see what craziness is being reported. The headlines are real, although the stupidity of many will make you wonder. Sign up to receive a free joke every day via email, or request a more targeted joke, such as a sports joke, college joke, or Osama bin Laden joke.

The Onion

http://www.theonion.com

These guys succeed the same way every other great newspaper does: by making stuff up. This faux newspaper includes headlines such as "Raccoon Leaders Call for Loosening of Garbage-Can Lids" and "Sentient Couch Thinks It Would Look Good Over by the Window."

SatireWire

http://www.satirewire.com

More sarcastic than satirical, this site provides a tongue-in-cheek view of current events that will keep you laughing for hours. No subject is safe; SatireWire will even poke fun at itself.

Spam Haiku Archive

http://pemtropics.mit.edu/~jcho/spam/

Learn how to create poetry in the rigorous haiku/Spam format. You'll find more than 19,000 Spamkus, most of which aren't so funny as they are curiously silly.

A
B
C
D
E
F
G
H
I
J
K
L
M
N
O
P
Q
R
S
T
U
V
W
X
Y
Z

Cabela's

http://www.cabelas.com/

Shop this outfitter for apparel, footwear, or equipment before your next hunting outing.

Field & Stream Online

http://www.fieldandstream.com/

The outdoorsman's bible has a site on the Internet. The current issue is here with features, articles, and editorials. You can even pick an area of the country and find out what's in season and where to hunt.

Hunting.Net

http://www.hunting.net/

The ultimate hunting site on the Web covers everything from turkey hunting to elk hunting, bowhunting, sporting dogs, hunting outfitters, and hunting gear. Chat areas, message boards, auctions, and swaps put you in touch with other hunters online.

A
B
C
D
E
F
G
H
I
J
K
L
M
N
O
P
Q
R
S
T
U
V
W
X
Y
Z

National Rifle Association

http://www.nra.org/

Keep up to date with the latest in gun legislation at this site. The NRA is one of the strongest advocates of the Second Amendment to the Constitution, guaranteeing the right to bear arms in the United States. The NRA offers programs benefiting gun safety, marksmanship, personal safety, hunting, and more. Find out about their services, latest news, and legislative activities at this site. This site also has a new online store where you can buy hats, shirts, and other NRA merchandise.

U.S. Fish and Wildlife Service

http://www.fws.gov/

Dedicated to conserving nature in the United States, this site helps hunters get appropriate permits, learn more about safe hunting, and aims to teach kids what it means when a species is endangered.

U.S. Sportsmen's Alliance

http://www.wlfa.org/

This is the place to go if you want to get serious about wildlife management and the future of hunting, fishing, and trapping. This is the only organization whose sole mission is the conservation of natural resources. Learn about their mission and how to join.

A
B
C
D
E
F
G
H
I
J
K
L
M
N
O
P
Q
R
S
T
U
V
W
X
Y
Z

[Best] BugBios.com

http://www.insects.org

Bug fans will consider this insect heaven. The colorful and information-packed site offers incredible pictures and descriptions of insects. The digest section offers information on how insects are present in every facet of our life. You'll also find an ordinal key to help you identify insects. Explore this site's links to other Web sites and resources. They've even taken the time to categorize and review them. The site is very eye-appealing and well organized, making it an easy best of the best pick.

eNature.com

http://www.enature.com/guides/select_Insects_and_Spiders.asp

National Wildlife Federation's eNature.com is a comprehensive encyclopedia of animal life. This site provides thorough coverage of common and uncommon insects. For each insect, eNature.com displays a picture, a physical description, and information about the insect's food, life cycle, habitat, and range.

Insecta

http://www.insecta.com/

Although the Spencer Entomological Museum has been closed since 1993, caretakers have posted lots of insect photos and information here, as well as designated a Bug of the Month and offered insect lore.

Insects Hotlist

http://sln.fi.edu/tfi/hotlists/insects.html

More information than you probably ever thought you needed about insects—beetles, butterflies, ants, moths, roaches, and more, from the Franklin Institute.

A
B
C
D
E
F
G
H
J
K
L
M
N
O
P
Q
R
S
T
U
V
W
X
Y
Z

INSURANCE

⟦Best⟧ Insure.com

http://www.insure.com

If you're trying to decide which insurer to go with, visit this site first. Insure.com provides free ratings from Standard & Poor's and Duff & Phelps Credit Rating Co. Their ratings will help you evaluate the quality and financial soundness of the insurers you are considering. You'll also find in-depth articles, and insurance tips on auto, homeowners, health, life, and business insurance. Perhaps best of all, this site does not sell insurance, and is not owned or operated by an insurance company.

AUTOMOBILE

Quotesmith.com

http://www.quotesmith.com/

Get insurance quotes from hundreds of different insurance companies. Compare prices and coverage at one site. Also provides a great collection of articles and tools to help you make well-informed decisions when selecting a particular policy.

COMPANIES

Farmers Insurance

http://www.farmers.com/

Calculate your need for auto, flood, home, life, business, or healthcare professional liability insurance at Farmers' site. Excellent collection of online calculators to help you determine your insurance needs and better manage your personal finances. Checklists for bicycle safety, home inventory, and emergencies. Lots of great information and tools. Plus you can get an insurance quote or file a claim right online.

RESOURCES

Insurance Institute for Highway Safety

http://www.hwysafety.org/

Learn more about vehicle ratings, find out which cars are rated safest, and read the latest crash test results online.

A
B
C
D
E
F
G
H
I
J
K
L
M
N
O
P
Q
R
S
T
U
V
W
X
Y
Z

CHATS. CLUBS. AND CONFERENCES

CyberTown

http://www.cybertown.com/

Cutting-edge, 3D virtual community where you can settle down online and become a citizen. Think of it as an online version of The Sims. You select a 3D character to represent you. You can then build a house, get a dog, find a job, create your own clubs, dance in the Black Sun nightclub, gamble at casinos, and much more. Very innovative online-community site. Not the easiest site to navigate if you have a standard modem connection.

evite

http://www.evite.com

Online gathering place for friends, relatives, and colleagues. To start an Evite session, you enter your online identity, name the event, pick a theme, and invite your friends and family to join in. Features a reminder service, polling, payments collection, restaurant and concert listings, and event shopping (sponsored by Ticketmaster).

ICQ: World's Largest Internet Online Communication Network

http://web.icq.com/

Download ICQ's time-limited beta for chatting, sending messages and files, and setting up other real-time communication. Developed by Mirabilis Ltd., this is a very comprehensive site, offering lots of valuable information on the ICQ suite of Internet tools. Site also features message boards, chat rooms, a search directory, and tools for communicating with cellular phones and other wireless devices.

Worlds 3D Ultimate Chat Plus

http://www.worlds.net/3dcd/

Provides a 3D multiuser chatting system. Allows you to use images and sound while you chat with others, interacting through your computer instead of with it. Links to online shopping, too.

Yahoo! Groups

http://groups.yahoo.com/

Enables family members, graduating classes, organizations, and other groups of people to organize on the Web. Group moderator can broadcast messages, alerts, and newsletters to group members, and all members can post messages, digitized photos, and other information to the group.

A
B
C
D
E
F
G
H

J
K
L
M
N
O
P
Q
R
S
T
U
V
W
X
Y
Z

CONNECTING FREE

Free ISP Directory

http://www.findanisp.com/
free_isps.php?src=findwhatfree

Use this site to find free and low-cost Internet connection services.

The Free Site

http://www.thefreesite.com/
Free_Internet_Access/

This is a listing of a variety of free Internet connections, as well as other free Internet services. Worth a look.

NetZero

http://www.netzero.net/

One of the few truly free ISPs that survived the great Internet bust. Users can get totally free Internet access, email, chat, and instant messaging for 10 hours per month. For about ten bucks a month, you get unlimited connect time and fewer pop-up ads.

INSTANT MESSAGING AND INTERNET PHONE

America Online Instant Messenger

http://aim.aol.com/

Get the most popular instant messaging program on the planet, register for a screen name, and start chatting online with all your friends and relatives who already use AOL's Instant Messenger.

ICQ.com

http://www.icq.com

Download the free trial ICQ (I Seek You) software so that you can immediately identify when a friend or family member logs onto the Internet. The software eliminates the need to regularly search for people you want to talk to. After you find someone you want to chat with, you can send text or voice messages in realtime.

MSN Messenger Service

http://messenger.msn.com/

The free MSN instant messaging software allows you to see which of your friends are online and then send instant messages to them. You can also have group meetings or play a real-time game.

Net2Phone

http://www.net2phone.com/

Free PC-to-PC "phone calls" to anywhere in the world and free limited time PC-to-phone calls to any phone in the nation, plus low rates on PC-to-phone calls to other countries. With Net2Phone, users can talk to each other over Internet connections and phone lines using their PC's sound card equipped with a microphone.

PRIVACY

TRUSTe

http://www.truste.com

A site for Web publishers and consumers, advising everyone on privacy issues. Consumers can learn how to best protect themselves from sharing too much information when online and publishers can learn how to safeguard information provided by visitors.

SAFETY FOR KIDS

Parenthood Web

http://www.parenthoodweb.com/
articles/phw557.htm

This site is the home of a parenting e-zine article titled Child Safety on the Information Superhighway (April 19, 1999), provided by the National Center for Missing and Exploited Children and the Interactive Services Association.

SafeTeens.com

http://www.safekids.com/
safeteens/

A guide to teen safety on the Internet. This site not only offers ways to keep teens safe while using the Internet, it also supplies many good Web sites that teens will find interesting or helpful. You can also subscribe to a free newsletter when you visit this site.

Web Wise Kids

http://www.webwisekids.com/
advice.html

Internet safety and computer usage tips from Tracey O'Connell-Jay, founder and director of Web Wise Kids. She offers some really good tips, such as keeping your computer in an easily supervised area, and establishing rules for computer use and Internet surfing.

Search Engines

About.com
http://www.about.com

AltaVista.com
http://www.altavista.com

Big Hub
http://www.thebighub.com

C4 TotalSearch Technology
http://www.c4.com

Dogpile
http://www.dogpile.com

Go2Net
http://www.go2net.com

Google.com
http://www.google.com

Hotbot.com
http://hotbot.lycos.com

Lycos.com
http://www.lycos.com

Mamma
http://www.mamma.com

MSN.com
http://www.msn.com

Northern Light
http://www.northernlight.com

Profusion
http://www.profusion.com

Yahoo!
http://www.yahoo.com

Child-Safe Search Engines

Ask Jeeves for Kids:
http://www.ajkids.com/

Yahooligans:
http://www.yahooligans.com/

http://www.searchengines.com/
kids/

http://www.lycoszone.com/

OneKey:
http://www.onekey.com/live/

Kids Click!:
http://sunsite.berkeley.edu/
KidsClick!/

SECURITY/VIRUS HOAXES

McAfee Antivirus

http://www.mcafee.com/

Home of McAfee VirusScan, one of the most popular antivirus programs on the market. Here, you can learn about the latest virus scares, find out if a reported virus is really a hoax, and download the latest

A B C D E F G H I J K L M N O P Q R S T U V W X Y Z

virus definitions. You can also check out McAfee's firewall program to protect your system from hackers.

Symantec AntiVirus Research Center

http://www.symantec.com/avcenter/index.html

Download detailed information on the latest virus definitions, find out what to do about them, browse the encyclopedia of online viruses and hoaxes, and visit the reference area

for answers to commonly asked questions. If someone sends an email to you, warning you of a new virus, be sure to check this site to make sure the virus warning isn't a hoax. This is a very extensive listing. You can purchase Symantec products here, from firewalls to virus scanners, as well as purchase updates to your existing Symantec products. You can also purchase a family Internet security system that helps defend your PC against Internet threats and protects your children against inappropriate online content.

Inventors Online Museum

http://www.inventorsmuseum.com/

Well-organized, visually pleasing, and full of useful information, this site was built as an online museum so people from all over the world could explore the world of invention and innovation. Sign up as a Museum affiliate and you will be kept informed about the museum, inventors' issues, new features, and news. Inventors, students, and teachers visiting this site will soon realize why it's our top pick in this category.

A
B
C
D
E
F
G
H
I
J
K
L
M
N
O
P
Q
R
S
T
U
V
W
X
Y
Z

360degrees

http://www.360degrees.org

Collection of interviews and taped audio diaries gathered from inmates, correctional officers, lawyers, judges, parole officers, parents, victims, and others whose lives have been affected by the criminal justice system.

As you listen to each individual's story, you can take a 360-degree tour of the individual's personal space—the jail cell, office, living room, or other environment in which the person spends most of his or her time.

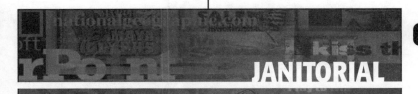

Janitor USA

http://www.janitorusa.com/

Whether you want to start your own janitorial business or train a crew of janitors and maids, this best of the best site provides access to the reference materials you need. Some great articles on specific janitorial issues, plus a link to subscribe to the Janitor USA newsletter.

JETSKI

Sea-Doo

http://www.sea-doo.com/

Home of some of the most popular lines of jetskis and waverunners on the market. Visit the virtual showroom to check out the current offerings. From the showroom, you can click a jetski or waverunner to view a brief description of it and check out the manufacturer's suggested retail price, check out the specs, view photos of the craft from different angles, check out reviews, or download a printable brochure. Site is very sleek and easy to navigate.

JEWELRY

Blue Nile

http://www.bluenile.com/

Fine jewelry with a focus on wedding and engagement rings. Great place to shop for that special gift. Some excellent information on how to select quality jewelry, evaluate diamonds and pearls, and understand the differences of various precious metals.

Diamond-Guide

http://www.diamond-guide.com/

From the home page, click the learning center link to access illustrated tutorials that show you how to evaluate diamonds, pearls, jewelry, and colored stones. Also provides tips on caring for and traveling with jewelry.

⎡Best⎤ DiamondReview.com

http://www.diamondreview.com/

Providing independent, unbiased research on diamond jewelry, this site is the favorite hangout for many diamond jewelry enthusiasts. Features a four-step process to be-coming an enlightened buyer: read the tutorial, ask questions, find a jeweler, and then research prices. Easy to navigate and packed with useful information for consumers, this site is an easy best of the best pick.

Mondera

http://www.mondera.com/

Collection of fine jewelry worn by royalty and celebrities worldwide. Here, you can create your own custom ring by selecting a stone and setting. Get expert advice on how to choose quality jewelry and spot the phony stuff.

DESIGNERS

Abrasha's Gallery

http://www.abrasha.com/

Intriguing gallery of jewelry created from combinations of precious and nonprecious metals, stones, and other materials.

CareerJournal from The Wall Street Journal

http://www.careerjournal.com/

(\$)

Excellent collection of articles and tips on finding the dream job. Salary and hiring information, job search tool, résumé database, discussion groups, and more.

 Best JobStar--Specific Career Information

http://jobsmart.org/tools/career/spec-car.htm

This site offers career guides packed with information about planning your career. What kind of training or education is required for a particular career? What can you earn? What kind of environment will you work in? What's hot? What's not? Some career guides include personal stories from folks working in the field: How did they move (or stumble) into their current work situation? What advice would they give newcomers? Whether you're planning for college, trying to select a career after graduating, or planning a career change, you'll find the information you need at this site, our unanimous choice for best career site.

COMPANY INFORMATION

Jobstar.org

http://www.jobstar.org

If you're looking for a job in California, this is a great starting place. Learn about putting together a good résumé, networking, and interviewing, as well as accessing databases of available jobs across the state.

JOB HUNTING

6Figurejobs.com

http://www.6figurejobs.com

Research jobs, find recruiters, and have your résumé seen by some of the top companies at this site for experienced professionals.

A
B
C
D
E
F
G
H
I
J
K
L
M
N
O
P
Q
R
S
T
U
V
W
X
Y
Z

A
B
C
D
E
F
G
H
I
K
L
M
N
O
P
Q
R
S
T
U
V
W
X
Y
Z

Career Builder

http://www.headhunter.net/index.htm

Billed as a "Mega Job Search," careerbuilder.com has an active, continuously updated database of more than 300,000 jobs from more than 25,000 companies. Search the database, post your résumé, and build your career.

FlipDog.com

http://www.flipdog.com/

Featuring a database of more than 400,000 jobs from more than 50,000 employers, FlipDog has become one of the most popular sites for jobhunters. Search the database, post your résumé, or contact a headhunter. Useful tutorials on résumé writing and distribution.

Monster.com

http://www.monster.com

Receive daily emails of job summaries that match what you're looking for, from part-time to full-time in a range of career fields. You can

search up-to-date databases for job openings nationwide in virtually any field and make online applications to those jobs. Post your résumé on the site and have prospective employers come to you! This site's popularity is enough to warrant it the best of the best designation, but it also features an easy-to-use interface and some of the best career information around.

JOB SHARING

Jobsharing.com

http://www.jobsharing.com/

Created by a company called Job Sharing Resources, this site is devoted to helping companies make job sharing part of their corporate culture by making it easier for companies to find job share partners. Here, businesses can search for employees who desire a job sharing arrangement, and job seekers can add their names to a database.

JOURNALISM

[Best] High School Journalism

http://www.highschooljournalism.org/

Presented by the American Society of Newspaper Editors, this site is designed to encourage and support high school journalists and journalism teachers. Students can find articles on journalism, post questions

to professional journalists, take a journalism quiz, and find links to high school newspapers. Teachers will find journalism lesson plans, links to support organizations, and other resources for teaching the craft. Visitors can also check into scholarships and colleges that offer journalism degrees. This best of the best site has something to offer anyone interested in journalism.

Poynter.org

http://www.poynter.org

Home of the Poynter Institute, "a school for journalists, future journalists, and teachers of journalism." Here, you can learn more about the Poynter Institute's many seminars, find out about journalism conventions across the country, access online journalism tutorials, read award-winning reports and commentary, and much more.

Society of Professional Journalists

http://www.spj.org/

Dedicated to the preservation of the free press as a cornerstone of democracy in the United States, this site is maintained to help defend the First Amendment rights and to promote high standards in journalism. Here you can catch the top news stories regarding journalism topics, find out more about careers in journalism, learn about SPJ's programs for journalists, and even enter a contest for a chance to win a prestigious SPJ award in journalism.

KIDS

ACTIVITIES

Bill Nye the Science Guy's Nye Labs Online

http://www.billnye.com

A companion site to the educational television show Bill Nye the Science Guy, Nye Labs Online features daily home science demonstrations, a forum for asking Bill questions, episode guides, teaching materials, and related show resources.

BONUS.com

http://www.bonus.com/

This supersite for kids features a huge range of games and activities, from word games to alien combat to pictures to print and color, and much more. Brainteasers and sports information are also part of this "busy" site. There is even a parent/teacher page that offers curriculum enhancers and homework help. But most importantly, your kids will be entertained for hours at this site.

Cartoon Network

http://www.cartoonnetwork.com/

The Web home of this cable cartoon channel features a viewer poll, a games library, and a refrigerator that showcases kids' artwork. You can also buy Cartoon Network clothing and merchandise, sorted by show or category.

A B C D E F G H I J K L M N O P Q R S T U V W X Y Z

A
B
C
D
E
F
G
H
I
J
K
L
M
N
O
P
Q
R
S
T
U
V
W
X
Y
Z

Channel One

http://www.channelone.com

Online version of the popular Channel One broadcasting service that pipes news and current events into classrooms across America. At this site, kids can find information and commentary on various issues that relate to their generation. Check out the latest headline news, listen to music, find out the latest sports scores and highlights, play online games, enter contests, and much more.

Children's Television Workshop

http://www.sesameworkshop.org/

Kid city! This site features stickers, games, gadgets, and puzzles. The Parent's Toolbox offers tips and tactics from Sesame Street Parents, plus email from Elmo, games, stories, coloring, Muppet profiles, show information, and trivia. You'll also find activities, crafts, and recipes.

CollegeBound Network

http://www.collegebound.net/

Working in partnership with colleges, universities, corporations, military branches, and educational companies, CollegeBound Network has created a stimulating community for teenagers to hang out and expand their horizons. Great resource for high school students who are considering college.

The Crayola Home Page

http://www.crayola.com/

Everything you always wanted to know about crayons and all the fun things you can do with them. You can buy Crayola products, from crayons and markers to clothing items you can color. There is also a gift idea link to help you choose the right gift for the right age. Great site!

Disney

http://disney.go.com/

Great place for young kids to explore, this site is packed with online games, information about Disney TV shows and movies, kids' clubs, family crafts and party planners, vacations, and more.

FunBrain

http://www.funbrain.com/

Fun games that train the brain, this site focuses on the K–8 crowd, but offers games for high schoolers, as well. Great place for teachers and parents to go for resources, too.

Just 4 Girls

http://jfg.girlscouts.org/

This Girl Scout–sponsored page helps girls learn how to do things, such as building their own Web page, as well as how to become a scout. And they can chat with friends online at the site.

MaMaMedia.com

http://www.mamamedia.com/

A kid-safe, entertaining site that offers kids the chance to create Web site collections, design their own multimedia characters and stories, and enjoy computer clubs and interactive chat with other kids.

OLogy

http://www.ology.amnh.org

If you think science is no fun then check out this site sponsored by the American Museum of Natural History. Here, you can study genetics, astronomy, and paleontology in a fun-filled environment, and learn some interesting facts by playing a robust selection of trivia games.

PBS Kids

http://pbskids.org/

Sing and dance to PBS tunes with your favorite characters, play any of the 47 different games available, or print out pages to color featuring more PBS characters. This site is rich with PBS characters and activities.

SFS Kids

http://www.sfskids.com

Created and maintained by the San Francisco Symphony, this site is dedicated to providing a place for kids and families to learn more about music. Here, you can check out a selection of instruments, learn the basics of reading music, compose your own tunes, and send audio postcards to your friends and family via email.

TIME for Kids

http://www.timeforkids.com/TFK/

This online magazine is written and produced by the Time Magazine folks. This is a site where your kids can get the latest on their favorite music, film, or TV artists, as well as get the latest news on current events. They can also add their opinions in Kids' Views on the News.

Wild World of Wonka

http://www.wonka.com/

Willie Wonka and his chocolate factory have built a home on the Web.

Visit the wacky Wonka, take a tour of the Chocolate Factory, read the joke of the day, play several games, or download the free screensaver or wallpaper. You and your kids both will love this best of the best site!

The Yuckiest Site on the Internet

http://yucky.kids.discovery.com/

Yuckiest is not a distinction many Web sites would want, but Wendall the Worm and Ralph the Roach take great pride in introducing you to their world. Read all the exciting facts about the creepy crawlers; then, take the Roach Quiz. Let Ralph give you the lowdown on all his friends, including the earthworm and the bearded worm. This site is a lot of fun, as well as informative. Parents should check out the Just for Adults section for lots of great resources and links.

KIDS' INTERNET GAMES

Epic Games

http://www.epicgames.com/

Includes the best pinball game, online or offline. Terrific graphics, sounds, and speed, as well as a ton of other games.

Seussville Games

http://www.randomhouse.com/seussville/games/

Some of the best games on the Internet can be found in Seussville, which features interactive games that are all about your children's favorite characters! They're all here—Horton, Mayzie, and, of course, the Cat in the Hat.

A
B
C
D
E
F
G
H
I
J
K
L
M
N
O
P
Q
R
S
T
U
V
W
X
Y
Z

A
B
C
D
E
F
G
H
I
J
K
L
M
N
O
P
Q
R
S
T
U
V
W
X
Y
Z

PEN PALS FOR KIDS

AltaVista Translation Site

http://babelfish.altavista.com/
translate.dyn

This amazing site lets you write a letter to someone in eight popular languages. You cut and paste what you wrote and translated, and "translate it" back to English to see how it reads in another language. Hilarious! Send someone a romantic letter in French, and include the URL to this site so they can figure out your message.

SAFE SURFING SITES BY KIDS

Awesome Math Stuff

http://www.geocities.com/
EnchantedForest/5411/math.html

Test your math skills at Annie's home page while you enjoy some cool tunes.

Brianna

http://hometown.aol.com/
ydb739094/brianna.html

Learn all about Brianna and the medical challenges she has faced since birth. You'll get to know her and gain an appreciation for all that she faces on a daily basis. A cute girl, and a touching site that can teach kids about children who are different.

Elizabeth's Snow White Page

http://www.ecnet.net/users/
gjmuzzo/lizzie1.htm

Elizabeth has Down Syndrome and cerebral palsy but that doesn't slow her down. Come see her Snow White Page. Elizabeth also has added many cool links to her site, from Disney links to other children's sites.

Artfibers Fashion Yarn

http://www.artfibers.com/

Displays hundreds of unique fashion yarns in knit swatches, and offers ideas for using these yarns to create stylish projects.

Coats Patons

http://www.coatsandclark.ca/

Canada's leading supplier of knitting, crochet, sewing, and craft products. Be sure to check out the newly designed patterns and yarn section of this colorful Web site.

Frugal Knitting Haus

http://www.frugalhaus.com/

This online knitting store offers a wide selection of knitting and crocheting patterns, as well as needles and supplies. In addition, you can find knitting pattern books that give ideas for the use of leftover yarn. They also offer free patterns.

Knitting Tutorials

http://www.sweaterscapes.com/
instruc1.htm

Excellent collection of online knitting tutorials to help you learn various techniques. Some tutorials even come with a free pattern.

Knitting Universe

http://www.knittinguniverse.com/

This is a comprehensive site for anyone interested in knitting. Learn about yarns, get tips, tricks, and techniques, and shop for yarns and patterns online. Download free patterns, too. You can also subscribe to Knitter's Magazine. Excellent resource for beginners and experts alike!

A
B
C
D
E
F
G
H
I
J
K
L
M
N
O
P
Q
R
S
T
U
V
W
X
Y
Z

LANGUAGES/LINGUISTICS

American Sign Language Linguistic Research Project

http://web.bu.edu/ASLLRP/

This is a collaborative research project involving researchers at Boston University, Dartmouth College, Rutgers University, and Gallaudet University. Information is provided at this site on the two main parts of this project: investigation of the syntactic structure of American Sign Language (ASL) and development of multimedia tools for sign language research.

Center for Applied Linguistics

http://www.cal.org/

CAL is dedicated to "improving communication through better understanding of language and culture." Here, you can find a comprehensive list of past and ongoing projects at CAL, plus a database packed with language resources and an online store for purchasing books. Some CAL publications are free.

English As a Second Language Home Page

http://www.rong-chang.com/

This home page is a starting point for ESL learners who want to learn English through the World Wide Web. Many people have created ESL learning materials for the Web. This home page links you to those ESL sites and other interesting places. The variety of materials will allow you to choose something appropriate for you.

Ethnologue: Languages of the World

http://www.sil.org/ethnologue/

If you've ever wanted to know what people are saying all over the world, this is the place to come. This site includes a detailed study of the names, number of speakers, location, dialects, linguistic affiliation, multilingualism of speakers, and much more information on more than 360 languages currently spoken on this planet. A searchable database and clickable maps are provided to help you find just the language you are looking for.

⟦Best⟧ ILoveLanguages

http://www.ilovelanguages.com/

There are more than 1,800 links to language resources, such as online language lessons, translating dictionaries, native literature, translation services, software, and language schools. This frequently accessed tool for students and teachers of foreign languages is a unanimous selection as the best language and linguistics site.

Loglan

http://www.loglan.org/

Loglan is an artificial human language originally designed/invented by the late James Cooke Brown in the late 1950s. This site details the construction and usage of this language. An HTML primer to learn Loglan is also available.

Model Languages

http://www.langmaker.com/

The electronic newsletter contains discussions and articles on made-up languages. Includes subscription information and a software package (Windows) for making your own language.

University of Virginia Foreign Languages & Cultures: Teaching Technologies

http://www.virginia.edu/ ~asmedia/flitig.html

Devoted to helping faculty and interest groups successfully incorporate various technologies into their curriculum to teach foreign languages. Faculty can swap ideas, discuss issues that arise in their courses, and share multimedia presentations and software. Email the Webmaster to join the group.

CONSTRUCTED LANGUAGES

The Klingon Language Institute

http://www.kli.org/

This site is for "scholars" wanting to study the Klingon language from the Star Trek TV series. Lots of information is available on the language, and you can even learn to speak Klingon using the site.

ENGLISH LANGUAGE

BritSpeak

http://martinamis.albion.edu/britspeak.htm

Have you ever heard anyone say, "I'll knock you up tomorrow morning"? This statement would be shocking only if you didn't realize that, to the British, the term knock up means to awaken someone by knocking on that person's door. This site attempts to clear up these miscommunications, and provides a dictionary that converts British words and phrases to American and vice versa. Includes a link to the Dictionary of British Cultural References.

The Collective Nouns

http://www.ojohaven.com/ collectives/

If a group of fish is called a school, and a group of lions equals a pride, then what is the name of a group of whales? Would you believe a pod? This fun site catalogs many collective nouns—many of them humorous. For example, you might see a colony of penguins, a siege of herons, a bunch of things, or a giggle of girls.

Cyberbraai

http://www.fortunecity.com/ marina/cyprus/125/cyberbraai/ cyberi.htm

A collection of lists of words and phrases in South African English, with explanations of their meanings. A very humorous and entertaining site.

Grammar and Style Notes

http://andromeda.rutgers.edu/ ~jlynch/Writing/

Quick! What's the difference between affect and effect? Jack Lynch has the answer, and he's offered it up on this site, an online guide to the complexities of English grammar. Lynch clearly explains the differences between commonly confused words, defines terms such as dangling participle, and offers his own opinions on a variety of style issues.

A B C D E F G H I J K L M N O P Q R S T U V W X Y Z

A
B
C
D
E
F
G
H
I
J
K
L
M
N
O
P
Q
R
S
T
U
V
W
X
Y
Z

GENERAL LANGUAGE AND LINGUISTICS

Gaelic and Gaelic Culture

http://www.ibiblio.org/gaelic/

This site contains a good introduction to the Gaelic languages spoken in Ireland, Scotland, and Wales. Information on Gaelic culture and history can also be found here. Many of the resources listed here are actually in Gaelic, so non-Gaelic speakers/readers beware.

Hindi: The Language of Songs

http://www.cs.colostate.edu/~malaiya/hindiint.html

Spoken by millions around the world, Hindi is one of the major languages of India. As the site's title implies, there is a large archive of Hindi songs available through this site. There are also links to Hindi language and literary resources.

LEARNING LANGUAGES

CLAP: Chinese Learner's Alternative Page

http://www.sinologic.com/clas/

CLAP offers the Chinese learner great resources. In addition to the standard fare of vocabulary words and dictionaries, CLAP offers information on the latest happenings in Chinese language and culture. For example, there is a section detailing English words in common Chinese usage.

CyberItalian

http://www.cyberitalian.com/

Free trial tutorials from their Italian with Pinocchio course. To continue your studies, you must become a member.

French Language Course

http://www.jump-gate.com/languages/french/

An online course in the French language. The course consists of nine lessons and some additional vocabulary. In addition to the lessons, there is a section describing French expressions and idioms. Also included are pointers to other French language and culture sites.

Foreign Languages for Travelers

http://www.travlang.com/languages/

A useful site featuring phrases in several languages that can be used by people who are planning trips abroad. Languages covered include Spanish, Portuguese, German, French, and Dutch. Sound clips demonstrating pronunciation can also be found on the site. Markets a line of text-based and voice-recognition translating devices and other translation tools.

Learn Spanish

http://www.studyspanish.com/

Learn some basic Spanish vocabulary, grammar, and phrases. Premium pay services are available for the more serious language student. CDs and audiotapes are also available.

LAW CRIME AND CRIMINAL LAW

Federal Bureau of Investigation

http://www.fbi.gov/

Take a look at the FBI's most wanted list, or the monthly list of new criminals at their site, where you can also learn about the agency's activities, and where kids can have fun finding out more about crime detection and law enforcement. Up-to-date information on the FBI's mission to combat terrorists, as well. A well-organized, comprehensive site.

 ## National Crime Prevention Council

http://www.ncpc.org/

Most famous for its McGruff, the crime dog, campaign to prevent crime, the NCPC provides information about its programs and upcoming public service announcements. It has a section just for kids, as well as training tools and program ideas to help keep you and your family safe. Excellent site design combined with relevant information for regular people make this an easy best of the best pick.

CYBER LAW AND CYBERSPACE ISSUES

Copyright Website

http://www.copyrightwebsite.com

Learn the basics of copyright law and how it applies to Web-based media. You can even register here to have your entire Web site copyright protected, for a fee.

GENERAL RESOURCES

ClassActionAmerica.com

http://www.classactionamerica.com/

Learn about ongoing and upcoming class action lawsuits and see whether you're eligible to cash in on the billions of dollars a year that go unclaimed.

FreeAdvice

http://www.freeadvice.com/

Explore a wide range of legal topics, research a particular issue, post a message in one of the many Q&A forums, or join a legal chat. Great place for the general public to find information on legal issues.

Law Books

http://www.claitors.com/

Purchase law books as well as legal products and supplies at this site. Claitor's also offers one of the largest inventories of government books and papers available for purchase.

A B C D E F G H I J K L M N O P Q R S T U V W X Y Z

LawGuru.com

http://www.lawguru.com/

Have a legal question you'd like the answer to? You'll probably find it at this site in the FAQs section, by searching more than 15,000 legal questions and answers in the bulletin board section (BBS), by searching the more than 500 search engines at the site, or by asking an attorney directly on the BBS system.

Laws.com

http://www.laws.com/

You'll find a select list of legal links culled by a private California business attorney, whose office seeks out the most useful sites, rather than trying to list all of them. Start by searching the resources section to find what you're looking for and expand from there if you're not successful.

LAW SCHOOLS

Columbia Law School

http://www.law.columbia.edu/

Learn more about the resources, students, and faculty at Columbia through their law school's Web site. A scrolling Columbia Law news function enables you to click on a story to learn more.

Harvard Law School

http://www.law.harvard.edu/

Whether you're considering a legal career and want to know more about attending the oldest law school in the country or are interested in finding out about jobs at Harvard Law School, the Web site can tell you just about anything you need to know. Learn more about the admissions process, career counseling, students, faculty, facilities, programs, and publications.

Kaplan Test Prep and Admissions

http://www.kaptest.com/

From Kaplan, everything you need to know about the LSAT and law school—including scoring, sections, and dates and registration—is available. The site also includes links to help you through law school admission and financial aid. Access to law schools and law student resources can also be found on the page.

LawSchool.com

http://www.lawschool.com/

Impressive collection of news reports, articles, and resources relating to law schools. Find law school rankings, tips on preparing for exams, law reviews, bar exam information, and more. Links to additional resources on prelaw and other topics.

LEGAL ORGANIZATIONS

ACLU Freedom Network

http://www.aclu.org/

The home page for the American Civil Liberties Union takes you to the latest happenings from Congress, and what's happening in the nation's courts. You can also join the ACLU, browse their cyberstore, and read about current events. Other links take you to highlights of cases that the ACLU has involvement in.

American Bar Association

http://www.abanet.org/

The ABA network connects you to any information you need pertaining to this world's largest voluntary professional association. Links to information about the various entities of the ABA (each entity has its own link), a calendar of events, and public information are just a few starting points on this Web site that is ranked in the top five percent.

Association of Trial Lawyers of America

http://www.atlanet.org/

Exchange information and ideas with fellow members of the ATLA, look into conferences and professional development opportunities, get up-to-date information on recent decisions, and learn more about the member benefits at this site.

ElderWeb

http://www.elderweb.com/

ElderWeb was established to provide guidance and resources to professionals and family members grappling with the issue of long-term care and its legal ramifications. The site has nearly 4,500 links to senior resources with information constantly being added.

LEGAL PUBLICATIONS

Hieros Gamos

http://www.hg.org/

Comprehensive resource for legal professionals, law students, and persons seeking law-related information. Links include bar associations, legal associations, law schools, publishers, law firms, law sites, government sites, vendors, and online services. The site is available in English, Spanish, German, French, and Italian. There are more resources than can be listed.

[Best] Nolo Press

http://www.nolo.com/

Publishing legal information in plain English for over 30 years, Nolo Press has empowered average citizens to understand and fight for their rights. Here, you'll find Nolo's Legal Encyclopedia, a law FAQ, financial calculators, resources for various types of cases and legal issues, and a wide selection of Nolo Press books, which you can purchase online. Because this site provides legal information for average people in an easily accessible format, this site is a hands-down winner as the best legal site on the Web.

A
B
C
D
E
F
G
H
I
J
K
L
M
N
O
P
Q
R
S
T
U
V
W
X
Y
Z

A
B
C
D
E
F
G
H
I
J
K
L
M
N
O
P
Q
R
S
T
U
V
W
X
Y
Z

Best Asimov, Isaac

http://www.asimov.com/

A wonderful site for Asimov fans! Comprehensive booklists, stores, and publishers that sell his work, transcripts of reviews and interviews, galleries, and lively discussion groups make this the best of the best for sci-fi fans and Asimov fans alike.

Bibliomania

http://www.bibliomania.com/

Thousands of searchable texts of classic fiction and nonfiction presented in their entirety. You can also purchase books from this site.

Brautigan, Richard

http://www.riza.com/richard/

One of the few sites dedicated to this truly American surrealist, this page has a library and a "Trader's Corner." Configured for Netscape-compatible browsers. This site links to Amazon.com so you can order Brautigan titles.

Burroughs, William S.

http://www.hyperreal.org/wsb/

Whenever a person begins to study William S. Burroughs, there are usually words of warning or at least a caveat lector. This site keeps with that tradition but gives great insight into the life of the writer of books such as Naked Lunch and Junky. This site offers a Web memorial to Burroughs.

Candlelight Stories

http://
www.candlelightstories.com/

This award-winning site is a repository for children's online literature. From Rumpelstiltskin to Thumbelina, you can read your children these online classics. Included is a bookstore, international gallery, and spelling machine game. Story and illustration submissions are welcome. This site links to Amazon.com where you can purchase books.

Christie, Agatha

http://www.nd.edu/~rwoodbur/christie/christie.htm

Provides a chronological listing of most of Christie's works, grouped optionally by featured detective. This site also offers a collection of plays and short stories. The maintainer of the page promises that all the books and plays listed will eventually have complete descriptions (including whodunit, for the impatient!).

Dickens, Charles

http://lang.nagoya-u.ac.jp/~matsuoka/Dickens.html

The home page includes a painting of Charles Dickens by William Powell Frith (1859). This site is absolutely exhaustive in resources about Dickens, author of such fabulous books as The Pickwick Papers and Great Expectations. The site's dynamic quality is that it is constantly being updated to include new information about Dickens.

You can link to archives back to April of 1997—and all the historical information is very up to date and useful.

Dostoevsky Research Station

http://www.kiosek.com/
dostoevsky/contents.html

Great site, brought to you by Christiaan Stange, about the stellar Russian author of books including Crime and Punishment and The Brothers Karamazov. Covers the life of Dostoevsky, bibliography of his works, quotations about him, online versions of the text, an image gallery, and more.

The Electronic Text Center at the University of Virginia

http://etext.lib.virginia.edu/

This site contains thousands of texts, in modern, early modern, and middle English, plus French, German, Japanese, and Latin. Here you will find fiction, science fiction, poetry, theology, essays, histories, and many other types of materials. This site is excellent and thorough. Although a huge number of these texts are freely available, some texts are available only to users at the University of Virginia—the licensors of these texts have not permitted the university to make them widely available.

Eliot, T.S.

http://virtual.park.uga.edu/~232/
eliot.taken.html

This site provides information on American poet T.S. Eliot. Includes a biography, bibliography, and poetry by Eliot. Also includes links to other related sites.

Faulkner, William

http://www.mcsr.olemiss.edu/
~egjbp/faulkner/faulkner.html

The site to visit for any sort of information about William Faulkner. John B. Padgett, currently a graduate student at the University of Mississippi (located at Oxford, whence Faulkner hailed), maintains this comprehensive site with so much information that anyone could find what they wanted to know. You can find information on his letters, novels, poetry, speeches, interviews, screenplays, and essays. You can also find commentaries and complete synopses on his writings.

Fitzgerald, F. Scott

http://www.sc.edu/fitzgerald/

Based at the University of South Carolina, this site is dedicated to F. Scott Fitzgerald in celebration of the centennial of his birth. The mission statement of the page states that "this site celebrates his writings, his life, and his relationships with other writers of the 20th century." True to this, you'll find biography, writings, and beautiful photos of the famous author from the Roaring '20s.

Fleming, Ian: Mr.KissKissBangBang Web Page

http://www.ianfleming.org/
index.shtml

The premier site of James Bond and Ian Fleming, his creator. Here, you'll find current articles and analysis of 007 themes, news clips, upcoming events, and new items to hit the market. Sign up for the newsletter to keep abreast of the most current information.

A
B
C
D
E
F
G
H
I
J
K
L
M
N
O
P
Q
R
S
T
U
V
W
X
Y
Z

Joyce, James

`http://www.2street.com/joyce/`

There are many joys to this site: pictures of the author, his family, and those people mentioned in his work; important songs and readings by Joyce himself; links to articles and Internet groups who study Joyce; and maps of the places mentioned in his work.

Kerouac, Jack

`http://www.charm.net/~brooklyn/People/JackKerouac.html`

A Literary Kicks page that provides a biography, a bibliography, excerpts, and pictures of beat author Jack Kerouac. Kerouac is known as the person who coined the term beatnik. His prose and style are still popular among the Bohemian culture today. This site includes a guide to character names, publications, and much more.

King, Stephen

`http://www.simonsays.com/subs/index.cfm?areaid=21`

Read an autobiography of Stephen King, see a complete listing of all his books, and join in discussion groups about this well-known horror and suspense novelist.

Koontz, Dean

`http://dkoontz.freshlinks.net/fanclub/index.htm`

This site is written and maintained by a Koontz fan club, so you know they are really charged with the excitement of his writing. This is not just a static Web experience (although there are some great links to other Koontz sites and online information). From this site you can chat with Koontz fans, join a club, send a Koontz postcard, join a discussion group, or play a trivia contest.

Morrison, Toni

`http://www.luminarium.org/contemporary/tonimorrison/toni.htm`

Anniina Jokinen's Toni Morrison page provides a biography, bibliography, and interviews of 1993 Nobel Prize–winning author Toni Morrison. It includes articles about Morrison's books such as Tar Baby, Song of Solomon, Sula, Beloved, and many more. Links to Amazon.com to purchase these great books.

Nabokov, Vladimir (Zembla)

`http://www.libraries.psu.edu/iasweb/nabokov/nsintro.htm`

A formidable presence on the World Wide Web in terms of layout, content, and conciseness, Zembla offers a great amount of information concerning Vladimr Nabokov, the author of novels such as Lolita and Bend Sinister.

Nobel Laureates

`http://www.nobel.se/literature/laureates/`

Complete list of winners of the Nobel Prize in literature from 1901 to the present. Click an author's name to access the author's biography, bibliography, acceptance speech, and other resources.

Oates, Joyce Carol (Celestial Timepiece)

`http://storm.usfca.edu/~southerr/jco.html`

Celestial Timepiece gives a full view of author Joyce Carol Oates. You can find a great amount of information on Oates, who is the author of many novels including You Must Remember This and The Triumph of the Spider. This site features a well-laid-out table of contents that covers her life and gives access to resources for research on Oates and her writing.

Parker, Dorothy

http://www.users.interport.net/
~lynda/dorothy.html

Combining amusing quotes from
Dorothy Parker and art created by
the Webmistress, this site is both
interesting and entertaining. Visitors
will get a good sense of Parker's
personality and style simply through
the selected quotes.

Project Gutenburg

http://www.gutenberg.org/

This award-winning site contains a
collection of electronically stored
books, mostly classics, that can be
downloaded free and viewed offline.
Gopher searches for your favorite
author reveal various options for
downloading.

Pulitzer Prizes

http://www.pulitzer.org/

Search the archive to find out past
Pulitzer Prize winners since their
inception, read about the history of
the awards, and download entry
forms for consideration this year.

Rand, Ayn

http://www.aynrand.org/

Dedicated to Rand's novels and
philosophy, there are many links to
biographies, bibliographies, mission statements, and objectivism.
The philosophy of reason and self-
interest lives here.

Rice, Anne

http://www.annerice.com/

The official site of the horror writer
from New Orleans. Anne Rice's
books have become very popular in
the last few years, and this site is
testimony to that. There are pictures, biographies, bibliographies,
sounds, and even information
about Rice's house in New Orleans.

The Romance Reader

http://www.theromancereader.com/

Before you buy that next romance
novel, scan the more than 3,000
reviews available at this site, which
is dedicated to romance novel fans
worldwide. While you're at the site,
you can read biographical information, learn more about other members' interests and feedback, and
share your thoughts on the quality
of recent romance titles you've read.

Meet J.K. Rowling

http://www.scholastic.com/
harrypotter/

Read a biography of the author of
the Harry Potter series and listen to
an audio clip from a February 2000
interview with the author.

Wilde, Oscar

http://www.oscariana.net/
index.html

A textual and visual tour of Oscar
Wilde's biography. During this tour,
you will read about his life, see
photographs, and view letters and
telegrams to and from Wilde. When
you get to the end, select About
This Project to see other Wilde
links on the Web.

The Wonderful Wizard of Oz

http://www.literature.org/
authors/baum-l-frank/
the-wonderful-wizard-of-oz/

Part of the Knowledge Matters Ltd.
literacy series, this site offers the
complete text of The Wonderful
Wizard of Oz, linkable by chapter.
Also offered are other titles by
L. Frank Baum in the Wizard of Oz
series.

A B C D E F G H I J K **L** M N O P Q R S T U V W X Y Z

A
B
C
D
E
F
G
H
I
J
K
L
M
N
O
P
Q
R
S
T
U
V
W
X
Y
Z

MAGIC

Earth's Largest Magic Shop

http://www.elmagicshop.com/

You'll find lots of stuff for everyone, from the beginner to the professional. Check out the Beginner's section and the Free Trick area.

HappyMagic.com

http://www.happymagic.com/

At HappyMagic, they have done the sifting for you—you don't have to worry about getting a trick that you will just throw in a drawer and never use again.

International Conservatory of Magic

http://www.magicschool.com/

This site contains more than 2,000 pages of magic. I.C.O.M. Online provides comprehensive, first-class instruction in the art of being a magician, offering personal live instruction via lecture tours, 24-hour-a-day Web site–based text and virtual lessons, Internet chat, and live Web audio lectures. All aspects of magic are covered, including sleight of hand, illusion, presentation, showmanship, promotion, and theory.

Magictricks.com

http://www.magictricks.com/

Online magic store with many sources of magic history, museums, facts, and places to visit.

Best **World of Magic**

http://www.worldofmagic.net/magictricks.htm

Magic tricks for kids and so much more: clown supplies, Halloween costumes, gags, pranks, makeup, gifts, toys, juggling equipment, masks, hats, deluxe children's costumes, wigs, special-effect lighting, and FunPaks for kids and adults. This is definitely one-stop shopping for your magic needs!

MARKETING

Ad-Guide

http://www.ad-guide.com/

Internet advertising, marketing, and electronic commerce are all included in this site. Lots of comprehensive marketing information available here.

CommerceNet

http://www.commerce.net/

Provides its users with a list of more than 20,000 commercial Web URLs, an 800-number directory, and a list of Internet consultants. Daily news updates keep users informed of events on the Internet.

The GreenBook

http://www.greenbook.org/

Looking for a marketing research firm? Then, the GreenBook should be your first stop. It is the annual directory of marketing research firms that can be ordered in print form here, or searched free online.

Guerrilla Marketing

http://www.gmarketing.com/

Read daily or bimonthly material from Jay Conrad Levinson, Mr. Guerrilla Marketing, as well as search the site's archives for useful guerrilla marketing strategies detailed by other marketing pros. There is plenty of information here, as well as details on Jay's latest book.

Iconocast

http://www.iconocast.com/

Weekly newsletter that tracks trends in marketing and advertising. Links to archives and other resources.

JimWorld

http://www.virtualpromote.com/

JimWorld provides advice and strategies for promoting commercial Web sites. It includes tutorials on site promotion, articles on the effectiveness of banner advertising, and more. Over two million site reviews, plus links to GazetteWorld, NewsKlatsch, PrivacyWorld, TipWorld, and more.

⌜Best⌝ KnowThis.com

http://www.knowthis.com/

A reference site consisting of thousands of sites having to do with marketing, advertising, and promotion. Get a basic course in marketing or delve deep to find out what an effective Web site looks like. Whether you're a marketing student or professional, you'll find plenty of excellent, up-to-date information at this site, our best of the best selection in the Marketing category.

LitLamp

http://www.litlamp.com/

Learn how to promote your business by sponsoring an organization. LitLamp is a community of over 30,000 sponsors and agencies, that offer advertising in exchange for sponsorships.

A
B
C
D
E
F
G
H
I
J
K
L
M
N
O
P
Q
R
S
T
U
V
W
X
Y
Z

Marketing Basics

http://www.cbsc.org/osbw/
pppp.html

This how-to guide for starting a business covers several important topics including "Starting with a Good Idea," "Marketing Basics," and "Financing Your Business."

Microsoft bCentral

http://www.bcentral.com/

Microsoft's small-business center provides tools and services to help entrepreneurs start and manage a successful business. Excellent source for information and other resources designed to establish a business presence on the Web and market products and services online.

MRA: Marketing Research Association

http://www.mra-net.org/

Dedicated to "advancing the practical application, use, and understanding of the opinion and marketing research profession," MRA features research tools, publications about marketing and opinion polls, software tools, and more. Distance-learning programs, video training, and a career guide are also available.

Professional Marketing Resource Services

http://www.pmrs-aprm.com/

Home of PMRS, a nonprofit marketing organization for research professionals. Provides assistance in marketing, advertising, and social and political research. Founded in 1960, PMRS now serves more than 1,800 members across Canada from chapters in Halifax, Montreal, Ottawa, Toronto, Manitoba, Alberta, and Vancouver.

Reveries.com

http://www.reveries.com/

Available only online, this marketing magazine groups its content into one of the following categories: Discussions, White Papers, Experts, Surveys, Essays, and Archives. You'll find case studies, marketing ideas, celebrity profiles, and more.

Sales and Marketing Executives International

http://www.smei.org/

The world's largest association of sales and marketing managers. More than 200,000 searchable articles covering all areas of sales and marketing.

MARTIAL ARTS

GENERAL RESOURCES

Century Fitness

http://www.centuryfitness.com/

Mega-store for exercise and fitness products, this site features a martial arts section, where you can shop for everything from uniforms and sparring gear to weapons and nutritional supplements.

Danny Abramovitch's Martial Arts Home Page

http://www.labs.agilent.com/
personal/_Danny_Abramovitch/
ma_sites.html

Huge collection of links that covers nearly every martial-arts fighting style and topics relating to martial arts. Excellent place to start your exploration of martial arts.

Best Martial Arts Equipment

http://www.martialartsequip.com/

Good site to visit for martial arts clothing, books, and videos. You can also find an impressive assortment of sparring gear, training equipment, and weapons. Join the mailing list to get the latest martial arts news as well as special sales information. For a complete line of martial arts products, this best of the best site is the only site you need to visit.

MartialArtsMart.com

http://store.yahoo.com/
martialartsmart/

More than 3,000 pieces of martial arts equipment, accessories, and supplies are available here. Choose from Chinese, Japanese, Filipino, Korean, and Thai martial arts.

Qi: The Journal of Traditional Eastern Health and Fitness

http://www.qi-journal.com/

Features in-depth information on Chinese culture, traditional medicine, and research; links; a calendar of events; Qi Journal articles; and a very complete catalog of items related to the internal martial arts, Chinese culture, and the traditional healing arts.

TigerStrike.com

http://www.tigerstrike.com/

Whether you need uniforms, sparring gear, weapons, or other martial arts equipment or apparel, this site claims that it can provide it faster and cheaper than anyone else can.

JUDO

Judo Junkie Online

http://www.geocities.com/
Colosseum/3068/

Find out all you wanted to know about the sport and art of judo from this Web home that connects you to other international judo links.

A
B
C
D
E
F
G
H
I
J
K
L
M
N
O
P
Q
R
S
T
U
V
W
X
Y
Z

Kodokan Judo Institute

http://www.kodokan.org/

Home of the Kodokan Judo Institute, this site provides information about the institute and the origin of Kodokan Judo. Links to other Judo sites, information about upcoming events, and an online store are all featured here.

USA Judo

http://www.usjudo.org/

The national governing body for the sport of Judo in the United States, USA Judo is responsible for selecting and preparing teams for international competition. Here, you can learn more about the organization, its teams and coaches, tournament results, and more.

KUNG FU

Chinese Kung Fu Wu Su Association

http://www.kungfu-wusu.com/

One of the few martial arts academies in the West that offers instruction in traditional Chinese kung fu. View a schedule of events and FAQ and meet Grandmaster Alan Lee and other masters of the temple. Additional information on Chi-Kung, Shaolin, Bhodidharma, and Taoism is in the works.

SHOTOKAN

Shotokan Karate of America

http://www.ska.org/

A nonprofit karate organization founded in 1955 by Tsutomu Ohshima, who is also recognized as the chief instructor of many other national Shotokan organizations worldwide.

TAI CHI

ChiLel Qigong

http://www.chilel-qigong.com

Information about qigong and tai chi. This site lists instructors, workshops, and retreats, and offers books and videotapes.

International Taoist Tai Chi Society

http://www.taoist.org/

Founded by Master Moy Lin-Shin, this international society is dedicated to making Taoist tai chi available to everyone.

Taoism and the Philosophy of Tai Chi Chuan

http://www.chebucto.ns.ca/
Philosophy/Taichi/taoism.html

Comprehensive history of Taoism showing the connection between Taoism and tai chi.

Wudang.com

http://www.wudang.com

This beautiful site contains information about the history, practice, and philosophy of tai chi.

MATHEMATICS

American Mathematical Society

http://www.ams.org/

Home of the American Mathematical Society. Offers professional memberships. Publishes electronic journals, books on math, and the fee-based MathSci database, which features comprehensive coverage of research in mathematics, computer science, and statistics.

Chaos at Maryland

http://www-chaos.umd.edu/chaos.html

Provides information on the various applications of chaos theory, including dimensions, fractal basin boundaries, chaotic scattering, and controlling chaos. Includes online papers, a searchable database, and general references. Also offers the Chaos Gallery. Be sure to check here for dissertation help!

eFunda

http://www.efunda.com

Short for engineering fundamentals, eFunda provides more than 30,000 pages packed with basic information about engineering along with a collection of engineering calculators. Here, you will find information about materials, designs, manufacturing processes, along with unit conversions, formulae, and basic mathematical principles.

Eric Weisstein's World of Mathematics

http://mathworld.wolfram.com/

This comprehensive encyclopedia of mathematics, includes hundreds of definitions and explanations of topics ranging from algebra and geometry to calculus and discrete math. Excellent reference book for math students and teachers. Hosted and sponsored by Wolfram Research, Inc., makers of Mathematica, "the world's most powerful and flexible software package for doing mathematics."

Interactive Mathematics Online

http://library.thinkquest.org/2647/main.htm

Learn more about what you can do with algebra, geometry, trigonometry, and chaos theory at this fun site. Check out the Cool Java Stuff page, and also make your own stereograms.

Larson Interactive Math Series

http://www.meridiancg.com/

Math books and interactive software designed to help students K-12 learn basic math. At this site, you can learn about the various programs, order free teacher demos, get technical assistance, and more.

A
B
C
D
E
F
G
H
I
J
K
L
M
N
O
P
Q
R
S
T
U
V
W
X
Y
Z

S.O.S. Mathematics Algebra

http://www.sosmath.com/algebra/algebra.html

Get basic definitions and tools for various math topics, from integers to quadratic equations and factors. This is a very comprehensive site with lots of good information and links.

MEDIATION

 Best ## Conflict Research Consortium

http://www.colorado.edu/conflict/

The Conflict Research Consortium takes a multidisciplinary approach to conflict resolution, focusing on "finding more constructive ways of addressing difficult, long-term, and intractable conflicts, and getting that information to the people involved in these conflicts so that they can approach them in a more constructive way." Here you can find conflict resolution sites, databases, publications, conference information, and links. This comprehensive resource on the subject of conflict resolution for difficult situations is well deserving of its best of the best designation.

JAMS ADR

http://www.jamsadr.com

Learn about ADR (alternative dispute resolution), find out about JAMS, discover why you should use the JAMS service, determine when you should contact JAMS, and find an office or panelist near you.

Mediation Information and Resource Center

http://www.mediate.com/

Everything from defining mediation to guidelines for choosing a mediator. An international searchable directory with links to mediators' Web pages.

A
B
C
D
E
F
G
H
I
J
K
L
M
N
O
P
Q
R
S
T
U
V
W
X
Y
Z

DRUG INFO

FDA Drug Approvals List

http://www.fda.gov/cder/da/da.htm

Come to this site for weekly updates on recently FDA-approved health products. You can search as far back as 1996 for past approvals as well.

PharmWeb

http://www.pharmweb.net/

This site is a great resource for pharmaceutical professionals or students. It provides information on job openings, college degrees, and coursework, as well as discussion forums, chat rooms, a virtual library, and access to a directory of fellow pharmacists.

RxList.com

http://www.rxlist.com/

Excellent for researching specific prescription medications. Provides information on indications, dosages, side effects, warnings, interactions, and more.

StayHealthy.com

http://www.infodrug.com/

Learn more about a particular medication through this drug database. Search by the exact drug name or alphabetically by the beginning letter if you aren't sure of the drug name's complete spelling. Be sure to check out the Health Store where you can purchase monitoring devices and other products.

DRUGSTORES

AdvanceRx.com

http://www.advancerx.com/IM/advrx_main.jsp

Get your prescriptions filled, purchase cosmetics, and buy any other product that you would normally find in a traditional drugstore.

drugstore.com

http://www.drugstore.com/

Purchase health, beauty, and nutrition products, as well as prescription medicines, online at this site. A great selection of products, from shampoos to suntan lotion to vitamins, at reasonable prices. Helpful articles and tips help you improve your health and appearance.

Medicine Shoppe

http://www.medshoppe.com/

In addition to ordering health products at this site, you can learn more about various diseases and illnesses and how you can avoid them, read health news, and search the Reuters Drug Database. The emphasis is on learning to stay healthy rather than on product sales, which is nice.

A
B
C
D
E
F
G
H
I
J
K
L
M
N
O
P
Q
R
S
T
U
V
W
X
Y
Z

more.com

http://www.more.com

Get answers to health questions and scan buyers' guides in the Resource Center at this site, or look for health information based on your gender or age (there's a seniors section as well as sections for men and women). Order health and beauty products, too, after checking the coupon section for special deals.

Rite Aid

http://www.riteaid.com/

In addition to having a prescription filled, asking a pharmacist a question online, buying products and scanning health databases online, you can also locate a nearby Rite Aid location and check for current specials and discounts.

SavOn.com

http://www.americandrugstores.com/default.asp

A fully stocked online drug store. Get product information here, and then purchase the products online from this site. Lots of merchandise to choose from, including baby supplies, cosmetics, and vitamins.

Walgreen's

http://www.walgreens.com/

Search the Mayo Clinic Health information database for medical information and have your prescriptions filled online or at your local Walgreen's location.

FIRST-AID INFORMATION

1st Spot First Aid

http://1st-spot.net/topic_firstaid.html

Find out how to treat basic injuries or conditions, such as heatstroke or frostbite, with the help of this site. There is also basic first-aid guidance and answers to first-aid questions. This site also offers invaluable information about what to keep in a first- aid kit.

American College of Emergency Physicians

http://www.acep.org/

Everything you need to know about preventing emergencies and responding to emergencies when they happen. Find out what you need to pack in a first-aid kit for your home and learn how to prepare an emergency-response plan.

MEDICAL RESOURCES

The AAMC's Academic Medicine Web Site

http://www.aamc.org/

The Association of American Medical Colleges site lists and provides links to accredited United States and Canadian medical schools, major teaching hospitals, and academic and professional societies. _It provides the latest information on news and events, includes AAMC publications and information, and presents research and government relations resources. Also includes information and links to education, research, and healthcare.

American Academy of Pediatric Dentistry

http://www.aapd.org/

Parents can open and read 24 brochures that answer commonly asked questions on topics such as emergency care and diet and snacking. Includes E Today, the electronic newsletter of the AAPD. Also enables you to subscribe to several related magazines. Includes a directory of advanced education programs in pediatric dentistry, with links to each program. Kids can investigate the entertainment section provided just for them.

American Lung Association

http://www.lungusa.org/

Here, you can find information on the ALA (including research programs, grants, and awards), as well as the American Thoracic Society (the international professional and scientific society for respiratory and critical care medicine). Read the ALA's annual report. Check out information on asthma, emphysema, and other lung diseases; tobacco control; and environmental health. This is a great resource for parents of children with asthma. You'll also find information on volunteer opportunities, special events, and promotions, as well as an extensive list of related links.

CDC: Diabetes and Public Health Resources

http://www.cdc.gov/diabetes/

This division of the Centers for Disease Control and Prevention (CDC) is responsible for translating scientific research findings into health promotion, disease prevention, and treatment strategies. Learn about diabetes and what CDC is doing to reduce the burden of this disease. You'll want to investigate the diabetes articles from the CDC and the helpful FAQs.

Centers for Disease Control and Prevention Home Page

http://www.cdc.gov/

Provides links to the CDC's 12 centers, institutes, and offices, and a search engine to quickly locate your point of interest. Includes geographic health information and pinpoints certain disease outbreaks in the world. Also makes vaccine and immunization recommendations. Provides information on diseases, health risks, and prevention guidelines, as well as strategies for chronic diseases, HIV/AIDS, sexually transmitted diseases, tuberculosis, and more. Also offers information on specific populations, such as adolescent and school health, infants' and children's health, and women's health. Offers helpful links to publications, software, and other products. Also provides scientific data, surveillance, health statistics, and laboratory information.

Healthfinder

http://www.healthfinder.gov/

Healthfinder is an informational site from the United States government. It leads you to selected online publications, clearinghouses, databases, Web sites, and support and self-help groups. It also gives you access to government agencies and not-for-profit organizations that produce reliable information for the public. Includes FAQs on children, older adults, women, minority health, and more. Also includes FAQs on many conditions from AIDS to food and drug safety.

A B C D E F G H I J K L **M** N O P Q R S T U V W X Y Z

New England Journal of Medicine

http://content.nejm.org/

A comprehensive site from the famed journal. You can find present and past issues of the Journal here, as well as up-to-date medical information on a wide variety of topics. This site is a must for anyone interested in the medical field.

Three Dimensional Medical Reconstruction

http://www.crd.ge.com/esl/cgsp/projects/medical/

This site lets you view 3D MPEG-format movies of the human brain, skull, colon, lung, heart (and its arteries), and torso. It also provides a simulation of a baby delivery, MR particle flow visualization (in this case, the artery structure of the brain and a visualization of data flow captured by an MR scanner), and a focused ultrasound. Very cool stuff!

United States Department of Health and Human Services

http://www.os.dhhs.gov/

Browse through press releases and fact sheets, speeches, public service campaigns, congressional testimony, and policy forums. Also check out the information on the research, policy, and administration provided by HHS, as well as other federal government research. Use the search feature to find topics from the federal HHS agencies and the government information Xchange.

⟦Best⟧ WebMD

http://www.webMD.com

A site connecting consumers and health professionals, WebMD aims to provide patients with more information about their healthcare, as well as to help prevent problems with useful health-related articles and advice. Online support groups are also available here for topics such as quitting smoking and dieting. This essential medical encyclopedia makes it easy to research symptoms, diseases, prescription medications, and other health-related topics. An easy best of the best pick in the Medical Resources category.

PAIN MANAGEMENT

American Academy of Pain Management

http://www.aapainmanage.org

A site for healthcare professionals and consumers suffering from chronic pain, providing both with the opportunity to connect and learn more about pain management techniques. Consumers can search the database for a qualified pain management professional.

Pain Alliance

http://www.painalliance.com/

For sufferers of chronic pain, fibromyalgia, or related pain syndromes. Covers waterway therapy, information about relaxation, watsu, aichi, stretchys, magnets, and more. Also offers a Support and Motivation section, a Fibro-Specific section, a section on Products and Pools, a Services section, and workshop information.

Pain.com

http://www.pain.com/

This site offers a world of information on pain, including information about pain products and the companies that make them, pain resources, a collection of original full-text articles on pain and its management by noted pain professionals, and much more! Be sure to check out the message board for discussions on pain, pain management, and patients dealing with chronic pain.

MEN AND MEN'S ISSUES

Fathering Magazine

http://www.fathermag.com/

A site that indexes a huge range of father topics, from custody issues to second families, to a father's relationship with a son or daughter. News, information, and discussions galore. Well worth a visit.

The Mankind Project

http://www.mkp.org/

A nonprofit training organization that seeks to help men make better decisions about how they live their lives, to help them connect with their feelings, and to lead lives of integrity. The site provides information on upcoming Warrior training weekends and the organization's mission.

⟦ Best ⟧ Men Stuff

http://www.menstuff.org/

An educational Web site with information on more than 100 topics related to men's issues, such as circumcision, divorce, fathers, and sexuality. Provides a nonjudgmental environment where men can learn more about becoming better fathers, husbands, and human beings. Find out more about male health issues, including testicular cancer and sexual dysfunction, and stay informed about other current issues relating to male health and well-being. When dealing with just about any issue related to being a man, there's no better site in this category.

MEN'S HEALTH

Plainsense.com–Mens Health

http://www.plainsense.com/Health/Mens/

Guides to men's health and lifestyle issues, organized alphabetically, that provide no-nonsense, helpful observations and suggestions for how men can best handle certain situations, from baldness to curvature of the penis to marriage and fatherhood.

A
B
C
D
E
F
G
H
I
J
K
L
M
N
O
P
Q
R
S
T
U
V
W
X
Y
Z

MENTAL HEALTH

Bipolar Disorders Portal

http://www.pendulum.org/

If you need information about bipolar disorder (manic-depression), then this is the site where you should start. Links to diagnostic criteria, psychotropic medications, alternative treatments, articles, and dozens of other resources on the Web.

The Center for Mental Health Services

http://www.mentalhealth.org/

The CMHS National Mental Health Services Knowledge Exchange Network (KEN) provides information about mental health via toll-free telephone services, an electronic bulletin board, and publications. KEN is for users of mental health services and their families, the general public, policy makers, providers, and the media. It gives you information and resources on prevention, treatment, and rehabilitation services for mental illnesses.

[[Best]] Internet Mental Health

http://www.mentalhealth.com/

Find what you need to know about mental health, including the most common mental health disorders, diagnoses, and most-prescribed medications. Also check out the several links to related sites and information. This site also has an online magazine that has editorials, articles, letters, and stories of recovery. If you or a loved one is suffering from a mental illness, and you need

information and hope, this best of the best site offers both in an easily accessible format.

Mental Health InfoSource

http://www.mhsource.com/

This site contains sections regarding disorders and drugs, 600 links on mental health, a mental health professional directory, and more. Use the search tool to track down information on the particular mental health topic in which you're interested.

mentalwellness.com

http://www.mentalwellness.com/

An online resource for people suffering from schizophrenia or other mental illnesses, where you can find a support group, locate other community resources available to assist you, as well as read about the disorder and others who are afflicted with it.

National Alliance for the Mentally Ill (NAMI) Home Page

http://www.nami.org/

Browse through a host of articles brought to you by NAMI. Learn about the latest treatments and therapy; health-insurance issues; the role of genetics; typical Q&As; and related bills, laws, and regulations. Look into NAMI's campaign to end discrimination against the mentally ill and how you can help. Take advantage of Helpline Online, where volunteers talk with you about mental illnesses and the medications that treat them. Examine the scientific aspects of mental illness. Get the facts on depression, schizophrenia, brain disorders, and several more.

Online Dictionary of Mental Health

http://www.shef.ac.uk/~psysc/psychotherapy/

Global information resource and research tool covering all the disciplines contributing to our understanding of mental health.

Who's Who in Mental Health on the Web

http://wwmhw.com/

A database of more than 2,000 mental health professionals around the world, and their practice and networking interests.

PSYCHOLOGY

Community Psychology Net

http://www.cmmtypsych.net/

Educators, undergrad and graduate students, and faculty members will find that the Community Psychology Network site is full of information regarding professional membership societies, graduate schools, community psychology course materials, funding sources, position announcements, books and suggested reading material, as well as links to other related sites.

PSYbersquare

http://www.psybersquare.com/

A site for worriers to come to acquire skills and tools they need to be more satisfied with their lives. "Whether you need help at home or at work, in the bedroom or the boardroom, the exercises and

events at PSYbersquare can help you achieve and win in the game of life," claims Dr. Mark Sichel, an experienced therapist and the originator of the site. Links to Amazon.com where you can purchase recommended books.

Psychology.com

http://www.psychology.com/

Find a therapist or ask a therapist a question online at this site, which also offers tests and games to help you learn more about yourself, articles on useful concepts and techniques, and tips on dealing with stress and other issues.

Psychology.net

http://www.psychology.net/

Headline news about current events and issues relating to psychology. Links to Amazon.com to search for books on various psychology topics.

School Psychology Resources Online

http://www.schoolpsychology.net

Good resource for school-related psychology programs. The links are vast and include mental retardation, eating disorders, substance abuse, the gifted and talented, mood disorders, and much more. This site also offers links to journals and articles, as well as many links to related sites.

Self-Help Magazine

http://www.shpm.com/

E-zine that has more than 75 professionals who contribute to its issues. Offers articles, classifieds, reviews, banner ads, and many links to related information. This site also has psychtoons and postcards. You can subscribe to a free newsletter, too.

A
B
C
D
E
F
G
H
I
J
K
L
M
N
O
P
Q
R
S
T
U
V
W
X
Y
Z

MOTIVATIONAL AND SELF-IMPROVEMENT INFORMATION

Deepak Chopra

http://www.chopra.com/

This is a one-stop shopping Web site for those seeking self-improvement. Pick up the tip of the day, the quote of the day, the vegetarian recipe of the week, and plenty of other spiritual guidance at Deepak Chopra's site, which includes information about his personal growth workshops and materials. You can also ask him a question and learn more about the Center for Well Being. You can also order books, candles, spices, and food supplements here.

InnerSelf Magazine: Behavior Modification

http://www.innerself.com/
Magazine/Behavior_Modification/

This site offers an extensive list of behavior modification articles. From here, you can click on the link to the InnerSelf Magazine home page and find lots of other articles and topics to explore. The entire premise behind this site is to "assist in creating the life you want."

Invisible Path To Success

http://www.invisiblepath.com/

Discover the next generation in personal success systems. Produce more powerful and consistent results in less time, with less effort and a lot more fun. Success, personal growth, and spirituality books, tapes, and personal seminars are available, as well as personal coaching.

John Gray

http://www.marsvenus.com/

Take John Gray's Personal Success Block Buster questionnaire to get feedback on what areas of your life are holding you back from total success. Then, read about all of his books, upcoming conferences, and recent magazine columns on relationships and parenting. Purchase books, audio and video tapes, CDs, and games at this site.

MotivationalQuotes.com

http://
www.motivationalquotes.com/

Huge collection of motivational quotes, prayers, and positive affirmations. Site is devoted to promoting positive thinking.

Personal Success Radio Network

http://
www.personalsuccessradio.com/

Internet radio station that focuses on "personal success, positive living, and self-improvement." Features top motivational speakers giving free advice.

Self-Worth.Com

http://www.self-worth.com/

A motivational mailer that arrives via email, delivering motivational messages, upbeat humor, and personal affirmations that can help you make it through the day.

Successories.com

http://www.successories.com/

Successories is dedicated to helping organizations and individuals realize their full potential. This company believes that motivation originates with attitude, grows in response to goals, and endures when reinforced through exposure to insightful ideas in your environment. The unique collection of themed merchandise is designed to promote a positive outlook, celebrate human achievement, and inspire excellence in your career, your business, and your life.

Tony Robbins: Resources for Creating an Extraordinary Quality of Life

http://www.tonyrobbins.com/

Home page of motivational guru Anthony Robbins. Learn about upcoming events, browse through his products and order them online, read the results he's achieved, visit daily for the day's "Daily Action," find out about coaching support, and more.

2WF.com

http://www.2wf.com/

Huge resource for everything related to motorcycles, this site covers racing, culture, bike tests, repair and maintenance, stunt riding, and more. Staffed by motorcycle owners and enthusiasts, dedicated to providing the best information in an irreverent and entertaining format. Discussion groups are also available.

AMA Superbike

http://www.amasuperbike.com

An unofficial AMA superbike site containing news, feature articles on racers, point summaries, and a racing calendar for the upcoming year.

American Motorcyclist Association

http://www.ama-cycle.org/

Promotes the interests of motorcycle enthusiasts. The site includes AMA pro and amateur racing information, travel, and more.

BMW Motorcycles

http://www.bmwmotorcycles.com/

As the official BMW motorcycles Web site, this is a visually appealing site—full of fun animation and solid information about BMW motorcycles. Learn about the complete line of BMW bikes, check out the gear and accessories, find a local dealer, and get financing information.

A B C D E F G H I J K L M N O P Q R S T U V W X Y Z

A
B
C
D
E
F
G
H
I
J
K
L
M
N
O
P
Q
R
S
T
U
V
W
X
Y
Z

Buell American Motorcycles

http://www.buell.com

Learn all about the history of bikes made by Buell, part of the Harley-Davidson family. The site also includes a locator for finding a local dealer and information about clothing and other accessories.

〚Best〛 Harley-Davidson

http://www.harley-davidson.com/

Official site of Harley-Davidson—the products, the company, and the experience. Check out the current models, find a dealer, and see what kind of new clothing, accessories, and gifts are available. You can even get information about investing in the Harley-Davidson company. This site's sleek design and comprehensive offerings make it the best commercial motorcycle site on the Web.

Indian Motorcycles

http://www.indianmotorcycles.com/

Home of America's oldest brand of motorcycle. Check out the latest line of Indian motorcycles, view a history of the company from 1900 to present, find a dealer, or copy free ride maps.

motogranprix.com

http://www.dorna.com/

If you follow the Motorcycle Grand Prix, you'll want to bookmark this page. Features calendar of races, race results, current standings, news, information about the riders and teams, and much more.

Motorcycle Riders Foundation

http://www.mrf.org/

This Washington, D.C.–based bikers' advocacy site offers news from D.C., MRF reports, a message board, national motorcycle laws, and links for information and research.

Motorcycle Tips and Techniques

http://www.msgroup.org/TIPS.asp

A collection of tips to keep the potentially dangerous hobby of motorcycling as safe as possible. There is also a case study on women motorcyclists, and links to a variety of other motorcycle pages.

Yamaha

http://www.yamaha-motor.com/

Home of Yamaha Motor Company, makers of motorcycles, snowmobiles, jetskis, boats, golf carts, and other popular recreational motor vehicles. Here, you can check out the latest motorcycle models and find a dealer near you.

MUSEUMS

Devices of Wonder

http://www.getty.edu/art/
exhibitions/devices

Sponsored by the Getty Museum, this site features the Devices of Wonder exhibit, a unique collection of the ancestors of modern cinema, cyborgs, computers, and optical devices.

Exploratorium

http://www.exploratorium.edu

Web site of the Exploratorium, a unique museum housed inside San Francisco's Palace of Fine Arts, which features more than "650 science, art, and human perception exhibits." Founded by noted physicist Dr. Frank Oppenheimer, this site is devoted to nurturing people's curiosity about the world around them. Here you can check out various online exhibits and learn more about the museum.

MUSÉE

http://www.musee-online.org/

International directory of museums which visitors can search by type of museum, alphabet, or geographical location. Rates each museum on a scale of one to five and provides information about each museum, including its hours of operation, educational materials, fun stuff to do, and visual content.

ARCHITECTURE

National Building Museum

http://www.nbm.org/

The National Building Museum presents permanent exhibitions about the world we live in, from our homes and offices to our parks and cities. This site has online excerpts of exhibits past and present, as well as information about books that complement them. There are also summaries from "The Urban Forum," a program designed to explore issues related to the design, growth, and governance of American cities. Stop by this site to find the museum's hours of operation and location.

Wharton Esherick Museum

http://www.levins.com/
esherick.html

This site features the life and work of this "Dean of American Craftsmen." Photos include the world-famous spiral oak staircase from his studio in Pennsylvania, and Esherick's regional influences are discussed.

ART

The African/Edenic Heritage Museum

http://www.kingdomofyah.com/
museum.htm

This traveling exhibit highlights the indigenous African presence in the Holy Land. Exhibit features "450 square feet of informative maps, provocative text, and exclusive photographs of the indigenous African/Edenic people of Israel." Here, you can learn more about the museum and how to contact the organizers.

Agung Rai Museum of Art

http://www.nusantara.com/arma/

This Indonesian museum houses a collection of works by Balinese, Javanese, and foreign artists. Select works are shown on the site, which are an intriguing display of history and culture.

The Andy Warhol Museum

http://www.warhol.org/

This site is part of the Carnegie Museums of Pittsburgh, which features a guided tour of the museum itself (opened in 1994), which features images and biographical information regarding Andy Warhol. It also describes the work of the Archives Study Center, which collects and preserves anything to do with Warhol's life and work. A calendar details upcoming exhibitions and events. Links to various Andy Warhol stores, where you can purchase T-shirts, posters, prints, and more.

The Art Institute of Chicago

http://www.artic.edu/

Comprising both a museum and an art school, the institute's site contains everything you always wanted to know about the museum, including information about exhibits and collections, the history and layout of the museum, publications and press releases, gift shop items, and institute membership information. You can also view art and play games related to art here.

Cincinnati Art Museum

http://www.cincinnatiartmuseum.com/

This site features a virtual tour of the museum's collections, children's activities, general information, and much more. Be sure to check out the museum's online gift store for gift items.

The Columbia Museum of Art

http://www.colmusart.org/

The museum's exhibits contain European and American fine and decorative art representing a time period of nearly seven centuries. Its public collections of Renaissance and Baroque art include works by Botticelli, Boucher, Canaletto, Tintoretto, and many others. The museum's online magazine, Collections, will alert you to recent acquisitions, a calendar of events, staffing changes, and additional newsworthy tidbits about the museum, located in Columbia, South Carolina.

Guggenheim Museums

http://www.guggenheim.org/

Site contains information about five museums: the Solomon R. Guggenheim Museum on Fifth Avenue in New York City; the Guggenheim Museum SoHo on Broadway in New York City; the Guggenheim Museum in Bilbao, Spain; the Peggy Guggenheim Collection in Venice, Italy; and the Deutsch Guggenheim Berlin. Includes some great photos of the museums and their exhibits.

J. Paul Getty Museum

http://www.getty.edu/museum

Learn about the Getty Museum's collection of works of art, which include antiquities, decorative arts, medieval manuscripts, European paintings, sculptures, drawings, and photographs. Get an overview of the exhibitions and check out the calendar of upcoming events. The online gift store offers everything from hats and T-shirts to calendars, cards, and posters. This site's excellent design, superior graphics, and exquisite content make it an easy choice as best of the best.

Le Louvre

http://www.louvre.fr/

This official site of the famous museum, the home of the Mona Lisa, includes information about the museum's seven departments: Oriental Antiquities (with a section dedicated to Islamic Art); Egyptian Antiquities (with a section dedicated to Coptic Art); Greek, Etruscan, and Roman Antiquities; Paintings; Sculptures; Objets d'Art; and Prints and Drawings. The site includes many details (small sections of paintings, enlarged so you can see them better) from the museum's collections. Take some cool QuickTime virtual tours of the museum.

Metropolitan Museum of Art, New York

http://www.metmuseum.org/

One of the largest art museums in the world, The Met's collections include more than 2,000,000 works of art—several hundred thousand of which are on view at any given time—spanning more than 5,000 years of world culture, from prehistory to the present. Stay updated on upcoming exhibitions and buy museum products online.

Museum of Fine Arts, Boston

http://www.mfa.org/

This museum prides itself on exhibiting art that is "past and present, old and new, plain and fancy," including masterpieces by Renoir, Monet, Sargent, Turner, Gauguin, and others. The site hosts an online exhibition and contains links to samples from upcoming exhibits. Learn about upcoming exhibitions and purchase museum products online.

Museum of Fine Arts, Houston

http://mfah.org

The Museum of Fine Arts, Houston site, includes visuals and information about the permanent collection, traveling exhibitions, events, and educational programs. Collections with online links include African sculpture, American painting, ancient art, decorative arts, Impressionist painting, and 20th-century sculpture.

Museum of Modern Art, New York

http://www.moma.org/

This site displays samples from current and future exhibits, as well as from the MOMA's permanent collection, which includes paintings and sculptures, drawings, prints and illustrated books, architecture and design, photographs, and film and video. The collection includes exceptional groups of work by Matisse, Picasso, Miró, Mondrian, Brancusi, and Pollock. It also contains links to online projects as well

A
B
C
D
E
F
G
H
I
J
K
L
M
N
O
P
Q
R
S
T
U
V
W
X
Y
Z

A
B
C
D
E
F
G
H
I
J
K
L
M
N
O
P
Q
R
S
T
U
V
W
X
Y
Z

as other Web sites created in conjunction with the Museum of Modern Art and its exhibits. A wealth of information is available about this New York City landmark. Be sure to check out the online gift store.

National Gallery of Canada

http://national.gallery.ca/

The National Gallery of Canada is the permanent home of Canada's exceptional national art collection, which includes Canadian art, Inuit art, contemporary art, as well as European, American, and Asian art. With text descriptions in both French and English, this well-designed site showcases this large gallery housing the Canadian national art collection.

The San Francisco Museum of Modern Art

http://www.sfmoma.org

Information about the museum's collection of modern and contemporary artwork is available, including exhibition details, a calendar of events, and educational programs. Information about the rental gallery can also be found here.

The Smithsonian Institution

http://www.si.edu/

The 150-year-old Smithsonian Institution comprises the National Portrait Gallery, the National Museum of American Art, the National Air and Space Museum, the Sackler Gallery, the Cooper-Hewitt Museum of Design, the National Museum of American History, the National Museum of Natural History, and more. You can search this comprehensive site using an A–Z subject index and learn about events and activities.

HISTORY AND CULTURE

Online Museum of Singapore Art and History

http://www.museum.org.sg/

This site contains links to the National Archives of Singapore, the National Museum of Singapore, the Asian Civilizations Museum, the Singapore History Museum, and the Singapore Art Museum. Details about each of these museums are provided, along with calendars, photos, and a plethora of information.

United States Holocaust Memorial Museum

http://www.ushmm.org/

This museum is an international resource for the development of research on the Holocaust and related issues, including those of contemporary significance. Includes a photographic, film, and video archive. The site contains links to museum resources and activities, as well as to related organizations and an internship program.

Wright Brothers Aeroplane Company and Museum of Aviation

http://www.first-to-fly.com/

Enjoy hands-on aviation fun at this museum, which offers virtual adventures and expeditions in four Wright brothers' planes, as well as historical information. There is a lot of information about planes and aviation that is perfect for students.

NATURAL HISTORY

American Museum of Natural History

http://www.amnh.org/

The museum's collections include the world's largest collection of fossil mammals, dinosaurs, insects, invertebrates, and more. The site lists a few of its thousands of research projects, along with some photos. The museum displays a wide range of temporary exhibits, which also can be explored at this site. Search the site to find specific information about animals of interest.

The Carnegie Museum of Natural History

http://www.carnegiemuseums.org/cmnh/

Founded in 1895, the Carnegie Museum of Natural History is one of the nation's leading research museums and is renowned for its Dinosaur Hall. This page was established to provide news of the museum's events, as well as developments in the field of natural history in general. It is divided into 13 different and wide-ranging scientific sections, from anthropology and birds to minerals and nature reserves.

The Field Museum

http://www.fmnh.org/

Use this site to find out what's new at Chicago's Field Museum, which has featured Sue, the largest, most complete T-Rex exhibit in the world, the Dead Sea Scrolls, and maneless tigers, called Tsavos. This is one of the largest and most diverse museums in the world.

Smithsonian National Museum of Natural History

http://www.mnh.si.edu/

This extensive site has everything you ever wanted to know about this museum. Read about museum exhibitions, such as the return of Ishi, Echinoderms, and the giant squid. There are also online exhibits that relate to global warming, hologlobes, and crossroads of continents, among others.

PAPERMAKING, PRINTING, AND TYPESETTING

Melbourne Museum of Printing

http://home.vicnet.net.au/~typo/

This is a working and teaching museum of type and printing. Its collection includes machines, information about fonts, and other printing items. It also has links to books and records that have to do with printing and businesses of that type (no pun intended).

PHOTOGRAPHY AND FILM

Berkeley Art Museum/Pacific Film Archive

http://www.bampfa.berkeley.edu/

The visual arts center of the University of California at Berkeley, the UAM/PFA is noted for its thought-provoking exhibitions of both art and film. The museum Web site contains online versions of current and former exhibitions.

A
B
C
D
E
F
G
H
I
J
K
L
M
N
O
P
Q
R
S
T
U
V
W
X
Y
Z

California Museum of Photography

http://www.cmp.ucr.edu/

This site contains photos, descriptions, and other information from exhibits at this museum, as well as links to a museum store, with copies of featured photos from the exhibit for sale. (Items in the store link to Amazon.com, where you can place your order.)

International Center of Photography

http://www.icp.org/

Established to collect 20th-century works, this center has a special emphasis on documentary photography. The center, located in New York City, also teaches all levels of photography. Site contains photos from special exhibits.

National Museum of Photography, Film, and Television

http://www.nmpft.org.uk/

This museum contains varied displays, interactive features, large and small screens, and constantly changing special exhibitions, events, theater, and education. Catch up on online research projects and learn about upcoming exhibitions here.

ORGANIZATIONS SCIENCE AND TECHNOLOGY

The Exploratorium

http://www.exploratorium.edu/

The Exploratorium is a collage of 650 interactive exhibits in the areas of science, art, and human perception. It provides access to and information about science, nature, art, and technology. The site has online versions of exhibits and tons of other scientific information.

The Museum of Contemporary Ideas

http://toolshed.artschool.utas.edu.au/moci/home.html

This unique museum delves into the worlds of the visual arts, the philosophy of science, architecture, technology, performing arts, and off-planet systems.

The Museum of Science and Industry, Chicago

http://www.msichicago.org/

This site contains online exhibits that provide a sample of the experiences available at the museum. It also provides Omnimax film clips and educational resources for teachers, as well as exhibit schedules and general information about the Chicago area.

National Museum of Science and Technology, Canada

http://www.science-tech.nmstc.ca/

This museum was created to explore "the transformation of Canada." Different subjects of the museum include agriculture, communications, energy, forestry, graphic arts, transportation, and many others. Links and descriptions are provided for all subjects as well as for behind-the-scenes information such as restoration.

Oregon Museum of Science and Industry

http://www.omsi.edu/

Observe vibrations and sound waves in the museum's Electronics Lab, or weave your own piece of the Web in the Computer Lab. This site provides links to all the museum's main areas, complete with photos and descriptions of many exhibits. There is a lot of great information at this site.

Shedd Aquarium

http://www.sheddnet.org/

Find out about animals and exhibits at this Chicago aquarium, where you can Ask Shedd about an aquatic topic, such as caring for a home aquarium, or a particular animal at the aquarium.

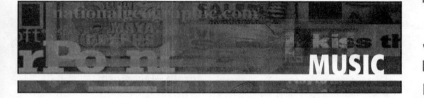

MUSIC

BUYING RESOURCES

Barnes & Noble.com

http://music.barnesandnoble.com/

This popular bookstore has been selling CDs for quite some time, check out their selection and prices and place your order online.

BestBuy.com

http://www.bestbuy.com/

The largest consumer electronics store in the nation now delivers a huge collection of CD and DVD titles at competitive prices.

Blue Vision Music

http://members.aol.com/JamesBVM/homepage.html

Specializing in original contemporary music for kids, this online store offers a small collection of tapes, CDs, and books featuring the work of James Coffey. Sample some of the songs directly from the site (in AU format—requires a plug-in or player). The Kid's Club section offers some interesting activities for the younger set (QuickTime or other movie viewer required).

Buy.com

www.buy.com

Pick a category of music and then search for particular artists or albums. On the right side of the site, you can find out which albums and singles are at the top of the charts. Buy.com provides free shipping, too.

A
B
C
D
E
F
G
H
I
J
K
L
M
N
O
P
Q
R
S
T
U
V
W
X
Y
Z

A
B
C
D
E
F
G
H
I
J
K
L

M
N
O
P
Q
R
S
T
U
V
W
X
Y
Z

CD Baby

http://www.cdbaby.com/

Online music store specializing in CDs from independent artists. If you recorded a CD, CD Baby can help you sell it online. You can even sample one or two songs from a CD before you decide to purchase it.

CD Universe

http://www.cduniverse.com/

CD Universe promises the most music at the best prices. The interface is particularly easy to use, with graphics augmented by text to explain the purpose of each section (you don't need to spend as much time roaming around to find the section you want). Interested in the top-flight artists in each genre? Check out the Charts section.

CDnow

http://www.cdnow.com/

CDnow claims to be the world's largest music store, and this site seems to back up that statement, with an amazing number of titles available. Plenty of RealAudio sound clips. Gift certificates for those who have everything; the personalized gift program can also recommend 10 gift ideas based on the names of four artists.

Sam Goody Music

http://www.samgoody.com/

Just about every type of music for every possible taste is available here. This online extension of Sam Goody's brick-and-mortar stores offers CDs, tapes, and videos, as well as sheet music.

SonyMusicDirect.com

http://www.sonymusicdirect.com/

A division of Sony Music Entertainment, Inc., that's dedicated to delivering thousands of CD and DVD titles directly to the consumer at bargain prices.

TowerRecords.com

http://www.towerrecords.com/

Search for particular bands or types of music, or just browse the listings to find something of interest. There are CDs for under $7 and new releases you'll want to pay attention to. You can also listen to tracks before you buy them.

Virgin Megastore

http://www.virginmega.com/

Get digital downloads and exclusive music news and clips, as well as a huge selection of music for sale in just about every category, at Virgin Records.

INFORMATION, NEWS, AND REVIEWS

Artistdirect.com

http://www.artistdirect.com/

This site represents a network of music-related offerings: MP3 and more, UBL.com, imusic.com, and the Artistdirect superstore. Visitors will find an overview of what each category has to offer and links to connect directly to anything that appeals. Find out what your favorite artists are listening to, read the latest music news, preview new music, buy official merchandise, and lots more.

Billboard Online

http://www.billboard.com/

This site offers fast and easy access to Billboard Magazine's huge electronic library. Charts and articles from the current issue are available to visitors.

Black Beat Magazine

http://www.blackbeat.com/

Online version of Black Beat magazine, the magazine for urban music and culture, primarily rap music.

iMUSIC

http://imusic.artistdirect.com/

News, features, CD reviews, bulletin boards, chat rooms, and even an online music store—this site has it all. Tons of links to individual artists and bands grouped by musical category.

IUMA

http://www.iuma.com/

At the Internet Underground Music Archive, bands can post information and MP3s free using their own URL with the band name first. You can also sell CDs, create message boards, fan lists, and most importantly, get email from your fans. The site is designed to help unknown bands get recognition, or at least get heard.

⟦Best⟧ MTV

http://www.mtv.com/

Weigh in with your vote for who should be cast in the next Real World/Road Rules crew, read interviews with top groups and artists, skim reviews of upcoming releases, and get the music news of the day here, where you can also find out about the TV schedule. Buy digital music on this site. One of the first of its kind, MTV's Web site remains the best of its kind.

NME

http://www.nme.com/

The online home of NME (New Musical Express) magazine, this site features music news, reviews, concert information, charts, and much more. Bulletin boards and chat provide a means of interacting with fellow fans, and NME Radio plays in the background, so you can listen while you explore the site.

SonicNet.com

http://www.sonicnet.com

Whether you're a jazz fan, hip-hop nut, or you like opera, pop, rap, or just about any other music genre, you'll find reviews of recent albums and releases, as well as music you can download and listen to here.

VH1.COM

http://www.vh1.com/

Read daily reviews at the online version of this cable station, where you can also get music news, find concerts coming to your area, and learn what's on tap tonight on VH-1.

A
B
C
D
E
F
G
H
I
J
K
L
M
N
O
P
Q
R
S
T
U
V
W
X
Y
Z

World Café

http://worldcafe.org/

Home of the World Café, a public radio show that provides an avenue for up-and-coming musicians to showcase their stuff. Hosted by David Dye, the show consists of a low-key interview intermixed with songs. Links to interviews that you can listen to online. Search for artists, buy CDs, enter contests, or find a local radio station that plays the show.

Worldwide Internet Music Resources

http://www.music.indiana.edu/
music_resources/

Hosted by the William and Gayle Cook Music Library at Indiana University. Contains links to almost every imaginable music-related site—artists/ensembles, composers, genres, publications, the music industry, general and miscellaneous resources, Usenet groups, research, and more.

LYRICS

Bob Dylan Music

http://orad.dent.kyushu-u.ac.jp/
dylan/song.html

Are you sometimes not sure what the words are when Bob sings? Here are the lyrics to just about every Dylan song ever recorded, alphabetized by song title.

The Cyber Hymnal

http://www.cyberhymnal.org/

At this site, you'll find the lyrics to hundreds of gospel songs and hymns. With a sound card and speakers, you can hear the music, too. There are special areas of children's, Christmas, and Easter songs, along with biographies of song writers and hymn trivia.

A House Is Not a Home Page

http://studentweb.tulane.edu/
~mark/bacharach.html

Provides lyrics, biography, audio files, chord sheets, and news about songwriter Burt Bacharach. Includes articles, pictures, and a list of hit songs. Also provides links to sites where Bacharach's music can be purchased.

Musicnotes.com

http://musicnotes.com/

Download digital sheet music to your PC for a small fee, print it, and play it. Choose from a huge selection of today's pop hits to classical selections. Search by title or artist, or composer, to find exactly what you're looking for.

Phil's Home Page

http://www.iinet.net.au/~pgb/

Phil has chosen quite a few songs to provide lyrics for, and they're all meaningful. He even suggests certain times when each song would be appropriate. Want to tell someone how you feel, but you're at a loss for words? Check these lyrics.

MP3—RESOURCES

Artist Direct Free MP3

http://listen.artistdirect.com/

Register at DownloadsDirect and be able to download the hottest music from every conceivable genre for a small fee. Some of it is even available at no charge. There is a huge selection of music. You can also read columns written by critics.

emusic

http://www.emusic.com/

Download music tracks for one low monthly fee. Try it free for one month. More than 200,000 MP3s to choose from.

KaZaA

http://www.kazaa.com

Internet file-sharing program enables users to swap files, including games, audio clips, video clips, and shareware over the Internet. Relies on the honor system to prevent users from breaking copyright laws.

listen.com

http://www.listen.com/

Listen.com provides a music-on-demand subscription service. You pay a monthly subscription fee and then pick the artists and songs you want to hear. Listen.com provides you with unlimited playback time for the selected songs.

MP3 Nexus

http://www.bigg.net/

Download players, search other MP3 sites for music, get the latest digital music news, and download songs for your personal enjoyment.

MP3.com

http://www.mp3.com/

The leader of the MP3 phenomenon that has more than 200,000 songs available for you to enjoy. Service costs about $10 per month, but MP3.com offers a free 14-day, 50-clip trial period.

MP3Nut

http://www.mp3nut.com/

Huge, searchable database of MP3 files. A little difficult to maneuver at first, but read the screens and follow the instructions, and this might just turn out to be your favorite MP3 site on the Web.

Music City

http://www.musiccity.com/

Devoted to leveling the playing field for musicians and artists, this site helps artists and bands distribute their music in order to establish an audience. Music City also features Morpheus, a program, similar to Napster, that allows users to swap MP3 files.

Napster

http://www.napster.com

Originally, the most popular place on the Internet for swapping MP3 music clips with other music lovers, this site is currently undergoing renovation to make its service legal.

MP3—SEARCH ENGINES

AudioGalaxy

http://www.audiogalaxy.com/

Excellent MP3 search site lets you browse for MP3 clips by category or search by keyword.

MUSIC EVENTS

Blues Festivals

http://www.bluesfestivals.com/

A fantastic site full of listings and links to blues festivals nationwide. Bookmark this one—it is a must for any true blues fan.

A B C D E F G H I J K L **M** N O P Q R S T U V W X Y Z

A
B
C
D
E
F
G
H
I
J
K
L
M
N
O
P
Q
R
S
T
U
V
W
X
Y
Z

CC.com

http://sfx.com/

Formed through the merger of Sunshine Promotions and SFX Entertainment, this site provides information about some of the hottest live shows on the circuit, including Nick Cave, The Cranberries, Paul McCartney, U2, and Jamie Foxx.

Pollstar: The Concert Hotwire

http://www.pollstar.com/

This online weekly media magazine geared for the concert industry publishes several industry directories, performer tour histories, mailing labels, and directories on disk. Search the site for upcoming concert information by band name or venue.

Ticketmaster.com

http://www.ticketmaster.com/

Find music and sporting events, as well as upcoming theater and comedy performances, by searching the Ticketmaster site by keyword, artist, or location. You can then charge your tickets by phone or purchase your tickets online.

TicketWeb

http://www.ticketweb.com

Online box office that simplifies the process of obtaining tickets to concerts, plays, museums, and other interesting and entertaining places and events.

MUSIC GENRES— ALTERNATIVE

Alien Ant Farm

http://www.alienantfarm.com/

Features spiffy Flash presentation of the band, showcasing their unique sounds and performances. Fans can read the latest news headlines, check out concert information, access biographies, check out links to related sites, and even shop for memorabilia online.

Angel in Devil's Boots: Nick Cave's Unofficial Web Site

http://
www.angelindevilsboots.org/

This unofficial site dedicated to the gothic blues rock music of Nick Cave and the Bad Seeds includes current news, articles, interviews, and links to other related sites in a well-organized format.

The Color Red

http://www.thecolorred.com/

Sample music from the latest album of this West Coast rock band, read about how they got together, and find out where some of their upcoming shows are.

Creed

http://www.creednet.com/

Check out Creed's home page, where you'll find music and video clips, a well-stocked photo gallery, concert information, and much more.

D'CuCKOO

http://home.earthlink.net/
~sabean2/bandlife.html

The techno-tribal band is made up of six women from Oakland who build and play their own percussion instruments, including 6-foot bamboo "trigger sticks." This site features information about the band, its famous MidiBall, and RiGBy, the computer-generated puppet. Their music mixes sophisticated pop vocals and lyrics with techno, dance, and world music influences.

Dave Matthews Band

http://www.dmband.com/

Join the announcement list to receive word of news and updates regarding this popular band. You can also investigate the band's history, check their tour schedule, read about the members and view their photos, or order Dave Matthews Band merchandise.

does not

http://www.doesnot.com/

Very high-tech site plays multimedia clips of several of the bands songs. Also features music videos, audio clips, bios, and more.

GreenDay.com

http://www.greenday.com/

The official site of Green Day. Here, you can find news about the band and its upcoming tours, check out its CDs and video clips, visit the photo gallery, and even join the "Idiot Club."

Korn

http://www.korn.com/

Watch KornTV—a.k.a. Kornography—at their site, read the transcripts from any online chat

sessions they've had, look at more than 70 photos from a recent performance, and find out when they'll be playing near you. You can also find which shows are going to be rescheduled.

Limp Bizkit

http://www.limp-bizkit.com/

Take a look at tour pictures, use the lyrics section to double-check those lyrics you weren't sure of, order merchandise, and link to their site.

Lou Reed and the Velvet Underground

http://www.rocknroll.net/loureed/

You'll find information about Lou Reed, the Velvet Underground, and more here. Includes, among other things, a bootleg gallery, a discography, an image gallery, and comments on the latest tour.

No Doubt

http://www.nodoubt.com/

Home of No Doubt, creators of the smash hit "Hey Baby," this site features a huge collection of tidbits about the band and its members, plus several music and video clips, a photo gallery, tour information, links to related sites, and more.

The Offspring

http://www.offspring.com/

Tons of information about the rock band The Offspring. Includes pictures, videos, lyrics, discography, articles, images, sound clips (in WAV and RealAudio), and interviews, plus chat rooms and message boards where you can stay in touch with fellow fans.

A
B
C
D
E
F
G
H
I
J
K
L
M
N
O
P
Q
R
S
T
U
V
W
X
Y
Z

A
B
C
D
E
F
G
H
I
J
K
L
M
N
O
P
Q
R
S
T
U
V
W
X
Y
Z

Pearl Jam

http://www.pearljam.com/

Pearl Jam's official home page, this site features news about the band, a discography, tour information, message boards, and even a Pearl Jam store where you can purchase "consumables" online.

Phish

http://www.phish.com

Find out everything you need to know about the band, Phish, from where they'll be playing to when their next album will be released. Band news also includes information about individual members, and where they'll be showing up live, onstage.

Red Hot Chili Peppers

http://redhotchilipeppers.com

Get on the official Red Hot Chili Peppers email list for updates regarding albums, tours, and news. Read Flea's messages from the road and listen to Chili Peppers' music at the site.

The R.E.M. Home Page

http://www.remhq.com/

This official R.E.M. Web site includes news and reviews, a link to the official fan club, discography, videography, and a "Thriftstore," where you can purchase CDs, T-shirts, and other memorabilia.

Smashing Pumpkins

http://www.smashingpumpkins.com/

Leaning toward the heavy side of alternative rock, this site is packed with free samples divided into three

categories: Sound (audio clips), Images (a photo gallery), and Movement (video clips). Visit the discussion forum to read and post messages about the band and its concerts.

Stone Temple Pilots

http://www.stonetemplepilots.com/

Official home page of the hard-hitting alternative rock band, Stone Temple Pilots, this site features news, tour dates, discography, biographies of the band and its members, multimedia shows, a photo gallery, and more. Purchase memorabilia online.

Sunhawk.com

http://www.sunhawk.com/

Download, print, and play back engraving-quality sheet music! This site offers Free Solero interactive music software, and a new free song every week. Thousands of best-selling titles to choose from! Digital alternative music is just one option of many.

Third Eye Blind

http://www.3eb.com/

Information about the band, albums, articles, tour dates, sound and video clips, and email. Interesting graphics, by the way.

Tom Waits

http://www.officialtomwaits.com/

This official Tom Waits site features background information and insights into this enigmatic artist. Not much in the way of audio and video clips, but if you'd like to know more about Tom Waits and his variety of creative projects, this is the place to go. Provides a complete list of Waits' albums, movies in which he acted, and interviews.

Violent Femmes

http://www.vfemmes.com/

Check out Violent Femmes interviews, lyrics, discography, photo gallery, tour information, and more at their official home site.

MUSIC GENRES— BLUEGRASS

The Bluegrass Connection

http://www.gotech.com/

Online resource where you can locate festivals and bluegrass music products and information. Also find out about record companies, manufacturers of bluegrass equipment, and instrument-supply companies.

Bluegrass Music Listings: The Country Grapevine

http://www.countrygrapevine.com/music/bluegrass/listings.htm

Florida country music fans will enjoy tracking down their favorite bluegrass bands at this site, where you can find out about upcoming auditions, check the schedule of local bands, and join in country chat.

Bluegrass World

http://www.bluegrassworld.com

You'll find bluegrass musicians, festivals, merchandise, record companies, catalogs, radio stations, and bluegrass music links all in one place.

BlueGrassRoots Master Catalog Search

http://members.tripod.com/~kc4vus/roots.html

Enormous database of bluegrass musicians and record labels. Search the database for your favorite musician, band, or album. You can also search by the label or the year. A master catalog is available for download.

Top 100 Bluegrass Sites

http://www.bluegrassrules.com/top100.asp

Directory of the "best" 100 bluegrass sites is a great place to start looking for information about various bands and festivals.

Welcome to Planet Bluegrass!

http://www.bluegrass.com/

Blue Planet Music, organizers of the legendary Telluride Bluegrass Festival, is now online. The site contains a festival schedule and information, as well as information about Blue Planet recordings and its mail-order operation. You can also buy posters, T-shirts, tickets, and other merchandise from their secure server.

MUSIC GENRES— CHRISTIAN MUSIC

Christian Music Resources

http://www.guitarsite.com/christian.htm

Excellent collection of links to various Christian music resource sites on the Web.

A
B
C
D
E
F
G
H
I
J
K
L
M
N
O
P
Q
R
S
T
U
V
W
X
Y
Z

A
B
C
D
E
F
G
H
I
J
K
L
M
N
O
P
Q
R
S
T
U
V
W
X
Y
Z

Jamsline: The Christian Music Info Source

http://www.jamsline.com/

Cool-looking site that offers hundreds of titles for purchase, including Amy Grant, Jars of Clay, Anointed, and more.

Jars of Clay

http://www.jarsofclay.com/

Official site of the Christian rock group Jars of Clay. Here you'll find band and tour information, sound bites, and more. Links to Amazon.com and other online retailers where you can purchase related materials. Great-looking page! Be sure to sign up for the mailing list!

MUSIC GENRES— CLASSICAL

BMG: Classics World

http://www.getmusic.com/ classical/bmg/

A large online store where you can order almost any classical recording currently in print.

Classical USA

http://classicalusa.com/

This site features reviews of more than 1,000 CDs, 4,800 files, and more than 2,600 links to other classical music Web sites. Very comprehensive directory to all things classical on the Web, including film and video, opera theater and song, and music publications.

Gramophone

http://www.gramophone.co.uk/

Online version of the internationally acclaimed magazine, this site features incisive articles on current classical music recordings, orchestras, and performances. Interviews, profiles, editor's choice top 10 recordings, information about competitions and industry news, and more. Also provides online discussion forums.

Klassiknet

http://www.culturekiosque.com/ klassik/

An online magazine for classical music fans, including articles, performer and composer interviews and biographies, reviews, and schedules. Some articles appear in both French and English. Don't leave without checking out the list of the 101 best vintage recordings.

Leonard Bernstein

http://www.leonardbernstein.com/

Here you can learn more about Bernstein's life and his work, find books about him, listen to excerpts from his recordings, look at photos of Bernstein and his family and friends, scan music from his personal collection, and read about some of his philanthropic projects. You can also purchase recording and sheet music, as well as books written by the famous composer/ conductor.

Medieval and Renaissance Music

http://home.hkstar.com/~mulcheng/

This is a site for beginners rather than scholars, and provides history and a timeline for both medieval and Renaissance music. Includes lists of literature and manuscript resources for more information about this music.

MusicOnline Classical Music Directory

http://www.musicalonline.com/

Comprehensive directory to classical music resources on the Internet, including schools, museums, journals, music theory, scholarly works, competitions, scholarships, and much much more.

National Association of Composers, USA

http://www.music-usa.org/nacusa/

NACUSA, founded in 1933, is devoted to the promotion and performance of music by Americans. The site includes member links, recent and upcoming concert schedules, chapter information, and a plethora of links to other music-related sites.

New York Philharmonic

http://www.nyphilharmon.org/

Information for fans and friends of the New York Philharmonic, including educational guides, historical information, ticket information, and news releases.

Piano Nanny

http://www.pianonanny.com/index. html

Always wanted to learn how to play the piano, but never had the time to learn? This site provides piano lessons online. Each lesson takes about 35 minutes to complete (you must have QuickTime installed).

Sony Classical

http://www.sonyclassical.com/

Sony Entertainment's classical music site, where you can learn about Sony's classical artists, check out their CDs, listen to sample sound clips, view photos, and find out about upcoming tours.

MUSIC GENRES— COUNTRY

Alan Jackson

http://ajackson.com/

Official site for fans of this popular entertainer. Offers tour and fan club information, and introduces you to his band. Check out the Alan Jackson merchandise available, from clothing to beanie bears. Did you know his favorite TV show is The Andy Griffith Show?

Brooks & Dunn Online

http://www.brooks-dunn.com/

Provides tour information and the opportunity to order merchandise and albums. Also provides an email address.

The Clint Black Web Site

http://www.clintblack.com/

See what this dimpled crooner has been up to lately and when he'll be appearing near you. Listen to sound clips, brush up on your lyrics, watch videos, or read recent articles about him.

A
B
C
D
E
F
G
H
I
J
K
L
M
N
O
P
Q
R
S
T
U
V
W
X
Y
Z

A
B
C
D
E
F
G
H
I
J
K
L

M
N
O
P
Q
R
S
T
U
V
W
X
Y
Z

CMT.com

http://www.cmt.com/

Read feature articles on country music stars, find new albums slated for release, download country music clips from your favorite artists, and read country music news. Also features audio and video clips.

Faith Hill

http://www.faithhill.com/

See Faith's latest album cover, read about her most recent awards, scan music and tour reviews, and learn more about this superstar performer at her official site. You can also buy apparel, mousepads, keychains, and other Faith Hill–related products. This is truly a lovely site, well-constructed, and easy to navigate.

Garth Brooks: Planet Garth

http://www.planetgarth.com/

Provides the latest on country sensation Garth Brooks. Includes tour information, reviews, chord chart positions, song lyrics, pictures, and downloadable songs in RealAudio format. This site also has an extensive store where you can purchase all kinds of Garth Brooks merchandise.

Johnny Cash: The Official Page

http://www.johnnycash.com/

Contains a long list of career highlights and a summary of Johnny Cash's biography (published in October of 1997). Check out the selection of classic audio clips from this legendary country performer.

Oak Ridge Boys

http://www.oakridgeboys.com/

This award-winning group has had members come and go in its 50-year history, but most people know the current members whose hits include Elvira and Y'All Come Back Saloon. Site contains tons of photos, clips, group history, and everything a fan could want.

Patty Loveless

http://www.sonynashville.com/PattyLoveless/

Listen to some of Patty's songs, read through her detailed bio, and join the fan club. This CMA Female Vocalist of the Year winner has earned her following by producing hit after hit. Check out this site to see why.

Reba McEntire

http://www.reba.com/

The official site for devotees of the country music singer. Links include the album, chat, the book, and off the record. Check out the store to see what CDs and videos are available for sale. You can even shop for your favorite Reba movies and videos. Online shopping available through Amazon.com.

Tim McGraw

http://www.timmcgraw.com/

Become a mcgrawfunaddict (in other words, join the fan club) at this site. Contains all the latest information about this hunky singer and his wife, country singer Faith Hill. You can also buy T-shirts and other "McGrawWear" items here.

Trace Adkins Official Website

http://www.traceadkins.net

Listen to a message from Trace or
the songs from his latest album.
Also contains the usual bio, tour
dates, gift shop, and fan club information.

The Trisha Yearwood Fan Page

http://www.totallytrisha.com

Track the singer's hits as they travel
the record charts. Post to the fan
page message board and take a fan
survey. Also includes current news,
a biography, photos, audio clips,
clothing and other merchandise for
purchase, and more—all dedicated
to fans of this powerfully voiced
country star.

MUSIC GENRES— ETHNIC

Temple Records

http://www.templerecords.co.uk

Provides home site and online
ordering for Temple Records, which
specializes in Scottish traditional
music. Includes an online catalog,
artist descriptions, and ordering
information.

The Unofficial Clannad Website

http://www.empire.net/
~whatmoug/clanhome.htm

Excellent site, organized into sections with a discography, lyrics,
images, interviews, sound bytes,
and information about the Irish
band Clannad. You'll also find links
to other Clannad sites.

Welcome to Bali & Beyond

http://www.balibeyond.com/

Bali & Beyond is a Los Angeles–
based performing arts company
inspired by the culture of Indonesia.
The ensemble tours nationwide,
featuring a variety of music, theater,
and educational presentations.
Their colorful site contains lots of
information about upcoming concert schedules and events. Check
out the Kechat section for background on the Indonesian culture
and music, and Maria's Corner for
all kinds of interesting gift items.

MUSIC GENRES— JAZZ

52nd Street Jazz

http://www.52ndstreet.com/

In addition to reading about featured "CDs in the Spotlight," here
you can find reviews of the latest
CDs featuring every kind of jazz—
from contemporary to avant garde.
There is also a searchable archive of
more than 1,000 previous reviews
and a bulletin board to share and
learn the latest jazz news. Links to
CDNOW, where you can purchase
jazz music online.

Down Beat Magazine

http://www.downbeat.com/

The place to go for the latest news,
reviews, and information about
your favorite jazz bands and artists.

A
B
C
D
E
F
G
H
I
J
K
L
M
N
O
P
Q
R
S
T
U
V
W
X
Y
Z

A
B
C
D
E
F
G
H
I
J
K
L
M
N
O
P
Q
R
S
T
U
V
W
X
Y
Z

Jazz Corner

http://www.jazzcorner.com/

This comprehensive jazz kiosk provides links to individual artists' home pages, a calendar of jazz events for most states, a photo gallery, interviews, reviews, news, and a discussion area.

The Jazz Review

http://www.jazzreview.com/

Listen to audio reviews, post your own review of particular pieces, read others' reviews, check out a featured artist, and listen to featured performers as part of the "CD of the Week."

Miles Davis

http://www.milesdavis.com/

Official home page of the famous jazz trumpet player and composer, this site features a biography of Miles Davis, a brief history of his musical career, a sampling of MP3 clips.

MUSIC GENRES— OPERA

Báthory Erzsébet: Elizabeth Báthory

http://bathory.org/

If you're at all interested in how an opera came to be, visit this site. In the Cologne Journal section, Dennis Báthory-Kitsz describes the plans for this semihistorical opera in progress. Check out the history, the bibliography, and, of course, the castle photos.

FanFaire

http://ffaire.com/

A Web-zine by and for fans of opera and classical music, updated quarterly, with reviews, slideshows, pictures, and embedded sound files. For best viewing, you'll need a fairly fast modem and a recent version of Netscape or Internet Explorer. Be prepared for sound at a substantial volume—the Java applets might reset your volume levels.

The Metropolitan Opera

http://www.metopera.org/

Before you head out to see Aida or Carmen—or any other major opera, for that matter—turn to the Stories of the Operas section at this site to get the lowdown on what's going to happen. You can also check the Metropolitan Opera's concert schedule, take the Met quiz, and learn more about the Met's history.

Opera News Online

http://www.operanews.com/

An electronic publication of the Metropolitan Opera Guild, Inc. Historical and musical analyses, performance reviews, profiles and interviews, and more. Visitors are welcome to pop in and scope out selected news and articles before subscribing. A subscription gives you access to the full magazine online and via mail.

Opera Works

http://patriciagray.net/operahtmls/works.html

This unusual site, a production of Rhodes College in Memphis, Tennessee, provides a pronunciation dictionary, complete with a brief description and a sound file, for dozens of names associated with opera—names of composers, names of operas, and so on. Also connects to the Opera Memphis home page.

Opera World

http://www.operaworld.com/

Sign up for a distance learning class to learn more about opera, or order educational material about operas to study on your own, and pick up information on upcoming opera broadcasts you can tune into. You can also search for and purchase opera CDs and merchandise, such as performance posters.

Sydney Opera House

http://www.soh.nsw.gov.au/

Learn more about this Australian cultural landmark, its history, and its future performances. This site also sports a nice shopping site where you can purchase CDs, videos, and Australian-related music gifts.

MUSIC GENRES— POP MUSIC

Backstreet Boys

http://www.backstreetboys.com/

Be the first to hear about the Backstreet Boys' upcoming projects, such as a book and comic, as well as check out photos and bios of the members, and sign up for their free fan newsletter. Free music clips and music videos. Check out the shopping site for Backstreet Boys merchandise.

The Beatles: Songs, Pictures, and Stories of the Beatles

http://www.rarebeatles.com/

Find out what that Beatles memorabilia is worth by taking a look at information and links at this site. Trying to locate that album cover that's missing from your collection? You're likely to find it here, where Beatles fans gather.

Bee Gees Main Page

http://www.beegees.net/

The ultimate disco group. A great site for true fans to enjoy the Brothers Gibb. Don't forget to order your Bee Gees calendar.

Britney Spears

http://www.britneyspears.com/

Check out the moves of this pop star maven, check out her latest CD, preview her movie Crossroads, and keep up on the latest tour dates and concert information. A good collection of photos, audio clips, video clips, and other entertaining material will keep fans busy for hours. Also features online shopping for Britney Spears apparel and memorabilia.

Buddy Holly

http://www.cmgww.com/music/holly/holly.html

Learn more about the career and music of Buddy Holly, through photos and a bio page here. There are also links to other music sites.

A
B
C
D
E
F
G
H
I
J
K
L
M
N
O
P
Q
R
S
T
U
V
W
X
Y
Z

A
B
C
D
E
F
G
H
I
J
K
L
M
N
O
P
Q
R
S
T
U
V
W
X
Y
Z

Chicago

http://www.chicagotheband.com/

The official Web site for the legendary music group Chicago. Learn about their music, what's new, talk to the band, look at images, and so on. You can also order band merchandise from this site.

Christina Aguilera

http://www.christina-a.com/

Check out the official site of Christina Aguilera and find out just how this sexy superstar has skyrocketed to fame in the world of pop. Here, you can listen to audio clips, view video clips, tour Christina's photo gallery, read her biography, join the fan club, and much more.

Janet Jackson

http://www.janet-jackson.com/

This site focuses on Janet Jackson, and includes the latest news, tour information, sounds, image gallery, lyrics, and more. Links to Artist Direct, where you can purchase Janet merchandise ranging from tour buttons to autographed CDs.

Jimmy Buffett's Margaritaville

http://www.margaritaville.com/

This is truly the quintessential Jimmy Buffett site. You can find current tour information, learn the lyrics to every Buffett tune, shop online for Jimmy Buffett apparel and other memorabilia, learn about the band members, and keep in touch with fellow Parrot Heads! Great site for hard-core Buffett fans!

Kid Rock

http://www.kidrock.com

Visit the official Web site of the bad boy of pop, Kid Rock. Check out the latest headline news concerning the band, check tour dates, read Kid Rock's biography, check out the photo gallery, listen to free audio clips, and more. Free Kid Rock desktop wallpaper and AOL chat icons available.

Madonna

http://www.madonnafanclub.com/

Catch up on the history of this pop icon, learn the lyrics to her most popular songs, listen to sample audio clips, view music videos, check out the photo gallery, or shop online for Madonna memorabilia.

Mariah Carey

http://www.mariahcarey.com/

For some time, the hottest performer in pop, Mariah may not hold the top spot, but her voice and her performances are still top-quality material. Check out her official Web site and sample her latest cuts, video clips, and information about upcoming projects and performances.

Michael Jackson

http://www.michaeljackson.com/

Hi-tech site from the legend of pop showcases this incredible performer's career. View MJ's biography, check out his discography and list of short films, and keep abreast of the latest news regarding Michael Jackson.

NSYNC.com

http://www.nsync.com/

Very cool site! Get a look behind the scenes at an NSYNC concert, or find out when and where the next one is. You can also review bios and pictures of band members, and check out new music and videos.

The Official Hootie and the Blowfish Web Site

http://www.hootie.com/

This site gives you a whole lotta Hootie! A good site with a distinctly collegiate feel. Check it out for more information on this longtime college party band. You can see latest tour photos, find song lyrics, and stop by the Hootie store for Hootie merchandise.

Pop-Music.com

http://www.pop-music.com

Check the charts to see how your favorite group is doing, search for information about pop groups, chat with fellow fans, and get the latest news here. You'll find just about everything you want to know about your group here, whether it's Nsync, the Backstreet Boys, or Madonna.

Ricky Martin

http://www.rickymartin.com/

This Ricky Martin site, which is full of photos, details the former Menudo performer's background and music. Good collection of audio and music video clips. You can also sign up to be on his mailing list.

Shakira

http://www.shakira.com/

Official home page of one of the hottest new pop stars, Shakira. Read her biography, check out the latest headlines, listen to audio clips, view video clips, and keep abreast of concert news and information. Site also features chat and message boards to keep in touch with fellow fans.

MUSIC GENRES— RAP/HIP-HOP

Busta Rhymes

http://www.bustarhymes.com/

This official home page of Busta Rhymes features his biography, news and information about upcoming tours, a photo gallery, sample audio clips, and more. Send an e-card to a friend or download free Busta Rhymes desktop wallpaper.

Da Brat

http://www.dabrat.com/

Visit Da Brat online and learn about her career and music. Check out audio and music video clips and the tour calendar, or subscribe to the free newsletter. Online bulletin board feature helps fans keep in touch.

Destiny's Child Fan Club

http://www.dc-unplugged.com/

The Official Destiny's Child Fan Club, this site features news about the group, biographies of the girls, a photo gallery, downloadable wallpaper and AOL chat icons, and a few music videos. Check out the online store for apparel and memorabilia.

A B C D E F G H I J K L M N O P Q R S T U V W X Y Z

A
B
C
D
E
F
G
H
I
J
K
L

M
N
O
P
Q
R
S
T
U
V
W
X
Y
Z

Eminem

http://www.eminem.com

Official home of Eminem, multi-platinum hip-hop artist and Grammy award winner, this site showcases Eminem's music and performances. Check out his biography and discography, play audio and video clips, tour the photo gallery, exchange messages with other fans in the discussion forums, and much more. Online store links to Artist Direct, where you can shop for Eminem memorabilia.

Lil' Kim

http://www.lilkim.com/home.html

Lil' Kim fans will want to bookmark this page to keep abreast of the latest news, concert information, audio and video clips, and hot photos of this sexy hip-hop star. Message board available for fans who want to keep in touch with one another and share their enthusiasm for Lil' Kim.

Public Enemy

http://www.publicenemy.com/

Official hi-tech site of one of Rap's most notorious bands features a photo gallery, an archive of song lyrics, band member bios, links to videocasts and Webcasts, an enemy board (for reading and posting messages), and more. Shop online at the pe shop for books, caps (hats), and T-shirts.

Will Smith

http://www.willsmith.net/

Sony Entertainment's official Will Smith Web site features the trailer for Men in Black II, plus links to Will Smith's discography, where

you can listen to some of his tunes from the Willenium and Big Willie Style CDs. Links to the Sony Music store, where you can purchase CDs online.

MUSIC GENRES— ROCK AND ROLL

Aerosmith

http://www.aerosmith.com/

This official Aerosmith site features tour dates, biographies of the band members, audio and video clips, a discography, and a chat room. Very imaginative, interactive site.

Blink 182

www.blink182.com

A ton of information about the band, from tour dates to personal information about band members. Watch their videos and hear the latest releases from this site. Lots of free audio and video clips for downloading.

Bob Dylan

http://www.bobdylan.com/

Visit Bob Dylan's official home on the Web to learn more about his albums, read lyrics to his songs, and check out links to other Bob Dylan sites. Features a great collection of audio clips and lyrics, so you can read along as Dylan sings.

Eric Clapton

http://www.repriserec.com/eric-clapton/

Sign up to receive advance notice of Eric Clapton's releases and be able to buy his music and videos at pre-release prices. You can also check out tour information as well as upcoming television appearances. Chat with other Clapton fans at the interactive fans page.

Grateful Dead

http://www.dead.net/

The official site for the Grateful Dead provides information about the band and its music, an online store of band paraphernalia, and sections created and maintained by individual band members.

Kiss

http://www.kissonline.net/

Win tickets to see Kiss live, read the transcript of interviews with band members, buy and sell Kiss memorabilia, listen to audio clips, view video clips, and just generally get to know the band better at this site. Contests, clubs, message boards, and other features make this a prime site for Kiss fans.

The Original (Unofficial) Elvis Home Page

http://metalab.unc.edu/elvis/elvishom.html

Listen to songs from early rock-and-roll star Elvis Presley. Includes a tour of Graceland, photos, lyrics, articles, and much more. Also includes links to related sites and an Elvis TV schedule. You'll also find an extensive list of Elvis pen pals you can hook up with. You can read Elvis's last will and testament, and—of course—keep up to date on all the latest Elvis sightings.

Plugged: The Unofficial Paul McCartney Home Page

http://www.mcbeatle.de/macca/

A personal home page dedicated to rock icon Sir Paul McCartney. The site has current news, pictures of McCartney, details on his investiture, a complete discography, links to many other McCartney and Beatles-related pages, and much more.

Best Rock+Roll Hall of Fame

http://www.rockhall.com/

This is the Web site for the Rock and Roll Hall of Fame and Museum, located in Cleveland, Ohio. Take a virtual tour of the museum to meet the legends of rock. Read about the songs that made them superstars and the events that made them notorious. Learn how the inductees are chosen, and find out who is being inducted this year. You can also view a list of all the past inductees by induction year. Click on any inductee to get a bio, description of impact, song clips, and musical influences. This is a great source of information on all the major influences in rock. And be sure to check out the online shop for some great gift ideas!

RollingStone.com

http://www.rollingstone.com/

This is the online home of Rolling Stone magazine. The site contains most of the news, reviews, charts, and interviews available in the print edition. It also includes an area where users can comment on movies, music, and more. Free downloadable MP3 clips, video clips, and a huge photo gallery make this one of the best hangouts for rock fans.

A
B
C
D
E
F
G
H
I
J
K
L
M
N
O
P
Q
R
S
T
U
V
W
X
Y
Z

A
B
C
D
E
F
G
H
I
J
K
L

N
O
P
Q
R
S
T
U
V
W
X
Y
Z

Santana

http://www.santana.com/

Listen to music by Santana, learn more about the man and the musicians who support him, as well as awards and news about the band's tour schedule here. The official Santana store offers autographed posters, jewelry, apparel, and other band-related items.

Sting

http://www.sting.com/

Try to keep up with Sting at his site, which features information and the sounds of his latest album, as well as details of his career and background. You can buy T-shirts, music, tour merchandise, and other Sting stuff from this Web site.

Stones.com

http://www.stones.com/

This official Web site of the Rolling Stones contains a vast collection of sounds, pictures, video, and interviews. Check out the discography, chronology, and biography. Also gives you a place to chat with other Stones fans. Links to online retail sites where you can purchase Stones music, books, and more.

Teenage Wildlife: The Interactive David Bowie Fan Page

http://www.teenagewildlife.com/

Chronicles the life of David Bowie. Get information and ratings about his albums, movies, and videos, and purchase merchandise at the online store. Find out where you can chat with other David Bowie fans. Also, learn about where he'll be touring and making appearances. Includes

a search engine so that you can locate the lyrics of specified David Bowie songs.

Official Site
http://www.davidbowie.com/

Tom Petty

http://www.tompetty.com/

A fantastic site featuring tons of information about Tom Petty and the Heartbreakers. Get bio information about all band members, check out the most current tour information, and learn the lyrics of all Tom Petty songs. Plenty of sample audio and video clips. Links to Artist Direct to shop for memorabilia.

zappa.com

http://www.zappa.com/

Browse through the complete discography, articles, and answers to FAQs. Get information about Frank's sons'—Dweezil and Ahmet—musical endeavors. Listen to the "Frank Zappa: American Composer" audio page, a two-hour radio documentary that originally aired on United States radio in the summer of 1996. Includes a brief biography and interview with Gail Zappa (Frank Zappa's wife) from SECONDS Magazine. Also includes an online store for Zappa's label, Barfko Swill Records.

MUSIC SOFTWARE

Media Player

http://www.microsoft.com/windows/mediaplayer

Download Windows Media Player here so that you can play virtually any format of music file, including MP3, WAV, AVI, MPEG and

Windows Media, as well as accessing streaming radio stations and improving the quality of videos you view onscreen. You can also get the latest upgrade and technical support at this site, if you've downloaded previous versions and need assistance.

MusicMatch

http://www.musicmatch.com/

Home of one of the most popular MP3 players, rippers, and burners around. With Music Match, you can transform audio clips on CDs into MP3 clips, arrange MP3 clips to create your own playlists, and burn your playlists to CDs to create custom CDs.

QuickTime

http://www.apple.com/quicktime/

Download QuickTime at this site so that you can view videos on your computer. You'll also find some of the top music videos available for download and viewing here.

RealPlayer

http://www.realplayer.com

Get 2,500 radio stations, clear audio and bright video, free upgrades, and more when you purchase RealPlayer from realplayer.com. This site also offers other Real products that can enhance your listening and viewing experience. Check it out!

Roxio

http://www.roxio.com

Home of Roxio's popular Easy CD Creator software, which allows you to duplicate CDs, copy data files to recordable discs, transform CD

tracks into MP3 clips, play MP3 clips on your PC, and burn your own custom playlists to audio CDs. Excellent program for managing your digital music collection, and very easy to use.

Shockwave.com

http://www.shockwave.com

Download Shockwave and Flash Player here, so that you can view games, presentations, and animation in all its glory on other sites. The software is free, too.

MUSIC: INSTRUMENTS

The Ethnic Musical Instruments Co.

http://www.mid-east.com/

This site offers a large selection of ethnic musical instruments: sitars, bagpipes, lyres, ocarinas, doumbeks, and many others. Specials, seconds, and repairs—some at great prices—have their own page. Addresses of regional showrooms and related links are also included.

Guitarsite.com

http://www.guitarsite.com/

If you're into guitar music—playing, recording, or listening—check out this site. You'll find hundreds of listings for guitar shops, guitar chords, guitar dealers, guitar publications, guitarists...you get the idea. But it's not just guitars—everything musical seems to be included. (Note: The screen colors might be a little extreme on some browsers.)

A B C D E F G H I J K L M N O P Q R S T U V W X Y Z

A
B
C
D
E
F
G
H
I
J
K
L
M
N
O
P
Q
R
S
T
U
V
W
X
Y
Z

Hubbard Harpsichords, Inc.

http://www.hubharp.com/

Hubbard sells complete harpsichords, but also sells kits. Their weekend workshops can help you to put together your own kit, with their help, at a price that's substantially reduced from that of a completely assembled instrument. This site offers details about all the Hubbard products and services, as well as books, CDs, news, events, and general information.

LOOPLABS

http://www.looplabs.com

Featuring an online music mixer, this site enables visitors to mix their own collection of recorded sounds to create original recordings. You'll feel like you're in a professional recording studio! Once you have recorded your tune, you can upload it to share with others online.

Rhythm Fusion—Musical Instruments from Around the World

http://www.rhythmfusion.com/

Looking for sound makers from around the world? Then, this is your site. You can purchase doumbeks, African drums, rattles, wind instruments, gongs, and much more by clicking on the icon of each type of instrument.

Things Musical

http://www.thingsmusical.com/

More than 18,000 musical instruments are available at this site, at prices up to 40% off. Search by clicking on the first letter of the type of instrument you're interested in, or scroll down to look at the long list of items available.

ORGANIZATIONS AND CLUBS

CD Club FAQ

http://www.blooberry.com/cdfaq/

If you're considering joining (or rejoining) a music club such as Columbia House or BMG, read this FAQ first. It provides details on the best deals from the various clubs, strategies on how to get the most for your money, and rules/restrictions of club memberships. Answers to most-asked questions are available in a brief yes/no format, as well as a detailed listing.

Grammy.com

http://www.grammy.com/

Home of the Grammy Awards, the premier awards organization in the recording industry. This site provides information about the National Academy of Recording Arts & Sciences, Inc., also known as the Recording Academy. This group is "dedicated to improving the quality of life and cultural condition for music and its makers." Here, you can find out about the upcoming Grammy Awards, check out the nominees, and look up the winners.

Wolverine Antique Music Society

http://www.shellac.org/wams/

Presents the Wolverine Antique Music Society. Focuses on the preservation of music originally recorded for 78rpm records. Offers much to the 78 collector and early jazz aficionado. Contains many articles on the music, collecting, and all sorts of technical and resource information pertaining to antique audio. Also contains information on the early record labels, 78 album cover art, and sound clips.

Women In Music

http://www.womeninmusic.com/

Women In Music (WIM) is a non-profit organization with the goal of supporting the efforts and careers of women in the music industry. Quite a number of programs are offered at this site, including referrals, newsletters, seminars and workshops, insider's tips, and more. Events and industry news sections provide useful updates on music-related activities. You can also order apparel and other merchandise from this site, join the organization, and make donations online.

RADIO SITES

all songs considered

http://www.npr.org/programs/asc

Home of National Public Radio's music broadcasts, this site provides an on-demand archive of musical pieces featured on NPR's popular radio show. Features a handful of music videos, as well.

BBC Radio 4

http://www.bbc.co.uk/radio4

The British Broadcasting Company is famous worldwide for its news coverage as well as in-depth reports on science, nature, history, religion, and more. Its comedy specials and dedication to preserving drama and the other arts also add to its allure. At this site, you can access much of what the BBC has to offer via its radio programming, plus you can quickly link to its television offerings, as well.

BRS Radio Directory

http://www.web-radio.com/

Directory of thousands of radio stations that broadcast on the Web. You can view the complete directory or browse stations by call letters, states, countries, or format, or view a list of stations that broadcast exclusively over the Internet.

Hearts of Space

http://www.hos.com

Home of Hearts of Space, a combination record label and radio show syndication company. Here you can sample the works of various recording artists, listen to Internet radio stations, and learn more about the company and its services.

KAOS: Welcome to KAOS!

http://www.kaosradio.org/

KAOS is a radio station located at Evergreen State College in Olympia, Washington. It offers traditional and popular music of America and the world, including jazz, classical, swing, blues, soul, rap, R&B, Celtic, new acoustic and electronic music, Native American, Spanish language, rock, and Broadway music. You'll also hear comedy, radio theater, stories from Pacifica News and the Monitor Press, and news on public affairs. The site includes an on-air schedule, bios of the programmers, and descriptions of the programs. You'll also see KAOS's listing of the current top 30 songs.

KPIG Radio Online

http://www.kpig.com/

Tune into the Web version of this California radio station that aims to be a throwback to the '60s and '70s when DJs added personality to

A
B
C
D
E
F
G
H
I
J
K
L
M
N
O
P
Q
R
S
T
U
V
W
X
Y
Z

A
B
C
D
E
F
G
H
I
J
K
L
M
N
O
P
Q
R
S
T
U
V
W
X
Y
Z

their broadcasts. Check the site for the station's playlist, which varies from '50s music forward, information on DJs, and an active community of fans you can chat with. Be sure to check out the calendars and T-shirts available for purchase from this site.

Live365

http://www.live365.com

Live365 features the largest network of Internet radio stations on the Web providing everything from music stations to talk radio and special broadcasts. To start browsing, simply click the link for the desired genre, including Alternative, Comedy, Hip Hop, Classical, Reggae, Pop, and Rock. Click the More link for a complete offering of links, including Talk and Government. When you don't know where to tune in, stop here for a complete directory.

NPR: National Public Radio Online

http://www.npr.org/

This site lets you listen to NPR news on the hour. View summaries of programs and then listen to them, or check out some of the special highlighted stories that you might have missed. Check out the information on the news magazines, talk shows, and cultural and information stories you can listen to—among them, All Things Considered, Morning Edition, Car Talk, and Jazz from Lincoln Center.

Transom

http://www.transom.org

Billing itself as "A Showcase & Workshop for New Public Radio," Transom features a diverse collection of in-depth, behind-the-scenes reports about real-life events and concerns. When you're tired of hearing the same old news reports and nightly specials, check out Transom for some more unique offerings. You can even record your own stories and submit them for inclusion on this site.

World Radio Network Online

http://www.wrn.org/

WRN offers a global perspective on current world events, and updates you on news from your homeland. It also covers arts and culture, music, sports, science, and more. WRN via cable, satellite, local AM/FM, and the Internet is used as an educational resource by schools, colleges, and universities. You'll also find WRN schedules and learn how to listen to live newscast audio streams in RealAudio and StreamWorks 24 hours a day from 25 of the world's leading public and international broadcasters.

Youth Radio

http://www.youthradio.org

Youth Radio is dedicated to providing young people with the training and opportunities to become successful as radio producers, broadcasters, and in other radio broadcasting roles. Here, you can check out the work of some of the talented individuals involved with Youth Radio.

BBC Nature Site

http://www.bbc.co.uk/nature/

The British Broadcasting Company's Nature site is packed with articles and presentations about animals and the environment. Check out this week's nature special, take the daily quiz, subscribe to the newsletter, check out the birdcam, or browse the site for nature information that catches your eye.

Becoming Human

http://www.becominghuman.org

Documentary, news, commentary, and reference library designed to help visitors more fully comprehend human evolution.

eNature

http://www.enature.com

This for-profit site, owned and operated by the National Wildlife Federation, features a huge collection of wildlife resources for novice and expert alike. Find field guides for a wide range of animal and plant species, learn about birding, find out how to create your own nature habitats in your yard, get answers from the experts, and much more.

Nature

http://www.nature.com/

This online version of Nature journal provides free access to many of the features and articles covered in the journal. Subscribers obtain full access to the site. Covers the latest

nature news, giving a more scientific perspective.

Best Ocean.com

http://www.ocean.com/

Dive into this site for the latest news, studies, and warnings about the condition of the earth's oceans. Here, you'll find information about ocean travel, a gallery of ocean photos, Poseidon's library of sea stories, and links to hundreds of sites featuring everything from ocean gear to conservation groups. Well-designed, easy to navigate, and packed with useful information and links to other resources, this site represents the best of the best.

Oceans Alive

http://www.abc.net.au/oceans/alive.htm

Focusing on marine life in the waters surrounding Australia, this site provides information on whale watching and marine biodiversity hot spots. Also provides general ocean information, including a list of ocean facts, seal training, links to schools that offer studies in marine biology, and links to other oceanic resources.

PBS Nature Site

http://www.pbs.org/wnet/nature/

For more than 20 years, the PBS Nature series has informed and entertained its viewers through its premier nature programming. You can now access much of the information presented in these shows online. Site features a searchable

A
B
C
D
E
F
G
H
I
J
K
L
M

N
O
P
Q
R
S
T
U
V
W
X
Y
Z

database of past programs, information on upcoming programs, a video database, puzzles, interactive games, and e-postcards you can send to friends and relatives.

RainforestWeb.org

http://www.rainforestweb.org/

Concerned about the preservation of rainforests? Then visit this site to learn more about rainforests and the projects that threaten their very existence. Learn why rainforests are important, what's happening to them, why they're being destroyed, and what you can do to help.

Sierra Club

http://www.sierraclub.org/

The Sierra Club is one of the oldest grassroots environmental activist groups. Its Web site encourages you to enjoy the great outdoors, take action to preserve our natural resources, and join or donate to the Sierra Club to help the organization fight for environment-friendly legislation. Great place for environmental activists to keep abreast of current issues.

NETWORKING

3Com

http://www.3com.com/

3Com Corp., a manufacturer of networking hardware, allows people who visit their site to learn about employment opportunities, browse company products, and get customer support.

About Computer Networking

http://compnetworking.about.com/

About's computer networking directory provides links to hundreds of resources on the Internet that provide information on networking. Links to sites that cover everything from basic networking terminology to setting up a network.

ATM Forum

http://www.atmforum.com/

This group seeks to accelerate the use of asynchronous transfer mode technology in computer networks. Included at this site are answers to frequently asked questions about ATM technology, a glossary of terms, and membership criteria for the organization.

Cable Datacom News

http://www.cabledatacomnews.com/

Tracks the development of high-speed cable data services and contains monthly news reports. Users can also subscribe to CDN's email newsletter.

Cable Modem University

http://www.catv.org/

Resource devoted to cable modems and high-speed access to computer networks. Includes industry news updates, a list of manufacturers, and information on communications standards for this hardware.

Cisco Connection Online

http://www.cisco.com/

Cisco Systems, Inc., is the worldwide leader in networking for the Internet. Cisco products include routers, LAN and ATM switches, dial-up access servers, and network management software. Cisco Systems news and product/service information are available on this site. An opening page that's packed with links for information, products, services, technology, and training, and its one-stop approach to networking make this site the best of the best.

Digital Tool Group

http://www.dtool.com/

Learn more about networking and system security through troubleshooting tips provided at the site, as well as networking resources and support information offered by the site's "wizardlettes."

Emulex Network Systems

http://www.emulex.com/

This company designs and produces hardware and software for network access, communications, and time management. Products specialize in the managing of data between computers and peripheral equipment. The site includes detailed product listings, upgrade programs, technical support, and a company profile.

HELIOS Software

http://www.helios.de

Developers of color-management and client/server software, including Helios EtherShare, PCShare, EtherShare OPI, and Helios ColorSync 2 Xtension. Check out the FAQ section, read their latest news, and see the specials they are offering.

Hitachi Data Systems (HDS)

http://www.hds.com

Learn about Hitachi Data Systems products and services targeting the IT needs of large enterprises.

Hughes Network Systems

http://www.hns.com/

Hughes Network Systems' home page presents the company's networking and telecommunications products and services. Job listings, general corporate information, and online customer support are also provided.

IBM Networking Hardware

http://www.networking.ibm.com/

Read IBM's Networking Primer to learn more about the basics of computer networking, and then get information about their Token Ring Network products and upgrades.

Intel Networking and Telecommunications

http://www.intel.com/products/comm/

A site with links to Intel products and information for your business. Networking, workstation computing, mobile computing, and server solutions are just some of the options.

A
B
C
D
E
F
G
H
I
J
K
L
M
N
O
P
Q
R
S
T
U
V
W
X
Y
Z

A
B
C
D
E
F
G
H
I
J
K
L
M
N
O
P
Q
R
S
T
U
V
W
X
Y
Z

Interphase Corporation

http://www.iphase.com/

Products for mass storage and high-speed networks. There are links to products, support, news, and employment opportunities.

InterWorking Labs

http://www.iwl.com/

Offers Test Suite software products that test SNMP network hardware, such as routers, printers, hubs, servers, and UPSs. Find out about their products, download a free SNMP test suite demo, and contact IWL staff.

Intranet Journal

http://www.intranetjournal.com/

Visitors to this site can learn about current intranet standards, intranet security and software, planning, tools, and more. Intranet FAQ, message boards, and an events calendar keep you abreast of what's happening in the world of intranet technology and development.

Jini Connection Technology

http://wwws.sun.com/software/jini/

Official page of Sun Microsystems' networking technology, Jini. This site features technical specifications, white papers, and tutorials. Jini? network technology provides a simple infrastructure for delivering network services and for creating spontaneous interaction between programs that use these services. The site has many articles and stories about Jini, as well as more extensive definitions.

KarlNet

http://www.karlnet.com/

Bridges and routers to solve your network security problems. Pictures and links to products and information, applications, and pricing are available.

Kinesix

http://www.kinesix.com/

Manufacturer of Sammi, which enables you to integrate network applications without writing any network or graphical user interface code. The site has several links to learn more about Sammi, including current users, tech support, employment opportunities, and more.

Lancom Technologies

http://www.lancom-tech.com/

Lancom Technologies provides all the courseware you need to become CNA or CNE certified. Provide this courseware for your students or your at reduced costs.

LANology Enterprise Network Solutions

http://www.lanology.com/

Networking and IT staffing service, LANology is a headhunting service for computer professionals. If you need a networking guru or IT professionals, and you don't know where to look, visit this site.

Linksys Online

http://www.linksys.com/

This site is the home page for Linksys, a manufacturer of high-speed networking and connectivity products, specializing in wireless networking configurations. Visitors to this site may learn about company products and receive technical support and free software upgrades.

Linux Mall

http://www.linuxmall.com

One of the more favorable places to seek out Linux software, books, novel items, and information on the world's best operating system. If you want to install a networking system using Linux or you need information on networking, this is the ultimate place to find it.

Microsoft Servers

http://www.microsoft.com/servers/

Interested in Microsoft's networking products? Then visit this site, where Microsoft showcases its network server software. Here you can find information about Microsoft's .Net Enterprise family of servers, including BizTalk, Commerce, Exchange, Internet Security, and Mobile Information servers. Obtain product information, find out where you can purchase products, get technical support, download patches, and much more.

Netgear

http://www.netgear.com

Whether you have a large corporate network or just a home or small office network you will find what you need here. This site complements itself with many useful and informative articles and documents on the subject of networking.

NETiS Technology, Inc.

http://www.netistech.com/

NETiS is a manufacturer and service provider for all your individual, business, and institutional computer needs. Check out their corporate profile, services and support, product info and press releases, promotions, and more.

NetMagic Systems

http://www.netmagicinc.com/

At this site is a full-service network integrator and ISV that develops and markets help desk, security, and administrative management software for networks. NetMagic Systems, Inc., produces NetMagic Pro, a Password Management and Security Automation Tool for Call Centers, Help Desk, and End User Self Service.

Network Buyer's Guide

http://
www.networkbuyersguide.com/

Reviews products and services relating to computer networks. Storage devices, routers, repair companies, and other items are listed and rated. The site also provides technical documentation.

Network Engineer's Toolkit

http://www.wanresources.com/

On this Web site you'll find reference material on different data communications protocols and technology commonly used in wide area networks, some estimators to help you with quick and dirty network management, and other useful information.

Network World Fusion

http://www.networkworld.com/

A huge online community that provides networking product reviews and buyers guides, online chat and discussion forums, headline news and networking-specific news, as well as columnists and career info.

A
B
C
D
E
F
G
H
I
J
K
L
M
N
O
P
Q
R
S
T
U
V
W
X
Y
Z

A
B
C
D
E
F
G
H
I
J
K
L
M
N
O
P
Q
R
S
T
U
V
W
X
Y
Z

Networking Enterprises

http://www.netenterprises.com/

Networking Enterprises offers network-based solutions to corporations wishing to deploy the latest in Internet technologies. This is an information–integration systems consulting firm offering such services as LAN and WAN implementation and also has some useful information about networking.

NetworkMagazine.com

http://www.networkmagazine.com/

Read the current issue of the online version of this print publication for networking professionals, or search the archives for back issues. The resource section contains helpful news and information for individuals looking for a new job.

Nortel Networks

http://www.nortelnetworks.com/index.html

Nortel offers secure networks to ensure privacy. Check out their networking solutions and their training programs to benefit your organization.

Novell, Inc.

http://www.novell.com

A leader in networking software provides information on new products, online technical support, and different networking solutions for business and government.

Paradyne Corporation Power Pages

http://www.paradyne.com/

Paradyne Corporation manufactures network access products. This Web site contains information about the company and its products and services, as well as support. An interactive form for checking on the status of an order is also provided at the site.

SoftLinx, Inc.

http://www.softlinx.com/

Provides network fax and Internet messaging products for midsize to large corporations and service providers.

TechFest–Networking Protocols

http://www.techfest.com/networking/prot.htm

Read reference material on networking, from the basic to the very advanced, here. And find out which books are recommended references through the Good Book listings.

Telindous

http://www.k-net.co.uk/

UK networking and telecommunications consultants, trainers, and service. Features manufacturer-independent solutions.

TENET Computer Group, Inc.

http://www.tenet.com

A Canadian Novell NetWare network reseller and installer. Find out about Tenet, its products, certifications, and more. Also, it offers IT links.

Vicomsoft

http://www.vicomsoft.com/

This software company develops and markets several products for networking PCs, primarily in a home- or small-business environment. Click Resources and then click KnowledgeShare to access some interesting tutorials on basic networking topics.

NEW AGE

A
B
C
D
E
F
G
H
I
J
K
L
M
N
O
P
Q
R
S
T
U
V
W
X
Y
Z

ConsciousNet

http://www.consciousnet.com/

Dedicated to mind-body-spirit development, this site provides a huge directory to New Age information, services and products. Think of it as a referral service for the best in New Age services and products.

Full Circle New Age Book Shop

http://members.tripod.com/
~vijaykumarjain/

Contains an extensive list of books on spirituality, Janism, Hinduism, self-realization, and meditation. Order the books through Amazon.com.

How to Talk New Age

http://www.well.com/user/mick/
newagept.html

Learn the New Age lingo, from a humorous standpoint. Serious followers of New Age disciplines probably should avoid this site.

New Age Books

http://www.newagebooks.com/

Browse a catalog of more than 30,000 books or their wide selection of incense, tarot cards, pendants, cards, and calendars.

[[Best]] New Age Online Australia

http://www.newage.com.au/

This site contains a huge amount of free-to-read New Age and spiritual information covering astrology, Wicca and Pagan, UFOs and ETs, ascension, earth changes, channelings, crystals, dreams, divination, angels, magic, karma, meditation, healing, and much, much more. With icons for just about every New Age topic you can imagine, great graphics, a clean design, and an easy-to-navigate interface make this site the best of the best.

New Age Page

http://www.newagepage.com/

Lists links to sites including angels, dreams, films, and the environment.

New Age Web Works

http://www.newageinfo.com/

A site that provides information about New Age, UFO, Pagan, Occult, and Alternative Spirituality communities. At the site, you can buy products, and read articles and newsletters, as well as share ideas.

Planet Earth Music

http://
www.planet-earth-music.com/

Well-presented online vendor of New Age music. Listen in RealAudio. They claim to offer a selection of more than 3,500 titles in 14 musical genres including many not carried by the "big" stores.

Ranch Rainbow Press

http://www.ranchrainbowpress.com/

This New Age publisher offers a newsletter, books, and seminars about the hands-on Japanese healing art of Reiki.

Salem New Age Center

http://www.salemctr.com/newage/

Offers FAQs on the New Age movement and meditation, lists of popular New Age books, articles on ET human origins, and a free email newsletter.

NEWS

MAGAZINES

Arts & Letters Daily

http://www.aldaily.com

Comprehensive digest and directory of news, book reviews, essays, and opinions gathered from the top newspapers, magazines, radio programs, news services, and other media sources around the world. Features gobs of information in an easy-to-access format.

Asia Pacific News

http://www.asia-pacific-news.com/
s/Links-Newspapers.asp

Browse through the top 50 news agencies and newspapers in the Asia Pacific region. Also offered are links to shopping and employment sites.

Atlantic Unbound

http://www.theatlantic.com/

Sample in-depth articles on politics, society, arts, and culture from this print magazine. Back issues are archived.

Congressional Quarterly

http://www.cq.com/

Comprehensive news and analysis of what's happening in the corridors of power. The site follows Congress, the federal government, and political events.

The Earth Times

http://www.earthtimes.org/

This daily newspaper focuses on the environment, business, health, population, and human rights. It also contains book and movie reviews.

Harper's

http://www.harpers.org/

Aims to provide readers with a window on the world by exploring nonmainstream topics. Find a magazine index and subscription details here.

Intellectual Capital

http://www.speakout.com/

Weekly bipartisan magazine covering politics and current affairs. Its roster of writers includes well-known commentators and policymakers.

National Journal

http://nationaljournal.com/

Formerly PoliticsNow, National Journal contains many of the features that made PoliticsNow one of the most popular sites on the Web, including the Poll Track database, the "Buzz" insider columns, and the Almanac of American Politics. Also, it contains Earlybird, an early morning digest of hot political news; Buzz Columns, a "daily dose of analysis and commentary on Congress; and Daybook, a daily planner for upcoming political and policy events in the capitol.

National Review

http://www.nationalreview.com/

This site is filled with opinions and features from the popular United States conservative magazine, with commentary from William F. Buckley, Jr.

[Best] Newsweek

http://www.msnbc.com/news/
NW-front_Front.asp

Read this week's top stories, check daily news updates, log in with your questions for upcoming Live Talk segments on controversial topics, as well as read regular columns about international issues, business, society, Campaign 2004, and more. You'll definitely be caught up on current events after visiting this best of the best site!

A
B
C
D
E
F
G
H
I
J
K
L
M
N
O
P
Q
R
S
T
U
V
W
X
Y
Z

A
B
C
D
E
F
G
H
I
J
K
L
M
N
O
P
Q
R
S
T
U
V
W
X
Y
Z

Popular Science

http://www.popsci.com/

This Web site comes to you compliments of the editors of Popular Science magazine. Find out what's new in the automotive, computer, electronics, home technology, and science fields. Plus, get other articles from the magazine, various buying guides, and helpful links.

Salon.com

http://www.salon.com/

An intelligent, provocative online magazine that presents the latest news, reviews, and analysis in a variety of content areas including Arts & Entertainment, Life, News, People, and Politics. Winner of several awards for site design and content as well as journalism.

Slate

http://slate.msn.com/

Hard-hitting online magazine that pulls no punches when it comes to criticizing politicians and policies. Behind-the-scenes reviews of international happenings and their effects on life in the United States. Features business, sports, and technology sections, as well.

The Smoking Gun

http://www.thesmokinggun.com

This online tabloid masquerading as the home of an investigative journalism site provides background reports covering the latest celebrity and political scandals. Check out the day's featured document or click the Archives link for a list of previous investigations.

Time

http://www.time.com/

Puts the news in context with full text of the print magazine each week. It is updated throughout the day and cross-referenced. Like the magazine, this site is more focused on celebrities, entertainment, science, and the human-interest viewpoint than on more serious news events and investigative journalism.

U.S. News

http://www.usnews.com/usnews/home.htm

Online version of the popular current affairs magazine. The Washington Connection is included for the latest political news and election coverage.

USA Weekend

http://www.usaweekend.com/

This Gannett magazine is carried by nearly 500 United States newspapers; and it features entertainment, fitness, finance, and current events.

The Utne Reader

http://www.utne.com/

The reader's digest of the alternative press, The Utne Reader wanders off the mainstream track to provide articles about topics you won't find covered in Time or Newsweek.

Veterans News and Information Service

http://www.vnis.com/

Browse through this comprehensive news and information resource for military veterans. It includes news from the Navy, the Marines, and the Coast Guard.

ZDNet–PC Magazine

http://www.pcmag.com/

You will find all kinds of current information about computers on this site including the late-breaking news, articles, product reviews, free downloads and by becoming a registered member, free email, software, and the free magazine. The site is very well designed with the information presented in a way that makes it easy to find and easy to navigate.

 RESOURCES

 Best **BBC News**

http://news.bbc.co.uk/

Updated every minute, the British Broadcasting Channel (BBC) site has a definite international slant to its reporting, which runs the gamut from international politics to sports and celebrities. Its balanced coverage, comprehensive approach, excellent design, and easy-to-navigate layout make this site the best of the best.

E&P Media Links

http://www.editorandpublisher.com/_editorandpublisher/index.jsp

Editor and Publisher has collected a vast listing of newspapers available on the Web, accessible via a clickable map or the Quick Links option.

EmergencyNet News

http://www.emergency.com/ennday.htm

An international news source reporting on worldwide incidents that pose potential threats to safety and security. Search the archives for past reports, link to other news channels, and find out what's going on in countries across the world. Recent articles reported on bomb scares, Internet security breaches, and child kidnapping, among others.

The Feedroom

http://www.feedroom.com/

Picture yourself surrounded by monitors, each broadcasting a different news story from around the world. You click a monitor to tune in to the story you want. News on demand? This is the closest thing, although you might get more in-depth coverage at some of the "print" news sites.

indianz.com

http://www.indianz.com/

You'll find news, information, and entertainment provided from a Native American perspective. In addition to national news, there are headlines from tribes across the country, as well as more in-depth reports on issues that directly impact Native American communities.

Mirror Syndication International

http://www.mirpix.com/

Features more than 250,000 newspaper pictures online plus an offline library of more than 3 million pictures, which it offers for sale to businesses and private customers. The site accepts credit cards.

News Express

http://www.foreignmedia.com/

Providers of foreign books, newspapers, and magazines. If you are doing research, this is a good place to find material on every news-related subject in many countries.

A
B
C
D
E
F
G
H
I
J
K
L
M
N
O
P
Q
R
S
T
U
V
W
X
Y
Z

A
B
C
D
E
F
G
H
I
J
K
L
M
N
O
P
Q
R
S
T
U
V
W
X
Y
Z

News365

http://www.news365.com/

Browse through this large Internet library of news, world headlines, and links to international news. Also, find classifieds from your local city.

oneworld.net

http://www.oneworld.org/news/today/

This supersite of information is dedicated to reporting on global development issues, such as education, migration, or children's rights. In addition to news reports, there are searchable archives, and opportunities for chat and discussion forums. Links to various editions worldwide in several different languages.

Slashdot

http://slashdot.org/

"News for Nerds," that covers topics ranging from computer bugs to censorship, American Online, BSD, encryption, and Linux—just to name a few. Editorials are supplied in droves, with some getting posted for everyone to enjoy and potentially respond to.

TotalNEWS

http://www.totalnews.com/

Comprehensive, searchable directory of news sites, covering everything from entertainment and sports to international news and business. Local news, weather, politics, human interest stories, and opinions are also covered.

SERVICES

allAfrica.com

http://allafrica.com/

This leading provider of African news and information posts over 700 stories daily in English and French and features a searchable archive of more than 400,000 articles. Visit this site to access the latest African headline news, sports, and editorials, along with business and stock market reports, currency information, health alerts, and more.

Associated Press

http://www.ap.org/

The Associated Press online offers full access to the AP news wires.

Business Wire

http://www.businesswire.com/

Business News distributes news to the media locally, nationally, and worldwide. This wire service offers customized news-release distribution to the news media, online services, the Internet, and the investment community.

CNN Interactive

http://www.cnn.com/

Get all the top news stories at your fingertips, or delve into weather, sports, science and technical news, travel, style, show business, health, and Earth topics. Many stories have accompanying QuickTime video segments. This site also lets you in on what CNN has to offer on television.

Crayon

http://crayon.net/

Nifty free tool for managing news on the Web. Create your own newspaper with links to sources that interest you.

Desktop News

http://www.desktopnews.com/

Get streaming news, weather, sports, and stock information on your Windows desktop. Download the free Desktop News Ticker Toolbar and customize it to view just the news you want.

ForeignWire

http://www.foreignwire.com

This is the U.K.-based international affairs news service offering free news, comments, and analysis on world-important issues.

HotBot: News Channel

http://news.lycos.com/

Wired News' search service looks at some major newspapers and a variety of other news sources.

IMEDIAFAX

http://www.imediafax.com

This online news distribution service faxes your business message to the media. Users create a proprietary media list from a vast selection of magazines, newspapers, syndicates, and broadcast stations. Click on industry and classification, key editors, states, market area, or circulation, and then enter your news release and click to send. IMEDIAFAX news releases can contain graphics, letterheads, logos, or pictures. The cost is 25¢ per faxed page (minimum order of $50). News releases are better targeted, and another bonus is that there are no international phone or fax charges.

InfoBeat

http://www.infobeat.com/

Find out about InfoBeat's personalized news service. They will deliver email news customized to your stated preferences.

Media Monitors

http://www.mediamonitors.com.au/

Learn about Australia's leading provider of customized news and information services, read today's top stories, and join the mailing list.

The Paperboy

http://www.thepaperboy.com/

Check this service's "top drawer" to find top news sources, or browse their newspaper listings by country. Excellent collection of the world's most popular newspapers, plus the search tools you need to track down the stories you want.

PBS: Online NewsHour

http://www.pbs.org/newshour/

News features and analysis complete with online forums for discussion of the issues of the day, and subscriptions for email news delivery are available.

The Positive Press

http://www.positivepress.com/

This online service posts positive news stories from publications around the United States, plus positive quotations, affirmations, stories, and more. The site is updated frequently and is free.

Reuters: Home Page

http://www.reuters.com/

Reuters, a leading news and information company, fulfills the business community's and news media's financial, multimedia, and professional information needs. At this site, you can get online news or learn more about Reuters.

A
B
C
D
E
F
G
H
I
J
K
L
M
N
O
P
Q
R
S
T
U
V
W
X
Y
Z

South African Broadcasting Corporation

http://www.sabc.co.za/

The South African Broadcasting Corporation (SABC) is South Africa's national public service broadcaster. This site gives details on the company, its services, answers to FAQs, and more.

WebClipping.com

http://www.webclipping.com/

Monitor Web and newsgroups for name, brand, or trademark. Prices, services, and research tools are listed.

World Radio Network

http://www.wrn.org/

The World Radio Network, WRN, provides you with access to the world's leading broadcasters which includes constant news flow and current events. WRN carries live newscast audio streams in RealAudio, WindowsMedia, and StreamWorks 24 hours per day. Listeners can hear the news live in English and other languages direct from the source.

WorldNetDaily

http://www.worldnetdaily.com/

Compiles stories from wire services, networks, and international papers, plus offers some original reporting. Asks some of the more probing questions that the mainstream news media avoid.

U.S. NEWS MEDIA

abcNEWS.com

http://abcnews.go.com/

This home site of ABC's award-winning World News Tonight with Peter Jennings puts the day's top stories within reach of a single mouse click. Check U.S. and international news, stock market updates, politics, weather, sports, and more. Links to other ABC news shows, including Good Morning America, 20/20, and Primetime.

CBS News

http://www.cbsnews.com/

Visit Dan Rather's home on the Web to check out today's headline news. Focuses mainly on U.S. news but covers international issues, business and stock market news, and investigative stories, as well. Use the navigation bar at the top of the home page to find more information on World news, Science and Technology, HealthWatch, and Entertainment. Links to 60 Minutes, 48 Hours, and The Early Show.

Christian Science Monitor

http://www.csmonitor.com/

Comprehensive national and international coverage from the online version of this award-winning newspaper. Use the navigation bar at the top of the page to check out World news, US news, Commentary, Work & Money, Learning, Living, and more. This newspaper provides a very balanced view on most issues.

Disaster News Network

http://www.disasternews.net/

Comprehensive source of primarily United States disasters, response news, and volunteer needs. Some coverage of international disasters and relief efforts, as well. Organization links, how to help, and the latest stories are included.

ESPN.com

http://espn.go.com/

You can view game scores and statistics, get sports news, participate in fan polls, interact with other sports lovers, buy tickets online for sports events, visit the training room, and much more.

FoxNews.com

http://www.foxnews.com/

For a more conservative approach to the news and editorials of the day, visit the FoxNews Web site. Here, you can check out national and international news, get weather forecasts for your area, keep abreast of the current political scene, and check in on entertainment options. Hardcore conservatives should check out the link to the O'Reilly Factor.

⟦Best⟧ Los Angeles Times

http://www.latimes.com/

Includes local news as well as national coverage of major stories, in-depth features, pictures, and classifieds. This Web site's no-frills approach to headline news, coupled with a comprehensive list of links to various feature articles, make it our choice as best of the best. However, there are so many excellent candidates in this category that we had a tough time selecting only one site.

MSNBC

http://www.msnbc.com/news/

You can personalize the MSNBC news page to get the news you want, the way you want it—or stick with the standard page for a wide variety of news options. You can also choose news audio headlines to hear the news read to you by newscasters (some video and illustrated audio are also available).

New York Times

http://www.nytimes.com/

Home of one of the world's most famous broadsheets, featuring local and national sports and news, as well as coverage of international issues. Covers the entire range of news, including national and international news, business, sports, weather, politics, science, technology, entertainment, education, health, and editorials.

Top 100 Newspapers

http://www.interest.com/top100.html

Composed by a leading home finance company, this site offers direct access to many popular United States newspapers on the Web.

United Press International (UPI)

http://www.upi.com/

Avoid the middlemen and get the news where the news services get their news, the UPI wire service. This site posts up-to-the-minute news on business, sports, current events, politics, science, technology, and more.

A
B
C
D
E
F
G
H
I
J
K
L
M
N
O
P
Q
R
S
T
U
V
W
X
Y
Z

USA Today

`http://www.usatoday.com/`

The first full-color national paper to hit the market, this online version of USA Today features the top news, money, sports, and life reports across the nation. When you'd rather look at pictures than read lengthy reports, USA Today is the place for you.

Wall Street Journal Interactive

`http://online.wsj.com/public/us`

If you think the Wall Street Journal is for guys who wear expensive suits, visit this site to have your preconceptions erased. WSJ features some of the best investigative reporting, analysis, and writing of any newspaper in the United States, and you can access much of it online. You must subscribe, for about $60 per year, but you can check it out for free.

Washington Post

`http://www.washingtonpost.com/`

Includes most of the print features from this daily, which is known for its political coverage. It also offers weather, style, technology, and a place for chat.

NONPROFIT AND CHARITABLE ORGANIZATIONS–RESOURCES

A B C D E F G H I J K L M **N** O P Q R S T U V W X Y Z

Adobe Community Relations

`http://www.adobe.com/`
`aboutadobe/philanthropy/`
`main.html`

This corporate philanthropy arm of Adobe is primarily interested in supporting nonprofit health and human service organizations that in turn provide help to disadvantaged youth, the homeless, victims of abuse, and so on.

The Alliance

`http://www.allianceonline.org/`

The Alliance for Nonprofit Manage-ment is devoted to helping nonprofits fulfill their missions by providing them with the information, resources, and leadership they need.

American Express

`http://www6.americanexpress.com/`
`corp/philanthropy/`

Promotes its own philanthropic goals in areas where they do business or where their employees live. They service three programs: community service, cultural heritage, and economic independence. They make grants to nonprofit organizations within and outside of the United States.

American Institute of Philanthropy

`http://www.charitywatch.org/`

Find out about this organization, the charities they track, and their philosophy on rating. You'll also find articles on charitable giving. Request a free copy of their Tips for Giving Wisely.

Benton Foundation

http://www.benton.org/

Concerned with the information infrastructure. Among their projects: communications policy and practice, a report on public opinion of library leader's visions of future, children's programs, the arts, and public interest organizations.

Canadian Charitable Organizations

http://www.charityvillage.com/ charityvillage/main.asp

This Charity Village page has Canadian nonprofits listed by type. Click on your choice, and you are taken to more links. From there, you can connect directly to the organization of your choice.

[Best] Carnegie Foundation

http://www.carnegie.org/

Grant-making foundation dedicated to enhancing knowledge. Currently supports education and healthy development of children and youth, preventing deadly conflict, strengthening human resources in developing countries, and other special projects. Learn how to submit a proposal, search for grant opportunities, and check out the proposal guidelines. If you're planning on writing a grant proposal, check out this best of the best site before you start. You'll save yourself some time and frustration.

Charitable Choices

http://www.charitablechoices.org/

Look here for information on more than 250 nonprofit organizations. Most of the charities listed are based in the Washington, D.C., area. Many international organizations are also represented.

Charity Watch

http://www.charitywatch.com/

Before you make your mind up about charitable organizations or if you have sincere questions about them visit the Charity Watch site to find out about all types of charitable organizations including donations and contributions.

The CharityNet

http://www.charitynet.org/

This supersite provides resources for the international nonprofit community and its contributors.

The Chronicle of Philanthropy

http://philanthropy.com/

Summaries of articles published in the Chronicle's print version. Browse the site to find information on gifts and grants, fund raising, management, and technology of interest to nonprofit organizations.

Commonwealth Fund

http://www.cmwf.org/

Conducts research on health and social policy issues. Programs include improving healthcare services, improving the health of minority Americans, the well-being of the elderly, developing the capacities of children and young people, and improving public spaces and services.

Council on Foundations

http://www.cof.org/

A membership association composed of more than 1,300 nonprofit foundations (independent, corporate, and public). Its programs are issues such as education, health, human services, science and research, and so on. The site also promotes accountability among member foundations.

A
B
C
D
E
F
G
H
I
J
K
L
M
N
O
P
Q
R
S
T
U
V
W
X
Y
Z

A
B
C
D
E
F
G
H
I
J
K
L
M
N
O
P
Q
R
S
T
U
V
W
X
Y
Z

FIU Volunteer Action Center

http://www.fiu.edu:80/~time4chg/

Sponsored by Florida International Center, this site provides opportunities for volunteers, service learning, and advocacy in southern Florida. It includes lists of nonprofit agencies in the area. In addition, it enables students to assist faculty in service learning programs. It also links to the Volunteer Action Center reading room.

Foundation Center

http://www.fdncenter.org/

For grant seekers and grant makers, this site contains information on libraries and locations, training and seminars, funding trends and analyses, the fundraising process, and publications and CD-ROMs. Also, it includes a searchable database and an online reference desk.

Foundation News and Commentary

http://www.cof.org/newsroom/index.htm

A Council on Foundations publication with feature articles about foundations and funding. Only selected articles are available online.

Fund$Raiser Cyberzine

http://www.fundsraiser.com/

Fundraising ideas, information, and resources. Only the current issue is online. Back issues may be ordered on disk.

Global Volunteers

http://www.globalvolunteers.org/

Global Volunteers is an effort to achieve worldwide peace by partnering volunteers with local hosts and sponsors, who all work together on a project. The site provides information on the work of this organization and includes an application to be considered as a volunteer.

Glossary of Terms

http://www.cof.org/glossary/index.htm

Helpful definitions of foundation and nonprofit terms from the Council on Foundations.

Goodwill Industries International

http://www.goodwill.org/

Provides employment and training services, and removes barriers for people with disabilities. The site contains information on the THAP Project, current news, and more. Also, it enables you to find a donation center, a retail location, and a Goodwill in your area.

GuideStar

http://www.guidestar.org/

Links to the latest articles in the popular press about nonprofits and philanthropy. Also, access their Search For A Nonprofit database, which contains more than 600,000 nonprofit organizations. You can search by type, city and state, revenue range, or keyword.

Habitat for Humanity International

http://www.habitat.org/

Learn about the efforts of this organization to build free homes for the needy. You'll find information on where the organization builds, how it works, and how you can support their work—either by volunteering locally or donating.

The Hunger Site

http://www.thehungersite.com/
cgi-bin/WebObjects/CTDSites/

By just visiting the site and clicking on a button you can help donate food to needy areas and countries. The site's sponsors fund the work of the group—so there is no cost to you. The site has delivered millions of tons of food through the United Nations World Food Program.

Idealist

http://www.idealist.org/

Global clearinghouse of nonprofit and volunteering resources. Search or browse through 26,000 organizations in more than 150 countries. Find volunteer opportunities worldwide, particular programs, services, books, videos, articles, or materials for nonprofits, and more. Idealist is a project of Action Without Borders.

Independent Charities of America

http://
www.independentcharities.org/

A nonprofit organization that pre-screens high-quality national and international charities and presents them for your giving consideration. Click on a category (Children, Animals, Environment) or click on Charity Search to search by name or keyword.

Internet Nonprofit Center

http://www.nonprofits.org/

Based on an IRS database, the Internet Nonprofit Center is a project of the Evergreen State Society of Seattle, Washington. It offers information for and about nonprofit organizations in the United States.

Junior Achievement

http://www.ja.org/

Find out more about Junior Achievement's efforts to introduce students in grades K–12 to the free enterprise system by establishing for-profit businesses in local communities. Search the site to find a JA chapter near you.

National Committee on Planned Giving

http://www.ncpg.org/

The National Committee on Planned Giving is the professional association for people whose work includes developing, marketing, and administering charitable planned gifts. Those people include fundraisers for nonprofit institutions and consultants and donor advisers working in a variety of for-profit settings.

Network for Good

http://www.networkforgood.org/

Network for Good aims to be a central resource connecting individuals who want to volunteer or donate financially to local organizations of interest. Search for a charity from among the 850,000 listed at the site based on your location or the type of work you want to do.

Nonprofit Genie

http://www.genie.org/

Sponsored by C-MAP, the California Management Assistance Partnership, this site is dedicated to providing the nonprofit community the information and resources it needs to succeed. Features a hot topic and cool site of the week, a useful collection of nonprofit FAQs, a monthly newsletter, and links to other nonprofit resources on the Web.

A B C D E F G H I J K L M N O P Q R S T U V W X Y Z

A
B
C
D
E
F
G
H
I
J
K
L
M
N
O
P
Q
R
S
T
U
V
W
X
Y
Z

Nonprofit Online News

http://www.gilbert.org/news/

Excellent news digest from the Gilbert Center, updated daily with links to articles and sites mentioned.

The NonProfit Yellow Pages

http://www.nweinc.net/testbays/bay3/index.html

The NonProfit Yellow Pages provides the person(s) searching for assistance or for information about charitable organizations with a wealth of information and directions for finding these types of organizations. In their own words, it is described as the Internet Directory of Human Services.

NPO-NET

http://npo.net/

This site is primarily a resource for Chicago-area nonprofit organizations, but also enables you to search for grants and grant makers, information on fundraising and philanthropy, training for nonprofit management, nonprofit discussions, and more.

Philanthropy Roundtable

http://www.philanthropyroundtable.org/

This site offers articles of interest to donors and observers of the philanthropic world.

Planned Giving Design Center

http://www.pgdc.net/pub/

This is a site offering research and planning resources to planned giving specialists and financial advisers. It is sponsored by a group of charitable organizations and requires registration. There is no charge for using the site.

Policy Action Network

http://www.movingideas.org/

An advocacy association for hundreds of nonprofit organizations. It contains links to current requests for proposals (RFPs), information on upcoming conferences, legislative actions, and other governmental relations, along with books and publications, education resources, and more.

PRAXIS

http://www.ssw.upenn.edu/~restes/praxis.html

From Richard J. Estes, professor at the University of Pennsylvania. This is a page of resources for social and economic development. It contains a reference room and links to development assistance agencies, organizations, policies, descriptions of levels of social development practice, home pages, news services, and more.

Tax Exemption Information

http://www.irs.ustreas.gov/prod/bus_info/eo/index.html

This IRS page is a good place to begin learning about tax-exempt nonprofit organizations.

UK Fundraising

http://www.fundraising.co.uk/

This site offers a lot of information about fundraising in the U.K. It offers information on charity and nonprofit fundraising in the U.K. and beyond.

United Way of America

http://national.unitedway.org/

An organization embracing local community-based United Ways, made up of volunteers, charities, and contributors. It contains information on several of their programs, including Sky Wish and United Way. The site also includes news, a United Way FAQ sheet, and a description of how United Way works.

Urban Institute

http://www.urban.org/

Studies policies surrounding social and economic problems. At this site, you'll find their annual report, text of current and back issues of publications (for example, Future of the Public Sector), and a list of the institute's sites. This site is also searchable.

World Vision

http://www.worldvision.org/world vision/master.nsf/

Sponsor a child, read about disaster relief opportunities, and check out the WV annual report. Features a newsletter and a domestic projects database.

VOLUNTEERING

20 Ways for Teenagers to Help Other People by Volunteering

http://www.bygpub.com/books/ tg2rw/volunteer.htm

This page shows teenagers 20 ways to volunteer their time to help other people. Have you ever thought of giving some of your time to helping others? There is a lot to be gained from doing this. For one thing, you can gain valuable experience that will help you in later life and better yet, you will make someone else happier. The world will be a better place to live with your contribution. Imagine yourself working at a homeless shelter, for the Red Cross, or the Salvation Army. When you get

older, you can travel the world by joining the Peace Corps.

Advice for Volunteers

http://www.serviceleader.org/ advice/index.html

Information on finding the right volunteer opportunity and making the most out of your volunteer activities and efforts can be found on this site.

America's Charities

http://www.charities.org/

This site features an index of U.S. charitable organizations, searchable by charity type (education, environment, health, human services, civil and human rights, and so on).

Child Net Volunteers

http://www.child.net/ volunteer.htm

Interested in volunteering to help children in your community? This site has ideas and helpful advice.

Corporation for National and Community Service

http://www.cns.gov/

Official site of the AmeriCorps, Senior Corps, and Learn and Serve America, this government site is dedicated to encouraging and supporting volunteerism in America.

Idealist

http://www.idealist.org/

Extensive directory of nonprofit and volunteering resources and organizations.

[[Best]] Peace Corps

http://www.peacecorps.gov/

U.S. government–supported volunteer organization with participants involved in projects in more than 80 countries. President Kennedy

A
B
C
D
E
F
G
H
I
J
K
L
M
N
O
P
Q
R
S
T
U
V
W
X
Y
Z

A
B
C
D
E
F
G
H
I
J
K
L
M
N
O
P
Q
R
S
T
U
V
W
X
Y
Z

founded the Peace Corps in 1961 to provide help and assistance to underdeveloped countries. Since then, thousands of people from diversified cultural groups have served in the Peace Corps. The Peace Corps has three main goals: to help people in countries that are interested, to promote a better understanding of Americans, and to promote a better understanding of other people in other countries and societies. On this site you can find out how and why you might want to volunteer.

SERVEnet

http://www.servenet.org/

Enter your ZIP Code at the SERVEnet site to post and find volunteer and career opportunities in your local area. In addition to searching for volunteer opportunities that make the best use of your interests and skills, you can find service news, events, best practices, and other resources.

Virtual Volunteering Project

http://www.serviceleader.org/vv/

Allows anyone to contribute time and expertise to nonprofit volunteer organizations via the Internet. Offers a project profile, news, and resources.

VISTA–Volunteers in Service to America

http://www.friendsofvista.org/

One of America's oldest volunteer organizations, founded during the Kennedy years, this site provides the volunteer with useful information about what the organization does and how you can join. A great way to volunteer your time.

Volunteer Today

http://www.volunteertoday.com/

This monthly gazette features news, articles, event schedules, and an archive, as well as recruiting, retention, and training information.

Volunteering and Service Learning

http://web.missouri.edu/~cppcwww/vsl.shtml

This site details some things to think about before volunteering, and some links to volunteering.

VolunteerLink

http://www.volunteerlink.com/

Dedicated to connecting volunteers with organizations. Offers a database, a talk list, community resources, and FAQs.

VolunteerMatch

http://www.volunteermatch.org/

This ambitious project has more than lived up to its potential, enabling volunteers to find many thousands of volunteer opportunities all over the United States. Organizations might post both ongoing and one-time projects, allowing volunteers from several key cities to find just the opportunity they are looking for.

VolunteerMatch–Find a City Near You Needing Volunteers

http://www.impactonline.org/citymatch

Learn about local opportunities you can volunteer with online and sign up now. You can search a huge database to find a city near you that has such organizations in need or search the nonprofit database. The VolunteerMatch organizations service utilizes the power of the

Internet to help individuals nationwide find volunteer opportunities posted by local and public sector organizations. You can locate an organization needing you and then sign up automatically by email. Makes the process informative, fun, and easy.

Volunteers of America

http://www.voa.org/

Services, news, and policy positions from one of America's largest and most comprehensive charitable nonprofit human service organizations.

Wilderness Volunteers

http://www.wildernessvolunteers.org/

This nonprofit organization promotes volunteer service in U.S. wildlands, parks, and reserves. The site details registration information, leadership qualities, meals, and activities.

A
B
C
D
E
F
G
H
I
J
K
L
M
N
O
P
Q
R
S
T
U
V
W
X
Y
Z

4Nurses.com

http://4nurses.4anything.com/

Buy uniforms and other nursing apparel at this site. Also, find nursing schools, placement services, publications, links, and associations.

AANN

http://www.aann.org/

American Association of Neuroscience Nurses is a specialty organization serving nurses worldwide. Its site offers membership info, bulletin board, resources, and more.

American Association of Colleges of Nursing

http://www.aacn.nche.edu/

Overview of the American Association of Colleges of Nursing. Upcoming conferences, educational standards and special projects, CCNE accreditation and publications, position statements, and a CareerLink are all included.

American Nurses Association

http://www.nursingworld.org/

The ANA represents the nation's 2,600,000 registered nurses. The site lists addresses of state nursing associations, meetings and events, and links to important reference sources.

A
B
C
D
E
F
G
H
I
J
K
L
M
N
O
P
Q
R
S
T
U
V
W
X
Y
Z

Cybernurse.com

http://www.cybernurse.com/

Resource page for nurses, with extensive information related to careers, a search function, and related links.

Healthcare Innovations

http://www.hcinnov.com/

Displays openings for nurses in hospitals, doctors' offices, schools, businesses, and homes. Examine the vacancies and submit a profile.

Interfaith Health Program (IHP): The Carter Center

http://www.interaccess.com/ihpnet/

This site explains IHP and offers a searchable database to access real-life examples of the healthcare model they support. You'll also find an archive of articles, news on their research, and health resource links.

National NurseSearch

http://www.nursesearch.net/

Fills a wide variety of nursing positions in hospitals nationwide. Subscribe to the job announcement newsletter or register with the firm.

NP Central

http://www.nurse.net/

Information for and about nurse practitioners, including a directory of links to sites, job announcements, education resources, and professional bodies.

Nurse Options USA

http://www.nurseoptions.com/

Sign up for an email listing of positions for RNs and nurse management or learn about extra income opportunities. Submit your profile.

⌈Best⌉ NursingCenter.com

http://www.nursingcenter.com/

Packed with articles, inside information, and links to the best nursing resources on the Web, this site lives up to its billing as "The Web's most comprehensive resource for nurses." Includes recommended reading, information on professional development and continuing education, career guides, a job center, links to the nursing community, and links to online stores where you can purchase nursing apparel and other nursing-related items.

Nursing Desk Software

http://www.community.net/~sylvan/MacNursing.html

Offers shareware and freeware, nursing links, and hospital unit information systems.

Nursing Education of America

http://www.nursingeducation.org/

This site offers info on NEA and their accredited continuing education programs for nurses.

Nursing Management Services

http://www.nms-nursing-usa.com/

International healthcare recruitment service, staffing hospitals throughout the United States on long- and short-term contracts.

NurseWeek.com

http://www.nurseweek.com

This site contains nursing articles, editorials, continuing education programs, nursing events, career advancement information, and employment opportunities. Excellent place for nurses to go for career information, information on continuing education courses, and news relating to the nursing field.

Procare USA

http://www.procareusa.com/

Places American and Canadian RNs throughout the United States. Read about the employment search and hiring packages.

StarMed Staffing Group

http://www.healthtour.com/

Family of companies that specialize in the placement of nursing and allied health professionals nationwide. The site provides info for specific job types.

WholeNurse

http://www.wholenurse.com/

Provides information to nurses, patients, and medical personnel of all types in an effort to keep up with the growing amount of information posted online.

OFFICE MANAGEMENT

OFFICE EQUIPMENT

Better Buys for Business

http://www.betterbuys.com/

Guides to the major types of office equipment relating to the printing, copying, transmission, and storage of documents. Each year, they publish a series of 10 guides covering subjects such as copiers, fax machines, multifunctional equipment, color devices, printers, duplicators, and electronic filing systems. You can pay for the subscription for this service online using secure credit card resources.

⟦Best⟧ BuyerZone.com

http://www.buyerzone.com/office_equipment/

Resources for becoming a more-informed purchaser of office equipment, focusing primarily on electronic equipment, including copiers, printers, fax machines, and shredders. Features buyer's guides, articles, and newsletters. Obtain free quotes on equipment purchases from several online stores. Whether you manage your own small office or offices for a large corporation, you'll find plenty of excellent information and deals on this best of the best site.

A
B
C
D
E
F
G
H
I
J
K
L
M
N
O
P
Q
R
S
T
U
V
W
X
Y
Z

A
B
C
D
E
F
G
H
I
J
K
L
M
N
O
P
Q
R
S
T
U
V
W
X
Y
Z

Buysmart.com

http://www.buysmart.com/

This site is devoted exclusively to helping companies at all stages of office equipment purchasing—from getting you up to speed on what you need to know before you buy to allowing you to compare products and to shop online. You'll find product category guides, reviews, and hot buys at this online shopping site. It seems that most of the shopping features are actually links to other sites but the result is the same, great shopping and convenient. There is a variety of things you can shop for to make your office more efficient. These include, but are not limited to, gifts, computers, real estate, home furniture, cars, travel, and information about mortgages.

Home Office Direct

http://www.homeofficedirect.com/

Online office furniture warehouse features wide selections of desks, computer desks, computer carts, office chairs, and accessories.

OfficeFurniture.com

http://www.officefurniture.com/

Search for modular furniture, filing cabinets, seating, and accessories for your office at OfficeFurniture.com, where you should have no problem finding an office furniture solution that fits your budget.

PriceSCAN.com

http://www.pricescan.com/home_office.asp

Get free price quotes from several companies, so you can comparison shop for office equipment online.

SOHO Consumer

http://www.sohoconsumer.com/

A collection of useful, objective information about products and services for the small office/home office.

OFFICE SUPPLY STORES

Dr. Shredder's

http://www.dr-shredders.com/

Dr. Shredder is the cartoon icon for A&W Business Machines, which supplies equipment to the print community—folders, letter openers, cutters, trimmers, shredders, and all kinds of other goodies. Used equipment is also available. Lines from a number of manufacturers are represented.

Independent Stationers Online

http://www.office-plus.com/

This online newsletter promises to keep you up to date on the latest in the office products industry—hot topics, products, reviews, and more. Also, get the details on the OP Office Plus cooperative and its network of dealers.

Levenger

http://www.levenger.com/

This Web site features quality stationery, pens, desks, chairs, reading lamps, and desk accessories. Other office supplies for sale include leather goods and corporate gifts. It bills itself as the site "for serious readers." You can order online using secure credit card services.

Office Depot

http://www.officedepot.com/

Office Depot offers a wide range of office supplies including office furniture, office stationery, and mailroom supplies. Shoppers can search for items by Office Depot's product number, the manufacturer's model number, or the UPC or barcode number found on products. The site also features an online Office Depot credit card application and a store locator to help shoppers find the Office Depot closest to them.

Office Helper

http://www.officehelper.com/

This online office supply superstore is divided into two "aisles": Organization Ideas and Find Your Printer Supplies. Click Organization Ideas to read articles and tips on how to organize your office more effectively and to shop for organizational products, such as filing cabinets and folders. Click Find Your Printer Supplies for printer cartridges and other related items. Free next-day delivery on all orders over $25.

OfficeMax OnLine

http://www.officemax.com/

Register at this business-to-business secure site. (Registration is required, and you must supply name, address, and billing information to enter the site.) Shop through various categories of office equipment, supplies, and services in the OfficeMax, CopyMax, and FurnitureMax sections. If your business has more than 50 office employees, you can sign up to join the OfficeMax Corporate Direct program for perks and savings.

onlineofficesupplies.com

http://www.onlineofficesupplies.com/

No-frills office warehouse packed with all the office supplies and equipment you may ever need. With a very basic home page that groups various office supplies and equipment into categories which makes it easy to browse the store to find what you need.

Quill Office Products

http://www04.quillcorp.com/Default.asp

Quill Corporation is a business-to-business direct marketer of office supplies, computer supplies, and office machines. They serve schools, businesses, associations, institutions, and professional offices in the United States.

⟦Best⟧ Staples, Inc.

http://www.staples.com/

While most are familiar with this office-products superstore, not as many are aware of their Web site. Locate the store nearest you, look over their special deals for contract and commercial customers (government, healthcare, and educational accounts), and don't forget to check out the job postings! Fill in your snail mail info for a copy of the Staples catalog or order all your supplies and equipment online and have them shipped to your door. Reasonable prices, a wide selection, and easy-to-use order forms combine to make this the best office equipment site on the Web.

A
B
C
D
E
F
G
H
I
J
K
L
M
N
O
P
Q
R
S
T
U
V
W
X
Y
Z

A
B
C
D
E
F
G
H
I
J
K
L
M
N
O
P
Q
R
S
T
U
V
W
X
Y
Z

USPS Shipping Supplies Online

http://supplies.usps.gov/

If you have a busy home office or even for commercial purposes, this site will save you a lot of time. You can order supplies and packing materials and you can order Priority Mail, Express Mail, Global Mail, and even Global Express Guaranteed. This provides a convenient way to do your shipping and receiving functions.

U.S. Office Products

http://www.usop.com/

This company is into all sorts of things related to business: office furniture and products, school supplies, and travel—even coffee! (Click Locations to see the amazing list of divisions, involving more than 19,000 employees.) Click the icon for the product or service that interests you to get details on local suppliers as well as overall services available in that area.

Viking Direct

http://www.viking-direct.co.uk/

If you are visiting Europe on a frequent basis, perhaps on business trips or you live in the area, this is a great place to order your supplies. You can also order from any other country but just keep in mind that if you are traveling, this resource is available to you. Viking is an online mail order facility offering everything from office supplies to office machines.

123 Sort It

http://www.123sortit.com

If you feel as though you could use some help in organizing your home or office, you'll definitely want to visit this site. Here you'll find some great ideas for getting more organized—finding your desk, reducing clutter, and managing your paperwork more efficiently. You can also buy some tools to help you stay on top of your mess.

Boise—Worldwide Office Supply Services

http://www.boiseoffice.com/

If you travel a lot or you need to order products while you are at different locations, this is a good resource to know about. Even if you order locally, there may be a need to know about this company if you can't find it locally. They have just about every office supply and any office equipment you need. They are a worldwide distributor of business supplies and services, computer supplies, office furniture, and promotional products. It's a valuable resource you can't ignore.

CheckWorks.com

http://www.checkworks.com/

Order your business or personal checks straight from the printer and get a huge selection of styles at a very reasonable price.

Eletter.com

http://www.eletter.com

Download templates from this site to create professional-looking letters, postcards, flyers, and brochures; then, have them printed, folded, and mailed, all by Eletter. You design it; and then leave it to the experts at the site to get it out quickly and economically.

Office.com

http://www.office.com/

A site that pulls together news specific to your industry, how to network with your peers, business management advice, and which suppliers to use. With this site's help, you can save time and money looking for qualified vendors. You can also learn more about getting started with e-commerce.

seeuthere.com

http://www.seeuthere.com/default.asp

Managing special events or parties is now easier with seeuthere.com. This site enables you to create and distribute invitations, accept event registrations (including payment), or process RSVPs online.

United States Postal Service ZIP Code–Look-Up

http://www.usps.gov/ncsc/lookups/lookups.htm

Type in the address, city, or office location and the U.S. Postal Service's ZIP Code look-up software will provide the ZIP-plus-four code. It's much easier than using the print directory—and you can be sure it's always up to date.

A
B
C
D
E
F
G
H
I
J
K
L
M
N
O
P
Q
R
S
T
U
V
W
X
Y
Z

A
B
C
D
E
F
G
H
I
J
K
L
M
N
O
P
Q
R
S
T
U
V
W
X
Y
Z

PARENTING

ADOLESCENTS

ABC's of Parenting

http://www.abcparenting.com/

This site contains a parenting and pregnancy index with reviews of thousands of sites, articles on child, infant, health, and women's issues. You can shop online and it has great gift ideas and links to other related sites.

About Parenting Teens

http://parentingteens.about.com/mbody.htm

You can learn a lot about parenting on this site from expert human guides and get hot news, helpful advice, and invaluable links to other sites that contain similar information.

ADOL: Adolescence Directory On-Line

http://education.indiana.edu/cas/adol/adol.html

This electronic guide to information on adolescent issues is a service of the Center for Adolescent Studies at Indiana University.

Being a Teenager

http://www.fcs.wa.gov.au/templates/being_a_teenager/

Great site for teenagers to learn more about themselves, their rights, and their responsibilities. Good place for parents to go to learn more about what's on the minds of their teenagers.

Canadian Parents Online

http://www.canadianparents.com/

This excellent resource covers everything from preconception tips to raising tweeners and teenagers. Chat rooms and message boards help parents join forces in the challenging field of parenting. Online experts offer tips and hints on topics such as packing a healthy lunch and raising children with special needs. Links to stores where you can purchase products online.

Child.net

http://www.child.net/

Sponsored by the National Children's Coalition, this site is an excellent resource for parents and kids. Features three sections: For Kids, For Teens, and For Parents & Teens. The Kids section offers safe search tools, kids chat, games, and more. The Teens section covers everything from drug and alcohol avoidance to study tips and free classifieds. The Parents section provides a directory to resources on tough love, how to volunteer to help kids, and drug and alcohol awareness.

Dear Lucie

http://www.lucie.com/

Lucie Walters writes a syndicated teen advice column. This site offers advice to teens on subjects such as sexuality, depression, alcohol, pregnancy, romance, eating disorders, and parents. The site contains an archive of past columns.

Drug Testing: PDT-90.com

http://www.drugtesting.net/

Are your kids on drugs? This site offers a drug testing collection kit for parents, which involves collecting hair samples for lab analysis. The site includes FAQs and details of the procedure.

Facts for Families

http://www.aacap.org/
info_families/

The American Academy of Child and Adolescent Psychiatry (AACAP) developed Facts for Families to provide concise and up-to-date information on issues that affect children, teenagers, and their families. Find out about depression in teens, helping your teen with stress, manic-depressive illness in teens, normal adolescent development, dealing with teens and eating disorders, and so on.

Girl Power! Campaign Home Page

http://www.girlpower.gov/

This is the official site of Girl Power, a national public education campaign sponsored by the Department of Health and Human Services to encourage 9- to 14-year-old girls to make the most of their lives.

KidsHealth.org: For Teens

http://kidshealth.org/teen/

Brought to you by AI duPont Hospital for Children in Delaware. Teens can come here and get answers to questions or concerns that they haven't wanted to talk about. Topics include issues such as health, sex, food, sports, and school. A separate section has been created for parents who need a resource for concerns about their own teen.

National Families in Action

http://www.emory.edu/NFIA/

National Families in Action is a national drug education, prevention, and policy center based in Atlanta, Georgia. The organization was founded in 1977. Its mission is to help families and communities prevent drug abuse among children.

National Parent Information Network

http://www.npin.org/

The National Parent Information Network is a clearinghouse of educational resources for parents and those who work with parents. This site offers links to news and resources.

Parenting Q&A

http://www.parentingqa.com/
teens.html

Answers to common questions bugging parents that are provided by parents who have already experienced them. Parents of teens confronting issues of sex, home schooling, and skateboarding, as well as death and loss, teen pregnancy, and many others, will find the Q&As helpful.

ParentsPlace.com

http://www.parentsplace.com/

Lots of parenting info for children of all ages. From birth to teenage years, select the Age/Stages option and follow the prompts to get to the topic that interests you. There is also some information to help parents after the great event such as how to put the spice back into your romance after the baby is born.

A B C D E F G H I J K L M N O P Q R S T U V W X Y Z

A
B
C
D
E
F
G
H
I
J
K
L
M
N
O
P
Q
R
S
T
U
V
W
X
Y
Z

Positive Parenting

http://www.positiveparenting.com/

The Positive Parenting site is dedicated to providing resources and information to make parenting more rewarding, effective, and considerably easier. It also offers some advice about how to put the spice back into your romantic life after the baby is born.

Talking with Kids About Tough Issues

http://www.talkingwithkids.org

Tips and resources for talking with your kids about tough issues, especially violence, alcohol, sex, HIV/AIDS, and terrorism. Request booklets and read Q&As to see how it is recommended you help teens deal with these important issues.

Teen Hoopla

http://www.ala.org/teenhoopla/

An Internet guide for teens. Links to sites on topics such as teen magazines, homework help, music, art, comics, sports, and library services.

Teens Today

http://www.thefamily.com/teens/teenindex.html

Articles written by parents who have successfully raised their teen and want to share their experience and wisdom with you.

The WholeFamily Center: Teen Center

http://www.wholefamily.com/aboutteensnow/index.html

Forum for learning strategies for resolving the tensions arising in family life. Each center has real-life dramas you can listen to on RealAudio. The site features just about all the information that families and teens, especially, have questions about. There are sections on school, sexuality, a crisis center, dealing with relationships, feelings and emotions, substance abuse, and what kids like to do, just hanging out. This best of the best site is easy to navigate and well designed and offers something of interest to everyone in the family.

BABIES AND TODDLERS

ABCs of Parenting

http://www.abcparenting.com/

Extensive Web directory with links to sites about parenting subjects, including pregnancy, childcare, health, safety, and education. Find chats, forums, and reviews.

Baby Bag Online

http://www.babybag.com/

This Web site is a resource for parenting and childcare. Visitors can post birth announcements, read stories, and access articles and links on topics ranging from health and safety to pregnancy and childbirth. Some excellent advice from experts.

Baby Catalog of America

http://www.babycatalog.com/

Baby supply store with online catalog and ordering, shower registry, and gift certificate ordering. Books, videos, furniture, toys, skin care, and safety items are featured.

BabyCenter

http://www.babycenter.com/

Offers information on pregnancy, baby care, and nutrition as well as a guide to baby names and a pregnancy timeline. Users can personalize the page by entering their baby's due date or birth date.

babyGap

http://www.gap.com/

Gap store designed for babies/ toddlers. Buy clothes online, locate a store near you, or see what's on sale. To get to the babyGap, open the Gap's home page and click the BABYGAP link.

BabysDoc.com

http://www.babysdoc.com/

Online healthcare resource for sick babies. Parents can visit to look up information about common symptoms, illnesses, and remedies. Check growth charts, body mass indexes, and development charts. Find out which vaccinations your baby needs and when baby should get them. Poison center, Parents Q&A, and articles from pediatricians make this one of the prime sites for parents of babies and toddlers.

CareGuide

http://www.careguide.net/

CareGuide provides child- and elder-care information. Find child and senior care centers, preschools, nursing homes, and other services anywhere in the United States by using the indexes or searchable databases at this site.

Dr. Greene: Toddlers

http://www.drgreene.com/toddlers.html

A pediatrician dispenses advice on handling temper tantrums, the terrible twos, teaching sharing, stopping biting, and all sorts of other questions and concerns that specifically apply to toddlers.

Early Childhood Educators' and Family Web Corner

http://users.stargate.net/~cokids/

Provides resources for both teachers and families on the subject of early childhood education. Resources include articles, Web sites, a calendar of events, and more.

eToys

http://www.etoys.com/

Huge online toy store, featuring recommendations, bargains, a catalog, and a searchable database. Items are sorted by age group and by category: dolls, collectible toys, video games, and so on.

Family Education Network: A Parenting and Education Resource

http://www.familyeducation.com/home/

Articles and advice from experts. Psychologists and pediatricians answer questions from parents. Users can find schools in their area that are online by using the search feature at this site.

FamilyTime

http://www.familytime.com/

Articles and advice from experts on how to better organize your family and the time you spend together. Tools for meal planning, keeping a calendar, and saving money are featured, along with plenty of useful tips.

iParenting.com

http://www.iparenting.com/

From conception to birth to teen years, you'll find helpful articles and guidance from other parents who've dealt with similar issues.

A
B
C
D
E
F
G
H
I
J
K
L
M
N
O
P
Q
R
S
T
U
V
W
X
Y
Z

KidSource: Toddlers

http://www.kidsource.com/
kidsource/pages/toddlers.html

Advice and reference material on health, learning, and development. The site also includes information on positive discipline.

Live and Learn

http://www.liveandlearn.com/

Contains links to education resources, free software, and online games, plus information on age-appropriate toys and child safety. In addition, the site provides a good list of teaching sites.

The National Parenting Center

http://www.tnpc.com/

Founded in July of 1989, The National Parenting Center (TNPC) has become one of America's foremost parenting information services. Dedicated to providing parents with comprehensive and responsible guidance from the world's most renowned child-rearing authorities, The National Parenting Center invites parents to expand their parenting skills and strengths. Also learn about product recalls at this site.

Pampers Parenting Institute

http://www.pampers.com

Advice for parents about child development, health, and skincare—plus a guide to the Pampers range of diapers.

ParenTalk Newsletter: Toddlers

http://www.tnpc.com/parentalk/
toddlers.html

Choose from all sorts of articles on toddler topics: How you can survive the terrible twos, advice on potty training, age appropriate learning and development, and more.

Parenthood.com

http://www.parenthood.com/

Lots of articles on parenthood, as well as chat, shopping, and special offers. There is also a useful how-to section that teaches even the newest parents the basics of caring for a child.

Parents.com

http://www.parents.com

Feature articles from this print publication cover topics such as parents-to-be, travel, development, health & safety, fun, and food. "Ask the Expert" gives you the chance to have your specific question answered.

K–6

About Child Parenting

http://childparenting.about.com/

About's Child Parenting section covers just about every topic imaginable that's related to raising children K–6. Learn some arts and crafts ideas, get help for raising children with special needs, and learn how to deal with specific problems that commonly arise.

AdvanceAbility Speech Therapist

http://www.aability.com/

Submit questions to a practicing speech/language pathologist. The site also includes a section for parents on teaching children to read.

America Links Up

http://www.americalinksup.org/

This group provides information for parents on safe surfing on the Internet for kids, links to tools and tips, a list of kid-safe Web sites, and a schedule of local classes.

Boy Scouts of America

http://www.bsa.scouting.org/

This organization's home page describes the Cub Scouts and Boy Scouts and their programs. The site also covers joining and volunteering for parents and kids, and offers a catalog of merchandise. Find a BSA council in your area using the locator provided.

Child Development from Elaine Gibson

http://www.elainegibson.net/parenting/index.html

This site outlines what to expect, needs, and a discipline approach for each age. This should ease your mind about some of your child's behaviors and also help you recognize whether your child's behaviors are outside of the normal range.

Childhood Years: Ages Six Through Twelve

http://www.nncc.org/Child.Dev/child6_12.html

This is a National Network for Child Care article reprinted by the North Carolina Extension Service.

ClubMom

http://www.mom.com/

Read interesting articles on raising children today, chat with moms facing similar situations as you, and get and give advice on parenting subjects. Also, tune in to live chats with experts.

Developmental Assets: An Investment in Youth

http://www.search-institute.org/assets/

The Search Institute promotes investing time in our youth. They offer ideas for families, communities, churches, and schools.

Expect the Best from a Girl

http://www.academic.org/

Provides ways to encourage your daughter to develop competence and self-confidence—particularly in science, math, and technology.

FamilyFun

http://family.go.com/

Lots of helpful information for running a household. The site gives problem-solving advice, tools, recipes, crafts, and gift suggestions.

Good Housekeeping: The Latchkey Solution

http://www.homearts.com/gh/family/10lachf1.htm

This site addresses self-care as an option for school-aged children, along with suggestions about preparing your child for being on his or her own and what you should know before leaving your child home alone.

HELP for Parents

http://www.helpforfamilies.com/frameparent.htm

A great resource from Dr. Tim Dunnigan, where you can learn effective discipline techniques. Visiting this site is just like going to a good parenting class—without having to leave your house.

KidsHealth.org

http://www.kidshealth.org/

Looking for expert health information for the entire family? KidsHealth.org has the latest on everything from chicken pox to dyslexia, in easy-to-read articles for kids, teens, and parents.

A
B
C
D
E
F
G
H
I
J
K
L
M
N
O
P
Q
R
S
T
U
V
W
X
Y
Z

A
B
C
D
E
F
G
H
I
J
K
L
M
N
O
P
Q
R
S
T
U
V
W
X
Y
Z

Kids Camps

http://www.kidscamps.com/
special_needs/
learning_disab_add.html

The Internet's most comprehensive directory of traditional and specialty overnight camps. The camps cater to those with learning difficulties and offer tours and experiences for children, teenagers, and families.

The Kotex Guide to Menstruation for Girls and Women

http://www.kotex.com/

This is a great commercial site. Take your daughter here when the time is right, or let her explore it on her own.

Looking After Kids

http://www.fcs.wa.gov.au/
templates/looking_after_kids/
default.cfm

Thorough discussion of your school-age child's development. This attractive site from Australia's Family and Children Services covers all stages of development from babies to teenagers. Includes tips on having fun together, protecting kids, and foster care.

National Network for Child Care: School Age Child Development

http://www.nncc.org/Child.Dev/
child.dev.page.html

Excellent collection of articles on all stages of childhood development from infant to primary school, plus groupings of articles on special topics, such as brain development, aggression, social skills, depression, and assessing a child's abilities.

NCF—National Center for Fathering

http://www.fathers.com/

The NCF mission is to inspire and equip men to be better fathers through fathering research and inspiration.

Parent News

http://www.parent.net/

Parent News provides a parenting tip of the day, family movie reviews, articles about childcare, a section on children's health, and links to educational Internet resources.

Parent Soup: Chat Descriptions

http://www.parentsoup.com/chat/

This site offers access to dozens of chat rooms, such as question-and-answer sessions with pediatricians and chats for parents of elementary school-age children.

Parenting Pipeline

http://www.ext.nodak.edu/extnews/
pipeline/

Online newsletters from the North Dakota State University Extension Service. Very good developmental information for elementary-age children.

Raising Our Children Free of Prejudice

http://familyeducation.com/
article/0,1120,1-1530,00.html

Dr. Alvin Pouissant has great advice for parents of all ethnicities at the Family Education Network.

SINGLE PARENTING

Divorce Online

http://www.divorceonline.com/

A well-organized Web site with articles on different aspects of divorce such as financial and legal issues.

Federal Child Custody Laws

http://wwwsecure.law.cornell.edu/topics/child_custody.html

Information about federal statutes and judicial decisions from the Legal Information Institute at Cornell University.

Making Lemonade

http://makinglemonade.com/

Read articles in the archives, check out single parent-related links, and share your war stories with other single parents at this site.

MotherLinC: Mothers Without Custody

http://users.ev1.net/~lavietes/momlac.htm

A support and resource organization for this much-overlooked segment of the single-parent population.

Power Parenting Tools

http://www.parentingtoolbox.com/timecush.html

Learn time-management and child-rearing tips for nontraditional families. The site is updated regularly.

Single and Custodial Father's Network

http://www.scfn.org/

Support organization for single and remarried fathers with custodial care. Find information on work and parenting issues, a mailing list, and chat.

Single Parent Central

http://www.singleparentcentral.com/

Get news and information about trends in single parenting families, share advice and wisdom, learn about ways to save money, and find links to other related sites.

Single Parents Association

http://www.singleparents.org/

Single Parents Association (SPA) is a nonprofit organization devoted to providing single-parent families educational opportunities and fun activities through its national headquarters and local chapter network.

Single Parents World

http://parentsworld.com/

Explore commentary on child support, dating, and parenting. Visit the site's bookstore. Also find a forum for meeting and talking with other parents.

SPECIAL NEEDS

ADDHELP

http://www.addhelp.com

For parents and teachers of ADD/ADHD children. The site helps you in getting an accurate diagnosis and providing strategies for managing your child's difficult behaviors. Find out how to reinforce positive behavior and discourage bad behavior, along with many other tips and ideas.

Alliance of Genetic Support Groups

http://www.geneticalliance.org/

This organization helps individuals and families with genetic disorders. The site includes publications and membership forms.

A
B
C
D
E
F
G
H
I
J
K
L
M
N
O
P
Q
R
S
T
U
V
W
X
Y
Z

A
B
C
D
E
F
G
H
I
J
K
L
M
N
O
P
Q
R
S
T
U
V
W
X
Y
Z

Arc

http://www.thearc.org/

Formerly the Association for Retarded Citizens, this national organization provides support for children and adults with mental retardation and their families.

Asperger/Autism: On the Same Page

http://amug.org/~a203/

This autism/Asperger's syndrome resource offers links to independent living, employment, medical information, and much more.

Asperger's Syndrome Parent Information Environment

http://www.aspie.org/

Information and resources about diagnosis and treatments for Asperger's syndrome. Provides behavior charts, school management tips, information about support groups and medications, a recommended reading list that links to Amazon.com, and more.

Attention Deficit Disorder

http://attn-deficit-disorder.com/

Information and help on ADD, one of the most misunderstood issues facing families today.

Autism Society of America

http://www.autism-society.org/

This organization offers information and referral packages for parents and educators. Membership and society details are included.

BandAids and Blackboards

http://funrsc.fairfield.edu/
~jfleitas/contents.html

Designed to help children cope with the stigma and isolation that a chronic medical condition can sometimes bring.

Center for the Study of Autism

http://www.autism.org/

This Oregon-based center provides information to parents and professionals. It also conducts research into various treatments.

Child Amputee

http://www.amp-info.net/
childamp.htm

New mailing list giving information and support contacts. The site includes a host of links to prosthetic technology sites.

Children with AIDS Project

http://www.aidskids.org/

Services for children infected and affected by AIDS. Kids can chat online and get support. Adults can read about becoming an adoptive parent.

Children with Spina Bifida

http://www.waisman.wisc.edu/
~rowley/sb-kids/index.htmlx

Promotes information sharing between parents. The site provides news and research updates, details of problems, and a list of related organizations.

Cleft Lip: Wide Smiles

http://www.widesmiles.org/

Formed to ensure that parents of cleft-affected children do not have to feel alone. Chat online with parents or read the files.

Cleft Lip and Palate Surgery

http://www.plasticsurgery.org/
surgery/cleftlp.htm

Introduction for parents to common palate surgery procedures. The site is sponsored by the American Society of Plastic and Reconstructive Surgeons.

ConductDisorders.com

http://www.conductdisorders.com/

You can join their parents' support group here. Also, read articles that may help you understand and better deal with your child's conduct difficulties. Find out about treatment programs, and scan the bookstore for suggested resources you may want to read.

Council for Exceptional Children

http://www.cec.sped.org/

The Council for Exceptional Children is an organization dedicated to improving educational outcomes for students with disabilities. Users can access a database of professional literature, information, and resources.

Down Syndrome

http://www.downsyndrome.com/

This forum for sharing experiences and information about Down syndrome features a family chat area, a bulletin board, and an online magazine.

Dyslexia: The Gift

http://www.dyslexia.com/

Provides information about the positive side of learning disabilities and remedial teaching methods suited to the dyslexic learning style.

Family Village

http://www.familyvillage.wisc.edu/

Virtual community for persons with mental retardation and other disabilities, their families, and those who provide services and support. From their shopping mall you can buy anything from canes and walkers to clothing, computers, software, and footwear.

Internet Resources for Special Children

http://www.irsc.org/

This site features a catalog for parents and professionals in relation to child disabilities, disorders, and health care. Huge collection of links broken down into categories including Adaptive Equipment & Technologies, Diseases & Conditions, Sports & Recreation, Learning Disabilities, and more than a dozen more. Great place to start researching any topics relating to children with special needs.

Make-a-Wish Foundation of America

http://www.wish.org/

This site outlines the history of this organization, which grants wishes to children with life-threatening medical conditions. You'll also find details about activities in the works.

Mountain States Genetics Network: MoSt GeNe

http://www.mostgene.org/

An A-to-Z listing of online groups and organizations providing information and support for those who live with or treat genetic illnesses. Focusing primarily on Arizona, Colorado, Montana, New Mexico, Utah, and Wyoming.

National Academy for Child Development (NACD)

http://www.nacd.org/

The NACD provides data and support for learning disorders, including ADD and mental retardation. Find out more about the organization and its products and services at this site. You may order CDs, audio tapes, and special software from their site.

A
B
C
D
E
F
G
H
I
J
K
L
M
N
O
P
Q
R
S
T
U
V
W
X
Y
Z

A
B
C
D
E
F
G
H
I
J
K
L
M
N
O
P
Q
R
S
T
U
V
W
X
Y
Z

National Information Center for Children and Youth with Disabilities (NICHCY)

http://www.nichcy.org/

The National Information Center for Children and Youth with Disabilities provides facts about referrals, education, and family issues. Their site can help you locate the organizations and agencies within your state that are working on disability-related issues.

National Organization of Mothers of Twins Clubs

http://www.nomotc.org/

Find facts and figures related to the incidence of multiple births as well as local support organizations and resources to aid in meeting the distinctive developmental needs of twins. Information on the organization's annual conference is also available.

Network on Disabilities

http://www.npnd.org/

The National Parent Network on Disabilities provides a national voice for parents of those with special needs.

STAY-AT-HOME PARENTS

Bizy Moms: A Complete Resource for Work-at-Home Moms

http://www.bizymoms.com/

Business ideas for moms working from home. Also included are FAQs and insights into the book The Stay at Home Mom's Guide to Making Money from Home.

Chat: Stay-at-Home Parents

http://homeparents.about.com/ mpchat.htm?once=true&

Meeting place for stay-at-home parents. The site has so many features it would be impossible to list them here but they have articles, a forum, a chat room, a contact guide, newsletter, and a nice FAQ. You can find extensive information on Arts & Crafts, links to other family sites, scrapbooks, home schooling, and a lot more. You can order a wide variety of products such as books and baby-related items from their online shopping mall.

Dr. Laura

http://www.drlaura.com/

This is the official Dr. Laura Schlessinger site. She is a controversial radio and TV talk host who believes strongly in stay-at-home parents.

The Entrepreneurial Parent

http://www.en-parent.com/

Tips on how to manage your career and your family from your home, with resources and links.

Feeling Respected As a Stay-at-Home Mom

http://www.suite101.com/ article.cfm/home_mom/17880

From Suite101, author Kelli Cole discusses her life as a stay-at-home mom.

Home-Based Working Moms

http://www.hbwm.com/

Association for mothers and fathers working from home. Find out about membership and get tips and ideas for your business.

HomeEcon Research

http://www.homeecon.com/
research.html

Lots of links to help parents. While there are definitely links oriented strictly to stay-at-home parents, there are even more that parents in general will find useful.

Main Street Mom

http://www.mainstreetmom.com/

An online network for stay-at-home moms. Lots of good articles and links are available.

Mothers and More

http://www.mothersandmore.org/

Find local chapters, advocacy efforts, and more. Particularly well suited to the mother who is neither a working mom nor an at-home mother but rather a mix of both.

Slowlane.com

http://www.slowlane.com/

Searchable online resource for stay-at-home dads and primary caregivers and their families. Includes articles primarily written by stay-at-home dads. Also includes media clips and links to hundreds of other resources on the Web. Online chat and discussion groups to help stay-at-home dads keep from becoming agoraphobic.

STEPPARENTING

 **FamilyFusion**

http://www.familyfusion.com/

Everything you need to know to survive and succeed as a stepparent. Learn your role in raising the children, find out how to deal with the biological parents and grandparents, get tips on how to deal with legal and financial issues, and even check out some stepparenting humor. This site's well-balanced and humorous approach to stepparenting makes it an easy selection for best of the best parenting site on the Web.

ParentsPlace: Stepfamilies

http://www.parentsplace.com/
family/archive/
0,10693,239452,00.html

Ask the family counselor a question or read previous Q&A columns about stepchildren and stepparents. It includes stepfamily discussion forums.

Shared Parenting Information Group

http://home.clara.net/spig/

Find guidelines for separated parents, parenting plans, and FAQs about joint custody. The site includes articles and resources on shared parenting.

Stepfamily Association of America

http://www.stepfam.org/

Support organization for stepfamilies and blended families. The site includes featured articles, book reviews, and some interesting facts.

The Stepfamily Bookstore

http://www.concentric.net/
~Lismith/STEP.HTM

Find links to books about stepfamilies that can be purchased through Amazon.com. Send comments or suggest other books via email.

Stepfamily Network

http://www.stepfamily.net/

Includes some useful links on how to get support. Find info on their volunteer network, and get your questions answered at this site.

A
B
C
D
E
F
G
H
I
J
K
L
M
N
O
P
Q
R
S
T
U
V
W
X
Y
Z

The Stepparenting Connection

http://www.tsconnection.org/

Use the stepparent directory to track down someone in your area who may be a resource and sounding board for you as you face the challenge of stepparenting. Read the diary of a stepparent and nominate someone for Stepparent of the Month. You'll also want to check out the entertainment section of the site, which has nothing to do with stepparenting but can reduce your stress level.

PARKS

Canyonlands

http://www.canyonlands-utah.com/

Utah's largest national park is profiled at this site. You'll find accommodations, various area destinations, tours, campgrounds, and travel resources via the site.

Colorado State Parks and Outdoor Recreation

http://parks.state.co.us

Information on parks in Colorado, including recreational activities and fees. This site also provides information on seasonal jobs, a park finder, trail maps, news, and online kids' activities.

Death Valley National Park

http://www.desertusa.com/dv/ du_dvpmain.html

Visitors to this Web site will find a virtual visitor's center for Nevada's Death Valley National Park. Information on weather, temperature, activities, accommodations, and fees is included, as are maps and a guide to desert wildlife. You can also communicate with others at the Desert Talk message board and mailbag. Be sure to visit the Trading Post for some shopping fun!

Discover Banff

http://www.discoverbanff.com/

A comprehensive guide to travel in Banff, Canada, is available at this site. It offers information on Banff and Jasper Parks, dining, tours, accommodations, equipment rentals, seasonal activities, and links to related sites.

Fodor's National Parks

http://www.fodors.com/parks

Information on lodging, camping, and dining facilities at America's national parks from Fodor's, featuring maps and photos of each park.

GORP: Great Smoky Mountains National Park

http://www.gorp.com/gorp/ resource/US_National_Park/ tn_great.HTM

Your first stop for information on the Great Smoky Mountains and the park. Find out about

A
B
C
D
E
F
G
H
I
J
K
L
M
N
O
P
Q
R
S
T
U
V
W
X
Y
Z

accommodations, traveling through the Smokies by car, cycling, camping, fishing, hiking and backpacking, horseback riding, the mountain people, and naturalist activities. Also access information on trips and other Internet resources.

GORP: U.S. National Parks and Reserves

http://www.gorp.com/gorp/resource/US_National_Park/main.htm

Features a state-by-state list of national parks in the United States. Users can click on a park to obtain specific information on visitor centers and facilities such as hiking, climbing, and camping.

GORP: Wilderness Area List

http://www.gorp.com/gorp/resource/US_Wilderness_Area/main.htm

Tourist information and tips about U.S. national forests and wildlife refuges.

Grand Canyon Official Tourism Page

http://www.thecanyon.com/

This site provides all the tourism information you'll need when visiting Grand Canyon National Park. You'll get all the standard information on what to do and where to go, stay, eat, and shop. Plus, read news bits, get weather info, see photographs, read anecdotes, and learn all about the local area. A great resource. They really have a great shopping mall where you can buy everything from wonderful jewelry to Native American art and you can shop online as well as at the park.

Maps of United States National Parks and Monuments

http://www.lib.utexas.edu/maps/national_parks.html

The University of Texas at Austin has put its map collection online. Maps are listed alphabetically or by park region. The site also contains maps of national historic and military parks, memorials, and battlefields.

Mesa Verde National Park

http://www.mesaverde.org/

This site provides a wealth of information on the Mesa Verde National Park in Colorado, delves into the archaeology of the ancestral Puebloans, and covers the ancient—as well as the modern—culture of the area. Check out the electronic bookstore, which sells park-related materials.

Mount Rainier National Park

http://www.mount.rainier.national-park.com/

This unofficial guide to Mount Rainier National Park features information on the park's history, visitor services, trails, and more.

New Hampshire Resource Listings

http://www.gorp.com/gorp/location/nh/nh.htm

Visitors to this Web site can explore New Hampshire's natural attractions, such as scenic drives, parks, and national forests. Purchase books about New England's outdoor activities.

A
B
C
D
E
F
G
H
I
J
K
L
M
N
O
P
Q
R
S
T
U
V
W
X
Y
Z

New Mexico State Parks

http://www.emnrd.state.nm.us/
nmparks

The New Mexico State Parks site contains information on and a detailed map of each park, as well as month-by-month listings of park events, fees, and regulations for park and boating use.

North Cascades Conservation Council

http://www.northcascades.org

This site is the unofficial guide to North Cascades National Park, in northwestern Washington, providing basic park facts and visitor services. Learn about the natural history of the area, obtain park management information, and link to related Web sites; get everything from the latest conditions, to boating information, to details on the alpine plants.

Olympic National Park

http://www.northolympic.com/onp/

This site provides dozens of links to information on Olympic National Park in the Pacific Northwest, which has 4,000,000 visitors annually. Also included is a link to a virtual tour of the park. All the information you need in one spot.

 ### PARKNET: The National Park Service Place

http://www.nps.gov/

A mandatory stop for anyone interested in our national parks. This is the National Park Service's home page, a searchable site that links to NPS sites for all the parks. Besides finding data on any individual park, you can read special travel features and learn about such topics as natural resources in the parks and America's histories and

cultures—plus visit the Park Store. If you're planning a nature vacation, be sure to check out this best of the best site.

Passport to Your National Parks

http://www.geocities.com/
Yosemite/4434/passport.html

Visit this site to learn about obtaining and using the Passport to Your National Parks, an information book and personal travel scrapbook available at national parks. The Passport offers color-coded maps, illustration, visitors' information, and photos—and it can be stamped with an official park "cancellation mark" each time you visit.

Petrified Forest National Park

http://www.gorp.com/gorp/
resource/US_National_Park/
az_petri.HTM

The Petrified Forest National Park protects one of the largest, most spectacular tracts of petrified wood in the nation. This site gives a history of the area as well as other useful information.

South Carolina State Parks

http://www.discoversouthcarolina.
com/sp.asp

Listing of state parks in South Carolina with photos, descriptions, and recreational information on each. This site also has listings of bed and breakfasts and other lodging, and a calendar of events.

The Total Yellowstone Page

http://www.yellowstone-natl-park.
com/

This is a one-man tour de force of information about Yellowstone National Park. Absolutely a must-visit site if you are planning a trip to Yellowstone National Park!

U.S. National Parks

http://www.us-national-parks.net/

List of national parks in the United States with photos and information on each, including the address; camping, hiking, and lodging guides; park details; maps; and skiing, rafting, and visitors' guides.

Wyoming State Parks and Historic Sites

http://spacr.state.wy.us/

Information on Wyoming State Parks, historic sites, and the State Trails program. Includes snowmobile regulations, regional trails, campground locations, a trading post, and a listing of annual events and things to do.

Yellowstone Net

http://www.yellowstone.net/

Site recommended by USA Today and others. Visit Yellowstone Net for all kinds of information on the park, news, photos, specialty stores, reservations, related links, and access to the Yellowstone Net community. Check it out.

Yosemite Park

http://www.yosemitepark.com/

Official Web site of Yosemite National Park in central California. This appealing site offers a park overview, information about Yosemite lodging, park activities, dining and shopping, special events, gifts and memories, special offers, news releases, and search/index categories for you to explore.

PEDIATRICS

 American Academy of Pediatrics

http://www.aap.org/

Established primarily for pediatricians seeking to provide the best care for their patients, the AAP site provides research papers, free access to Medline, the medical database, as well as information on professional opportunities. Parents will find the section on You and Your Family particularly useful; it's packed with safety information, product recalls, parenting guidelines, and tips to help make your parenting experience more fulfilling and successful.

Children with Diabetes

http://www.childrenwithdiabetes.com/index_cwd.htm

Anyone who has diabetes or who has a child with diabetes needs to visit this site. It is packed with information and has real-time chat rooms. They strive to be "the online community for kids, families, and adults with diabetes."

DISHES Project for Pediatric AIDS

http://www.dishes.org/

The DISHES Project is the modeling industry's first 501(c)(3) nonprofit

A B C D E F G H I J K L M N O P Q R S T U V W X Y Z

A
B
C
D
E
F
G
H
I
J
K
L
M
N
O
P
Q
R
S
T
U
V
W
X
Y
Z

foundation. At the heart of the project is the desire to raise funds and awareness for direct care, education, and emotional support for pediatric AIDS.

DocsOnline

http://www.docsonline.com/

Enables you to locate dentists, physicians, health care providers, and hospitals in your area based on your specific health care needs.

Dr. Greene's HouseCalls

http://www.drgreene.com/

Get helpful hints from this pediatrician. Need some advice from a kid pro? Submit a question online, search through topics relating to developmental stages, or just read up on Dr. Greene's featured articles. This site is a friendly resource for any parent.

Dr. Plain Talk

http://www.childrenshc.org/fp/default.asp

This site is maintained by Dr. Rob Payne, who has been a pediatrician for more than 20 years. At this site, you can find plain and simple information about complex medical issues relating to babies and children.

Journal of Pediatrics

http://www.harcourthealth.com/scripts/om.dll/_serve?action=searchDB&searchDBfor=home&id=pd

The Journal of Pediatrics site describes the contents and what is covered in the journal as well as offering other pertinent information. Everything from preventive health care, to treatment of childhood diseases, to emergency care is covered in the journal. It serves as a practical guide for the continuing

education of physicians who diagnose and treat disorders in infants and children. There are many useful articles that anyone can derive helpful information from. Abstracts are available for free, but to access full-text articles, you must subscribe (for about $150 per month).

kidsDoctor

http://www.kidsdoctor.com/

This site's for you if you like expert opinions on how to keep your kid(s) healthy. You'll find a list of topics written by a doctor, parents' Q&As, and a searchable database so you can zero in on the specific health information you want.

KidsMeds

http://www.kidsmeds.com/

Provides pediatric drug information to parents of infants and children. A pediatric pharmacist is online at this site to answer specific questions.

National Childhood Cancer Foundation

http://www.nccf.org/

This site gives details of the programs and activities of this organization which supports pediatric cancer treatment and research projects.

OncoLink

http://www.oncolink.com/

Sponsored by the University of Pennsylvania Cancer Center, this site acts as an information guide to all topics relating to pediatric and adult cancer, including leukemia. Excellent source for information on the latest treatments.

PETS

AllPets.com

http://www.allpetsmarket.com/

Well-stocked online pet store offers just about everything any pet owner needs, from beds and bones to pet ramps and training aids. The only thing this store doesn't carry is food. Shop online and have your order shipped to your home, so you can spend more time with your pet.

mypetstop.com

http://new.mypetstop.com/

This multilingual site provides more information than you can shake a tail at. Pick your country, click the species (Dogs, Cats, Fish, Birds, Horses, or Other Animals), and you're on your way to learning everything you need to know to properly care for your pet and enjoying your time together. You can ask questions ranging from ailments to nutrition. There's also some information on animal psychology.

CATS

American Cat Fanciers Association

http://www.acfacat.com

Rated one of Links2Go's top feline sites, this site showcases ACFA, a national cat registry sponsoring shows internationally and annually ranking top-scoring cats. ACFA also records Household Pets. The site guides you to local cat shows and breeders and contains photos and forms to register and join this ever-growing organization.

Cat Fanciers Association

http://www.cfainc.org/

The world's largest purebred cat registry features its top award-winning felines and information on each recognized breed. This site encourages responsible cat ownership and advises how one can show purebred and household pet felines and participate in local CFA cat clubs and shows throughout the world.

Cat Fanciers Home Page

http://www.fanciers.com/

Provides cat-related information. This site offers numerous FAQs on different cat breeds, feline health, and care issues. It also offers links to show schedules, cat organizations, FTP and gopher sites, as well as links to commercial sites, picture sites, and cat owners' home pages.

Cat House (EFBC/FCC) Home Page

http://www.cathouse-fcc.org/

Contains pictures and some audio clips straight from the cat's mouth. The Cat House (a.k.a. the Feline Conservation Center) is a desert zoo that contains a variety of wild cat species. More than 50 cats, representing 13 species, live at the compound. Photos of recent births are included.

Cats Protection League

http://www.cats.org.uk/

Learn more about caring for cats through online guides at this non-profit organization's site that is dedicated to providing new homes

A
B
C
D
E
F
G
H
I
J
K
L
M
N
O
P
Q
R
S
T
U
V
W
X
Y
Z

for cats throughout the U.K. At the site you can track down a location near you and find out how to adopt a kitten or cat that's been rescued.

Catsbuzz Bookstore

http://members.aol.com/catsbuzz/

Books, books, and more books about cats. On this site, you'll find books about specific breeds, books with general information, books for kids, and books for Christmas. Link over to Catsbuzz Central and check out cats in the news, great cat links, and cat poetry.

Best CatToys.com

http://www.cattoys.com/

Check the list of recommended toys for your particular breed of cat and then purchase it online here. You'll want to visit frequently to see what the new specials are each week. One of the most fun things you can do with cats is to watch them play with that new toy you just bought them and this site will allow you to order many types of toys for them online. If you're a cat lover, this best of the best site is a must site for you.

DOGS

Adopt a Greyhound

http://www.adopt-a-greyhound.org/

Greyhounds may have been famous for their speed and grace on the track, but recently, people have begun to adopt them upon retire-ment from the races—saving them from euthanasia or worse. This site provides a huge amount of informa-tion, as well as links to other sites. Check out the many adoption agen-cies specializing in greyhounds.

American Kennel Club (AKC)

http://www.akc.org/index.cfm

Find out more about this organiza-tion, read about different breeds, and locate an AKC near you. You'll also enjoy their information brochures covering everything from boarding your dog to showing your dog. This site is packed with infor-mation! Besides the great graphics layout, ease of use and all the infor-mation, you can purchase every-thing concerning dogs from books, videos, and apparel to artwork.

Best Dog Breed Info Center

http://www.dogbreedinfo.com/

Before investing in a new pet, visit this site to select the best breed for your family situation, temperament, living space, or whatever criteria you want to use. It's a good place to assess whether you're ready for the responsibilities of being a dog owner. This site is very well organ-ized and offers the information you need to have before taking that big step of owning a dog. The site has great graphics, is easy to navigate, and will help you in the selection process which is important because you want to make sure you select an animal you will be happy with.

Dog Owner's Guide

http://www.canismajor.com/dog/

Read up on articles about choosing the right breed, caring for a dog, training him, selecting a vet, as well as learning about the law and dogs, and how to stay out of trouble. The site has plenty of information on a wide range of topics.

Dog Term Glossary

http://www.ecn.purdue.edu/~laird/
dogs/glossary

Presents terminology both common and uncommon to the canine field. It provides many links to additional sites, as well as pointers to other parts of the glossary. Also, it contains contact information for Humane Societies and the American Kennel Club. Great place to go to for a description of most dog breeds plus links to other sites that focus on specific breeds.

Dog.com

http://www.dog.com/

Search more than 17,000 dog-related sites to find the information you need, including details of a breed's personality. You can also catch up on the latest dog news headlines and shop for the dog lover in your life.

Dog-Play

http://www.dog-play.com/

Literally an A–W (no X, Y, or Z) of fun things to do with your dog, as well as giving pet owners something different to think about: Animal-assisted therapy. The author of this site details the experience of using dogs to help reach out to the elderly and confined individuals. The site includes links to organizations involved in animal-assisted therapy, books and publications on therapy dogs, and links to other dog-related sites.

GORP: Great Outdoor Recreation Pages

http://www.gorp.com/gorp/
eclectic/pets.htm

Tired of walking the dog just around the block or to the local park? These pages detail countless destinations that will cater to you and your canine. Complete lists by activity, region, interest, and lodging are provided.

Index of Famous Dogs, Cats, and Critters

http://www.citizenlunchbox.com/
famous/animals.html

A surprising number of dogs and other animals have important roles in TV and movies or are owned by famous people. This site is dedicated to listing most if not all of them. You'll even find the obscure ones. For example, what is the name of the dog who pulls down the bikini of the little girl in the old Coppertone ads? What was the name of Santa's Little Helper's wife? How about all their puppies? You can get the answers at this Web site.

k9web

http://www.k9web.com/

This is a resource for the canine community. Find breeders, groomers, clubs, info on boarding, pet care, trainers, and more.

PET CARE

American Animal Hospital Association (AAHA)

http://www.healthypet.com/

AAHA offers pet care tips, answers to FAQs on care and illnesses, and a library of articles on topics from behavior to nutrition. At first glance, the site looks a little sparse, but click on the Pet Care Library link, and you'll see links to all sorts of tutorials and articles on pet care and training. Click the Coloring link to view printable posters for kids to color. Check the FAQ for answers to common questions, or subscribe to the Pet Planet newsletter.

A
B
C
D
E
F
G
H
I
J
K
L
M
N
O
P
Q
R
S
T
U
V
W
X
Y
Z

American Pet Association

http://www.apapets.com/

The American Pet Association is dedicated to promoting responsible pet ownership through action, services, and education. You will find lots of useful information here to help you assist your pet in leading a more peaceful, safe, and enjoyable coexistence with you. There is lots of information here that is interesting, informative, and useful for pet owners of all types.

Animal Health Information

http://www.avma.org/care4pets/
avmaanim.htm

Get info on dental care, pet population control, and vaccinations. Learn how to deal with diseases such as heart disease, heartworm disease, cancer, Lyme disease, parasites, toxoplasmosis, and rabies.

The AVMA (American Veterinary Medical Association) Network

http://www.avma.org/

The American Veterinary Medical Association answers questions on pet care, selection, and loss, and how your veterinarian helps you enjoy your pet. The Kids' Korner includes pictures you can print out and let your kids color. Each picture includes an activity or advice on feeding, training, or basic care. This site is extremely attractive, well organized, and offers a wealth of information.

I Love My Pet

http://www.ilovemypet.com/

The I Love My Pet site offers tips, a pet club, online vet, specialty foods, discounts, and a breeder registry. Both pet owners and pet fans will find useful information here. If you're looking for information on pet diets, healthcare, or just fun and games, this is the place to find it. While you're there, check out all the selections from their online catalog.

NetPets

http://www.netpets.com/

A resource for dog, cat, horse, fish, and bird owners. The site includes information about pet health and nutrition, and offers an events calendar, a library of articles, and a list of animal shelters by state.

OncoLink: Veterinary Oncology

http://www.oncolink.com/
templates/types/section.
_cfm?c=22&s=69

This veterinary hospital of the University of Pennsylvania has information for owners about the diagnosis and treatment of cancer in animals.

Online Animal Catalog

http://www.blarg.net/~critter/
index.html

Offers articles, pictures, and links relating to all kinds of animals.

Pet Care and Wildlife Information

http://www.klsnet.com/

This reference provides information on caring for all sorts of pets, including exotic fish, reptiles, and amphibians. Also provides information about caring for dogs, cats, and other furry creatures.

Pet Columns from University of Illinois College of Veterinary Medicine (CVM)

http://www.cvm.uiuc.edu/ceps/

Search by keyword or by most recent to least recent for authoritative articles on pet care, common problems, and their management. Also, the site provides links to the University of Illinois CVM and their Continuing Education Public Extension Service.

PetEducation.com

http://www.peteducation.com/

This site was created by vets to provide information on caring for your pet, so there are tons of articles you'll want to scan. There are also pet services directories, a veterinary dictionary, answers to frequently asked questions, quizzes, and the latest pet news.

Pets Need Dental Care, Too

http://www.petdental.com/

This site makes you aware of potential problems with your pets caused by dental situations just as with humans. Dental problems can cause serious health problems in addition to painful tooth loss or gum disease. If your pet is acting strangely or seems to be ill for no apparent reason, then you should check out this site.

Professor Hunt's Dog Page

http://www.cofc.edu/~huntc/dogpage.html#Message

Get info on rescues, animal health, and socially responsible activities. This site has a special emphasis on herding (working) breeds.

Purina Pet Care Center

http://www.purina.com/

More than just nutrition from this pet-food company. Pet care advice, training, kennel management, and some fun games. Their hope is that you'll find this site to be a very useful resource and the goodwill generated will translate into lots more sales of Purina products.

Veterinary Mall

http://www.veterinarymall.com/

Excellent resource for pet owners, as well as for veterinarians, this site provides dozens of links to articles ranging from basic pet care and training to diagnosis and treatment of specific illnesses. Search the directory for animal hospitals, breeders, trainers, and other pet services organized by state; post a question for a licensed veterinarian; chat online; or check out some recommended pet products.

Waltham World of Pet Care

http://www.waltham.com/

This pet nutrition company provides advice on caring for dogs, cats, birds, and fish. Provides excellent information about each animal that's covered, including how to select the proper breed, basic care instructions, training and feeding tips, and more.

PET SUPPLIES

Doolittle's

http://www.doolittles.com/

At Doolittle's, you will find a unique combination of distinctive gifts for pets and pet lovers, fine quality pet supplies, premium pet foods, gourmet treats, and a full-service pet grooming salon.

A
B
C
D
E
F
G
H
I
J
K
L
M
N
O
P
Q
R
S
T
U
V
W
X
Y
Z

A
B
C
D
E
F
G
H
I
J
K
L
M
N
O
P
Q
R
S
T
U
V
W
X
Y
Z

Noah's Pet Supplies

http://noahspets.com

This site offers more than 6,000 items for pets. You'll also find a Q&A section where you can get answers to your pet questions. Their selection is so large they even offer a section that highlights the newest product additions.

Pet Experts

http://www.pet-experts.com/

About pets, animals, wholesale pet products, and discount animal supplies. Dog, cat, bird, fish, reptile, iguana, and even ferret supplies can be found here.

Pet Warehouse

http://www.petwarehouse.com

A mail-order catalog company that specializes in aquatic, bird, dog, cat, reptile, small animal, and pond products at factory-direct prices.

PetFoodDirect.com

http://www.petfooddirect.com/store/

Order pet foods and accessories online and have them shipped to your doorstep. Food, health products, toys, and treats are all found here.

Petopia.com

http://www.petco.com/

Read articles about dog care, such as how to safely trim your pooch's nails. Learn whether putting your pet in a kennel is harmful, and search for pet services and products all at this one place.

PETsMart

http://acmepet.petsmart.com/

Huge online pet store and pet information kiosk. Whether you own a dog, cat, bird, fish, reptile, or rodent, you can find all the supplies and accessories you need right here. Features basic care instructions, feeding calculators, information on illnesses and treatments, instructions on choosing the right animal for you, and much more.

ThatPetPlace.com

http://www.thatpetplace.com/

This pet supply superstore carries everything for almost every pet imaginable at great prices. Features accessories for dogs and cats, fish, birds, reptiles, and other small creatures. Includes a few articles on caring for and training pets. Easy to navigate.

PHOTOGRAPHY

CAMERAS

Abe's of Maine

http://www.abesofmaine.com/

Promising prices of up to 50% off retail, Abe's specializes in selling camera equipment and supplies online and from their Brooklyn, New York, store.

AGFA Digital Cameras

http://www.agfahome.com

Which digital camera is right for you? Check out AGFA's product line. They have a search feature that allows you to search for information and they offer commercial services such as those they offer to the newspaper industry.

Apogee Photo: The Internet Photo Magazine

http://www.apogeephoto.com/

Dedicated to entertaining and informing photographers of all ages, this site offers high-quality articles and columns about photography. Features basic instructions on taking pictures, techniques for novice and advanced photographers, information about digital imaging, and more. Also provides links to workshops, books, and schools that may be of interest to readers.

B&H Photo

http://www01.bhphotovideo.com/

A discount photography equipment dealer with a large selection of digital cameras, video equipment, lighting, traditional cameras, and accessories.

Beach Photo & Video

http://beachphoto.com/

Whether you need a photo restored or are in the market for a used camera, Beach Photo is likely to provide the services you need. Buy new or used equipment here, and have film processed or printed, too.

Bender Photographic

http://www.benderphoto.com

Thinking about making your own camera? Benders sells kits for 4·5 and 8·10 view cameras from kiln-dried cherry and brass hardware. By building your own camera, you can invest more on a good lens, which will improve the quality of your photos. Learn more about building a camera and then order the kit at this site.

A
B
C
D
E
F
G
H
I
J
K
L
M
N
O
P
Q
R
S
T
U
V
W
X
Y
Z

Camera.com

http://www.camera.com/

A complete digital camera resource that carries information about hundreds of digital cameras and accessories, adds new cameras and accessories, and updates their prices daily to remain competitive.

Camera Review.com

http://www.camerareview.com/

Specify the features you're looking for in a camera and the database will provide a list of camera models that meet your criteria. You can also take a look at the online rankings of the most popular cameras, according to people who own and use them. And compare features side-by-side of two or more cameras to help in making your purchase decision.

Cameras Etcetera

http://www.cameras-etc.com/

This site focuses on selling "quality used photo equipment at fair prices." The site is updated regularly, and you can find out what is currently available by clicking on a category featured on the home page. They encourage you to attend their Trade Shows and direct you to check their schedule to see whether one will be in your area. You can place your order via email, phone, or fax. You pay for the call, and for shipping, too.

CameraWorld

http://www.cameraworld.com/

This enormous online camera warehouse is stocked with everything a novice or expert photographer needs: digital cameras, film cameras, a wide variety of camcorders, lenses, film, light meters, books, and more.

Complete Guide to Digital Cameras and Digital Photography

http://www.shortcourses.com/

A free online course on digital photography. A gallery of images taken with a digital camera is included. It is an information-packed site!

Digital Camera Imaging Resource Page

http://www.imaging-resource.com/

Digital cameras, features, specs, reviews, and sample images for most brands and models are available at this site.

Focus Camera & Video

http://www.focuscamera.com/

Bills itself as the #1 deep discount source for every photographic, sports optic, astronomical, and video camera item for more than 30 years. One of America's largest-stocking photo and optics dealers, with more than 32,000 items in stock.

Kodak Digital Cameras

http://www.kodak.com/global/en/
digital/cameras/DCSGateway.jhtml

The Kodak family of digital cameras and related products.

PC Photo Review

http://www.pcphotoreview.com/

Digital camera site offers news, reviews, guides, tips, and forums.

Photo.net

http://www.photo.net/

Pages and pages of camera-related commentary. For example, "What Camera Should I Buy?" explores some options (view cameras, medium-formats, SLRs, and even lowly point-and-shoots are covered) and some opinions. It contains a ton of handy tips: recommended films, ritzy frame shops, where to shop for cameras, where to send your slides for processing, and so on.

Ritz Camera

http://www.ritzcamera.com

A network of e-commerce Web sites, including Ritz Camera, Wolf Camera, Photography.com, and other businesses, this site offers a huge selection of cameras and provides easy browsing. Stop by the Learning Center to learn more about various photographic products and services and then check out the special coupons and deals available at Ritz Camera.

TECHNIQUES

American Museum of Photography

http://www.photographymuseum.com/

This site has a beautifully displayed collection along with information and services for researchers and collectors. It also contains information on preservation and a newsletter.

Apogee Photo

http://www.apogeephoto.com

Check Apogee's buyer's guide and product reviews before making another camera equipment purchase, and enjoy the free online magazine to learn more about the art and process of taking good photos. Industry news, articles, columns, and other tidbits round out the site, which is for professionals and amateurs.

Best BetterPhoto.com

http://www.betterphoto.com/home.asp

This excellent source for novice photographers features scads of information about photography basics, plus online workshops that lead you step-by-step through the process of learning new techniques. Created and maintained by Jim Miotke, author of Absolute Beginner's Guide to Taking Great Photos, this site also provides a Q&A section, discussion forums, and a buyer's guide. Links to Amazon.com, where you can purchase cameras and accessories online.

City-Gallery.com

http://www.city-gallery.com/

Post information and ask questions about old photography methods and materials.

Focus on Photography

http://www.azuswebworks.com/photography/

Lots of information on the processes and techniques of modern photography. A wealth of technical information is available. This site is wonderful in its simplicity because the information is easy to find. This makes it a gem for the amateur and professional alike. You will find everything from the basics to the more complicated techniques such as lighting and composition. They have a section on sample pictures, reference, and an excellent FAQ.

FotoForum

http://www.fotoforum.com

FotoForum is an online forum where amateur photographers can share tips, ask questions, sell items, and post and view photos. Take a

A
B
C
D
E
F
G
H
I
J
K
L
M
N
O
P
Q
R
S
T
U
V
W
X
Y
Z

A
B
C
D
E
F
G
H
I
J
K
L
M
N
O
P
Q
R
S
T
U
V
W
X
Y
Z

look at the online gallery, join a discussion group, or purchase a photography book while you're here.

George Eastman House: Timeline of Photography

http://www.eastman.org/
5_timeline/5_index.html

An overview of the history of photographic images from the 5th century B.C. until the present. It is presented in list style or by time periods. The site is from the George Eastman House.

Getty Images

http://creative.gettyimages.com/
photodisc

Looking for high-quality digital images for use in an upcoming marketing campaign? Then search this site by keyword to find images that may fit your needs. You can purchase more than 34,000 images on disc using secure card services.

International Center of Photography

http://www.icp.org

ICP's mission is to "present photography's vital and central place in contemporary culture, and to lead in interpretation issues central to its development." View online exhibitions and learn more about the work of this organization.

KODAK: Taking Great Pictures

http://www.kodak.com/US/en/nav/
takingPics.shtml

This handy guide to taking better pictures provides tips, techniques, and "problem picture remedies," for

any level photographer. Online tutorials discuss fundamentals of photography, including lighting, composition, and basic darkroom techniques. Sample photos show you how the pros do it, and a selection of reference materials are always on-hand to help you with technical terminology and concepts.

Photography Review

http://www.photographyreview.com/

Learn photography skills from fellow photographers, check out product reviews of cameras by consumers and professionals, as well as other photography equipment, and then scan the online swap sheet to find good used gear. The site is "By photographers for photographers," leaning more toward an advanced audience.

PhotoWorks.com

http://www.photoworks.com/

Send your photos in to PhotoWorks for processing and have them store the pictures on a personalized, password-protected Web site for view by anyone you like—at no charge. The photos can be either digital or film-based. From their online store you can purchase anything from photographic supplies and cameras to T-shirts and mugs with your photos on them.

A
B
C
D
E
F
G
H
I
J
K
L
M
N
O
P
Q
R
S
T
U
V
W
X
Y
Z

Contacting the Congress

http://www.visi.com/juan/congress/

Find a congressperson's email address, Web site, or ground address by typing in that person's name, or clicking on the state they represent. You can also key in your ZIP Code to identify your representative and find their email address. There are more than 500 email addresses on the site and 500 more Web page addresses.

Council on Foreign Relations

http://www.cfr.org

Are you interested in United States foreign relations? Then check out this official site of the Council on Foreign Relations, where you can find out the latest information on the United States's relationships with other countries, including Russia, Britain, Egypt, Saudi Arabia, Pakistan, and others. Learn what current and former presidents, national security advisors, and other leaders are thinking about U.S. foreign policy and politics.

The Hill

http://www.thehill.com

Web home of The Hill, "a non-partisan, non-ideological weekly newspaper that describes the inner workings of Congress, the pressures confronting policy makers and the many ways—often unpredictable—in which decisions are made." If you're interested in the inner workings of Congress and other government leaders and are looking for behind-the-scenes coverage of current political events, this is the site for you.

National Political Index

http://www.politicalindex.com/

Designed to be a one-stop shop for substantive political information, this site provides ways to contact federal and local politicians. It also provides access to think tanks, news media, contests, and areas for discussions and debates.

Office of the Clerk On-line Information Center

http://clerkweb.house.gov/

Take a virtual tour of the House Chamber, obtain copies of bills and House documents, and find historical information about the House of Representatives.

opensecrets.org

http://www.opensecrets.org

Are your senators and congressional leaders in the pockets of large corporations and special interest groups? Check this site to find out. This site is created and maintained by the Center for Responsive Politics, a watchdog group that follows the money in Washington D.C. to find out where it's going and why, and to keep citizens informed.

A
B
C
D
E
F
G
H
I
J
K
L
M
N
O
P
Q
R
S
T
U
V
W
X
Y
Z

Political Money Line

http://www.fecinfo.com

Home of the Federal Election Commission, this site provides citizens with information on campaign contributions from corporations, PACs, and other sources. If you're wondering where the money flows in Washington, check out this site.

Politics1.com

http://www.politics1.com

A bipartisan site that aims to inform Americans regarding the political process and issues being discussed. Get campaign information, updates on current debates, and sign up for the Politics1 newsletter.

 ### SpeakOut–Politics, Activism, and Political Issues Online

http://www.speakout.com/

SpeakOut.com is an opinion research company started by Ron Howard, a guy who wanted to speak out and make his opinions known to the government, but didn't have a clear idea about how to go about expressing himself to the people who could really help him. So, Ron started this site to help other aspiring activists figure out how to make their voices heard. SpeakOut gives you an opportunity to let your thoughts and opinions be known using the site's online polls. The site provides you with the information and activism tools you need to speak out on such subjects as political and social issues, elections, political parties, the government, and democracy. When you feel like you can't sit still and remain silent while other people are making decisions that affect your life, check out this best of the best site and get involved!

washingtonpost.com/OnPolitics

http://www.washingtonpost.com/politics

Home of the Washington Post, one of the most popular newspapers on Capitol Hill, this site provides headline news about what's going on in the Capitol. In addition, you can find out about upcoming elections, election results, lobbying efforts, campaign contributions, and other political topics. You can even cast your vote in the daily poll.

POLITICAL CAMPAIGNS

C-SPAN Networks

http://www.c-span.org

Check out the C-SPAN schedules (C-SPAN and C-SPAN2) and content, explore the Public Affairs Video Archives, or listen to the show, Washington Journal. Explore today's headlines from papers such as the Washington Post, San Francisco Examiner, Chicago Sun-Times, and more. C-SPAN in the Classroom is a great link for teachers and students. C-SPAN's Majic Bus travels on tours such as one chronicling the history of civil rights in the Deep South. C-SPAN Online Live lets you watch events as they are happening (such as news conferences). Check out the Booknotes program, which presents America's finest authors discussing reading, writing, and the power of ideas. Get information on the U.S. House schedule and weekly committee hearings.

California Voter Foundation

http://www.calvoter.org

If you're a California citizen and you feel obligated to cast your vote in the next election, visit this site first to get the information you need to make an informed choice. Here, you can find the most current voter guide along with information about the latest initiatives. Pull up the campaign promises archive to see whether your local politicians are delivering on their word.

Campaign and Elections

http://www.campaignline.com/

Campaigns and Elections Online is a magazine for political professionals. You can check out the changing odds on major national, state, and local races across the country. Browse any of the following sections: National Directory of Public Affairs; Lobbying; and Issues Management Consultants, Products, and Services. Or, check out the political analysis section. Get a subscription to Campaign Insider—a weekly newsletter for political consultants and committees. The site also includes C&E's Buyers Guide, information on telephone services, media placement, direct mail services, fundraising, and more.

Campaign Finance Reform

http://www.brookings.org/GS/CF/CF_HP.HTM

This site's goal is to improve the quality of debate on campaign finance reform so that a workable approach can be passed by Congress and signed into law by the president. Examine new approaches to reform. Check out articles analyzing the proposed reforms, related opinion pieces, and proposals to Congress. Go to the Public Forum on Campaign Finance Reform to view others' ideas, analyses, and opinions.

Elections

http://www.multied.com/elections/

This presidential elections statistics site is presented by MultiEducator. Check out colorful graphs of the electoral votes cast in presidential elections from 1789 to the present. Download photos of scenes from American history and read selected documents (such as the Articles of Confederation and the Civil Rights Act of 1957). The MultiEducator American History product lets you access events chronologically, alphabetically, or by topic. Access facts about major events in U.S. history and get extensive information about each of the presidents. Audiovisuals highlight major periods in U.S. history, and video clips showcase achievements and tragedies. It links to HistoryShopping.com, where you can purchase learning materials online.

Electronic Activist

http://gemini.berkshire.net/~ifas/activist/

An email address directory of members of Congress, state governments, and media entities. Excellent site for political activists and concerned citizens to go to learn how to make their voices heard in their state legislatures and in Washington, D.C.

A
B
C
D
E
F
G
H
I
J
K
L
M
N
O
P
Q
R
S
T
U
V
W
X
Y
Z

A
B
C
D
E
F
G
H
I
J
K
L
M
N
O
P
Q
R
S
T
U
V
W
X
Y
Z

Federal Election Commission (FEC)

http://www.fec.gov/

This is the official site for the Federal Election Commission (FEC), which was established to administer and enforce the Federal Election Campaign Act (FECA). The site is filled with tons of useful information that can be searched by state, party, office, or name. Very useful for research on political subjects, for entertainment, or just for informative reading on how the political system works.

MotherJones.com

http://www.mojones.com/

Mother Jones is a magazine of investigation and ideas for independent thinkers. Provocative articles inform readers and inspire action toward positive social change. Colorful and personal, this magazine challenges conventional wisdom, exposes abuses of power, helps redefine stubborn problems, and offers fresh solutions. The discussion forum encourages visitors to share their views with one another on a variety of issues. Winner of several awards for excellence in publishing and journalism.

The National Journal

http://nationaljournal.com/

The National Journal provides commentary, news, and resource materials on politics and policy. It offers online delivery of most National Journal Group daily publications—CongressDaily, The Hotline, American Health Line, Greenwire, and Technology Daily. It includes a database of polling results and trends. It also offers the Almanac of American Politics, as well as schedules for Congress.

OnPolitics.com

http://www.washingtonpost.com/wp-srv/politics/talk/talk.htm

On Politics.com is a site that provides you with the "Free Media" weekday political talk show from the washingtonpost.com site. Post reporters and editors and the people they cover put the news of the day in perspective. The site also has a huge article archive, graphics photo library, cartoons, and political news. Great for entertainment or just to be informed.

Project Vote Smart

http://www.vote-smart.org/

Project Vote Smart tracks the performance of more than 12,000 political leaders—the president, Congress, governors, and state legislatures. Get information on issue positions, voting records, performance evaluations, campaign finances, and biographies. Enter your ZIP Code, and the search engine looks up who represents you and gives you the relevant details and statistics. Alternatively, track the performance of the Congress. Find out how candidates stood on issues before they were elected and see how your congressperson voted on a bill. Track the status of legislation as it works its way through Congress; read the text of a bill; and find out whether a bill has had committee action, whether it is scheduled for a hearing or a vote, and whether your congressperson is a cosponsor.

Votenet

http://www.votenet.com/

Search the Votenet site using its search engine and find just what you're looking for in the world of politics. Find out who's giving what to different campaigns, read today's headlines, and use political content provided here to inform and educate others.

POLITICAL PARTIES

The American Party

http://www.theamericanparty.org/

Home of the American Party, a very conservative organization devoted to free trade, clean living, and strong families. Visit this site to learn more about the party and its principles, read their platform for the upcoming election, view a calendar of events, and check out their list of officers.

The Christian Coalition

http://www.cc.org/

CC members fight for laws they feel promote the Christian agenda and fight against those that do not. Their site has reports on every relevant law, as well as how each member of Congress voted. The pages include family resources, articles on American Christians, and more.

College Republican National Committee

http://www.crnc.org/

Home of the nation's largest, oldest Republican student organization, this site features information about the CRNC, news related to the organization, and membership information. Use the online form to register to vote.

The Democratic National Committee

http://www.democrats.org/index.html

Read news from the DNC, browse through the archives, and learn about where the Democratic Party stands on various issues. You can also read through the current year of DNC press releases. It includes information on various Senate hearings, as well as a guide to Republican campaign finance abuses. The site also includes Democratic National Committee FAQs. The Get Active! section tells you how to join the DNC, volunteer, and register to vote.

New Party

http://www.igc.apc.org/newparty/

A grassroots, progressive political party running candidates for local elections around the country. They fight for living wage jobs, campaign finance reform, and public education.

Reform Party Official Web Site

http://www.reformparty.org/

If there's an aspect to politics and government that can be reformed, this party wants to reform it. Their platform is wide, but highlights include disallowing all gifts and junkets, requiring the White House and Congress to have the same retirement and healthcare plans as the rest of us, shortening campaigns to four months, changing Election Day to a Saturday or Sunday so working people can vote more easily, and more.

Republican National Committee

http://www.rnc.org/

The RNC has a pretty interesting home page. It looks like a small town main street and the icons are the storefront windows. You can link with candidates and get their email addresses and, of course, join the party.

A
B
C
D
E
F
G
H
I
J
K
L
M
N
O
P
Q
R
S
T
U
V
W
X
Y
Z

A
B
C
D
E
F
G
H
I
J
K
L
M
N
O
P
Q
R
S
T
U
V
W
X
Y
Z

Workers World Party

http://www.workers.org/

This anticapitalist, prosocialist party believes that capitalism rests on the foundation of the wealthy few oppressing the multitudes of poor. The party basically calls for the workers of the world to unite against imperialist policies worldwide.

Young Democrats of America

http://www.yda.org/

This site offers a map of the United States that you can click to find the contact information and upcoming Young Democrats events for your area.

PREGNANCY

INFERTILITY

About Infertility

http://infertility.about.com/

Directory of articles and resources relating to infertility and techniques and drugs that can increase your chances of conceiving.

American Infertility Association

http://www.americaninfertility.org/

Dedicated to increasing the awareness and understanding of infertility and related issues, AIA features support groups for couples who have trouble conceiving. AIA also advocates health insurance to cover infertility. At this site, you can learn more about the AIA support groups, join discussion forums, chat with other couples who are dealing with infertility, and read the Facts and FAQs for additional information.

Ask Fertilitext

http://www.fertilitext.org/

A guide to getting pregnant. This site contains a comprehensive guide to conception and pregnancy. Excellent information on reproductive health, ovulation, and the male factor.

BabyMed

http://www.babydata.com/

Everything you need to know to get pregnant and stay pregnant: a fertility calendar, discussion groups, an interactive BBT curve, fertility tools and Q&As, and more. An online ticker displays a running count of the world's ever-increasing population.

Child of My Dreams—Infertility Community & Support Center

http://www.childofmydreams.com/infertility/community/

This site's focus is to offer people struggling with infertility a place to find online support. Visitors are invited to participate in chats, read message boards, find infertility resources, and read about adoption.

Fertility Plus

http://www.fertilityplus.org/toc.html

Read articles about basic fertility issues, such as low-tech ways to conceive and ovulation predictor kits, as well as more advanced topics. Check out fertility FAQs, see the fertility resource list, and chuckle at the humor section.

From Infertility to Adoption

http://myria.com/relationships/parenting/infertadopt.htm

Author Brook Dougherty maintains her humor as she walks you through tests, procedures, and more tests, before deciding to adopt. The site is from Myria Magazine.

Infertility: A Couple's Survival Guide

http://www.drdaiter.com/table.html

Learn the basics regarding infertility, ovulation, the pelvis, and sperm here—in order to up your odds of getting pregnant.

Infertility Treatments

http://www.ihr.com/infertility/treatmnt.html

Take a quick online tour of infertility treatments and options. Or gather more in-depth information on the various options. You can also get book references and check out links. There are lots of useful medical overviews.

[Best] The InterNational Council on Infertility Information Dissemination (INCIID)

http://www.inciid.org

This nonprofit consumer advocacy group aims to inform couples of their options regarding infertility treatments. Features essays, articles, commentaries, and fact sheets on infertility, plus a searchable directory of fertility experts. The site also includes interactive discussion forums and chat rooms. This site's excellent information and straightforward presentation help it rein in the honor of the best site in its category.

National Library of Medicine's Infertility Resources

http://www.nlm.nih.gov/medlineplus/infertility.html

Reading room packed with news and articles pertaining to infertility divided into categories including News, General Overviews, Anatomy/Physiology, Clinical Trials, Diagnosis, Treatment, and much more. Excellent place to start researching infertility and finding ways to treat it.

Oxygen's Infertility Page

http://www.oxygen.com/family/issues/infertility/

This site features expert articles on infertility, its impact on relationships, and more. Find out how others cope, and learn about adoptions.

A
B
C
D
E
F
G
H
I
J
K
L
M
N
O
P
Q
R
S
T
U
V
W
X
Y
Z

A
B
C
D
E
F
G
H
I
J
K
L
M
N
O
P
Q
R
S
T
U
V
W
X
Y
Z

MIDWIFERY

Doulas of North America

http://www.dona.org/

This site explains what doulas are, how to find one, what their role is, certification/training information, and more.

Midwife Archives

http://gentlebirth.org/archives/

Offers a midwife perspective on pregnancy, childbirth, and women's healthcare. You'll also find links to other related sites.

Midwifery Information

http://www.moonlily.com/obc/midwife.html

Whether you're interested in becoming a midwife or are one already, you'll enjoy this site's wealth of information on the topic. It offers articles, links, current news and information, and lots of resources.

Midwifery, Pregnancy, Birth and Breastfeeding

http://www.moonlily.com/obc/

Lots of information about being a parent, keeping your child safe, and the benefits of breastfeeding.

Midwifery Resources on the Internet

http://www.users.globalnet.co.uk/~ics/midwifery.htm

This site features FAQs, mailing lists, chat, newsgroups, links, a bulletin board, visitor pictures and stories of their experiences.

MISCARRIAGE

Hygeia

http://www.hygeia.org/

Hygeia is an international community of families grieving from the loss of a child. Here you'll find original poetry of loss and hope, medical information about maternal and child health, and the opportunity to share your stories and share your experience of lost parenthood with thousands of registered families, worldwide.

PREGNANCY/ BIRTH

Ask NOAH

http://www.noah-health.org/english/pregnancy/_pregnancy.html

A very thorough guide to all aspects of pregnancy from the New York Online Access to Health.

BabyZone

http://babyzone.com/drnathan/glossary.htm

A handy reference tool from preconception to parenting. You can also shop online with a large selection of baby clothes, educational toys, and some baby gift ideas for you in case you can't make your mind up about what to get. You can also read about adoption, birth stories, and baby names and you can ask an expert.

Breastfeeding.com

http://www.breastfeeding.com/

Wow, you'll be amazed at all the information you can find here on breastfeeding. Answers to questions about supply, technique, development, working while breast-feeding, and much more, is all provided here. You can buy breast pumps, watch video clips of babies, find a local lactation consultant, and join discussions with other moms and dads.

Childbirth.org

http://www.childbirth.org/

Search this huge site to get answers to all your questions about child-birth, including subjects on avoiding an episiotomy, doulas, depression, and diapering. It's all here.

ePregnancy.com

http://www.epregnancy.com/

As this site claims, "from before pregnancy to after birth," you'll find helpful articles, interactive features to chat with and meet other women like you, links to useful resources, as well as shopping solutions for you and your baby.

Parenthood.com

http://www.parenthood.com/

Parenthood.com brings you a one-stop source for articles, expert advice, and feedback from other parents on issues related to preg-nancy, labor, and baby care.

Pregnancy Daily

http://pregnancydaily.com/

Sign up to receive your pregnancy daily update, telling you how old your fetus is in days and what's going on with your pregnancy that day. More than 500 entries guide you from pregnancy to birth.

Pregnancy Information

http://www.w-cpc.org/pregnancy/

Pregnancy help, fetal development, health tips, and resources are avail-able here.

Pregnancy Today

http://pregnancytoday.com/

Pregnancy information including news, discussion boards, resources, lifestyle issues, expert advice, and more.

Womb.com

http://www.womb.com/

Visit Womb.com to find a variety of links to information about preg-nancy, birth, and parenting. There are sites listed to help you find just about any information you need including information on teenage pregnancy, Cesarean births, and infertility.

A
B
C
D
E
F
G
H
I
J
K
L
M
N
O
P
Q
R
S
T
U
V
W
X
Y
Z

PUBLICATIONS

JOURNALS AND E-ZINES

BestEzines – Choose Your Ezines Wisely

http://www.bestezines.com/

Why waste time searching for e-zines on the Internet when you can find them on BestEzines.com? This site offers you hundreds of free e-zine subscription opportunities. You can choose from the best ones and there are many articles and advice on the subject. Don't clutter your mailbox with worthless junk when you can have the best and most useful to you.

De Proverbio

http://www.utas.edu.au/docs/flonta/

This is an electronic journal of international proverb studies. Several issues are available to be accessed and read, and there are other links available to reach the editors and editorial board of the periodical.

Dimension2

http://members.aol.com/germanlit/dimension2.html

This is a journal of contemporary German-language literature. It is available in both the original German and in English. Also present at this site is original artwork by a contemporary German artist.

E-zineZ

http://www.e-zinez.com/

The E-ZineZ site is dedicated to helping you produce and publish an Internet email newsletter. It begins by offering an online tutorial and individual articles on planning, producing, and promoting your e-zine. It is very helpful!

Early Modern Literary Studies

http://www.shu.ac.uk/emls/emlshome.html

Dedicated to the English language, literature, and literary culture from the 16th and 17th centuries, this journal is very interactive, featuring the capability to respond to its published papers in a reader's forum.

Exemplaria

http://web.english.ufl.edu/exemplaria/

A journal of theory in medieval and Renaissance studies, Exemplaria is based at the University of Florida. Read articles concerning literature and culture from the formative Middle Ages.

Ezine-Universe.com

http://ezine-universe.com/

Searchable and browsable directory of e-zines. E-zines are grouped into categories including Arts and Humanities, Business and Economy, Entertainment, Government, Health, and more.

Pet Bird Magazine

http://www.birdsnways.com/
wisdom/

Pet Bird Magazine is an e-zine about exotic birds and pet parrots, including magazine articles on the care and breeding of pet birds.

Best Science Fiction Weekly

http://www.scifi.com/sfw/

This electronic sci-fi magazine covers books, movies, TV, games, artwork, and merchandise, and even some interviews. This popular site among sci-fi buffs includes a "news of the week" feature which informs readers about current events in the sci-fi world. The site is very easy to navigate and features interesting letters from readers and other visitors. Although the site design is not stellar for a science-fiction site, the content here is top notch, earning this site our best of the best designation.

WebMedLit

http://
webmedlit.silverplatter.com/

This site scans medical journals daily and compiles them into reports on specific medical topics that are then emailed to individuals who've requested them. Sign up here to be on the list for the most up-to-date medical information on AIDS, women's health, cardiology, and several other topics.

MAGAZINES

Advertising Age

http://www.adage.com/

This site presents images for viewing and contains archives, ad market information, and a daily top story. It also enables you to join the AdAge mailing list.

Astronomer Magazine

http://www.theastronomer.org/
index.html

A British publication online that targets the advanced amateur but still contains items for the beginner. It also contains information on comets, asteroids, supernovae, and a variety of other topics that pertain to astronomy.

BYTE Magazine

http://www.byte.com/

Contains a five-year, searchable archive of BYTE Magazine. Enter a search term, and presto! Articles that include the term you entered appear in an easy-to-retrieve format. You can download files and shareware mentioned in BYTE articles and download BYTE's benchmark tests. It's a valuable site worth a bookmark in your browser software.

Computer Games Online

http://www.cdmag.com

This site (which also publishes a print magazine) keeps up with the daily happenings in the computer games industry. It contains everything from in-depth previews and reviews of the latest games to daily news. Dialogue forums, where readers can discuss their favorite titles for any genre, are also available.

Computer Shopper Online

http://shopper.cnet.com/

Check out the top stories for the latest edition of Computer Shopper. It is considered to be the monthly computer Bible for computer buyers. To access the magazine, go to cnet's shopping page, using the link above, and then click the link for Computer Shopper Magazine.

A
B
C
D
E
F
G
H
I
J
K
L
M
N
O
P
Q
R
S
T
U
V
W
X
Y
Z

Computerworld Online

http://www.computerworld.com/

Stay current on all the news of the computer industry with this rich site.

Cosmopolitan

http://www.cosmomag.com/

Pick up weekly tips to improve your love life and career, check your horoscope, and offer advice to other readers facing agonizing situations. It is an encapsulated version of the print magazine, but entertaining nonetheless.

Discover Magazine

http://www.discover.com

Discover Magazine online is a science magazine that includes text of issues, photos, links related to articles, and a subscription service.

Editor & Publisher

http://www.editorandpublisher.com/

Editor & Publisher Magazine online offers selected articles from the printed version of the magazine, as well as Web-only content. It also offers comprehensive coverage of new media news and trends affecting the newspaper industry.

Electronic Green Journal

http://egj.lib.uidaho.edu/

This environmental journal online contains information about environmental issues. It also lists the contents of the recent issues of the journal.

Esquire

http://www.esquireb2b.com

Online version of one of the most popular men's magazines—Esquire. Find out what's stylish and what's not and who's hot and who's not.

Forbes

http://www.forbes.com

Stay up to date on the day's financial and investing news with Forbes.com, analyze your holdings, get stock advice from Streetwalker, and play the Forbes Investment Challenge to earn a chance at a new laptop computer.

Fortune

http://www.fortune.com

Daily business reports and articles from the print magazine. Get company profiles, tips on investing, small-business information, and career leads. Also features top executives, top companies, and a list of the best companies to work for.

Gigaplex

http://www.gigaplex.com

Presents an arts and entertainment Web magazine with departments for film, TV, music, books, theater, photography, food and restaurants, and more. It includes celebrity interviews with actors, musicians, authors, playwrights, directors, and photographers.

Glamour

http://us.glamour.com/

Read some of this month's articles online, check out fashion do's and don'ts, and post your opinion for the benefit of Glamour's editors.

HotWired

http://hotwired.lycos.com/

The slickest magazine in the industry has a Web page with articles on the arts, politics, and technology. Before you can access much of anything, however, you have to join (free of charge). If you decide to sign up and are looking for something to do, check out the Arts and Renaissance articles first.

Internetweek Online

http://www.internetweek.com

A colorful site with news for corporate network managers. This publication provides testing, reviews, industry news, and funny tidbits on the world of networking and information management.

MacWorld Online Web Server

http://www.macworld.com/

MacWorld is the premier magazine for Macintosh computers, users, and buyers. MacWorld online enables you to search past issues and read articles. It also provides Internet tips, product reviews, industry news, newletters, forums, and a pricefinder. If you own a Mac, bookmark this site.

Magazine City.net

http://www.magazinecity.net

Search to find your favorite magazines or locate ones in subject areas of interest and then subscribe at the "guaranteed lowest price."

Magazine CyberCenter

http://www.magamall.com

Get information on magazines, such as where to buy them locally, how to subscribe, and how to get back issues. Search by magazine name or topic to find what you're looking for.

Magazine Rack – Free Online Magazines

http://www.magazine-rack.com/

Find hundreds of magazines online, all free at this site that allows you to click and read magazines on just about any subject. Why pay when you can read for free?

Magazines A-Z

http://www.magazinesatoz.com/

This site has a directory of Magazines Online including automotive, arts & entertainment, bridal, business and finance, computers, and a few other subjects. Find your favorite magazine here for sure. You can use their shopping feature to shop dozens of online stores such as Amazon and each of the magazine offerings which are presented in a more orderly fashion than normal.

Millennium Whole Earth Catalog

http://www.wholeearthmag.com/
market/index.cfm?FuseAction=
foreword

A limited edition of Howard Rheingold's Whole Earth Catalog online. It provides many online excerpts from the catalog book.

Mother Jones Interactive

http://www.mojones.com/

Mother Jones online provides insightful information with a Mother Jones slant.

Motorcycle Online

http://www.motorcycle.com/

This online magazine covers all aspects of motorcycles, including new model reviews, daily news, technical help, pictures, and tours.

NewsLink

http://newslink.org/

Find online versions of many of the most popular newspapers and magazines or search for a topic to find articles in one or more of the online publications.

A
B
C
D
E
F
G
H
I
J
K
L
M
N
O
P
Q
R
S
T
U
V
W
X
Y
Z

A
B
C
D
E
F
G
H
I
J
K
L
M
N
O
P
Q
R
S
T
U
V
W
X
Y
Z

Newsweek

http://redirect.msnbc.com/
newsweek.asp

Catch this week's news on the Newsweek online site, which contains articles and commentary.

People

http://people.aol.com/people/

Get a rundown of the articles in this week's issue of the popular entertainment magazine, People, as well as special subscription offers.

PM Zone

http://popularmechanics.com/

Popular Mechanics online provides movies, pictures, and information about new and useful products and technology.

Popular Science

http://www.popsci.com/

Articles from the magazine's current issue, links, and message forums are available here.

Rolling Stone

http://www.rollingstone.com/

Stay in tune to top musical acts, read music news, and even upload your demo tape for review by Rolling Stone critics! You'll also find video-on-demand of stars you love and a schedule of upcoming music Webcasts.

Runners World

http://www.runnersworld.com/

Race results, tips from top athletes, info on biomechanics and injury prevention, and articles from the print magazine are at this site.

Science Magazine Home

http://www.sciencemag.org/

You will find many interesting articles from this magazine and learn how to subscribe to the magazine. There are current articles and an archive of previous articles.

ScienceDaily Magazine–Your Link to the Latest Research News

http://www.sciencedaily.com/

ScienceDaily is a free, advertising-supported online magazine that presents you with late-breaking news about the latest discoveries and hottest research projects in everything from astrophysics to zoology. They also have a nice search feature and a picture of the day.

Scientific American

http://www.sciam.com/

Scientific American is the premier science magazine for the general public. Features the latest news in the world of science, covering everything from Anthropology to Zoology. Good collection of articles on recent discoveries in space, on earth, and undersea. Covers medical breakthroughs, environmental debates, strange phenomena, and daily occurrences that you might not understand, such as what happens when you get a sunburn. If you're a scientist at heart, this is the site for you.

SciTech Daily Review

http://www.scitechdaily.com

Comprehensive digest and directory of science and technology articles pulled from the top scientific publications around the world. Covers everything from the latest feats accomplished by computer hackers to how a doctor's bedside manner can affect the recovery rates of his or her patients. This publication takes no sides and presents a balanced selection of the latest data in science, technology, and medicine.

Scientific Computing and Instrumentation Online

http://www.scamag.com/scripts/default.asp

A colorful Web site for a magazine devoted to computer analysis software for scientists and engineers. Read articles from the latest issue, link to related sites and to sites of software developers such as IBM and National Instruments, or access chemical databases.

Sky & Telescope Online

http://www.skypub.com/

Sky Publishing Corporation provides astronomical news and calendars, product reviews, viewing tips, and special pages.

Tai Chi

http://www.tai-chi.com/

Some general information about Chinese internal martial arts and information on subscribing to the magazine.

Time Magazine

http://www.time.com/time/

Time Warner's site offers links to Time online, Sports Illustrated online, Money Magazine online, and more.

TravelASSIST Magazine

http://travelassist.com/mag/mag_home.html

This online magazine contains articles on travel and travel spots around the United States and the world. It includes back issues for online reading.

Twins Magazine

http://www.twinsmagazine.com/

This site includes tidbits, resources, articles, and more from the magazine's current issue.

Typofile Magazine

http://www.will-harris.com/type.htm

This online magazine focuses on type and its uses. The site includes articles and links to other type and desktop publishing sites.

U: The National College Magazine

http://www.colleges.com/

News, sports, fun, and special offers for college students, including contests and scholarship money.

Videomaker's Camcorder and Desktop Video Site

http://www.videomaker.com/scripts/index.cfm

Videomaker Magazine online includes a product search engine, back issues, and information about camcorders and video.

Windows and .NETMagazine

http://www.winntmag.com/

Lab and book reviews, features, and other exclusive stories are available on the magazine's Web site. These Web-exclusive articles will not be published in the print edition.

A
B
C
D
E
F
G
H
I
J
K
L
M
N
O
P
Q
R
S
T
U
V
W
X
Y
Z

A
B
C
D
E
F
G
H
I
J
K
L
M
N
O
P
Q
R
S
T
U
V
W
X
Y
Z

The AIDS Memorial Quilt

http://www.aidsquilt.org/

Description of the AIDS Memorial Quilt project, including its history, purpose, and display schedule. They have a nice gift shop or online store from which you can purchase clothes, videos, books, posters, postcards, and other such items. The site is very well designed and easy to navigate and features information about the AIDS Memorial Quilt project.

American Quilts

http://www.americanquilts.com

Search the database to find an Amish or antique quilt from among the 1,500 in inventory. Large, small, finished, and custom are available.

The Antique Quilt Source

http://www.antiquequiltsource.com/

Browse the current catalog and order quilts online. Based in, and inspired by, Pennsylvania's famed quilt country.

Applewood Farm Publications

http://applewd.com/

Offers quilting patterns, classes, seminars, and mystery quilts by Beth Ferrier.

Canadian Quilters' Association

http://members.tripod.com/~cqaacc/

Learn about this association, check out the schedules for upcoming events, paste a message on the quilting board, and peruse their extensive list of quilting links.

Cats (and People) Who Quilt

http://www.catswhoquilt.com/

Sew a cat on your quilt! This site has no patterns or instructions, but lots of images and links to Net resources, all featuring cat quilts.

The Cozy Home Page

http://www.erols.com/cozy/

Elegant home page of this Pennsylvanian textile artist includes a quilt gallery and instructions for Shibori fabric dyeing.

David Walker—Artist, Teacher, Quiltmaker

http://w3.one.net/~davidxix/

Gallery of work by this artist and quiltmaker, as well as a workshop and lecture schedule. Also features an artist of the month.

Down Under Quilts Online

http://www.duquilts.com.au/

Discover something new in quilting from down under. Find out everything that you wanted to know about Australian quiltmaking. The site opens the door to the world of Australian quilts, quiltmakers, guilds, and tutors. There is also information on their magazine and a door to online shopping.

ElectricQuilt.com

http://www.tvq.com/topten.htm

This commercial site sells software and books for quilters, including quilt design software, patterns, fabric selection guides, and print enhancement software for printing the patterns you design.

Favorite Quilting Magazines

http://www.quiltmag.com/

Information on five U.S. quilting magazines, with article abstracts and notes from the editors, plus subscription information. The site has a lot of links to other sites which allow you to order quilting supplies.

From the Heartland

http://www.qheartland.com

Share ideas and information with other quilters in the online discussion forum at the site, and learn more about upcoming TV and online specials hosted by Sharlene Jorgenson. You also can search for local quilting shops.

Grandmothers' Quilts

http://www.womenfolk.com/
grandmothers/

History and heritage, includes images of heirloom quilts, and a comprehensive article about the Victorian crazy quilt.

Jinny Beyer Studio

http://www.jinnybeyer.com/

quilters' showcase as well as Jinny Beyer's own range of quilting fabrics.

Keepsake Quilting

http://www.keepsakequilting.com/

Online warehouse packed with a wide selection of fabric, batting, patterns, books, and other quilting supplies. Project corner features free patterns. Before you leave, check out a picture of the shop, inside and out, and say hello to Cisco.

Kwik Squares

http://www.mwaz.com/quilt/
patterns.htm

Quilting site with free lessons, patterns, a free product demo, and links to related sites.

Martingale & Company

http://www.patchwork.com

Looking for books on quilting? Then, here is your source. Search for a particular book or scan their database of titles. There are also free quilting patterns for download.

McCall's Quilting Magazine

http://www.quiltersvillage.com/
mccalls/

You can get free quilting patterns, articles, and information about quilting shows, as well as find out how to subscribe to the magazine.

Piecemakers

http://www.piecemakers.com/

You'll definitely want to check out the calendar quilts this group designs and sells—they're extraordinary. At their site you can buy quilting supplies and kits, pick up free stuff, and just learn more about quilting. California residents might want to find their location and class schedule.

A
B
C
D
E
F
G
H
I
J
K
L
M
N
O
P
Q
R
S
T
U
V
W
X
Y
Z

A
B
C
D
E
F
G
H
I
J
K
L
M
N
O
P
Q
R
S
T
U
V
W
X
Y
Z

Planet Patchwork

http://planetpatchwork.com/

This comprehensive site for quilters includes reviews of quilting software, books, and products, plus links and excellence awards.

Planet Patchwork's Web Excellence Awards

http://www.tvq.com/topten.htm

Looking for the best quilting sites? Check out Planet Patchwork's picks. Read a brief description for each site, and then link directly to it.

Quilt Care FAQs

http://www.bryerpatch.com/faq/storage.htm

Learn how to hang, store, and clean quilts of any age. Get workshop information or look at the free quilting pattern.

The Quilt Channel

http://www.quiltchannel.com/

This quilting hub provides a searchable database for quilting related queries, or you can click on one of the subject categories to get started. You'll find connections to anything quilting related you could desire: people, sites, tips, organizations, shopping resources, and more.

The Quilt Emporium

http://www.quiltemporium.com/

This shop in California offers classes, patterns, quilting supplies, and a selection of books.

Quilt Gallery Magazine

http://www.quiltgallery.com/

This monthly magazine features profiles, articles about technique and design (backdated and indexed), and a gallery with quilts for sale.

QuiltArt

http://www.quiltart.com/

View images from the gallery, find out about online chat groups for quilters, and more.

QuiltBiz

http://www.nmia.com/~ozzg/quiltbiz.htm

Comprehensive quilting site with links to supplies and software, publications, groups, and pattern archives.

⟦Best⟧ Quilters Online Resource

http://www.nmia.com/~mgdesign/qor/

Meet pen pals, look at patterns, scan project ideas, read software reviews, or enjoy the photo gallery. Check out the beginners' section. If you are a busy quilter, this site is probably your best bet as it is quick loading, with not a lot of graphics, but the ones they have are effective in leading you to the information you need. It is easy to navigate and has many useful features. These features include, but are not limited to, a section for beginners (well-suited for a general quilting audience), a project section, pen pals section, send an email card, quilting styles, and a pattern page. There are links to where you can make online purchases, too.

Quilting and Sewing with Kaye Wood

http://www.kayewood.com

Quick and easy, accurate quilting with Kaye's strip-piecing techniques and tools. This site has a lot of information on quilting and sewing books, tools, and notions for sale. All designed to make your quilting a pleasure, not a pain.

Quilting Guilds Around the World

http://quilt.com/QuiltGuildsPage.html

This site features a listing of quilting guilds and clubs in U.S. regions and some international locations.

Quilting with a Passion

http://quiltingpassion.com/

Comprehensive directory of free patterns and other quilting resources on the Web. Find more than 2,100 free patterns! Subscribe to the Quilting Passion newsletter, check out the forum gallery, download a free quilted calendar Windows desktop, or take a quilting class. You'll find plenty to keep you busy (and interested) at this site!

QuiltWear.com

http://www.quiltwear.com/

Advertises women's and children's clothing patterns and embellishments of interest to quilters, sewers, and crafters.

World Wide Quilting Page

http://quilt.com/Quilt

This, the oldest and largest quilting site on the Web, has hundreds of pages of instructions, patterns, show listings, store listings, guild listings, famous quilters' pages, a bulletin board, a trading post, classifieds for quilters, and lots more.

QUOTATIONS

Ability.org

http://www.ability.org/quotat.html

Many links to famous and not-so-famous quotes.

Advertising Quotes

http://advertising.utexas.edu/research/quotes/

Jef Richards, associate professor of Advertising at the University of Texas at Austin, has collected here a set of quotations about the world of advertising. The index includes more than 60 subcategories. Highlights along the way include Billboards, Critics, Evil, Fantasy and Dreams, Honesty, Manipulation, Morality and Ethics, Puffery, Sex, and Value.

Annabelle's Quotation Guide

http://www.annabelle.net/

Browse quotes by topic or author, sign up to receive a weekly featured quote, and check out the quotation bookstore to find just the right book of sayings.

Bartlett's Familiar Quotations

http://www.bartleby.com/100/

The 10th edition of John Bartlett's famous book, published in 1901, has been converted to HTML format and posted to the Web by Project Bartleby, an extensive Web-based literature library established by Columbia University.

A
B
C
D
E
F
G
H
I
J
K
L
M
N
O
P
Q
R
S
T
U
V
W
X
Y
Z

A
B
C
D
E
F
G
H
I
J
K
L
M
N
O
P
Q
R
S
T
U
V
W
X
Y
Z

Creative Quotations

http://creativequotations.com/

A comprehensive quotation site that can be searched/perused in multiple ways: by different thematic concepts, keyword, or author. Also included are areas for quotational poetry, a thematic quotation calendar, quotations from famous individuals born on the current date, and a "Test your QQ (Quotational Quotient)" section. Well worth a visit.

Cyber Quotations

http://www.cyberquotations.com/

The site's focus is on anything inspirational. Find quotes, poems, products, stories, photographs, and more. Subscribe to their email quote service or check out one of their many inspirational categories. Also includes a career center.

Daremore Quotes

http://www.daremore.com/
quosoft.html

This site offers daily inspirational messages for women, providing a different quote on the users' desktops every day. New messages can be downloaded monthly, or you can drop by the site at any time to peruse the entire list.

Famous Quotations

http://www.famous-quotations.com/

Search quotations alphabetically, by author, or by subject, or browse the category listings. You can find proverbs here, too. Learn about the lives of select authors, check out the top 10 quotation sites, and even get free email for life.

Follow Your Dreams

http://www.followyourdreams.com/
food.html

Inspirational quotations. Includes hundreds of quotations about courage, persistence, happiness, the purpose of life, and more from famous people throughout history.

Freality Search

http://www.freeality.com/
phrases.htm

Search for words, phrases, and quotations at a list of sites, which should provide a wide range of quotes to choose from.

MemorableQuotations.com

http://www.memorablequotations.
com/blake.htm

Huge collection of quotations categorized by discipline (or profession), country, historical period, and author. No search tool to zero in on a specific quote, but a great place to browse for wise tidbits and sage advice.

Quotation Center

http://cyber-nation.com/
victory/quotations/subjects/
quotes_subjects_a_to_b.html

Provided by Cyber Nation, this collection of more than 13,000 quotes meant to empower and motivate is quite impressive. Alphabetized by category, you can choose from just about any topic available.

Quotation Search

http://www.starlingtech.com/
quotes/search.html

Search this site for quotations from famous people with more than 10,000 quotes to choose from. You can browse by subject, author, or keywords.

Quotations Home Page

http://www.geocities.com/
~spanoudi/quote.html

Another good site that enables you to find quotes by category. With more than 21,000 entries in 30 collections, this is a site you'll need to visit more than once to enjoy them all.

Quotations Page

http://www.quotationspage.com/

This searchable collection of quotations includes quotes of the day, links to other quotation resources, and the opportunity to submit quotations.

Quotegeek.com

http://www.quotegeek.com/

Find quotes for term papers or school work, or just for fun, from Literature and Personalities to Movies and TV. Scan quotes relevant for the season and find which are the most popular.

quoteland.com

http://www.quoteland.com/

Identify who said it, or ask for help in tracking down an appropriate quote. There are databases to be searched and discussion groups to turn to for assistance.

Best QuoteWorld.org

http://www.quoteworld.org/

Tens of thousands of famous quotations. Search for a specific quote by author or subject, check out the quotation of the day, browse the quotations by topic or author, see quotes in context, or check out the discussion area to post a quote or ask someone for help in tracking down a quote. This site's comprehensive collection of famous quotes, combined with its powerful search tools, make it the best of the best quotations sites on the Web.

Quotez

http://www.geocities.com/Athens/
Oracle/6517/

This site features more than 5,000 quotations arranged into more than 500 subjects by some 800 authors (including more than 100 by Shakespeare alone). Can't find what you are looking for? Fill out the form provided; they'll conduct a search for you and post your request to the alt.quotations newsgroup for quotation nuts to respond to as well.

TPCN – Quotation Center

http://www.cybernation.com/
victory/quotations/
directory.html

You will find more than 12,000 great quotations on this site indexed by author and by subject. You will be inspired by these words of wisdom designed to empower you to achieve your dreams and fantasies.

Women's Quotes

http://wisdom_quotes.tripod.com/
blqulist.htm

Free online database of quotations by historic and contemporary women. Browse by subject or author.

Zappa Quote of the Day

http://www.science.uva.nl/
~robbert/zappa/quote/

Offers a new random quote each day from one of the geniuses of rock music, Frank Zappa.

A
B
C
D
E
F
G
H
I
J
K
L
M
N
O
P
Q
R
S
T
U
V
W
X
Y
Z

RAILROADS

AAR: Association of American Railroads

http://www.aar.org/

Representing North America's freight railroads and Amtrak. Strives to help make the rail industry increasingly safe, efficient, and productive. Examine statistics, position papers, and links collections.

Amtrak

http://www.amtrak.com

Check departure and arrival times for Amtrak trains, find the nearest station to you, check fares and schedules, plan a trip, and search for specials. If you like riding the train, you'll love the convenience of this site.

Federal Railroad Administration

http://www.fra.dot.gov/site/index.htm

Home of the United States government's organization for ensuring and improving railroad safety. Visit this site for a brief history of the administration and see what it's doing to make train travel safer.

Freightworld

http://www.freightworld.com/railroads.html

Provides links to Web sites for railroad companies throughout the world, organized by region.

⟦Best⟧ Gateway Division NMRA

http://www.gatewaynmra.org/library.htm

This online modeler's reference library of tips, techniques, photos, clinics, and articles is sponsored by the Greater St. Louis area chapter of the National Model Railroad Association, host of the 2001 NMRA National Convention. One of the most useful sites I've found for information about model railroading with a complete online library and a section on modeling topics as well as recent news about the subject. The site is well organized with easily searched topics. There is even a section on the annual train show. Novices and experts will both agree that this site is well deserving of its best of the best designation.

Great American Station Foundation

http://www.stationfoundation.org/

Dedicated to fostering community growth and enhancing railroad travel, the Great American Station Foundation is responsible for organizing the restoration and rebuilding of many train stations in major metropolitan areas across America. Visit this site to learn more about the organization and its ongoing projects.

The Historical Web Site

http://www.rrhistorical.com

If you are interested in railroading, this is the first site you should visit, as it contains extensive information about railroading including information about the history of railroading, clubs, organizations, and technical societies.

Hobbees.com: The World's Hobby Shop

http://www.hobbees.com/

Your source for model railroading products. You'll also find r/c cars, model cars, model rockets, military models, and slot cars. They double manufacturers' warranties and offer great prices and price guarantees, free or flat-rate shipping, and secure online ordering.

Interactive Model Railroad

http://rr-vs.informatik.
uni-ulm.de/rr/

If you enjoy model railroads, you will love this site. It allows you to run and operate the model railroad on the site and interact with the other users. There is a gallery of pictures you can explore, a help feature, statistics, awards, a guestbook for you to sign, and some railroad and link pages. You can also send the Webmaster a comment about the site.

Model Railroading Magazine

http://www.
modelrailroadingmag.com

A model train magazine by modelers, for modelers. Includes prototype and modeling information. The site offers several books that you can order online using secure credit card resources. The site is

beautifully designed and easy to navigate using the convenient and easy-to-understand menus.

NMRA on the Web: The National Model Railroad Association

http://www.nmra.com/

Claims to be the "largest organization devoted to the development, promotion, and enjoyment of the hobby of model railroading." Find out all about the NMRA and also enjoy their Directory of World Wide Rail Sites featuring more than 3,700 links.

NYO&W WebTrain

http://nyow.railfan.net/webtrain/

Operated by the New York, Ontario, and Western Modelers Special Interest Group, this site serves to connect Web sites that either feature the NYO&W and the railroads that served the NYO&W's territory or companies that offer products related to these railroads. All stations on the NYO&W WebTrain are family friendly and child safe.

Pacific Northwest LEGO Train Club

http://www.pnltc.org/

The Pacific Northwest LEGO Train Club (PNLTC) is a great resource for model train builders that prefer the LEGO medium. Read articles about creating the perfect layout or view galleries of past club displays.

RailServe

http://www.railserve.com/

A railroad site's catalog that enables visitors to search by a specific keyword to find all rail-related sites, or to browse by category, such as antiques, newsgroups, or passenger transit. Thousands of links.

A
B
C
D
E
F
G
H
I
J
K
L
M
N
O
P
Q
R
S
T
U
V
W
X
Y
Z

A
B
C
D
E
F
G
H
I
J
K
L
M
N
O
P
Q
R
S
T
U
V
W
X
Y
Z

Train Pictures and Wallpaper Images

http://www.snap-shot.com/

More than 1,000 free pictures and desktop wallpaper images. After opening the home page, click the Transportation and Aviation link and then click Trains to view the selection of train images.

Trains.com

http://www.trains.com/

Incredible collection of articles, specs, and other resources concerning model trains, railroading, rail travel, and railroads for kids. Even provides links to railroading magazines and online stores where you can purchase model railroads, tracks, and accessories.

Union Pacific Railroad

http://www.uprr.com/

The official Union Pacific site, containing service reports, the INFO Online magazine, facts, and figures and history, as well as plenty of corporate information regarding getting a job here and doing business with the company.

Walthers Model Railroad Mall

http://www.walthers.com

Brings you the best in model railroading, including a searchable catalog, containing more than 70,000 items, plus online ordering from your local hobby shops.

Z-World

http://www.z-world.com

Provides information about Z scale (1:220) model railroading for collectors, operators, and dealers.

REAL ESTATE

BUYING/SELLING

Ads4Homes

http://www.ads4homes.com/

Find homes listed by state, enabling you to locate ads for homes that might interest you. Provides links to relocation information. Also, you can place an ad for your home, get the latest interest rate listings, and find a bank.

Americas Virtual Real Estate Store

http://
www.americas-real-estate.com/

In their own words, this is the Internet's most complete source for finding homes for sale and free home valuations.

Apartments for Rent Online

http://www.forrent.com/

Apartments for Rent Online is a listing of apartments and homes available across the United States. Users can search alphabetically, by amenities, or by state, city, and neighborhood. Visitors also can submit online ads.

Buying a Home in Arizona

http://www.burtonc.com/buying.htm

Although the properties on display are located in Arizona, this page contains lots of advice from an experienced realtor. You'll find tips for making the move easier on children; hazards to watch out for, such as lead paint; a glossary of real estate terms; mortgage rates; a loan calculator; and more.

Century 21

http://www.century21.com

Aimed at property buyers and sellers. An online Property Search lets you search by state, city, or ZIP Code. You provide input, and every listing matching your criteria pops up. Click on Tips and Terms and find answers to FAQs and their Real Estate Glossary, which defines more than 900 real estate–related terms.

Coldwell Banker

http://www.coldwellbanker.com/
coverpage.asp

Before you invest time in searching for a new home, try out Coldwell Banker's Personal Retriever service that assists you in determining what features of a home you need. Then, search the Coldwell Banker database of more than 200,000 homes and make use of the online concierge service to get you settled with less hassle.

The Commercial Network

http://www.tcnre.com/

A comprehensive resource for securing corporate real estate and facility requirements worldwide, including North America, the Pacific Rim, Latin America, and Europe, among others. In addition to listing properties for sale or lease in more than 150 locations, the site offers an online referral information service and a database that helps members pinpoint market values and property trends worldwide.

Consumer Information Center

http://www.pueblo.gsa.gov/

Free federal consumer publications covering mortgages, mobile homes, inspections, buying, insurance, and many other topics. Most of the online versions of the publications are free, but you can order the print versions of most publications for 50¢ to $3.00. After you reach the home page, by entering the address given above, click the Housing link to view a list of publications relating to housing.

Domania.com

http://www.domania.com/

Before selling or buying a home, do your homework at this site. Check comparable home prices, determine how much equity you have built up in your home, check mortgage rates, use the online calculators, and much more. Cool tool helps you find out the actual sales price of recently purchased homes in your area.

A B C D E F G H I J K L M N O P Q **R** S T U V W X Y Z

A
B
C
D
E
F
G
H
I
J
K
L
M
N
O
P
Q
R
S
T
U
V
W
X
Y
Z

HomeBuilder.com

http://www.homebuilder.com/

Find a new home, or a home builder, from the database of builders at this site. You also can make arrangements for financing, moving, and many other home-buying–related activities at the site.

HomeFair.com

http://www.homefair.com

The calculators and research tools available at this site will be a big help to anyone looking for a home, including crime statistics, moving estimates, and school reports, to name just a few. You also can get information on home-related services, such as decorating, home improvement, financing, gardening, and more.

HomeGain

http://www.homegain.com

Use HomeGain's Valuation Tool to find out what your home's worth and then select an agent that's just right for you using the Agent Evaluator. There are also consumer guides to home buying and selling in the site's library. Please note that you will have to register to use the site's resources.

Homeseekers.com

http://www.homeseekers.com/

Search for a home in a particular city or region and track down an agent to assist you in finding a new home, or use the information pulled from 175 multiple listing services to assess the value of your home before deciding to put it on the market. You also can shop for a mortgage and other home-related services.

HUD: U.S. Department of Housing and Urban Development

http://www.hud.gov/

Created and maintained by the U.S. government, HUD's online site provides some valuable information for anyone who's planning to buy or sell a home. Check out a list of questions you should ask before purchasing a home, learn your rights as a home buyer, find out how much house you can afford, and much more.

[Best] International Real Estate Digest

http://www.ired.com

Looking for an independent and all-inclusive source of real estate information? This mega-site is it. The IRED Real Estate Directory offers nearly 10,000 links to real estate Web sites worldwide and can be searched by state, country, or category. If you are buying a home, selling a home, or just interested in real estate information in general, this site offers just about everything you want to know. Some of the topics are Appraisers, Builders, Buyer's Agents, Foreclosures, Inspectors, International Real Estate, and Prime Locations. The site is very easy to navigate and well designed for your ease of use.

Land.Net

http://www.land.net/

Very extensive real estate site. Offers lots of interactivity. Buyers can search for homes and also post their requests so they can be contacted when a property matches their requirements. Special sections cater to real estate professionals.

LoopNet

http://www.loopnet.com

This site is geared for commercial realtors, offering a commercial listing service, marketing program, financing assistance, and buyer/seller matching service. More than 94,000 professional realtors are members, making it one of the largest commercial real estate sites.

MSN HomeAdvisor

http://homeadvisor.msn.com/

HomeAdvisor provides a searchable database of U.S. real estate listings, complete with neighborhood demographics. It contains information on the home-buying process, including negotiating and financing. Visitors can prequalify or apply for a loan online.

NewHomeNetwork.com

http://www.newhomenetwork.com/

A site for new home builders and buyers, visitors can search the database of available homes in cities across the country. In addition to basic home and community information, you can learn about school districts and mortgage estimates and see floor plans and photos.

Nolo.com–Real Estate

http://www.nolo.com/category/
re_home.html

This self-help legal site can assist you in learning more about the process of buying and selling real estate, as well as commercial space and rental property. Read articles, do research, and turn to Aunti Nolo, with questions you can't seem to find the answer to. Features online mortgage calculators, as well.

Owners.com

http://www.owners.com/

Owners.com provides a searchable, national database of homes for sale by owners. It also provides reports on school districts, real estate glossaries, and mortgage calculators.

Real Estate Center Online

http://recenter.tamu.edu/

This is the comprehensive source for all things related to Texas real estate. An excellent site design allows viewers to browse efficiently through myriad materials, including numerous publications, statistical data, an extraordinary collection of real estate articles—even annual and monthly building permit statistics for all 50 states.

realtor.com

http://www.realtor.com

Home buying is broken down into a well-organized, six-step process: Getting Started, Buying, Selling, Offer/Closing, Moving, and Owning. Lots of tools, tips, and advice within each step.

REMAX Real Estate Network

http://www.remax.com/index.html

The corporate site of this nationwide real estate agency offers a lot of material useful to both agents and consumers. Browsers can search a listing of home properties or REMAX agents, review commercial or mortgage information, or find out about relocation services.

San Diego County Real Estate Library

http://www.realestatelibrary.com/

A collection of real estate articles of interest to buyers and sellers. Includes links to other high-content sites. Focuses primarily on real estate in the San Diego area.

A
B
C
D
E
F
G
H
I
J
K
L
M
N
O
P
Q
R
S
T
U
V
W
X
Y
Z

SchoolMatch

http://www.schoolmatch.com

Find a school or system anywhere in the United States using the free online directory here, or buy an instant school evaluation.

Wine Country Weekly Real Estate Reader

http://www.rereader.com/

A delightful online magazine with a wealth of information on California wine country real estate. Beyond its extensive listings (recreational, commercial and estate properties, vacation rentals, developments, and homes), the magazine offers real estate articles and sales data.

REFERENCE

DICTIONARIES AND THESAURI

Acronym Finder

http://www.acronymfinder.com/

The Acronym Finder provides more than 148,000 common acronyms, abbreviations, and initialisms for a wide range of subjects in a searchable database.

Acronyms and Abbreviations

http://www.ucc.ie/cgi-bin/
acronym

Can't remember an acronym's meaning, like whether you should call AA or AAA when your car won't start? This easy-to-use site can help you out of your dilemma. Just type in the letters you're trying to decipher, and the acronym lookup site gives you an immediate definition.

ARTFL Project: Roget's Thesaurus Search Form

http://humanities.uchicago.edu/
orgs/ARTFL/forms__unrest/
ROGET.html

The ARTFL (American and French Research on the Treasury of the French Language) Project, located at the University of Chicago, has provided this online version of Roget's Thesaurus. The interface is simple—type the word you want, and the form will return synonyms and antonyms. Back up to http://
humanities.uchicago.edu/orgs/
ARTFL/ for more resources.

The Astronomy Thesaurus

http://msowww.anu.edu.au/library/
thesaurus/

This is an extensive thesaurus of words related to astronomy. Just click a word and the list of synonyms appears onscreen. The thesaurus is available in English, French, German, Spanish, and Italian.

AVP Virus Encyclopedia

http://www.avp.ch/avpve/

The makers of AntiViral Toolkit Pro present this encyclopedia, featuring descriptions of hundreds of computer viruses. Search by virus name or type.

Dictionary of Cell and Molecular Biology

http://www.mblab.gla.ac.uk/ ~julian/Dict.html

Searchable cell biology index. The online counterpart to The Dictionary of Cell and Molecular Biology, Third Edition, plus some additions.

Dictionary.com

http://www.dictionary.com/ translate/

Translate any word, phrase, or sentence from English to a long list of languages, including French, German, Italian, Spanish, and Portuguese, or to English from the same languages.

Martindale's Reference Desk: Language Dictionaries

http://www-sci.lib.uci.edu/ ~martindale/ Language.html

Comprehensive directory of language dictionaries complete with links for accessing the various dictionaries. Includes links to translation dictionaries, multilingual dictionaries, sign language guides, and much more.

Merriam-Webster Online

http://www.m-w.com/

In addition to a dictionary and a thesaurus, you'll find a word of the day, a game to play, and other interesting word-related items. Check out Words from the Lighter Side if you enjoy knowing the latest slang terms and their meanings.

On-line Dictionaries and Glossaries

http://www.rahul.net/lai/ glossaries.html

Access dictionaries to assist in translating documents in foreign languages to English, or from English to something else. A long list of languages covered.

RhymeZone

http://www.rhymezone.com/

Trying to write a poem? Stymied for a word that rhymes with hungry? Check out this page. Simply type the word you want to find a rhyme for, and click the Submit button. RhymeZone also features other fun and educational sections, including a section on Shakespeare, grammar quizzes, nursery rhymes, and quotations.

Thesaurus.com

http://www.thesaurus.com/

This is the complete thesaurus. You can browse alphabetically, choose one of the six classes of words, or type in a word to search for. Then, click the word and receive a list of synonyms.

travlang's Translating Dictionaries

http://dictionaries.travlang.com/

Access a long list of translating dictionaries at this site, offering translations to and from many foreign languages.

A Web of Online Dictionaries

http://www.yourdictionary.com/

Whoa, you're likely to find just about any answer to a translation or language question through the online translating dictionaries, thesauri, grammar checkers, and linguistic tools.

A
B
C
D
E
F
G
H
I
J
K
L
M
N
O
P
Q
R
S
T
U
V
W
X
Y
Z

A
B
C
D
E
F
G
H
I
J
K
L
M
N
O
P
Q
R
S
T
U
V
W
X
Y
Z

Webopedia.com

http://www.webopedia.com/

Is there a computer acronymn, term, or concept that has you stumped? Then turn to the Webopedia to decipher it. Just type the entry and press enter to find a complete definition. Most definitions also include a collection of links to other resources where you can find additional information.

The Word Wizard

http://wordwizard.com/

Not a dictionary in the strictest sense, but a site where words are celebrated. You must register to participate, but there are contests with prizes and just plain fun stuff to do with words. You also can Ask the Word Wizard for help with definitions, usage, or word origins.

The World Wide Web Acronym and Abbreviation Server

http://www.ucc.ie/info/net/
acronyms/acro.html

As simple as it sounds, this site offers a dictionary of acronyms and abbreviations.

LIBRARIES

The American War Library

http://members.aol.com/veterans/

This library contains data on every military conflict in which the United States has been involved since the founding of the country. There is also a veterans' registry, a photo archive section, and many other areas of benefit to veterans and their families.

Berkeley Digital Library SunSITE

http://sunsite.berkeley.edu/

This site contains "digital collections and services while providing information and support to others doing the same." Essentially an online library.

Bibliomania: The Network Library

http://www.bibliomania.com/

With more than 40 complete classic novels in HTML and PDF formats, plus reference works such as Gibbon's Decline and Fall of the Roman Empire (work in progress), this is a great place to get that classical education you always wanted but never found the time for. You can purchase some of these books online using secure card resources.

The Campus Library

http://www.go-campus.com/
campus/library.htm

A virtual library for a virtual college campus, called The Campus, the library is a great source of links to all sorts of information services, such as DunsLink from Dun & Bradstreet, lots of news services, and magazine sites from CNN to Sports Illustrated to Cosmopolitan. There are book links sorted by topic—poetry, science fiction, mystery, and so forth. In fact, the entire Campus site is a great resource for sites on all sorts of topics.

Center for Research Libraries

http://wwwcrl.uchicago.edu/

An international not-for-profit consortium of colleges, universities, and libraries that makes available scholarly research resources to users everywhere.

Internet Public Library

http://www.ipl.org/

Includes resources for children, teenagers, and adults. The reference center allows you to ask questions of a real librarian (not a computer). The youth services and teen divisions have links to both books and other resources, such as writing contests, college information, science projects, and author question-and-answer sessions. A section is also devoted to information for librarians and other information professionals. Other features include tutorials, an exhibit hall, a reading room with browsable full-text resources, links to Web search engines, and a MOO (multiuser object oriented) environment for browsing the library.

The Library of Congress

http://www.loc.gov/

Provides access to the Library of Congress's online catalog and other databases. For librarians, this site includes valuable information about Library of Congress standards for cataloguing, acquisitions, and book preservation. There are frequently asked reference questions; links to international, federal, state, and local government information; links to Internet search engines and metaindexes; a link to the U.S. Copyright Office home page; and information about Library of Congress special events and exhibits.

Library Spot

http://www.libraryspot.com/

This online reference desk provides access to libraries, as well as answers to questions about a host of subjects, organized into categories. Established for students and teachers, but accessible to everyone.

Libweb–Library Servers on the WWW

http://sunsite.berkeley.edu/Libweb/

Find information from libraries in more than 100 countries. Use a keyword to locate a particular library location or system, or scan the long list.

Medical/Health Sciences Libraries on the Web

http://www.lib.uiowa.edu/hardin-www/hslibs.html

A state-by-state listing of all medical and health science libraries on the Net. There are also sections for foreign countries, plus an extensive listing of links.

National Archives and Records Administration

http://www.nara.gov/

Includes both searchable and browsable services for locating government information via the Government Information Locator Service (GILS). Has links to the Federal Register, the National Archives and Records Administration Library, and the presidential libraries. The presidential libraries' page also includes the addresses, phone numbers, fax numbers, email addresses, and links to the home pages for the presidential libraries. Also has links for genealogical research.

North American Sport Library Network

http://www.sportquest.com/naslin/

NASLIN was developed to facilitate the spread of sports information among sports librarians, archivists, and others through publications, conferences, and educational programs. SPORTDiscus Online, the

A
B
C
D
E
F
G
H
I
J
K
L
M
N
O
P
Q
R
S
T
U
V
W
X
Y
Z

A
B
C
D
E
F
G
H
I
J
K
L
M
N
O
P
Q
R
S
T
U
V
W
X
Y
Z

largest database of its kind, offers coverage of sports, fitness, and recreation-related publications. SPORTDiscus contains more than 400,000 bibliographic citations and "a wide range of information published in magazines and periodicals, books, theses, and dissertations, as well as conference proceedings, research papers, and videotapes." Click the Sports link to access a huge directory of links for nearly every sport imaginable.

OCLC Online Computer Library Center, Inc.

http://www.oclc.org/

Contains information that is especially useful for librarians and other information professionals. Has links to OCLC documents and forms, a search engine for searching OCLC information, and demonstrations of OCLC services. Actual logon to some OCLC services is available by subscription only.

Perry-Castañeda Library Map Collection

http://www.lib.utexas.edu/maps/united_states.html

An online map library, with one of the most extensive collections of maps in the world. The online collection is more than just a listing of maps in the library—the maps can be viewed, downloaded, and printed out as the user requires. Be sure to read the FAQ before viewing or printing any of the maps to be sure that your machine is capable of the task (some of the maps are very large). The site also has links to other map-related sites around the world.

Portico: The British Library

http://www.bl.uk

Portico is the online information server for the British Library. From this point, you gain access to the online catalogs, lists of services, collections, and digital library. The site is beautifully rendered, with some documents (including images of actual pages) already available or in progress.

Smithsonian Institution Libraries

http://www.sil.si.edu/

Includes links to the various Smithsonian Museums, a search engine for locating information within the Smithsonian, information about visiting Washington, D.C., information about how to become a member of the Smithsonian, a map showing the locations of most of the Smithsonian Museums, and a browsable shopping area.

StudyWeb

http://www.studyweb.com/

This site provides quick access to an encyclopedia, dictionary, and thesaurus plus maps, calculators, converters, and categorized information. There are more than 141,000 research topics available. Your school must subscribe to the StudyWeb, for a fee, in order for you to access its resources.

The Sunnyvale Center for Innovation, Invention & Ideas

http://www.sci3.com/

Established by a unique arrangement between the United States Patent and Trademark Office and the City of Sunnyvale, California, the center is able to provide patent and trademark information and research to the entire western United States as well as to Pacific Rim countries. This is the only office of its kind in the western United States that can provide PTO information outside the Washington, D.C., area.

U.S. Department of Education (ED) Home Page

http://www.ed.gov/index.jsp

Explore the U.S. Department of Education's Home Page and discover information about their offices, programs, and information about how to get assistance from the department. Lots of information and resources for research and education.

U.S. National Library of Medicine

http://www.nlm.nih.gov/

Search the library's free online health information library, Webline, or clinical trials information database for a better understanding of issues surrounding your personal health.

WWW Library Directory

http://www.webpan.com/msauers/libdir/

Click a country name to be presented with a list of links to libraries in that country. Most of the countries currently represented are European (both East and West) and North American, although there are a few Asian, Middle Eastern, and South American countries, also. Also has links to other library-related resources.

RESEARCH HELP

555-1212.com Area Code Lookup

http://www.555-1212.com/

Search by city or state name for U.S. or Canadian area codes, or browse by area code or state name. Returns area code and corresponding city/state. Area code links lead to a business directory that can be browsed by category or searched by business name.

Academic Info

http://www.academicinfo.net/

A subject directory of Internet resources tailored to the university community. Each subject entry contains an annotated list of links to general Web sites for the field and links to more specialized resources.

Academy of Achievement

http://www.achievement.org/

The Academy of Achievement features the stories of influential figures from the 20th century who have been successful in their fields. Video and sound clips are included, inspirational books are cited, and an online mentor program is available.

American Sign Language Browser

http://commtechlab.msu.edu/sites/aslweb/browser.htm

Click on a word to get a short description of the motion of the sign, which is also illustrated by a video clip.

A B C D E F G H I J K L M N O P Q R S T U V W X Y Z

A
B
C
D
E
F
G
H
I
J
K
L
M
N
O
P
Q
R
S
T
U
V
W
X
Y
Z

AnyWho Toll Free Directory

http://www.tollfree.att.net/tf.html

Toll-free phone number directory set up by category or by company name, city, state, and/or category. Also includes information about AT&T.

Ask Jeeves

http://www.ask.com/

Ask a question of the Internet butler in plain English and get references to sites that are likely to be able to answer it.

AskERIC

http://www.askeric.org/

The Educational Resources Information Center provides an online question-and-answer service, plus access to the ERIC database. A virtual library of lesson plans, project materials, and other educational resources are also included.

Biography.com

http://www.biography.com/

Search a database of biographical information on more than 20,000 famous people and historical figures at this site. A program guide, trivia games, discussion forums, and an online store are also available.

Britannica.com

http://www.britannica.com/

Search the complete Encyclopedia Britannica at this site, as well as learn historical information and catch up on the day's news. Browse topics of interest or search for specific nuggets of knowledge.

Car Talk

http://cartalk.cars.com/

The online version of NPR's radio show provides advice and information on cars, mechanics, and repairs. The site also features Car Talk trivia, a puzzler, virtual postcards, online classifieds, and Car Talk hate mail.

Central Notice

http://www.notice.com/

Central Notice posts listings of product recalls, class action lawsuits, and missing children. It also offers help and answers to consumer problems, finding a lawyer, and more.

CIA World Factbook

http://www.odci.gov/cia/publications/factbook/

The CIA World Factbook provides ethnographic, scientific, political, and geographic information about the world's countries and regions.

The Consumer Information Center

http://www.pueblo.gsa.gov/

Federal consumer publications are available at this site. Choose from eight categories or view those most recently featured by the media. Full-text versions are available online and can be viewed at no charge. You also can purchase printed copies. The site also offers a search option to make retrieving information easier.

The Cook's Thesaurus

http://www.switcheroo.com/

Search this database for more information about ingredients and cooking tools. You'll find definitions, uses, pictures, and common substitute information for each category.

Dismal Scientist

http://www.dismal.com/

If you're looking for global economic news and analysis, this is the site to visit. Here you'll find tools, analyses, and message boards to share your thoughts and opinions with others.

eHow

http://www.ehow.com/

Interesting search tool that helps you track down instructions on how to perform more than 15,000 tasks. Covers everything from checking the oil in your car to delivering puppies.

eLibrary

http://ask.elibrary.com/

This unique library assistant, made up of partnerships with newspapers and magazines, provides a searchable index of articles from both current and past issues. You simply enter a keyword or phrase, and the e-librarian tracks down the resources for you. Provides free abstracts; to access entire articles, you must subscribe to the service (about $20 per month or $80 per year). Free seven-day trial.

Encarta Online

http://encarta.msn.com/

Microsoft's Encarta Concise Free Encyclopedia is available at this site. The encyclopedia is available in several languages and includes more than 16,000 articles. Lesson plans featuring Encarta content and other teaching resources are also provided. For a monthly fee, you can have access to articles from encyclopedias, magazines, reference books, and so on.

FedWorld.gov

http://www.fedworld.gov/

This site provides a list of links to various United States Federal offices and administrations to make it easier for citizens to find the information they need.

FinAid: The Financial Aid Information Page

http://www.finaid.org/

A clearinghouse of information on college funding. Learn about loans, scholarships, grants and fellowships, and prepaid tuition plans. You also can calculate future college costs and estimate financial aid awards.

The Flag of the United States of America

http://www.usflag.org/toc.html

Provides flag etiquette, a history of the U.S. flag, text of the Declaration of Independence, and words to the national anthem and the Pledge of Allegiance to the flag (in English, German, and Spanish). Information about obtaining a flag that was flown over the U.S. Capitol, and links to other flag-related sites, poetry, songs, and more.

Geographic Nameserver

http://geonames.usgs.gov/pls/
gnis/web_query.gnis_web_query_
form

This index is searchable by ZIP Code or city name. Results returned include city, county, state, country, and ZIP Code; latitude, longitude, population, and elevation are returned if available. If more than one city matches the search criteria then information on all matching cities is returned.

A
B
C
D
E
F
G
H
I
J
K
L
M
N
O
P
Q
R
S
T
U
V
W
X
Y
Z

A
B
C
D
E
F
G
H
I
J
K
L
M
N
O
P
Q
R
S
T
U
V
W
X
Y
Z

How Stuff Works

http://www.howstuffworks.com/

Learn how everyday machines and contraptions work. This site provides in-depth explanations, illustrations, and answers to frequently asked questions.

infoplease.com

http://www.infoplease.com/

Comprehensive, searchable research library provides convenient access to various almanacs, a dictionary, an encyclopedia, and an atlas. Research history and geography and look up information on any country in the world. Also features biographies, weather reports and information, business and entertainment news, and more.

InfoSpace.com

http://infospace.com

An information portal that gives you access to several information resources, from White and Yellow Page listings to maps and directions, city guides, weather, and many shopping options, all in one spot.

The Internet 800 Directory

http://inter800.com/

Searchable by keyword and state. Returns businesses matching the search criteria and their corresponding 800 telephone numbers, up to a maximum of 100 businesses.

Internet Public Library

http://www.ipl.org/

Links to thousands of online resources, including electronic texts and online serials. Stories for children, college help for teens, a reading room with information about thousands of books, special exhibits on topics such as African-American history and dinosaurs, and much

more. Former reference-library giant Argus Clearinghouse is currently in the process of adding its assets to this site, beefing it up with some substantial new material.

iTools.com

http://www.itools.com/

Using fill-in-the-blank forms, you can search through dictionaries and thesauri; find acronyms or quotations; translate words between English and French and English and Japanese; find maps, area codes, and 800 numbers; look up currency exchange rates and stock quotes; and even track packages through the United States Postal Service, UPS, and FedEx.

Library of Congress

http://www.loc.gov/

This site includes virtual exhibits, publications, congressional information, and online catalogs from the Library of Congress in Washington, D.C. The American Memory section offers collections of documents, photos, and sound clips from America's history.

MegaConverter

http://www.megaconverter.com/

A collection of calculators and converters of measures, weights, and units is available at this site. For instance, users can convert miles to kilometers, gallons to liters, and years to seconds. Ancient measuring systems also can be converted.

ModemHelp

http://www.modemhelp.com/

Installation instructions, upgrade information, and links to various modem resources. There is also a great tutorial on how to set up and install a home network or a small office.

Morse Code and the Phonetic Alphabets

http://www.soton.ac.uk/~scp93ch/morse/

Contains the phonetic alphabets in British English, American English, international English, international aviation English, Italian, and German—and the Morse code equivalent for all letters plus some punctuation marks.

MRX: Morse Receive and Transmit Training

http://www.mrx.com.au/

MRX Morse Code for Windows 9x/NT is a program designed to teach Morse code. Receive and transmit using the benefits of multimedia PC technology. Download a copy of MRX from this Web site.

National Address and ZIP+4 Browser

http://www.semaphorecorp.com/

Searchable by company name, street address, city, state, and ZIP Code. Returns closest matches along with ZIP+4 Code. After information is returned, you are given the option to browse addresses in the same geographical location. Also includes list of state code abbreviations.

National First Ladies' Library

http://www.firstladies.org/

Explores lives of our first ladies and their contributions to history. Contains bibliographies, press releases, a newsletter, a photo album, and Saxton McKinley house information.

The Nobel Foundation

http://www.nobel.se/

In addition to offering a list of present winners, this official site presents a searchable database for past winners. Also offers a bio of Alfred Nobel and discusses his motivations for founding the prizes, in addition to explaining how Nobel laureates are nominated and selected.

Old Farmer's Almanac

http://www.almanac.com/

The Old Farmer's Almanac is North America's oldest continuously published periodical, providing information on weather and soil conditions since 1792. The online version offers weather forecasts, agricultural reports, and other seasonal features.

Period.Com Airlines

http://www.period.com/airlines/

Airline toll-free 800 phone numbers and links to airline Web sites. Click on any letter, A–Z, to get started. Coming soon: a Travel Specials section and City/Airport Database.

PhoNETic

http://www.phonetic.com/

Enter a phone number to receive all possible letter combinations for that phone number, or enter letters to receive the phone number corresponding to those letters. Also includes information about obtaining phonetic telephone numbers and an explanation for why calculator and telephone keypads are different.

A
B
C
D
E
F
G
H
I
J
K
L
M
N
O
P
Q
R
S
T
U
V
W
X
Y
Z

A
B
C
D
E
F
G
H
I
J
K
L
M
N
O
P
Q
R
S
T
U
V
W
X
Y
Z

▌Best▐ refdesk.com

http://www.refdesk.com/

This site bills itself as a "one-stop reference for all things Internet." Although it is mainly a collection of links, it maintains a thorough and comprehensive database of references on a vast array of subjects. This site is one of my favorites, especially since I am a writer and it provides quick reference to everything from grammar usage to the Library of Congress. Reported to be used by many professional people as well as just about everyone else including government officials. If you need to do some quick and accurate research, I would highly recommend this site as being your first stop.

Reference Tools

http://www.washington.edu/tools/

An extensive collection of links to a variety of reference materials from libraries to encyclopedias.

Researchpaper.com

http://www.researchpaper.com/

Educators, students, and anyone engaged in basic research will want to give an apple to the folks at Researchpaper.com. Here, students can find a plethora of assistance in finding a research topic and developing essays and reports on a wide variety of topics.

Retire Early Home Page

http://www.geocities.com/
WallStreet/8257/reindex.html

Aided by software and spreadsheets, this magazine offers details on ways to retire early. News, articles, and a planner are listed.

RxList: The Internet Drug Index

http://www.rxlist.com/

Users can search this site for prescription drugs by brand or generic name. There is also a Top 200 list, and information on side effects, toxicity, and other concerns related to the use of specific drugs.

Smithsonian Institution Research Information System

http://www.siris.si.edu/

SIRIS searches the research catalogs of the Smithsonian Institution that include the institution's libraries, art collections, archives, manuscripts, and specialized research bibliographies.

SuperPages.com

http://www.superpages.com/

Find the names and locations of businesses using this search engine, which accepts the business name, category, city, and/or state. Search also can be narrowed by using the ZIP Code, area code, street name, or map location. Search returns the name, address, and telephone number of businesses matching search criteria. Option is available for seeing business locations on a map.

Switchboard

http://www.switchboard.com/

Search for either businesses or people. For people searches, enter the last name, first name, city, and/or state to receive the name, address, and phone number of all people matching the search criteria. For business searches, enter the company name, city, and/or state to return the name, address, and phone number of all businesses matching the search criteria. Registered users might also personalize and update their own listings. This is another highly recommended site for researchers and those persons interested in finding quick information about companies and businesses.

THOR: The Virtual Reference Desk

http://thorplus.lib.purdue.edu/reference/index.html

This information-rich site at the Purdue University Library provides references to many Web resources, including government documents, information technology, dictionaries and language references, phone books and area codes, maps and travel information, science data, time and date information, and ZIP and postal codes.

U.S. Census Bureau

http://www.census.gov/

The U.S. Census Bureau provides population figures, economic indicators, and demographic information at this site. The site features an internal search engine to allow users to find census data more easily.

United States Postal Service

http://www.usps.com/

Includes information about stamp releases, pictures of stamps available, a searchable index for ZIP+4 Codes, state and address abbreviations, preferred addressing methods, size standards for mail, postage rates for both domestic and international mail delivery, history of the USPS, news releases, a calendar of events, and other postal-related information. The business section of this Web site includes information addressing the mailing needs of businesses and the purchasing needs of the USPS.

Virtual Reference Desk

http://www.vrd.org/

Developed primarily for K-12 educators, the Virtual Reference Desk is an Internet-based question-and-answer service that connects users with subject matter experts who respond to questions personally. What makes this type of site unusual is that an actual person answers a question, rather than relying on the results posted by a computer database.

Vital Records Information: United States

http://vitalrec.com/

This page contains information about where to obtain vital records from each state, territory, and county of the United States. You can also search public records (birth, death, marriage certificates, divorce decrees, and so on) for just about any citizen of the United States. To obtain records, you must pay up front for the search.

World Population

http://metalab.unc.edu/lunarbin/worldpop/

This site offers an estimate of the current world population at the time you access it.

The WWW Virtual Library

http://vlib.org/Overview.html

This Web-based library offers hundreds of subjects in science, mathematics, art, literature, music, culture, museums, religion, spirituality, sports, finance, and transportation.

A
B
C
D
E
F
G
H
I
J
K
L
M
N
O
P
Q
R
S
T
U
V
W
X
Y
Z

RELIGION AND PHILOSOPHY

Academic Info: Philosophy

http://www.academicinfo.net/
phil.html

An extensive directory of sites on the study of philosophy. Includes sections on specific philosophical topics and general reference sources.

Academic Info: Religion

http://www.academicinfo.net/
religindex.html

This site contains an extensive directory of Web sites devoted to world religions. Especially useful for the academic study of comparative religions.

Adherents–Religion Statistics and Geography

http://www.adherents.com/

This site offers an insight into the growing collection of church memberships and religion inherent statistics. They have more than 50,000 statistics for more than 4,200 faith groups from all major and most minor religions. Very statistical.

BBC World Service–Religions of the World

http://www.bbc.co.uk/
worldservice/people/features/
world_religions/

Learn more about the major religions of the world at this site, which brings together information about Islam, Hinduism, Christianity, Buddhism, Judaism, and Sikhism.

beliefnet

http://beliefnet.com/

Nonsectarian religious site devoted to keeping believers and nonbelievers informed. Covers everything from atheism and Christianity to earth-based (pagan) religions. Additional sections explore the links between religions and marriage, sexuality, politics, and more. Take online quizzes, check out the message boards, or join a meditation or prayer group online.

Religion and Philosophy Web Sites

http://www.chowan.edu/acadp/
Religion/websites.htm

There are links to many religion and philosophy Web sites compiled by Chowan College.

ANCIENT

⟦Best⟧ Antiquity Online

http://fsmitha.com/h1/

Search this site or scan the major subcategories for information about ancient history, philosophy, and religions, with an emphasis on historical significance and events of the times. The site has many documents and other information tracing the religious philosophy from ancient times to later years. The site is easy to navigate and has maps, images, and testimonials about the information on the site. You can read about how religious ideas more than likely developed in "cavedweller" days of ancient persons to later times. Although not one of the "flashier" sites, it provides an intriguing look at the historical aspects of religion.

ATHEISM

American Atheists

http://www.atheists.org/

Information about atheism, separation of church and state, legal battles, school prayer, and Biblical contradictions. Features an online store and a magazine.

Atheism Central for Secondary Schools

http://www.eclipse.co.uk/thoughts/

This excellent introduction to atheism explains the basis for most atheist's beliefs in the nonexistence of God (or of a god who intervenes in our lives).

Atheist Alliance

http://www.atheistalliance.org/

Reach out to other atheists through this site, which aims to educate the public about the dangers of authoritarian religions through articles, books, links to other Web sites, and reference material.

The Secular Web

http://www.infidels.org/

A page of interest to atheists, agnostics, humanists, and freethinkers. Links to a variety of Internet resources, including Usenet newsgroups, IRC channels, and other Web pages. The library contains several documents, historical and otherwise.

BUDDHISM

Buddhanet.net

http://buddhanet.net/

This site, affiliated with a nonprofit organization, has a huge amount of information about the teachings of Buddha, links, chat, books about Buddhism, articles, and much more. You're likely to find everything you wanted to know about Buddhism here.

DharmaNet International

http://www.dharmanet.org/

An online clearinghouse for Buddhist study and practice resources. It is home to DharmaNet's own in-house databases and collections, as well as providing links to all online Buddhist resources, large and small.

Journal of Buddhist Ethics

http://jbe.gold.ac.uk/

The Journal of Buddhist Ethics is a free online publication that promotes academic research in Buddhist ethics. Offers current and back issues.

New Kadampa Tradition

http://www.kadampa.net/

This Mahayana Buddhist organization aims to preserve and promote the essence of Buddha's teachings in a form suited to the Western mind and way of life. This site offers information on books, meditation programs, and a directory of NKT centers.

Resources for the Study of Buddhism

http://online.sfsu.edu/~rone/Buddhism/Buddhism.htm

Learn about basic Buddhist teachings through links and Web references offered at this site, which contains helpful sites for children and adults.

A
B
C
D
E
F
G
H
I
J
K
L
M
N
O
P
Q
R
S
T
U
V
W
X
Y
Z

A
B
C
D
E
F
G
H
I
J
K
L
M
N
O
P
Q
R
S
T
U
V
W
X
Y
Z

tharpa.com

http://www.tharpa.com/

Online bookstore for some of the best books on Buddhism and meditation. Site also features weekly snippets of wisdom, informative articles, and 500 glossary terms with definitions.

Zen@MetaLab

http://www.ibiblio.org/zen/

Created as an online home for the Gateless Gate, a collection of koans. Features other Zen sites, including links to the Zen Hospice Project and to Zen and Taoist texts.

CHRISTIANITY

About.com–Christianity

http://christianity.about.com/

This site culls the latest news and information about Christianity, centralizing on this one site. Information is organized by subtopic, making it easy to track down what you're looking for. You'll also see headline news and chat and discussion opportunities linked to each.

American Baptist Churches USA Mission Center Online

http://www.abc-usa.org/

Contains information about local American Baptist churches, and American Baptist Green Lakes Conferences, as well as national, international, and educational ministries.

Augustine

http://ccat.sas.upenn.edu/jod/augustine.html

Contains translations and texts of Augustine, one of Christianity's most gifted and disciplined thinkers. Also includes other research materials and reference aids, and papers from an online seminar and images.

The Best Christian Links

http://www.tbcl.com/

Comprehensive directory of the best Christian sites on the Web divided into categories including Art & Culture, Churches, Fellowship & Fun, and Spiritual Growth.

Bible Gateway

http://bible.gospelcom.net/

This award-winning site provides a search form for the Bible and handles many common translations. Lets you conduct searches and output verses in French, German, Swedish, Tagalog, Latin, or English.

Catholic Online

http://www.catholic.org/

Bills itself as the "world's largest and most comprehensive Roman Catholic information service." Provides message centers, forums, and research materials related to Roman Catholicism. There is also information about Catholic organizations, dioceses and archdioceses, publications, software, and doctrines.

Center for Paleo-Orthodoxy

http://capo.org/

This consortium of scholars, think tanks, and publications is committed to shedding ancient (hence "Paleo") light on modern issues. Links to their award-winning e-journal, Premise. Also links to various institutes (Calvin, Kuyper, Van Til), and PCA (Presbyterian Church in America) mail.

Center for Reformed Theology and Apologetics (CRTA)

http://www.reformed.org/

A nonprofit organization committed to the dispersal of online resources for the edification of believers of a Calvinist leaning. Links to articles on apologetics, the Bible, reformed books and commentaries, Calvinism/soteriology, Christianity and science, and so on. Searchable.

Christian Interactive Network

http://www.cin.com/

A huge Web resource for Christians. Contains links to information on various ministries, missions, publishing, family issues, radio/TV, education, sports, business, shopping, and more. Enables you to enter your business into their directory freely.

The Christian Missions Home Page

http://www.sim.org/

This site offers the Great Commission Search Engine which gives you the ability to search for Christian Missions all over the world.

Christianbook.com

http://www.christianbook.com/

Huge online bookstore specializing in books and other publications dealing with Christianity and related topics. Sells CDs, videos, and Christian gifts, as well.

Christianity Online

http://www.christianitytoday.com/

Christianity Online is a Christian service featuring news about current events and politics, interviews with Christian musicians, and links to other Christian magazines. Visitors also can search a database of more than 5,400 Christian Web sites.

crosswalk.com

http://www.crosswalk.com/

Crosswalk offers Christians access to a directory of more than 20,000 Christian sites, news, information, Bible study tools, chat and discussion forums, a Bible search directory, and much more. But there's also a community to join, and entertainment to be had here through the learning and sharing taking place.

Fire and Ice: Puritan and Reformed Writings

http://www.puritansermons.com/

In this case, the name is highly suggestive of the contents. Contains many works of various Puritan writers, from John Owen to Cotton Mather. Also contains history and biography, poetry, new and recommended works, and a quote of the week.

First Church of Cyberspace

http://www.godweb.org/

In an effort to bring together an online Christian congregation, this site offers sermons, scripture studies, a multimedia Bible, and movie reviews.

The Five Points of Calvinism

http://www.gty.org/~phil/dabney/5points.htm

R.L. Dabney discusses Calvinism without making use of the well-known acrostic. He discusses original sin, effectual calling, God's election, particular redemption, and perseverance of the saints. Footnotes follow.

A
B
C
D
E
F
G
H
I
J
K
L
M
N
O
P
Q
R
S
T
U
V
W
X
Y
Z

Glide Memorial Church

http://www.glide.org

San Francisco's "church without walls" has a long history of serving the downtrodden outcasts of our society from the hippies and Black Panthers in the sixties, Vietnam protestors in the seventies, AIDS victims in the eighties, crack addicts in the nineties, all people suffering from socioeconomic problems into the 21st century. Here you can learn more about Glide and how you can help.

GraceCathedral.org

http://www.GraceCathedral.org

Visit San Francisco's Grace Cathedral Episcopal Church online, listen to services via its Webcast, check out the media center, read interviews with spiritual leaders, and even take a virtual tour of the church without stepping foot in San Francisco.

Greater Grace World Outreach

http://www.ggwo.org/

An international ministry with links to associated ministries such as The Grace Hour International Radio Show, missionary outreaches, and the Maryland Bible College and Seminary. This site also contains daily faith thoughts and information about upcoming conferences.

Harvest Online

http://www.harvest.org/

Provides the history of the Harvest Christian Fellowship. Includes dates for upcoming Harvest Crusades, along with information about A New Beginning with Greg Laurie broadcasts.

Jesus Army

http://www.jesus.org.uk/

What is the Jesus Revolution? Find out on this award-winning British-based site. Contains an electronic magazine and many pictures.

Jesus Fellowship Home Page

http://jf.org/

A family church, a Christian teaching center, a covenant community, a worldwide outreach center, a campus ministry, a neighborhood Bible fellowship, and much more. Links to Miami Christian University, where you can earn theological degrees online.

Jesus Film Project

http://www.jesusfilm.org/

Presents the Campus Crusade for Christ's Jesus Film project. Includes well-designed graphics pages. Offers links to other Campus Crusade for Christ sites in the United States and abroad.

Leadership U

http://www.leaderu.com/menus/truth.html

An interdisciplinary, nonspecialized journal for the academic community (students, professors, scholars) with a distinctly Christian perspective. Seeks to provide a critical analysis of crucial contemporary intellectual issues. The issues discussed are scientific, philosophical, literary, historical, or theological in nature.

Logos Research Systems

http://www.logos.com/

An electronic publishing firm that offers CD-ROMs of biblical translations, ranging from the King

James to the Revised Standard Version. Also includes many other titles.

Monastery of Christ in the Desert

http://www.christdesert.org/pax.html

Benedictine monks share their monastery via a beautiful Web site. Read up on their lives, listen to their chants, research their monastic studies, and even shop at the online gift store for books, prints, and other items.

Orthodox Christian Page

http://www.ocf.org/OrthodoxPage/

What is Greek Orthodox Christianity all about? This site tells you and provides links to European and American Orthodox sites. There are pages covering scriptures and liturgy, icons, prayers, readings, and links to other resources.

Orthodox Ministry ACCESS

http://goa.goarch.org/access/

Provides information about Orthodox Christianity, the Greek Orthodox Archdiocese, the Orthodox Ministry ACCESS bulletin board system (accessible via the Internet), Orthodox Christian resources, Orthodox Christian organizations, and more.

Presbyterian Church USA

http://www.pcusa.org/

Contains news from the Presbyterian News Service, reports and proceedings of the General Assembly, mission news, religious humor, and the PresbyNet conferencing system. There also are links to other Presbyterian-related sites, such as the Web pages of local churches.

Project Wittenberg

http://www.iclnet.org/pub/resources/text/wittenberg/wittenberg-home.html

This award-winning site provides the thought of Martin Luther online. Plans to accumulate all of Luther's work, along with that of other theologians.

Religion News Service

http://www.religionnews.com/

The Religion News Service provides a daily newsletter featuring unbiased coverage of religion, ethics, and Christian spiritual issues from a secular viewpoint.

Religious Society of Friends WWW site

http://www.quaker.org/

Offers a list of links about Quakers on the Web. Includes links to sites focusing on Quaker schools, journals, the American Friends Service Committee, genealogy sites, Quaker history, newsgroups, and more.

Scrolls from the Dead Sea

http://www.ibiblio.org/expo/deadsea.scrolls.exhibit/intro.html

This exhibit from the Library of Congress (reorganized by Jeff Barry) is a great scholastic site, containing the published text of the Quamran scrolls, commonly known as the Dead Sea Scrolls. Bible scholars have extensively studied these works. The site offers a link to the Expo Bookstore where a printed copy of the exhibition catalog can be purchased.

The Spurgeon Archive

http://www.spurgeon.org/

This award-winning site is a collection of resources by and about Charles H. Spurgeon, the English

A
B
C
D
E
F
G
H
I
J
K
L
M
N
O
P
Q
R
S
T
U
V
W
X
Y
Z

preacher and theologian. Contains information on his personal library, the full text of his sermons, his writings, and excerpts from The Sword and the Trowel and The Treasury of David.

Vatican

http://www.vatican.va

Online home of the Roman Catholic Church, this site takes you on a virtual tour of the Vatican, where you can access the latest news, perform research in the Vatican library and secret archives, tour the Vatican museums, read about past popes, and much more.

World Religions Index

http://wri.leaderu.com/osites.html

This site provides you with an insight into the many religions and religious organizations of the world and offers to answer many interesting questions that you may have such as, do all religions point to the same truth and do all religions lead to God?

CULTS

Cults "R" Us

http://www.mayhem.net/Crime/cults1.html

This "hit list" from the pages of the Internet Crime Archives gives general information about a number of cult figures whose cultish practices included murder, human sacrifice, and suicide.

F.A.C.T.Net

http://www.factnet.org/

Read news reports and suggestions of mind control and cult activity at this site, which aims to protect the freedom of the mind. Learn about

psychological coercion, cult groups, and mind control here.

Ms. Guidance on Strange Cults

http://www.t0.or.at/msguide/devilgd1.htm

A plethora of links to all sorts of cult subjects. Several cult categories are addressed, including generic magic, paganism, freemasons, Gnostics, and many more.

DEISM

United Deist Church

http://www.deism.org/

Learn what Thomas Jefferson thought about traditional religions, including Christianity, and the theology of deism. Read the basic tenets of deism and research its history.

World Union of Deists

http://www.deism.com/

Excellent introduction to deism, the belief that there is a God, but that God does not directly intervene in the world through revelations or actions. Read thought-provoking essays by Thomas Paine, read a comparison of deism to Christianity and Atheism, and research some of the beliefs of this humanist approach to spirituality.

HINDUISM

Bhagvat Gita

http://www.iconsoftec.com/gita/

For students of Hinduism's most revered scripture, this site offers the Bhagvat Gita in the original Sanskrit (requires a PostScript viewer, such as GhostScript). Also offers Arnold's complete English translation.

Friends of Osho

http://www.sannyas.net/

Introduction to the work of Osho (Bhagwan Shri Rajneesh), popular and controversial teacher of Tantra Yoga.

Hare Krishna Home Page

http://www.webcom.com/~ara/

Official ISKCON site, detailing the religion of Krishna Consciousness founded by A.C. Bhakti-vedanta Swami Prabhupada. Identifies spirit as primary and matter as secondary.

Hindu Universe: Hindu Resource Center

http://www.hindunet.org/

Learn about upcoming events, get the latest Hindu and India news, and stay connected to Hindu practices and teachings.

Hinduism Online

http://www.himalayanacademy.com/

Created and maintained by the Himalayan Academy, this site provides a basic introduction to Hinduism, plus links to Hinduism Today magazine, Hindu books and art, the Hawai'i Ashram, and other resources.

Hinduism Today

http://www.hinduismtoday.kauai.hi.us/

Learn all the basics of Hinduism at this informative site, which also offers books and other resources on the subject. Shopping mall provides links to stores where you can shop online for everything from books to gemstones.

ISLAM

Al-Islam

http://www.al-islam.org/

This site serves as a means of introducing Islam to you, and provides you with options for exploring this religion further. If you are a Muslim, this site serves as a repository for advancing your knowledge about Islam.

Haqqani Foundation

http://www.naqshbandi.net/haqqani/

Offers a look into the teachings and precepts of Sufism. Offers many pages of information, pictures, and links intended to spread Sufi teachings of the brotherhood of man. Focuses on Sufi leader Shaykh Muhammad Nazim al-Haqqani. Navigate the site in any of 12 different languages.

Islam in the United States

http://usinfo.state.gov/usa/islam/

Maintained by the U.S. Department of State, this site is dedicated to promoting a greater understanding of Islamic people in the United States and elsewhere. Features a photo gallery, electronic journals, and links to other Web sites and publications.

Islam World

http://www.islamworld.net/

Islamic Studies

http://www.arches.uga.edu/~godlas/

With the ongoing turmoil in the Middle East, more and more people are becoming interested in the Islamic faith. To learn about Islam for yourself, check out this site.

A
B
C
D
E
F
G
H
I
J
K
L
M
N
O
P
Q
R
S
T
U
V
W
X
Y
Z

A
B
C
D
E
F
G
H
I
J
K
L
M
N
O
P
Q
R
S
T
U
V
W
X
Y
Z

Here you can find the basic beliefs and traditions explained and explore some of the teachings of one of the world's largest religions. This site also describes the various Islamic sects, provides statistics about some of the more populous Islamic areas around the globe, and provides galleries of Islamic art and architecture.

IslamiCity in Cyberspace

http://www.islam.org/

Includes overview of doctrine, Qur'an; news, culture, education, and political information; down-loadable radio/TV broadcasts (free software download); online shopping; a chat room; a virtual Mosque tour; Web links; and a matrimonial service. Heavy coverage of Middle East politics.

Online Islamic Bookstore

http://www.sharaaz.com

Provides information about the books, tapes, and software. Offers links to Islamic sites and book reviews of important books. Its aim? "To encourage the Muslim community to read again. To assert the importance of spiritual knowledge especially in this modern age."

JUDAISM

Chabad-Lubavitch in Cyberspace

http://www.chabad.org

Offers information pertaining to Chabad philosophy and Chassidic Judaism. Includes Kosher recipe and children's links, multimedia, a LISTSERV, and Gopher resources.

Jewish America

http://www.jewishamerica.org/ja/index.cfm

Links to Jewish sites, humor, and news are available through this site, which aims to connect Jewish people to each other.

Jewish Theological Seminary

http://www.jtsa.edu/

Represents this conservative seminary online. Provides a wealth of resources and links to conservative Jewish synagogues and institutions.

Judaism 101

http://www.jewfaq.org/

This site is an online encyclopedia of Judaism, covering "Jewish beliefs, people, places, things, language, scripture, holidays, practices and customs." The purpose is simply to inform and educate Jews and non-Jews about the religion.

Judaism and Jewish Resources

http://shamash.org/trb/judaism.html

Quite possibly the most complete source of Jewish information and Jewish-related links on the Web. Lists of links include media, singles groups, communities, newsgroups, reading lists, and museums, as well as commerce sites.

MavenSearch

http://www.maven.co.il/

Searchable directory for links to all things Jewish. Type a keyword or phrase to search the directory or browse by category. Categories include Communities, Travel and Tourism, Israel, Holocaust, Shopping & Gifts, and much more.

ORT

http://www.ort.org/

Coined from the acronym of the Russian words Obschestvo Remeslenovo i zemledelcheskovo Trouda, meaning The Society for Trades and Agricultural Labour, ORT is a worldwide education and training organization. At this site, you can learn more about ORT and its programs and schools.

Project Genesis–Torah on the Information Superhighway

http://www.torah.org/

This site provides Jewish educational material through article and reference archives, program and speaker information, and popular email classes.

Shamash

http://shamash.org/

This award-winning site run by the Jewish Internet Consortium offers links to various Jewish religious organizations ranging from Hillel to the World Zionist Organization. Includes FAQs pertaining to various facets of Judaism.

Shtetl: Yiddish Language and Culture Home Page

http://metalab.unc.edu/yiddish/shtetl.html

"Shtetl" means "small town" in Yiddish. This site aims to be a virtual small town on the Web. Provides information on Yiddish culture, as well as resources that point toward a wide range of links ranging from recommended books to kosher recipes.

Virtual Jerusalem

http://www.virtualjerusalem.com/

Virtual Jerusalem offers updated news and information about Judaism and Israeli life, with departments for news, travel, technology, holidays, and entertainment. Bulletin boards and a Jewish email directory.

Zipple.com

http://www.zipple.com/

This "Jewish SuperSite" provides Jewish information, news, chat, discussions, a business directory, an events calendar, and much more. Shopping links point to stores where you can purchase products online.

PHILOSOPHY

Dictionary of Philosophy of the Mind

http://www.artsci.wustl.edu/~philos/MindDict/

Exhaustive glossary of philosophical terms and brief biographies of the most famous philosophers, along with explanations of what made them famous. Enables you to submit entries and error corrections. Also contains philosophy links.

EpistemeLinks.com: Philosophy Resources on the Internet

http://www.epistemelinks.com/

Site features thousands of sorted links to philosophy-related sites. Links are divided into categories including philosophers, philosophy texts, publications, newsgroups, and job postings. Shop for books via a link to Amazon.com. Excellent starting point for any philosophical research project.

Exploring Plato's Dialogues

http://plato.evansville.edu/

Brief biography of Plato's life, including his works, plus English translations of Plato's dialogues,

A
B
C
D
E
F
G
H
I
J
K
L
M
N
O
P
Q
R
S
T
U
V
W
X
Y
Z

A
B
C
D
E
F
G
H
I
J
K
L
M
N
O
P
Q
R
S
T
U
V
W
X
Y
Z

including The Crito, The Phaedo, The Phaedrus, The Symposium, and The Republic.

Here, Madame

http://library.thinkquest.org/3075/frames.htm

Tries to answer man's nagging questions ("Does God exist?" "Do I have a free will?" "How do I know I exist?") through the writings of various philosophers. Has information on the various components of philosophy (metaphysics, epistemology, logic, aesthetics, ethics), the history of philosophy, as well as many of the philosophers themselves.

Internet Enclyclopedia of Philosophy

http://www.utm.edu/research/iep/

Search this philosophy encyclopedia by keyword or by clicking on the first letter of the topic you want to explore. Entries cover most philosophers, philosophies, and philosophical terms.

Nietzsche Page at Stanford

http://plato.stanford.edu/entries/nietzsche/

Excellent overview of Friedrich Nietzsche's life, publications, and ideas. Features a substantial bibliography plus links to other useful Nietzsche sites. Part of Stanford's Encyclopedia of Philosophy.

Philosophy Around the Web

http://users.ox.ac.uk/~worc0337/phil_index.html

Striving to be a central gateway to philosophy information on the Web, users can learn the basics of philosophy, find useful links, check out sites by topic, scan educational institution and individual Web pages, and much more.

PSYCHE

http://psyche.cs.monash.edu.au/

PSYCHE is an interdisciplinary journal of research and consciousness. The site provides direct access to PSYCHE's archives. Also contains a FAQ associated with the journal.

Stanford Encyclopedia of Philosophy

http://plato.stanford.edu/

Features an indexed dynamic encyclopedia in which each entry is maintained and kept up to date by an expert or group of experts in the field of philosophy. This is a work in progress, and many of the philosophers and concepts listed in the comprehensive index are not covered in the encyclopedia. However, the coverage that is provided is exceptional.

Theosophical Society

http://www.theosociety.org/

The society was founded in 1875 in an effort to promote the expressed awareness of the Oneness of Life. This site links to descriptions of foundational, esoteric texts by Blavatsky and others. Acts as a guide for personal exploration of truth.

The Thinking Man's Minefield

http://www.theabsolute.net/minefield/index.html

Contains all kinds of worldly insights, including philosophic works, male and female psychology, poetry, quotations, travel in India, atheist archives, and links to articles from Life and Death Magazine.

PRAYER

Book of Common Prayer

http://justus.anglican.org/
resources/bcp/

A comprehensive resource for the Book of Common Prayer, including sections formatted as the original.

Catholic Prayers

http://www.webdesk.com/catholic/
prayers/

A treasury of Catholic prayers.

International Prayer Network

http://www.victorious.org/
needpray.htm

The 24-hour International Prayer Network is one of the world's largest Christian prayer fellowships, with worldwide volunteers interceding for prayer requests from all over the globe.

Presidential Prayer Team

http://www.
presidentialprayerteam.org/

Join the Presidential Prayer Team and pray with others for the president of the United States.

The Prophet's Prayer

http://www.qss.org/articles/
salah/toc.html

This Islamic Society provides information on the Prophet's Prayer and other Islamic prayers and practices.

Sacred Space

http://www.jesuit.ie/prayer/

Visit this site for an invitation to pray along with a group of Irish Jesuits. Features a prayer of the day in 11 languages plus a link to a site where you can pray with the Pope.

US Christian Resource Center

http://www.usprayertrack.org/

This site contains many interesting articles and materials concerning prayer and offers support through prayer.

World Ministry of Prayer Home Page

http://www.wmop.org/

This site allows you to pray with a live person over the telephone or by email. It also has a prayer requests section as well as a catalog from which you can order from a large selection. Offers support through prayer.

World Prayer Network

http://www.worldprayer.org/

This site is interested in uniting the world in prayer. Offers you the opportunity to pray with thousands of others with the same concerns and problems.

A
B
C
D
E
F
G
H
I
J
K
L
M
N
O
P
Q
R
S
T
U
V
W
X
Y
Z

RELOCATION SERVICES

[Best] America Mortgage Online

http://amo-mortgage.com/relocate.htm

This site focuses on offering you mortgage information and tools in addition to relocation services. You'll find relocation links for all 50 states and you can register to receive a free relocation package. Just some of the things you can do here is to look through their Mortgage Library, read the Real Estate News, order your Credit Report, do a Home Inspection, search for Homes, and look at other Real Estate links. The site is very well designed and easy to navigate and the information is very useful.

Employee Relocation Council (ERC)

http://www.erc.org/

This site covers myriad relocation and human resource issues, from transfer costs to family concerns. Sections include a Relocation Career Hotline, information on ERC, Research and Publications, and more.

ExecuStay Inc.

http://www.rent.net/ads/execustay/

Find temporary housing accommodations nationwide at this site. ExecuStay (by Marriott) offerings range from fully furnished apartments to private homes, complete with linens, electronics, and cable television.

MonsterMoving.com

http://www.monstermoving.com/

MonsterMoving.com, from the same folks who created MonsterJobs.com, is an online relocation guide that contains more than 100,000 links. Users can find links to real estate, careers, education, travel, taxes, insurance, mortgage, and rental sites. The database can be searched by subject, city, or state. You'll even find resources for child care information and links for making the move easier for children. If an international move is in your future, this site can help with that, too.

The Relocation Wizard

http://homefair.com/wizard/?NETSCAPE_LIVEWIRE.src=

Answer the questions and submit your information to the wizard and receive a suggested timeline. Find out what to do to help make your move go smoothly. Good selection of calculators for analyzing salary issues, moving costs, home affordability, and more. Links to school reports, city reports, and crime reports for most cities and towns.

RelocationCentral.com

http://www.relocationcentral.com/

Comprehensive directory to everything you need to know to make wise relocation decisions. The home page is minimal, offering four main links: State Selector, National Relocation Directory, Tools & Tips, and Search. Click State Selector to begin your research, and then pick the destination state and city.

RelocationCentral displays links for all sorts of services in the specified city, including apartment locators, real estate agents, local phone companies, moving and storage companies, and much more.

Rent.net

http://www.rent.net/

This site offers a variety of rental and relocation resources broken into different categories of interest. Visitors will find a section geared to seniors, another on vacation rentals, one on furnished suites, and more. There are also sections on movers, truck rental, furniture rental, city guides, insurance and auto information, and lots more.

RentCheck

http://www.rentcheck.com/

Search listings of more than 300,000 apartment units, temporary furnished suites, houses, condominiums, and vacation rentals for floor plans, photos, and customized neighborhood views at this site.

The School Report

http://www.homefair.com/sr_home.html

Offers school comparisons by city or county. Pick a state and a city or county, and up pops a report listing the various school districts along with information about the total number of students, average student-teacher ratio, and average class size.

TIMESHARES

Century 21 TRI-Timeshares

http://www.tri-timeshare.com/

Bid on timeshare auctions here, or search through available timeshare

opportunities for more information. There's also a timeshare advisor to assist you in finding a good vacation match.

ERA Stroman

http://www.stroman.com/

Search this site to learn more about available timeshares for sale, by looking through the catalog of properties and reading up on the buying and selling process. Thousands of resort timeshares are also available.

Holiday Group Timeshare Resales

http://www.holidaygroup.com/

The Holiday Group offers an enormous inventory of foreclosed or liquidated timeshares. In addition to discounted properties, the site offers a number of timeshare articles. Excellent way to buy timeshare properties without having to attend hardsell sales presentations.

Hotel Timeshare Resales

http://www.htr4timeshare.com/index.html

This site's entire focus is Marriott hotel timeshares. This site offers listings to browse and information on why you should choose them to buy a timeshare property.

RCI vacationNET

http://www.rci.com/

Resort Condominiums International (RCI) offers a searchable online directory of more than 3,000 resorts around the world affiliated with its timeshare exchange program. The site also includes travel tips, a tour of featured resorts, and a section explaining vacation ownership.

A
B
C
D
E
F
G
H
I
J
K
L
M
N
O
P
Q
R
S
T
U
V
W
X
Y
Z

A
B
C
D
E
F
G
H
I
J
K
L
M
N
O
P
Q
R
S
T
U
V
W
X
Y
Z

TimeLinx

http://www.timelinx.com/

Fully searchable database, containing information on more than 3,500 timeshare resorts worldwide for exchange, resale, and rental. Includes membership details and featured resorts.

TimeSharing Today

http://www.timesharing-today.com/

The online edition of this magazine includes extensive classifieds, sample articles, and resort reviews.

RETIREMENT

401K Center for Employers

http://401kcenter.com/

Helps employers formulate a 401K plan by providing information on the six plan functions. Features plan overviews, Q&As, and contact numbers.

401Kafe.com

http://www.mpowercafe.com/

Participants in 401Ks with questions or concerns about their investments will want to stay up to date regarding 401K news, as well as tips, reports, and useful information about this particular investment vehicle.

〖Best〗 AARP WebPlace

http://www.aarp.org/

The home page for. the American Association of Retired Persons provides information on the group's membership benefits, public policy positions, and volunteer programs. It also includes fact sheets on health, money, retirement, and

other topics. As soon as you retire (possibly even before you retire), become a member of AARP and start taking advantage of what it has to offer. AARP is one of the most vocal advocates of senior citizen rights in the country.

The Advisor

http://finance.americanexpress.com/finance/fshub.asp

This instructional site, maintained by American Express, provides information on retirement savings, tax planning, and insurance buying.

American Association of Homes and Services for the Aging

http://www.aahsa.org/

The American Association of Homes and Services for the Aging is an advocacy group composed of more than 5,600 nonprofit nursing homes, retirement communities, and other senior housing facilities. This site features a database of available senior housing.

ElderNet

http://www.eldernet.com/

This comprehensive Web index offers links to sites for the elderly, along with descriptions of each site. Incorporates health, finance, law, retirement, and lifestyle advice for seniors. Use tutorials, find activities, search resources, and read tips.

Maple Knoll Village Retirement Home

http://www.mapleknoll.org/

Web home of Maple Knoll Village Retirement Home, one of the top 20 retirement communities in the nation. Here, you can learn more about Maple Knoll and what it has to offer. Explore the history of the home or request more information online. Maple Knoll Village Retirement Home is located just outside Cincinnati, Ohio.

Quicken.com Retirement

http://www.quicken.com/
retirement/

Use the online financial planner to find out how much you'll have for retirement given your current savings plan and asset-base, or update your portfolio. You also can get the basics regarding many different retirement planning tools, such as Roth IRAs and SEPs.

Retire.net

http://www.retire.net/

Offers retirees links, articles, and a chat room.

Retirement Calculators

http://www.bhbt.com/pgs/
calc_frame.html

What will your expenses be after you retire? Are you saving enough to retire comfortably? What will your income be after you retire?

Find answers to all of these questions and more by using Bar Harbor Bank and Trust's online retirement calculators.

Retirement Research Foundation

http://www.rrf.org/

This is the nation's largest private foundation devoted to aging and retirement issues. Explore funding interests, guidelines, FAQs, and what's new.

Seniors-Site.com

http://www.seniors-site.com/

Features information and bulletin boards on topics for seniors, including finance, education, death and dying, retirement, nursing homes, and nutrition.

SeniorsSearch

http://www.seniorssearch.com/

This directory provides links to more than 5,000 sites geared toward the over-50 age group. Topics include history, health and fitness, hobbies, grandparenting, genealogy, travel, senior discounts, retirement, volunteering, and more.

Social Security Online

http://www.ssa.gov/

This official site includes an online earnings and benefit statement, a guide for employers, and many other resources.

Third Age

http://www.thirdage.com/

An e-zine aimed at those baby boomers who are starting their fifth decade. It includes articles on investing, love and relationships, health and fitness, hobbies, and technology. It also includes a chat room, discussion forums, and advice columns.

A
B
C
D
E
F
G
H
I
J
K
L
M
N
O
P
Q
R
S
T
U
V
W
X
Y
Z

A
B
C
D
E
F
G
H
I
J
K
L
M
N
O
P
Q
R
S
T
U
V
W
X
Y
Z

ROCK CLIMBING

About.com: Rock Climbing

http://rockclimbing.about.com/

Advice and links on mountain and rock climbing, including locations, photography, training techniques, and gear reviews.

Big Wall Climbing Web Page

http://www.bigwalls.net/

Diehard climbers will appreciate a home page dedicated to intense, multiday climbs; read about different walls, as well as stories of individual climbs. Answers the big question: What about when you need to go?

Bouldering

http://www.bouldering.com/

Read interviews with master climbers, take a look at photos from amazing vantage points, and stay in touch with the rock-climbing community through news and information here.

Climb New Hampshire

http://climbnh.com/

Provides information on where to climb in the Granite State as well as listing places to eat and stay plus a bibliography of guide books for the region.

⟦Best⟧ Climbing Online

http://www.climbing.com/

Climbing magazine's home on the Web features the latest climbing news, feature stories, product reviews, and online tutorials. Learn the basics or go beyond the basics with the latest techniques. Special

how-to sections on dealing with rock and dealing with ice, plus dozens of technical tips and links to other rock climbing resources on the Web make this site the pinnacle of sites in this category.

Climbing Quotes

http://www.gdargaud.net/Humor/QuotesClimbing.html

Inspirational and not-so-inspirational climbing quotes, plus stunning photos of conquered summits from around the world.

GORP–Climbing

http://www.gorp.com/gorp/activity/climb.htm

Read articles organized by topic, such as gear, know-how, and location, to improve your skill level and prepare for your next climb. There is also information on trips you might want to consider. Lots of inspiring photos and helpful tips.

Himalayas: Where Earth Meets Sky

http://library.thinkquest.org/10131/

Learn all about the world's tallest mountain range: its geologic past, flora and fauna, environmental concerns, countries that touch these wonders of nature, and more. Other pages have maps, wonderful stories, and quizzes.

Joshua Tree Rock Climbing School

http://www.rockclimbingschool.com/

Learn how to climb from some of the top climbers in the world at one of the most popular climbing sites in the world, Joshua Tree National Park, located in southern California. This site provides information on the various rock climbing courses offered at the school, plus brief biographies of the instructors and information about accommodations.

Nova Online: Lost on Everest

http://www.pbs.org/wgbh/nova/everest/

PBS's Nova followed an expedition up the world's highest mountain, and every aspect of the climb can be found on this site, which originally followed them live in real-time.

Online Climbing Guide

http://www.onlineclimbing.com/

This site, created by rock climbers for rock climbers, represents a community effort by climbers to provide a comprehensive directory of places to climb. Includes directions to favorite climb sites, photos, difficulty ratings, and more. Search for sites by state. Also features a directory of climbing gyms organized by state.

RockClimbing.com

http://www.rockclimbing.com/

A super climbing Web site complete with climbing routes, gear shopping, partner connecting, discussions, photos, and information on climbing techniques to improve your skill.

RockList

http://www.rocklist.com/

Long lists of cliffs, climbing gyms, alpine clubs, e-zines, literature, expeditions (including Everest), gear manufacturers, mountain information, and more. Search by geographical area anywhere in the world. Great site for finding places to climb.

Thedeadpoint.com

http://www.thedeadpoint.com

Read about climber triumphs, take a look at the photo gallery, read articles on rock climbing and bouldering, join in discussions, and post reviews.

A
B
C
D
E
F
G
H
I
J
K
L
M
N
O
P
Q
R
S
T
U
V
W
X
Y
Z

A
B
C
D
E
F
G
H
I
J
K
L
M
N
O
P
Q
R
S
T
U
V
W
X
Y
Z

RODEO

American Junior Rodeo Association

http://home1.gte.net/ajra/

The AJRA was begun when its founder went to rodeos and thought how unfair it was that kids were competing with adults, and so would never win, despite giving it their all. This page has a history of the AJRA, information about the coliseum they use, a schedule, and more.

Billy Joe Jim Bob's Rodeo Links Page

http://www.gunslinger.com/rodeo.html

Perhaps the most complete rodeo index on the Web. Billy Joe Jim Bob takes great care to include links for every rodeo, rodeo association, and rodeo site he could find, which numbers at least 191 links.

Janet's Let's Rodeo Page

http://www.cowgirls.com/dream/jan/rodeo.htm

Janet's page has pictures, links to other rodeo sites, a long list of articles, and countless answers to her question, "What do cowgirls dream about?"

Playdays Rodeos and Teampenning

http://www.playdays.com/

Center for rodeo information of all kinds, with links to local and regional events. Includes rodeo lingo, a horse sale, and more related info.

Pro Rodeo Home Pages

http://www.prorodeohome.com/

This site houses personal Web pages for any rodeo personnel who wants one. It has categories for clowns and bullfighters, announcers, cowboys and cowgirls, ropers, bronco riders, and more.

[Best] Pro Rodeo Online

http://www.prorodeo.com/

The Professional Rodeo Cowboys Association's official Web site, ProRodeo.com provides up-to-date information about the latest rodeo competitions across the country. Read about your favorite rodeo riders, find the tour standings and scoreboard, check out the injury reports, learn of upcoming televised events, and even flip through some action photos. For novice fans, the Sport link introduces you to the sport of rodeo, describes the various events and how they are scored, and provides an online record book and a link to the ProRodeo Hall of Fame. You can shop online at ProRodeo Merchandise, become a member, and even check out the media library. Packed with useful information in an easy-to-navigate format, this site is the hands-down winner of the best of the best award.

ReadTheWest.com

http://www.readthewest.com/rodeo
.html

Check on the standings of your favorite rodeo cowboys and girls, find out about the schedule of upcoming events, learn about rodeo books you might want in your library, and get results from recent competitions here.

Sarah's Rodeo Page

http://mama.indstate.edu/
prentice/sarah/

Nice rodeo and horse links resource. Choose from Rodeos & Associations, Cowfolk, Horse & Ag Info, or General Store, in addition to a discussion group and information on upcoming rodeo events.

SLAM! Sports Rodeo

http://www.canoe.ca/SlamRodeo/
home.html

Interested in what happened at rodeo tournaments last night or want to know more about your favorite rodeo stars? Check Slam! Sports Rodeo for all your rodeo news needs. Slam also covers other sports.

SCI-FI AND FANTASY

Analog Science Fiction and Fact

http://www.analogsf.com/

The popular Analog magazine is online here, offering samples of its columns and stories. Analog places equal emphasis on the terms "science" and "fiction," in an attempt to provide a more realistic view of how science might develop in the future and be applied to improve the human condition. At this site, you can check out some columns and story excerpts from the magazine.

Asimov's Science Fiction

http://www.asimovs.com/

Home of Asimov's Science Fiction magazine, which reviews the best of the best new science fiction publications and presents some of its own. Learn about the awards it has won, its authors, and other information about the magazine. Read some science fiction short stories from some of the best sci-fi writers in the business.

A
B
C
D
E
F
G
H
I
J
K
L
M
N
O
P
Q
R
S
T
U
V
W
X
Y
Z

Broadsword

http://www.broadsword.org/

The Web page for Doctor Who, the New and Missing Adventures. This e-zine includes interviews with actors, a writer's guide, articles on the missing adventures, and a list of books published about Doctor Who. Don't click New Adventures if you don't want to know what happens in these stories.

Buffy the Vampire Slayer

http://www.buffy.com/

This shrine to Buffy the Vampire Slayer has excellent photos of all the stars, brief character bios, and extensive information on Sarah Michelle Gellar, who plays Buffy.

Caroline's Hercules Page

http://www.angelfire.com/co/greekbard/

This fan's Hercules site has an interesting page where she compares the TV character to the one in classical mythology. Includes games based on the show, plus upcoming episodes. Has links to other Hercules and Xena pages.

The Centre

http://www.enteract.com/~perridox/pretender/

Based on the TV show The Pretender, this site has episode guides, bios on the staff, and an excellent FAQ that answers most of the questions you might have if you haven't watched every episode. Lots of photos of the program and some audio files.

Dark Planet Science Fiction Webzine

http://www.sfsite.com/darkplanet/

The official site of the Dark Planet Science Fiction, Fantasy, and Horror Webzine. This e-zine accepts submissions from writers and has a nice archive of stories and articles. The graphics are great and the site is very well worth the visit if you like to read science fiction and horror stories.

Dark Shadows

http://members.aol.com/darkkshad/super/natural.htm

Premiering in 1966 on ABC television, this show was a soap opera based on ghouls, goblins, vampires, and the like. There are story lines, photo galleries, fan fictions, and other points of interest for Dark Shadows fans at this Web site.

FANDOM–Star Trek central

http://www.cinescape.com/0/Fanspeak.asp

Star Trek fans will love this site, which provides actor interviews, Trek news, show and movie information, photos, polls, discussion forums, and products for sale.

FanGrok

http://www.roblang.demon.co.uk/fangrok/

A U.K. online e-zine that satirizes sci-fi television. The site essentially reprints an article or two from the paper magazine FanGrok. Some of the articles are very funny—be sure to check out the Spice Docs issue. And, naturally, you can get instructions on how to subscribe to FanGrok so you can get the complete issue.

Lord of the Rings Movie Site

http://www.lordoftherings.net/

This site provides a virtual tour of the film(s) and the legend. Check out movie trailers, learn more about the cast and crew, find late-breaking news and upcoming events, explore the well-stocked photo library, and even download free screensavers, desktop wallpaper, and other goodies.

The Matrix Reloaded

http://
whatisthematrix.warnerbros.com/

Fans of The Matrix will want to enter this virtual tour of the movie set to experience The Matrix in a completely new way. Read interviews with the cast and crew, view photos from the set, take 3D tours of the deck of the Neb, flip through the comics, and more.

Mystery Science Theater 3000

http://www.mst3kinfo.com/

Have your friends been talking about the weird TV show where they make fun of old sci-fi and horror movies from a space station? Would you like to know what they're talking about? Then come to the MST3K site and see what all the hype is about. The site has audio and video files, a FAQ, plus information on the stars and writers and lots of other goodies.

The Netpicker's Guide to The X-Files

http://bedlam.rutgers.edu/
x-files/

This site points out the netpicks in each episode. A netpick is "a writing/research error, a technical glitch, or a continuity error that made it through post production." A very interesting site, but it covers only the first three seasons.

Poltergeist: The Legacy

http://members.aol.com/
legacymemb/legacy.htm

This site is presented as the Seattle Legacy House Web site. Not only does it have information on the show itself, but includes fan fiction, character and actor bios, and a Legacy Handbook for aspiring members.

The Sci-Fi Experience

http://www.geocities.com/
Hollywood/Boulevard/4090/

A well-done Star Trek site with an emphasis on Voyager and Deep Space Nine (with The X-Files thrown in for flavor). Episode listings, convention information, crew bios, fan fiction, some great photos, and audio files.

The Sci-Fi Site

http://www.sfsite.com/

Book reviews, news, and resources. This is a great site with lots of book reviews, opinion pieces, author interviews, fiction excerpts, author and publisher reading lists, and a variety of other wonderful features. There is a comprehensive list of links to author and fan tribute sites, SF conventions, movies, TV, magazines, e-zines, writer resources, publishers, and small press sites.

Sci-Fi.Net

http://www.sci-fi-net.com/

In addition to finding reasonably priced videos and DVDs of sci-fi programming and movies, you can search the Sci-Fi.Net database to read up on story lines of your favorite sci-fi TV shows, buy sci-fi merchandise, chat with fellow sci-fi fans, and link to other sites of interest. Please check to see whether your VCR is PAL compliant before ordering videos from this site.

A
B
C
D
E
F
G
H
I
J
K
L
M
N
O
P
Q
R
S
T
U
V
W
X
Y
Z

A
B
C
D
E
F
G
H
I
J
K
L
M
N
O
P
Q
R
S
T
U
V
W
X
Y
Z

Science Fiction and Fantasy World

http://www.sffworld.com/

Featuring more than 10,000 pages of science fiction and fantasy, this is one of the largest science fiction sites on the Web. Read some of the latest short stories and poems, check out the interviews, or visit the discussion forums to share your science fiction enthusiasm with other fans. Also provides a directory of TV and movie listings, book reviews and excerpts, e-zines, and more. You can even submit your own writings for consideration.

Science Fiction and Fantasy Writers of America (SFWA)

http://www.sfwa.org/

Sci-fi writers will find this site, and this nonprofit organization, a big help in improving their writing skills and improving the financial rewards of writing science fiction. The site provides writing tips as well as model contracts to follow, document formatting guidance, and a regular bulletin for members.

Science Fiction Resource Guide

http://www.sflovers.org/SFRG

An extensive collection of links to sci-fi resources on the Net. Subject areas include other archives and resource guides, authors, bibliographies, movies, and more.

Science Fiction Weekly

http://www.scifi.com/sfw/

Weekly news, articles, features, interviews, and reviews. The site also features a games column, letters from fans, On Screen information about programs on television and in the movies, a Cool Stuff column, and a site-of-the-week feature.

SciFan

http://www.scifan.com/

SciFan offers science fiction fans plenty of reading material, from magazine subscriptions and books. Search the sci-fi author database to track down those titles you haven't read yet, and then link to a bookstore to order it.

[Best] SCIFI.COM

http://www.scifi.com/

Lots of sci-fi adventures to choose from here; between online programming and TV and movie reviews, you'll find plenty of unique and fascinating story lines to follow. You can also get sci-fi news, clips of animated features, and movie trailers, and connect with other sci-fi fans through chat or bulletin board postings. With so much to offer, this site is an easy pick as the best sci-fi site on the Web, although there are plenty of outstanding competitors.

SF Site

http://www.sfsite.com/

Nominated for a Hugo award, this is one of the best sites on the Web covering science fiction and fantasy. Features book reviews, author interviews, information on upcoming conventions, and more.

Smallville Ledger

http://www2.warnerbros.com/web/
smallville/ledger/_home.jsp

Smallville, the latest TV series based on the Superman legend, has its own neighborhood newspaper on the Web. Check out the front-page news, the community calendar, the local classifieds, and more. You can even check out the Smallville Torch, the Smallville high school newspaper.

Very entertaining stuff, especially for Smallville fans.

Songs of the Blue Bird

http://members.iquest.net/~jeneric/songs.html

An e-zine and news source for fans of the former CBS television drama Beauty and the Beast. Includes unaired scripts, images, and paintings by fans, back-issue catalogs, and information about conventions for this cult TV show.

Star Trek

http://www.startrek.com/

Provides a good amount of information and links to many sites that cover the television, film, and cultural phenomenon that is Star Trek. This site includes pictures, sounds, quotes, fan information, and much more. Links to Amazon.com for online shopping.

Star Wars Official Site

http://www.starwars.com/

Star Wars fans will want to bookmark this site. This site serves up everything you need to know about the Star Wars series. Features movie clips, well-stocked photo galleries, interviews with the creators and cast, and much more. Material is organized by episode, making it easy to find what you want. You can even shop online for Star Wars apparel and collectibles.

Starship Store

http://www.uncomyngifts.com/Main/Recreation_Room/_StarTrek/

Includes collectors' items, memorabilia, and clothing of every Star Trek series. Order T-shirts of your favorite characters, keychains, toys, and other items.

The TV Sci-Fi and Fantasy Database

http://www.pazsaz.com/scifan.html

If you can't remember the name of a particular episode, or when it ran, just check with the database. It lists the name and original air date of more than 70 different shows. Please note that no information about the episode is given. Comes in full graphical and less graphical versions.

The Ultimate Science Fiction Web Guide

http://www.magicdragon.com/UltimateSF/SF-Index.html

If you are looking for Web sites about science fiction, you will be in the right place at the Ultimate Science Fiction Web Guide because they feature more than 6,000 links to such resources.

Virus

http://www.virusthemovie.com/

This official site offers information on the cast and crew of this action–science fiction movie. Photos, movie trailer, and games.

A
B
C
D
E
F
G
H
I
J
K
L
M
N
O
P
Q
R
S
T
U
V
W
X
Y
Z

AARP

http://www.aarp.org/

This very user-friendly site contributes to AARP's goal of allowing senior citizens to lead the rich and fulfilling lives that they are accustomed to—not only by staying well informed, but also by staying active.

Administration on Aging (AOA)

http://www.aoa.dhhs.gov/

AOA is a federal agency serving as an advocate for older Americans and issues that concern them. The site provides a lot of background information on the Older Americans Act, as well as practical information for senior citizens and their caregivers—a resource directory, list of local agencies providing senior services, news, and health information.

Age of Reason Recommended Senior Living Facilities

http://www.wiredseniors.com/ageofreason/

Complete information, including online experts about living and vacationing in several senior-friendly facilities.

[Best] AgeNet

http://agenet.agenet.com/

Seniors and their family members will find information at this site interesting and useful. Topics covered include health, insurance, finance, drugs, and caregiver support. You can use the Social Security estimator, for example, to estimate the value of benefits you should receive at retirement, or try

out some brain exercises to improve your mental faculties. This site's comprehensive collection of resources for seniors combined with a very inviting presentation makes this our choice as the best of the best senior sites on the Web.

Alliance for Retired Americans

http://www.retiredamericans.org/

The Alliance is a new national organization for retired citizens of the United States. Created by the AFL-CIO, the Alliance works to promote legislation that "protects the health and economic security of seniors, rewards work, strengthens families and builds thriving communities." Think of it as a union for retired workers, a way for retired workers to fight for their rights and have their voices heard.

Alzheimer's Association

http://www.alz.org/

This national nonprofit organization provides support to those afflicted with Alzheimer's as well as their caregivers. AA funds Alzheimer's research, which is reported on at the site, and offers support and resources to help families cope with this illness.

Alzheimer's Disease Education & Referral Center

http://www.alzheimers.org

This site has a wealth of information for anyone interested in assessing their risk of being afflicted with the disease, researching treatments, as well as learning to cope with caring for someone with the disease.

American Association of Homes and Services for the Aging

http://www.aahsa.org

Visit this site for a listing of member facilities. Includes assisted living, nursing homes, and retirement communities.

Assisted Living Described

http://www.alfa.org/

Detailed description from the Assisted Living Federation of America. The Assisted Living Federation of America (ALFA) represents more than 7,000 for-profit and not-for-profit providers of assisted living, continuing care retirement communities, independent living, and other forms of housing and services. Founded in 1990 to advance the assisted living industry and enhance the quality of life for the approximately one million consumers it serves, ALFA broadened its membership in 1999 to embrace the full range of housing and care providers who share ALFA's consumer-focused philosophy of care. They have an online bookstore from which you can order their books and other related items.

Caregiver Network Inc.

http://www.caregiver.on.ca/

The Canadian woman who maintains this site became a caregiver overnight. She is very aware of what resources you need to take care of someone you care about. Most links are in the United States, and many will refer you to services in your own area.

Choosing an Assisted Living Facility

http://www.aahsa.org/public/al.htm

What assisted living is, how to choose, costs, and standards. American Association of Homes and Services for the Aging.

Elderhostel

http://www.elderhostel.org/

With the fundamental belief that no one should ever stop learning, this site provides access to resources around the world to continue your education (for adults age 55 and over). Currently, you must register through postal mail, but all the registration information is at the site.

Friendly4Seniors Web Sites

http://www.friendly4seniors.com/

This site simply offers links to sites that are of interest to seniors. Choose your topic—Government, Financial, Housing, Medical, and many more—click and find what you're looking for. More than 2,000 senior-related listings that are reviewed and approved before being added to the list.

HomeStore.com Senior Living

http://www.springstreet.com/seniors/

This site has gathered a wide range of lifestyle options so family members and seniors can easily sort through retirement communities, assisted living, nursing homes, and home health care. Search through more than 55,000 listings!

A
B
C
D
E
F
G
H
I
J
K
L
M
N
O
P
Q
R
S
T
U
V
W
X
Y
Z

A
B
C
D
E
F
G
H
I
J
K
L
M
N
O
P
Q
R
S
T
U
V
W
X
Y
Z

HUD for Senior Citizens

http://www.hud.gov/groups/seniors.cfm

The United States Department of Housing and Urban Development has created this section specifically to inform senior citizens of their housing options and help them find suitable places to live. Information to help seniors stay in their current homes, find apartments to rent, find retirement or nursing homes, locate organizations to stay active, and much more. Features related information on senior jobs, links to other resources on the Web, and links to other government agencies that address the needs of seniors.

Life Extension Foundation

http://www.lef.org/

Anyone looking to slow the aging process will want to visit this site for research and medical news regarding life extension and aging. You can also purchase products and learn about membership in LEF.

LivOn

http://www.livon.com/

Look for senior housing, care, and services in the United States and abroad.

Maple Knoll Village—Pioneer in the Alzheimer's Experience

http://www.mapleknoll.org/

Web home of Maple Knoll Village Retirement Home, one of the top 20 retirement communities in the nation. Here, you can learn more about Maple Knoll and what it has to offer. Explore the history of the home or request more information online. Maple Knoll Village Retirement Home is located just outside Cincinnati, Ohio.

The National Senior Citizens Law Center

http://www.nsclc.org

The National Senior Citizens Law Center advocates, litigates, and publishes on low-income elderly and disability issues including Medicare, Medicaid, SSI, nursing homes, age discrimination, and pensions.

New LifeStyles

http://www.newlifestyles.com/

New LifeStyles Online, a complete guide to senior housing and care options, lists all state-licensed senior housing facilities in the major metropolitan areas nationwide.

Senior Center

http://www.seniorcenter.com/

Excellent collection of information for seniors organized by categories including News, Living, Health, Money, Travel, Services, and Weather.

The Senior Citizens' Website

http://www.intecon.com/senior/

This Web site for active seniors features sections on Crisis & Grief, Education, Financial, Recreation, Government, Health, and more. Complete directory of organizations and places of interest for seniors organized by state.

Senior Cyborgs

http://online96.com/seniors/

Extensive listing of online resources for adults age 50 and older. Includes information about health, medicine, legal issues, housing, retirement, and finance.

The Senior Information Network

http://www.senior-inet.com/

This site has everything you need to know about being a senior. The Senior-inet (Senior Information Network) site is the premier high-tech source in obtaining information about Senior Support Services across the United States. The body of the community Web pages is designed to provide you with a list of those people and agencies who can provide services for seniors in each community. The Web site has a lot of information about seniors for seniors.

Senior Sites

http://www.seniorsites.com/

This site lists more than 5,000 non-profit housing and services for senior citizens in the United States, Guam, and Puerto Rico. Also includes national and state resources.

Senior.com

http://www.senior.com/

There's lots of interest to seniors on this site, including a chat room and message center devoted to the senior citizen community. You'll find articles of interest and links to other pages. Unique features of this page are the chat room and message board. Be sure to read the Solutions column and definitely check the Personals.

SeniorJournal.com

http://www.seniorjournal.com/

This news and information kiosk for seniors covers everything from health to politics. Check here for information on healthcare for seniors, legislation, social security and Medicaid information, and much more.

SeniorNet

http://www.seniornet.org/

SeniorNet's mission is to "provide older adults education for and access to computer technology to enhance their lives and enable them to share their knowledge and wisdom." The site supports this effort through online programs, discussions, news, and special offers available only on the Internet.

seniorresource.com

http://www.seniorresource.com/

A resource for seniors considering all their housing options, with information about alternatives and links to supporting services, such as financing, mortgages, and retirement communities.

The Seniors Page–FirstGov for Seniors

http://www.seniors.gov/

The senior citizen is not only the fastest-growing element of the population but also the fastest-growing user base on the Internet. This site gives these seniors information on everything from the specifics of Alzheimer's to how to prepare your income taxes. There are also dozens of links of interest to seniors.

SeniorsSearch.com

http://www.seniorssearch.com/

A comprehensive search engine developed specifically for the over-50 crowd. Find merchants, information sources, and services organized by category. There are also senior media, such as senior radio, that provide programming information.

Social Security Online

http://www.ssa.gov/

Official Web site of the Social Security Administration. Includes announcements and reports on

A
B
C
D
E
F
G
H
I
J
K
L
M
N
O
P
Q
R
S
T
U
V
W
X
Y
Z

A
B
C
D
E
F
G
H
I
J
K
L
M
N
O
P
Q
R
S
T
U
V
W
X
Y
Z

issues related to Social Security, contact information, and regular updates.

Third Age

http://www.thirdage.com/features/healthy/resource/

Third Age editors, researchers, and producers have compiled a resource locator showing you the way to the Web's most reliable sources of information. You can purchase everything from cameras to binoculars to clothes from their online store using a secure card resource.

Transitions, Inc. Elder Care Consulting

http://www.asktransitions.com/

Transitions locates and arranges services for older adults and their caregivers. Company representatives assess needs, hold seminars, and provide eldercare counseling.

Wired Seniors

http://www.wiredseniors.com

This is a directory of businesses and services that are geared to the senior or that offer special senior citizen discounts. There are hundreds of links to businesses you'll want to know about.

SEWING

Cranston Village

http://www.cranstonvillage.com/

Home of the oldest fabric printing company in the United States, this site features suggestions for crafts and quilts, plus a history of the Cranston Print Works Company.

The Fabric Club

http://www.fabricclub.com/store/

Order a wide variety of fabrics from this site, which advertises wholesale prices. Search by type of fabric or use, such as home decorating or quilting, and order as many or as few yards as you need.

Fabrics.net

http://www.fabrics.net

An information resource for sewers in search of particular fabrics, as well as individuals and vendors who have fabrics to sell. You can learn all about various types of fabrics and then look for sources in the database or shop online.

Fashion Fabrics Club

http://www.sewingfabrics.com

Looking for unique, high-quality fabrics for your next sewing project? Then visit the Fashion Fabrics Club and check out their selection.

Fashion Supplies

http://www.umei.com/

Fashion accessories, supplies, buckles, buttons, trims, chains, lace, fittings, zipper pulls, and more.

Fiskars

http://www.fiskars.com/

You'll find plenty of information about the many types of Fiskars brand scissors at their site, which also has many project ideas and tips. There are also links to related sites, such as crafts, special rebates or deals, and news about Fiskars.

 Home Sewing Association

http://www.sewing.org/

Dedicated to "Get People Sewing," this site encourages visitors to take up a needle and thread and start stitching their own clothes. This site is packed with tutorials covering sewing techniques for both novice and intermediate stitchers, plus plenty of sewing projects, tips, and advice. Excellent place for both children and adults to learn how to start sewing. With its appeal to such a wide audience, and its comprehensive sewing information and instructions, we couldn't help naming this site best of the best in the Sewing category.

Jo-Ann etc.

http://www.joann.com/

If you're looking for a sewing project, come to the Jo-Ann etc. site for free craft, sewing, home decorating, and quilting projects to choose from. After you've selected a project, you can search the Jo-Ann catalog for the supplies you need. There's also

a discussion forum to connect you with fellow sewers who might have the advice you need.

Lily Abello's Sewing Links

http://www.lilyabello.com

For sewing links and books, or button crafts, visit Lily's simple but abundant site.

Nancy's Notions

http://www.nancysnotions.com/

A catalog of sewing, serging, and quilting notions. Also the home of Sewing with Nancy (the longest-running sewing show on PBS) and Nancy's Video Library, your rental source for sewing and other creative arts ideas.

Patternshowcase.com

http://www.patternshowcase.com/

Huge collection of sewing patterns listed by manufacturer, style, or size. Shop online for your patterns and have them delivered to your door.

Sew News

http://www.sewnews.com

Read articles from this sewing magazine, share information and ideas with others through the discussion forums, and link to other sewing sites through this one.

A Sewing Web

http://www.sewweb.com/

Provides quality industrial sewing supplies to professional sewers all over the world, including industrial sewing thread, sewing machine presser feet, sewing accessories, and more.

A
B
C
D
E
F
G
H
I
J
K
L
M
N
O
P
Q
R
S
T
U
V
W
X
Y
Z

A
B
C
D
E
F
G
H
I
J
K
L
M
N
O
P
Q
R
S
T
U
V
W
X
Y
Z

Sewing.com

http://www.sewing.com/

Find sewing instruction from other sewing community members as well as links to sites providing lessons, as well as book reviews, articles, and discussions. Comprehensive sewing dictionary, too.

Threads Magazine

http://www.taunton.com/threads/index.asp

Threads is the creative forum where people who sew and love to work with fabrics and fibers share their knowledge. The Feature Library offers links for Sewing Basics, Garment Construction, Fabric, Fitting, and more. Packed with step-by-step instructions, tips from the experts, and online videos that show you how it's done.

Vy's Sewing Site

http://www.geocities.com/Heartland/4456/sewing.html

Find new sewing projects, learn about sewing machine maintenance, and surf more than 600 sewing sites at this rich site.

Wild Ginger Software

http://www.wildginger.com/

Home of Wild Ginger Software, a company that develops sewing software for customizing patterns. You can download a free demo at this site.

MACHINES

Baby Lock

http://www.babylock.com/

Learn more about Baby Lock brand machines, find projects you can complete with your Baby Lock, and local dealers and events.

Bernina USA

http://www.berninausa.com/

Official corporate site for Bernina sewing machines. Product information, dealer listing, new products, and more.

Creative Feet

http://www.creativefeet.com/

Founder of the company, Clare Rowley-Greene, invented Creative Feet in order to enable visually impaired individuals to sew using a standard sewing machine. Since creating the first presser feet designs, Clare has widened her focus to create presser feet that simplify the sewing of specialized stitches. The site offers information about the presser feet designs, as well as other sewing products, such as books and videos.

Elna USA

http://www.elnausa.com/

Developers of sewing machines, sergers, embroidery machines, presses, and sewing accessories. Product information, dealer locations, and more.

Husqvarna Viking

http://www.husqvarnaviking.com/

Learn more about Husqvarna, its products, and dealers, as well as educational retreats and free projects available at the site.

Pfaff Sewing Machines

http://www.pfaff.com/

Official corporate site for Pfaff sewing machines.

Sewing Machine Outlet

http://
www.sewingmachineoutlet.com/

Source for new and used sewing
machines, needles, sewing machine
parts, and more.

Singer Machines

http://www.singersew.com/

Wide variety of Singer-brand
sewing machines, prices, product
information, and more.

PATTERNS

Angel Baby Designs – Sewing Patterns for Your Home

http://www.angelbabydesigns.com/

You will find all kinds of information
about sewing and various patterns
for your family, children and pet
beds, and for just about everything
else.

Butterick Home Catalog

http://www.butterick.com

Preview the Butterick Home Catalog
or subscribe from their site.

Free Patterns Online

http://sewing.about.com/hobbies/
sewing/msubfree.htm

Visit this Mining Company site to
find a number of free patterns
available for downloading.

McCall's Pattern Catalog

http://www.mccall.com/
catalog.html

Order your own copy of McCall's
catalog and receive free patterns.

Simplicity

http://www.simplicity.com/

Flip through the latest Simplicity
pattern book for ideas for this season's fashions and get sewing help
online here.

Vogue Patterns

http://www.voguepatterns.com/

Online catalog, pattern magazine,
tech center, and a listing of retail
shops that sell Vogue patterns and
craft patterns.

A
B
C
D
E
F
G
H
I
J
K
L
M
N
O
P
Q
R
S
T
U
V
W
X
Y
Z

A
B
C
D
E
F
G
H
I
J
K
L
M
N
O
P
Q
R
S
T
U
V
W
X
Y
Z

SEXUALITY

AltSex

http://www.altsex.org/

A Web site dedicated to sharing and exploring information related to sexuality and sexual issues, such as homosexuality, sexual conduct, and transgender issues.

Australian Love & Sexuality

http://www.sexualitybytes.com/

A wide range of text and graphical information intended to provide a greater understanding of sex and sexual health.

Coalition for Positive Sexuality

http://www.positive.org/Home/

Subtitled "sex ed for your head," this site is an honest affirmation of safe sex between consenting individuals.

Dr. Ruth Online!

http://webcenter.drruth.aol.com/DrRuth/

Ask Dr. Ruth a question that's been bugging you, or read her responses to others who've written in for sex guidance. There are daily tips, too.

Gender and Sexuality

http://eserver.org/gender/

This page publishes texts that address gender studies and homosexuality studies, with a particular focus upon discussions of sex, gender, sexual identity, and sexuality in cultural practices.

Go Ask Alice!: Sexuality

http://www.goaskalice.columbia.edu/Cat6.html

Read frequently asked questions about male and female anatomy and sexual response at this site.

Guide to Love and Sex

http://www.loveandsex.com/

Tips on love, sex, romance, dating, and birth control. Offers free stuff such as product samples and electronic post cards.

HisandHerhealth.com

http://www.hisandherhealth.com/

Read current research findings regarding male and female reproductive health and sexuality, as well as joining in chat, asking the doctor for guidance, and scanning articles and news.

Impotence Specialists

http://www.impotencespecialists.com

Find an impotence specialist online, read through FAQs about impotence and potential treatments, or post a question for a doctor on the bulletin board and check back for an answer.

intimategifts.com

http://www.intimategifts.com/

Order sex toys, books, lubricants, videos, and other accessories and gifts for loving couples here.

Nerve.com

http://www.nerve.com

Online magazine that celebrates the beauty and absurdity of sex through thought-provoking, and very funny articles on various topics relating to human relationships and sexuality. View photographs, read personal essays, check out Nerve's fiction and poetry, check out the personals, get advice, or check out the message boards to view questions and opinions from other fans of Nerve.

Oxygen's Relationships and Sex

http://www.oxygen.com/sex

Articles on all topics of sexuality, plus chat, message boards, quizzes, polls, and contests.

 ### Sexual Health infoCenter

http://www.sexhealth.org/

Online reading room and multimedia center for everything related to human sexuality. Guides on how to have better sex, sex and aging, STDs, safe sex, sexual dysfunction, and birth control. Discussion forums for having your questions answered. Links to intimategifts.com for online shopping. With its extensive coverage of nearly every topic relating to human sexuality, this site is well deserving as one of our best of the best sites.

SexualHealth.com

http://www.sexualhealth.com/

You'll find lots of questions regarding sex, as well as answers from professionals, to help you understand your own issues and options. You can post your own questions, get recommended reading, and scan articles on sex topics.

Sexuality Database

http://www.sexualitydata.com

Search the online sexuality database to get more information about topics you're interested in, or concerned about. There are also FAQs and the opportunity to ask a question of a doctor. Created and maintained by the Sinclair Intimacy Institute.

Sexuality Forum

http://www.askisadora.com/

Check the article archive for sexuality subjects you're interested in and, if you don't find what you're looking for, post a question to the public forum. You can also buy products that have been carefully selected by Isadora, the site's host.

Sexuality Information and Education Council of the U.S.

http://www.siecus.org/

SIECUS is a national, nonprofit organization that affirms that sexuality is a natural and healthy part of living. Provides information for parents and teens in an easy-to-understand format that's designed to educate visitors about sexuality and safe sex practices.

Sexuality.org

http://www.sexuality.org/

You'll find articles and material designed to educate and inform visitors regarding sexuality issues. There are technique tips, book reviews, and event information.

A
B
C
D
E
F
G
H
I
J
K
L
M
N
O
P
Q
R
S
T
U
V
W
X
Y
Z

308

A
B
C
D
E
F
G
H
I
J
K
L
M
N
O
P
Q
R
S
T
U
V
W
X
Y
Z

SHOPPING

Amazon.com

http://www.amazon.com/

This well-known online bookstore offers just about every title under the sun, as well as videos, music, software, electronics, gardening equipment, toys, kitchen paraphernalia, and more. The Amazon auction site provides a wide variety of items available from Amazon members.

BargainDog

http://www.bargaindog.com/

Bargain Dog hunts down the best bargains on the Internet and sends you an email notice, so you'll never miss a deal you can't pass up.

Buy.com

http://www.buy.com/

Buy videos, music, software, books, games, computers, electronics, and travel services at a discount from this site. Pick a category and search the database to find the product you're looking for.

CatalogLink

http://www.cataloglink.com/

Select the catalogs you want to receive from the categories at this site to help you with your home shopping. There are also several links to the companies' home pages for online shopping.

Half.com

http://half.ebay.com/

Buy used items at 50% off or more from individuals who have them available. Unlike auctions, you're guaranteed to get the product if it's advertised. Books, music, movies, and games are available.

Inshop.com

http://www.inshop.com/

Search online for products you want, check to find the best deal, and then visit your local store to buy it. You can also learn about upcoming local special events and sales.

iQVC

http://www.qvc.com/

The granddaddy of home shopping networks. You can buy clothing, jewelry, electronics, home decor items, office supplies, fitness equipment, and more at this site.

Lycos Shopping Network

http://shop.lycos.com/

A good point of entry, this site includes an impressive list of shopping categories as well as special features such as Aardvark, the online shopping experience with gifts for pets and the people who love them, and Andy's garage, gift ideas for men. Find the department store you are looking for from here.

Netmarket.com

http://www.netmarket.com/

Search this database of more than 800,000 items to find what you're looking for. Daily special deals offer great prices, and you can sign up for a personal shopper to take care of your shopping for you. The site's goal is to save you time by bringing together tons of merchandise. Because it achieves both goals and does it with style, we award it our best of the best designation.

Outlets Online

http://www.outletsonline.com/

Provides nationwide information on outlet and factory store shopping. Includes Virtual Outlets, which allow you to order merchandise or request catalogs from online outlet stores. An online magazine and Q&A from other readers let you get in touch with fellow shoppers.

Shopping the World

http://www.shoppingtheworld.com/

Shop some of the biggest names in designer fashion, located around the world, through this site. Click on the city you want to shop in, and then skim the current merchandise in search of what you want—all without an airline ticket. In addition to NYC and Los Angeles, you can visit shops in London, too.

CLOTHING

Bloomingdale's

http://www.bloomingdales.com/

Includes online shopping, shopping by catalog, and shopping by personal shopper. The events page tells about upcoming sales and seasonal happenings in its various stores. Get design and style tips from the home design experts page.

DELiAs.com

http://www.delias.com

Request a catalog or shop online referring to catalog pages or a clothing item. You can also hang out in the lounge and chat, look at pictures, and enter contests. Popular with high school girls.

Designer Outlet.com

http://www.designeroutlet.com/

Every two weeks new designer fashions are made available at this site, which aims to bring designer samples and overstocks to the world. Search by category, look at photos of items for sale, or sign up for a personal shopper to keep her eyes open for that perfect item.

Eddie Bauer

http://www.eddiebauer.com/eb/default.asp

Search the site to check out Eddie Bauer's latest casual wear for men and women, request a catalog, or see what's on sale this week.

A
B
C
D
E
F
G
H
I
J
K
L
M
N
O
P
Q
R
S
T
U
V
W
X
Y
Z

A
B
C
D
E
F
G
H
I
J
K
L
M
N
O
P
Q
R
S
T
U
V
W
X
Y
Z

Fashionmall.com

http://www.fashionmall.com/

Shop by brand, category, or style for fashions from a wide variety of merchants online. You can also enter drawings for free merchandise, check out recommended purchases, and tune in for chats with designers and celebrities.

HerRoom.com

http://www.herroom.com/

No matter what kind of undergarment you prefer, underwire bras, thongs, or half-slips, this is the site you'll want to check out. Search for products by brand, style, or size.

L.L. Bean

http://www.llbean.com/

Search L.L. Bean's selection of apparel and sporting gear online.

Land's End

http://www.landsend.com/cd/frontdoor/

Land's End, recently purchased by Sears, Roebuck and Company, offers decorations, kids' stuff, pet gifts, home accessories, and more. A good-quality mail-order merchandiser with a nicely designed Web site.

NYStyle

http://www.nystyle.com

This Web site features articles on current events in fashion with a shopping service for clothing accessories and household items. In addition, there is an online magazine that features an archive of previous editions.

COMPARISON BOTS

BizRate

http://www.bizrate.com/

Comparison-shopping service that helps you find the best prices from online merchants who carry the products you want. Features customer ratings, too, to help you find online stores that offer reliable customer service.

DealTime.com

http://www.dealtime.com/

Choose a product and DealTime searches for the best prices among many online merchants and auctions. If you're not ready to buy right away, DealTime will keep you posted on specials and new options.

mySimon

http://www.mysimon.com

Search for products by keyword or brand and then let MySimon provide you with a list of online merchants who carry it and their quoted price.

NexTag

http://www.nextag.com

Unlike other comparison shopping sites, this site lets you negotiate with sellers after collecting total quoted prices from several. Sellers are online merchants and individuals.

Pricegrabber.com

http://www.pricegrabber.com/

Find the stuff you want for the best price on the Web. Search for specific products or browse through several categories. Pricegrabber finds the store that offers the item for the best price. Enter your ZIP Code to add shipping and handling charges.

PriceScan

http://www.pricescan.com/

Click on a category and then specify the particular product you're looking for and PriceScan will provide a list of all online merchants who have it, organized by total cost, which includes shipping and handling fees.

Productopia

http://www.productopia.com

Read user reviews and join in product discussions before searching the site for a purchase. You'll also find recommended gifts to get you started.

RoboShopper.com

http://www.roboshopper.com

Pick a category, pick a product, and RoboShopper presents you with the merchants carrying that product and the associated price. You can then jump from site to site, comparing total product cost information.

DISCOUNT STORES

Kmart

http://www.bluelight.com/

Get the latest Kmart corporate news, as well as information about the Kmart celebrities, community outreach programs, the Baby of Mine Club, the Kmart cash card, and the Kmart credit card. You can also take a virtual tour through Kmart, view the current sales circular, enter a sweepstakes, and locate a store near you. Their Find a Product option makes it easy to search their site.

Overstock.com

http://www.overstock.com

Search for brand-name bargains at this site, which offers just about everything—from computers to home décor to clothing—at a discount. Overstocked merchants mean great deals for consumers. But beware—the selection is limited.

Sam's Club

http://www.samsclub.com/eclub/main_home.jsp

Learn all about Sam's Club and member benefits, locate a Sam's Club near you, purchase a membership, and shop securely with Sam's Club Online. Also find out what's new at the club and join the Product Forum.

Target

http://www.target.com

A sharp site detailing all of Target's programs and offerings, such as the Lullaby Club, Club Wedd, Take Charge of Education, School Fundraising Made Simple, 5% Back to the Community, TREATSEATS, the Target Guest Card, and various guest services. You can even access sound clips of new music available at Target.

Wal-Mart Online

http://www.wal-mart.com/

Find Wal-Mart product and price information at this site, and order your goodies online. Search the store for what you want; you'll be rewarded with photos and details on each item. Also, locate the Wal-Mart nearest you.

A
B
C
D
E
F
G
H
I
J
K
L
M
N
O
P
Q
R
S
T
U
V
W
X
Y
Z

A
B
C
D
E
F
G
H
I
J
K
L
M
N
O
P
Q
R
S
T
U
V
W
X
Y
Z

JEWELRY

Ashford.com

http://www.ashford.com

Specializing in watches, but also offering other luxury goods, Ashford provides guidance in selecting gifts and gives customers access to some of the top brands, all in one place.

First Jewelry

http://www.firstjewelry.com

Search this designer jewelry site by typing in a keyword or clicking on a category to view images of a wide variety of pieces, including rings, necklaces, bracelets, earrings, and watches. You can also read articles and get gift ideas here.

Mondera

http://www.mondera.com/

Home of "Fine diamonds and timeless jewelry," this site features great deals on high-quality jewelry, plus advice from the experts. Great place to shop for wedding rings, anniversary gifts, or surprises for that special someone.

NetJewels.com

http://www.netjewels.com/

Excellent selection of rings, necklaces, bracelets, watches, and other jewelry at good prices. Use the navigation bar at the top of the screen to pick the type of jewelry you want. Shop online and have your order shipped to your home. Check back often for rebate deals and free gifts.

PERFUME

FragranceNet

http://www.fragrancenet.com/

FragranceNet boasts that it is "The world's largest discount fragrance store." With more than 1,000 genuine brand names at up to 70% off retail, it might well be. The attractive, well-designed site also offers free gift wrapping and free shipping, a gift reminder service, a search engine, and the chance to enter to win a $100 shopping spree, and more.

Perfume Center

http://www.perfumecenter.com/main.htm

This store offers more than 1,200 original brand-name fragrances for both men and women. You can place your order online or call their toll-free phone number, which is prominently featured on the opening page.

Perfumes Direct

http://www.perfumesdirect.com/

Offers an extensive selection of men's and women's perfumes. You can search their site or select a category (women's fragrances) to get started. Secure online ordering and toll-free phone orders make it easy to shop. Free shipping in the United States.

Smell This

http://www.smellthis.com/

They are not shy about their philosophy, which is, in a nutshell, "perfume sucks." Smell This is the alternative line of fragrance products for the mind, body, and home. These scents are based on familiar smells we all identify with such as baby powder, the beach, canned peaches, cut grass, soda pop fizz, fresh towels, chocolate brownies... you get the idea. You can order online, read through FAQs, find a store that carries the line, and more.

Uncommon Scents

http://uncommonscents.com/

In their 26th year of specializing in luxurious, natural, custom-scented body care products. Choose from more than 70 fragrances inspired by nature or shop for natural bath and body care products from around the world. Toll-free phone and fax ordering available in addition to the online shopping option. Most products can be custom scented at no additional charge to you!

SEARCH ENGINES

Buyer's Index

http://www.buyersindex.com/

Search 20,000 shopping sites and mail order catalogs offering more than 153 million products for consumers and businesses. Use keywords, product names, or company names to begin your search.

ShopGuide

http://www.shopguide.com/

When you search this site, which consists of more than 20,000 online store sites all rolled into one, you'll find what you're looking for and learn about specials, discounts, coupons, freebies, and incentives.

Shopnow.com

http://www.internetmall.com/

Comparison shop by searching through categories of products and services at this site, or link to other shopping sites of interest.

Yahoo! Shopping

http://www.shopfind.com/

A search engine devoted to making your online shopping experience more satisfying. You simply enter items you want to purchase, and ShopFind returns a detailed list of places to start. Site is simple and easy to use.

SPECIALTY

eBags.com

http://www.ebags.com/

This site specializes in bags of all types—for computers, clothes, and sporting gear. You can find wallets, duffel bags, and bags for kids in all materials.

Fogdog

http://www.fogdog.com

Basketball, baseball, and football fans will want to check out this site for the equipment they need to play well. But there is plenty of other gear for sports enthusiasts who like golf, badminton, tennis, and just about every other sport around. Apparel, equipment, and footwear can all be found here.

A
B
C
D
E
F
G
H
I
J
K
L
M
N
O
P
Q
R
S
T
U
V
W
X
Y
Z

A
B
C
D
E
F
G
H
I
J
K
L
M
N
O
P
Q
R

S
T
U
V
W
X
Y
Z

Harry and David

http://www.harryanddavid.com/

This site belongs to the company that has the best pears found anywhere in the world. Anything you order here will be appreciated and devoured.

House Mouse Specialty Shopping

http://www.housemouse.twoffice.com/

This specialty shopping site claims to have the lowest prices anywhere for Christmas decorations, jewelry, collector plates, porcelain collectibles, toys, and many other items, including spun-glass figurines.

Ikea.com

http://ikea.com/

Request a copy of this year's catalog of inexpensive but well-designed furniture from IKEA or search the online product listings. You can also locate a store nearest you and get technical assistance in assembling your purchases.

InnoGear

http://www.innogear.com/

Specializing in portable digital gear, InnoGear is focused on serving generation Next. This is a great place to check out the latest innovations, including MP3 players and handheld computer accessories.

Reel.com

http://www.reel.com/

Movie buffs will want to check out this site for access to more than 100,000 movies and DVD titles available for purchase through buy.com. The site provides lots of assistance in deciding which movies to buy through the use of reviews, interviews with stars, trailers, and synopses.

Soap Specialty Shop

http://www.soapspecialtyshop.com/

Carries all natural, organic soaps, including soap made from maize, oatmeal, bran, cocoa butter, lavender, and chamomile, just to name a few.

The SPORTS Authority

http://www.thesportsauthority.com

Brand-name sporting good merchandise is available at this site in more than 1,000 categories, for just about every activity imaginable. Apparel, equipment, and footwear are all here. There is also an auction section where you can bid on used equipment.

World Traveler Luggage and Travel Goods

http://www.worldtraveler.com/

A discount site for online ordering of sporting goods, luggage, business and computer cases, and travel accessories. Shop by product or by brand—whichever you find easier. Lowest, direct-to-consumer prices on major brands. Money-back guarantee.

SIGN LANGUAGE/ DEAF RESOURCES

Alexander Graham Bell Association for Deaf and Hard of Hearing

http://www.agbell.org/

Learn more about membership benefits of this international organization, which was established to serve parents of deaf and hard-of-hearing children. You'll find information on local chapters, publications, and financial assistance here.

ASL Access

http://www.aslaccess.org/

Information about American Sign Language videos and how to order them is available here, as well as information about supporting the group's efforts to get more ASL videos into public libraries.

ASL Fingerspelling

http://www.where.com/scott.net/asl/

A great finger spelling dictionary is available here, as well as a converter, which provides the correct finger spelling for any word you type into the directory. You can also take a quiz to test your knowledge.

Captioned Media Program

http://www.cfv.org/

CMP lends open captioned videos to members who complete an application form, enabling them to borrow videos on a wide variety of topics, for school, for entertainment, or information.

Communications Unlimited

http://www.communltd.net/

Communications Unlimited is a deaf-owned business that sells telecommunications (TTYs/TDDs—text telephones) equipment and notification alerts, amplified telephones, and assistive listening devices for the deaf and hard-of-hearing community. Search the online product catalog to find what you need.

Deaf Resources

http://www.deafresources.com/

This site offers a variety of home décor items and gifts using ASL as the theme. Baby blankets, for example, are embroidered with the ASL sign for "I love you." You'll find jewelry, jackets, videos, tote bags, and many other interesting items.

Gallaudet University

http://www.gallaudet.edu/

Get information about this university established for the deaf, learning about faculty, students, events, curriculum, and how to apply.

Handspeak.com

http://www.handspeak.com/

Complete resource for learning how to sign, this site includes a dictionary with video clips showing how to sign most words. Features a sight of the day and links to additional resources.

A
B
C
D
E
F
G
H
I
J
K
L
M
N
O
P
Q
R
S
T
U
V
W
X
Y
Z

Helen Keller National Center for Deaf-Blind Youth

http://www.helenkeller.org/national/

The Helen Keller Center provides evaluation and training in vocational skills, adaptive technology and computer skills, orientation and mobility, independent living, communication, speech-language skills, creative arts, fitness and leisure activities for deaf-blind youth. Learn more about the center and its work here.

 ### National Association of the Deaf (NAD)

http://www.nad.org

This national nonprofit organization provides grassroots advocacy and empowerment for deaf individuals, captioned media, certification of American Sign Language professionals and interpreters, deafness-related information and publications, legal assistance, and policy development and research. The group also works to improve awareness of issues specific to deaf individuals. This site's straightforward presentation and excellent information combine to make it the best resource for hearing-impaired people on the Web.

SignWritingSite

http://www.signwriting.org

Learn more about SignWriting, which enables people to read and learn using sign language, including taking lessons and joining in discussion forums about its use. There is a search engine and online library for further research and learning.

Zoos Software

http://www.zoosware.com/

Learning American Sign Language (ASL) is now easier with this software package for Palm devices. The software enables you to study the sign language alphabets and numbers at your own pace. After you're more familiar, you can type in the words and PalmASL will show you the words using American Sign Language.

SKATING

Riedell Skates

http://www.riedellskates.com

Get information about Riedell skates for hockey, figure skating, inline skating, speed or roller skating, and pick up some tips and techniques for improving your performance and caring for your skates.

SkatesAway.com

http://www.skatepro.com/catalog/

A huge selection of skates and parts are available at this site, as well as special deals and closeouts.

FIGURE SKATING

International Figure Skating Magazine (IFS)

http://www.ifsmagazine.com/

Get the scoop on the latest news in figure skating through the online version of this print magazine. Read about the stars, their challenges, results of recent competitions, sporting news, and chat online with other fans.

Stars On Ice

http://www.starsonice.com/

Learn more about the cast of skaters in the year's Stars on Ice performance and get news regarding the tour here. You can also get ticket information and performance dates.

INLINE SKATING

Get Rolling

http://www.getrolling.com/

Find out about skating books, classes, camps, workshops, magazines, and more through the resources section of this site, which was established to help all skaters improve their skill and enjoyment of the sport.

International Inline Skating Association

http://www.iisa.org/

Learn to skate, find places to skate safely, pick up rules of the road, meet fellow skaters—all through this site. In addition, you can get news and information about the sport. Lots of information you'll want to look into.

Skatepile.com

https://www.skatepile.com/

💲

One-stop shop for inline skates, parts, accessories, videos. Features advice from the masters, profiles of some of the best inline skaters around, videos, trick tips, setup tips, and a photo gallery. For skates, accessories, and tips, there's no better place on the Web.

Skating.com

http://www.skating.com/

A place for sharing information about where to skate, what you think of particular brands and models of skates, as well as a place to sell old equipment, ask questions of more experienced skaters, read profiles of skating legends, and read the latest skating news.

Zephyr Inline Skate Tours

http://www.skatetour.com/

Get information about skating tours and vacations here, where you can request a guide by mail or scan the basic details online.

A
B
C
D
E
F
G
H
I
J
K
L
M
N
O
P
Q
R
S
T
U
V
W
X
Y
Z

A
B
C
D
E
F
G
H
I
J
K
L
M
N
O
P
Q
R
S
T
U
V
W
X
Y
Z

SKIN CARE/COSMETICS

Acne Treatment

http://www.acnetreatment.com

Basic information about diet, prescription drugs, over-the-counter products, stress, and other factors.

Acne Treatment, Prevention, and Products

http://4acne.4anything.com/

This site offers you a chance to purchase books and other skin care products related to acne. You get information on skin care, acne removal, treatments, and how to prevent acne. There are various links relating to the subject and you can purchase an excellent book on the subject written by a dermatologist.

Dermatology Images: University of Iowa

http://tray.dermatology
.uiowa.edu/DermImag.htm

The Image Database of the Department of Dermatology of the University of Iowa provides you with information about common skin disorders and images of what they look like. This site will help you to identify most forms of skin problems but you should consult your dermatologist if you think you have a problem. Nevertheless, the site is very informative. Not for those with weak stomachs.

National Rosacea Society

http://www.rosacea.org

Information on the skin problem, including the Rosacea Review, a

hotline, links to Web sites, and other areas.

Neutrogena

http://www.neutrogena.com

Skin care products, special offers, and advice. S.O.S. section lists links to common skin problems; click a link to find solutions and products that can help. If the problem you have is not listed, click the Ask Neutrogena link to post the question to a dermatologist.

⟦Best⟧ Patient Resources on Skin Conditions

http://www.execpc.com/~stjos/
skin.html

Information on acne, contact dermatitis, scabies, and other conditions. This site isn't the usual "flashy" Web page that you would normally expect on the Internet but it does have all or most of the information you would need to know about skin care with many interesting articles on the subject. Probably its best feature is the fact that you can access it and find the information you need, and it is all quick and easy. Just a few of the many subjects discussed include Acne, AIDS, Rashes, Athlete's Foot, Dermatitis, and Eczema. Each subject is categorized alphabetically which makes it easy to find. When you need information about skin care and you don't know where to turn, turn to this site.

Problems and Diseases of the Skin

http://cpmcnet.columbia.edu/texts/guide/hmg28_0003.html

Prevention, causes, home remedies, alternative therapies, and related information on disorders such as acne, hair loss, and more.

Skin Culture Peel

http://www.skinculture.com

Manufactures and sells skin peel products. This site features an online form you can fill out to determine your skin type, information about skin peels, and an online store where you can purchase various skin peel products.

COSMETICS

Avon

http://shop.avon.com/

Having trouble finding the Avon Lady in your neighborhood? Then go directly to Avon online. Avon carries a complete line of beauty aids, cosmetics, and jewelry. Shop online and have your order shipped to your door.

beautyjungle.com

http://www.beautyjungle.com/beautyjungle/main.asp

Whether you like elite cosmetic brands or purely natural, you're likely to be able to find them here among the 10,000 products available. You can also learn more about celebrity beauty routines so you can copy them.

Cosmetic Connection

http://www.cosmeticconnection.com/

Read feature articles on beauty trends, techniques, application tips, and other seasonal information in the articles section, and then search for product reviews in the library before investing your hard-earned money in products that don't work as you want them to. Sign up for the free cosmetic report newsletter to get the skinny on the products you've been hearing about.

Cosmetic Mall

http://www.cosmeticmall.com

Shop by brand or department, such as face or aromatherapy, for your favorite products. Or get advice and tips on what you should be using.

drugstore.com

http://www.drugstore.com/

Search for skin care products by use or brand here and have them shipped directly to you. There are also fragrance and cosmetics available here.

eve.com

http://www.sephora.com/

Search for products to address your beauty challenges by typing in keywords, or looking by brand. There is advice, gift ideas, and product information galore. Sephora is the leading retail beauty chain in Europe. And now they're here in the United States. Discover more about the company and the innovative stores, and learn more about

A
B
C
D
E
F
G
H
I
J
K
L
M
N
O
P
Q
R
S
T
U
V
W
X
Y
Z

A
B
C
D
E
F
G
H
I
J
K
L
M
N
O
P
Q
R
S
T
U
V
W
X
Y
Z

Sephora's family of companies, including Sephora.com, Sephora USA, and the parent company, LVMH.

If you are looking for a Sephora store near you, take a look at their Store Directory and their new store openings. There is a nice store with areas on Fragrance, Makeup, Magazines, Bath & Body, Tools & Accessories, Gifts, and Treatments.

Faceart

http://www.faceart.com/

Created by makeup junkies for makeup junkies, this site features articles on creative makeup projects. Sections on eye art, lip art, hair art, and more. Read the feature articles, find answers to your makeup questions, or visit the Makeupshop for how-to videos.

iBeauty.com

http://www10.ibeauty.com/index.jsp

Here you can order beauty products as well as receive personalized answers to your beauty questions, and your horoscope.

Mary Kay

http://www.marykay.com/

Learn how to get the look you want with makeup through the Virtual Makeover section of this site, which shows you pictures of models having makeup applied in various ways. You can also learn more about various Mary Kay products and locate a local consultant, if you don't already have one.

SNOW SKIING

Altrec.com

http://www.altrec.com/shop/dir/ski/

Skiing, snowboarding, cycling, hiking, hunting, and fishing, and other outdoor adventure sports. Altrec carries all the gear you need for most adventure sports, including skiing. Site also features some articles and comparison shops.

Austria Ski Vacation Packages

http://www.snowpak.com/snowpak/resorts/austriaresorts.html

Part of the Snow Pak Online site. Get quotes for ski vacation packages in

Austria, and plan your dream vacation. Be sure to register for full-color brochures to be mailed to you and check out the live resort cams.

Boston Mills-Brandywine Ski Resort

http://www.bmbw.com/

Located in the Cleveland/Akron area of Ohio, these two ski resorts operate jointly. Check out their Web site for powder and weather reports, available services, rental fees, night skiing information, and lots more.

Cool Works' Ski Resorts and Ski/Snowboard Country Jobs

http://www.coolworks.com/
skirsrts.htm

Ever wondered how those ski instructors get such cool jobs? Check out this site. Pick a state. Pick a resort. Pick a job. Spend the winter playing at your dream job. There are links here to other cool jobs in state parks, on cruise ships, and in camps. Definitely check this out.

CRN: Colorado Resort Net

http://www.discovercolorado.com/
CRNMAIN.HTM

Serves as a guide to Colorado resort communities, including hotels, restaurants, arts, events, real estate, and shopping information.

GoSki.com

http://www.goski.com/

Get more information about ski resorts around the world, plan your next ski vacation, look at product reviews, check the weather, and check the headlines before you head out.

Hyperski

http://www.hyperski.com/

Find out about snow conditions and special packages. Also read the articles about picking the right pair of skis, snow-cat skiing, skid chains, and skiing in Austria. This page has a little more than the usual.

K2 Skis

http://www.k2skis.com/

Visit this site to check out the complete line of K2 skis or use the ski selector to find a pair that matches your needs. Use the Dealer Locator to find a dealer near you.

Las Lenas Ski Packages

http://www.snowpak.com/snowpak/
resorts/laslenas.html

Skiing in Argentina might not be something you've considered before. Check out this page to discover what's available. Get a quote for your vacation plans. Check this one out. It's a little different, but you might like it.

Outdoor REVIEW

http://www.outdoorreview.com/

Read or write your own reviews of skis, gear, and resorts. You can also pick up some basic skiing tips, chat with other skiers, check road reports, submit photos from mountains you've skied, and link to other hot sites.

Over the Hill Gang

http://www.skiersover50.com/

If you're over 50 and enjoy skiing and other outdoor activities, check out this site. The Over the Hill Gang provides discounts on everything from lift tickets to lodging and ski shop purchases. The group also plans trips to North American, South American, and European ski areas. In the summer, there's whitewater rafting, bicycling, hiking, and golf. If one spouse is over 50, you both qualify for membership.

Salomon Sports

http://www.salomonsports.com/

Home of some of the most popular skis and snowboards, this site provides product information, information about famous skiers, and links to Salomon ski magazines and sites.

A
B
C
D
E
F
G
H
I
J
K
L
M
N
O
P
Q
R
S
T
U
V
W
X
Y
Z

A
B
C
D
E
F
G
H
I
J
K
L
M
N
O
P
Q
R
S
T
U
V
W
X
Y
Z

⎡Best⎤ SkiCentral

http://www.skicentral.com/

Check out the #1 search and index site for skiers and snowboarders on the Internet. You'll find 8,000 snow sports sites, ski reports, resorts, snowcams, travel packages, equipment, and more. So, before planning your trip to the "white mountains of fun and pleasure," check out what this site has to offer.

They have categories on Snowsport Sites, Find Gear, Resort Lodging, Ski Packages, Free Ski Photographs, Resorts & Travel, Lodging, Trip Planning, Skiing, Snowboarding, Snow Reports, Snowcams, News & Views, Sites by Region, Contests, Employment, and even Trail Maps.

Skiing in Jackson Hole

http://www.jacksonholenet.com/ski/

Extensive information about travel and lodging, the usual weather and powder reports, and information about four different ski resorts: Snow King, Grand Targhee, Jackson Hole, and White Pine. There's also a unique bit of information about ski safety, road safety, and spring skiing safety—along with tips on keeping warm.

SkiNet

http://www.skinet.com/

The editors of Ski Magazine and Skiing Magazine present snow reports, resort profiles, gear information, and news.

St. Moritz Ski Page

http://www.ifyouski.fr/

Get an honest appraisal of the world's most luxurious ski accommodations. Find out what to really expect in St. Moritz, what's available to entertain the children, and what to do at night. There's also the usual information about trail conditions and weather, as well as links to other European ski areas.

Stowe Mountain Resort

http://www.stowe.com/

Find out about upcoming package deals at Stowe, Vermont. The latest weather and powder conditions are here, along with FAQs, information about lessons, and directions to the resort.

The U.S. Ski Home Team Page

http://www.usskiteam.com/

The official page for the U.S. Ski Team. Stay informed about all the doings of the ski team all the time, not just during the Olympics. There's also World Cup news, selection criteria, and more official news.

SNOWMOBILING

A
B
C
D
E
F
G
H
I
J
K
L
M
N
O
P
Q
R
S
T
U
V
W
X
Y
Z

American Snowmobiler Magazine

http://www.amsnow.com

Up-to-date information about snowmobiling and the snowmobile industry. Includes current news, a racing guide, a travel guide, and more.

Arctic Cat

http://www.arctic-cat.com

Arctic Cat company's official site, with product information on snowmobiles, watercraft, and ATVs—plus safety information and dealer links.

Greg's Comparison Page

http://www.odyssey.on.ca/
~gsmulders/snow/compare/
compare.htm

Snowmobile comparison charts. Categories include top performance, trail performance, sport, and mountain.

International Snowmobile Manufacturers Association

http://www.snowmobile.org

Timely information about the sport of snowmobiling in North America and Europe. Features articles, stats & facts, and information on snowmobile safety. Links to other sites, as well.

Maine Snowmobile Connection

http://www.sledmaine.com

Accommodations, trail reports, clubs, sled rentals, and other information for would-be Maine snowmobilers.

Northern Michigan Snowmobiling

http://www.michiweb.com/
snowmobile/

Northern Michigan snow and trail reports, featured regions, rentals, stops, and more.

Polaris Industries

http://www.polarisindustries.com

Maker of snowmobiles, watercraft, and ATVs. Product information, latest news, annual report, and employment opportunities.

Ski-Doo

http://www.ski-doo.com

Official site for Ski-Doo snowmobile manufacturer. Includes product information, safety tips, and links.

Best Snowmobile Online

http://www.off-road.com/
snowmobile/

Read the latest snowmobiling news, stay up to date on land use issues that threaten snowmobilers' access to parks and other areas, find places to ride, read product reviews and lots of other information about snowmobiling here. Snowmobilers will want to bookmark this best of the best snowmobiling site for quick return trips.

Snowmobiling.net

http://www.snowmobiling.net

Snowmobilers load up on links, classified ads, electronic shopping services, message boards, and news.

Yamaha Motor Corporation

http://www.yamaha-motor.com/

Official corporate site of Yamaha Motor Corporation, USA, maker of snowmobiles, watercraft, ATVs, boats, racing karts, and more. Includes product and competition information.

SOCCER

[Best] AlphaSoccer

http://www.alphasoccer.com/

This is your one-stop place to find out about soccer with various links to clubs, leagues, associations, players, and other interesting information about soccer. Convinced me and I'm not a sports fan. This comprehensive directory to everything related to soccer even provides links to various places online where you can purchase equipment, apparel, books, videos, and other soccer-related items. Although not the easiest soccer site to navigate, this site is the best directory of soccer information on the Web.

ATL World Soccer News

http://www.wldcup.com/

Offers world soccer news, commentary, statistics, and scores.

The Daily Soccer

http://www.dailysoccer.com/

The Daily Soccer e-zine features up-to-the-minute news, scores, and statistics from the world of soccer. Content is organized by country, although a searchable players database is available as well. The page also contains links to related sites.

ESPN Soccer

http://espn.go.com/soccer

Provides links to soccer's hot zone, Europe, but also to World Cup qualification coverage worldwide. As Major League Soccer grows in the United States, expect ESPN's current coverage to grow with it.

FIFA Online

http://www.fifa.com/

Official page of soccer's world governing body provides coverage of competitions, press releases, a newsletter, and rules updates.

FIFA World Cup

http://fifaworldcup.yahoo.com

Home of the biggest soccer tournament in the world, this site provides coverage of the most recent World Cup soccer games. Provides a preview of upcoming matches, scores and coverage of recent matches, video highlights, online message boards, and more.

InternetSoccer.com

http://www.internetsoccer.com/

Late-breaking soccer news and scores plus a searchable index of teams and players. Search for news by continents, countries, competitions, or leagues.

Major League Soccer (MLS)

http://www.mlsnet.com/

Get stats, schedules, results, rankings, team information, and images of some of the best shots this season.

Soccer Camps

http://www.soccer-camps.com/

Get the latest scores, schedules, recruiting, information on camps, and much more at this site. You can search for a soccer camp, find registration and pricing information, schedules, and just about anything else you need to know about soccer camps with dozens of camps listed.

The Soccer Home Page

http://www.distrib.com/soccer/

This cool page contains tons of information, from soccer clubs to current standings, events, and game information.

Soccer Information Systems

http://www.soccerinfo.com/

Contains a database of information relating to amateur soccer. Topics include high school soccer, coaching, recruiting, soccer writers, and camps.

Soccer Times

http://www.soccertimes.com/

Up-to-date news on the latest in U.S. and international soccer. Check on your favorite teams and players, explore NCAA soccer, get information on U.S. national teams, and keep abreast of the happenings at the World Cup Soccer tournament.

Soccer Yellow Pages

http://www.tdl.com/~chuckn/soc/soc.html

Lots of listings for soccer sites. This is a good place to go when searching for more information on soccer.

The Soccer-Sites

http://www.soccer-sites.com/

One of the best directory sites dedicated to thousands of soccer sites around the world.

SoccerLynx

http://www.soccerlynx.net/

SoccerLynx is an online resource for soccer gambling. Provides soccer game handicapping and predictions. Links to other sites for placing bets.

U.S. Youth Soccer

http://www.usysa.org/

History of the association, an events calendar, a catalog of U.S. Youth Soccer materials, and addresses of groups across the United States.

A
B
C
D
E
F
G
H
I
J
K
L
M
N
O
P
Q
R
S
T
U
V
W
X
Y
Z

United States Soccer Federation

http://www.ussoccer.com/

The official site of the United States soccer governing body. It provides a history of soccer in the United States, an Olympic recap, a quarterly soccer e-zine, and more. Coaches and referees will find training advice and tips here as well.

World Soccer Page

http://www.wspsoccer.com/

The world soccer page gives you plenty of information about U.S. and international soccer teams, players, games, news, and merchandise.

SOCIAL WORK/SERVICES

AAMFT

http://www.aamft.org/

American Association for Marriage and Family Therapy. Information on marriage and family therapists, and a practice strategy newsletter.

The Carter Center

http://www.cartercenter.org/

Atlanta, Georgia, is where former U.S. president Jimmy Carter and his wife have based their public policy institute. Visit the site to get information about their current and past work, as well as to find out what you can do to help.

Catholic Charities USA

http://www.catholiccharitiesusa.org/

Largest social services organization in America. Site provides description of programs and contact details for local agencies.

Centers for Disease Control and Prevention

http://www.cdc.gov/

Tells about the agency and its services. Links to public health officials and agencies nationwide. Warns travelers of disease outbreaks worldwide. Gives data and statistics. Very informative.

National Association of Alcoholism and Drug Abuse Counselors (NAADAC)

http://naadac.org/

Learn about the NAADAC and its membership, certifications, products, services, resource links, and more.

National Center for Missing and Exploited Children

http://www.missingkids.org/

Offers searchable database records by specific criteria. Short and long indexes of all missing children. Comprehensive site with photographs of some of the children. For even more, click the "Children at Risk" link. Service provided in an attempt to find missing children.

National Children's Coalition (NCC)

http://www.child.net/ncc.htm

Site contains information about National Children's Coalition membership, advocacy for kids and teens, KIDS N' NEED radio-thons, and the new WWW Youth and Children Resource Center and its work with street kids and runaways.

National Civic League

http://www.ncl.org/

When Theodore Roosevelt founded this group with the goal of improving communities, he surely didn't realize how helpful and accessible it would become. This site will link you to mission statements, recent progress in the area, and how you can assist your own community.

Native American Culture and Social System

http://www.greatdreams.com/native.htm

This site contains more information than you can read in one night on the Native American social system and philosophy. There is information on every tribe that has ever existed with detailed descriptions of their thoughts, beliefs, and the way they live. If you are doing research on Native Americans or you just want to understand their social system then this is a great place to start.

New York State Department of Family Assistance

http://www.dfa.state.ny.us/

Formerly the Department of Social Services. You have three categories to choose from: Office of Temporary and Disability Assistance,

General Department of Family Assistance, and Office of Children and Family Services.

SocialService.com

http://www.socialservice.com/

Social workers and other social service professionals looking for a job will want to start here to find a new position, whether you're looking for something in mental health, domestic violence, children, outreach, or just about any other specialty. Employers can also post openings for access by professionals nationwide.

Best Social Work and Social Services Web Sites

http://gwbweb.wustl.edu/websites.html

This directory of services, put together by Washington University in St. Louis, features a robust list of links to social work and social services sites on the Web, categorized into dozens of groups covering everything from Abuse and Violence to Women's Issues. This comprehensive list of resources addresses health issues, psychiatric illnesses, disabilities, family crises, counseling, housing, veteran issues, and much more. When you're looking for help, this is the best place to start.

U.S. Department of Health and Human Services

http://www.os.dhhs.gov

The government's principal agency for protecting the health of Americans and providing essential human services, especially for those who are least able to help themselves. They oversee more than 300 programs.

A B C D E F G H I J K L M N O P Q R S T U V W X Y Z

A
B
C
D
E
F
G
H
I
J
K
L
M
N
O
P
Q
R
S
T
U
V
W
X
Y
Z

VISTA Web

http://www.friendsofvista.org/

Volunteers in Service to America has been around since 1964, and it is now part of the larger AmeriCorps VISTA program. Find out about both groups' successes in the past, what they're planning to do in the future, as well as how to find someone with whom you might have worked in either group.

SOFTBALL

Amateur Softball Association

http://www.softball.org/

If it's information about the game of softball you're looking for—fast pitch, slow pitch, or modified, men's or women's, adult or youth—you've come to the right place. Lots of links to other softball sites too.

 ### ISF: International Softball Federation

http://www.internationalsoftball.com/

This bilingual site (English and Spanish) is the home of the governing body of international softball, "as recognized by the International Olympic Committee (IOC) and the General Association of International Sports Federations (GAISF)." This site features information about the organization, the rules it sets, and upcoming and ongoing tournaments it sponsors. Tournaments include the Olympic Games, the Slow Pitch World Cup, the Seniors Softball World Cup, and the World Masters Games. Free subscription to the ISF newsletter, plus online shopping for ISF merchandise. With all it has to offer, this site is the best of the best softball sites on the Web.

NCAA Softball Championships

http://www.ncaasoftball.com/

National Collegiate Athletic Association's official site for women's softball. Includes a schedule, ticketing information, results, and previews. This site is well designed and easy to navigate and has great graphics with lots of information about softball. Some of the many features are rankings, teams, history, where to purchase tickets, and information about NCAA championships. There is also an online store where you can purchase merchandise.

NZ Softball – New Zealand

http://www.softball.org.nz/

Get a new perspective on the old baseball game by visiting this site somewhere down under—namely, New Zealand. This is the official New Zealand Web site with plenty of interesting information and facts about softball.

Senior Softball

http://www.seniorsoftball.com/

Learn more about tournaments, rules, tours, and news regarding senior softball here.

Slow Pitch Softball History Page

http://www.angelfire.com/sd/slopitch/

This site features softball national championship and World Series history. Also contains links to other softball-related sites.

Softball on the Internet

http://www.softball.com/

Softball information and an online catalog with products. Facts about gear, an Ask the Umpire section, and a toll-free number for ordering. Enter tournament dates into the directory.

Softball.net

http://www.softball.net/

Offers a directory of 118 links related to softball. Find national and local Amateur Softball Associations (ASA), colleges and universities, commercial sites, fast pitch sites, general softball sites, non-ASA softball associations, slow pitch sites, and tournament information, too.

SoftballSearch.com

http://softballsearch.eteamz.com/

Tournament listings and results along with team announcements by state and country. Just click a state name to view current announcements.

U.S.A. Softball Official Site

http://www.usasoftball.com/

Fans of the U.S.A. Men's and Women's softball teams should bookmark this site to keep abreast of the latest news and developments. Provides information about and coverage of the Olympic Games, Pan American Games, and ISF World Championships. Includes "rosters, player and coach biographies, competition schedules, statistics and live play-by-play updates," when available.

United States Specialty Sports Association

http://www.usssasports.com/sports/

The site of this national organization features the history of slow pitch and fast pitch softball, major players and rankings, tournaments, state associations, and more.

WPSL: Women's Pro Softball League

http://www.prosoftball.com/

This official site of the Women's Pro Softball League provides information about the league, its president, and its future. League plans to relaunch in 2003, and then this site will include information about teams, players, standings, and more.

A
B
C
D
E
F
G
H
I
J
K
L
M
N
O
P
Q
R
S
T
U
V
W
X
Y
Z

International Stress Management Association

http://www.isma.org.uk/

Excellent resource for learning how to deal with stress. Features articles from Stress News, a complete list of recommended reading materials, a schedule of conferences and upcoming events, links to other useful sites, and some specific advice and suggestions on how to make your life more enjoyable and stress-free.

Lycos Health with WebMD–Stress

http://webmd.lycos.com/content/dmk/dmk_summary_account_1466

If you're feeling stressed, this site might help you better understand what you're feeling and how you can deal with it in the short and long term. You can determine whether the symptoms you're exhibiting are likely to be caused by stress and read articles about coping with it.

Optimum Health Resources

http://www.optimumhealth.ca/

Learn how to reduce your stress either at home or in the workplace to improve your health and well-being.

⟦Best⟧ Stress and Workstress Directory

http://web.inter.nl.net/hcc/T.Compernolle/strescat.htm

Dr. Theo Compernolle put together this catalog of noteworthy and award-winning sites on stress and coping. Sites are divided into categories. Actually, this is one of the best sites I've seen on stress management, how to find out whether you have a stress problem, and resources for coping with it. The site has numerous links to other sites and other information that is important to those seeking a solution to their particular problem. The site doesn't have a lot of graphics to slow you down, which will allow you to quickly find what you're looking for. The main reason I've selected this site as a best site is that it presents the information in a clear, concise manner and it is easily accessible.

The Stress Doc

http://www.stressdoc.com/

Mark Gorkin, a licensed psychotherapist, known as "The Stress Doc," offers a wealth of stress management resources. In addition to finding information about his speaking programs, visitors will also find lots of articles and links to help them get a handle on their stress.

Stress Less

http://www.stressless.com/

Learn about and purchase stress reduction products, such as tapes, videos, and books, here.

Stress Management

http://www.ivf.com/stress.html

This fact sheet from the Atlanta Reproductive Health Centre offers a definition of stress and several pointers on how to manage stress.

Stress Management & Emotional Wellness Page

http://www.imt.net/~randolfi/
StressPage.html

Well-stocked directory of links to various resources on the Web designed to help visitors reduce stress. Links point to sites covering everything from biofeedback and relaxation techniques to controlling stress in the workplace.

Stress Management and Stress Reduction

http://www.less-stress.com/

Stress management and information about the nature and causes of stress with online stress assessment service. The Web site provides an insight to the causes and effects of stress and offers a jargon-free understanding of the problems that arise from excessive levels of stress.

Most importantly, the Web site gives direct access to the Changing Times method of psychometric modeling and online stress reduction. The site provides a valuable tool for individuals who seek to tackle their own stress levels and to managers and executives who want to reduce stress in their organizations.

Stress Management for Patients and Physicians

http://www.mentalhealth.com/
mag1/p51-str.html

This book by David B. Posen, M.D., is for anyone with a busy lifestyle; it covers all the major approaches of stress management, including humor.

StressStop.com

http://www.stressstop.com/

Materials and ideas to make your stress management training the best it can be. Complete with tapes, articles, and online resources.

Wes Sime: Stress Management

http://www.unl.edu/stress/mgmt/

Dr. Wesley Sime teaches stress management at the University of Nebraska. Topics discussed include the physiology of stress and decision-making.

A
B
C
D
E
F
G
H
I
J
K
L
M
N
O
P
Q
R
S
T
U
V
W
X
Y
Z

Best Coaching Advice

http://www.tabletennis.gr/

Prematch, match, and postmatch tips by Dimosthenis E. Messinis, Ph.D. Huge collection of resources with an easy-to-use navigation bar on the left containing sections on Articles-Tips, Exercises, Basics, Equipment, Rules, and even video clips. Quizzes, FAQs, interviews, world rankings, awards, and more provide a one-stop kiosk for everything a table tennis enthusiast needs to know. The best of the best table tennis sites in the group.

English Table Tennis Association Limited

http://www.etta.co.uk/

Top resource for table tennis information in the U.K. Information and entry forms for the Butterfly Grand Prix, information on TV coverage of table tennis tournaments, an events calendar, the latest news, details on county and national championships, and more.

International Table Tennis Committee for the Disabled

http://www.ipttc.org/

The official governing body for the disabled table tennis—both wheelchair and standing disabled.

Megaspin.net

http://www.megaspin.net/

Check out table tennis rules, rankings, links, the picture gallery, news, and updates. Subscribe to the free newsletter to keep abreast of the latest news and upcoming events, or shop online for paddles, balls, and other table tennis accessories. This excellent site was barely edged out in the running for the best of the best prize, so be sure to check it out.

North America Table Tennis, Inc.

http://www.natabletennis.com/

Find out about the Stiga North American Teams Championships, one of the largest table tennis championships in the world, and about the Stiga North American Tour. Also provides information about the AAU Junior Olympics and the ACUI/NCTTA Collegiate events and other NATT events. Provides a calendar of events, plus an online store where you can register for tournaments, and purchase NATT apparel and used tables.

Ping Pong Mania & Sporting Goods Co.

http://www.pingpongmania.com/

At the time I was writing this book, the Ping Pong Mania & Sporting Goods site was undergoing a major renovation and was planning to reopen by August 2002. This site promises to provide coverage of the latest table tennis events and tournaments around the world as well as providing a wide selection of table tennis equipment and accessories. Check it out this fall.

The Sport of Table Tennis

http://library.thinkquest.org/20570/

Excellent information for anyone interested in taking up the game of table tennis organized in a Q&A format. Answers the questions: What is table tennis? How do I play? What do I need? Where do I play? Also provides tips, table tennis facts, table tennis terms, and a discussion board.

Table Tennis

http://tabletennis.about.com/

Find out lots of interesting facts from this complete table tennis community with an expert guide, forum, chats, links, bimonthly newsletter, weekly features, coaching tips, and much, much more.

Table Tennis Links

http://www.hal-pc.org/~canupnet/ttlinks.html

You will find thousands of links here relating to table tennis worldwide. Why waste time searching for this subject when you can do it from one convenient site?

Table Tennis World Championships Videos

http://www.reflexsports.com/wttcfrcopy.html

Offers videos of official table tennis world-class competition. Includes world and European table tennis championships, training, and Olympic competitions.

Table-Tennis.com

http://www.tabletennis1.com/

Comprehensive, searchable directory of table tennis sites organized by categories including Associations and Federations, Books and Videos, Clubs, Competitions, Leagues, Personal Web Sites, and more. Search by keyword or phrase or browse through the directory by category.

USA Table Tennis

http://www.usatt.org/

Check here for news on the USA Nationals, and browse through the Tournament Information Guide. Investigate the information on clubs, hot spots to play, equipment, dealers, USATT rules, upcoming tournaments, and results. Learn how to become a USA Table Tennis member. You can get information on table tennis rules in the Stump the Ump section, or browse through the current and past issues of USA Table Tennis e-zine.

World Wide Ping Pong

http://www.asahi-net.or.jp/~SZ4M-KS/wwpp.html

This site gives you a collection of links to table tennis home pages all over the world.

A
B
C
D
E
F
G
H
I
J
K
L
M
N
O
P
Q
R
S
T
U
V
W
X
Y
Z

A
B
C
D
E
F
G
H
I
J
K
L
M
N
O
P
Q
R
S
T
U
V
W
X
Y
Z

TAXES

Bankrate.com

http://www.bankrate.com/brm/itax/default.asp

Excellent income. tax information and tips for individuals and small-business owners. Articles on topics including tracking down your refund, estimating your withholding tax, claiming tax credits, the benefits of itemizing, how to deduct mortgage interest, and much more.

Citizens for an Alternative Tax System: CATS

http://www.cats.org/

Houses the national public interest group for an alternative tax system and tax reform. Talks mainly about the group's manifesto and related information, which basically consists of replacing the current federal income tax system with a retail sales tax.

Citizens for Tax Justice

http://www.ctj.org/

This is a nonprofit organization that does research to support its advocacy of a fairer tax code for middle- and low-income families, closing corporate tax loopholes, reducing the federal deficit, and requiring the rich to pay their fair share.

The Digital Daily

http://www.irs.gov/newsroom/index.html

The Digital Daily is the IRS's online newsletter. It provides news, where to go for help, online forms, links, information about record keeping, a commissioner's forum, and a site map.

eSmartForms

http://www.etaxforms.com/

Tired of filling out those paper forms and mailing your tax return? Then do it online. This site features two simple, inexpensive ways to file your tax return electronically: either complete the "paperwork" online using Web-based forms or download the forms you need, in Microsoft Word format. Complete the forms and upload to submit them. Cost is less than $20.

Essential Links to Taxes

http://www.el.com/elinks/taxes/

Taxpayer tips and information on income tax preparation assistance, rules, tax code, financial planners and tax preparers, forms (from W-2 to Form 1040), publications, instructions, deductions, and filing.

Fairmark Press–Tax Guide for Investors

http://www.fairmark.com/

There are pages and pages of material to guide you in making smart investment choices here in the Tax Guide section—more than 700 pages to be exact. Learn the essentials of Roth IRAs, the basics of computing capital gains, or the tax guide for traders, as well as several other tax-related subjects covered in depth.

H&R Block

http://www.hrblock.com/

Although there's plenty of information here to help you get better rates on credit cards, mortgages, and loans, the tax information is the most helpful. Use the Withholding Calculator to figure out how much you should be having taken out of your paycheck. Or find out the status of your refund check. And get answers to your basic tax questions here.

IRS: Internet Revenue Service

http://www.irs.gov/

The IRS site provides everything you need to become an informed taxpayer. Search the site for specific information or for downloadable, printable tax forms you might have trouble finding at your local post office or library. Site also provides news about the IRS and tax legislation, along with information specifically for individuals, businesses, nonprofit organizations, and tax professionals. Learn about the earned income tax credit, tax scams and frauds, and your rights as a taxpayer.

IRS.com

http://www.irs.com/index.htm

IRS.com is the Internet's first consumer-oriented source for federal, state, and local tax-related developments. You are provided with answers to general tax questions plus hyperlinks to current federal and state-sponsored tax information.

Kiplinger Online

http://www.kiplinger.com

Business forecasts, news of the day, financial advice, taxes, and investment and retirement information. Additional services for members.

MoneyCentral on Taxes

http://moneycentral.msn.com/tax/home.asp

Information on tax planning and preparation, tax estimators, deduction finder, tax IQ test, Q&A, and information on reducing your tax burden.

Quicken.com Taxes

http://www.quicken.com/taxes/

Download commonly used tax forms here and use tax tools to save money on taxes, such as the tax estimator and Roth IRA planner. You can also get 401K advice. There are also tax discussion forums and quick answers to frequently asked questions to help you.

SmartPros Accounting

http://accounting.smartpros.com/

Download federal and state tax forms and publications, file your taxes electronically, or find an accountant to handle your taxes for you.

State and Local Taxes

http://www.taxsites.com/state.html

State tax resource with general locators, current tax issues, organizations, and more. This site has dozens of useful and informative links to information about tax preparation, tax changes and updates and more.

A
B
C
D
E
F
G
H
I
J
K
L
M
N
O
P
Q
R
S
U
V
W
X
Y
Z

A
B
C
D
E
F
G
H
I
J
K
L
M
N
O
P
Q
R
S
T
U
V
W
X
Y
Z

Tax and Accounting Sites Directory

http://www.taxsites.com

Guide to tax resources on the Web. Includes tax forms, electronic filing preparation, articles, and accounting information.

Tax History Project

http://taxhistory.tax.org/

Visit the multimedia timeline of American taxation here and learn all about the history of taxation.

Tax Links

http://www.taxlinks.com

Online resource for IRS revenue rulings. Tax lawyers will find this site particularly useful for tracking down precedents that might help their clients or hinder their cases.

The Tax Prophet

http://www.taxprophet.com/

Read through helpful articles on taxes written by attorney Robert Sommers, as well as FAQs and tax-related links.

Tax Resources on the Web

http://pages.prodigy.net/agkalman/

A simple-to-navigate site, yet very comprehensive, that allows you to click on keywords, such as kiddy tax or dividends, and find links to sites with useful information on the subjects.

Tax Sites

http://www.taxsites.com

A site full of Web-based tax and accounting resources, accessed by clicking on a key word.

Tax.org

http://www.tax.org

This nonprofit for tax professionals provides lists of its publications and discussion groups about various tax issues. Also provides the Tax Notes Today, updated three times daily.

TaxFoundation.org

http://www.taxfoundation.org

Dedicated to translating the overly complex and cryptic income tax code into something the average taxpayer can understand, TaxFoundation.org publishes reports that explain in plain English what taxpayers need to know. The foundation also answers tax questions from individuals and the media. This site also features headline tax news and commentary.

TaxHelp Online.com

http://www.taxhelponline.com

Get tax help online to address your individual concerns and situation. Find out what to do if you owe back taxes, or if you haven't filed in years, as well as how to handle just about any situation, including the infamous audit.

[Best] TaxPlanet.com

http://www.taxplanet.com/

Everything a taxpayer needs to know to take full advantage of his or her tax breaks and stay within the legal limits. Features tax news and tips, a year-round tax planning guide, a tax calendar, information about new tax laws, a well-stocked library of tax forms and IRS publications, and hundreds of tax-saving tips. Very attractive site, easy to navigate, and packed with the best tax information you'll find on the planet or at least on the Web.

United States Tax Code Online

http://www.fourmilab.ch/ustax/ustax.html

Provides interactive access to the complete text of the United States Internal Revenue Code.

TEACHING

Activity Search

http://www.eduplace.com/activity/

A searchable database of 400 original K–8 classroom activities and lesson plans for teachers and parents.

American Federation of Teachers

http://www.aft.org/

Representing one million teachers and educational staff members, the AFT site (part of the AFL-CIO) provides teaching news, reports, and resources. This site also has many downloadable files concerning information that teachers will be interested in, plus information for parents.

Archive.edu

http://www.coe.uh.edu/archive/

A storehouse of instructional materials on a variety of topics, including language arts, math, science, social studies, and technology.

[Best] ArtsEdge

http://artsedge.kennedy-center.org/artsedge.html

ArtsEdge, sponsored by the Kennedy Center and maintained by Worldcom, is devoted to helping educators teach the arts more effectively. Teachers will find a pre-established curriculum, lesson plans, teaching materials, and activities available for download, as well as helpful Web links, publications, and professional development information. Site also features a NewsBreak section that provides current, up-to-date information on what's happening in the arts and education. Well-presented and packed with useful tools, this site is a hands-down winner of our best of the best award in Teaching.

AskERIC

http://ericir.syr.edu

Resources, info-guides, lesson plans, a Q&A service, and a searchable database from the Educational Resources Information Center (a branch of the U.S. Department of Education).

A B C D E F G H I J K L M N O P Q R S U V W X Y Z

A
B
C
D
E
F
G
H
I
J
K
L
M
N
O
P
Q
R
S
T
U
V
W
X
Y
Z

Classroom CONNECT

http://www.classroom.net/

This business unit within Harcourt, Inc., is dedicated to helping schools incorporate the Internet into their curricula. Provides professional development and online curriculum resources that foster the use of computers and the Internet in core subjects, including math, language arts, science, and social studies.

Collaborative Lesson Archive

http://faldo.atmos.uiuc.edu/CLA/

Forum for the creation, distribution, and archival of education curricula for all grade levels and subject areas.

EdLinks

http://webpages.marshall.edu/
~jmullens/edlinks.html

Annotated directory of education links. This site contains dozens of useful links.

Education Place

http://www.eduplace.com/

Focused on education for K-8 students, this site provides teachers with resources for professional development, as well as offering some lively activities for the classroom. Special sections for students and parents, as well.

Education Week on the Web

http://www.edweek.org

News, special reports, a teacher magazine, and discussion forums.

Education World

http://www.education-world.com

Education World is a powerful and free search engine focused on providing information to educators, students, and parents. Use their keyword search, browse by category, or join the Educators' Forum, a message board system to dialogue with educators around the globe. Reviews of 20 education sites are posted each month.

Education.com

http://www.education.com/

This learning site for teachers, parents, and students provides the tools needed to help parents and teachers better educate students. Well-stocked collection of resources for students broken down by age groups: ages 0-6, ages 6-9, and ages 9-12. Home schooling resources, including an online encyclopedia, are available, plus articles that teach parents what children should know at each stage of their educational careers. Register for access to additional features.

The Educator's Toolkit

http://www.eagle.ca/~matink/

The Educator's Toolkit is a great tool for busy educators. Here you'll find a monthly Internet newsletter, lesson plans, theme sites, teacher resources, and more.

Educators Net

http://www.educatorsnet.com

Interactive education directory serving the communications and information needs of educators and students at the secondary and post-secondary school levels. Search the directory of more than 10,000 entries by keyword or phrase or browse the categories for what you want.

ENC Online–Eisenhower National Clearinghouse

http://www.enc.org

Get K–12 math and science teaching support, including the newest ideas in approaches and material for teaching the subjects, and professional development support through publications and discussions.

Federal Resources for Educational Excellence (FREE)

http://www.ed.gov/free/

FREE makes hundreds of Internet-based education resources supported by agencies across the U.S. federal government easier to find.

Figure This!

http://www.figurethis.org

A site that encourages family involvement in supporting math skill development through challenging online quizzes that everyone can take part in.

Gateway to Educational Materials

http://geminfo.org

A project to provide teachers with one-stop access to Internet lesson plans.

Global SchoolHouse

http://www.gsh.org/

One-stop shopping for Internet-based projects of interest to K–12 educators. Encourages and assists teachers in working collaboratively no matter where they're located geographically.

Harcourt School Publishing

http://www.harcourtschool.com/

A site that blends interactive learning for kids in grades K–8 with resources for teachers and parents—all to complement Harcourt Brace school publications.

How Stuff Works

http://www.howstuffworks.com/

An innovative teaching tool that's fun, too. Want to know more about how something works? This is the site. From how car engines work to, Web pages, CDs, and TVs and toilets, there is plenty of interesting and instructional information to share.

History/Social Studies for K-12 Teachers

http://earth.execpc.com/~dboals/boals.html

K–12 teachers will find this history and social studies directory useful for tracking down lesson plans, collaborative projects with other classes and schools, newsgroups, links, and training resources. This site contains at least a couple of hundred links to resources of interest to teachers, parents, and students.

ICONnect

http://www.ala.org/ICONN/

Learn the skills necessary to navigate the information superhighway. Developed especially for school library media specialists, teachers, and students.

Intel Innovation in Education

http://www.intel.com/education/

Intel provides curriculum in support of math and science education, as well as information on competitions, scholarships, events, and more. Good information for teachers and students.

Lesson Plans Page

http://www.lessonplanspage.com

More than 1,500 lesson plans that are helpful for anyone in elementary education. Simply select your subject and your grade level to display a hefty list of links to lesson plans organized by category such as math, science, English, music, computers and the Internet, social studies, art, physical education, and other subjects.

McGraw-Hill School Division

http://www.mmhschool.com

Web-based teaching resources for reading/language arts, mathematics, health, social studies, music, bilingual, and professional development. This site is the brainstorm of Macmillan/McGraw-Hill, the elementary school publishing unit of McGraw-Hill, and is one of the better designed sites I've seen. McGraw-Hill is dedicated to educating children and to helping educational professionals by providing the highest-quality services. The site is divided up into sections called islands with one for Parents, Teachers, and Students. Very well designed and worth the click it takes to visit here.

National Education Association

http://www.nea.org/

The NEA site provides education statistics, reports, information on grants, events, legislative action, and much more information on the state of education.

New York Times Learning Network

http://www.nytimes.com/learning/

Challenge your students to the daily news quiz, or the word of the day. Science Q&A, Ask a Reporter, and a crossword puzzle are additional learning opportunities posted at this site. Teachers gain access to lesson plans and lesson plan archives.

Pitsco's Ask an Expert

http://www.askanexpert.com

Select from 12 categories with more than 300 Web sites and email addresses where you can find experts to answer your questions from the Amish lifestyle to facts about zoo keeping.

The Puffin House

http://www.puffin.co.uk

The Puffin House contains information about Penguin children's books. It includes activities for children, teachers' resources, and a searchable database of the full range of book titles.

Scholastic.com

http://teacher.scholastic.com/index.htm

Lots of great information to be incorporated into lesson plans as well as news regarding the latest teaching tools and methods, such as software and books.

TeacherServe

http://www.nhc.rtp.nc.us:8080/tserve/tserve.htm

Practical help in planning courses and presenting rigorous subject matter to students.

Teachers.net

http://www.teachers.net/

Self-described as "The ultimate teacher's resource," this site encourages and supports teacher communication and collaboration. Features message boards, chat rooms, a schedule of online teacher meetings, libraries of teacher-submitted lesson plans and curricula, and more. To stay in touch with other teachers worldwide and work together to improve education, check out this site.

U.S. Department of Education– Funding Opportunities

http://www.ed.gov/topics/
topics.jsp?&top=Grants+%26+
Contracts

Any teacher looking for funding will find it well worth their while to visit this site for information about funding sources, how to apply for an educational grant, contract information, and upcoming opportunities.

USA Today Education

http://www.usatoday.com/
educate/home.htm

Join Experience Today to get your students involved in reading and understanding issues covered in the media. A four-page lesson plan accompanies a subscription to USA Today to assist teachers in making use of editorial content.

About Teen Pregnancy

http://web.bu.edu/COHIS/
teenpreg/teenpreg.htm

The Community Outreach Health Information System answers questions about teen pregnancy, birth control, neonatal health, postnatal care, and more.

Alloy Online

http://www.alloyonline.com/

Online magazine and community dedicated to entertaining and informing teenage girls. Check up on your favorite celebrities or keep abreast of the latest fashion crazes at this site.

Bolt

http://www.bolt.com

Bolt is a popular hangout for high school and college kids, where they can express their opinion freely on virtually any topic. Sharing information can happen through forums, chat, or instant messaging. Almost all the content comes from members, not adults.

Consumer Education for Teens

http://www.wa.gov/ago/youth/

Information for teens, by teens, about becoming wise consumers. Includes sections on music clubs, car buying, and credit cards.

CyberTeens

http://www.cyberteens.com/

Contests, interviews, art, and chat. When the site is redesigned, you will be able to shop online but know how to use your credit card responsibly.

Girls Life Magazine

http://www.girlslife.com

A magazine for girls and teens, featuring entertainment, news, advice, and more. Subscription information is available. The site contains a one-stop shopping mall just for girls.

A
B
C
D
E
F
G
H
I
J
K
L
M
N
O
P
Q
R
S

U
V
W
X
Y
Z

High School Central

http://www.child.net/
hscentral.htm

A cool gathering environment for high school students.

⌜Best⌝ IPL Teen Division

http://www.ipl.org/teen/

A large collection of teen resources for doing homework, researching papers, career pathways, clubs, dating, health, and much more. If you are a teen, this site has information on all the things you would normally be interested in, such as arts & entertainment, college, high school, books, music, clubs, organizations, computers and the Internet, money matters, and homework. If you are looking for some easy answers and who isn't, here is the place you can come to and ease your mind. There is also a teen adviser that will help you with your problems. One of the more positive hangouts for teens on the Web.

The Junction

http://www.thej.co.uk

A European youth hangout aimed at ages 13–21, the focus is on sharing information through discussion forums and chatting about a wide variety of subjects, such as X-Files, dating, or homework help.

LIQUIDGENERATION.com

http://www.liquidgeneration.com/

Learn something new about getting into college, investing, or current events in the Absorb section, or chat about partying and after-hours entertainment. Edgy and irreverent, this site pokes fun at the establishment with its singing celebrity karaoke machine, disgusting how-to videos, and LiquidGeneration EXPOSED tabloid.

MyFuture

http://www.myfuture.com

Resources to help high-school students plan for their future. Includes information about saving money, careers, résumés, military opportunities, alcoholism, buying cars, finding scholarships, and dating.

React

http://www.react.com

Online teen magazine presents news, entertainment, contests, jokes, and bizarre factoids. The site has a nice shopping mall where you can purchase everything you need including music CDs.

TechnoTeen

http://technoteen.studentcenter.
org/

Super site for teens features a student center, relationship questionnaires, teen horoscopes and jokes, chat rooms and discussion forums, a date finder, and much more.

Teen Advice Online

http://www.teenadviceonline.org/

Counseling center where you can get help from a team of nonprofessional counselors age 13 years and older. Meet the volunteer counselors, read articles on various teenage-related issues, or post your question to get some free advice.

Teen Chat

http://www.teen-chat.net

Designed as a safe place for teens to chat on the Net, you can find pen pals from around the world, hop into chat, or join ongoing discussions.

TeenLink

http://www2.nypl.org/home/branch/teen/

Links from the New York Public Library.

Teenmag.com

http://www.teenmag.com/

This e-zine for teenagers features news about teen celebrities and musical groups, an advice column, style tips, online questionnaires, and much more. Primarily suited for teenage girls.

TeenPeople.com

http://www.teenpeople.com/teenpeople/

People magazine for teenagers is online with this sleek site that features news about celebrities most teens care about. Celebrity news, hot styles, online games, and chat rooms make this a great teen hangout.

TeenTalk

http://teentalk.com

Christian site where teens can post questions about problems and get advice from other teens. Topics include alcohol, appearance, dating, depression, school, and more.

Young Investor

http://www.younginvestor.com

A place to learn about money and maybe even earn some, too. Features a game room, where you can learn about money in a fun environment; a parent-to-parent section, where parents can have their questions answered; a survey where you can find out how you stack up against others in regard to how much you know about money; and an online college savings calculator you can use to determine how much money you need to save for college.

TELEVISION

BBCi

http://www.bbc.co.uk

Home of British Broadcasting Corporation's interactive Web site, BBCi provides the latest headline news and sports, TV and radio programming information, and information on concerts, nightclubs, and other entertainment offerings.

CSI:Crime Scene Investigation

http://www.cbs.com/primetime/csi/main.shtml

This interactive site, created and maintained by CBS, provides visitors with case files for the various episodes of the popular television series Crime Scene Investigation. Here, you can check the latest case file, obtain personnel records for the various investigators, access a handbook that explains many of the technical terms used on the show, tour the crime lab, and chat with other fans.

A
B
C
D
E
F
G
H
I
J
K
L
M
N
O
P
Q
R
S
T
U
V
W
X
Y
Z

A
B
C
D
E
F
G
H
I
J
K
L
M
N
O
P
Q
R
S
T
U
V
W
X
Y
Z

E! Online

http://www.eonline.com

TV fans will want to bookmark this site, home of E!, the source for the latest news about everything in the entertainment industry. Here you can find the latest news and gossip about your favorite celebrities and the hottest TV shows, movies, and recording artists. Read TV, movie, and CD reviews; take online quizzes and compete in trivia contests; check out the latest movie trailers and music clips; and find recent interviews with the top stars.

HBO: Home Box Office

http://www.hbo.com/

Home of the Sopranos, Sex and the City, Six Feet Under, and other award-winning shows, this site provides information about the various HBO original series, premier movies, sports specials, HBO documentaries and films, and much more. Here, you can get a sneak preview of your favorite shows and movies and go behind-the-scenes with your favorite HBO celebrities.

The Osbournes

http://www.mtv.com/onair/osbournes

Wondering what Ozzy Osbourne and his family are up to? Then drop in on them at their Web home and find out. Here, you can learn more about this popular reality-based, family-oriented sitcom, meet the family, take a virtual tour of their home, and check the TV listings for the next episode. You can even download a free screensaver and flip through the kids' personal diaries.

Best TV Guide Online

http://www.tvguide.com/

Can't find your television guide? Then tune in to the home page of one of the most popular magazines in the country, TV Guide. Click the TV Listings link, enter your ZIP Code, make a few other selections, and you get an on-screen listing of all the TV shows of the day. This site also features news about your favorite shows, gossip about your favorite stars, a movie guide, a guide to the soaps, and much more. Shop the online store for collector's items, special CDs and DVDs, and other items. If you spend more than an hour a day in front of the tube, you'll want to bookmark this best of the best site for your future reference.

TV Land

http://www.tvland.com

Do you miss those TV shows from yesteryears? Can't live without The Dick Van Dyke Show, Leave It To Beaver, and Get Smart? Then check out TV Land's home on the Web, where you can learn more about these shows, download complete TV listings, and even shop online for TV Land apparel and paraphernalia.

TV Party

http://www.tvparty.com/

Online museum of the best (and worst) in TV over the past 40 years. If you become nostalgic over the old TV shows, this is the site for you. Go behind-the-scenes with the site's creator and host, Billy Ingram, to listen to the gossip, explore the scandals, and view some of the best dancing, drama, comedy, and action clips from the shows that made TV what it is today.

Ultimate TV

http://www.ultimatetv.com/

Ultimate TV provides television shows on-demand by recording your favorite shows to disk. You simply set up a schedule of what you want to record and then play back the show when you're ready to view it. Visit this site to learn more about this revolution in TV viewing.

Who Wants to Be a Millionaire

http://abc.abcnews.go.com/
primetime/_millionaire/
millionaire_home.html

Home of the most popular game show on the planet, the Who Wants to Be a Millionaire Web site provides

information about the show, show highlights, and an online version of the game. Join Regis Philbin online, play fastest finger, and see how much play money you could win playing a sample round of the game. This site also provides information on how to get tickets to the show and how to become a contestant.

TV NETWORKS

ABC
http://abc.abcnews.go.com/

CBS
http://www.cbs.com/

FOX
http://www.fox.com/

NBC
http://www.nbc.com/

American Tennis Professionals

http://www.atptour.com

Tour news, events information, player profiles, and pro shop. In English and German. Links to the Tennis Warehouse (www.tennis-warehouse.com) for online shopping.

CBS SportsLine: Tennis

http://www.sportsline.com/u/
tennis/

Daily news and tournament results, plus special features and columns relating to the game of table tennis. Some areas require membership. The site has a shopping area where you can purchase tennis rackets and other tennis-related products.

A B C D E F G H I J K L M N O P Q R S T U V W X Y Z

A
B
C
D
E
F
G
H
I
J
K
L
M
N
O
P
Q
R
S
T
U
V
W
X
Y
Z

GoTennis

http://www.gotennis.com

Find tournament information, results, player profiles, tips and techniques for improving your game, tennis-related shopping links, and audio and video news. The site has a Pro shopping area just for all you pros where you can purchase tennis rackets, shoes, and just about everything else.

 ### International Tennis Federation Online

http://www.itftennis.com

Official site of the world governing body for tennis. Includes results and rankings. Want the latest news about tennis related events? This site has much to offer in the way of the latest news, rules and regulations, and even the latest facts and figures. Add all that to a great-looking site and you have the winner of our best of the best award for tennis sites.

Nando Sports Server: Tennis

http://www.sportserver.com/tennis/archive/

Daily updated news covering players and tournaments, statistics, a recap of the week in tennis, and world team tennis standings.

Steve G's ATP Tour Rankings

http://www.stevegtennis.com/

Current rankings and archives, tour calendar. Covers ATP, challengers, satellites, and futures.

Tennis Canada

http://www.tenniscanada.com

Canadian tennis rankings plus player information and tournament news. In French and English.

Tennis Server

http://tennisserver.com

Features, equipment tips, and links to other tennis sites. The site has a nice selection of tennis products with lots of links to other sites where you can continue to shop if you don't see what you want on the Tennis Server site.

Tennis: A Research Guide

http://gopher.nypl.org/research/chss/grd/resguides/tennis/tennisinstruct.html

Bibliography on general tennis works from the New York Public Library, with links to more specific bibliographies. References to biographies, histories of the game, tennis instruction and literature, and periodicals.

Tennis.com

http://www.tennis.com/

Get weekly tips and fitness advice, as well as information on instruction and camps. Find out when this week's tournaments will be aired on TV, and stay tuned for the latest match results.

TennisONE

http://www.tennisone.com

Tennis lessons, fitness information, and products. This site also has a Pro Shopping area where you will find most of the things you need to play tennis effectively.

United States Professional Tennis Association (USPTA)

http://www.uspta.org/

Find a pro in your area for instruction, find out when this year's conferences and conventions are being held, and learn all about being a USPTA member here.

United States Tennis Association

http://www.usta.com/index.html

Web home of the USTA, this site is dedicated to promoting and developing tennis. The USTA is the first governing body for tennis. At this

site, you'll find news about the latest tournaments, information about various tennis leagues, tennis rules and regulations, and even some online games.

USA Today: Tennis

http://www.usatoday.com/sports/tennis/tennis.htm

Includes ATP and WTA results, rankings, money leaders, archived stories, and the latest news.

WTA Tour

http://www.wtatour.com

Official site with schedule, rankings, news, profiles, pro shop, and multimedia clips.

THEATER AND MUSICALS

Actors' Page

http://www.serve.com/dgweb32/

An actor and member of the Screen Actors Guild and the American Federation of Television and Radio Artists has offered a practical and entertaining site for those interested in the acting arts, as well as finding some contacts in show biz. You can add your URL to the page, check out lists of talent agencies and casting directors in New York City, and join a discussion called "The Actors' Roundtable." Click the Links button at the bottom of the home page to view an exhaustive list of links to theaters and actors.

American Conservatory Theater

http://www.act-sfbay.org/

This acclaimed training institution and regional theater offers information on its upcoming schedule, performers, past productions, and mission here. You can purchase single tickets online to some productions.

American Repertory Theatre

http://www.amrep.org/

Interviews with casts and playwrights, previews of upcoming shows, and synopses of past productions.

A
B
C
D
E
F
G
H
I
J
K
L
M
N
O
P
Q
R
S
U
V
W
X
Y
Z

A
B
C
D
E
F
G
H
I
J
K
L
M
N
O
P
Q
R
S
T
U
V
W
X
Y
Z

American Variety Stage

http://lcweb2.loc.gov/ammem/
vshtml/vshome.html

Vaudeville and Popular Entertainment, 1870–1920. Online exhibition from the Library of Congress.

Annie: Long John Silver's Reference Website

http://www.anniethemusical.com/

Links to various articles and resources about Annie: The Musical, plus discussion forums for fans of this popular musical. Includes cast lists and biographies, cast member birthdays, audio clips, and links to other Annie sites.

Better Living Through Show Tunes

http://www.geocities.com/
Broadway/2685/

This site, devoted to Broadway show-tune fans, is a serious collection of information on Broadway musicals and their composers, with pictures, cast lists, discographies, CD reviews, links to related sites, and more.

Broadway Play Publishing, Inc.

http://www.BroadwayPlayPubl.com/
⑨

A company that adapts American plays, has a search engine and several related links. You can order their books, plays, musicals, one-act collections, and play anthologies. See their adaptations of American classics and check out the photo gallery.

Complete Works of William Shakespeare

http://tech-two.mit.edu/
Shakespeare/works.html

In addition to providing the complete text of every Shakespeare play and poem, this site includes a discussion area, chronological and alphabetical lists of the plays, Bartlett's familiar Shakespeare quotations, and a funeral elegy by the old man himself. An unbelievable site!

Current Theatre

http://www.nytimes.com/library/
theater

Theater reviews from the New York Times.

English Actors at the Turn of the Century

http://www.siue.edu/COSTUMES/
actors/pics.html

This very straightforward, interesting site provides colorful, full photographs of 20th-century actors in their roles. Just click an actor or movie, and you're there. See many old actors including Maud Jeffries in Herod, Sir Henry Irving in As You Like It, and George Alexander in If I Were King.

Grand Theatre

http://www.grandtheatre.com/

Check out this London, Ontario, Canada's theater Web site to learn more about the renovated theater and upcoming performances, and to catch a glimpse of the ghost of the theater's founder, Ambrose Small, who haunts the theater and the site, it seems. You can get ticket purchase information here and do a little shopping online.

London Theatre Guide Online

http://www.londontheatre.co.uk/

Use this handy page to find information on West End shows, the Royal National Theatre, and other London theaters. Includes addresses, seating arrangements, reviews of current shows, ballet and opera listings, and a monthly email update service. You can find out the current costs of tickets and where to purchase them as well as doing some shopping by linking to other sites such as Amazon.com.

MovieTunes

http://www.hollywood.com/movietunes/

Part of the Hollywood.com group of sites, this amazing site receives more than 40,000 hits per week. The Soundtracks section alone is worth a visit if you're a music fan. The databases are kept up to date with new films and productions being premiered. The site has a shopping area where you can purchase CDs, DVDs, and other items.

Musical (Dance) Films

http://www.filmsite.org/musical-films.html

This site is composed of a lengthy, incredibly detailed document that tells the history of musical films from Don Juan (1926) to Tarzan (1999). It includes pages on many of the films, with theatrical posters, pictures, and some synopses that tell in great detail the story of each film—including occasional song lyrics and dialogue.

Musicals.net

http://musicals.net

This site lists about 75 popular musicals and plenty of new ones coming up. Click a musical's name to list links, lyrics, media clips, notes, synopses, and tons of other information.

New York's Capital District Theater Page

http://www.danielnorton.net/capdist/theatre/

Lists all the plays currently running in Albany, New York. This page also includes audition information, class and workshop information, and active theater company schedules. The Other Related Web Sites and Theater-Related Newsgroup sections provide dozens of links and Usenet addresses.

Now Casting

http://www.laactorsonline.com/

Searchable database brings together actors, casting directors, managers, and agents to help filmmakers create films and to find appropriate jobs for actors.

Performing Arts Online

http://www.performingarts.net

The Performing Arts Network has put together a great site, with links to dozens of performers and companies, sorted by genre—musical theater lists of current shows in production. A clickable Featured Artists button changes every few seconds to connect you to performers' sites. Hundreds of links to related sites.

A
B
C
D
E
F
G
H
I
J
K
L
M
N
O
P
Q
R
S
T
U
V
W
X
Y
Z

A
B
C
D
E
F
G
H
I
J
K
L
M
N
O
P
Q
R
S
T
U
V
W
X
Y
Z

[Best] Playbill Online

http://www1.playbill.com/
playbill/

The electronic version of the famous print publication that focuses on Broadway and Off-Broadway theatres. You can purchase tickets online, read reviews, and learn about the stars behind the top productions. Excellent site with a strong content offering.

The Public Theater

http://www.publictheater.org/

The Public Theatre presents full seasons of new plays and musicals, as well as Shakespeare and other classics at its Manhattan location. Find out how to get there, what shows the troupe will be performing, who's in the cast, and how you can support this group.

Roundabout Theatre Company

http://www.roundabouttheatre.org/

Find out more about this classic theater group, upcoming shows, subscriptions that give members access to additional private performances (Theatre-Plus), its history, and how to subscribe.

Sam's Musical Box

http://members.ozemail.com.au/
~samoran/

Australian Sam Moran has put together a hefty collection of musical-related links across the world. You will find information on some of the most famous Broadway composers: Andrew Lloyd Webber, the Gershwin Brothers, Stephen Sondheim, and others, as well as links to sites about their shows and others. Also includes information on musical theater performers, as well as "wannabees."

Screen Actor's Guild

http://www.sag.com/

Online site of the Screen Actor's Guild, the largest professional actors' advocacy group. Read news about SAG and its events, view a calendar of upcoming events, and get leads on talent agents. Professional actors should bookmark it.

Shakespeare Theatre

http://shakespearedc.org/

Information about the Washington, D.C.–based Shakespeare Theatre, including upcoming performances, cast bios, job listings and internships, and acting classes.

SITCOM Home Page

http://www.dangoldstein.com/
sitcom.html

Information on the SITCOM program of improvised half-hour shows that mimic rehearsed and planned TV comedy. Provides a blend of structuralist literary criticism and artificial intelligence, a live show that converts audience suggestions into full-length, improvised TV sitcoms that unfold live on stage.

TenEyck Design Studio

http://www.inch.com/~kteneyck/

Web page for a set-design company in New York City. Be sure to enter the door to learn more about its designs for productions such as The Tempest and La Traviata. The Observatory includes information on all the productions for which TenEyck has designed sets.

Theatre Crafts International Magazine

http://www.etecnyc.net/tci/

Selected articles from the print version of the highly respected magazine for behind-the-scenes theater professionals, including lighting, sound, production designers, and costume and makeup professionals. The site has a nice selection of magazines that you can subscribe to on every subject including theater-related subjects.

Theatre Link

http://www.theatre-link.com

Comprehensive collection of links to theater-related resources.

Tony Awards Online

http://www.tonys.org/

It isn't strictly musicals, of course—plenty of wonderful dramas and comedies take awards in their own categories—but the Tonys are always a guide to what's good in musicals on stage. Go to this site for a variety of entertainment: contests, games, a chat page, lists of award winners (and nominees, depending on the season), theater news, and other interesting sections. The site is very well designed and has a variety of information about the Tonys.

Vintage Vaudeville and Ragtime Show

http://www.bestwebs.com/vaudeville/

Get back to the old ragtime days with this modern site about Vaudeville. First, check out the history of Vaudeville. Then, view some cool old pictures. Also, get some biographical data on stars such as Ada Jones and Len Spencer. Best of all, sit back and enjoy some actual music, such as Arthur Collins singing Ragtime. There are several RealAudio files to enjoy.

World Wide Arts Resources: Theater

http://wwar.com/categories/Theater/

Huge directory of theater-related resources on the Web covering everything from actors to musicals and from opera to theater companies. Search by keyword or phrase or browse through the many categories.

A
B
C
D
E
F
G
H
I
J
K
L
M
N
O
P
Q
R
S
T
U
V
W
X
Y
Z

TOYS

ALEX

http://www.alextoys.com

A fun and creative site offering art supplies and activity kits at its site, where children can also hear animals talk, read the Alex newsletter, and find out about featured products.

Archie McPhee

http://www.mcphee.com/

Home of the FUZZ action figure, tailless monkey T-shirts, and nerd supplies, this novelty store carries a good collection of fun stuff that's a little on the wild side.

AreYouGame.com

http://www.areyougame.com/interact/default.asp

Choose an age group, favorite type of activity—such as brain teasers—or game, such as Monopoly, and AreYouGame will recommend specific games and puzzles for your child, or child at heart. Learn about new games or order well-known favorites at this site. The site has an extensive collection of games for almost any age group.

Boardgames.com

http://www.boardgames.com/

A huge selection of board games is available here, from children's games to adult, strategy, or electronic handheld. You'll find current popular games such as Millionaire

and Scrabble, but there are many, many others to buy or give as gifts. This site is well designed and easy to navigate. Better and easier than shopping at the mall. If you are into games of all kinds and you would rather spend your time playing them than shopping in faraway crowded malls, then here is the place to get them. You can shop from the convenience of your own home, look at the games online, and read the descriptions at your leisure. There is also a lot of useful information about all the games here.

BRIO

http://www.briotoy.com/

Learn all about how BRIO wooden toys are constructed, about the many types, and the awards the toys have won. You can request a catalog be mailed to you or conduct an online toy search here to find what you're looking for. The site contains a feature where you can find out where to buy BRIO toys near you.

The Copernicus Home Page

http://www.copernicustoys.com

A store specializing in toys of the imagination for adults—optical illusions, craft kits, puzzles, and the like. You can email for a complete catalog.

Creativity for Kids

http://www.creativityforkids.com

A wonderful craft activities supplier. Choose craft projects by age or type—such as glass beads, ceramics, or stitchery—and be given a long list of products that match the criteria. Although you can't buy the products at this site, if you enter your ZIP Code you can be given a list of local stores that carry what you're looking for, as well as online merchants.

Discovery Toys

http://www.discoverytoysinc.com/

Check out the latest toys from this company, which creates toys appropriate for a child's age and developmental state. Learn more about which toys are appropriate and find a local educational consultant you can buy from.

Disney Online Store

http://disney.store.go.com/

Offers a full online catalog of Disney merchandise with secure online purchasing. The Disney Store "gift finder" service and a listing of Disney Store locations worldwide are also available.

Dr. Toy

http://www.drtoy.com

Find out which toys have been recommended by Dr. Toy, who has chosen more than 1,500 for your review. You can also ask Dr. Toy for advice, browse toy shop links, and scan the top 100 toys. You can also get the lowdown on all their latest toys.

The Dummy Doctor

http://homepage.mac.com/asemok/dummies2.html

A commercial site offering "handcrafted professional ventriloquial

figures," plus puppets and marionettes for both professionals and hobbyists. Also does repair and evaluation of vintage dummies and puppets.

EducationalToys.com

http://www.educationaltoys.com/

This site sells Quercetti Intelligent Toys, which are designed to stimulate reasoning, creativity, and mobility skills. They can be used over and over without being repetitive and inspire new discoveries and inventions. Choose by age, category, activity, or recommendations and shop online.

⟦Best⟧ EToys

http://www.etoys.com

Huge online toy warehouse featuring just about every toy imaginable. Shop for specific toys by keyword or phrase, or browse for toys by age, by category, or by brand name. eToys can even help you shop by providing a list of bestselling toys, video game reviews, and special offers. Order toys online and have your order shipped right to your door. If you need a hard-to-get toy and you need it soon, you'll find that this site is truly the best of the best.

FAO Schwarz

http://www.fao.com/

Order online in a secure shopping area. Read about the FAO Schwarz/Universal Pictures sweepstakes, and learn more about FAO, their stores, and events.

A
B
C
D
E
F
G
H
I
J
K
L
M
N
O
P
Q
R
S
T
U
V
W
X
Y
Z

A
B
C
D
E
F
G
H
I
J
K
L
M
N
O
P
Q
R
S
T
U
V
W
X
Y
Z

Firebox.com

http://www.firebox.com/

Toys for boys (older boys and men, that is). This site features an excellent collection of toys for older kids, including digital cameras, portable MP3 players, game pads, remote control vehicles, mini speakers, projection clocks, and all sorts of other gadgets. Shopping for the man who has everything? Then shop here.

Fisher-Price

http://www.fisher-price.com

Select the perfect product from the personal shopper, create your own online baby and gift registry, view more than 300 products in their showroom, and more.

The Gallery of Monster Toys

http://members.aol.com/raycastile/page1.htm

The creator of this site says it best: "Vintage monster toys are typically overlooked by collectors, largely because they seem obsolete in today's world. The toys in this gallery are not, for the most part, 'slick' or 'hyper-detailed.' They are humble and imperfect. They depict flawed, tortured creatures. These toys capture a time when horror was fun." After searching through all the "monsters" of past, present, and maybe the future, you may want one of these cuddly creatures for your very own. There is some information and links where you can purchase these prize creatures. This site is nice to visit if for no other reason. It is well-designed and shows some great "monsters" that you may want to own.

Genius Babies.com

http://www.geniusbabies.com/

Whether you're looking for an activity for your toddler or a baby shower gift, you're likely to find one in your price range here. Choose by age or type of toy, such as play mats or puzzles. You might want to find out what the top sellers are, which are listed at the site, too.

Hasbro World

http://www.hasbro.com

Home to the makers of Action Man, Battleship, Collector's Corner, Monopoly, Risk, Scrabble, Trivial Pursuit, Yahtzee, and many more favorites. There is a nice selection of Hasbro toys here such as G.I. Joe along with all his accessories and equipment. There is a search feature to help you locate where you can buy the toys.

Into The Wind

http://www.intothewind.com/

Claiming to be the world's largest kite seller, this site will teach you about flying a kite and give you lots of types to choose from for purchase. From flags and banners to wind socks to traditional or stunt kites, this site has them all. You can also join a discussion forum to chat with fellow kiters.

KBKids

http://www.kbkids.com/index.html

Shop by age, price, or brand for the toy you want, or find out about this week's sales before you decide. This online KB Toys site has a wide selection of toys for all ages.

Latoys.com

http://www.latoys.com/

A wide selection of toys and brands is available here with plenty of pictures to guide you.

Learning Curve International

http://www.learningcurve.com/

Learn about the toy product lines that build on your child's expanding mobility and development. Starting with soft Lamaze toys for infants, you can move to more solid Ambi toys, and into several other toy lines as your child ages. Select the product line you're interested in and then view all the available toys. The site has a feature where you can find out where to purchase these toys.

Little Tikes

http://www.littletikes.com/

View and listen to Little Tikes toys being used at this site, which shows you the complete 200+ toy line here. Then you can find out where your local store is that carries what you need. There is also a list of hot toys and those on sale.

Mattel

http://www.mattel.com

The official site of one of the worldwide leaders in the design, manufacture, and marketing of children's products including such brand names as Barbie, Hot Wheels, Tyco, Disney, and more. Guess what? You can conveniently shop online at this site for all those toys you couldn't find locally.

Nintendo

http://www.nintendo.com

Home of the king of video games, this site is packed with information about the company and its products. Here you can learn about the latest Nintendo game systems, explore the wide selection of available games, get technical support and customer service, and share your enthusiasm for Nintendo video games with other enthusiastic players. You can even play free online games, download free software, subscribe to the Nintendo newsletter, check out featured Nintendo sites, and get more information about Nintendo and its products than you could ever imagine. Very easy to navigate and packed with valuable resources for Nintendo fans.

The Official Lego World Wide Web Site

http://www.lego.com/default.asp

Aimed primarily at kids, this site lists the Lego toy groups (Lego, Duplo, and so on) and provides a parent guide, a Web surfer's club (so kids can list or make their own Lego sites), and games to play on the Internet. Also has listings of whom to contact to get the various toys in every country. You can also shop online if you prefer. One of the better sites on the Internet with great graphics and easy to navigate menus.

A
B
C
D
E
F
G
H
I
J
K
L
M
N
O
P
Q
R
S
U
V
W
X
Y
Z

A
B
C
D
E
F
G
H
I
J
K
L
M
N
O
P
Q
R
S
T
U
V
W
X
Y
Z

Only Toys

http://www.onlytoys.com/

Search this online toy store for stuffed animals, dolls, wooden toys, and more. And if you don't find exactly what you're looking for, send an email to the store and they'll tell you whether they have it in their Tennessee store. Buy more than $100 and shipping is free.

Rokenbok

http://www.rokenbok.com/

Rokenbok Toys are for kids aged five and up and are designed to be expanded. You can build with them, add cars and trucks, as well as radio-controlled pieces. Learn about the components and skills your child builds with each addition. There is a convenient deal locator to help you find your local source of toys and items for you to purchase.

Schylling

http://www.schylling.com/

If you're looking for classic toys such as tea sets or Curious George playthings, you'll want to scan this online store first.

Sega

http://www.sega.com

Games, contests, product news, an online store, technical support, and more.

SmarterKids.com

http://www.smarterkids.com/

Choose toys for your child according to their developmental stage, learning style, or grade expectation, or by teachers' and parents' recommendations. There are lots of toys to choose from, organized in many ways. And there are thousands of toys on sale at 50% off.

Toys for Tots

http://www.toysfortots.org/

The U.S. Marine Reserve program Toys for Tots is described in complete detail at this site. It goes into the history, the foundation that helps to support the program, its corporate sponsors, and most importantly, how you can help.

The Virtual Toy Store

http://www.uncomyngifts.com/

Targeted toward science fiction and fantasy enthusiasts. Offers a fully interactive toy store, complete with sound and video clips. Specializes in hard-to-find gifts, toys, T-shirts, and jewelry.

Zany Brainy

http://www.zanybrainy.com/

Web home of Zany Brainy, dedicated to providing toys that inspire minds as well as inspiring fun. Here, you can search for a specific toy or type of toy or browse the well-stocked shelves by categories, including Arts & Crafts, Dolls, Electronics, Science & Nature, and Trains. Buy books, software, videos, and CDs online; check for upcoming store events, and find out where the closest Zany Brainy store is located. Shop online and have your order shipped to your door. You can even have your gifts wrapped for you.

TRACK AND FIELD

Athens 2004

http://www.athens.olympic.org/

The official home pages of the 2004 Summer Olympics, to be held in Athens, Greece. You can view media releases, environmental guidelines, information about any of the events, and other information. Download free screensavers, desktop wallpaper, and e-cards. You can even learn about becoming one of the many volunteers who contribute to making the Olympics a success.

Athletics Canada

http://www.canoe.ca/Athcan/
home.html

As the governing body for Canadian track and field, Athletics Canada's page focuses on Canadian athletes, records, rankings, events, coaching, and news.

Athletics Home Page

http://hkkk.fi/~niininen/
athl.html

A book of records—every record known to the sport is listed here, or a link is provided. Want to know track records for Croatia, South Africa, or Bulgaria? Try this page first, and you'll know what to shoot for.

Kangaroo's Triple Jump Online

http://www.owlnet.rice.edu/
~riceroo/tjol/

Not just your casual jumper, this site's author has been studying the biomechanics of jumping since high school. The pages include triple jump and long jump

resources, articles, a poll of the best jumpers, and a media archive dedicated to the sport.

Kelly's Running Warehouse

http://www.cheapshoes.com/

With more than 75,000 running shoes in stock at prices up to $50 off, runners will want to at least check the inventory at this site before their next purchase. You can shop online using 100% secure shopping.

Masters Track and Field

http://www.mastertrack.com/
index.shtml

Young whippersnappers aren't the only people enjoying themselves on the track. This page is dedicated to running seniors, some of whom, into their nineties, are still breaking records.

Road Runner Sports Shoe Store

http://www.roadrunnersports.com

Research and buy sports shoes, including name brands such as Nike, Reebok, Adidas, and Puma. If you like to shop online, this site has a very nice, well organized and easy-to-navigate online store.

Runner's Web

http://www.runnersweb.com/
running.html

Information source for running competitions, news, and accessories.

A
B
C
D
E
F
G
H
I
J
K
L
M
N
O
P
Q
R
S
T
U
V
W
X
Y
Z

Runner's World Online

http://www.runnersworld.com/

Home of the popular Runner's
World magazine, this site features
some of the best articles about
track and field events, cross-country,
and marathons. Free training log
and workout regimens, training
plans, and calculators. Shoe and
treadmill reviews, treatments for
injuries, nutrition information, and
much more.

Running Network

http://www.runningnetwork.com/

Get running tips, news, and links,
as well as a track calendar and race
results. This e-zine is dedicated to
America's 3,600,000 track-and-field
participants from the high school
to the post-college club level. The
site has a nice list of stores in different states that you can shop from.

Best Track and Field News

http://www.trackandfieldnews.com/

Peruse past issues, and check up
on races, athletes, and records. The
countless articles will keep die-hard
runners busy until they're rested
and ready to start running again.
This site offers much for the online
shopper as well. You can shop in a
nice, easy-to-navigate online store
and purchase everything from
books to videos. You can review the
latest issue of the magazine, see the
men's world rankings by nation,
and search for articles of interest in
the archive, and it even has a calendar and several links to related sites.
With all it offers and its pleasing
presentation, this site grabs the gold.

Training for 400m/800m: An Alternative Plan

http://www.pnc.com.au/~stevebn/
plan.htm

This site shares information gathered by its author regarding better
methods to prepare an athlete to
run in either the 400- or 800-meter
medium sprints. The information
includes specific training regimens.

USA Track and Field

http://www.usatf.org/

The official site of track and field's
overseeing authority in the United
States. These pages contain news,
national and international records,
race walking resources, masters racing, and race numerology.

Vault World (Pole Vault Paradise)

http://www.polevault.com/

Get questions answered in the
Coaching Area, see who the top
vaulters are this year, link to related
sites, view pictures and videos, and
read articles about vaulting.

TRAVEL AND VACATION

ADVENTURE

Adventure Center

http://www.adventurecenter.com/

Adventure Center provides safaris, treks, expeditions, and active vacations worldwide in Antarctica, South America, Europe, Africa, Asia, and the South Pacific. Tribal encounters are common, and you can see images of past trips at this site, where you can find out more about upcoming travel opportunities.

Adventurous Traveler Bookstore

http://www.gorp.com/atbook.htm

The claim "The world's most complete source of outdoor adventure books and maps" pretty much says it all. You can search this bookstore's entire database from this site.

Mountain Travel Sobek

http://www.mtsobek.com/

There are a huge number of different types of adventure travel trips described at this company's site—from hiking adventures to river rafting, biking, small boat cruises, and many more. Look at photos from past trips and read the Travel Journal to hear from past travelers about some of their experiences.

Rod and Gun Resources

http://rodgunresources.com/

An international hunting and fishing adventure travel company offering trips around the world. See the site for information about destinations and to see comments from past travelers.

Silver Lining Tours

http://silverlining.pair.com/
chase.html

Ever wanted to see a storm up close? Then see this site for information on storm-chasing adventures planned for next year. Learn about what you might see and how you can sign up for this very popular tour. This site has a lot of information about tornadoes and severe storms if you are interested in that sort of thing. If you don't want to pay for a tour, just move to the Midwest if you don't already live there. The site has contact information you will need to sign up for the trip.

Storm Chasing Adventure Tours

http://storm-chaser.com/tour.html

Another storm-chasing travel operator that will tell you about upcoming trips and accommodations. Trips are 13 days long. The site has contact information for helping you plan your tour online.

A
B
C
D
E
F
G
H
I
J
K
L
M
N
O
P
Q
R
S
T
U
V
W
X
Y
Z

Best Tornado Alley Safari Tours

http://tornadosafari.com

Learn about the storms this travel company has encountered on its expeditions and get information on upcoming trips to witness serious storms and tornadoes. You can get contact information here for planning your tour. This site was featured on several top network news shows and is very well organized with lots of pictures and information about the tours. If you like tornadoes, lightning, and severe weather, this site is well worth a visit. Site also features numerous pictures of previous tours that have resulted in encounters with tornadoes and severe storms.

Travel Source

http://www.travelsource.com/

Use this travel search guide to find the adventure travel experience you're looking for with the activities and location you want.

The Veiled Voyage

http://www.vvoyage.com/

A mystery travel company that arranges special themed vacations based on your interests and budget. You pick the type of excursion you want—such as golf, romantic, or shopping—and the amount of money you want to spend. Then Veiled Voyage makes all the arrangements but doesn't tell you where you're headed until shortly before you're set to go. You can make reservations and sign up here using your credit card.

Walking Adventures International

http://www.walkingadventures.com/

Consider taking a walking tour of interesting places all around the world with this group, which travels through the United States, Europe, the Mediterranean, and many more places. Check the travel schedule to see when and where you might like to go. There is information on the site to help you conveniently sign up for the tour.

AIR TRAVEL

Air Charter Guide

http://inetserver.guides.com/acg/

The online edition of The Air Charter Guide, a limited version of the book. Serves as a guide for locating charter operators, arranged by state, name. Also includes tips on planning and pricing a charter.

Airlines of the Web

http://flyaow.com/

Provides information about airlines, organized by geographic region. Also provides information about cargo airlines, newsgroups, and airports.

AirlineSafety.com

http://www.airlinesafety.com/

Devoted to making airlines safer for passengers to fly, this site attempts to provide an open forum about airline safety that's free from special interests and politics. Here you can read articles on various airline safety topics that you won't see in the daily news.

Airpasses of the World

http://www.etn.nl/airpass.htm

> Links to airlines that offer airpasses. An airpass can be used only by a foreign visitor, and they are fabulous bargains. If you are planning to visit outside of your home country, check the possibility of using an airpass.

AirSafe.com

http://www.airsafe.com/

> If you're worried about airline safety and security, this is the site for you. Here you will find tips on how best to deal with safety issues, terrorist threats, airport security, and baggage issues. Loads of tips available to make your air travel safer and make it proceed with fewer hassles. Get the latest safety statistics for various airlines and airplane models, plus additional travel advice. Before you head to the airport, head to this site.

Flight Arrivals

http://www.flightarrivals.com

> Real-time arrival and departure times for flights throughout the United States and Canada. Just type in the flight information and learn whether it's on time.

AIRLINES

Aer Lingus

http://www.aerlingus.ie/

Air Canada

http://www.aircanada.ca/

Alaska Airlines

http://www.alaska-air.com

America West

http://www.americawest.com

American Airlines

http://www.aa.com/

Ansett Australia

http://www.ansett.com.au/

British Airways

http://www.british-airways.com/ecp_no_dhtml.shtml

Canadian Airlines International

http://www.cdnair.ca/

Cathay Pacific

http://www.cathaypacific.com/

Continental

http://www.continental.com

Delta

http://www.delta.com/

Hawaiian Airlines

http://www.hawaiianair.com

Lufthansa

http://www.lufthansa.com/

New England Airlines

http://users.ids.net/flybi/nea/

A
B
C
D
E
F
G
H
I
J
K
L
M
N
O
P
Q
R
S
T
U
V
W
X
Y
Z

A
B
C
D
E
F
G
H
I
J
K
L
M
N
O
P
Q
R
S
T
U
V
W
X
Y
Z

Northwest

http://www.nwa.com

Qantas Airlines

http://www.qantas.com/

(\$)

Southwest

http://www.southwest.com/

(\$)

TWA

http://www.twa.com

(\$)

United

http://www.ual.com

(\$)

US Airways

http://www.usairways.com

(\$)

BARGAIN TRAVEL

11th Hour Vacations

http://www.11thhourvacations.com

(\$)

Browse the available trips and cruises with departure dates in the next couple of weeks to find great deals. Whether you want to see New York City or Greece, there are a huge number of options to choose from. And the prices are very reasonable. You can also enter your email to be alerted to deals on a particular destination.

Bestfares.com

http://www.bestfares.com/

Sign up for the BestFares weekly email to be alerted to special discount opportunities for Thursday through Tuesday travel. Some great deals you wouldn't have found anywhere else.

Bidtripper.com

http://www.bidtripper.com

Learn about the opportunity to bid on travel bargains that meet specific criteria that you select.

CheapTickets

http://web.cheaptickets.com

Self-billed as "The Best Kept Secret in Travel," this site offers inexpensive air fares, car rentals, and hotel reservations. Simply specify your departure point, desired destination, and dates of travel, and CheapTickets can put together a package for you.

DiscountAirfares.com

http://www.discountairfares.com

Lots of links to low-cost airfare sites.

Expedia

http://www.expedia.com

Search for travel deals, make reservations, and shop around for special packages at Expedia.

LastMinuteTravel.com

http://www.lastminutetravel.com/

A site where you can find last-minute deals on airfare, hotels, cars, and cruises. Search by departure date or desired destination.

Lowestfare.com

http://www.lowestfare.com/

If you are planning a vacation, cruise, or just a short trip into the next state, you will find a travel guide and a reservation section here and all at the lowest fares. Check out the fares here before planning your trip.

Moment's Notice

http://www.moments-notice.com

Check the daily specials to find last minute travel deals at greatly reduced prices. Sign up for email alerts when travel bargains arise that meet your particular interests.

OneTravel.com

http://www.onetravel.com/index.cfm

This site tracks hot deals for airfare, cruises, resorts, and long weekends. You can search multiple departure cities at the same time, and you can request customized emails to be sent to you weekly to keep you posted of specials that matter to you. Some excellent travel advice from the experts, too.

priceline.com

http://www.priceline.com

Place a bid on airfare, hotels, and car rentals and see whether a company will accept it. If they do, you can save hundreds or even thousands of dollars.

SkyAuction.com

http://www.skyauction.com/

Bid on airfares, resorts, hotels, and car rentals starting at $1.

Travel Discounts

http://www.traveldiscounts.com/

A business travel–oriented site providing information about discounts on car rentals, railroads, tours, cruises, airlines, and specific tour packages arranged by region.

Travelairline.com

http://www.travelairline.com/

Free real-time booking! Rates up to 65% off—hotel rooms exclusively available online through Travelairline.com, even if they're sold out! Book your air, hotel, and car with them online.

Travelocity

http://www.travelocity.com

Full online travel service with information on destinations, travel bargains, and travel tips. Pager service provides flight information.

BUDGET TRAVEL

Arthur Frommer's Budget Travel Online

http://www.frommers.com

Features and resources for all types of vacations and travel. Includes a travel planner and tips on booking travel.

A B C D E F G H I J K L M N O P Q R S T U V W X Y Z

ArtofTravel.com

http://www.artoftravel.com/

Read this online book to learn how to backpack around the world for less than $25 a day. You'll find tips, commentary, and humor here about backpacking and world travel.

Backpack Europe on a Budget

http://www.backpackeurope.com/

Learn some of the strategies that can make it possible for you to backpack across Europe inexpensively. Find out about hostels, working abroad, and discount packages.

Budget Hotels

http://www.budgethotels.com

Find accommodations around the world at discount prices, as well as other travel bargains on cars and airfares here.

Busabout Europe

http://www.busabout.com/

The economical alternative to rail travel. Connects 66 cities in Europe by bus.

Council Travel

http://www.counciltravel.com/

Offers discount and budget airfares, rail passes, hostel memberships, international student ID cards, and more, for student, youth, and budget travelers.

Economy Travel

http://www.economytravel.com/

Lowest international airfares on the Web, booked online. Consolidator fares, private fares, and low published fares, all on one site.

Hostels.com

http://www.hostels.com/

Find a hostel or low-cost hotel near where you're traveling and learn more about what to expect from experienced travelers at this site.

CAR RENTAL

Alamo Rent A Car

http://www.goalamo.com/

Avis

http://www.avis.com

Budget Rent a Car

http://www.drivebudget.com/

Dollar Rent A Car

http://www.dollar.com/

Economy Car Rental Aruba

http://www.economyaruba.com/

Enterprise Rent-A-Car

http://www.enterprise.com/

Hertz

http://www.hertz.com

National Car

http://www.nationalcar.com

Rent-A-Wreck

http://rent-a-wreck.com/

Thrifty Car Rental

http://www.thrifty.com/

CAR TRAVEL

ASIRT: Association for Safe International Road Travel

http://www.asirt.org

Want to know which countries are the most dangerous to drive in? You'll find out here, as well as other road information and safety data.

Auto Europe Car Rentals

http://www.autoeurope.com/

Auto Europe offers auto rentals, discounted airfare, and hotel packages worldwide. Check the Travel Specials to find this week's bargains.

BreezeNet's Rental Car Guide and Reservations

http://www.bnm.com/

A one-stop car rental site for quick online reservations to auto rental companies with airport service. Also includes coupons, discounts, and phone numbers.

Route 66

http://www.historic66.com/

Get your kicks on the famous roadway Route 66. This site is packed with photos, stories, and a wealth of helpful information. Also features a locator map.

Scenic Byways and Other Recreational Drives

http://www.gorp.com/gorp/
activity/byway/byway.htm

Organized into categories such as Far West, Desert Southwest, Great Plains, and Great Lakes, this site helps you locate the scenic route to your destination. Contains links to a majority of the 50 states.

Traveling in the USA

http://www.travelingusa.com/

These pages will help the U.S. traveler find information on parks, campgrounds, resorts, and recreation. From relief maps to kiddie activities, you'll probably satisfy your travel needs here. Also features links for Traveling Australia, Canada, and New Zealand.

CRUISES

Carnival Cruises

http://www.carnival.com/

Home of one of the most popular cruise lines in the world, this site provides quick quotes on the cost of your cruise. Just select a destination, specify the desired length of the cruise (in days), and pick a month. Site also provides information about destinations and guest services, group travel rates, and ways to finance your cruise. Also learn about job openings at this site.

A
B
C
D
E
F
G
H
I
J
K
L
M
N
O
P
Q
R
S
T
U
V
W
X
Y
Z

A
B
C
D
E
F
G
H
I
J
K
L
M
N
O
P
Q
R
S
T
U
V
W
X
Y
Z

Cruise Specialists

http://www.cruiseinc.com/

Provides information and profiles about many different cruises and destinations. Includes company backgrounds, photo albums, cruise reviews, and ordering information, as well as links to cruise lines on the Web.

Cruise Value Center

http://www.cruisevalue.com/

Find great values in cruises throughout the United States and Caribbean here.

Cruise.com

http://www.cruise.com/

This site provides cruise reviews, statistics, and deals and offers to beat just about any offer you can find.

CruiseStar.com

http://www.cruisestar.com/

In addition to cruise reviews and FAQs, you'll find discount cruises, last minute deals, and bargains organized by cruise line.

Freighter World Cruises

http://www.freighterworld.com/

Advertises Freighter World Cruises, Inc., a travel agency that focuses on freighter travel. Provides information on various freighter lines and their destinations. Cruise in economy style.

Holland America Line

http://www.hollandamerica.com/

This site has information on Holland America Line's cruises to Alaska, the Caribbean, Hawai'i, Asia and the Pacific, South America, Canada and New England, and Europe. You might request literature and order a video on your desired cruise destination.

i-cruise.com

http://www.i-cruise.com/

Search for cruises by destination, travel date, or type of trip—singles, group, honeymoon, or linked with an adventure travel tour.

mytravelco.com

http://www.mytravelco.com

You'll find all sorts of travel deals and information on getting discounts on cruises, airfare, and group tours here.

Norwegian Cruise Line

http://www.ncl.com/

Read about Norwegian Cruise Line destinations and music theme cruises, such as a big band cruise. Sample destinations are Mexico, Hawai'i, Alaska, and the Caribbean. Find out about special deals.

Princess Cruises

http://www.awcv.com/princess.html

Cruise on the Love Boat to the Caribbean. Find out about special discounts, 50% or more. You can book your cruise online.

Schooner Mary Day

http://www.schoonermaryday.com/

The *Schooner Mary Day* is a sailing cruise ship (Windjammer) that carries couples, singles, and groups on three- to six-day cruises among the islands of Midcoast Maine. There is online contact information for booking a cruise.

INFORMATION/ TRAVEL TIPS

A&E Traveler

http://travel.aande.com/

Not your average travel agent, this travel site, maintained by A&E, the History Channel, and Biography, is designed to help you plan trips to some of the more interesting points on the globe. Pick a country and an interest to view a list of available tours.

Away.com

http://away.com/index.adp

Are you tired of the standard vacations to Florida, Hawai'i, and other popular tourist destinations? Then check out Away.com for some more unique ideas. Here, you can learn about trips to far out places ranging from Alaska to Zimbabwe; search by activity to find archaeological trips, windsurfing hot spots, or ecological adventures; or search by interest to find inspirational destinations.

biztravel.com

http://www.biztravel.com/

Business travelers can plan upcoming trips, get destination information, and track and manage account summaries for multiple frequent travel programs here.

The Compleat Carry-On Traveler

http://www.oratory.com/travel/

Learn how to travel light, with tips on what to pack and how to pack. You'll also find travel resource information and other tips on making travel easier.

Culture Finder.com

http://www.culturefinder.com/

Locate information on arts and cultural events in major cities nationwide. A handy resource to check before leaving town.

Ecotourism Explorer

http://www.ecotourism.org/

Official Web site of The International Ecotourism Society (TIES), this site provides information about finding and using ecology-friendly lodging and travel services. Learn how to make ecologically responsible travel decisions, check out some sample trips, and learn more about ecotourism.

Excite Travel

http://travel.excite.com

The first Web site stop any cyber-traveler should make. Contains a well-organized index of most features of more than 2,090 cities and 780 other locations worldwide. Take a virtual tour of Marseille, check the subway schedule for Philadelphia, or find out what types of entertainment are available in Victoria.

Fodor's Travel Online

http://www.fodors.com

Features guides to cities worldwide, travel chat, and resources. Also lets you custom-tailor a guide to more than 90 destinations worldwide.

A
B
C
D
E
F
G
H
I
J
K
L
M
N
O
P
Q
R
S

U
V
W
X
Y
Z

A
B
C
D
E
F
G
H
I
J
K
L
M
N
O
P
Q
R
S
T
U
V
W
X
Y
Z

Gimponthego.com

http://gimponthego.com

Pick up disabled travel news, tips, and suggestions for packing at this site, which aims to connect disabled travelers to aid in sharing information.

IgoUgo

http://www.igougo.com

Looking for travel advice from real people who traveled where you plan to go? Then look no further. IgoUgo features personal travel journals for more than 2,000 destinations written by regular people who have actually visited those places. Find out about the best places to stay, the top restaurants offering the best value, interesting sites, and much more. Links to other services to book flights and cruises, rent automobiles, reserve a room, and more. Also features a good collection of photos of various destinations.

Journeywoman

http://www.journeywoman.com

From where Queen Elizabeth buys her bras to how to stay healthy in Tibet, to girls-only fly-fishing in the United States, Journeywoman dispenses valuable travel tips gathered from around the world. Written entirely from a female perspective.

Lonely Planet Online

http://www.lonelyplanet.com/

Lonely Planet guidebooks have always catered to the budget traveler. At this site you can explore U.S. and world destinations. Simply click on a region, a country, or a city to get started. The Optic Nerve gives you pictures of the area you

are considering. Read a selection from a book related to a journey that might be of interest, post messages for other travelers to respond to, and lots more.

The North American Virtual Tourist

http://www.virtualtourist.com/North_America/

An incredible resource for North American travel! One click on the image map of North America will lead you to every WWW resource available for the selected state or region. This site is heaven for those looking for an all-encompassing site in the United States, Canada, and Mexico. Make a bookmark and visit frequently!

Parentsoup Family Travel

http://www.parentsoup.com/travel

Lots of tips for traveling with kids, finding great deals, and making your trip more pleasant. You can also chat with a travel expert each week.

Pets Welcome

http://www.petswelcome.com

Look through the Listings page to find hotels, bed-and-breakfasts, resorts, campgrounds, and beaches that are pet-friendly. Learn from other pet owners who've traveled with their friends, and share your advice with others in the discussion forums.

Rough Guides

http://www.roughguides.com

Read online articles at this publisher's site to find out more about traveling to exotic locations. Learn more about restaurants, landmarks, the people, and things to do for many cities.

Round-the-World Travel Guide

http://www.travel-library.com/
rtw/html/

Offers links to sites that help you
make travel decisions, choose transportation and accommodations,
and provide information on money
matters and communications.
Covers travel-related newsgroups.

The Savvy Traveler

http://www.savvytraveler.com/

This Minnesota Public Radio presentation, hosted by Diana Nyad,
provides traveling tips from seasoned travelers.

timeout.com

http://www.timeout.com/

Get the latest information about
bars, restaurants, night life, and
more for the top 33 cities in the
world. Just click on London,
Beijing, New York, Paris, or many
others, to get the inside scoop on
the scene.

Tourism Offices Worldwide Directory

http://www.towd.com/

Find tourism information about
countries around the world, or
locate U.S. offices in other countries as well. A useful resource to
check before you head out of town.

Travel Channel Online

http://travel.discovery.com/

Programming and schedules along
with travel resources and travel chat
from the folks who bring us the
Discovery Channel. Choose to
explore the site by destination or
idea. Check out the live Webcams
and the interactive gallery.

Travel Facts

http://www.travelfacts.com

Provides detailed information and
photos for dozens of destinations,
hotel and restaurant databases, a
chat room, feature articles, and
more.

Travel Medicine

http://healthlink.mcw.edu/
content/topic/Travel_Medicine

Provides information about diseases, environmental concerns, and
immunizations for travelers.
Includes tips on what to pack in
your travel medicine kit and concerns for pregnant women who are
traveling.

The Travel Page

http://www.travelpage.com/

A thorough travel-planning site for
visitors. Make hotel, airline, and
cruise reservations online. Provides
vacation recommendations ranging
from the more popular to the truly
unique.

Travel.com

http://www.travel.com/

Get travel advisories, weather information, as well as recreational,
shopping, and real-time flight
information at this site, which is
arranged as a travel search engine.

The Travelite FAQ

http://www.travelite.org/

Learn more than you probably ever
wanted to know about packing tips.
You'll find out about luggage, what
to bring, packing methods, electri-
cal appliances, accessories, and
more.

A
B
C
D
E
F
G
H
I
J
K
L
M
N
O
P
Q
R
S
T
U
V
W
X
Y
Z

Travelon

http://www.travelon.com

Travel resources ranging from trips offered by adventure and specialty travel companies to cruises and package vacations.

TravelSource

http://www.travelsource.com/

Includes information about different vacation packages and locations. Also provides links to travel agents and other travel resources to fine-tune your vacation plans. Whether you're looking to scuba dive, white-water raft, take a cruise, or simply kick back, this site is your one-stop vacation planner.

TravelWeb

http://www.travelweb.com

Search for flight and hotel information here.

Uniglobe.com

http://www.uniglobe.com/

Designed for individuals and small business travelers looking for a one-stop shop for airline, hotel, car rental, cruises, and vacation package information.

Virtual Tourist

http://www.virtualtourist.com/

Information and links about entertainment, media, business, culture, and traveling opportunities all over the world.

Zagat.com

http://www.zagat.com/splash.asp

You'll find more than 20,000 restaurant reviews for dining spots around the world. Choose a city and you'll get recommendations for where to dine that evening.

INTERNATIONAL TRAVEL

1000Tips4Trips

http://www.tips4trips.com/

More than 1,000 travel tips submitted by real travelers. Search for tips by keyword or browse by categories, which include Air Travel, Cruises, Just for Men, Just for Women, Traveling with Children, Traveling with Pets, and more.

AFRICANET

http://www.africanet.com/

Use the search feature to track down just what you're looking for in the way of Africa travel information. Get in-depth information on many African countries and learn about recommended African sites to check out.

Airhitch

http://www.airhitch.org/

This down-and-dirty site will help you learn how to travel to and within Europe for very little money, as well as telling you about other amazing travel deals. You might not have the coziest of accommodations, but you can get there cheaply.

Australia Travel Directory

http://www.anzac.com/aust/aust.htm

Offers links to information on tourism, visas, individual states, and transportation.

Bargain Travel Cruises–Cheap Cruises

http://www.bargaintravelcruises.com/

You can have a terrific vacation at the lowest possible cost by doing some research for the best possible deals available. You can take a bargain cruise by selecting from the best and cheapest available on this site. The site contains contact information on how to sign up for that trip of your dreams.

CDC (Centers for Disease Control and Prevention)

http://www.cdc.gov/travel/

This United States government health agency is dedicated to preventing the spread of infectious diseases. This site provides useful, up-to-date information about health risks and disease outbreaks in areas all over the world. Find out which vaccinations you should receive and treatments you should pack before you leave for your trip. Also provides up-to-date information about biological agents, such as anthrax.

China Travel Specialists

http://www.chinaexplorer.com/

Find out how to arrange group or individual travel to China, getting as little or as much assistance from this travel group as you'd like.

Czech Info Center

http://www.muselik.com/czech/frame.html

An incredibly well-organized guide to the Czech Republic. Includes general information, bulletin boards (such as finding an ancestor), helpful travel information, and a section on the city of Prague.

Europe Today Travel and Tourist Information

http://europe-today.com

Travel and tourist information covering 16 European countries, regions, resorts, travel tips, excursions, tours, hotels, and competitions.

European Visits

http://www.eurodata.com/

This "online magazine of European travel" offers articles on travel through Europe, as well as flight and hotel information. Get rail passes as well as guidebooks and maps online here, too.

Eurotrip.com

http://www.eurotrip.com

Anyone considering backpacking through Europe will want to start at this site for information on flying there cheaply, which hostels to stay in, what to see and do, packing, getting rail passes, and much more.

Help For World Travelers

http://www.kropla.com/

Find out the basics of electricity and phone usage in countries around the world. You'll want to know this stuff so you can use your modem and blow dry your hair after you get there.

Indonesia

http://www.sino.net/asean/indonesa.html

Serves as a guide to Indonesia—its customs, traveling within the country, entertainment, useful phrases, currency, and other traveler tips. Includes a recording of the National Anthem of Indonesia and a soon-to-be-available video clip.

A
B
C
D
E
F
G
H
I
J
K
L
M
N
O
P
Q
R
S
T
U
V
W
X
Y
Z

International Travel Guide for Mallorca and the Balearic Islands

http://www.mallorcaonline.com

Check out this international travel guide for Mallorca and the Balearic Islands to plan your next trip to Spain.

International Travel and Health

http://www.who.int/ith/

This World Health Organization's publication on world health and infectious diseases is an invaluable resource for world travelers. This site features information on traveling by air, environmental health risks, travel accidents, infectious diseases, and more. Search by country to determine specific health risks for a particular region.

Mexico: Travel Trips for the Yucatan Peninsula

http://www.geocities.com/
TheTropics/5087/

Travel advice for people wanting to go to Mexico or the Yucatan Peninsula. Advice on choosing an airline, resorts, shopping, the best places to see, and many other things.

The Monaco Home Page

http://www.monaco.mc/

Presents the Principality of Monaco and its tourism, business, and motor racing. Includes English and French versions.

MU-MU Travel Tips in Japan

http://www.
asahi-net.or.jp/~py3y-knd/

Many important tips for travelers to Japan. Don't worry about the culture difference, just visit this home page for advice on food, money, and more.

OANDA.com

http://www.oanda.com/converter/
classic

Quickly convert U.S. dollars into any other currency using this handy online converter. You can also convert into U.S. dollars by specifying the international currency.

Peru

http://www.travelspots.com/
peru.htm

Anything you want to know about travel through Peru is probably here. How to get there, what to see, what to do, what to eat, how to dress, and what to listen to. It's all here and easy to click to.

Planeta

http://www.planeta.com

Environmentally aware travelers will want to check out Planeta, which is a guide to ecologically and environmentally responsible travel through South America and the Caribbean. This site serves as a central repository for travel that explores conservation and local development issues. Contributors include travel operators, environmentalists, and fellow travelers.

Rick Steves' Europe Through the Back Door

http://www.ricksteves.com/

Learn what Rick Steves means about traveling Europe through the "back door," at his site, which contains information gleaned from his travel books, as well as information on upcoming trips through Europe that he manages.

A
B
C
D
E
F
G
H
I
J
K
L
M
N
O
P
Q
R
S
U
V
W
X
Y
Z

Salzburg, Austria

http://www.salzburg.com/holiday/
index_e.html

Provides seasonal tourist information about Salzburg, Austria, and its surrounding regions. Offers alternatives to traditional holiday plans when abroad (in German and English).

Sri Lanka Internet Services

http://www.lanka.net

The Sri Lanka Web server page with links to travel and business guides, maps, gems, news, and Internet access information.

Sydney International Travel Centre

http://www.sydtrav.com.au

Sydney International Travel is an integrated agency, combining corporate, wholesale, and retail departments, specializing in individual group arrangements and personalized tour programs. You will be able to plan and purchase your trip online.

Tour Canada Without Leaving Your Desk

http://www.cs.cmu.edu/Web/
Unofficial/Canadiana/
Travelogue.html

Take a virtual vacation in Canada and each of its provinces via the Web site links provided. This site is a good resource for anything you'd like to find out about Canada and what it has to offer for tourists.

United Kingdom Pages

http://uk-pages.net/

Provides information about the United Kingdom in many categories: Higher Education, Cities, Countryside, Culture, Government, Travel, Employment, and more. Provides more than a thousand links to other sites, primarily within the United Kingdom. Also lists bed-and-breakfast accommodations, picturesque pubs, and so forth. Offers several photo albums of downloadable images, including a page of photographs of the Royals.

United States State Department Travel Warnings and Consular Info Sheets

http://travel.state.gov/
travel_warnings.html

Provides up-to-date information for international travelers, including warnings, entry requirements, medical requirements, political status, and crime information for travel sites abroad. Also includes the location of the U.S. embassy in each country. Countries are easy to find in an alphabetical index.

Universal Currency Converter

http://www.xe.com/ucc/

Presents the exchange rate for 90 currencies. Don't be taken for an ignorant tourist and robbed blind when touring another country. If you need to know what Indian rupees are worth in Dutch guilders, this site will not let you down. Exchange rates are updated daily.

Vagabond Travel

http://members.shaw.ca/
vagabondtravel/

Your full-service travel agency based in Vancouver, Canada. Will take care of your travel and accommodation needs, from a cruise to an around-the-world trip.

A
B
C
D
E
F
G
H
I
J
K
L
M
N
O
P
Q
R
S
T
U
V
W
X
Y
Z

Vancouver, British Columbia

http://www.city.vancouver.bc.ca/

Provides FreeNet's information and links about Vancouver. Also offers links to the British Columbia home page and other Canadian home pages.

World Hum

http://www.worldhum.com

This unique travel site focuses less on commerce and more on human interaction, the stuff that makes most trips most memorable. Here, you'll find some of the best travel stories on the Web. This site encourages visitors to break out of their small, limited lives and expand their horizons through travel and human interaction.

World Travel Guide

http://www.wtgonline.com/navigate/world.asp

A quick worldwide reference guide from Sabre with top-line information on just about anyplace in the world.

World Travel and Tourism Web Sites on the Internet

http://bestofthenet.tv/wtravel.html

This site provides many links to other Web sites about world travel and tourism that you will find useful and all accessible from one central point.

ISLAND TRAVEL

All-Inclusives Resort and Cruise Vacation Source

http://www.all-inclusives.com/

This site offers information on Caribbean and Mexican cruises and resorts as well as vacation information about Alaska, the Panama Canal, and Hawai'i. Their offer is to give you all services with one payment and you can sit back and enjoy it without worrying about attached costs. Links to Magellan's, Amazon.com, and Sharper Image for online shopping.

America's Caribbean Paradise

http://www.usvi.net/

Provides information about the Virgin Islands, including wedding and vacation information, holidays, carnivals and other events, and weather forecasts. Also offers a section on real estate, vacation rentals, recipes, and Caribbean products.

Club Med

http://www.clubmed.com/

Locate a Club Med location that meets your needs for a particular type of vacation and activities, find out more about the atmosphere there, check on current deals, and even take a 360-degree look at some of the beaches.

Galveston Island Official Tourism Site

http://www.galvestontourism.com

Your official site for information about Galveston, including maps, weather reports, activities, attractions, restaurants, and entertainment. You can even reserve a room online!

Hideaway Holidays: Travel Specialists to the Pacific Islands

http://www.hideawayholidays.com.au/

Specialist tour wholesaler to the exotic islands of the South Pacific.

Air/land inclusive or land-only packages. Inquiries welcome from anyone.

Holman Travel Agency

http://visitmyweb.com/holman/

A travel service with links to travel specials and exotic travel, including Hawai'i, Tahiti, Fiji, and other islands. Airline, accommodations, and pricing information included.

Isles of Scilly Travel Centre

http://www.islesofscilly-travel.co.uk

Sea and air services to the Isles of Scilly from southwest U.K. Pictures and information about these sub-tropical islands.

NetWeb Bermuda Home Page

http://www.bermuda.com/

Offers links to Bermuda travel and cultural information. Also serves as an advertising site for Bermuda businesses.

Tybee Island Home Page

http://www.tybeeisland.com

The complete Tybee Island information center. Includes information on rental units, hotels and motels, restaurants, night life, shopping, and more.

Washington's Island Sampler

http://www.scenic-cycling.com/wa_is_samp.htm

This site gives you a 5-day, 4-night bicycling tour of Washington state's San Juan islands, which boast some of the best bicycling in the country. Check out the itinerary and take in the breathtaking photos.

World Beaches

http://www.surf-sun.com/worldbeaches.html

This site can help you to choose the perfect coastal destination. It links to sandy sites throughout the United States and around the world.

LODGING

Alaskan Cabin, Cottage, and Lodge Catalog

http://www.midnightsun.com

The Alaskan Cabin, Cottage, and Lodge Catalog is a comprehensive listing of all the wilderness cabins, cottages, and lodges in the state of Alaska. It includes a listing of 200 USFS recreation cabins in the Tongass and Chugach National Forests.

all-hotels.com

http://www.all-hotels.com/

A site that aims to provide a one-stop shop for hotel reservations, centralizing information about hotels worldwide at one site. Get information on available hotels and rooms for cities around the world, and book online when you find what you want. More than 60,000 hotels in 9,600 locations in the database.

Campground Directory

http://www.holipub.com/camping/director.htm

Look here for a place in the 50 states, Great Britain, or Canada to pitch a tent (or a camper). Searchable/browsable database of more than 10,000 campgrounds across these nations.

A
B
C
D
E
F
G
H
I
J
K
L
M
N
O
P
Q
R
S
T
U
V
W
X
Y
Z

Choice Hotels

http://www.hotelchoice.com/

More than 5,000 of the Choice Hotels International are available from this site, which includes branches of Econolodge, Clarion, Comfort Inn, and more. Reservations are available from this site.

Colorado Association of Campgrounds, Cabins, and Lodges

http://www.coloradoadventure.net/

The leading source for Colorado campgrounds, cabins, and lodges. Includes Colorado recreation, vacations, adventures, and fun things to do. Come and experience beautiful Colorado!

Cyber Rentals

http://www.cyberrentals.com/

Looking for a really "quiet" and private vacation spot? Why not rent a home, condo, or villa for your vacation and enjoy a home away from home? This site provides you with plenty of resources for just such a vacation and many of them at bargain prices. Features available accommodations worldwide.

Holiday Junction

http://www.holidayjunction.com/

Holiday Junction is an online accommodation directory focusing on resorts, lodges, and private cottage rentals.

Hotelguide.com

http://www.hotelguide.com/

Look at a map of most major cities worldwide here to find the locations of hotels before booking a room. Then search the database to find available rooms and book online at one of more than 65,000 hotels listed for savings of up to 50%. You can also get information on vacation packages, such as golf outings, and link to other vacation and travel sites.

InnSite

http://www.innsite.com/

Search more than 50,000 pages of bed-and-breakfast listings to find one in 50 countries worldwide that meets your needs. For more detailed feedback about locations, you might want to visit the discussion groups to chat with fellow travelers.

International Bed and Breakfast Guide

http://www.ibbp.com/

National and international B&Bs dot this site. Countries featured other than the United States include Canada, Great Britain, New Zealand, and Argentina.

Lake Tahoe's West Shore Lodging

http://www.tahoecountry.com/wslodging.html

Bed-and-breakfasts, guesthouses, and lodges along Lake Tahoe's tranquil West Shore offer visitors peaceful settings and a taste of Old Tahoe.

Lodging Guide World Wide

http://www.lgww.com/

It's not called the Lodging Guide World Wide for nothing. Reservations in most major cities around the world can be made here.

The National Lodging Directory

http://www.guests.com

The National Lodging Directory, a user-friendly site, contains listings for hotels, motels, bed-and-breakfasts, and vacation rental property located in the United States. You can make online reservations on most client sites.

Professional Association of Innkeepers International

http://www.paii.org/

You'll find more than just the Innkeeping Weekly at this site, but do look at that, too. The book So You Want to Be an Innkeeper is available from this site, as are stimulating articles such as "Cutting Deals with Unlikely Allies" and B&B management tips.

Travel Web

http://www.travelweb.com/

This huge travel monster will provide more information than just lodging. This site features a unique selection of independent hotels to help you keep away from the lodging machine of franchised establishments, if that is what you're looking for; however, you can find chain hotels here, too.

West Virginia Lodging Guide

http://wvweb.com/www/
travel_recreation/lodging.html

West Virginia Lodging, a visitors guide to WV accommodations in the West Virginia Web, includes bed-and-breakfasts, camping, hotels, motels, resorts, and vacation properties.

TRAIN TRAVEL

Abercrombie & Kent

http://www.abercrombiekent.com/
html/act_ltt.html

Luxury train travel at its best. Visit this site and see how the other half lives. Travel through Scotland on the Royal Scotsman, with tours through England and Wales. Or ride aboard the Venice-Simplon Orient Express. Enjoy gourmet dining and impeccable service. Go ahead—splurge!

Amtrak

http://www.amtrak.com/

The country's foremost train authority, Amtrak, is accessed through this page. Find everything from the latest high-speed train information to travel tips and reservations on this useful home page. Promotional offers, student discounts, senior discounts, child fares, disability discounts. Check the site regularly as their seasonal fare specials vary.

Grand Canyon Railway

http://www.thetrain.com/

Read about the historic Grand Canyon Railway. This site lists timetables and fares, travel packages, and weather information. The opening graphic is wonderful, and when you "climb aboard," listen for the train whistle blowing.

A
B
C
D
E
F
G
H
I
J
K
L
M
N
O
P
Q
R
S
T
U
V
W
X
Y
Z

Orient-Express Trains & Cruises

http://www.orient-expresstrains.com/

Watch a video of one trip on this train line, called the Road to Mandalay, to get a sense of the experience of traveling cross-country via train. You can also look at the route each train travels and get information on upcoming trips. Whether you want a luxury ride through the United Kingdom, Southeast Asia, Australia, or Europe, there are several train rides to choose from.

VIA Rail Canada

http://www.viarail.ca/en.index.html

Canada's rail system. Here you will find senior rates, student rates, a frequent traveler program, the CanRailPass, and 52 outdoor adventures in Canada.

U.S. TRAVEL

Access New Hampshire

http://www.nh.com/

A comprehensive guide to the state of New Hampshire, including information about tourism, historical legacy, local happenings, and everything else under the sun.

Alabama

http://www.eng.auburn.edu/alabama/map.html

A detailed clickable image map of Alabama by city or region. Provides information of interest to the cyber-traveler in the different regions of Alabama. Offers links to other Alabama-related sites. Awarded an America's Best! site award.

Alaskan Travel Guide

http://www.alaskan.com/

Find out all about travel in and around Alaska here, from where to stay, what to see, parks to visit, and much more. Use the travel planner to sketch out your visit, as well as consider specific types of vacations.

America's Land of Enchantment: New Mexico

http://www.newmexico.org/

A traveler's guide to New Mexico. Provides information about culture, outdoor activities, area ruins, regional events, and skiing. Also includes maps and historical tidbits for travelers.

⟦Best⟧ The Arizona Guide

http://www.arizonaguide.com/

The official site for the Arizona Office of Tourism organized by region in text and image-map format. Provides up-to-date weather information, maps, and state information. Features golf resorts and, of course, the Grand Canyon and the many touring packages for exploring it. Well worth visiting even if you're not planning a trip to Arizona any time soon. Extremely well done and beautiful site. The site contains a lists of destinations, things to do, activities, offers a travel service, trip planner, maps, and even a free travel kit. If you live in the United States and with the current cost of fuel, this would be a great mini-vacation for you to look forward to. If you live in another country then it is still worth saving your money and taking a vacation here, as Arizona has a lot to see. There are also many interesting things on the site you can learn about such as places to stay, eat, and sleep. If you are an Old West fan, you won't want to miss out on visiting such historical places as Tombstone and Fort Apache.

Arkansas: The Natural State

http://www.arkansas.com/

This exhaustive tourism guide of Arkansas provides information on state parts, outdoor recreation, history and heritage, arts and entertainment, lodging and dining, and a calendar of events. Features some free Arkansas screensavers and desktop wallpaper, plus an area for kids stuff, and information about group travel.

Blue Ridge Country

http://www.blueridgecountry.com/

Read the current issue of this travel magazine dedicated to the Blue Ridge Mountain region, see photos of the area, get advice on travel routes, and read the birding guide to learn more about native species. Lots of interesting articles that will pique your interest in this area.

Boston.com Travel Page

http://travel.boston.com/places/boston/

Just about everything you might want to know about Boston is here, from what to see, where to stay, where to eat, what it's like to live here, and more, is available on the site. Read articles about famous and not-so-famous landmarks and places to visit before you get into town.

California Smart Traveler

http://caltrans511.dot.ca.gov/

Find out which California roads are closed or are under construction at this site, which also features tourism information and frequently asked questions.

Cambridge, Massachusetts

http://www.ci.cambridge.ma.us/

Features Cambridge resources and more. Offers information on the city's art, entertainment, museums, tourism, and more general information for those looking to relocate.

Cincinnati Vacation Gateways

http://cincinnati.com/getaways

If you're thinking about traveling in the United States why not visit one of the most beautiful and exciting places in the Midwest—Cincinnati, Ohio, where you can spend a day at Kings Island with the kids, stay at one of dozens of luxury hotels, and dine in some of the finest restaurants in the country. Stay awhile and watch the Bengals football team play or maybe even spend a day watching a game of baseball with the world-famous Cincinnati Reds. In its own words, the service will customize an "à la carte" vacation that is just right for you. They can provide you with hotel accommodations, tickets to events and attractions, sporting events, museums, and much, much more. This is your complete online shopping mall for a wonderful vacation in Cincinnati.

Colorado.com

http://www.colorado.com/

Request the official Colorado state guide to what's going on there or search the site for activities, view the state map to choose a destination, or search the city directory to find items of interest by location. There's also a seasonal directory to activities statewide. You'll definitely want to stop here before finalizing your plans for a trip to Colorado.

A
B
C
D
E
F
G
H
I
J
K
L
M
N
O
P
Q
R
S
U
V
W
X
Y
Z

A
B
C
D
E
F
G
H
I
J
K
L
M
N
O
P
Q
R
S
T
U
V
W
X
Y
Z

TheGrandCanyon.com

http://www.thegrandcanyon.com

Need to know more about the Grand Canyon? You'll find maps, tour information, lodging and camping details, weather information, and more to help you get the most out of your trip here.

George Washington's Mount Vernon Estate

http://www.mountvernon.org/

Take a virtual tour of Mount Vernon, or get information on visiting the estate in person. You can also find out about information from the library and archaeological digs on the premises.

Idaho Home Page

http://www.state.id.us/

Provides information on regional attractions, state parks, national forests, a calendar of events, and more general information on the state of Idaho.

Iowa Virtual Tourist

http://www.jeonet.com/tourist/

A detailed clickable image map separated by region links you to any information resources available in Iowa. Take a cyber-tour before you go for real or just enjoy the wealth of information.

Las Vegas

http://www.vegas.com

Includes a wide range of vacation-planning information concerning Las Vegas, ranging from hotel information and reservations, to show schedules, sports, conventions, betting tips, employment opportunities, and business services.

Louisiana Travel Guide

http://www.louisianatravel.com/

Request a free travel kit to learn more about all there is to do and see in Louisiana, or search online for ideas for family outings, outdoor fun, landmarks, restaurants, and accommodations.

Minneapolis

http://www.minneapolis.org

The official site of the city of Minneapolis, the city of lakes. Contains a searchable database for narrowing the scope of your search for travel information whether you're in town for a convention or on vacation with the family. From accommodations to dining and entertainment, it's all right here.

Nashville Scene

http://www.nashscene.com/

An award-winning online newspaper providing the traveler a guide to dining and events in Nashville, Tennessee, in addition to offering some insight into the Tennessean mindset.

Nebraska Travel and Tourism

http://visitnebraska.org/

A well-presented documentation of the attractions, campgrounds, hotels, and tourist sites of Nebraska presented in a colorful interface organized by locale and topic.

New Jersey and You

http://www.state.nj.us/travel/

Explore New Jersey at this Web site to find out about the main attractions, events, and accommodations. Features sections on the arts, family recreation, romantic getaways, historical sites, outdoor recreation, shopping, and sports.

New York State

http://www.iloveny.com

Get travel ideas by region, as well as accommodation and activities suggestions at this site, where you'll see photos of the varied landscape in New York State. Check the schedule of state events and attractions, too.

Oregon Online

http://www.oregon.gov/

Provides information on the government, education, and commerce of Oregon. Of particular interest to the tourist is the section on communities, which provides links to the various regions of the state that might be more pertinent to your travel plans.

RING: Online Michigan's Electronic Magazine

http://www.ring.com/michigan.html

Offers comprehensive information on what Michigan has to offer, such as local news and events, sightseeing, travel, entertainment, and more. Be sure to visit this site before you find yourself in Michigan.

Santa Fe Station

http://www.santafestation.com/

Excellent guide for tourism and business travel for Santa Fe, New Mexico. Includes a directory of restaurants, art galleries, museums, motels, and more. Features a Kids Zone with points of interest for children.

Seattle

http://www.eskimo.com/
seattle2.html

Serves as a guide to events, restaurants, accommodations, shopping, sports, and nightlife in the greater Seattle area. Also includes a weather link and news information.

South Dakota World Wide Web Site

http://www.state.sd.us/

The official state page of South Dakota, replete with travel information including area attractions, available accommodations, events, state parks, outdoor recreation, and travel tips available from an accurate clickable image map. Also provides general information about South Dakota in addition to links to other South Dakota sites.

USA CityLink

http://www.usacitylink.com

A fantastic guide to touring the 50 U.S. states. This site is organized alphabetically by state and further broken down by city. Offers links to pertinent travel information for each city. A thoroughly indexed site for the virtual or planning tourist.

Utah! Travel and Adventure Online

http://www.utah.com/

Visit the Rocky Mountains, sand dunes, and Salt Lake of Utah via a virtual tour. This site also provides general tourist information including maps and travel tips. Find out about a selection of vacation packages ranging from guided adventures to traditional family adventures. A visually breathtaking site not to be missed.

Virginia Is for Lovers

http://www.virginia.org/home.asp

An eye-pleasing site containing general tourism in addition to recreational activities, where to stay, restaurants, local events, theme attractions, and other points of interest in the state for lovers.

A
B
C
D
E
F
G
H
I
J
K
L
M
N
O
P
Q
R
S
T
U
V
W
X
Y
Z

A
B
C
D
E
F
G
H
I
J
K
L
M
N
O
P
Q
R
S
T
U
V
W
X
Y
Z

Vista Alaska

http://www.ptialaska.net/
~vistatrv/main.html

$

A full-service Alaskan travel agency specializing in Alaskan tours and cruises. Guaranteed lowest rates for Princess Cruises in the United States.

Washington D.C.

http://www.district-of-columbia.
com

Take a look at some of the most popular attractions and activities in Washington, as well as getting the editor's picks for hotels and restaurants. Recreation and travel into the area are also covered at this comprehensive site.

The Yankee Traveler

http://www.newengland.com/yt/
yt.html

Provides a compilation of travel-related sources of New England. Includes state Web pages, information on Cape Cod and the islands, bed-and-breakfast inns, and map links. Also provides information about real estate, local businesses, and more.

WEEKEND GETAWAYS

123World Directory of Amusement Parks

http://123world.com/amusement/

Here you'll find links to amusement and theme parks, water parks, fun centers, roller coasters, and Disney parks. Choose a country and state or region to browse links for parks in the selected area.

1st Traveler's Choice

http://www.virtualcities.com/ons/
0onsadex.htm

Information on lodging across the United States, Canada, and Mexico. Search by state, province, type, or languages spoken by innkeepers. Includes Country Inns magazine, the Inn Times, virtual cities' trade show, and a gourmet directory of hundreds of recipes from innkeepers. New inns added weekly.

Balsam Shade Resort

http://www.balsamshade.com/

This country family resort is located in the foothills of the northern Catskill Mountains (Greenville, New York). Activities include springtime whitewater rafting down the Hudson River Gorge, bicycling, and hiking the trails of the Catskill Park. Several golf courses and museums are nearby. Other activities include horseback riding, visiting amusement parks, and taking a trip to Reptiland.

Concierge Travel

http://www.concierge.com/
travelfeatures/brides/
romanticgetaways/

Includes an interactive destination finder, information on 500 places, plus travel help and tips from the experts at both Fodor's and Conde Nast magazines.

GORP: California National Forests

http://www.gorp.com/gorp/
resource/US_National_Forest/
CA.HTM

GORP (Great Outdoor Recreation Pages) describes all the national forests in California. Click the city you're interested in to view details on activities such as hiking, fishing and hunting, camping, picnicking, mountain biking, and sightseeing. Also includes descriptions of canyons. You'll also find the locations and phone numbers of the district ranger stations.

GORP: Great Outdoor Recreation Pages

http://www.gorp.com/

Your guide to U.S. parks, forests, wildlife areas, wildernesses, monuments, rivers, scenic drives, national trails, beaches, recreation areas, historic sites, and archaeology sites. Get advice on equipment, apparel, and accessories; travel and lodging; maps and tours; and features and activities for each destination. Visit the photo gallery of beautiful outdoor scenes, get tips on staying healthy while you travel, and investigate ideas of where to take your kids and pets on your next outdoor adventure.

Mountain Villas

http://www.digitel.net/smokymtn/mtnvillas/

Nestled at the foothills of the Great Smoky Mountain Park, the Mountain Villas is a resort community consisting of 50 chalets and villas. The villas feature full kitchens and living rooms, and vary in size from one to four bedrooms (photos provided). The property includes a heated swimming pool, a workout room, an arcade, and several picnic areas with tables and barbecues. Mountain Villas is located seven miles from Pigeon Forge (home of the Dixie Stampede, Dollywood, and music theaters) and nine miles from Gatlinburg (entrance to the Great Smoky National Park).

Romantic America

http://www.romanticamerica.com

Features reviews of bed-and-breakfast inns, hotels, restaurants, romantic towns, plus love notes and recipes for romance.

Sandals Resorts

http://www.sandals.com

Features information on tropical hideaways on the enchanted isles of Jamaica, Antigua, St. Lucia, and the Bahamas, created exclusively for couples.

site59.com

http://www.site59.com

If you're not the type to plan your trip ahead of time, Site59 is the place for you. Named after the 59th minute, this site assumes that you've waited till the last minute to start planning your trip. Just choose the desired destination, and Site59 will assemble a travel package for you, including airline tickets, car rentals, and room reservations at a reasonable price. The departure points are limited to major cities, but except for that minor drawback, the site features an interesting approach to last-minute travel plans.

St. Paul Recommends: Destinations (Minnesota)

http://www.mspmag.com/

One of the 10 best Minnesota sites recommended in Minneapolis St. Paul Magazine, the Brainerd Lakes area is located 125 miles north of the Twin Cites in central Minnesota. It features 450 lakes within a 15-mile radius and access to some of the state's best resorts, golf courses, and fishing holes. This site recommends three places to

A B C D E F G H I J K L M N O P Q R S T U V W X Y Z

A
B
C
D
E
F
G
H
I
J
K
L
M
N
O
P
Q
R
S
T
U
V
W
X
Y
Z

stay, where to eat, what to see, what to buy, and which local amusements to check out. Don't miss the weekly turtle races during the summer. Also includes Brainerd International Raceway with drag, classic, and Formula One racing. And, hey—it's the home of Paul Bunyan.

This Week in the Poconos Magazine Online

http://www.thisweek.net/

This e-zine includes information about B&Bs, country inns, lodging, dining, hiking, and more. It lists airports, upcoming events, church services, libraries, movie theaters, museums and galleries, and points of interest. Also features a guide to searching for antiques, tips on shopping, and information on state parks.

TotalEscape

http://www.totalescape.com/

Get away from it all by traveling to the most interesting sites in and around California. TotalEscape is California's guide to "local adventures, area activities, and cool places" off the beaten track. Excellent collection of photos and links of the best places to go to and things to do to recharge your batteries.

Trip Spot

http://tripspot.com/

Travel planning central for your weekend getaways—airlines, hotels, maps, city guides, destination ideas, and much more!

Washington Post Weekend Getaways Guide

http://www.washingtonpost.com/wp-adv/specialsales/virtualvacation/weekend.html

Guide to weekend getaways in and around Washington, D.C. Provides information on scenic events, fun and educational activities, recreation, lodging, and restaurants. Features links to the most popular vacation spots in the Washington, D.C., area.

UFOS

Alien Abduction Experience and Research

http://www.abduct.com/

A page for and about abductees which has many nice features. Among these interesting items are a discussion group, news exclusively about UFOs, research reports, UFO book reviews, stories about personal experiences, and many other feature articles. Besides offering a wealth of information and interesting photos, the site also has some movie reviews of your favorite UFO-related movies.

Aliens and UFOs Among Us

http://www.bright.net/~phobia/

For those who wonder "Are we alone?" this site is for you. Take a look at the photos, participate in chats, and read through some of the information collected regarding UFOs.

Anomalous Images and UFO Files

http://www.anomalous-images.com/

The site contains a lot of information about such abnormal things as lost cities on Mars, crashed spacecraft on Mars, a secret cave in the Grand Canyon that is supposed to be UFO related, the famous faces of Mars, and the latest Lost Island City on Mars; and, all of this is documented and with pictures to prove it. There are many great graphics, pictures, and information to pique your interest. Good site for a cold, dark, and wet night. It also has some interesting music to listen to that will put you in the mood.

Art Bell Web Site

http://www.artbell.com/

This home of the famous talk-radio host, Art Bell, features program information, a comprehensive library and photo gallery, and additional information. Focuses on UFOs, extraterrestrial beings, paranormal phenomena, and conspiracy theories.

〖Best〗 Center for UFO Studies

http://www.cufos.org

This organization. is dedicated to exploring and studying reports of UFOs, and is asking for help in keeping its files current. You can search the archive of articles and UFO sightings, as well as add to them with your own stories and reports. You can also read about famous sightings here.

The Center for UFO Studies (CUFOS) is an international group of scientists, academics, investigators, and volunteers dedicated to the continuing examination and analysis of the UFO phenomenon. Their purpose is to promote serious scientific interest in UFOs and to serve as an archive for reports, documents, and publications about the UFO phenomenon.

A
B
C
D
E
F
G
H
I
J
K
L
M
N
O
P
Q
R
S
T
U
V
W
X
Y
Z

A
B
C
D
E
F
G
H
I
J
K
L
M
N
O
P
Q
R
S
T
U
V
W
X
Y
Z

Conspiracy Journal

http://members.tripod.com/
uforeview/

Conspiracy Journal will bring you the best UFO/conspiracy reports. The site also has a massive list of books and other items you can order online using a secure card resource as well as other interesting information about UFOs, Tesla, and other scientists and engineers who are interested in the UFO phenomena.

CSETI—The Center for the Study of Extraterrestrial Intelligence

http://www.cseti.org/

This is the site of the only world-wide organization dedicated to establishing peaceful and sustainable relations with extraterrestrial life-forms. The organization was founded in 1990 for this specific purpose.

Famous UFO Cases

http://ourworld.compuserve.com/
homepages/AndyPage/

All the classic UFO cases of the past, in date order. The site also contains a list of books, articles, and other items that are of great interest to those interested in this field.

International Center for Abduction Research

http://www.ufoabduction.com/

David Jacobs' International Center for Abduction Research (ICAR) is devoted to the dissemination of information about UFO abductions to help improve the understanding of such experiences.

Journal of Scientific Exploration

http://www.scientificexploration.
org/jse.html

"Advances are made by answering questions. Discoveries are made by questioning answers." The Journal of Scientific Exploration publishes articles about unusual scientific research in a scientific journal format.

Kidnapped by UFOs?

http://www.pbs.org/wgbh/nova/
aliens/

The Nova Online! program on abductions is very likely the best, most balanced presentation available on the topic of UFO abductions. Features a balanced view by providing expert opinions from the two conflicting camps: believers and skeptics.

MUFON

http://www.mufon.com/

Dedicated to the "systematic collection and analysis of UFO data with the ultimate goal of learning the origin & the nature of the UFO phenomenon." Here, you can report a sighting, get the latest UFO news and information, find out more about MUFON, join MUFON, and purchase UFO books and other publications online.

National UFO Reporting Center

http://www.ufocenter.com

The latest sightings reported to the National UFO Reporting Center. Have you seen a UFO? Then you can file a report at this site, too.

Secrets of the Hidden Universe

http://www.geocities.com/Area51/
Corridor/6280/

This site is dedicated to introducing the topic of UFOs and alien contact to those new to the subject. Discusses events and ideas that helped to shape the study known as UFOlogy, and also provides the latest news and information on the subject.

UFO Info

http://www.ufoinfo.com

Get updates regarding sightings and abduction reports, news from around the world, publications, books, TV and radio programs devoted to UFOs, links, and other related articles and information about the site and how it functions (with the help of volunteers around the world). You can purchase dozens of books, CDs, and DVDs related to this subject on their online e-store by using secure credit card ordering.

UFO Roundup

http://ufoinfo.com/roundup/

The latest weekly sightings roundup from Joseph Trainor. This is an Australian site that has lots of books, CDs, and videotapes you can purchase from their online store. Most of these are through such online retailers as Amazon.com. There are about 20 UFO-related reports for you to read. These are professional, authentic reports that are factual, straightforward, and interesting. This is an excellent source for UFO-related materials.

UFO Seek

http://www.ufoseek.com/

Comprehensive directory of UFO and paranormal information and resources. Search the directory by keyword or phrase or browse by categories including alien abductions, near death experiences, and millennium prophecies, to name just a few.

WWW Space and Mystery

http://spaceandmystery.tripod.ca
/mystery.htm

An excellent source for UFO news. This is a unique site because it has information on just about everything concerning UFOs and the unusual. There are articles, books, and news about the mysteries of Mars, the Roswell incident, the Egyptians and their culture, and much more. There are links where you can go to purchase books and other material on the subject.

A
B
C
D
E
F
G
H
I
J
K
L
M
N
O
P
Q
R
S
T
U
V
W
X
Y
Z

U.S. GOVERNMENT INFORMATION/SERVICES

Center for Defense Information: Terrorism Project

http://www.cdi.org/terrorism/responding.cfm

As a result of the 9-11 tragedy, the United States government has been working diligently to wage a war on terrorism and protect the United States homeland. The Center for Defense Information has been working just as diligently to keep track of the government's progress and to keep citizens informed. Here you can find information about the war on terrorism, including reports about Operation Enduring Freedom, the President's special orders and mandates, reports from known terrorist hot spots, homeland security issues, and much more.

Central Intelligence Agency

http://www.cia.gov

Learn all about the CIA, what it does, how to be considered for employment, which agencies report into it, what announcements the organization has made recently, and publications it has produced. There are also FAQs and related links here.

Consumer Information Center

http://www.pueblo.gsa.gov/

The folks with all the free publications. Most can be obtained online from their Web site. You can read these free publications or order them online. There are dozens of topics you can get information on including consumer help, education, employment, federal programs, food, health, housing, money, recalls, travel, and scams/frauds.

DefenseLINK

http://www.defenselink.mil/

The Department of Defense is responsible for providing the military forces needed to deter war and protect the security of our country. Visit this site to learn of the latest progress in the war on terrorism.

Department of Agriculture

http://www.usda.gov/

USDA enhances the quality of life for Americans by supporting agriculture, and ensuring a safe, affordable, nutritious, and accessible food supply.

Department of Commerce

http://www.doc.gov

Responsibilities include expanding U.S. exports, developing innovative technologies, gathering and disseminating statistical data, and predicting the weather.

Department of Education

http://www.ed.gov/

The mission of the Education Department is to ensure equal access to education and to promote educational excellence for all Americans.

Department of Energy

http://www.energy.gov/

DOE works to foster a secure and reliable energy system and to be a responsible steward of the nation's nuclear weapons.

Department of Health and Human Services

http://www.os.dhhs.gov/

Health and Human Services is responsible for protecting the health and well-being of Americans through programs such as Medicare, and disease research to aid in prevention. The Web site provides information about the wide range of HHS programs.

Department of the Interior

http://www.doi.gov/

The Department of the Interior protects and provides access to our nation's natural and cultural heritage. Part of this mission involves honoring our responsibilities to Native American tribes.

Department of Justice

http://www.usdoj.gov/

As the largest law firm in the nation, the Department of Justice serves as counsel for its citizens. It represents them in enforcing the law in the public's interest.

Department of Labor

http://www.dol.gov/

The Department of Labor helps to prepare Americans for work and attempts to ensure their safety while on the job.

Department of State

http://www.state.gov/

The Department of State is the institution for the conduct of American diplomacy, a mission based on the role of the Secretary of State as the president's principal foreign policy adviser.

Department of Transportation

http://www.dot.gov/

Serves as the focal point in the federal government for the coordinated national transportation policy and safety efforts.

Department of the Treasury

http://www.ustreas.gov/

The Department of the Treasury has a long history of managing the government's finances, promoting a stable economy, and helping to ensure a safer America by promoting a prosperous and stable American and world economy, managing the government's finances, safeguarding the financial systems, protecting government leaders, securing a safe and drug-free America, and building a strong institution.

Department of Veterans Affairs

http://www.va.gov/

The Department of Veterans Affairs (VA) Internet World Wide Web server is a resource of information on VA programs, benefits, and facilities worldwide.

Environmental Protection Agency

http://www.epa.gov

Learn about pending environmental legislation, recent reports and updates regarding hazardous substances, speeches and testimony, emerging environmental issues, and more at this site.

Federal Bureau of Investigation

http://www.fbi.gov

Learn all about the FBI. Read the FBI's Most Wanted Fugitives list, see what investigations are underway, learn about the Freedom of Information Act, and more.

A
B
C
D
E
F
G
H
I
J
K
L
M
N
O
P
Q
R
S
T
U
V
W
X
Y
Z

A
B
C
D
E
F
G
H
I
J
K
L
M
N
O
P
Q
R
S
T
U
V
W
X
Y
Z

Federal Trade Commission

http://www.ftc.gov/

Learn about what this agency does to protect consumers and educate yourself about protection through articles and publications, news releases, legal action reports, and other information about the inner workings of this organization.

FedStats

http://www.fedstats.gov/

Statistics from more than 100 government agencies. Many agencies provide statistical reports in the form of downloadable PDF files only.

FedWorld Information Network

http://www.fedworld.gov

Search for documents, reports, and forms generated by U.S. government agencies through this searchable site.

FirstGov

http://www.firstgov.org/

Billing itself as "Your First Click to the U.S. Government," this site acts as an information kiosk to help citizens, businesses, and other government agencies find their way around Washington. Here you can start your search to find out how to secure government benefits, find a government job, check your Social Security status, apply for student loans, and access other federal government services. This official site of the U.S. government is intended to put government within easy reach of its citizens and reduce some of the paperwork involved.

Health Statistics

http://www.cdc.gov/nchs/datawh/statab/pubd.htm

The National Center for Health Statistics (NCHS) presents a massive statistical study of the health of Americans. Categories include Obesity, Diseases, Births, and Deaths. Data is presented in easy-to-read tables.

Index to Government Web Sites

http://usgovinfo.about.com/newsissues/usgovinfo/blindex.htm

An alphabetically indexed list of links to more than 200 federal agencies, bureaus, commissions, and offices.

MarineLINK

http://www.usmc.mil

Learn what it takes to be a Marine, stay current on Marine news, read about commemorative events for veterans, current leadership, history and traditions, and how to be considered for the Marines.

Motor Vehicle Registration and Licensing

http://www.usps.gov/moversnet/motor.html

This handy page from the postal service gives links to the DMV Web sites of almost every state in the Union.

Peace Corps

http://www.peacecorps.gov

Read stories of true Peace Corps volunteer adventures, learn about what it means to be a volunteer, and apply for the opportunity online.

U.S. Army

http://www.army.mil

Read about the leadership and management of the Army, as well as news regarding current issues and events, what it means to be in the Army, where installations are, and get access to an archive of Army information you can search.

U.S. Navy

http://www.navy.mil

Learn all about the Navy, its ships and submarines, job opportunities, and news here, where you can also post a question to be answered by a naval officer. You can also view photos of ships and subs.

United States House of Representatives

http://www.house.gov

Find out what issues are being debated on the House floor this week, check on the voting histories of current representatives, and find out who your local representative is. You can also write to that individual through the site.

United States Senate

http://www.senate.gov

Search the site for your senator, or for the specifics of a bill recently passed or under consideration, and view images of fine art on display in the Senate Art Collection.

 ## Welcome to the White House

http://www.whitehouse.gov

Lots of information about the White House, the current president and vice president, access to White House documents, statistics and reports, and issues of the day, as well as information about how the government works and how to track down services you might be entitled to. There is information about touring the White House including a map and information for those who may be handicapped or have special needs. You will find information about the president and other government leaders, as well as news, history, and information for kids. Sorry, there isn't a virtual online tour just yet.

WhoWhere? People in U.S. Government

http://www.whowhere.lycos.com/GovtPages

Search this directory to find just about any government official, from municipal and state legislators to federal personnel. Just type the name and city or state and you'll be provided with contact information. Or just type in town or state information and you'll be given a long list of all the officials for that area. A handy resource!

A
B
C
D
E
F
G
H
I
J
K
L
M
N
O
P
Q
R
S
T
U
V
W
X
Y
Z

VETERAN AND MILITARY ORGANIZATIONS

Air Force Association

http://www.afa.org/

The AFA is "an independent, nonprofit, civilian aerospace organization that promotes public understanding of aerospace power and national defense." At the site, visitors can learn more about this organization, get information on legislative affairs, find out about membership, and access the online library, links, and event details.

〖Best〗 The American Legion

http://www.legion.org/

This site offers information about the Legion's patriotic programs, including education and scholarships, Boy Scouts, flag protection, and more. Also covers veteran health issues. The American Legion was chartered by Congress in 1919 as a patriotic, mutual-help, wartime veterans' organization. Since then, they have offered many services to their members such as making sure they are treated fairly in hiring, getting medical attention, and receiving their rights for serving their country. There are approximately 15,000 Legion posts worldwide with nearly three million members.

Army and Air Force Exchange Service

http://www.aafes.com/

💲

AAFES operates close to 11,000 facilities worldwide, supporting 25 separate businesses in 25 countries,

as well as in every state. Military personnel can access their account online, check out weekly specials, and find locations.

Department of Veterans Affairs

http://www.va.gov/

An up-to-the-minute report about where veterans can go to find out about benefits, facilities, and special programs available to them.

Disabled American Veterans

http://www.dav.org/

The DAV is a nonprofit organization of more than one million veterans disabled during war. The primary work of the DAV is fighting for and obtaining benefits from various government agencies on behalf of disabled veterans. Veterans need not be members to qualify for this free assistance. The Web site describes the work the organization does and how individuals can support it.

Federal Job Search Links

http://www.careers.iastate.edu/
Students/Job_Searching/
federal_job_search_links.htm

This site is offered by the Liberal Arts and Sciences Career Services of Iowa State University. It has links to employment Web sites of various federal departments and to other sites where you can learn more about employment opportunities in the government.

Gulf War Veteran Resource Pages

http://www.gulfweb.org

This site is focused on providing useful information for Gulf War veterans. There are links to FAQs about chronic fatigue syndrome, Veterans Affairs medical centers, and information about chemical warfare and mustard gas. You will also find a newsletter from Gulf veteran organizations and other support sources.

Military Order of the Purple Heart (MOPH)

http://www.purpleheart.org/

The only congressionally chartered veterans organization exclusively for combat-wounded veterans.

Military USA

http://www.militaryusa.com/

Military USA is an organization that locates veterans worldwide. The site includes the company's mission, a national reunion registry, and a Vietnam veteran database.

National Coalition for Homeless Veterans

http://www.nchv.org/

This site provides links to veteran and related organizations, including All Things Military, AMVETS Blinded Veterans Association, Disabled American Veterans, Gulf War Veteran Resource, Jewish War Veterans of the USA, Military Order of the Purple Heart, National Veterans Legal Service Program, and more.

National WWII Memorial

http://www.wwiimemorial.com/

Get a glimpse of this memorial to World War II veterans, find out who has been involved in supporting it, and how you can support it.

Office of the Inspector General

http://www.va.gov/oig/51/
51-home.htm

The Office of the Inspector General, Office of Investigations Web site. The office makes criminal investigations in veteran-related areas. The site includes a sample list of investigation areas.

Soldier City

http://www.soldiercity.com/

Online Army and Navy store. Scroll down the page and click Military Links to access dozens of military sites.

TROA

http://www.troa.org

A nonprofit organization dedicated to providing benefits to members of the uniformed services in the form of products and services, personal affairs assistance, and educational aid.

U.S. Department of Housing and Urban Development Veteran Resource Center (HUDVET)

http://www.hud.gov/offices/cpd/
about/hudvet/index.cfm

HUDVET provides assistance in securing home mortgages and receiving HUD services through local assistance centers. The Web site offers information on resources and publications of use to veterans.

A
B
C
D
E
F
G
H
I
J
K
L
M
N
O
P
Q
R
S
T
U
V
W
X
Y
Z

Veterans News and Information Service

http://www.vnis.com/

VNIS is a comprehensive Internet resource for military veterans who are searching for the latest news and information regarding the military veteran community, including Navy, Air Force, Marine Corps, and Army news.

VFW: Veterans of Foreign Wars

http://www.vfw.org/

Dedicated to remembering and supporting U.S. veterans, the VFW is the nation's oldest major veterans organization. At this site, you can learn more about the organization and its programs and find links to other veterans' organizations and support groups.

The Vietnam Veteran's Memorial Wall Page

http://thewall-usa.com/

This site contains a database of 58,195 names on The Wall in Washington, D.C., which is the most accurate database online.

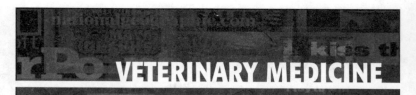

4Vets.com

http://4vets.4anything.com/

Designed primarily for practicing vets who want to connect with other vets, identify local hospitals and resources, gain access to vet trade publications, and professional development information, including a directory of colleges and universities with vet programs. There are also links to specific sites by type of animal.

AAHA HealthyPet.com

http://www.healthypet.com/

This association of veterinary care providers seeks to help consumers identify qualified hospitals to care for their pets, as well as provide basic pet care information through its online library. Kids will enjoy printing out and coloring in the coloring page, and owners will appreciate the newsletter and FAQs.

American College of Veterinary Surgeons

http://www.acvs.org/

Find out why your pet might need a specialist surgeon and what board certification means. Search the directory for a surgeon near you.

[Best] American Veterinary Medical Association

http://www.avma.org/

The association's official site presents articles from the Journal of American Veterinary Medical Association, along with an animal health database, veterinary industry information, and pet care advice. This site features a lot of news and stories about animals and animal care as well as vet resources and has a members center and a list of allied organizations. The site is very well designed and easy to navigate, and you won't have any problems in finding information about animal care here.

AVA Online

http://www.ava.com.au/

The Australian Veterinary Association provides online employment, education, and conference references on veterinary medicine. The site also has the latest news stories, current issues, articles on the rural sector, a search engine, and related links.

Care for Pets

http://www.avma.org/care4pets/

This American Veterinary Medical Association site contains pet care information, such as safety tips, breed statistics, articles on how to deal with death of a pet, tips for selecting a veterinarian, and pet stories.

Careers in Veterinary Medicine

http://www.avma.org/care4pets/morecare.htm

This site has extensive information on the veterinary profession and animal-related news. If you're considering a career as a vet, this site may be your best bet.

Center for Animal Health and Productivity

http://cahpwww.nbc.upenn.edu/

This site describes a research institution created by the School of Veterinary Medicine at the University of Pennsylvania. Here, laypeople and experts can find information on livestock diseases, new treatments, and reference materials in animal medicine.

Department of Animal Science: Oklahoma State University

http://www.ansi.okstate.edu/

This site provides information about the Oklahoma State School of Veterinary Science. A map of the campus, descriptions of current research, student resources, and course information is included.

Murdoch University: Division of Veterinary and Biomedical Sciences

http://wwwvet.murdoch.edu.au/vbs/vet/

This site, maintained by the Division of Biomedical Sciences at Murdoch University in western Australia, has information on the school, its programs, faculty, staff, students, studies, alumni, computer-aided learning, and activities, along with a search engine.

National Board Exam (NBE)

http://www.nbec.org

In-depth information for candidates preparing for the National (U.S.) Board Exam, from the Professional Examination Service. You can also order a sample exam to study.

A
B
C
D
E
F
G
H
I
J
K
L
M
N
O
P
Q
R
S
T
U
V
W
X
Y
Z

A
B
C
D
E
F
G
H
I
J
K
L
M
N
O
P
Q
R
S
T
U
V
W
X
Y
Z

OncoLink: Veterinary Oncology

http://www.oncolink.com/
templates/_types/section.
cfm?c=22&s=69

This site, provided by the veterinary hospital of the University of Pennsylvania, has information about the diagnosis and treatment of cancer in animals.

ProVet

http://www.provet.com/

Well-stocked online warehouse of products for veterinary clinics and veterinarians. Features products from more than 150 manufacturers and offers services to help veterinarians find the products they need and manage their inventories more efficiently.

TalkToTheVet.com

http://www.talktothevet.com/

Get quick information about your pet by reading the numerous articles and information on this site. For about $25 per month, you can consult with a veterinarian via email about various health-related issues for your pet(s).

Veterinary Medicine

http://vetmedicine.miningco.com

This site contains a lot of material pertinent to animal care such as information about diseases, pets, animals, vaccinations, vet schools, vet professional careers, and much more. If you are interested in becoming a vet, they have information about this, also.

Veterinary Medicine Libraries

http://duke.usask.ca/~ladd/
vet_libraries.html

This site offers extensive links to veterinary-related catalogs and libraries at many major universities, colleges, and other professional establishments. The collections are listed by geographic area such as Canada, USA, and Mexico. You can find information on just about every aspect of the subject here.

Veterinary Pet Insurance

http://www.petinsurance.com/

Find out why you might want to consider buying pet insurance, and the type of insurance products available, and then enroll online if you like.

Vetscape

http://www.vetscape.co.uk/

A veterinary resource site for professionals. Links to sites containing information on medical topics such as homeopathic medicine, exotic animals, professional journals, anesthesia, parasitology, and others.

Washington State University College of Veterinary Medicine

http://www.vetmed.wsu.edu/

This site provides a virtual tour of veterinary hospital and service units. Admissions, undergraduate and graduate programs, continuing education, and research are also covered at this site.

World Equine Health Network

http://www.wehn.com/

This site is a resource for equine veterinarians, featuring a bulletin board for exchanging ideas on equine health. Other resources include an archive of the journal World Equine Veterinary Review and a calendar of upcoming seminars.

World Organization for Animal Health

http://www.oie.int/

Databases on animal diseases and biotechnology. Online animal health texts are included.

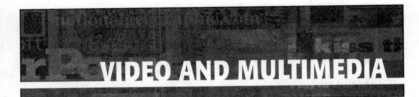

VIDEO AND MULTIMEDIA

DVD

bThere

http://www.bthere.tv

Hip, Web-based television station that gives you everything you can get on TV, including the commercials! Go behind the scenes with your favorite models and celebrities, cheer for the top athletes, or just kick back and listen to some tunes. See what the future of broadcasting has in store for you. You'll need a broadband Internet connection to fully experience this site, but it's well worth the visit.

DVD Price Search

http://www.dvdpricesearch.com

A site that compares the total cost of purchasing a particular DVD across several sites, telling you which merchant offers you the best deal. The site doesn't sell movies—it just tells you which online merchant has the lowest price.

DVDDigital.com

http://dvddigital.vstoredvds.com/

Search for DVD movies or read the reviews of new releases in order to select those you want to purchase from this site.

DVDExpress.com

http://www.dvdexpress.com/default.asp

If you're planning on starting your own video library, this is the place to be. Here, you can get a list of the DVDs no library should be without, the AFI's (American Film Institute's) top 100 list, plus lists and reviews of the best DVD videos on the market. You can also track down those hard-to-find cult flicks that give your collection character.

A
B
C
D
E
F
G
H
I
J
K
L
M
N
O
P
Q
R
S
T
U
V
W
X
Y
Z

A
B
C
D
E
F
G
H
I
J
K
L
M
N
O
P
Q
R
S
T
U
V
W
X
Y
Z

dvdfile.com

http://www.dvdfile.com/

Join in discussions about DVD movies, hardware, and software at this site, which also features industry news, movie release information, and a long list of movies currently available for rent or purchase in DVD format. Find out information on just about any movie, DVD, or software that you might have an interest in and order online. The site also has interesting information on the most current movies and music.

Netflix.com

http://www.netflix.com

This site offers a movie-recommendation search engine, and Cinematch, which enables you to see movie suggestions that are geared to your specific preferences. In addition to offering movie reviews, the site also offers online rentals, access to what's playing when at your local theater, ticket sales, and streaming movies.

Oddcast

http://www.oddcast.com

Oddcast is a multimedia service company that develops tools to help media moguls create and roll out interactive, on-demand media products for broadcasting over the Web. At this site, you can check out some of the many tools that Oddcast has developed, learn more about how the company has helped other media companies develop award-winning media products, and even enter some online contests.

Without a Box

http://www.withoutabox.com

Service designed for upcoming filmmakers, Without a Box helps aspiring filmmakers submit their films to various festivals, including Cannes. As a filmmaker, you can submit one video, one press kit, and a single application to Without a Box to have your film distributed to multiple film festivals around the world.

MOVIES

E! Online

http://movies.eonline.com/

You're sure to be up to speed on all the movie industry dirt with the help of this site, which offers celebrity news, movie release information and rankings, movie synopses, and box office reports.

Film.com

http://www.film.com/

Read reviews of top movies and new releases and watch clips and movie trailers, as well as read interviews with the stars and find out about upcoming projects.

Flicker

http://www.flicker.org

Flicker festivals have cropped up all around the nation, providing budding filmmakers the chance to produce their own short flicks (under 15 minutes) and show them to real live audiences. This site is the home of the Richmond Flicker, located in Richmond, Virginia. Here you can learn about upcoming festivals, check the schedule, and even download programs from past festivals. Do you have a movie you want to show? Click the SUBMIT

YOUR FILM link and learn where to mail your footage. Flicker is a great source of information about alternative films. You can read about filmmakers, find out what's showing where, and download images from films.

IFILM

http://www.ifilm.com

Online video library packed with short downloadable movies and movie clips broken down into several categories, including Action, Animation, Comedy, Drama, Erotica, Gay & Lesbian, and Sci-Fi. Check out the top short films and trailers, or browse the categories for a complete selection.

Internet Movie Database

http://www.moviedatabase.com/

The online authority for all things related to movies and film, this comprehensive directory allows you to track down movies and trivia by movie title, director, or actor. Want a list of all the movies in which Robert De Niro appeared, then search for "Robert De Niro" to pull up a list of this master's films. Check out the new releases, top videos on DVD and VHS, top-rated movies of all time in various categories, and independent movies. You can tour the photo gallery, play movie trivia games online, and visit the message boards to keep in touch with fellow movie buffs. With its no-frills presentation, excellent search tools, and comprehensive database of movie trivia, this site has no equal.

Metacritic

http://www.metacritic.com

Are you looking for a movie review for a newly released flick? Then look no further. For every movie featured on the site, Metacritic pulls together reviews from the top film critics, provides a brief synopsis of each critic's opinion of the flick, and provides a link for accessing the full review. Metacritic also tallies the ratings to determine a "metascore" that reflects the collective rating from all critics. Recently, Metacritic has started rating CDs and games, as well.

Waking Life

http://www.wakinglifemovie.com

An animated movie for young adults, Waking Life tackles some interesting issues regarding perception and reality and an individual's ability to control his or her own reality through dreams and passions. Here, you can view a trailer of the movie, learn about the director's concepts for the flick, and access biographies of the creators, animators, and actors. You can also play an online game to find out if you're a "dreamer."

MULTIMEDIA SEARCH ENGINES

Real.com

http://realguide.real.com/

Search for videos and music at this site, which offers a wide range of things to listen to and watch. For movies, you can catch trailers and information about the latest releases, view interviews and animated features, or watch business and

A
B
C
D
E
F
G
H
I
J
K
L
M
N
O
P
Q
R
S
T
U
V
W
X
Y
Z

A
B
C
D
E
F
G
H
I
J
K
L
M
N
O
P
Q
R
S
T
U
V
W
X
Y
Z

educational pieces. For videos, you can look for a particular title for download, or research top box office hits and site favorites.

Scour.com

http://www.scour.com/

This site lets you search for video, MP3, images, and radio selections at one site. Who's the most downloaded celebrity? Which radio clip is favored? These questions and more are answered with the top five listings for each category at the top of the site.

Search Engine Colossus

http://
www.searchenginecolossus.com/

The International Directory of Search Engines gives you quick, efficient access to hundreds of search engines from around the world with which you can search for the latest audio and video information as well as many other subjects.

VIDEO

Blockbuster

http://www.blockbuster.com/

Search Blockbuster's database of videos and DVDs for purchase, get news on upcoming releases, learn who won the latest video awards, and watch short films online. There's also a news section called Latest Scoop to keep you in the know regarding the movie industry.

Buy.com

http://www.us.buy.com/

Search for videos to buy at a discount here, and find out about new releases and top rentals before making your selection.

Reel.com

http://www.reel.com

Information kiosk for movies on DVD and VHS. Find out about new releases, check out the movie reviews, and even go behind the scenes in Hollywood to learn about your favorite celebrities and their latest projects. Links to Amazon.com for purchasing videos.

VITAMINS AND SUPPLEMENTS

A
B
C
D
E
F
G
H
I
J
K
L
M
N
O
P
Q
R
S
T
U
V
W
X
Y
Z

anti-oxidant.com–Quick Reference Guide

http://www.klsdesign.com/anti-ox/

Find up-to-date health and wellness information and research articles at this site. This particular section invites the user to use a pull-down menu to obtain information on every antioxidant from Alpha-lipoic Acid to Zinc.

Champion Nutrition

http://204.247.175.118/champion/index.jsp

Vitamins, minerals, and nutritional supplements for athletes.

eNutrition.com

http://www.enutrition.com

Get tips for managing your weight, improving your health, sports nutrition, body and senses, and vitamins through useful short articles at the site. And then buy the products you need to get the results you want, such as appetite suppressants, vitamins, meal replacements, and much more, organized by category.

healthshop.com

http://www.vitacost.com/healthshop.html

Use the site's Healthplanner to design a custom program for improving your health. Answer questions about medical history, lifestyle, and family history and receive an action plan to help overcome fatigue, illness, or other challenges, such as weight gain. The site provides information and products for sale that are all natural. You can also ask an expert or have an online chat with a nutritionist for more support.

Best MotherNature.com

http://www.mothernature.com/

This site offers a plethora of "natural" products and services aimed at helping you have a healthier lifestyle. You can research health issues, use their Supplement Planner to determine what vitamins are best for you, read customer reviews of products, and purchase vitamins and supplements online. With its huge product line, excellent search tools, and simplified order forms, this site earns its place in the best of the best club.

Pharmaton

http://www.pharmaton.com/

Features a collection of natural healthcare products and dietary supplements, including Ginsana, Ginkoba, and Prostatonin.

Puritan's Pride

http://www.puritan.com/

Shop online for vitamins, minerals, and other dietary supplements. This site includes health, fitness, and consumer information; a nutrient database; and a listing of live chat events.

Thriveonline.com

http://thriveonline.oxygen.com/

Thrive offers a searchable health library, feature articles on topics ranging from stress to vitamins, and a chance to email a doctor with health questions.

Vita-Web

http://www.vita-web.com

Everything you want to know about vitamins is here. Find out what your body needs, how it metabolizes different vitamins, what interferes with their absorption, effects of deficiencies, and more. The site also provides links to current research and resources.

VitaminShoppe.com

http://www.vitaminshoppe.com/

Shop by brand name or product to find vitamins, nutritional supplements, and herbal products here. You can also catch up on health and nutrition news in the Learning Center.

VOLLEYBALL

American Volleyball Coaches Association

http://www.avca.org/

The AVCA site provides up-to-date results, job openings, available playing dates, educational materials, and articles on sports medicine and coaching.

American Wallyball Association

http://www.wallyball.com/

Wallyball is volleyball played on a racquetball court. Use this site to read the game's rules, order supplies, find out where you can play, and get details about different leagues and tournaments.

Collegiate Volleyball Update

http://www.cvu.com/

Visit this site to keep abreast of the latest news, scores, stats, and standings in college volleyball. Covers both men's and women's volleyball, featuring dozens of stories about college teams, players, and coaches across the nation. Also provides some information on high school volleyball.

Best FIVB WWW Home Page

http://www.fivb.ch/

The FIVB (Fédération Internationale de Volleyball) is the governing body of international volleyball. Use their site to learn more about upcoming events and tournaments, worldwide beach volleyball, FIVB meetings, program development, and educational and promotional material. As the home for the governing body of international volleyball, this site has an edge over the other sites in this category, but its design and content also contribute to making it the best site in its class.

NCAA Men's and Women's Volleyball

http://www.ncaachampionships.com/

The National Collegiate Athletic Association's official site includes information about all NCAA sports, including volleyball. After you pull up the NCAA home page, click the Volleyball link in the navigation bar on the left and click the desired section: Men's Volleyball or Women's Volleyball. Each section provides a schedule, ticketing details, results, and previews.

Schneid's Volleyball Page

http://www.volleyweb.com/

Schneid's excellent content includes the normal links and rules, but also tips on strategy, drills to improve your game, nutritional information for athletes, and advice on training and flexibility.

Todd's Volleyball Page

http://vbref.org/

Todd provides comprehensive coverage of the game's rules, according to varying organizations. He also recommends his favorite equipment and discusses volleyball in the opposing towns of Austin, Texas, and Chicago, Illinois.

USA Volleyball Home Page

http://www.usavolleyball.org/

Links to youth and Junior Olympic teams as well as rosters for top men's and women's teams (U.S. and international).

Vball.com

http://www.vball.com/

Complete online resource for junior volleyball players, coaches, and fans. Information about tournaments, club programs, high school programs, and college programs. Features information on treating common injuries. Links to stores where you can purchase volleyball equipment and accessories.

Volleyball Hall of Fame

http://www.volleyhall.org/

Read the sport's and the hall's history, view photos, see who's been inducted into the hall, send feedback, buy a centennial volleyball, and study a map showing where the hall is located in Holyoke, Massachusetts.

Volleyball Magazine

http://www.volleyballmag.com/

Coverage of the sport from the beaches to the hardwood courts. Scores, player features, and forums for volleyball players are included in this site, along with information on subscription.

A
B
C
D
E
F
G
H
I
J
K
L
M
N
O
P
Q
R
S
T
U
V
W
X
Y
Z

Volleyball One

http://www.volleyballone.com/

With the slogan "work, play, shop," Volleyball One offers visitors lots of information about the game of volleyball, including improving your skills and understanding of game strategies, coaching opportunities, and a place to order the gear you need.

Volleyball Sites on the WWW

http://volleyball.org/www_sites/

Links to volleyball sites all over the world indexed by country.

Volleyball World Wide

http://www.volleyball.org/

This site includes a fact page and links for both indoor and beach volleyball (men's and women's), and provides information for all levels of volleyball (amateur, collegiate, and professional). Links to related associations such as the U.S. Disabled Volleyball Team home pages are also provided.

Volleyball.com

http://www.volleyball.com/

You'll find indoor and outdoor volleyball gear for sale here, as well as tips for improving your form, information on where to play locally, and rankings, schedules, bios, and stats on AVP, college, and Olympic volleyballers. The volleyball forum lets you express your opinion and get advice from fellow volleyball fans.

WATER SPORTS

DIVING/SCUBA DIVING

Beneath the Sea

http://www.beneaththesea.org/

BTS is a not-for-profit organization that works toward increasing awareness of the earth's oceans and the sport of scuba diving. BTS helps promote the protection of marine wildlife via grants to other nonprofit groups. Includes links to

seminars, workshops, mailing lists, and other diving-related sites.

Deep Sea Divers Den

http://www.divers-den.com/

Based in Far North Queensland, Australia, Deep Sea Divers Den includes scuba diving to the Great Barrier Reef. Offers scuba diving courses in Cairns, Australia, at all levels as well as one-day trips to the Great Barrier Reef for snorkelers and divers. PADI certification is available. You are asked to email them for information on registering or signing up for the courses and other activities.

Dive Connections

http://www.caldiveboats.com/

Home of the largest dive charter company in San Diego, this site provides a list of interesting dive sites around San Diego with a brief description of each site, plus a description of the various charter boats that are available.
Information about rental gear and hotels in the area is also available.

DiverLink

http://www.diverlink.com/

Pointers to dive sites on the Internet in categories such as clubs, manufacturers, and aquariums.

DiversDiscount.com

http://www.diversdiscount.com/

Shop the online scuba catalog for gear you might need, or ask the scuba experts for guidance. Read newsletter articles about diving and find resources and instruction here.

DiveWeb

http://www.diveweb.com/

Comprehensive resource for commercial diving, marine technology, underwater repair of vessels, and other underwater industries. Here you can find headline news stories about a wide range of water-related issues and events around the world. You can also join discussion groups, learn about commercial diving equipment, and check the online calendar for conferences and shows.

Doc's Diving Medicine

http://faculty.washington.edu/ekay/

Dedicated to undersea medicine and issues of diving safety for sport and professional divers.

The Franck Goddio Web Site

http://www.underwaterdiscovery.org/

Home of the Franck Goddio Society, an organization that "sponsors search and excavation projects around the world aimed at finding and recovering or preserving underwater shipwrecks and other underwater sites of special historical and cultural significance." Franck Goddio is the archaeologist version of Jacques Cousteau. Here you can learn more about Franck Goddio and his society, find out about upcoming events and ongoing projects, visit the photo gallery, and more.

HSA: Handicapped Scuba Association

http://www.hsascuba.com/

This organization is dedicated to making scuba more accessible to people with physical challenges, and its site appears to be updated frequently. It offers a quarterly journal, travel schedule, guides to wheelchair-accessible dive resorts, an HSA instructor locator page, and training course information for divers interested in becoming an HSA dive instructor.

Luis Cabanas Scuba Diving and Instruction (Mexico)

http://www.cozumel.net/diving/luis/

Luis, a PADI master scuba diver trainer, has logged in more than 250 dives to Punta Sur. His Web site includes quotes from satisfied customers, photographs of dives in

A
B
C
D
E
F
G
H
I
J
K
L
M
N
O
P
Q
R
S
T
U
V
W
X
Y
Z

A
B
C
D
E
F
G
H
I
J
K
L
M
N
O
P
Q
R
S
T
U
V
W
X
Y
Z

progress, and descriptions of basic dives for beginners. Also offers fishing trips, jungle adventure tours, underwater camera rentals, fast boat dive trips, and cave diving. Group discounts available. You are asked to send email for registration.

PADI: Professional Association of Diving Instructors

http://www.padi.com/

A fantastic site with current information. Updated daily—it offers the usual dive center listings, BBSes, product catalogs, news, and course listings, and a wide range of information beyond the usual. There is a fish quiz to test your knowledge, a map of the ocean floor from NOAA, dive insurance, and more.

Rodale's Scuba Diving–The Magazine Divers Trust

http://www.scubadiving.com/

The complete source for answers about diving including objective equipment evaluations, information on dive sites and dive medicine answers to help you dive safely. Visitors are offered a free trial subscription to SCUBA Daily News. Also supplies a guide to dive-related books available on the Web, a humorous top-10 list, and a helpful Scuba Divers Handbook. Purchase books mostly through Amazon.com and learn about tours worldwide.

Scuba Diving and Snorkeling Worldwide

http://www.batnet.com/see&sea/

Information about dive travel, liveaboard diving, marine life, and underwater photography. Features an excellent directory of diving

destinations around the world, complete with links to Web sites where you can learn more about each destination. Excellent photo gallery of Carl Roessler's diving adventures, plus tips on taking your own great underwater photos.

Scuba Radio

http://www.scubaradio.com/

Tune in online to the Internet radio show devoted to scuba diving. At the site you can also find information on learning to dive, archived shows, and lots of information on sites and guides.

Scuba Source

http://www.scubasource.com/

A huge source of information about diving, offering a diving-specific search engine, classified ads for equipment, a way to hook up with diving buddies, find an instructor, and read articles about scuba diving safely.

Best Scuba Yellow Pages

http://www.scubayellowpages.com/

Search this worldwide directory to find contacts and suppliers for all your scuba diving needs—from tour operators to airlines to clubs and certifications. The site also offers tons of information, a divers directory, a search feature to help you quickly locate information, email, and lots of divers' resources. If you are interested in diving for fun or profit, this is the place for location equipment you need and other resources to make your dive much more successful no matter what your reason for diving.

ScubaDuba

http://www.scubaduba.com/
index.html

Encourages active participation from divers. Requests that visitors submit diving-related articles or stories of interest. It offers classified ads, a buddy directory, a chat room, and photos.

Skin Diver Online

http://www.skin-diver.com/

With destination guides, gear info, instruction how-tos, and shopping options, you'll want to see what's here. The best feature is a Medical Center page with common questions and answers, tips, quizzes, and information from doctors who will answer divers' medical questions.

Sport Diver

http://www.sportdivermag.com/

Read feature articles from this magazine about dive spots, track down dive operators and hotels, as well as getting gear and instruction information. Learn about diving and the beautiful places you might want to experience.

Sub-Aqua Association

http://www.saa.org.uk/

This organization was founded more than 20 years ago by various British dive clubs to promote diving issues nationally. The site is extremely professional and detailed, including a URL minder service to notify you via email any time the site is updated.

United States Divers Aqua-Lung

http://www.aqualung.com/
snorkel.htm

A fun site with an island theme. Click the diver as it swims across your screen to see cool facts of interest to divers. Offers an in-depth look at the Jean-Michel Cousteau Institute, which was founded by the oldest son of the famous Jacques-Yves Cousteau. Also contains standard business information about the company's catalog, dealer locations, and company contacts.

United States Diving Online

http://www.usdiving.org/

The official Web site of United States Diving, the national governing body of Olympic diving in the United States.

YMCA Scuba Program

http://www.webcom.com/cscripts/
ymca/

A good source of general information such as a list of courses offered at the Y. This site also contains instructions on how to replace a lost C-card, which is a requirement for any diver. This site offers a quarterly journal, too.

RAFTING

ab257's Whitewater Page

http://home.epix.net/~ab257/

This site contains a cornucopia of information. You can visit the author's favorite rafting sites, view many thrilling photos, get satellite weather maps, and jump to ab257's great collection of links—including hot pages, local sites, online stores and resources, and club sites.

A
B
C
D
E
F
G
H
I
J
K
L
M
N
O
P
Q
R
S
T
U
V
W
X
Y
Z

A
B
C
D
E
F
G
H
I
J
K
L
M
N
O
P
Q
R
S
T
U
V
W
X
Y
Z

American Whitewater Resources Online

http://www.americanwhitewater.org/

Find out all the specifics about the rivers you will be rafting on before planning your experience. The mission of the AWA is to conserve and restore America's whitewater resources and to enhance opportunities to enjoy them safely. You'll find all kinds of help and information here, especially on safety and what is being done to save the whitewater ways.

Find-a-Guide: Rafting Guides and Trips

http://www.findaguide.com/raft.htm

Worldwide directory of links and contact information for professional rafting guides.

GORP: Paddlesports

http://www.gorp.com/gorp/activity/paddle.htm

GORP's paddlesports site is part of a larger network of sites devoted to outdoor recreation. Here, find out what is featured in the rafting news. Jump to river sites all over the country and the world. Learn how to keep from capsizing, get information on clubs, find books and other media about rafting, and join an online forum devoted to whitewater fans that have shared interests.

Grand Canyon River Running

http://www.azstarnet.com/grandcanyonriver/

This site gives information about private and commercial rafting trips through the Grand Canyon. Also shows beautiful pictures and helpful maps as it guides you through the beginning point, Lee's

Canyon, to the ending point, Lake Mead. This site is well designed, with a Native American motif and easy-to-follow icons.

Northwest River Supplies

http://www.nrsweb.com/

Shop the online rafting catalog or surf the online classifieds to locate used equipment. You can also join the discussions and check out other river rafting links here.

Rapid Shooters

http://rapidshooters.com/

A photographer's paradise. This site has a great photo gallery that features the South Fork American and Kings Rivers. It also offers a message board, a free screensaver for download, and a number of whitewater links. Searching is easy: Just click the Select Your Destination option, click Go, and you're off.

The River Wild

http://www.nationalgeographic.com/features/96/selway/

Offers a cyber tour of the Selway River in Idaho. From the home page, you get full access to a map that shows the course of rafting the Selway. Pictures give you a feel for the lovely mountain scenery. The tour offers hints for camping, navigating the river, speaking in river lingo, and observing the nearby wildlife. Features a QuickTime movie of a rafter running through Lava Falls.

RIVERSEARCH

http://www.riversearch.com/

Click on the online map to locate the best rivers for rafting near you, as well as outfitters equipped to guide you.

Vince's Idaho Whitewater Page

http://www.webpak.net/~rafter/

A charming example of a personal Web site, this offers everything from music for your listening pleasure to a photo gallery. In frames, this site is laid out well and easy to navigate. Plus, it has some extra information not found in most rafting sites, such as political issues surrounding Idaho's rivers. Find out about flow and weather conditions, and read about Vince's personal rafting experiences.

Wild and Scenic Rivers

http://www.nps.gov/rivers/

The Wild and Scenic River Act in 1968 called for preserving rivers and their natural environments. This site tells you the history of the act. An exceptional part of this site's information, however, is in the listings of rivers by state, which is fairly exhaustive. Also, find out how you can get involved with agencies whose goal it is to uphold the Wild and Scenic River Act.

Windfall Rafting

http://www.windfallrafting.com/

Learn more about rafting at this Maine outfitter, which also can provide accommodations and a travel planner. Get more information here or request a brochure.

ROWING

Amateur Rowing Association

http://www.ara-rowing.org/

Home of the governing body of the sport of rowing in Great Britain, this site features information on coaching, development, and competitions. Features a brief article on the history of rowing, plus water safety codes and guidelines.

iROW.com

http://irow.com/

Check the rowing calendar to find upcoming rowing regattas and competitions, read the Olympic diary of Chris Ahrens, learn more about the sport of rowing, including how the top schools rank, and join in online discussions.

NCAA Women's Rowing

http://www.ncaachampionships.com/row/wrow/

National Collegiate Athletic Association official site. Includes schedules, ticket information, TV coverage, results, and previews.

No Frontiers: A Year in the Life of Fermoy Rowing

http://ireland.iol.ie/~tops/

This video follows eight young rowers going for three Irish titles and an Olympic medal in 1996. Be sure to visit—the European scenery is beautiful.

Paddling@about.com

http://rowing.about.com/recreation/rowing/mbody.htm

This site offers comprehensive information about rowing that covers canoes, kayaks, and rafts. Features news, results, links, a chat room, a bulletin board, magazines, outfitters, stores, and more.

Regatta Sport

http://www.regattasport.ca/

The primary apparel maker for the Canadian National Rowing Team, Regatta Sport also makes jackets, jewelry, and other accessories for the crew enthusiast.

A
B
C
D
E
F
G
H
I
J
K
L
M
N
O
P
Q
R
S
T
U
V
W
X
Y
Z

A
B
C
D
E
F
G
H
I
J
K
L
M
N
O
P
Q
R
S
T
U
V
W
X
Y
Z

Row Works

http://www.rowworks.com/

The Row Works Clothing Company makes top-quality suits, shorts, winter gear, insulating Lifa Bodywear, and other fine rowing accessories.

Row2K.com

http://www.row2k.com/

Source of news, results, interviews, and general information about the sport of rowing.

Rower's World

http://rowersworld.com/

Comprehensive rower's resource contains news and regatta results, a glossary of terms and rules, images and email postcards, and classifieds. The site is well designed and easy to navigate which makes finding the information that you want almost as much fun as rowing itself. There is a nice search feature which will help you find what you want, a section with diaries and columns, and lots of stories, and you can even shop at an online store for items you may want to purchase.

Rowing FAQ

http://www.ruf.rice.edu/~crew/rowingfaq.html

Extensive collection of basic rowing information and terminology. Includes contact information for some of the larger rowing associations.

Rowing from an Oarsman's Perspective

http://library.thinkquest.org/3265/

This site is great for people new to the sport. You can learn about its history, study the glossary to understand all the terminology, view illustrations of the different kinds of boats, learn about the ergonomics of rowing, understand what the coxswain does, and more.

The Rowing Service

http://users.ox.ac.uk/~quarrell/

This British page offers news, crew notices, race reports, coaching and technical information, and more. Site is a little archaic and not the easiest to navigate, but it features a treasure trove of information and links to related resources on the Web.

RowingLinks–The Internet's Definitive Source for Rowing Links

http://www.rowinglinks.com/

You can find all kinds of links to sites about the fine art of rowing your boat. Offers information about the sport all around the globe.

Simply OarSome

http://www.oarsome.com.au/

This Australian company has been supplying the Australian Rowing Team since 1989. You can view their entire catalog and order all the gear online. You'll also find WWW rowing links, and results from major rowing events.

USRowing

http://www.usrowing.org/

Home of the organization that's dedicated to promoting and supporting the sport of rowing in the United States. Here you can learn more about the organization and its members, get the latest rowing news and results, view a list of upcoming USRowing events, obtain information about the national team, and more.

Vespoli USA

http://www.vespoli.com/

This is a commercial site promoting Vespoli racing shells. Their site discusses their shells' speed and value, as well as the company's quality assurance and service.

[Best] WorldRowing.com

http://www.fisa.org/

Home of FISA, the Fédération Internationale des Sociétés d'Aviron (in French), or the English equivalent International Federation of Rowing Associations. FISA is the international governing body of the sport of rowing. This site provides information about the organization, the events and competitions it sponsors, rowing news from World Rowing Magazine, competition results and standings, best times, and much more. Also features a photo gallery, a list of the top rowers, and an online version of FISA's rulebook. Links to stores where you can purchase FISA apparel online. Any rowing enthusiast should bookmark this page.

WWW Virtual Library: Rowing

http://archive.museophile.sbu.ac.uk/rowing/

Features a comprehensive rowing directory. It includes information about regattas, Olympic results, and links to rowing publications and newsgroups.

SURFING

Board Building

http://www.viser.net/~anthwind/

This library of links related to surfboard building includes links to board design, shaping, repair, tools, and fins. Includes a section on CAD.

Closely Guarded Secrets of the UK Surfing World

http://www.britsurf.org/UKSurfIndex/

A thorough and well-designed site for surfing in the U.K. Features include listings of surf clubs and schools, an online surf shop, links to surfing magazines and the British Surfers Association, and much more.

[Best] Coastal British Columbia

http://www.surfingvancouverisland.com/

This great site gives you all kinds of information about surfing. Even if you don't want to go surfing in British Columbia, you should check out the great pictures and information on this page. It has weather and wave information as well as good stories, photos, and other sporting information. If you like to surf and are interested in more information about some of the best surfing locations, enjoy a good story, and want to see photos of what you can expect when you get there, this is the site to find out about all that. It also has a free classified ad section for you.

International Surfing Museum

http://www.surfingmuseum.org/

At this site, visitors can view the collection of surf films, surf music, surfboards, and memorabilia. Visit the current exhibit, too. If you like this site, consider becoming a member.

OceanBlue

http://www.oceanblue.com/

This site offers a guide to the best beaches and sea sports, and to taking care of the environment. Also

A
B
C
D
E
F
G
H
I
J
K
L
M
N
O
P
Q
R
S
T
U
V
W
X
Y
Z

A
B
C
D
E
F
G
H
I
J
K
L
M
N
O
P
Q
R
S
T
U
V
W
X
Y
Z

contains information on windsurfing, body boarding, boogie boarding, and ocean kayaking. A picturesque site full of useful information.

Surf and Sun Beach Vacation Guide

http://www.surf-sun.com/

This site strives to be the ultimate resource for beach information and vacation planning on the Internet. It offers information on more than 500 beach destinations. Definitely check out their Surf the Beach Guide.

Surfermag.com

http://www.surfermag.com/

The Surfermag site features up-to-the-minute headlines and pictures, video clips of surfers in action, a bulletin board, product reviews, a surf report, an online surf shop, and subscription information.

Surfing in South Africa

http://www.wavescape.co.za/

This site offers you an extensive guide to surfing in South Africa with travel information, surfing spots, photos, daily surf reports, stories, cartoons, and a lot more.

Surfline

http://www.surfline.com

Billing itself as "The Best Place on the Net to Get Wet," this site provides up-to-date reports and live Web cams of the best places to surf worldwide. Site also features some product reviews and plenty of articles about surfing and the world's top surfers.

Surfrider Foundation USA

http://www.surfrider.org/

The Surfrider Foundation is a nonprofit group dedicated to

protecting, preserving, and restoring the world's oceans and beaches. Its site includes daily surf reports, Coastal Factoids, policy updates, and an online membership form.

Windsurfer.com

http://www.windsurfer.com/newsite/index.cfm

A thorough windsurfing database divided into organized categories. Board reviews, travel reviews, weather information, wind calculator, and links, too.

SWIMMING

D&J Sports

http://www.djsports.com/

Speedo, Tyr, and Dolfin competition and fashion swimwear, plus caps, clothing, accessories, and other equipment. Use the secure online shopping cart.

FINA

http://www.fina.org/

FINA is the international governing organization of amateur aquatic sports. FINA is based in Switzerland and is a worldwide policy maker in all swimming, diving, synchronized swimming, water polo, open water, and Masters swimming sports. Read articles on the latest developments in aquatic sports. Check out the FINA calendar of events, and find out the latest competition results. Learn about FINA's history, regulations, and members. You can also purchase related publications and videos from FINA.

International Swimming Hall of Fame

http://www.ishof.org/

The International Swimming Hall of Fame is a not-for-profit educational organization. It annually honors the world's greatest aquatic heroes and preserves the sport's history. It serves as a worldwide focal point of swimming, diving, water polo, and synchronized swimming. Learn about the history of the Swimming Hall of Fame, the membership, and how to make a donation. Includes a calendar of events and information on programs and activities.

NCAA Men's Swimming and Diving

http://www.ncaachampionships.com/swim/mswim/

National Collegiate Athletic Association official site. Includes schedules, ticket information, records, results, and previews.

NCAA Women's Swimming and Diving

http://www.ncaachampionships.com/swim/wswim/

Official guide to the three divisions of the National Collegiate Athletic Association championships.

SwimInfo

http://www.swiminfo.com/

Caters to recreational swimmers as well as world-class competitors. Includes water workouts for specific purposes, products, results, and records.

Swimmers Guide Online

http://www.swimmersguide.com/

Contains a database of international, accessible, full-size, year-round pools (6,000+ currently). Each listing includes the name and address of the facility, contact and admission information, and a description of the facility.

Swimming Science Journal

http://www-rohan.sdsu.edu/dept/coachsci/swimming/index.htm

This journal is divided into several parts, including the following: Swimming Science Abstracts, the Carlile Coaches' Forum, the Swimming Science Bulletin, DRUGS: The Crisis in Swimming, and How Champions Do It. The articles presented are drawn from the personal files of the editor. The contents usually are changed monthly and might or might not be thematic.

Swimming Teachers' Association

http://www.sta.co.uk/

The STA focuses on teaching aquatic skills, from basic water confidence to serious survival. Progressive challenges enable everyone—toddlers, teenagers, adults, the elderly, the handicapped, and the disabled—to get used to the water, enjoy it safely, and increase their fitness and water skills. Ambitious, able swimmers can proceed to competition lifeguard and teaching levels. The STA discusses new ideas on coaching in swimming, diving, water polo, and lifesaving. Read a history of the STA and learn about the examinations, certificates, and awards available. Learn about becoming an STA member, the membership goals, and the fees.

A
B
C
D
E
F
G
H
I
J
K
L
M
N
O
P
Q
R
S
T
U
V
W
X
Y
Z

A
B
C
D
E
F
G
H
I
J
K
L
M
N
O
P
Q
R
S
T
U
V
W
X
Y
Z

SwimNews Online

http://www.swimnews.com/

This e-zine of the printed version presents breaking news, meet results, world rankings, and special events. Read the current issue of the magazine or browse through the archives of back issues. Use the search engine to specify a swimmer's last name or country and then view that swimmer's biography. Check out the swimming calendar of events or visit the Shopping Mall to order clothing, equipment, accessories, or training software.

United States Masters Swimming

http://www.usms.org/

An organized program of swimming for adults. Anyone can join USMS. It has grown to more than 40,000 men and women from age 18 to over 100 and offers a variety of programs for the swimming enthusiast.

USA Swimming

http://www.usswim.org/

USS is the national governing body for competitive swimming in the United States. Get information on the USS; it formulates the rules, implements policies and procedures, conducts the national championships, disseminates safety and sports medicine information, and chooses athletes to represent the United States in international competition. You'll also get the latest swimming news, meet results, records, Olympic Games information, and several swimming discussion forums you can participate in.

WebSwim

http://www.webswim.com/

Excellent directory of swimming resources on the Web as recommended by Donncha, the site's creator and maintenance crew. Site includes a FAQ that Donncha updates regularly based on questions asked and answered in the newsgroup rec.sport.swimming. Site also features links to online swim stores, a discussion of drugs in the sport of swimming, and a short list of Masters clubs and events around the world.

WATERSKIING

American Barefoot Club

http://barefoot.org/

A division of USA Water-ski, ABC is dedicated to promoting the sport of barefoot skiing for individuals at all ability levels. Here, you can learn more about the organization, get the latest news, check up on United States competitions, hang out in the Barefoot chat room, check rankings, and more.

International Water Ski Federation

http://www.iwsf.com

Includes information on the IWSF World Cup, a calendar, World Junior Championships, and more.

National Show Ski Association

http://showski.com/

If waterskiing with one foot hooked on the bar or as part of a pyramid sounds like fun to you, consider joining the NSSA. Their site has a schedule of events, results of the Nationals tournament, show ski humor, news, photos, links, and more.

National Water Ski Racing Association

http://www.nwsra.net/

News, schedule of events, results, and more. Sport division of the American Water Ski Association.

Planet Waterski

http://www.planetwaterski.com/

Up-to-date list of upcoming water-skiing competitions around the world covers events in racing, bare-foot, kneeboard, wakeboard, cable, and tournament events. Features event results and recommended places to ski, plus links to other ski resources on the Web.

USA Water Ski/American Water Ski Association

http://www.usawaterski.org/

The official site of the United States waterskiing's governing body. Keep up to date on upcoming competitions and read the latest news on who's making headlines in this sport.

Water Skier's Web

http://waterski.net/

Every type of water-skimming sport is listed in this links page, including barefoot, air chair, wake boarding, and knee boarding. You can check out the Water Skier's Mall and follow Usenet discussions.

WaterSki Online

http://www.waterskimag.com/

Home of the world's leading water-skiing magazine, this site features news, product reviews, links to ski equipment stores and manufacturers, a photo gallery, a Q&A area, discussion forums, and much more. Waterskiing enthusiasts should be sure to bookmark this page, as its contents are ever changing.

WEATHER AND METEOROLOGY

AccuWeather.com

http://www1.accuweather.com/

Watch the animated weather map of the United States to see what patterns might affect your plans. You can also type in your ZIP Code to get your local forecast. This site is the world's weather authority for weather information in your area including five-day forecasts. Not only that but you can get weather forecasts for almost any city that you might be interested in traveling to. Lots of weather news and information using cool graphics.

A
B
C
D
E
F
G
H
I
J
K
L
M
N
O
P
Q
R
S
T
U
V
W
X
Y
Z

Atlantic Tropical Weather Center

http://www.atwc.org/

Provides the latest hurricane information and other weather information dealing with tropical cyclones. Also offers images, data, pictures, meteograms, models, and satellite loops.

Automated Weather Source Nationwide School Weather Network

http://www.aws.com/corp/
default.asp

Provides national weather information from images to textual data. Also presents a photo gallery of severe weather by storm chasers throughout the country. Download the WeatherBug to have up-to-the-minute weather forecasts and information beamed to your desktop.

Climate/Weather/Earth Hotlist

http://space.rice.edu/~streutke/
hotlist.html

Huge online directory of various weather information resources on the Web divided into several categories, including Severe Events, Current Weather, Climate, Pollution, and Movies.

CNN Weather

http://www.cnn.com/WEATHER/

Get your weather from CNN with full weather-related stories, information, and maps.

Current World Weather

http://www.emulateme.com/
weather.htm

Offers many links to current United States and world weather conditions, other weather-related sites, and AccuWeather information. This site gives information provided by major weather organizations, such as CNN weather, the Weather Channel, and Earthwatch Communications, Inc.

Defense Meteorological Satellite Program

http://web.ngdc.noaa.gov/dmsp/
dmsp.html

Two satellite constellations of near-polar orbiting, sun-synchronous satellites that monitor meteorological, oceanographic, and solar-terrestrial physics environments. Features currently occurring meteorological phenomena.

EarthWatch Weather on Demand

http://www.earthwatch.com/

Contains many images of 3D satellite views from space. Also plugs its 3D software package that integrates 3D weather visualization with a global database to create a virtual world.

El Niño

http://www.enn.com/
specialreports/elnino/

Tells what El Niño is, what past El Niños were like, and how they affect our weather. Also gives news reports on the current status of El Niño and discusses how El Niño systems are measured.

Florida Weather Monitor

http://www.tropicsweather.com

Florida weather, radar, and satellite images; tropical weather information; and surf reports.

Intellicast

http://www.intellicast.com/

Serves as guide to weather, ski reports, and ocean conditions. Provides information for weather novices and professionals. New to

A
B
C
D
E
F
G
H
I
J
K
L
M
N
O
P
Q
R
S
T
U
V
W
X
Y
Z

Intellicast are health and travel reports. Also, check out its forecasts for national parks.

The Internet Weather Report

http://www.mids.org/weather/

More like an Internet traffic report, this site gauges the lag time of Internet connections for various areas of the world.

National Hurricane Center Tropical Prediction Center

http://www.nhc.noaa.gov/

Contains resources for the researcher, advanced student, and hobbyist interested in the latest information on tropical weather conditions, as well as archival information on weather data and maps. Provides links to other NOAA information and satellite data.

National Severe Storms Laboratory

http://www.nssl.noaa.gov/

Provides information about the laboratory, including current research and programs. Does not offer specific information on severe weather but does provide links to sites that do. Also includes an extensive list of links to Web literacy sites.

National Weather Center: Interactive Weather Center

http://iwin.nws.noaa.gov/iwin/gr aphicsversion/bigmain.html

A user-friendly interface to the weather, with raw data from a telecommunications gateway, satellites, and other multilayered links.

⌐Best⌐ National Weather Service

http://www.nws.noaa.gov/

Provides all information output by the NWS, including national and international weather in graphical and textual formats, and information about regional offices. Also offers links to NOAA and other NWS programs. This is the official site of the National Weather Service, which is part of the National Oceanic and Atmospheric Administration. The site is clean, well organized, and easy to navigate. You don't have to wait for the latest weather bulletins from all around the country. The National Weather Service (NWS) provides weather, hydrologic and climate forecasts, and warnings for the United States and adjacent waters and oceanic areas. This is a good site to bookmark for quick weather forecasts and urgent bulletins such as tornado and severe storms information. This site can provide you with excellent information for such purposes as knowing when you are in danger from severe weather, planning trips, and for general interest.

Ocean Weather

http://www.oceanweather.com/

Uses a unique hindcasting approach to forecast ocean weather including winds, waves, and surf. At this site, you can obtain current ocean data for various areas worldwide.

Seismological Laboratory

http://www.gps.caltech.edu/ seismo/

Southern California site that provides seismology-related resources, including the record of the day, recent earthquake activity, and

A
B
C
D
E
F
G
H
I
J
K
L
M
N
O
P
Q
R
S
T
U
V
W
X
Y
Z

A
B
C
D
E
F
G
H
I
J
K
L
M
N
O
P
Q
R
S
T
U
V
W
X
Y
Z

publications. A new feature of this site is its Terrascope section, in which you can plot data or get EQ information for recent large earthquakes.

Storm Chaser Home Page

http://www.afn.org/~afn09444/
weather/spotchas.html

Includes information about storm chasers, a photo gallery of storms, and the latest news about the Storm Chasers group. Also provides information about storm chasing at home, including how to contact the NWS.

UM Weather

http://cirrus.sprl.umich.edu/
wxnet/

Tries to list every weather-related link on the Internet. Includes not only WWW sites, but FTP sites, Gophers, and Telnet sites. Includes commercial sites as well as educational and governmental sites.

Vantage Point Network

http://vp.accuweather.com/
vantagepoint/wx/cur_radar/

Information kiosk for the agriculture industry, this site features online weather forecasts, powered by AccuWeather, plus updated futures prices.

Weather Channel

http://www.weather.com/

Includes information about the Weather Channel and also provides novice weather enthusiasts with simple weather maps. Provides up-to-date flight information, travel forecasts, and storm watches.

Weather Site

http://www.weathersite.com

Maps, radar, forecasts, and special pages for marine, aviation, agricultural, hurricane, and travelers' weather.

The Weather Underground

http://www.wunderground.com/

Nationwide weather forecasts and information, including temperatures, visibility, wind strength and direction, heat index, windchill factor, humidity, dew point, and more. Click the desired state on the map or find forecasts by city or ZIP Code.

Weather World

http://www.ems.psu.edu/
WeatherWorld/

Forecasts and special features about how weather works. From Penn State University.

WeatherOnline!

http://www.weatheronline.com/

Get forecasts complete with weather graphics for any part of the United States. Just type in a ZIP Code, city, or state to be provided with plenty of weather and condition information and forecasts for the region.

After I Do

http://www.afterido.com

Learn more about an alternative to the standard wedding registry, which includes registering for a dream honeymoon that your guests can contribute to as their wedding gift. Work with travel planners to select your desired honeymoon and direct guests here to contribute. You'll also find links to other wedding service companies to help you plan your wedding day.

The Best Man

http://www.thebestman.com/

Has your buddy designated you to be the best man at his wedding? If you've never done it before, you may be wondering just what you're supposed to do. This site provides a list of your duties as best man, help for planning the bachelor party, information on tuxedos, and tips on how to compose a successful toast.

Bridalink Store

http://www.bridalink.com/

The Bridalink site is an online store known to have low prices on accessories, such as wedding cameras. In addition, visitors can register for monthly giveaways.

Brides and Grooms

http://www.bridesandgrooms.com

Marriage and wedding guide with information on everything from honeymoons to marriage counseling.

Great Bridal Expo

http://www.greatbridalexpo.com/

This site features information about the Great Bridal Expo, a bridal show that tours to various cities throughout the United States. From this site you can find out more about the Expo's exhibitors, special events, dates, and locations throughout the United States. You can even order tickets for the show online!

Best The Knot: Weddings for the Real World

http://www.theknot.com

This site is the ultimate wedding resource: 3,000+ wedding-related articles, 6,000 searchable gown pictures, how-tos, plus daily hot tips, a 24-hour chat room, and special personalized planning tools. This is definitely one of the most comprehensive, useful bridal planning sites on the Web. The site offers much in the way of helping you to plan your wedding and helpful hints; and, you can even shop online for just about everything you probably will need.

A
B
C
D
E
F
G
H
I
J
K
L
M
N
O
P
Q
R
S
T
U
V
W
X
Y
Z

A
B
C
D
E
F
G
H
I
J
K
L
M
N
O
P
Q
R
S
T
U
V
W
X
Y
Z

Marrying Man

http://www.marryingman.com/

The ultimate wedding site for men, the Marrying Man home page provides a forum where men can discuss various wedding issues. It also provides helpful wedding information written in a tone especially designed for men.

Modern Bride

http://www.modernbride.com/

Features a peek at the current issue of Modern Bride magazine. Contains sections covering just about anything wedding-related, plus a chat room and a tip of the day. You can subscribe to the magazine online using secure credit card resources.

Ten Top Honeymoon Destinations

http://honeymoons.miningco.com/
travel/honeymoons/msub8.htm?

The Mining Company has investigated and ranked the top 10 honeymoon locations for brides to consider. Links to each country (most are in the Caribbean) are right here on the page.

Time Out City Guides

http://www.timeout.com/

The latest (and hippest) word on what to do and where to go in major domestic and international cities.

Today's Bride Online Magazine

http://www.todaysbride.com/

Picked as a Yahoo! Pick of the Week, Today's Bride magazine's Web site is very user friendly, including a search engine to help you find specific topics. There is even an online bridal consultant to help you with your toughest questions.

Town & Country Weddings

http://tncweddings.com/

From Town & Country Magazine, this site contains not only their special wedding issue, but also a wealth of other wedding information. A Registry section allows couples to specify where they are registered, and friends and family can access this information. Overall, this site is a complete source for wedding fashion, planning, and much, much more!

Ultimate Internet Wedding Guide

http://www.ultimatewedding.com

Comprehensive information for those planning a wedding in California. Includes products and services, bridal shows, engagement announcements, upcoming bridal shows, and links galore.

USA Bride

http://www.usabride.com

Wedding planning help for brides and grooms including gift and shower ideas, wedding songs, frugal wedding tips, and more.

Wedding Bells

http://www.weddingbells.com/
unitedstates/

Wed-zine that takes a thorough and stylish approach to wedding planning.

The Wedding Channel

http://www.weddingchannel.com

The Wedding Channel is an all-encompassing wedding resource. It contains the following wedding-related sections: Fashion and Beauty, Local Businesses, Honeymoon Suite, Home and

Registry, Wedding Planner, and Groom's Corner. The Wedding Planner section has tips from wedding planning expert Beverly Clark, author of the best-selling book, Planning a Wedding to Remember.

Wedding Photography—Advice for the Bride and Groom

http://members.aol.com/anorama/

This site offers some advice about selecting a wedding photographer for the special event. You should choose with care because you only get one shot at it and you want the best pictures possible.

Weddings on Hawaii, Kauai, Maui, and Oahu

http://www.creativeleisure.com/hawaii/weddings/

Are you thinking of marrying in the Hawai'ian Islands? This site offers special wedding packages for each of the islands. Your dream wedding could be only a Web site away!

WedNet

http://www.wednet.com/

Contains numerous wedding-related articles with tips for every aspect of wedding planning. In addition, you can search for other Internet resources and wedding vendors, visit the WedNet library, and even register for a free subscription to their monthly newsletter.

Your Formal Wear Guide

http://www.tuxedos4u.com/

A complete guide to men's tuxedos. You can view the latest styles in tuxedos, and use the "store finder" to locate the closest place to rent your tuxedo. In addition, the site has a Q&A section to help you select the appropriate tux for your occasion, and a worksheet to help organize your tuxedo needs.

A
B
C
D
E
F
G
H
I
J
K
L
M
N
O
P
Q
R
S
T
U
V
W
X
Y
Z

WEIGHT LOSS

American Dietetic Association

http://www.eatright.org

Healthy lifestyle tips, nutrition resources, how to find a dietitian, and more. Includes information on food irradiation.

Best of Weight Loss

http://bestofweightloss.com/

The Best of Weight Loss is a new directory maintained by specialists in weight-loss physiology, weight management, exercise programs, and Internet research.

A
B
C
D
E
F
G
H
I
J
K
L
M
N
O
P
Q
R
S
T
U
V

X
Y
Z

CyberDiet

http://www.cyberdiet.com

Access a daily food planner and assessment tools, find your nutritional profile, grab recipes and exercise tips, and much more.

Doctor's Guide to Obesity

http://www.docguide.com/news/content.nsf/PatientResAllCateg/Obesity?OpenDocument

The latest medical news and information for patients or friends/parents of patients diagnosed with obesity-related disorders.

eDiets.com

http://www.ediets.com/

Meal plans and fitness programs designed to help you lose weight and keep it off. Enter your email address, age, sex, height, weight, for a free profile and newsletter.

Fast Food Facts–Interactive Food Finder

http://www.olen.com/food/

Click on a fast food restaurant name and type in a product to find out the breakdown of calories, fat, sodium, carbohydrates and more. Or find out what products fit your diet by selecting a restaurant and setting limits on calories or sodium. Warning: You might lose your appetite after seeing how fattening some items are.

Jenny Craig

http://www.jennycraig.com/

Home of one of the most popular weight loss programs, this site features Jenny Craig's story, success stories of people who have followed the program, weight-loss programs and support for members, and online shopping.

Natural Nutrition

http://www.livrite.com/

Learn all about natural nutrition, its basic philosophy and how to eat better with whole grains. There are lots of articles to read, recipes to copy, and directories of natural food stores and merchants online.

Nutrisystem

http://www.nutrisystem.com/

Home of the popular Nutrisystem weight loss program. Here you can learn more about the program, sign up for a free membership, and shop online for products.

Prevention.com–Weight Loss and Fitness

http://www.prevention.com/cda/channel/1,1207,2,00.html

With 71 weight-loss tips, a meal planner, calorie calculator, and workout and weight quizzes, you're sure to be inspired to start that weight-loss program you've been meaning to. Lots of helpful advice and strategies from the publishers of *Prevention Magazine*.

⟦Best⟧ Shape Up America

http://www.shapeup.org

Safe weight management and physical fitness programs for one and all. Although not one of the flashier sites on the Internet, this site does have a lot of helpful information that will assist you in losing and controlling weight. If you are serious about this undertaking then you can visit their Body Fat Lab to find out about how to control your diet, exercise, and use other methods to control your weight. There is a handy BMI (Body Fat Lab),

Library, Cyber Kitchen, Professional Help, Fitness Center, and an area for support.

Thriveonline: Nutrition

http://www.oxygen.com/health/diet/archive.html

Get advice on heart-healthy diets, low-cal eating, and recipe makeovers here. There's also a 1,000-recipe database of healthy meals and an Ask the Dietitian feature to answer those nagging questions.

Weight Watchers

http://www.weightwatchers.com

Learn about Weight Watchers programs around the world at this site, which will also tell you about their proprietary 1-2-3 Success Plan. Find local organizations by searching their database.

Ask Dr. Weil

http://www.askdrweil.com

Learn more about Dr. Andrew Weil's approach to health by combining Western thinking and traditional medical perspectives. At the site you can learn about eating healthier, how vitamins and herbs can improve your health, and where to find natural foods.

The Black Health Network

http://www.blackhealthnetwork.com/

Find out more about conditions that frequently affect African-Americans and what you can do about them. There's plenty of medical news, preventive approaches, and helpful tips for living longer here.

Health Ink & Vitality Communications

http://www.healthink.com

Publisher of consumer health newsletters provides this informative site with articles on children, teen, and adult health. Includes an Ask the Doctor section.

Best | HealthCentral

http://www.healthcentral.com

If you're looking for health and wellness information, it's very likely you'll find it here, along with just about anything else you need to know about nutrition, health, eating right, vitamins, and more. There are columns, library articles, and many tools available to treat your body better.

A
B
C
D
E
F
G
H
I
J
K
L
M
N
O
P
Q
R
S
T
U
V
W
X
Y
Z

This site has just about everything that you need to know and to purchase in the area of health care. Besides being well designed and easy to navigate, the site offers a full online drugstore, a library, drug interaction center, facts about vitamins, prescriptions, beauty products, and many health products. You can place a prescription at the drugstore or purchase other products. There is a lot of helpful information and access to professional help here.

HealthGate

http://www.healthgate.com

Read about health issues affecting consumers today and steps you can take to prevent serious illness or treat conditions you already have. Columns, news, and articles are all available to you.

StayHealthy

http://www.stayhealthy.com

Links to a health resource directory, a drug information database, healthcare topics, expert advice, an American hospital directory, and more.

Wellness Junction

http://www.wellnessjunction.com/

For consumers and healthcare professionals who want to stay on top of the research and trend information regarding wellness. Read the headlines for this week, learn more about wellness at home or office, and link to other useful sites. Professionals will also find professional development and networking opportunities.

WellnessWeb

http://www.wellnessweb.com/

Find information about clinical trials and community health, how to select a health care provider, reports on illnesses and conditions, and more topics.

A
B
C
D
E
F
G
H
I
J
K
L
M
N
O
P
Q
R
S
T
U
V
W
X
Y
Z

WOMEN/WOMEN'S ISSUES

The Ada Project

http://tap.mills.edu/

Provides resources and information for women in the computer sciences.

AFL-CIO: Working Women Working Together

http://www.aflcio.org/women/

Working women will want to check out the AFL-CIO's site devoted to supporting working women for facts and figures regarding working women and the children they support, as well as getting information on how to become more active in supporting legislation for working women. Fill out the survey and find out more about upcoming conferences, too.

American Association of University Women (AAUW)

http://www.aauw.org/

The American Association of University Women is a national organization that promotes education and equity for all women and girls. This Web site describes AAUW issues, research programs, grants and fellowships, membership information, and much more.

Amnesty International USA Women's Human Rights

http://www.amnestyusa.org/women/

Read about the poor conditions and situations women around the world face, as well as learning more about what you can do to change it.

Artemis Search for Women's Studies Programs

http://users.rcn.com/
kater.interport/

A database of 324 United States women's studies programs, listed alphabetically with brief descriptions and the opportunity to link to the specific college or university for more information.

AWARE

http://www.aware.org

Learn more about the importance of self-protection and defense, strategies you can use, and where to go for instruction.

BizWomen

http://www.bizwomen.com/

BizWomen provides the online interactive community for successful women in business to communicate, network, exchange ideas, and provide support for each other via the Internet. BizWomen also provides you with an Internet presence with your online business card, a colorful online brochure, or interactive catalog to make your products and services available online.

A
B
C
D
E
F
G
H
I
J
K
L
M
N
O
P
Q
R
S
T
U
V
W
X
Y
Z

[Best] The Business Women's Network Interactive

http://www.bwni.com/

The Business Women's Network Interactive acts as an umbrella organization to unite, network, and promote the 2,300 women's business and professional organizations and Web sites profiled in the directory—a constituency representing more than 10,000,000 women throughout the United States and Canada. BWN serves as a liaison between the executive branch, Small Business Administration, Congress and other government divisions and working women—with an emphasis on women's business ownership.

CatalystWomen.org

http://www.catalystwomen.org/

Catalyst reports on the state of women in business, providing research summaries and reports to help companies improve conditions and opportunities for women. Learn more about recent reports and recommendations made by Catalyst.

Center for Reproductive Law and Policy

http://www.echonyc.com/~jmkm/wotw/

This site provides a review of women's reproductive freedom in six countries around the world: Brazil, China, Germany, India, Nigeria, and the United States. Each country's pertinent laws and policies are discussed on a wide range of topics.

Centre for Women's Studies in Education (CWSE)

http://www.oise.utoronto.ca/webstuff/departments/cwse1.html/

This Web server in Toronto is run by the Ontario Institute for Studies in Education. Among its many pages you will find project descriptions, research papers, information on CWSE publications, and links to women's studies sites worldwide.

Christian+Feminist

http://www.users.csbsju.edu/~eknuth/xpxx/

Many articles, reviews, and directories that support the premise that feminism can coexist peacefully with the historically patriarchal Christian religion.

Cybergrrl

http://www.cybergrrl.com/

Informing, inspiring, and celebrating women. Includes articles, movie and book reviews, family information, and more. The server for this site also houses many other feminism-related sites.

Diotima: Women and Gender in the Ancient World

http://www.stoa.org/diotima/

This Web site is intended to serve as a resource for anyone interested in patterns of gender around the ancient Mediterranean and as a forum for collaboration among instructors who teach courses about women and gender in the ancient world. Includes research articles, course materials, a comprehensive bibliography, and more.

Expect the Best from a Girl

http://www.academic.org/

This site prepared by the Women's College Coalition contains information about what parents and others can do to encourage girls in academic areas, particularly math and the sciences. Includes a listing of programs and institutes that can be contacted.

Feminist Arts-Music

http://www.feminist.org/arts/linkmusic.html

An annotated list of feminist musicians, with links to the artists' home pages and fan club pages where you can get more information.

Feminist Majority Foundation Online

http://www.feminist.org/

This site contains information on government actions for and against women, an online discussion group, publication information, and much more. There is also a shopping area where you can purchase feminist gifts, clothing, and other items.

Feminist.com

http://feminist.com/

Feminist.com is a site aimed at helping women network more effectively on the Internet. Includes the abridged text of articles and speeches, women's health resources, women-owned businesses, links, and lots more!

Forum for Women's Health

http://www.womenshealth.org/

Health and wellness page that focuses exclusively on women's health issues.

Girl Power!

http://www.health.org/gpower/

The national public education campaign sponsored by the Department of Health and Human Services to help encourage and empower 9- to 14-year-old girls.

Girl Scouts of the USA

http://www.girlscouts.org/

For every girl who enjoys scouting and every adult woman whose life was enhanced by scouting. Girl Scouts can find out about special events and activities, order uniforms and equipment, and read about the history of Girl Scouting; adults can participate in an alumni search, and learn how to volunteer.

Girls Incorporated

http://www.girlsinc.org/

An organization dedicated to "Helping girls become strong, smart, and bold." This site includes research and advocacy information, membership information, and more.

Global Fund for Women

http://www.globalfundforwomen.org/

The Global Fund for Women is an international organization that focuses on female human rights. Includes information on supported programs, news articles, a FAQ sheet, and describes what you can do to help.

Good Vibrations

http://www.goodvibes.com/

Good Vibrations is a worker-owned cooperative with two retail stores, a publishing company called Down There Press, and two catalogs: Good Vibrations and The Sexuality

A B C D E F G H I J K L M N O P Q R S T U V **W** X Y Z

Library. They sell quality sex toys, books/audio, and videos at reasonable prices, in a straightforward, nonsleazy environment.

Herspace.com

http:// www.we-womensentertainment.com/

An interactive creative place on the Web that promotes and supports female artists. Check out the works of some up-and-coming female artists and authors or recharge your creative batteries with a few fun exercises.

Inventors Museum

http://www.inventorsmuseum.com/ women.htm

Take the inventors quiz to find out how knowledgeable you are about women inventors. Then read all about women inventors and their inventions. Lots of interesting information, as well as details about the museum operations if you'd like to tour.

iVillage.com: The Women's Network

http://www.ivillage.com/

Find information about many subjects of interest to women, including getting pregnant, relationships, money, work and career, raising children, and more here.

Library Resources for Women's Studies

http://metalab.unc.edu/cheryb/ women/librcws.html

As the site title indicates, this page provides links to university and research center libraries across the United States that contain "useful or unique collections" related to women's studies. Includes Telnet, Gopher, FTP, and Web addresses.

Lifetime Online

http://www.lifetimetv.com/

This is the World Wide Web extension of Lifetime Television, the women's network. Provides information about Lifetime's television schedule and programs, as well as articles on health and fitness, parenting, sports, and more. Includes a searchable index of topics covered.

Machon Chana

http://www.machonchana.org/

A women's institute for the study of Judaism. This nicely done site helps educate Jewish women about their religion and culture.

National Association for Female Executives

http://www.nafe.com/

Offers links to online career and business resources as well as contacts for networking. The site also offers articles on entrepreneurial issues and information on the mission and benefits of the National Association for Female Executives.

National First Ladies' Library

http://www.firstladies.org/

Explores lives of our first ladies and their contributions to history. Contains bibliographies, press releases, a newsletter, a photo album, and Saxton McKinley house information.

National Museum of Women in the Arts

http://www.nmwa.org

Home of the only museum in the world dedicated to recognizing the contributions of women artists, this site provides a history of the organization, an online gallery complete with biographies of each featured artist, a library and research center, and much more.

The National Organization for Women (NOW)

http://www.now.org

This home page for NOW offers press releases and articles, issues NOW is currently involved in, information on joining (with email or Web addresses for many local chapters), and the history of NOW. Also provided is a search form if you're looking for a specific topic at NOW's site.

National Partnership for Women & Families (NPWF)

http://www.nationalpartnership.org/

Test your knowledge of work and family issues by taking the short online quiz here. Then find out more about public policy issues facing families and watch a video about NPWF.

National Women's Hall of Fame

http://www.greatwomen.org/

Find out who this year's Hall of Fame inductees are, play games and participate in exercises to increase your knowledge of the contribution great women have made, learn more about the work of this organization, and buy Hall of Fame merchandise here.

National Women's History Project

http://www.nwhp.org

Official Web site of the National Women's History Project which originated Women's History month. Many interesting features here about the history of women and what they have contributed in the past. Educators might benefit

from learning more about the significant impact women had on history that they have not received credit for. This project aims to bring their contributions to light. The site offers information and resources, as well as an online catalog of products for sale.

NBCC–National Breast Cancer Coalition

http://www.natlbcc.org/

Learn more about this nonprofit advocacy organization and its efforts to eradicate breast cancer through action and public policy change. Join the organization or just learn more about breast cancer here through the breaking news section.

NWSA–National Women's Studies Association

http://www.nwsa.org/

The NWSA supports and promotes feminist teaching, learning, research, and many other projects. They provide professional and community service at the pre-K through postsecondary levels. They provide information about the interdisciplinary field of Women's Studies for those outside the profession. They publish a newsletter called NWSAction and other publications. The NWSA Journal is an official publication of the National Women's Studies Association, that publishes the most up-to-date interdisciplinary, multicultural feminist scholarship linking feminist theory with teaching and activism. They have an annual conference that provides opportunities for teachers, students, activists, and others to share research findings, strategies, and ideas for effecting social change.

A
B
C
D
E
F
G
H
I
J
K
L
M
N
O
P
Q
R
S
T
U
V
W
X
Y
Z

A
B
C
D
E
F
G
H
I
J
K
L
M
N
O
P
Q
R
S
T
U
V
W
X
Y
Z

Office of Women's Business Ownership

http://www.sbaonline.sba.gov/womeninbusiness/

Produced by the United States Small Business Association, this page provides information and resource links for women currently running or seeking to run small businesses in the United States.

OWBO Online Women's Business Center

http://www.onlinewbc.gov/

OWBO promotes the growth of women-owned businesses through programs that address business training and technical assistance. There's a wealth of information here if you are in business or thinking about it.

Oxygen.com

http://www.oxygen.com/

The online site with information for, by, and about women. Discuss issues of great importance, such as making the world a better place, to less important but perhaps equally interesting, shopping, relationships, learning, and more. Lots of chat and discussion opportunities, as well as interactive elements. The site also supports a shopping area for things you might need.

Shescape Online

http://www.shescape.com/

Shescape is a dance show that celebrates lesbian culture. This site provides information about the show and includes an advice column, interviews, schedules of upcoming concerts and events, monthly horoscopes, health and fitness advice, and links to related sites.

Sports Illustrated for Women

http://sportsillustrated.cnn.com/siwomen/

Stay up-to-date on hot women's sports stars and learn more about getting and keeping your body in shape.

UnderWire

http://underwire.msn.com/

Women take a spirited look at social issues, relationships, fitness, and politics in this interactive magazine.

The United Nations and the Status of Women

http://www.un.org/Conferences/Women/PubInfo/Status/Home.htm

This site from the United Nations provides information about what the UN has done during its 54-year history to further the status of women. Included are conference findings, general articles, and commission reports.

Voices of Women Online

http://www.voiceofwomen.com/

In these pages, women are telling their stories, discussing real issues, and sharing hard-won wisdom. Offers articles on a wide variety of topics, a calendar of events, bridges to other destinations on the Web, a directory of woman-friendly businesses, and a marketplace as tools to empower you on your journey.

WE: Women's Entertainment

http://www.we-womensentertainment.com/

Home of the Women's Entertainment broadcasting company which features programming specifically addressed to the female audience. Here, you can learn more about WE's various TV programs.

Web by Women, for Women

http://www.io.com/~wwwomen/

Lots of solid, unbiased, nonsleazy information about sexuality, pregnancy, contraception, and more.

The Women and Politics Home Page

http://www.american.edu/oconnor/wandp/

Women and Politics is an academic journal published at West Georgia College in Carrollton, Georgia. The goal of the journal is to foster research and the development of theory on women's political participation, the role of women in society, and the impact of public policy upon women's lives. Included online are article abstracts, calls for papers, and subscription information.

Women in Islam

http://www.usc.edu/dept/MSA/humanrelations/_womeninislam/

Interesting basic information about how women fit into the Islamic religion, mostly oriented toward those unfamiliar with Islam.

Women Leaders Online (WLO)

http://wlo.org/

WLO is an organization dedicated to stopping the Radical Right/Contract with America agenda. This Web site contains information about Women Leaders Online and a variety of other women-related issues.

Women's Human Rights Net

http://www.whrnet.org/

A beautiful site designed with women's rights in mind. Lots of useful information for you to read and benefit from.

Women's History

http://socialstudies.com/c/@0/Pages/womenindex.html

This Web site, part of the Social Studies School Service, provides teachers with several lessons, student exercises, and reviews of special materials that present exciting ways to bring women's history into their classrooms. Topics include Women in Wartime, American Women at Work, Amelia Earhart, and others.

Women's Human Rights Resources

http://www.law-lib.utoronto.ca/Diana/

A collection of Web sites, online documents, and bibliographies about women's human rights issues.

Women's Sports Network

http://www.wsnsports.com

Get women's sports updates and results, order sporting equipment and gear, and read articles that keep you informed regarding women's sports stars and teams.

WomanOwned.Com–Business Information for Women Entrepreneurs

http://www.womanowned.com

Learn how to start your own business, get it financed, and get support for your business. There are pages of helpful information as well as links to other related sites.

Working Moms Refuge

http://www.momsrefuge.com/

Pick up tips and strategies for making the most of your time, from quick recipes to ideas for choosing a financial planner, at this site. Much of the content is geared to

A
B
C
D
E
F
G
H
I
J
K
L
M
N
O
P
Q
R
S
T
U
V
W
X
Y
Z

moms juggling childcare and work responsibilities, with chat and discussions forums available for commiserating and advice.

WWWomen!

http://www.wwwomen.com/

A comprehensive search directory for information on issues of interest to women. WWWomen links users to chats, advice, site reviews, message boards, and Web sites about topics including health, religion, education, and feminism.

Yale Journal of Law and Feminism

http://www.yale.edu/lawnfem/law&fem.html

The Yale Journal of Law and Feminism is committed to publishing pieces about women's experiences, especially as they have been structured, affected, controlled, discussed, or ignored by the law. This Web site contains subscription information, Telnet access to past issues, and the chance to submit your own article or even order a T-shirt.

WRESTLING

IronSilk Wrestling Scoops

http://www.scoopscentral.com/partners/wrestling.html

Get information on pro wrestlers, matches, news, and opinions here.

ProWrestling.com

http://www.prowrestling.com/

Locate information on upcoming pro wrestling matches and TV programming, and read articles, get headline news, and stay up to date regarding your favorite wrestler's career here.

TheMat.com

http://themat.com/

Whether you're looking for collegiate, high school, youth, or women's wrestling, you'll find Olympic trial information, archives, results, and links here.

World Wrestling Federation

http://www.wwf.com/

Home of the World Wrestling Federation (WWF) and the most popular professional wrestling league in the world. Here, you can read the latest news, find out about upcoming events, and learn more about your favorite celebrity wrestlers. Details on pay-per-view offerings, TV appearances, videos, magazines, sweepstakes, and more. If you're a big fan of professional wrestling, be sure to bookmark this page.

WOW (World of Wrestling) Magazine

`http://www.wowmagazine.com/`

Published monthly by H&S Media, Inc., WOW is "the only magazine that covers the complete world of wrestling," including the WWF and ECW. Go behind the scenes to find out the real scoop on the wrestlers you love and the wrestlers you love to hate. Preview the current issue of WOW magazine, check out WOW's links to other wrestling sites, or contact the editors to voice your opinion or make a suggestion.

WrestleZone

`http://www.wrestlezone.com/`

Read the extensive list of headline wrestling news, stay updated on results and upcoming fights, and check out pics of your favorite guys and gals here.

Wrestling Threat

`http://wrestlingthreat.com/`

Wrestling news, inside information, and discussion forums help you keep abreast of what's happening in the world of professional wrestling and put you in touch with other fans.

⟦Best⟧ Wrestling USA Magazine

`http://www.wrestlingusa.com/`

Take a look at action photos, see results from college and high school matches, read articles, and find out about wrestling camps and just about anything else you might want to learn about junior high, high school, and collegiate wrestling. You can subscribe to their magazine, Wrestling USA, using a secured credit card connection. For coverage of real wrestling, this site has no match.

WRITING

11 Rules of Writing

`http://www.junketstudies.com/rulesofw/`

Concise and practical tip list for punctuation, grammar, and writing clearly. Also has links to other writing resources.

A+ Research and Writing

`http://www.ipl.org/teen/aplus/`

This resource for high school and college students includes guides for researching and writing academic papers. Also has research links.

About.com—Freelance Writers

`http://freelancewrite.about.com/careers/`

A great site for experienced and new freelance writers, providing writing gigs, tips for improving your writing abilities, contract help, and discussion opportunities. Go to the Jump Start section if you're new to freelancing or just jump right in to look for potential assignments. Find out what editors expect and learn from fellow writers based on their experiences.

A
B
C
D
E
F
G
H
I
J
K
L
M
N
O
P
Q
R
S
T
U
V
W
X
Y
Z

A
B
C
D
E
F
G
H
I
J
K
L
M
N
O
P
Q
R
S
T
U
V
W
X
Y
Z

 Best **AuthorLink!**

http://www.authorlink.com/

A Web site dedicated to authors, literary agents, and publishers. Contains book reviews, business news, competition info, links to publishers and agents, and insights into writing. Very comprehensive.

Authorlink is an award-winning Internet news/information/marketing service for the publishing industry that has been around for several years which proves its viability. They provide editors and agents fast access to prescreened professional fiction and nonfiction manuscripts that have been submitted by authors. Readers and writers can quickly order any titles from the secure e-store. Their titles are available at major bookstores and online bookstores such as Amazon. They also have their own publishing imprint, Authorlink Press, which offers all the standard services including electronic press, short-run publishing services, and other services. If you are a writer or just interested in reading a good book, this is the site for you.

Bartleby.com

http://www.bartleby.com/

This site bills itself as "The preeminent publisher of literature, reference and verse providing students, researchers, and the intellectually curious with unlimited access to books and information on the Web, free of charge."

BookLocker.com–Online Bookstore and Publisher

http://www.booklocker.com/

BookLocker sells print and ebooks on all subjects, from everyday to unusual and eclectic, by new authors and published authors. This is a great site for the first time author to get exposure and to learn about writing from the many articles, books, and links.

Children's Writing Resource Center

http://www.write4kids.com/

Articles and recommendations for becoming a successful writer for children. Chat with other children's writers and illustrators.

Computer Book Café

http://www.studiob.com/content.asp

StudioB is a literary agency for computer book authors. It sponsors and maintains the Computer Book Café to offer computer book writers articles about the computer book industry, its publishers, fellow writers, financial information, tax advice, and a mailing list. StudioB also presents information on the organization and how to become represented.

The Editor's Eye

http://home.worldnet.att.net/~DReleford/index.html

This site contains information of interest to writers, potential writers, editors, publishers, the general reading public, and many links to other writers' resources. Click on links to download free software such as Red Hat Linux and StarOffice. The site also offers information about the authors' books and has a bookstore where you can link to sites such as Amazon and Barnes & Noble where you may purchase the books. The site also attempts to offer information and help to other writers. Worth a look if you're interested in books, writing, and free software.

FreelanceWorkshop.com

http://www.freelanceworkshop.com/

A very rich graphical site providing links to the workshop materials, a chat room, and information on how to take the online magazine's Article Writing Workshop.

Guide to Grammar and Writing

http://webster.commnet.edu/HP/
pages/darling/original.htm

A great refresher regarding sentence structure and grammar, as well as a resource to turn to regarding correct usage of various parts of speech.

IAAY Expository Writing Tutorial

http://www.cty.jhu.edu/writing/

Home to John Hopkins' Institute for the Academic Advancement of Youth. This cool site provides expository writing instructions for kids in grades 6–12. Kids get to work with a more experienced writer as they explore the writing process. To participate, they must be enrolled in the tutorial to access the pages containing the assignments. Financial aid is available.

Paradigm Online Writing Assistant

http://www.powa.org/

This excellent site by Chuck Guilford provides extensive instruction on how to write essays for different

purposes. Each essay type is presented via a link. A discussion group is provided for sharing writing ideas.

Purdue Online Writing Lab (OWL)

http://owl.english.purdue.edu/

Improve your writing with help from this online resource, where you'll also find handouts that might answer lots of your questions. But if not, turn to the Purdue experts for help.

RoseDog.com

http://rosedog.com/

Post your work and get feedback or just exposure that might help boost your career. You'll also find information on literary agents here, too.

storybay

http://www.storybay.com/

Online meeting place for writers, editors, and consumers, this site features tools to help writers fast-track their careers by developing and showcasing their talents. Provides executives the opportunity to find and recruit writers for their various projects. For consumers, the site features novels, screenplays, and other literary works.

Waterside Productions

http://www.waterside.com/

Waterside Productions Inc., an electronic rights, software, and literary agency, was founded in 1982. Since that time, more than 5,000 contracts have been negotiated with more than 100 publishers. The site hosts links to agents, writers' resources, sample contracts, publishers, conferences, and information about how to be represented.

A
B
C
D
E
F
G
H
I
J
K
L
M
N
O
P
Q
R
S
T
U
V
W
X
Y
Z

A
B
C
D
E
F
G
H
I
J
K
L
M
N
O
P
Q
R
S
T
U
V
W
X
Y
Z

The Write News

http://writenews.com/

This site presents everything you ever wanted to know about the publishing business. An online industry newsletter with more than 1,000 links for writers, agents, and publishers.

The Writer's Place

http://www.awoc.com/
AWOC-Home.cfm

Searchable writer's guidelines database of paying markets (currently 637 markets). Find advice for making money as a writer, publications, and writing resources.

Writer's Write

http://www.writerswrite.com/

Find writing jobs, improve your craft, and mingle with fellow authors here.

Writers on the Net

http://www.writers.com/

Pay-for-use tutoring and editing classes, and workshops led by experienced, published writers.

Writing Assessment Services

http://members.aol.com/
cmarsch786/

These writing assessments are offered to home schoolers to help evaluate children's writing progress from a woman who was a college English instructor, and is a current instructor for America Online's Online Campus. She's also a home schooler herself.

Writing for the Web

http://www.useit.com/papers/
webwriting/

People read differently on the Web than they do when reading printed publications, so writers need to adapt their material to the Web. Here, John Morkes and Jakob Nielsen publish the findings of their research on how people access information on the Web. Some excellent writing guidelines for Web authors.

Writing-World.com

http://www.writing-world.com/

News articles, tips, and online classes for aspiring writers and for writers who want to further develop their talents.

Young Authors Workshop

http://www.planet.eon.net/
~bplaroch/

Resource for middle school students has sections for getting ideas, writing, editing, and publishing their work. Also has teacher resources.

Asana Sequences

http://www2.gdi.net/~mjm/
sequence.html

One sequence for each day of the week, complete with small graphic images for demonstration. From the site of YOGAaahh.

Body Trends

http://www.bodytrends.com/
strech.htm

You can order all your yoga-associated products from the BodyTrends.com site to get you started off on the right stretch. They offer such products as mats, bags, wedges, blocks, sandbags, straps, and numerous yoga-related videos.

Hatha Yoga: Yoga Synergy

http://www.yogasynergy.com.au/

Yoga Synergy was established in Newtown, Australia, in 1984. The teaching represents a synthesis between traditional hatha yoga and modern medical science.

INDOlink: Health and Fitness

http://www.indolink.com/Health/
main.htm

Find detailed information about yoga, along with other aspects of health and fitness such as herbal remedies.

Sahaja Yoga Meditation

http://www.sahajayoga.org/

Created by Shri Mataji Nirmala Devi in 1970, Sahaja Yoga is a "method of meditation which brings a breakthrough in the evolution of human awareness." At this site, you can learn more about Sahaja meditation, read testimonials and health benefits, view a list of Q&As, check out the book reviews, and much more.

Siddha Yoga Meditation

http://www.siddhayoga.org/

Learn what Siddha Yoga is, find out about courses, news, and reading that might be of help, as well as centers that specialize in this type of yoga. The site also provides information on upcoming events and programs for youth. They also have a nice online bookstore from which you may order related books.

Sivananda Yoga "Om" Page

http://www.sivananda.org/

A clearinghouse for information on yoga and vedanta. The site has yoga exercise tips, a guide to higher consciousness, and biographies of Swami Vishnu and his guru, Swami Sivananda.

A B C D E F G H I J K L M N O P Q R S T U V W X **Y** Z

 Step by Step Yoga Postures

http://www.santosha.com/asanas/

This site has a lot of useful information. One of the highlights is the listing of both the Sanskrit name and English translation. Choose from a long list of asanas and read step-by-step directions on how to achieve these yoga positions. Also read about meditation.

This site represents the presence of Yoga Anand Ashram, a nonprofit organization founded in 1972 by Gurani Anjali, whose goal is to educate and uplift humanity through each individual's understanding, practice, and embodiment of the yoga path. To accomplish this, they offer such things as an online community, a beginners' guide, articles, a forum, a section on philosophy, a section for children's yoga, and an online bookstore for your convenient shopping.

A World of Yoga

http://www.yogaworld.org/

At this site, you'll learn more about yoga techniques and how it can help you reach a higher state of consciousness, according to the site's host, Graham Ledgerwood. Find out about the eight main types of yoga and how they relate to an individual's spiritual path.

The Yoga Directory

http://www.yogadirectory.com/

The Yoga Directory contains a list of yoga teachers, yoga centers, organizations, music, yoga therapists, health products, and yoga retreats which gives you just about everything you need to practice yoga.

Yoga Journal

http://www.yogajournal.com/

Read online articles about Hatha Yoga here, as well as learn about other publishing products you might be interested in. There is also a directory of yoga teachers you can consult to find a local instructor. You can subscribe to their magazine online.

Yoga Site

http://www.yogasite.com/

Great instructional material that tells and shows you, through drawings, about basic yoga positions. You also can read about yoga styles, review questions and answers posed regarding yoga, identify yoga-related organizations, and read about yoga therapy news. And if you still find you have unanswered questions about yoga, there are links to other yoga sites that might help.

YogaClass

http://www.yogaclass.com/welcome.html

Online yoga instruction including breathing, exercises, stretches, and chants. Includes a chat room.

YogaFinder

http://www.yogafinder.com/

Use this national search system to find classes, facilities, and general information about yoga.

YREC: Yoga Research and Education Center

http://www.yrec.org/

This "Gateway to Traditional Yoga" provides information on yoga education and research as well as the therapeutic application of yoga in healthcare. Here, you can check on daily classes and teacher training, sign up for a yoga correspondence course, and learn how to give something back to yoga. The illustrated beginner's tour is especially helpful for novices and those interested in finding out more about yoga.

YOUTH ORGANIZATIONS

Boy Scouts of America

http://www.bsa.scouting.org/

If you're a scout, you can use this site to learn about scouting programs, events, publications, merchandise, and awards, as well as to play fun games online. Anyone considering becoming a scout, which includes boys age 7–20, or a scout leader, will find this site informative.

Boys and Girls Clubs of America

http://www.bgca.org/

The Boys and Girls Club Movement is a nationwide affiliation of local, autonomous organizations working to help youth from all backgrounds (with special concern for those from disadvantaged circumstances) develop the qualities needed to become responsible citizens and leaders.

B'nai B'rith Youth Organization

http://www.bbyo.org/

B'nai B'rith is a "youth-led, worldwide organization which provides opportunities for Jewish youth to develop their leadership potential, a positive Jewish identity and commitment to their personal development."

The CityKids Foundation

http://www.citykids.com/

A multicultural organization dedicated to the survival, education, and self-expression of today's youth. Based out of New York City.

CYO: Catholic Youth Organization

http://www.cyocamp.org/

Home of the Catholic Youth Organization–sponsored camps. Learn more about the CYO camps, meet the staff, check up on employment opportunities, and learn how to contact personnel via email.

A
B
C
D
E
F
G
H
I
J
K
L
M
N
O
P
Q
R
S
T
U
V
W
X
Y
Z

A
B
C
D
E
F
G
H
I
J
K
L
M
N
O
P
Q
R
S
T
U
V
W
X
Y
Z

[Best] Girl Scouts

http://www.girlscouts.org/

Learn all about the world's largest organization for girls, its programs, research activities, traditions, publications, and, of course, Girl Scout cookies. The site also has a nice shopping mall where you can securely shop for most of the things any young woman would be interested in. There is also a helpful FAQ if you have unanswered questions. The Girl Scouts are where girls turn to discover fun, friendship, and the power of girls together. They promote the theory that Girl Scouting gives girls opportunities to build skills for lifetime success in sports, science, and even in a Girl Scout cookie sale.

Little League Baseball Online

http://www.littleleague.org/

Find out more about Little League baseball programs in your area, the history of the program, divisions, summer camp, forms and policies, equipment, and merchandise.

National 4-H Council

http://www.fourhcouncil.edu/

Whether you're considering joining 4-H, or if you're a 4-H alumnus, this site has information for you about their current programs and initiatives, getting involved, and reconnecting with past 4-Hers. 4-H is dedicated to helping youth develop leadership skills while understanding and addressing important community issues.

National PTA

http://www.pta.org/

Work for one of America's oldest organizations working on behalf of youth. The site offers facts, photographs, archives, and officers.

YMCA

http://www.ymca.int/

Locate YMCA offices and hotels at this site, where you'll also learn more about the mission of this Christian organization and its programs. You can review the online magazine, YMCA World, and catch up on organizational news. There is also a directory of national and local associations.

Youth and Children's Resource

http://www.child.net/

Extensive list of links to support networks and services. Includes resources for parents and national hotlines.

YouthLink

http://www.youthlink.org/

This is a division of the Foundation of America that is geared toward youths, and encourages their participation within their own communities by rewarding those who are selected with Youth Action Award grants.

A
B
C
D
E
F
G
H
I
J
K
L
M
N
O
P
Q
R
S
T
U
V
W
X
Y

The Albuquerque Aquarium

http://www.cabq.gov/biopark/
aquarium/index.html

Take a fascinating journey through the marine habitats of the oceans at this fantastic aquarium in New Mexico. There are many other features available here such as information about the zoo, the city, and other items you may be interested in.

American Zoo and Aquarium Association

http://www.aza.org/

This is the flagship membership organization for zoological parks, aquariums, oceanariums, and wildlife parks in North America. Find out what they are all about, their members, publications, conferences, how to support their conservation and animal welfare work, and more.

Arizona-Sonora Desert Museum

http://www.desertmuseum.org/

A zoo, a natural history museum, and a botanical garden make up this complex. Find information about visiting this Tucson institution and view exhibits at this site.

Big Cats Online

http://dialspace.dial.pipex.com/
agarman/bco/ver4.htm

Find out everything you ever wanted to know about the world's wild cat species. No matter what question you have about these beautiful cats, you're likely to find it here.

There are great pictures and lots of detailed information.

Brevard Zoo

http://www.brevardzoo.org/

Visitors to this site can take a virtual tour of the Brevard Zoo in Melbourne, Florida. The site also includes general information and news updates from the zoo.

The Bronx Zoo

http://wcs.org/zoos/

The Bronx Zoo is home to more than 6,000 animals, including some of the world's most endangered species. The zoo has more than 265 wooded acres devoted to spacious naturalistic habitats. The site is almost as impressive with abundant information about the zoo, what it provides, and other useful information.

Calgary Zoo

http://www.calgaryzoo.ab.ca/

Learn about the zoo (in Calgary, Alberta, Canada), conservation programs, special events, and employment and volunteering opportunities.

Best Cincinnati Zoo and Botanical Garden

http://www.cincyzoo.org/

Wander through this site to experience the Cincinnati Zoo and the world of nature. Get current events and discover what's new, learn about conservation and how you can help, get information on exotic travel programs, get educated about wildlife, and participate in the weekly animal/plant guessing game. With its excellent site design and wealth of useful

A
B
C
D
E
F
G
H
I
J
K
L
M
N
O
P
Q
R
S
T
U
V
W
X
Y

information, this site is well-deserving of its ranking as the best online zoo on the Web.

Cleveland Metroparks Zoo

http://www.clemetzoo.com/

Want to visit the rain forest? Tour the zoo? Learn about conservation? Get educated about the natural world? Read about research being conducted by zoo staff? You can do all this and more at the site of the Cleveland Metroparks Zoo.

The Cyber Zoomobile

http://www.primenet.com/ ~brendel/

This kid-oriented virtual zoo focuses on the curator's own favorite animals: the canidae (dogs), the ursidae (bears), and the felidae (cats), as well as sea life, primates, lizards, snakes, boas, and more. Big cats are the clear favorites, but you'll find lots of photos and facts exploring any of the categories that have been included. By signing in and providing feedback, you are registering to win a prize from their monthly drawing. This site also offers lots of good links and activities in their Stuff section. Definitely browse through the photomosaic images of animals, too.

The Dallas Zoo

http://www.dallas-zoo.org/home/home.asp

One of the best-looking Web sites and featuring all the main attractions you can find at most zoos plus an aquarium. There's tons of information about the zoo and related subjects. Be sure to visit here before you go to the zoo. It's worth the effort just to visit the site and after you do, you'll probably want to visit the zoo in person.

Denver Zoo

http://www.denverzoo.org/

Visitors can take a zoo tour and view short video clips of the animals, find operating hours and admission prices, or read about the conservation efforts of the Denver Zoo.

Fort Worth Zoo

http://www.fortworthzoo.com/

Zoo hours, a zoo map, educational opportunities, and special events are presented here. Visitors also can print games and puzzles from the Delta's Kids Page.

Fort Worth Zoo

http://www.fortworthzoo.com/

Zoo hours, a zoo map, educational opportunities, and special events are presented here. Visitors also can print games and puzzles from the Delta's Kids Page.

The Good Zoo Guide Online

http://www.goodzoos.com/

This site offers you an exciting guide to all the zoos on the entire planet. It features the best zoos, wildlife parks and animal collections, and more than 200 pages of zoo reviews and discussions.

The Indianapolis Zoo

http://www.indianapoliszoo.com/

Go to the Information Center for who, what, when, where details on the Indianapolis Zoo, or visit the virtual zoo for photos and information on the zoo's many inhabitants—both plants and animals. In the Virtual Zoo, you can use the search utility to put the information you want at your fingertips. Includes one of the few baby elephants born in captivity.

Kids World 2000: Animals, Zoos and Aquariums

http://now2000.com/kids/zoos.shtml

A place where young cyber-travelers can find 50+ links to animals, zoos, and aquariums in the United States and overseas. Just click a link to jump to the site of your choice and learn all about the flora and fauna.

Lincoln Park Zoo

http://www.lpzoo.com/

This site provides an index of the more than 1,000 animals featured at this free Chicago zoo. You also can find information on adopting animals; endangered species; and educational programs for schools, families, and adults. A special feature is an online tour of the zoo.

The Los Angeles Zoo

http://www.lazoo.org/

Opened in November 1966, the Los Angeles Zoo is home to more than 1,200 animals. This site includes a history of the zoo as well as visitor information, animal facts, excerpts from the zoo's quarterly magazine, and a list of job opportunities.

Memphis Zoo Home Page

http://www.memphiszoo.org/

This site provides basic information about the Memphis Zoo, such as hours and prices, educational programs, special events, membership, the gift shop, the animal hospital, and the zoo's history. Good information mainly for those interested in visiting in person.

The North Carolina Zoological Park

http://www.nczoo.org/

If you'd like to get a glimpse at this zoo, click Visit the Zoo to get a park overview, a park map, visitor's hints, and gift and food information. One tip for real-world visitors: Wear good walking shoes, because the zoo spans more than 1,400 acres and takes an estimated five hours to walk through.

Oregon Zoo

http://www.zooregon.org/

You can search this Portland, Oregon, zoo's site or just jump to one of the offered areas: About our Zoo, About our Animals, Visitor Information, What's Happening, Get Involved, Saving Species, Teachers and Educators, No Adults Allowed!, and more. There's something for everyone here.

Perth Zoo

http://www.perthzoo.wa.gov.au/

Find out about upcoming events and exhibits at this West Australia zoo, as well as conservation efforts, research, and zoo schedules and operations at this site.

Philadelphia Zoo Online

http://www.phillyzoo.org/

Besides the home page, this site offers an education page, a conservation page, an animals list, the PhillyZoo News page, and an online search engine. You also can enter the site index to get all kinds of information on animals, conservation activities, zoo facts, and more.

A
B
C
D
E
F
G
H
I
J
K
L
M
N
O
P
Q
R
S
T
U
V
W
X
Y

The Phoenix Zoo

http://www.phoenixzoo.org/zoo/

Offers zoo trails to explore, a cool stuff section especially for kids, a calendar of events, animal information, zoo stats, general information, and links to other sites.

The St. Louis Zoo

http://www.stlzoo.org/home.asp

You can do everything from plan your visit to the zoo to adopt an animal and much more. A beautiful site consisting of many rich features to make your visit more enjoyable.

The San Antonio Zoo

http://www.sazoo-aq.org/

At this site, you can get a word from the director, learn what's new at the zoo, get general zoo information, tour the zoo, learn about the "adopt an animal" program, find out about zoo membership and employment opportunities, and access links to related sites.

San Diego Zoo

http://www.sandiegozoo.org/

Known for its housing of some of the rarest pandas, the San Diego Zoo takes full advantage of this, creating Panda Central on its site. Here you can view video clips of baby panda Hua Mei or look at the photo album, as well as check in on the panda family through Panda cam. Panda facts help educate children on the lives of these special animals. You also can get information on visiting the zoo and supporting its panda initiatives here.

San Francisco Zoo

http://www.sfzoo.org/

At the time this was being written, the San Francisco Zoo was undergoing a major renovation. The site was well-designed and graphical but suffered from a lack of content. However, the site promises to include a virtual tour of the zoo and features about animal conservation and preservation.

Sea World/Busch Gardens Animal Information Database

http://www.seaworld.org/

Contains a searchable animal information database maintained by the Sea World Busch/Gardens theme parks. Find out how your classroom can take advantage of the Shamu TV series. The Animal Bytes section includes "Ask Shamu," a column that features answers to animal-related questions. The site offers a wealth of animal information, images, and resources. It also has sections devoted to camps, study trips, and zoological career information.

Wildlife Conservation Society

http://www.wcs.org/

This society, founded in 1895 in New York City, works to save wildlife around the world. It also maintains five wildlife parks in New York, including the Bronx Zoo. This site provides information on the society, its wildlife parks, and other programs.

Woodland Park Zoo (Seattle, WA)

http://www.zoo.org/

The Woodland Park Zoo in Seattle, Washington, maintains this site with a virtual tour, information on admission, conservation and education, special events, the zoo store, and exhibits.

WWW Virtual Library: Zoos

http://www.mindspring.com/zoonet/www_virtual_lib/zoos.html

A comprehensive site with links to zoos, related organizations, and sites with pictures and sound. The links are too numerous for us to vouch for all of them, but the site is well worth a visit.

Zoo Boise

http://www.animalpark.org/zoo/

This site features Zoo Boise (in Idaho), and details the events, animals, education center, upcoming projects, Critter College, and animal adoption aspects of the zoo. It also offers a list of zoo-related links.

ZooWeb.net

http://www.zooweb.net/

Your comprehensive. directory to zoos, aquariums, and conservation organizations on the Web.

A
B
C
D
E
F
G
H
I
J
K
L
M
N
O
P
Q
R
S
T
U
V
W
X
Y
Z

A

abortion, 1-2

About.com, 111

    Christianity, 276

    Freelance Writers, 433

    Homework Help, 62

    Rock Climbing, 290

    Table Tennis, 333

ACLU (American Civil Liberties Union), 39

    Freedom Network, 126

    Reproductive Rights, 1

acne. *See* skin care/cosmetics

activism

    CorpWatch.org, 2

    Gay and Lesbian Alliance Against Defamation (GLAAD), 87

    Idealist.org, 2

    National Organization for Women (NOW), 429

    Sierra Club, 180

    tolerance.org, 2

activities for kids, 117-119

actors/actresses

    Actor's Page, 347

    Now Casting, 349

    Screen Actor's Guild, 350

    Tony Awards Online, 351

acupuncture, 8

ADD/ADHD (attention deficit disorder/ attention deficit hyperactivity disorder)

    ADDHELP, 215

    Canadian Parents Online, 208

    National Attention Deficit Disorder Association, 3

addictions, 3-4

addresses (residential/business)

    InfoSpace.com, 270

    National Address and ZIP+4 Browser, 271

adolescents, 208-210

adoption

    Adoption Benefits - Employers As Partners in Family Building, 5

    From Infertility to Adoption, 241

    Infertility@Thrive, 241

    International Adoption Resource, 5

adventure travel, 359-360

advertising

    Advertising Quotes, 253

    classified ads, 39

advice (personal)

    All Experts, 5

    drDrew, 5

    eHow, 6

    Teen Advice Online, 342

African-Americans

    AFRICANET, 370

    African/Edenic Heritage Museum, 150

    Black Health Network, 423

    Internet Public Library, 270

agriculture

    Agriculture Online, 6

    Center for Animal Health and Productivity, 395

    DirectAg.com, 6

    Economic Research Service (USDA), 6

    Gemplers.com, 6

    John Deere Agricultural Equipment, 7

    National Agricultural Library (NAL), 7

    Old Farmer's Almanac, 271

    U.S. Department of Agriculture, 388

    Vantage Point Network, 418

    Weather Site, 418

AIDS (acquired immune deficiency disorder)

    AIDS Memorial Quilt, 250

    Children with AIDS Project, 216

    DISHES Project for Pediatric AIDS, 224

Gay Men's Health Crisis, 86

Marty Howard's AIDS Page, 94

Air Force

Air Force Association, 392

Army and Air Force Exchange Service, 392

Veterans News and Information Service, 394

air travel resources, 360-361

airlines

Aer Lingus, 361

Air Canada, 361

Airlines of the Web, 360

Alaska Airlines, 361

America West, 361

American Airlines, 361

Ansett Australia, 361

Boeing, 30

British Airways, 361

Canadian Airlines International, 361

Cathay Pacific, 361

Continental Airlines, 361

Delta Airlines, 361

DiscountAirfares.com, 362

Hawaiian Airlines, 361

Lufthansa, 361

New England Airlines, 361

Northwest Airlines, 362

Period.Com Airlines, 271

Qantas Airlines, 362

Scuba Yellow Pages, 406

Southwest Airlines, 362

TWA Airlines, 362

U.S. Department of Transportation, 389

United Airlines, 362

US Airways, 362

Weather Channel, 418

Alaska

Alaska Airlines, 361

Alaskan Cabin, Cottage, and Lodge Catalog, 375

Alaskan Travel Guide, 378

All-Inclusives Resort and Cruise Vacation Source, 374

Vista Alaska, 382

alcohol recipes, 77

alcoholism

Alcoholics Anonymous, 4

National Association of Alcoholism and Drug Abuse Counselors (NAADAC), 326

alien abductions, 385-387

allergies, 7

alternative medicine, 8-9

Alzheimer's disease

Ageless Design, Inc., 9

Alzheimer's Association, 9, 298

Alzheimer's Disease Education & Referral Center, 298

Health and Age.com, 9

Maple Knoll Village Retirement Home, 289

amusement and theme parks, 10-11, 382

animals. *See also* pets

Animal Health Information, 228

Big Cats Online, 441

Brevard Zoo, 441

Bronx Zoo, 441

Calgary Zoo, 441

Center for Animal Health and Productivity, 395

Cincinnati Zoo and Botanical Garden, 442

Cleveland Metroparks Zoo, 442

Cyber Zoomobile, 442

Dallas Zoo, 442

Denver Zoo, 442

Fort Worth Zoo, 442

horses, 103-104

Index of Famous Dogs, Cats, and Critters, 227

Indianapolis Zoo, 442

Kids World 2000: Animals, Zoos and Aquariums, 443

Lincoln Park Zoo, 443

Los Angeles Zoo, 443

Memphis Zoo, 443

Murdoch University: Division of Veterinary and Biomedical Sciences, 395

National Board Exam (NBE), 395

National Wildlife Federation, 66

A
B
C
D
E
F
G
H
I
J
K
L
M
N
O
P
Q
R
S
T
U
V
W
X
Y
Z

North Carloina Zoological Park, 443

OncoLink: Veterinary Oncology, 396

Oregon Zoo, 443

Perth Zoo, 443

Philadelphia Zoo Online, 443

Phoenix Zoo, 444

San Antonio Zoo, 444

San Diego Zoo, 444

San Francisco Zoo, 444

Sea World/Busch Gardens Animal Information Database, 444

St. Louis Zoo, 444

Veterinary Medicine, 396

Vetscape, 396

Wildlife Conservation Society, 444

Woodland Park Zoo (Seattle, WA), 445

World Equine Health Network, 397

World Organization for Animal Health, 397

WWW Virtual Library: Zoos, 445

Zoo Boise, 445

ZooWeb.net, 445

antiques

Antique Quilt Source, 250

Antiques Roadshow (PBS), 11

Antiquity Online, 275

Circline, 11

CollectiblesNet.com, 40

Maine Antique Digest, 12

Newel, 12

RailServe, 257

Steptoe & Wife Antiques, Ltd., 101

antivirus software, 46

apartments

Apartments for Rent Online, 259

RentCheck, 287

Apple Computer

Apple Corps, 82

Home Page, 44

aquariums, 441-443

architecture

Architecture Magazine, 12

Design Basics Home Online Planbook, 12

Frank Lloyd Wright, 12

museums

National Building Museum, 149

Wharton Esherick Museum, 149

area code directories

555-1212.com Area Code Lookup, 267

THOR: The Virtual Reference Desk, 273

Argentina

International Bed-and-Breakfast Guide, 376

Las Lenas Ski Packages, 321

Arizona

Arizona Guide, 378

Arizona-Sonora Desert Museum, 441

Buying a Home in Arizona, 259

Phoenix Zoo, 444

Army (U.S.), 391-394

art

ALEX, 352

Crayola Home Page, 118

National Museum of Women in the Arts, 428

WWW Virtual Library, 285

art museums, 150-152

arts and culture

Arts & Letters Daily, 186

ArtsEdge, 60, 337

Benton Foundation, 195

Culture Finder.com, 367

Gigaplex, 246

HotWired, 246

ASL (American Sign Language), 315

assisted living, 299-300

associations

AAR: Association of American Railroads, 256

American Cat Fanciers Association, 225

American Lung Association, 141

Appraisal Institute, 102

Association of Trial Lawyers of America, 127

Cat Fanciers Association, 225

Closely Guarded Secrets of the UK Surfing World, 411

A
B
C
D
E
F
G
H
I
J
K
L
M
N
O
P
Q
R
S
T
U
V
W
X
Y
Z

Knitting Tutorials, 121

Marketing Research Association (MRA), 134

National Education Association, 340

National Rifle Association, 106

National Show Ski Association, 414

NWSA—National Women's Studies Association, 429

Rotary International, 13

Sales and Marketing Executives International, 134

Single Parents Association, 215

U.S. Youth Soccer, 325

United States Tennis Association, 347

Volleyball World Wide, 404

astronomy

Amazing Space, 13

American Astronomical Society, 13

Astro!nfo, 13

Astronomer Magazine, 245

Astronomy Thesaurus, 262

Constellation X, 14

Earth & Sky, 14

NASA Earth Observatory, 14

NASA HumanSpaceflight, 14

Sky & Telescope Online, 249

atheism, 275

auctions, 15

audio books, 26-27

Australia

Australia Travel Directory, 370

Australian Love & Sexuality, 306

AVA Online, 395

Deep Sea Divers Den, 405

Down Under Quilts Online, 251

Media Monitors, 191

Murdoch University: Division of Veterinary and Biomedical Sciences, 395

New Age Online Australia, 185

Perth Zoo, 443

Qantas Airlines, 362

Simply OarSome, 410

Sydney International Travel Centre, 373

Sydney Opera House, 169

Austria

Austria Ski Vacation Packages, 320

Hyperski, 321

Salzburg.com, 373

authors

11 Rules of Writing, 433

About.com—Freelance Writers, 433

Agatha Christie, 128

Anne Rice, 131

AuthorLink!, 434

Ayn Rand, 131

Bibliomania, 128

BookLocker.com—Online Bookstore and Publisher, 434

Candlelight Stories, 128

Charles Dickens, 129

Children's Writing Resource Center, 434

Computer Book Café, 434

Dean Koontz, 130

Dorothy Parker, 131

Editors Eye, 435

Electronic Text Center at the University of Virginia, 129

F. Scott Fitzgerald, 129

FreelanceWorkshop.com, 435

Fyodor Dostoevsky, 129

Ian Fleming, 129

Jack Kerouac, 130

James Joyce, 130

Joyce Carol Oates (Celestial Timepiece), 130

Meet J.K. Rowling, 131

Nobel Laureates, 130

Oscar Wilde, 131

Project Gutenburg, 131

Pulitzer Prizes, 131

Richard Brautigan, 128

Romance Reader, 131

RoseDog.com, 435

Science Fiction and Fantasy Writers of America (SFWA), 296

Stephen King, 130

storybay, 435

T.S. Eliot, 129

Toni Morrison, 130

A B C D E F G H I J K L M N O P Q R S T U V W X Y Z

Vladmir Nabokov (Zembla), 130
Waterside Productions, 435
William Faulkner, 129
William S. Burroughs, 128
Wonderful Wizard of Oz, 131
Writer's Place, 436
Writer's Write, 436
Writers on the Net, 436
auto racing, 16
automobiles
buying online, 17
Car Talk, 268
Carfax Lemon Check, 17
Carprice.com, 17
classic cars, 17
Consumer Education for Teens, 341
information, 17
insurance, 108
Insurance Institute for Highway Safety, 108
manufacturers, 17
Microsoft Carpoint, 17
Motor Vehicle Registration and Licensing, 390
Popular Science Magazine, 188
repair, 18
U.S. Department of Transportation, 389
aviation
Air Combat USA, 18
Air Safe, 18
NASA, 18
National Air and Space Museum, 18
Weather Site, 418
Wright Brothers Aeroplane Company and Museum of Aviation, 152
awards
Nobel Foundation, 271
Tony Awards Online, 351

B

babies and toddlers
ABC's of Parenting, 210
Babies Today Online, 19
Baby Bag Online, 210

Baby Catalog of America, 210
BabyCenter, 211
babyGap, 211
CareGuide, 211
Dr. Greene: Toddlers, 211
Dr. Plain Talk, 224
Early Childhood Educators' and Family Web Corner, 211
eToys: The Internet's Biggest Toy Store!, 211
Fisher-Price, 354
Family Education Network: A Parenting and Education Resource, 211
Genius Babies.com, 354
iParenting.com, 211
KidSource: Toddlers, 212
Learning Curve International, 355
Little Tikes, 355
Live and Learn, 212
National Parenting Center, 212
Pampers Parenting Institute, 212
ParenTalk Newsletter: Toddlers, 212
Parenthood, 212
Parents.com, 212
banks
Bank of America Corporation, 30
Bankrate.com, 334
Chase Manhattan Corporation, 30
Citigroup, 30
bargain travel, 362-363
bargains (household)
BargainDog, 308
Cheapskate Monthly, 81
coupons, 20
eSmarts Newsletter, 81
freebies, 20
Overstock.com, 20
baseball
Baseball Links, 22
Little League Baseball Online, 440
basketball, 22-23
BBC (British Broadcasting Corporation)
BBCi, 343
Nature Site, 179

A
B
C
D
E
F
G
H
I
J
K
L
M
N
O
P
Q
R
S
T
U
V
W
X
Y
Z

News, 189

Radio 4, 177

World Service—Religions of the World, 274

beaches, 412

bed-and-breakfasts, 376-377

beverages

alcohol, 77

Coca-Cola, 76

coffees and teas

Cafe Maison Coffee Roasters, 77

Peet's Coffee & Tea, 77

MixedDrink.com, 77

Wet Planet Beverages, 77

wines

Food & Wine Magazine, 78

Gruppo Italiano Vini, 78

Into Wine, 78

K&L Wine Merchants, 78

Robin Garr's Wine Lovers, 78

Wine Searcher, 78

Wine Spectator, 78

Wine.com, 79

Wines on the Internet, 79

Bible

Bible Gateway, 276

First Church of Cyberspace, 277

Logos Research Systems, 279

bicycles, 24

bing, 25

biographies

Academy of Achievement, 267

Biography.com, 96, 268

birds

Bird Watchers Digest, 25

National Audubon Society, 66

NetPets, 228

Pet Bird Magazine, 245

Waltham World of Pet Care, 229

Wild Birds Unlimited, 25

bluegrass music, 163

boats and sailing

Internet Boats, 26

Weather Site, 418

books

Adventurous Traveler Bookstore, 359

Amazon.com, 308

audio books, 26-27

authors

Agatha Christie, 128

Anne Rice, 131

Ayn Rand, 131

Charles Dickens, 129

Dean Koontz, 130

Dorothy Parker, 131

F. Scott Fitzgerald, 129

Fyodor Dostoevsky, 129

Ian Fleming, 129

J.K. Rowling, 131

Jack Kerouac, 130

James Joyce, 130

Joyce Carol Oates, 130

L. Frank Baum, 131

Oscar Wilde, 131

Richard Brautigan, 128

Stephen King, 130

T.S. Eliot, 129

Toni Morrison, 130

Vladmir Nabokov, 130

William Faulkner, 129

William S. Burroughs, 128

BargainDog, 308

Bibliomania: The Network Library, 128, 264

BookLocker.com—Online Bookstore and Publisher, 434

bookstores, 27

Buddhanet.net, 275

Buy.com, 308

Candlelight Stories, 128

Catsbuzz Bookstore, 226

City Lights Bookstore, 26

Good Vibrations, 428

Half.com, 308

Hinduism Online, 281

Hinduism Today, 281

Internet Public Library, 265

Library of Congress, 270

Martingale & Company, 251

New Age Books, 185
News Express, 189
Nolo Legal Press, 127
Online Islamic Bookstore, 282
Puffin House Publishers, 340
Ranch Rainbow Press, 186
Salem New Age Center, 186
Scholastic.com, 340
SciFan, 296
Stepfamily Bookstore, 219
stores
    Barnes & Noble.com, 27
    Best Book Buys, 27
    Borders.com, 27
    WordsWorth Books, 27
Stress Less, 330
Stress Management for Patients and
  Physicians, 331
TechFest—Networking Protocols,
  184
botanical gardens, 441-442
bowling, 28
boxing, 28-29
breast cancer
  Avon – The Crusade, 35
  Breast Cancer Action, 35
  Faces of Hope, 35
  NBCC—National Breast Cancer
    Coalition, 429
Buddhism, 274-276
budget travel, 363-364
budgeting tips, 81
bulletin boards
  LawGuru.com, 126
  Midwifery Resources on the
    Internet, 242
  SCIFI.COM, 296
  Virtual Jerusalem, 283
business
  American International Group, Inc.,
    30
  Ameritech, 30
  AT&T Corporation, 30
  Bigfoot, 29
  BizWomen, 425
  CatalystWomen.org, 426

Coca-Cola Company, 30
CorporateInformation, 29
Dismal Scientist, 269
e-commerce, 60
Fast Company, 29
Federal Express Corporation, 30
Forbes Digital Tool, 29
Ford Motor Company, 30
Fortune, 246
franchising, 31
General Electric Company, 30
General Motors, 30
Goodyear Tire and Rubber
  Company, 30
Hewlett-Packard Company, 30
home-based business, 31
IBM Corporation, 30
Intel Corporation, 30
international business, 31, 63
Internet 800 Directory, 270
Junior Achievement, 197
Kmart Corporation, 30
Lucent Technologies, 30
marketing, 133-134
MCI WorldCom, Inc., 30
Merck & Co., 30
Merrill Lynch, 30
Microsoft Corporation, 30
Mobil, 30
Motorola, 30
National Association for Female
  Executives, 428
office equipment
  Better Buys for Business, 203
  BuyerZone.com, 203
  BuySmart.com, 204
  Home Office Direct, 204
  OfficeFurniture.com, 204
  PriceSCAN.com, 204
  SOHO Consumer, 204
office management resources
  123 Sort It, 206
  Checkworks.com, 206
  Eletter.com, 207
  Office.com, 207

A
B
C
D
E
F
G
H
I
J
K
L
M
N
O
P
Q
R
S
T
U
V
W
X
Y
Z

A
B
C
D
E
F
G
H
I
J
K
L
M
N
O
P
Q
R
S
T
U
V
W
X
Y
Z

seeuthere.com, 207

USPS Zip Code Lookup, 207

office supplies

   Dr. Shredder's, 204

   Independent Stationers Online, 204

   Levenger, 204

   Office Depot, 205

   Office Helper, 205

   OfficeMax OnLine, 205

   onlineofficesupplies.com, 205

   Quill Office Products, 205

   Staples, Inc., 205

   U.S. Office Products, 206

   USPS Shipping Supplies Online, 206

   Viking Direct, 206

OWBO Online Women's Business Center, 430

Procter & Gamble Company, 30

Prudential Insurance Company of America, 30

SBC Communications, 30

Sears, Roebuck & Company, 30

Small Business—Products and Services, 32

State Farm Insurance Companies, 30

SuperPages.com, 272

Switchboard: The Internet Directory, 29, 273

Texaco, 30

TIAA-CREF, 30

U.S. Department of Commerce, 388

United Parcel Service of America, Inc. (UPS), 30

Wal-Mart Stores, Inc., 30

Wall Street Journal Interactive, 194

Walt Disney Company, 30

WomanOwned.com—Business Information for Women Entrepreneurs, 431

C

California

   California Museum of Photography, 154

   California Smart Traveler, 379

   California State Science Fair, 62

   California Vacation Rentals, 376

   California Voter Foundation, 237

   GORP: California National Forests, 383

   Los Angeles Zoo, 443

   San Diego County Real Estate Library, 261

   San Diego Zoo, 444

   San Francisco Zoo, 444

   TotalEscape, 384

   Ultimate Internet Wedding Guide, 420

   Wine Country Weekly Real Estate Reader, 262

   Yosemite Park, 223

Calvinism, 277

cameras, 231-233

camping

   Altrec.com, 33

   Benz Campground Directory, 33

   Camp Channel, 33

   Campground Directory, 33, 375

   Camping Source, 33

   Coleman.com, 33

   Cool Works' Ski Resorts and Ski/Snowboard Country Jobs, 321

   hiking, 33-34

   Kids Camps, 214

   Soccer Information Systems, 325

Canada

   1st Traveler's Choice, 382

   Air Canada, 361

   Athletics Canada, 357

   Business Women's Network Interactive, 426

   Calgary Zoo, 441

   Campground Directory, 375

   Canada.com, 34

   Canadian Airlines International, 361

   Canadian Charitable Organizations, 195

   Canadian Parents Online, 208

   Canadian Quilters' Association, 250

   Centre for Women's Studies in Education (CWSE), 426

   Coastal British Columbia, 411

Coats Patons, 121
Discover Banff, 220
Flight Arrivals, 361
Grand Theatre, 348
International Bed-and-Breakfast Guide, 376
National Gallery of Canada, 152
National Museum of Science and Technology, 154
Regatta Sport, 409
Tennis Canada, 346
Tour Canada Without Leaving Your Desk, 373
Vancouver, British Columbia, 374
VIA Rail Canada, 378

cancer
American Cancer Society, 34
Avon: The Crusade, 35
Breast Cancer Action, 35
Cancer411.com, 35
Faces of Hope, 35
National Cancer Institute, 35
National Childhood Cancer Foundation, 224
NBCC—National Breast Cancer Coalition, 429
OncoLink:
University of Pennsylvania Cancer Center Resources, 35
Veterinary Oncology, 228, 396
Pediatric Leukemia, 224
Terry Fox Foundation, 68

candy, 36
car rental, 364-365
car travel, 365

careers
Career Builder, 116
Career Journal.com, 115
Careers in Veterinary Medicine, 395
company information, 115
IPL Teen Division, 342
job hunting, 115-116
JobStar—Specific Career Information, 115
National Association for Female Executives, 428
Veterinary Medicine, 396

caregivers, 298-299, 302

Caribbean vacations
All-Inclusives Resort and Cruise Vacation Source, 374
Planeta, 372
Sandals Resorts, 383

catalogs
Baby Catalog of America, 210
BizRate, 310
Buyer's Index, 313
CatalogLink, 308
Copernicus Home Page, 352
DELiAs.com, 309
Disney Online Store, 353
eders.com, 76
First Aid Products Online, 140
Home School World, 103
Northwest River Supplies, 408
Pet Warehouse, 230
Softball on the Internet, 329
Walthers Model Railroad Mall, 258

Catholicism
Catholic Charities USA, 326
Catholic Online, 276
Catholic Prayers, 285
Catholic Youth Organization (CYO), 439
Sacred Space, 285

cats
American Cat Fanciers Association, 225
Big Cats Online, 441
Cat Fanciers Association, 225
Cat Fanciers Home Page, 225
Cat House (EFBC/FCC) Home Page, 225
Cats (and People) Who Quilt, 250
Cats Protection League, 226
Catsbuzz Bookstore, 226
CatToys.com, 226
Index of Famous Dogs, Cats, and Critters, 227
NetPets, 228
PetCat, 225
Waltham World of Pet Care, 229

A B C D E F G H I J K L M N O P Q R S T U V W X Y Z

CDs (compact discs). *See also* music
CD Universe, 156
CDNow, 156
Logos Research Systems, 279
MovieTunes, 349
UFO Info, 387

celebrities
E! Online, 398
Film.com, 398
Internet Movie Database, 399
Scour.com, 400
WrestleZone, 433

charitable organizations, 194-199

chat rooms
ABC's of Parenting, 210
About.com Table Tennis, 333
Bolt.com, 341
Buddhanet.net, 275
Chat: Stay-at-Home Parents, 218
CyberTeens, 341
CyberTown, 109
Darts Directory, 51
DeafZONE, 53
ICQ.com, 109
International Conservatory of Magic, 132
Just 4 Girls, 118
The Knot: Weddings for the Real World, 419
LIQUIDGENERATION.com, 342
MaMaMedia.com, 118
Midwifery Resources on the Internet, 242
Modern Bride, 420
Mom.com, 213
oneworld.net, 190
Oxygen.com, 307, 430
Parent Soup: Chat Descriptions, 214
Parenthood, 212
PharmWeb, 139
Retire.net, 289
SCIFI.COM, 296
ScubaDuba, 407
Senior.com, 301
Stay-at-Home Parents, 218
TechnoTeen, 342
Teen Chat, 342
Third Age, 289
Travel Facts, 369
Worlds 3D Ultimate Chat Plus, 109
WWWomen!, 432
Yahoo! Groups, 109
Zipple.com, 283

Chicago, Illinois
Chicago Bears (NFL), 79-80
Chicago Field Museum, 153
Chicago Shedd Aquarium, 155
Lincoln Park Zoo, 443

children. *See also* special needs children
AAHA HealthPet.com, 394
ALEX, 352
Amateur Softball Association, 328
American Academy of Pediatric Dentistry, 141
American Junior Rodeo Association, 292
Archie McPhee, 352
B'nai B'rith Youth Organization, 439
Benton Foundation, 195
books, 128
Boy Scouts of America, 213, 439
Boys and Girls Clubs of America, 439
camps, 33
Carnegie Foundation, 195
Catholic Youth Organization (CYO), 439
Child Amputee, 216
Child of My Dreams—Infertility Community & Support Center, 241
Child Net Volunteers, 199
Child.net, 208
Children with AIDS Project, 216
Children with Diabetes, 223
Children with Spina Bifida, 216
Children's Rights Council, 59
Children's Writing Resource Center, 434
CityKids Foundation, 439
Crayon, 190
Creativity for Kids, 353
Cyber Zoomobile, 442

drSpock.com, 38

eBags.com, 313

Facts for Families, 209

games, Kids Domain Online Games, 83

Girl Scouts of America, 440

Health Ink & Vitality Communications, 423

IAAY Expository Writing Tutorial, 435

International Softball Federation (ISF), 328

Internet Public Library, 265, 270

Internet safety
  Parenthood Web, 111
  SafeTeens.com, 111
  Web Wise Kids, 111

Junior Achievement, 197

K-6, 212-214

Kids World 2000: Animals, Zoos, and Aquariums, 443

KidsHealth, 95

Little League Baseball Online, 440

National 4-H Council, 440

National Center for Missing and Exploited Children, 327

National Children's Coalition (NCC), 327

National Parenting Center, 212

NYO&W WebTrain, 257

Resources for the Study of Buddhism, 275

SOC-UM (Safeguarding Our Children – United Mothers Organization), 37

St. Moritz Ski Page, 322

U.S. Youth Soccer, 325

USA Volleyball Home Page, 403

WordsWorth Books, 27

Writing Assessment Services, 436

Writing for the Web, 436

YMCA, 440

Young Authors Workshop, 436

Youth and Children's Resource, 440

Zany Brainy, 356

China
  Center for Reproductive Law and Policy, 426
  China Travel Specialists, 371
  Chinese Kung Fu Wu Su Association, 136
  CLAP: Chinese Learner's Alternative Page, 124

Christianity
  About.com—Christianity, 276
  American Baptist Churches Mission Center Online, 276
  Augustine, 276
  BBC World Service—Religions of the World, 274
  Best Christian Links, 276
  Bible Gateway, 276
  Catholic Online, 276
  Center for Paleo-Orthodoxy, 276
  Center for Reformed Theology and Apologetics (CRTA), 277
  Christian Interactive Network, 277
  Christian Missions Home Page, 277
  Christian+Feminist, 426
  Christianbook.com, 277
  crosswalk.com, 277
  Fire and Ice: Puritan and Reformed Writings, 277
  First Church of Cyberspace, 277
  Five Points of Calvinism, 277
  Greater Grace World Outreach, 278
  Harvest Online, 278
  International Prayer Network, 285
  Jesus Army, 278
  Jesus Fellowship Home Page, 278
  Jesus Film Project, 278
  Leadership U, 278
  Logos Research Systems, 279
  Monastery of Christ in the Desert, 279
  music
    Jamsline – Christian Music Info Source, 164
    Jars of Clay, 164
  Orthodox Christian Page, 279
  Orthodox Ministry ACCESS, 279
  Presbyterian Church USA, 279

Project Wittenberg, 279

Religion News Service, 279

Religious Society of Friends, 279

Scrolls from the Dead Sea, 279

Spurgeon Archive, 280

TeenTalk, 343

US Christian Resource Center, 285

World Religions Index, 280

Cincinnati, Ohio

Cincinnati Art Museum, 150

Cincinnati Bengals (NFL), 79-80

Cincinnati Vacation Gateways, 379

Cincinnati Zoo and Botanical Garden, 442

cities, 269-270

classical music, 164-165

classified ads

automobiles, 268

Classifieds2000, 39

Microsoft Carpoint, 17

Northwest River Supplies, 408

Rower's World, 410

ScubaDuba, 407

Snowmobiling.net, 324

Trader Online, 39

Cleveland, Ohio

Cleveland Browns (NFL), 79-80

Cleveland Metroparks Zoo, 442

clothing

Bloomingdale's, 309

D&J Sports, 412

DELiAs.com, 309

Designer Outlet.com, 309

Eddie Bauer, 309

Fashionmall.com, 310

Fogdog, 313

HerRoom.com, 310

L.L. Bean, 310

Land's End, 310

NYStyle, 310

QuiltWear.com, 253

Regatta Sport, 409

Row Works, 410

SPORTS Authority, 314

clubs

Closely Guarded Secrets of the UK Surfing World, 411

Pacific Northwest LEGO Train Club, 257

Quilting Guilds, 253

coffees and teas, 77

coins, 40

collecting, 40-41

colleges and universities

4Vets.com, 394

Academic Info, 267

American Association of Colleges of Nursing, 201

American Association of University Women (AAUW), 425

Artemis Search for Women's Studies Programs, 425

Center for Research Libraries, 264

CollegeBound Network, 118

Columbia Law School, 126

Department of Animal Science: Oklahoma State University, 395

FinAid: The Financial Aid Information Page, 269

financial aid and scholarships

eStudentLoan.com, 75

FinAid!, 75

United Negro College Fund, 75

Gallaudet University, 315

graduate schools, 42

Harvard Law School, 126

Internet Public Library, 270

LIQUIDGENERATION.com, 342

Mapping Your Future, 41

Murdoch University: Division of Veterinary and Biomedical Sciences, 395

Princeton Review Rankings, 41

Purdue Online Writing Lab, 435

Softball.net, 329

U: The National College Magazine, 249

Washington State University College of Veterinary Medicine, 396

Colorado

Colorado Association of Campgrounds, Cabins, and Lodges, 376

A B C D E F G H I J K L M N O P Q R S T U V W X Y Z

Colorado State Parks and Outdoor Recreation, 220

Colorado.com, 379

CRN: Colorado Resort Net, 321

Denver Zoo, 442

Mesa Verde National Park, 221

Pro Rodeo Hall of Fame, 292

comedy. *See* humor

comics, cartoons, and animation, 42-43

comparison bots, 310-311

computer games and puzzles, 82-84

computers

    AVP Virus Encyclopedia, 263

    Buy.com, 308

    buying/information resources

        egghead, 44

        Gadget Boy Gazette, 44

    BYTE Magazine, 245

    Center for Applied Linguistics, 122

    Computerworld Online, 246

    hardware and software

        Apple Computer Home Page, 44

        Gateway, 44

        IBM Corporation, 45

        Intel, 45

    Macintosh, 45

    MacWorld Online Web Server, 247

    ModemHelp, 270

    NETiS Technology, Inc., 183

    PCs, 45

    Popular Science, 188

    programming languages, 46

    reference

        Family Tree Maker Online, 47

        International Data Corporation, 47

        Laurie McCanna's Photoshop, Corel, Painter, and Paintshop Pro Tips, 47

        Network ICE Corporation, 47

        SlaughterHouse, 47

    SeniorNet, 301

    Slashdot, 190

    software

        antivirus, 46

        downloads, 46

    troubleshooting, 47

    ZDNet, 189

Congress, U.S.

    Congressional Quarterly, 187

    Contacting the Congress, 235

    Library of Congress, 265, 270

    Office of the Clerk On-line Information Center, 235

    U.S. House of Representatives, 391

    U.S. Senate, 391

conservation

    Arbor Day Foundation, 66

    National Audubon Society, 66

    National Oceanic and Atmospheric Administration, 66

    National Wildlife Federation, 66

    Ocean.com, 179

    Oceans Alive, 179

    PBS Nature, 179

    RainforestWeb.org, 180

    SierraClub, 180

consumer electronics stores, 64-65

consumer issues

    Consumer Information Center, 259, 268, 388

    Consumer World, 48

    Federal Consumer Information Center, 48

    Federal Trade Commission, 390

    National Fraud Information Center, 48

cooking and recipes

    Art of Eating, 48

    CheeseNet 95, 48

    Christiane's Cooking Recipes of Chemists and Physicists, 49

    Cook's Thesaurus, 268

    Cookbooks Online Recipe Database, 49

    Cooking.com, 49

    Cooks Online, 49

    Fabulous Foods, 49

    Food TV Network, 49

    Good Cooking, 49

    Official French Fries Page, 49

A
B
C
D
E
F
G
H
I
J
K
L
M
N
O
P
Q
R
S
T
U
V
W
X
Y
Z

cosmetics, 319-320. *See also* skin care/cosmetics

country music artists, 165-167

crafts
Creativity for Kids, 353
hobby shops, 50
knitting
Afrugal Knitting Haus, 121
Artfibers Fashion Yarn, 121
Coats Paton, 121
Knitting Tutorials, 121
Knitting Universe, 121
QuiltWear.com, 253
sewing, 302-305

credit counseling
About Credit, 71
Consumer Education for Teens, 341
Credit Counseling by Springboard, 54
iVillage Personal Finance, 54
Money Magazine Money 101 Tutorial, 72

crime and criminal law
FBI, 125, 389
National Crime Prevention Council, 125

cruises
All-Inclusives Resort and Cruise Vacation Source, 374
Bargain Travel Cruises- Cheap Cruises, 371
Carnival Cruises, 365
Cool Works' Ski Resorts and Ski/Snowboard Country Jobs, 321
Cruise Specialists, 366
Cruise Value Center, 366
Cruise.com, 366
CruiseStar.com, 366
Freighter World Cruises, 366
Holland America Line, 366
i-cruise.com, 366
mytravelco.com, 366
Norwegian Cruise Line, 366
Princess Cruises, 366
Schooner Mary Day, 367

cults, 280

culture
Atlantic Magazine Unbound, 187
Culture Finder.com, 367
WWW Virtual Library, 285

current events, 188-191

D

Dallas, Texas
Dallas Cowboys (NFL), 79-80
Dallas Mavericks (NBA), 23
Dallas Zoo, 442

dance, 51

dating
Fantasy Generator, 52
Guide to Love and Sex, 306
IPL Teen Division, 342
Match.com, 52

deafness
American Sign Language Browser, 267
American Sign Language Linguistic Research Project, 122
Animated ASL Dictionary, 52
Deaf Resources, 315
DeafZONE, 53
GG Wiz's FingerSpeller, 53
National Institute on Deafness and Other Communication Disorders, 53

death and dying
Hospice Foundation of America, 53
Hospice Net, 53
Seniors-Site.com, 289

Deism, 280

dentists
American Academy of Pediatric Dentistry, 141
Pets Need Dental Care, Too, 229

Denver, Colorado
Denver Broncos (NFL), 79-80
Denver Nuggets (NBA), 23
Denver Zoo, 442

depression, 55

dermatology, 318-319

diabetes
ADA (American Diabetes Association), 56

Centers for Disease Control Diabetes Resources, 141

Children with Diabetes, 223

Joslin Diabetes Center, 56

dictionaries and thesauri

A Web of Online Dictionaries, 263

Acronym Finder, 262

Acronyms and Abbreviations, 262

ARTFL Project: *Roget's Thesaurus* Search Form, 262

Astronomy Thesaurus, 262

AVP Virus Encyclopedia, 263

Dictionary of Cell Molecular Biology, 263

Dictionary of Philosophy of the Mind, 283

Dictionary.com, 263

iTools.com, 270

Martindale's Reference Desk, 263

Merriam-Webster Online, 263

On-Line Dictionaries and Glossaries, 263

RhymeZone, 263

StudyWeb, 266

Thesaurus.com, 263

travlang's Translating Dictionaries, 263

Webopedia.com, 264

Word Wizard, 264

World Wide Web Acronym and Abbreviation Server, 264

diets and nutrition

Best of Weight Loss, 421

CyberDiet, 422

DietSite.com, 56

eDiets.com, 422

eNutrition.com, 401

Fast Food Facts—Interactive Food Finder, 422

Jenny Craig, 422

Nutrisystem, 422

nutrition

American Heart Association, 56

Center for Science in the Public Interest, 56

Mayo Clinic Nutrition Center, 57

Meals for You, 57

Natural Nutrition, 422

NutriBase, 57

Nutrition.gov site, 57

Prevention Magazine Healthy Ideas, 57

Virtual Nutrition Center, 57

Prevention.com—Weight Loss and Fitness, 422

Shape Up America, 423

Weight Watchers, 423

digital cameras, 231-232

dinosaurs

Discovering Dinosaurs, 58

Dr. Internet on Dinosaurs, 58

Internet Public Library, 270

NMNH Dinosaur Home Page, 58

Sue at the Field Museum, 58

directories

Christian Interactive Network, 277

Climbing Archive, 290

Conscious.net, 185

CorporateInformation, 29

crosswalk.com, 277

Darts Directory, 51

EdLinks, 338

Educators Net, 338

Electronic Activist, 237

Home School World, 103

Magazines A-Z, 247

New Kadampa Tradition, 275

Softball.net, 329

StayHealthy, 424

Stepparenting Connection, 220

Stress and Workstress Directory, 330

Virtual Jerusalem, 283

Voices of Women Online, 430

Wired Seniors, 302

Yoga Directory, 438

ZooWeb.net, 445

disabilities

Alexander Graham Bell Association for Deaf and Hard of Hearing, 315

American Sign Language Browser, 267

ASL Access, 315

A
B
C
D
E
F
G
H
I
J
K
L
M
N
O
P
Q
R
S
T
U
V
W
X
Y
Z

ASL Fingerspelling, 315

Captioned Media Program, 315

Communications Unlimited, 315

Council for Exceptional Children, 217

Deaf Resources, 315

Disabled American Veterans, 392

Gallaudet University, 315

Gimponthego.com, 95, 368

Goodwill Industries International, 196

Handspeak.com, 315

Helen Keller National Center for Deaf-Blind Youth, 316

HSA: Handicapped Scuba Association, 405

International Table Tennis Committee for the Disabled, 332

National Association of the Deaf (NAD), 316

Network on Disabilities, 218

SignWritingSite, 316

Zoos Software, 316

discount stores, 311

discussion groups

Actor's Page, 347

Complete Works of William Shakespeare, 348

Education Week on the Web, 338

Feminist Majority Foundation Online, 427

Oxygen.com, 430

Paradigm Online Writing Assistant, 435

Tax.org, 336

Teen Chat, 342

Water Skier's Web, 415

diseases

American Lung Association, 141

cancer, 34-35

Centers for Disease Control and Prevention, 326

Down Syndrome WWW Page, 94

Gulf War Veteran Resource Pages, 393

U.S. Department of Health and Human Services, 389

Disney.com, 10, 42, 118

Disney Online Store, 353

Disney Schoolhouse Rock, 62

diving/scuba diving, 404-407

divorce and child custody

Children's Rights Council, 59

Divorce Online, 215

DivorceNet, 59

domestic violence, 59

dogs, 226-229

domestic violence, 59

drugs

AgeNet, 298

DrugTestNow.com, 209

FDA Drug Approvals List, 139

KidsMeds, 224

National Association of Alcoholism and Drug Abuse Counselors (NAADAC), 326

National Families in Action, 209

PharmWeb, 139

RxList: The Internet Drug Index, 272

StayHealthy, 424

Swimming Science Journal, 413

drugstores, 139-140

DVDs (digital versatile discs)

Blockbuster, 400

DVD Price Search, 397

DVD.com, 397

DVDDigital.com, 397

dvdfile.com, 398

MovieTunes, 349

Netflix.com, 398

Reel.com, 314

Sci-Fi.Net, 295

UFO Info, 387

E

e-zines (electronic magazines). *See also* magazines

Broadsword, 294

Dark Planet Science Fiction Webzine, 294

e-ZineSearch, 244

E-zineZ, 244

FanGrok, 294

Marketing Online, 134

Running Network, 358

Songs of the Blue Bird, 297

Teenmag.com, 343

Third Age, 289

This Week in the Poconos Magazine Online, 384

United States Soccer Federation, 326

USA Table Tennis, 333

earth science

Climate/Weather/Earth Hotlist, 416

Earth & Sky, 14, 177

Earth Times, 187

EarthWatch Weather on Demand, 416

Seismological Laboratory, 418

eating disorders, 3-4

ecology, 66

economics

Dismal Scientist, 269

Economic Research Service (USDA), 6

U.S. Census Bureau, 273

U.S. Department of the Treasury, 389

education

A+ Research and Writing, 433

American Association of University Women (AAUW), 425

AskERIC, 268

Bibliomania: The Network Library, 264

Centre for Women's Studies in Education (CWSE), 426

College Bound Network, 118

colleges and universities, 41-42

continuing education, 60

Department of Animal Science: Oklahoma State University, 395

Education Index, 61

Education Place, 338

Education Week on the Web, 338

Education World, 63, 338

EducationalToys.com, 353

Educator's Toolkit, 338

Educators Net, 338

Expect the Best from a Girl, 427

Girl Power!, 427

Helen Keller National Center for Deaf-Blind Youth, 316

home schooling, 103

International Swimming Hall of Fame, 413

Jesus Fellowship Home Page, 278

K–12, 60-61

  educational television, 61-62

  homework help, 62, 272

  private education, 63

Lancom Technologies, 182

Lincoln Park Zoo, 443

Live and Learn, 212

Nursing Education of America, 202

Nursing Excellence, 202

NWSA—National Women's Studies Association, 429

preschool, 63

Project Genesis—Torah on the Information Superhighway, 283

resources

  infoplease.com, 63

  Peterson's Education Center, 63

  Web of On-line Dictionaries, 64

  Web66: K–12 Schools Registry, 64

Seniors-Site.com, 289

TROA, 393

U.S. Department of Education, 267, 388

Veterinary Medicine, 396

Washington State University College of Veterinary Medicine, 396

WholeNurse, 203

Women's History Month, 431

WWWomen!, 432

Young Authors Workshop, 436

elderly, 298-302

electronics

Best Buy, 64

Buy.com, 308

Circuit City, 64

Electronics.cnet.com, 65

Popular Science, 188

Radio Shack, 65

A
B
C
D
E
F
G
H
I
J
K
L
M
N
O
P
Q
R
S
T
U
V
W
X
Y
Z

ShopNow, 65

Tek Discount Warehouse, 65

emergency services

American Red Cross, 65

EmergencyNet News, 189

employment

3Com, 180

Careers in Veterinary Medicine, 395

Cool Works' Ski Resorts and
Ski/Snowboard Country Jobs, 321

Federal Job Search Links, 392

Healthcare Innovations, 202

Hughes Network Systems, 181

Interphase Corporation, 182

Kinesix, 182

National NurseSearch, 202

Now Casting, 349

NP Central, 202

Nurse Options USA, 202

Nursing Excellence, 202

Nursing Management Services, 202

Polaris Industries, 323

Procare USA, 203

Social Security Online, 289

Social Work and Social Services, 327

SocialService.com, 327

StarMed Staffing Group, 203

U.S. Department of Labor, 389

encyclopedias

Britannica.com, 268

Encarta Online, 269

Herbal Encyclopedia, 95

Internet Encyclopedia of Philosophy,
284

Judaism 101, 282

Stanford Encyclopedia of
Philosophy, 284

StudyWeb, 266

England. *See* United Kingdom

English

Astronomy Thesaurus, 262

Bible Gateway, 276

BritSpeak, 123

Collective Nouns, 123

Cyberbraai, 123

Dictionary.com, 263

Dimension2, 244

Electronic Text Center at the
University of Virginia, 129

English As a Second Language Home
Page, 122

Grammar and Style Notes, 123

Hieros Gamos, 127

Morse Code and the Phonetic
Alphabets, 271

entertainment

Gigaplex, 246

Stars On Ice, 317

USA Weekend, 188

World Wrestling Entertainment
(WWE), 432

WOW (World of Wrestling), 433

Wrestling Threat, 433

Wrestling USA Magazine, 433

environment

conservation, 66

Earth Times, 187

ecology, 66

Ecotourism Explorer, 367

Electronic Green Journal, 246

Environmental Protection Agency
(EPA), 389

nature

BBC Nature Site, 179

Nature Journal, 179

Ocean.com, 179

Oceans Alive, 179

PBS Nature Site, 179

preservation, 67

RainforestWeb.org, 180

Sierra Club, 180

U.S. Department of the Interior, 389

ethnic music, 167

etiquette, 67

Europe

Airhitch, 370

Backpack Europe on a Budget, 364

Busabout Europe, 364

ESPN Soccer, 324

Europe Today Travel and Tourist
Information, 371

European Visits, 371

Eurotrip.com, 371

A
B
C
D
E
F
G
H
I
J
K
L
M
N
O
P
Q
R
S
T
U
V
W
X
Y
Z

International Snowmobile Manufacturers Association, 323

Rick Steves' Europe Through the Back Door, 372

exercise

Best of Weight Loss, 421

CyberDiet, 422

fitness, 68

Herspace.com, 428

Prevention.com—Weight Loss and Fitness, 422

running, 68

Shape Up America, 423

weightlifting and bodybuilding, 68

yoga

Asana Sequences, 437

Body Trends, 437

Hatha Yoga, 437

INDOlink, 437

Sahaja Yoga Meditation, 437

Siddha Yoga Meditation, 437

Sivananda Yoda Om Page, 437

Step by Step Yoga, 438

World of Yoga, 438

Yoga Directory, 438

Yoga Journal, 438

Yoga Site, 438

YogaClass, 438

YogaFinder, 438

extraterrestrials and aliens, 385-387

extreme sports, 69

F

fabrics

Fabri-Centers, 50

Fabrics.net, 302

Fashion Fabrics Club, 302

Fashion Supplies, 303

families

Cybergrrl, 426

Family Education Network, 63, 211

Family Tree Maker Online, 47, 89

Family Village, 217

Family.com, 213

Figure This!, 339

genealogy

Ellis Island, 88

Everton's Genealogical Helper, 88

FamilyTreeMaker.com, 89

Genealogy Portal, 89

National Partnership for Women & Families (NPWF), 429

New York State Department of Family Assistance, 327

fashion, 71, 310

feminism

Feminist Arts-Music, 427

Feminist Majority Foundation Online, 427

WWWomen!, 432

figure skating, 317

finance and investment

bonds, Bond Market Association, 72

credit

About Credit, 71

Money Magazine Money 101 Tutorial, 72

Forbes Magazine, 246

investment clubs, Motley Fool's Guide to Investment Clubs, 72

investment information

Hoover's Online, 72

Investor's Business Daily, 72

Kiplinger, 73, 335

Motley Fool, 73

Silicon Investor, 73

Wall Street City, 73

mutual funds

Brill's Mutual Funds Interactive, 73

Dreyfus Corporation, 73

Janus Funds, 73

Putnam Investments, 74

online trading

American Express Financial Direct, 74

Ameritrade, 74

Datek Online, 74

E*Trade, 74

Morgan Stanley Dean Witter, 75

A B C D E F G H I J K L M N O P Q R S T U V W X Y Z

U.S. Department of the Treasury, 389

USA Weekend, 188

Wall Street Journal Interactive, 194

WWW Virtual Library, 285

financial aid and scholarships, 75, 269

first-aid, 140

fish

Albuquerque Aquarium, 441

NetPets, 228

Ocean.com, 179

Oceans Alive, 179

Sea World/Busch Gardens Animal Information Database, 444

Shedd Aquarium, 155

Waltham World of Pet Care, 229

fishing

Altrec.com, 320

eders.com, 76

Luis Cabanas Scuba Diving and Instruction, 406

Rod and Gun Resources, 359

United States Fish and Wildlife Service, 76

fitness. *See also* **exercise**

Fitness Online, 68

SeniorsSearch, 289

Third Age, 289

USA Weekend, 188

Florida

Brevard Zoo, 441

FIU Volunteer Action Center, 196

Florida Weather Monitor, 416

Sea World/Busch Gardens Animal Information Database, 444

Universal Studios Florida, 10

food and drink

alcohol, 77

Coca-Cola, 76

coffees and teas, 77

Food TV Network, 49

Fulton Street Lobster & Seafood Co., 76

groceries

At Your Service, 93

Marsh Supermarket, 93

NetGrocer, 93

Your Grocer.com, 93

Live Lobsters and Clambakes, 76

organic foods, GAIAM.org Lifestyle Company, 77

Pickles, Peppers, Pots & Pans, 77

Wet Planet Beverages, 77

wines

Food & Wine Magazine, 78

Gruppo Italiano Vini, 78

Into Wine, 78

K&L Wine Merchants, 78

Robin Garr's Wine Lovers Page, 78

Wine Searcher, 78

Wine Spectator, 78

Wine.com, 79

Wines on the Internet, 79

foreign policy, 80, 389

forums

ABC's of Parenting, 210

ATM Forum, 180

Chat: Stay-at-Home Parents, 218

FANDOM—*Star Trek* Central, 294

FotoForum, 234

GORP: Paddlesports, 408

Intranet Journal, 182

Jo-Ann etc., 303

Motley Fool, 73

oneworld.net, 190

PharmWeb, 139

Popular Science, 248

Quicken.com Taxes, 335

Sam's Club, 311

Sew News, 303

Sexuality Forum, 307

Silicon Investor, 73

Single Parents World, 215

franchising, 31. *See also* **business**

free Internet connections, 110

freelancing, 433-435

French language sites

Alcoholics Anonymous, 4

Astronomy Thesaurus, 262

Bible Gateway, 276

Dictionary.com, 263

Electronic Text Center at the University of Virginia, 129

Foreign Languages for Travelers, 124

French Language Course, 124

Hieros Gamos, 127

Tennis Canada, 346

fruit, 314

G

games and puzzles, 82-84, 211, 354

gardening and landscaping, 84-85

gay/lesbian issues, 86-88

genealogy
Ellis Island, 88

Everton's Genealogical Helper, 88

Family Tree Maker Online, 47

FamilyTreeMaker.com, 89

Genealogy Portal, 89

National Archives and Records Administration, 265

SeniorsSearch, 289

geography
CIA World Factbook, 268

Geographic Nameserver, 269

Geography World, 89

How Far Is It?, 89

maps, 90

TIGER Mapping Service, 90

WorldAtlas.com, 89

Georgia
The Carter Center, 326

Wild Adventures, 11

German language sites
Astronomy Thesaurus, 262

Bible Gateway, 276

Dictionary.com, 263

Dimension2, 244

Electronic Text Center at the University of Virginia, 129

Foreign Languages for Travelers, 124

Hieros Gamos, 127

Morse Code and the Phonetic Alphabets, 271

gifts
Ashford.com, 312

Deaf Resources, 315

Doolittle's, 229

First Jewelry, 312

Gifts.com, 90

giftsplash.com, 91

Hammacher Schlemmer, 91

Lycos Shopping Network, 308

MarthaStewart.com, 91

Mondera, 312

MuseumShop.com, 91

NetJewels.com, 312

Sharper Image, 91

Spencer Gifts, 91

girls
Alloy Online, 341

cheerleading, 37

Expect the Best from a Girl, 213

Girl Scouts of the USA, 427, 440

Girl Power! Campaign Home Page, 209, 427

Girls Incorporated, 427

Girls Life Magazine, 341

Glamour Magazine, 246

Just 4 Girls, 118

Kotex Guide to Menstruation for Girls and Women, 214

golf, 92

GORP (Great Outdoor Recreation Page), 34
California National Forests, 383

Climbing, 290

Great Outdoor Recreation Pages, 227, 383

Great Smoky Mountains National Park, 221

Paddlesports, 408

U.S. National Parks and Reserves, 221

Wilderness Area List, 221

government agencies
Centers for Disease Control and Prevention (CDC), 371

Department of Veterans Affairs, 392

FedStats, 390

FedWorld Information Network, 390

A B C D E F G H I J K L M N O P Q R S T U V W X Y Z

FedWorld.gov, 269

Food and Drug Administration (FDA), 139

HUD – Department of Housing and Urban Development, 260

Index to Government, 390

IRS, 335

NASA, 18

National Archives and Records Administration, 265

National Cancer Institute, 35

Peace Corps, 200

Social Security Online, 302

THOR: The Virtual Reference Desk, 273

U.S. Department of Education, 267

U.S. Department of Health and Human Services, 142, 327

VISTA, 328

grammar

Grammar and Style Notes, 123

Guide to Grammar and Writing, 435

Grand Canyon

GrandCanyon.com, 380

Official Tourism Page, 221

Railway, 377

River Running, 408

groceries, 93

H

hardware

Emulex Network Systems, 181

Network Buyer's, 183

Hawaii

All-Inclusives Resort and Cruise Vacation Source, 374

Hawaiian Airlines, 361

Holman Travel, 375

Weddings on Hawaii, Kauai, Maui, and Oahu, 421

healing (New Age), 185-186

health

AgeNet, 298

American Dietetic Association, 421

anti-oxidant.com—Quick Reference Guide, 401

Ask Dr. Weil, 423

Black Health Network, 423

Centers for Disease Control and Prevention, 326

Champion Nutrition, 401

Commonwealth Fund, 195

diseases and conditions, 94

ElderNet, 289

eNutrition.com, 401

Forum for Women's Health, 427

Health and Age.com, 9

Health Ink & Vitality Communications, 423

Health Statistics, 390

healthcare, 95

HealthCentral, 424

Healthfinder, 141

HealthGate, 424

healthshop.com, 401

HealthSquare.com, 7

herbs, 95

HisandHerhealth.com, 306

HIV/AIDS treatment and prevention, 94

institutes, 95

Intellicast, 417

IPL Teen Division, 342

kidsDoctor, 224

KidsHealth.org, 209, 213

Medical/Health Sciences Libraries on the Web, 265

MotherNature.com, 401

Optimum Health Resources, 330

Pharmaton, 401

Planned Parenthood Federation of America, Inc., 1

Puritan's Pride, 401

SeniorsSearch, 289

SexualHealth.com, 307

Society for Medical Decision Making, 95

StayHealthy, 424

Third Age, 289

Thriveonline.com, 402

Travel Medicine, 369

travel resources, 95

U.S. Department of Health and Human Services, 389

U.S. National Library of Medicine, 267

Vita-Web, 402

VitaminShoppe.com, 402

Wellness Junction, 424

WellnessWeb, 424

WWWomen!, 432

herbs

Ask Dr. Weil, 423

Herbal Encyclopedia, 95

hiking

Altrec.com, 320

America's Roof, 33

GORP—Great Outdoor Recreation Page, 34

Hinduism

BBC World Service—Religions of the World, 274

Bhagvat Gita, 280

Friends of Osho, 281

Full Circle New Age Book Shop, 185

Hare Krishna Home Page, 281

Hindu Universe: Hindu Resource Center, 281

Hinduism Online, 281

Hinduism Today, 281

The Language of Songs, 124

history

American Variety Stage, 348

Biography.com, 96, 268

Elections, 237

English Actors at the Turn of the Century, 348

Flag of the United States of America, 269

Great American Station Foundation, 256

historical documents and landmarks, 97

History Channel, 96

History Matters, 96

History Net, 96

History of Photography, 96

History On-Line, 96

History/Social Studies for K-12 Teachers, 339

HyperHistory, 96

Library of Congress, 270

museums

Guggenheim Museum, 97

Online Museum of Singapore Art and History, 152

United States Holocaust Memorial Museum, 152

Wright Brothers Aeroplane Company and Museum of Aviation, 152

National Women's History Project, 429

Office of the Clerk On-line Information Center, 235

Smithsonian National Museum of American History, 97

Smithsonian Natural History Museum, 97

Tax History Project, 336

Union Pacific Railroad, 258

Vintage Vaudeville and Ragtime Show, 351

Women's History Month, 431

hobbies

collecting, 40-41

Hobbees.com: The World's Hobby Shop, 257

HOBBYLINC, 50

SeniorsSearch, 289

shops and stores

Fabri-Centers, 50

Scentmasters Candles, 50

Third Age, 289

hockey, 98-99

home schooling, 103

homeopathy

Homeopathy Online, 8

Vetscape, 396

homes

Ads4Homes, 258

America Mortgage Online, 286

American Association of Homes and Services for the Aging, 288

Americas Virtual Real Estate Store, 258

A
B
C
D
E
F
G
H
I
J
K
L
M
N
O
P
Q
R
S
T
U
V
W
X
Y
Z

Apartments for Rent Online, 259

Buying a Home in Arizona, 259

Century 21, 259

Coldwell Banker, 259

Commercial Network, 259

Consumer Information Center, 259

decorating/renovation

> Ace Hardware, 101
>
> Ask The Builder, 100
>
> Ballard Design, 101
>
> Baranzelli Home, 101
>
> Building Industry Exchange, 100
>
> Home and Garden Television (HGTV), 101
>
> Longaberger Baskets, 101
>
> Lowe's Home Improvement Warehouse, 102
>
> Popular Science, 188
>
> SmartHome.com, 101
>
> Steptoe & Wife Antiques, Ltd., 101

Domainia.com, 259

Employee Relocation Council (ERC), 286

ERA Stroman, 287

home building, 100

home decorating/painting, 101

home improvement and restoration, 101-102

HomeBuilder.com, 260

HomeFair.com, 260

HomeGain, 260

Homeseekers.com, 260

HUD – Department of Housing and Urban Development, 260, 393

International Real Estate Digest, 260

Land.Net, 260

MonsterMoving.com, 286

mortgages and financing, 102

MSN HomeAdvisor, 261

NewHomeNetwork.com, 261

Nolo.com-Real Estate, 261

Owners.com, 261

plumbing, 102

Real Estate Center Online, 261

realtor.com, 261

RelocationCentral.com, 287

REMAX Real Estate Network, 261

San Diego County Real Estate Library, 261

Wine Country Weekly Real Estate Reader, 262

homosexuality. *See* **gay/lesbian issues**

honeymoons, 419-421

horoscopes, 320

horses

American Saddlebred Horse, 103

Art of Classical Riding, 104

NetPets, 228

World Equine Health Network, 397

hotels. *See also* **travel**

all-hotels.com, 375

Choice Hotels, 376.

Hotel Timeshare Resales, 287

Hotelguide.com, 376

housing. *See also* **homes**

Age of Reason Recommended Senior Living Facilities, 298

New LifeStyles, 300

seniorresource.com, 301

Transitions, Inc. Elder Care Consulting, 302

how-to guides, 269-270

human rights

Global Fund for Women, 427

Human Rights Campaign, 87

Women's Human Rights Resources, 431

Women's Rights Net, 431

humor

Centre for the Easily Amused, 104

Cursing in Swedish, 104

Despair.com, 104

How to Talk New Age, 185

HumorSearch, 104

Jokes.com, 105

The Onion, 105

SatireWire, 105

SITCOM Home Page, 350

Spam Haiku Archive, 105

hunting

Altrec.com, 320

Cabela's, 105

A B C D E F G H I J K L M N O P Q R S T U V W X Y Z

Field & Stream Online, 105
Hunting.Net, 105
National Rifle Association, 106
Rod and Gun Resources, 359
U.S. Fish and Wildlife Service, 106
U.S. Sportmen's Alliance, 106
hurricanes, 416-418

I

Idaho
Idaho Home Page, 380
Zoo Boise, 445
income taxes. *See* taxes
India
Center for Reproductive Law and Policy, 426
Hindi: The Language of Songs, 124
International Adoption Resource, 5
Indiana
Indianapolis Colts (NFL), 79-80
Indianapolis Zoo, 442
Marsh Supermarket, 93
infertility, 240-241
inline skating, 317
insects, 107
inspiration
Positive Press, 191
quotations, Follow Your Dreams, 254
instant messaging
AOL Instant Messenger, 110
Bolt.com, 341
ICQ.com, 110
MSN Messenger Service, 110
Net2Phone, 110
insurance
AgeNet, 298
automobile insurance, 108
companies, 108
Insurance Institute for Highway Safety, 108
Insure.com, 108
PADI: Professional Association of Diving Instructors, 406
Veterinary Pet Insurance, 396

Intel Corporation, 30, 45
Innovation in Education, 339
Networking and Telecommunications, 181
international interests
Adventure Center, 359
Amnesty International USA Women's Human Rights, 425
ArtofTravel.com, 364
ASIRT: Association for Safe International Road Travel, 365
BBC News, 189
business
Infonation, 31, 63
Internationalist, 31
NEWSWEEK International Business Resource, 31
Climbing Archive, 290
Commercial Real Estate Network, 259
Economy Travel, 364
Elderhostel, 299
EmergencyNet News, 189
Ethnologue – Languages of the World, 122
FINA, 412
FIVB WWW Home Page, 403
Freightworld, 256
Global Fund for Women, 427
Good Zoo Guide Online, 442
International Adoption Resource, 5
International Bed-and-Breakfast Guide, 376
International Center for Abduction Research, 386
International Center of Photography, 154, 234
International Conservatory of Magic, 132
International Data Corporation, 47
International Figure Skating Magazine (IFS), 317
International Inline Skating Association, 317
International Powerlifting Federation, 68
International Prayer Network, 285
International Real Estate Digest, 260

International Snowmobile Manufacturers Association, 323

International Softball Federation (ISF), 328

International Stress Management Association, 330

International Surfing Museum, 411

International Swimming Hall of Fame, 413

International Table Tennis Committee for the Disabled, 332

International Tennis Federation Online, 346

Internationalist, 31

Kids World 2000: Animals, Zoos and Aquariums, 443

Libweb—Library Servers on the WWW, 265

News365, 190

oneworld.net, 190

Orient-Express Trains & Cruises, 378

RCI vacationNET, 287

Shopping The World, 309

Teen Chat, 342

Time Out City Guides, 420

Tourism Offices Worldwide Directory, 369

Virtual Tourist, 370

Walking Adventures International, 360

World Soccer Page, 326

World Wide Ping Pong, 333

WorldRowing.com, 411

WWW Library Directory, 267

international travel, 370-374

Internet

America, 212

chats, messaging, and conferences, 109

child safety

Parenthood Web, 111

SafeTeens.com, 111

Web Wise Kids, 111

e-commerce, 60

evite, 109

free connections, 110

ICONnect, 339

instant messaging

AOL Instant Messenger, 110

ICQ.com, 110

MSN Messenger, 110

Net2Phone, 110

Internet 800 Directory, 270

Internet Movie Database, 399

Internet Public Library, 265, 270

Internet Underground Music Archive, 157

Internet Weather Report, 417

Internetweek Online, 247

marketing, 133-134

privacy, TRUSTe, 110

search engines, 111

security/virus hoaxes

McAfee Antivirus, 111

Symantec AntiVirus Research Center, 112

Switchboard: The Internet Directory, 29

technologies, Networking Enterprises, 184

Teen Hoopla, 210

inventors and inventions, 267, 428

investments

401k Center for Employees, 288

401Kafe, 288

Fairmark Press—Tax Guide for Investors, 335

Forbes Magazine, 29, 246

information

About Credit, 71

Hoover's Online, 72

Investor's Business Daily, 72

Kiplinger, 73, 355

Money Magazine Money 101 Tutorial, 72

Motley Fool, 73

Silicon Investor, 73

Wall Street City, 73

Motley Fool's Guide to Investment Clubs, 72

Young Investor, 343

Ireland

Aer Lingus, 361

Gaelic and Gaelic Culture, 124

No Frontiers: A Year in the Life of Fermoy Rowing, 409

Islam
Al-Islam, 281
BBC World Service—Religions of the World, 274
Haggani Foundation Home Page, 281
Islam in the United States, 281
Islam World, 281
IslamiCity in Cyberspace, 282
Online Islamic Bookstore, 282
Prophet's Prayer, 285
Women in Islam, 431

island travel, 374-375
Italian language sites
Astronomy Thesaurus, 262
CyberItalian, 124
Dictionary.com, 263
Hieros Gamos, 127
Morse Code and the Phonetic Alphabets, 271

J

Japanese language sites
Electronic Text Center at the University of Virginia, 129
MU-MU Travel Tips in Japan, 372

jazz, 167-168
jewelry
Abrasha's Gallery, 115
Ashford.com, 312
Blue Nile, 114
Diamond-Guide, 114
DiamondReview.com, 114
First Jewelry, 312
Mondera, 114, 312
NetJewels.com, 312

jobs
6Figurejobs.com, 115
Career Builder, 116
Careers in Veterinary Medicine, 395
Federal Job Search Links, 392
FlipDog.com, 116
Hughes Network Systems, 181

JobStar: Specific Career Information, 115
Monster.com, 116
U.S. Department of Labor, 389

journals
Cyber Boxing Zone, 28
Homeopathy Online, 8
Journal of American Veterinary Medical Association, 395
Journal of Buddhist Ethics, 275
Journal of Pediatrics, 224
Journal of Scientific Exploration, 386
The National Journal, 238
Nature Journal, 179
New England Journal of Medicine, 142
PSYCHE, 284
Qi: The Journal of Traditional Eastern Health and Fitness, 135
Swimming Science Journal, 413
Women and Politics Home Page, 431
World Equine Health Network, 397
Yale Journal of Law and Feminism, 432
Yoga Journal, 438

journals and e-zines, 244-245
Judaism
BBC World Service—Religions of the World, 274
Chabad-Lubavitch in Cyberspace, 282
Jewish America, 282
Jewish Theological Seminary, 282
Jewish War Veterans of the USA, 393
Judaism 101, 282
Judaism and Jewish Resources, 282
Machon Chana, 428
MavenSearch, 282
ORT, 283
Project Genesis—Torah on the Information Superhighway, 283
Shamash, 283
Shtetl: Yiddish Language and Culture Home Page, 283
Virtual Jerusalem, 283
Zipple.com, 283

judo, 135-136`

A
B
C
D
E
F
G
H
I
J
K
L
M
N
O
P
Q
R
S
T
U
V
W
X
Y
Z

K

K-6 development
 AdvanceAbility Speech Therapist, 212
 America Links Up, 212
 Boy Scouts of America, 213
 Child Development from Elaine Gibson, 213
 Childhood Years: Ages Six Through Twelve, 213
 Developmental Assets: An Investment in Youth, 213
 Expect the Best from a Girl, 213
 Family.com, 213
 Good Housekeeping: The Latchkey Solution, 213
 HELP for Parents, 213
 Kids Camps, 214
 KidsHealth.org, 213
 Mom.com, 213
 National Network for Child Care: School Age Child Development, 214
 NCF—National Center for Fathering, 214
 Parent News, 214
 Parent Soup: Chat Descriptions, 214
 Parenting Pipeline, 214
 Parenting Tips for Primary Schoolers (6-12), 214
 Raising Our Children Free of Prejudice, 214
K-12 education
 ArtsEdge Network, 60
 Discovery Channel School, 61
 Education Index, 61
 Microsoft K-12 , 61
 Scholastic.com, 61
 Science Source, 61
 educational television
  Discovery Channel, 61
  Learning Channel, 61
  Schoolhouse Rock, 62
  Stephen Hawking's Universe, 62
 homework help
  Algebra Online, 62
  California State Science Fair, 62
  Dictionary.com, 62
  Homework Help, 62
  Homework Helper Page, 62
  Researchpaper.com, 62, 272
 private education, 63
kids
 activities for kids, 117-119
 Channel One, 118
 Internet games, 119
 Kids Camps, 214
 Kids Click!, 111
 Kids Domain Online Games, 83
 KidsHealth.org, 95, 209, 213
 KidsMeds, 224
 OLogy, 119
 pen pals for kids, 120
 sites by kids, 120
knitting, 121

L

languages/linguistics
 A Web of Online Dictionaries, 263
 American Sign Language Linguistic Research Project, 122
 Center for Applied Linguistics, 122
 constructed languages, 123
 English As a Second Language Home Page, 122
 Ethnologue: Languages of the World, 122
 foreign courses
  CLAP: Chinese Learner's Alternative Page, 124
  CyberItalian, 124
  Foreign Languages for Travelers, 124
  French Language Course, 124
  Web Spanish Lessons, 124
 general language and linguistics, 124
 iLoveLanguages, 122
 learning languages, 124
 Loglan, 122
 Martindale's Reference Desk, 263
 Model Languages, 123
 Morse Code and the Phonetic Alphabets, 271

THOR: The Virtual Reference Desk, 273

translation

On-Line Dictionaries and Glossaries, 263

travlang's Translating Dictionaries, 263

University of Virginia Foreign Languages & Cultures, 123

Latin

Bible Gateway, 276

Electronic Text Center at the University of Virginia, 129

law

ACLU Reproductive Rights, 1

American Civil Liberties Union – Lesbian and Gay Rights, 87

Copyright, 125

crime and criminal law, 125

ElderNet, 289

general resources, 125-126

law schools, 126

legal organizations, 126-127

legal publications, 127

Office of the Inspector General, 393

organizations

ACLU Freedom Network, 126

American Bar Association, 127

Association of Trial Lawyers of America, 127

resources

ClassActionAmerica.com, 125

FreeAdvice, 125

Law Books, 125

LawGuru.com, 126

Laws.com, 126

schools

Columbia Law School, 126

Harvard Law School, 126

Kaplan Law, 126

LawSchool.com, 126

U.S. Department of Justice, 389

Yale Journal of Law and Feminism, 432

libraries

American War Library, 264

Berkeley Digital Library SunSITE, 264

Bibliomania: The Network Library, 264

Campus Library, 264

Center for Research Libraries, 264

eLibrary, 269

Gateway Division NMRA, 256

infoplease.com, 270

Internet Public Library, 265

Library of Congress, 265

Library Resources for Women's Studies, 428

Library Spot, 265

Libweb—Library Servers on the WWW, 265

Medical/Health Sciences Libraries on the Web, 265

National Archives and Records Administration, 265

National First Ladies' Library, 271

News365, 190

North American Sport Library Network, 266

OCLC Online Computer Library Center, 266

Perry-Castaneda Library Map Collection, 266

Secular, 275

SignWritingSite, 316

Smithsonian Institution Libraries, 266

StudyWeb, 266

Sunnyvale Center for Innovation, Invention & Ideas, 267

Thriveonline.com, 402

U.S. Department of Education, 267

U.S. National Library of Medicine, 267

Veterinary Medicine Libraries, 396

WedNet, 421

WWW Library Directory, 267

literary agents, 434-435

literature

authors, 128-131

WWW Virtual Library, 285

lodging, 375-377

Los Angeles, California

Los Angeles Clippers (NBA), 23

Los Angeles Lakers (NBA), 23

Los Angeles Times, 193
Los Angeles Zoo, 443
love
Guide to Love and Sex, 306
Third Age, 289
Lycos.com, 111
Health with WebMD—Stress, 330
Shopping Network, 308
lyrics, 158

M

Macintosh computers
Mac Design Online, 45
MacWorld Online Web Server, 247
Ultimate Mac, 45
magazines
1st Traveler's Choice, 382
Advertising, 245
AJR NewsLink, 247
American Atheists, 275
Analog Science Fiction and Fact, 293
Apogee Photo, 233
Architecture Magazine, 12
Asia Pacific News, 186
Asimov's Science Fiction, 293
Astronomer Magazine, 14, 245
Atlantic Magazine Unbound, 187
Bouldering, 290
BYTE Magazine, 245
Campaign and Elections, 237
Computer Games Online, 245
Computerworld Online, 246
Congressional Quarterly, 187
Conspiracy Journal, 386
Cosmopolitan, 246
Discover Magazine, 246
Down Beat, 167
Earth Times, 187
Editor & Publisher, 246
Esquire, 246
European Visits, 371
Fast Company, 29
Favorite Quilting Magazines, 251
Field & Stream Online, 105

Food and Wine Magazine, 78
Forbes, 246
Fortune, 246
FreelanceWorkshop.com, 435
gay/lesbian, 88
Girls Life Magazine, 341
Glamour, 246
Harper's, 187
HotWired, 246
InnerSelf Magazine, 146
Intellectual Capital, 187
International Figure Skating Magazine (IFS), 317
Internetweek Online, 247
Intranet Journal, 182
Investor's Business Daily, 72
Journal of Scientific Exploration, 386
MacWorld Online Web server, 247
Magazine City.net, 247
Magazine CyberCenter, 247
Magazine Rack - Free Online Magazines, 247
Magazines A-Z, 247
Maine Antique Digest, 12
McCall's Quilting Magazine, 251
Millennium Whole Earth Catalog, 247
Model Railroading Magazine, 257
Modern Bride, 420
Mother Jones Interactive, 247
Motorcycle Online, 247
National Journal, 187
National Review, 187
NetworkMagazine.com, 184
News Express, 189
Newsweek, 187, 248
NME Magazine, 157
NYStyle, 310
Outlets Online, 309
People, 248
PM Zone, 248
Popular Science, 188, 248
Prevention, 422
Quilt Gallery Magazine, 252
React, 342

Retire Early Home Page, 272

Reveries.com, 134

RING: Online Michigan's Electronic Magazine, 381

Rodale's Scuba Diving - The Magazine Divers Trust, 406

Rolling Stone, 248

Runners World, 248, 358

Salon.com, 188

Science Magazine, 248

ScienceDaily Magazine—Your Link to the Latest Research News, 248

Scientific American Editors' Selections, 248

Scientific Computing and Instrumentation Online, 249

SciFan, 296

Self-Help Magazine, 145

Sew News, 303

Sky & Telescope Online, 249

Slate.com, 188

Sport Diver, 407

Sports Illustrated for Women, 430

Surfermag.com, 412

SwimNews Online, 414

Tai Chi, 249

TeenPeople, 343

Theatre Crafts International Magazine, 351

Threads Magazine, 304

TIME for Kids, 119

Time Magazine, 188, 249

TimeSharing Today, 273

Today's Bride Online Magazine, 420

Town & Country Weddings, 420

Track and Field News, 358

TravelASSIST Magazine, 249

Twins Magazine, 249

Typofile Magazine, 249

U.S. News & World Report, 188

UnderWire, 430

USA Weekend, 188

Utne Reader, 188

U: The National College Magazine, 249

Veteran News and Information Service, 188

Volleyball Magazine, 403

Volunteer Today, 200

Wedding Bells, 420

Wine Country Weekly Real Estate Reader, 262

Wrestling USA Magazine, 433

magic, 132

Maine

Maine Antique Digest, 12

Maine Snowmobile Connection, 323

Schooner Mary Day, 367

Windfall Rafting, 409

maps

AccuWeather.com, 415

Adventurous Traveler Bookstore, 359

CIA World Factbook, 268

Geography World, 89

iTools.com, 270

MapBlast, 90

MapQuest, 90

Maps of United States National Parks and Monuments, 221

National Geographic, 89

Perry-Castaneda Library Map Collection, 266

StudyWeb, 266

THOR: The Virtual Reference Desk, 273

TIGER Mapping Service, 90

WorldAtlas.com, 89

Marines (U.S.)

MarineLINK, 390

Toys for Tots, 356

Veterans News and Information Service, 188, 394

marketing, 133-134

martial arts, 135-136

Massachusetts

Boston Museum of Fine Art, 151

Boston.com Travel Page, 379

Cambridge, Massachusetts, 379

mathematics

Algebra Online, 62

American Mathematical Society, 137

Awesome Math Stuff, 120

Chaos Gallery at University of Maryland, 137

eFunda, 137

ENC Online—Eisenhower National Clearinghouse, 339

Eric Weisstein's World of Mathematics, 137

Expect the Best from a Girl, 427

Intel Innovation in Education, 339

Interactive Mathematics, 137

Larson Interactive Math Series, 137

MegaConverter, 270

S.O.S. Mathematics Algebra, 138

WWW Virtual Library, 285

medical resources

AAMC's Academic Medicine, 140

American Academy of Pediatric Dentistry, 141

American Academy of Pediatrics, 223

American Lung Association, 141

Centers for Disease Control and Prevention, 141

Doctor's Guide to Obesity, 422

Healthfinder, 141

Medical/Health Sciences Libraries on the Web, 265

Medicare

  National Senior Citizens Law Center, 300

  U.S. Department of Health and Human Services, 389

New England Journal of Medicine, 142

Three Dimensional Medical Reconstruction, 142

United States Department of Health and Human Services, 142

WebMD, 142

medicine

allergies, 7

American Diabetes Association (ADA), 56

Doc's Diving Medicine, 405

drug info, 139

drugstores, 139-140

first-aid info, 140

medical resources, 140-142

Medical/Health Sciences Libraries on the Web, 265

nurses

  4Nurses.com, 201

  AAAN, 201

  American Association of Colleges of Nursing, 201

  American Nurses Association, 201

  Cybernurse.com, 202

  Healthcare Innovations, 202

  Interfaith Health Program (IHP), 202

  National NurseSearch, 202

  NP Central, 202

  Nurse Options USA, 202

  NurseWeek.com, 202

  Nursing Desk Software, 202

  Nursing Education of America, 202

  Nursing Management Services, 202

  NursingCenter.com, 202

  Procare USA, 203

  StarMed Staffing Service, 203

  WholeNurse, 203

pain management, 142-143

RxList: The Internet Drug Index, 272

Skin Diver Online, 407

Travel Medicine, 369

U.S. National Library of Medicine, 267

WebMedLit, 245

men's interests

Amateur Softball Association, 328

Best Man, 419

electronic gadgets, 354

Fathering Magazine, 143

Go Ask Alice!: Sexuality, 306

health, 143

HisandHerhealth.com, 306

International Softball Federation (ISF), 328

Mankind Project, 143

Marrying Man, 420

Men Stuff, 143

NCF—National Center for Fathering, 214

Perfumes Direct, 312

Plainsense.com—Men's Health, 143

Single and Custodial Father's Network, 215

United States Masters Swimming, 414

USA Volleyball Home Page, 403

Volleyball World Wide, 404

Your Formal Wear Guide, 421

mental health, 144-145

Mexico

1st Traveler's Choice, 382

All-Inclusives Resort and Cruise Vacation Source, 374

Luis Cabanas Scuba Diving and Instruction, 406

Mexico: Travel Trips for the Yucatan Peninsula, 372

Michigan

Northern Michigan Snowmobiling, 323

RING: Online Michigan's Electronic Magazine, 381

Microsoft Corporation, 30

bCentral, 32, 134

Carpoint, 17

K–12 resources, 61

MoneyCentral on Taxes, 335

midwifery, 242

military. *See also* **veteran and military organizations**

American War Library, 264

DefenseLINK, 388

MarineLINK, 390

Military Links, 393

Military Order of the Purple Heart, 393

Military USA, 393

U.S. Army, 391

U.S. Department of Veterans Affairs, 389

U.S. Navy, 391

Minnesota

Minneapolis.org, 380

Minnesota Timberwolves (NBA), 23

Minnesota Vikings (NFL), 79-80

St. Paul Recommends: Destinations, 384

Missouri

Blue Ridge Country, 379

Gateway Division NMRA, 256

St. Louis Zoo, 444

model railroads, 256-258

mortgages and financing

America Mortgage Online, 286

Appraisal Institute, 102

H&R Block, 335

LendingTree.com, 102

PlanetMortgage.com, 102

mothers

MotherLinC: Mothers Without Custody, 215

Mothers and More, 219

Working Moms Refuge, 432

motivational and self-improvement resources, 146-147

motorcycles, 147-148, 248

movies

Alien Abduction Experience and Research, 385

Berkeley Art Museum/Pacific Film Archive, 153

Blockbuster, 400

BuyVideos.com, 400

DVDDigital.com, 397

DVDs, 397-398

E! Online, 398

Film.com, 398

Flicker, 399

Half.com, 308

International Surfing Museum, 411

Internet Movie Database, 399

Lord of the Rings Movie Site, 295

Matrix Reloaded, 295

MovieTunes, 349

Netflix.com, 398

Poltergeist – The Legacy, 295

Real.com, 400

Reel.com, 314, 400

Screen Actor's Guild, 350

Star Wars Official, 297

Virus The Movie, 297

A
B
C
D
E
F
G
H
I
J
K
L
M
N
O
P
Q
R
S
T
U
V
W
X
Y
Z

moving services. *See* relocation services
MP3 resources
    Artist Direct Free MP3, 158
    AudioGalaxy, 159
    emusic, 159
    listen.com, 159
    MP3 Nexus, 159
    MP3.com, 159
    MPEG.ORG, 175
    Music City, 159
    Napster, 159
    Scour.com, 400
MSN (Microsoft Network), 111
    Game Zone, 83
    HomeAdvisor, 261
    Messenger Service, 110
multimedia
    DVDs, 397-398
    movies, 398-399
    search engines, 400
museums
    architecture museums, 149
    Arizona-Sonora Desert Museum, 441
    art museums, 150-152
    Devices of Wonder, 149
    directories, 149
    Exploratorium, 149
    Guggenheim Museum, 97
    history and culture museums, 152
    Insecta, 107
    International Surfing Museum, 411
    Inventors Museum, 428
    Museum of Contemporary Ideas, 154
    Museum of Fine Arts, Boston, 151
    Museum of Fine Arts, Houston, 151
    Museum of Modern Art, New York, 152
    Museum of Science and Industry, Chicago, 154
    MuseumShop.com, 91
    National Air and Space Museum, 18
    National Museum of Natural History, 58

    natural history museums, 153
    papermaking, printing, and typesetting museums, 153
    photography and film museums, 153-154
    Pro Rodeo Hall of Fame, 292
    science and technology museums, 154-155
    Smithsonian Institution Libraries, 266
    Smithsonian National Museum of American History, 97
    Smithsonian Natural History Museum, 97
    WWW Virtual Library, 285
music
    all songs considered, 177
    BBC Radio 4, 177
    Buy.com, 308
    buying resources, 155-156
    Feminist Arts-Music, 427
    Half.com, 308
    Hearts of Space, 177
    Hindi: The Language of Songs, 124
    information, news, and reviews
        Artistdirect.com, 157
        Billboard Online, 157
        iMUSIC, 157
        IUMA, 157
        MTV, 157
        NME Magazine, 157
        SonicNet.com, 157
        VH1.COM, 157
        World Café, 158
        Worldwide Internet Music Resources, 158
    International Surfing Museum, 411
    KaZaA, 159
    Live365, 178
    LOOPLABS, 176
    lyrics, 158
    MovieTunes, 349
    MP3s
        resources, 158-159, 175
        search engines, 159
    musical instruments, 175-176

A
B
C
D
E
F
G
H
I
J
K
L
M
N
O
P
Q
R
S
T
U
V
W
X
Y
Z

organizations and clubs, 176-177

Planet Earth Music, 186

radio sites, 177-178

Real.com, 400

Rolling Stone, 248

software, 175

TicketWeb, 160

Transom, 178

Vintage Vaudeville and Ragtime Show, 351

WWW Virtual Library, 285

Zappa Quote of the Day, 255

music events, 159-160

music genres—alternative, 160-163

music genres—bluegrass, 163

music genres—Christian music, 163-164

music genres—classical, 164-165

music genres—country, 165-167

music genres—ethnic, 167

music genres—jazz, 167-168

music genres—opera, 168-169

music genres—pop music, 169-171

music genres—rap/hip-hop, 171-172

music genres—rock and roll, 172-174

music software, 175

musical instruments, 175-176

mutual funds, 73-74

N

NASA (National Aeronautics and Space Administration), 14, 18

Native Americans

indianz.com, 189

Native American Culture and Social System, 327

natural history museums

American Museum of Natural History, 153

Arizona-Sonora Desert Museum, 441

Carnegie Museum of Natural History, 153

Field Museum, 153

Smithsonian National Museum of Natural History, 153

nature, 179-180

Navy (U.S.)

Military Links, 393

U.S. Navy, 391

Veterans News and Information Service, 188, 394

NCAA (National Collegiate Athletic Association)

Men's and Women's Volleyball, 403

Men's Swimming and Diving, 413

Softball Championships, 328

Women's Rowing, 409

Women's Swimming and Diving, 413

networks

3Com, 180

About Computer Networking, 180

ATM Forum, 180

Cable Datacom News, 180

Cable Modem University, 181

Cisco Connection Online, 181

Digital Tool Group, 181

Emulex Network Systems, 181

HELIOS Software, 181

Hitachi Data Systems (HDS), 181

Hughes Network Systems, 181

IBM Networking Hardware, 181

Intel Networking and Telecommunications, 181

Internetweek Online, 247

Interphase Corporation, 182

InterWorking Labs, 182

Intranet Journal, 182

Jini Connection Technology, 182

KarlNet, 182

Kinesix, 182

Lancom Technologies, 182

LANology Enterprise Network Solutions, 182

Linksys Online, 182

Linux Mall, 183

ModemHelp, 270

Netgear, 183

NETiS Technology, Inc., 183

NetMagic Systems, 183

Network Buyer's Guide, 183

Network Engineer's Toolkit, 183

Network World Fusion, 183

A
B
C
D
E
F
G
H
I
J
K
L
M
N
O
P
Q
R
S
T
U
V
W
X
Y
Z

Networking Enterprises, 184

Nortel Networks, 184

Novell, Inc., 184

Paradyne Corporation Power Pages, 184

SoftLinx, Inc., 184

TechFest-Networking Protocols, 184

Telindous, 184

TENET Computer Group, Inc., 184

Vicomsoft, 185

Nevada

Lake Tahoe's West Shore Lodging, 376

Las Vegas.com, 380

New Age, 185-186

New England area

New England Airlines, 361

New England Journal of Medicine, 142

New England Patriots (NFL), 79-80

New Hampshire

Access New Hampshire, 378

Climb New Hampshire, 290

New Hampshire Resource Listings, 221

New Mexico

Albuquerque Aquarium, 441

America's Land of Enchantment: New Mexico, 378

New Mexico State Parks, 222

Santa Fe Station, 381

New York (state and city)

Bronx Zoo, 441

Capital District Theater Page, 349

I Love NY, 381

Manhattan Public Theater, 350

Metropolitan Museum of Art, 151

Museum of Modern Art, 152

New York City Ballet, 51

New York City Marathon, 68

New York Giants (NFL), 79-80

New York Jets (NFL), 79-80

New York Philharmonic, 165

New York State Department of Family Assistance, 327

New York's Capital District Theater Page, 349

Playbill Online, 350

Wildlife Conservation Society, 444

New Zealand

International Bed-and-Breakfast Guide, 376

NZ Softball - New Zealand, 329

news

Arts & Letters Daily, 186

magazines, 186-189

resources

BBC News, 189

E&P Media Links, 189

EmergencyNet News, 189

The Feedroom, 189

indianz.com, 189

Mirror Syndication International, 189

News Express, 189

News365, 190

oneworld.net, 190

Slashdot, 190

TotalNEWS, 190

services

ABC News.com, 192

Associated Press, 190

Business Wire, 190

CBS News.com, 192

Christian Science Monitor, 192

CNN Interactive, 190

Crayon, 190

Desktop News, 191

ESPN.com, 193

ForeignWire, 191

FoxNews.com, 193

IMEDIAFAX, 191

InfoBeat, 191

Los Angeles Times, 193

Media Monitors, 191

MSNBC.com, 193

New York Times, 193

The Paperboy, 191

PBS Online NewsHour, 191

Positive Press, 191

Reuters, 191

A B C D E F G H I J K L M N O P Q R S T U V W X Y Z

South African Broadcasting Corporation Welcome Page, 192

Top 100 Newspapers, 193

United Press International (UPI), 193

Wall Street Journal Interactive, 194

Washington Post, 194

WebClipping.com, 192

World Radio Network, 192

WorldNetDaily, 192

Smoking Gun, 188

TechnoTeen, 342

U.S. news, 193-194

Veterans News and Information Service, 394

newspapers

Asia Pacific News, 186

Christian Science Monitor, 192

E&P Media Links, 189

Editor & Publisher, 246

High School Journalism, 116

Los Angeles Times, 193

Mirror Syndication International, 189

New York Times, 193

News Express, 189

The Onion, 105

The Paperboy, 191

Top 100 Newspapers, 193

USA Today, 194

Washington Post, 194

nonprofit and charitable organization resources, 194-201

nursing, 201-203

nursing homes, 288-289, 300

nutrition

American Dietetic Association, 421

CyberDiet, 422

eNutrition.com, 401

Fast Food Facts—Interactive Food Finder, 422

HealthCentral, 424

healthshop.com, 401

Jenny Craig, 422

Natural Nutrition, 422

Nutrisystem, 422

Nutrition.gov, 57

Seniors-Site.com, 289

Thriveonline: Nutrition, 423

O

oceans

American Zoo and Aquarium Association, 441

Beneath the Sea, 404

Franck Goddio, 405

Intellicast, 417

National Weather Service, 417

Ocean Weather, 417

Ocean.com, 179

OceanBlue, 412

Oceans Alive, 179

Surfrider Foundation USA, 412

office management

office equipment

Better Buys for Business, 203

BuyerZone.com, 203

BuySmart.com, 204

Home Office Direct Consumer, 204

SOHO Consumer, 204

resources

123 Sort It, 206

CheckWorks.com, 206

Eletter.com, 207

Office.com, 207

seeuthere.com, 207

USPS Zip Code Lookup, 207

supply stores

Dr. Shredder's, 204

Independent Stationers Online, 204

Levenger, 204

Office Depot, 205

Office Helper, 205

OfficeMax OnLine, 205

onlineofficesupplies.com, 205

Quill Office Products, 205

Staples, Inc., 205

A
B
C
D
E
F
G
H
I
J
K
L
M
N
O
P
Q
R
S
T
U
V
W
X
Y
Z

U.S. Office Products, 206

USPS Shipping Supplies Online, 206

Viking Direct, 206

office supply stores, 204-206

Ohio

Cincinnati Art Museum, 150

Cincinnati Vacation Gateways, 379

Cincinnati Zoo and Botanical Garden, 442

Cleveland Metroparks Zoo, 442

Olympics

Athens 2004 Games, 357

iROW.com, 409

No Frontiers: A Year in the Life of Fermoy Rowing, 409

North American Table Tennis, Inc., 332

Table Tennis World Championships Videos, 333

TheMat.com, 432

U.S. Ski Home Team Page, 322

United States Diving Online, 407

USA Basketball, 23

USA Swimming, 414

USA Volleyball Home Page, 403

Volleyball.com, 404

online games, 118-119

online trading, 74-75

opera, 168-169

Oregon

Oregon Museum of Science and Industry, 155

Oregon Online, 381

Oregon Zoo, 443

organizations

Air Force Association, 392

Alexander Graham Bell Association for Deaf and Hard of Hearing, 315

All Things Military, 393

Alliance of Genetic Support Groups, 215

American Federation of Teachers, 337

American Kennel Club (AKC), 226

American Legion, 392

American Veterinary Medical Association, 395

American Zoo and Aquarium Association, 441

AMVETS Blinded Veterans Association, 393

ATM Forum, 180

Beneath the Sea, 404

Business Women's Network Interactive, 426

Carnegie Council on Ethics and International Affairs, 80

Catholic Charities USA, 326

Cats Protection League, 226

Citizens for Tax Justice, 334

Computer Book Café, 434

Disabled American Veterans, 392-393

Gulf War Veteran Resource Pages, 393

International Center of Photography, 234

Jewish War Veterans of the USA, 393

Mankind Project, 143

Military Order of the Purple Heart (MOPH), 393

Military USA, 393

National Association of the Deaf (NAD), 316

National Coalition for Homeless Veterans, 393

National Organization for Women (NOW), 429

National PTA, 440

National Veterans Legal Service Program, 393

NMRA on the Web: The National Model Railroad Association, 257

Sexuality Information and Education Council of the U.S., 307

Shamash, 283

Shotokan Karate of America, 136

Sub-Aqua Association, 407

TROA, 393

United States Specialty Sports Association, 329

USA Judo, 136

Women Leaders Online (WLO), 431

outdoors

camping, 33

A
B
C
D
E
F
G
H
I
J
K
L
M
N
O
P
Q
R
S
T
U
V
W
X
Y
Z

fishing
  eders.com, 76
  *United States Fish and Wildlife
    Service, 76*
GORP: Paddlesports, 408
hiking, 33-34
hunting, 105-106
Outdoor REVIEW, 321

P

pain management, 142-143
parenting
  ABC's of Parenting, 208
  About Parenting/Family, 208
  Activity Search, 337
  adolescents, 208-210
  babies and toddlers, 210-212
  Education.com, 338
  K-6, 212-214
  KidsHealth.org: For Teens, 209
  National Parent Information
    Network, 209
  National PTA, 440
  Parenting Pipeline, 214
  Parenting Q&A, 209
  Parenting Tips: Primary Schoolers
    (6-12), 214
  Parents, Families, and Friends of
    Gays and Lesbians (PFLAG), 87
  Parents.com, 212
  Parentsoup Family Travel, 368
  ParentsPlace.com, 209, 219
  single parenting, 215
  special needs children, 215-218
  stay-at-home parents, 218-219
  stepparenting, 219-220
parks, 220-223
patterns (sewing), 304-305
PBS (Public Broadcasting System)
  Nova Online: Lost on Everest, 291
  Online NewsHour, 191
  PBS Kids, 119
  PBS Nature, 179
pediatrics
  American Academy of Pediatrics,
    223

Babies Today Online, 19
Children with Diabetes, 223
DISHES Project for Pediatric AIDS,
  224
DocsOnline, 224
Dr. Greene's HouseCalls, 224
Dr. Plain Talk, 224
Journal of Pediatrics, 224
kidsDoctor, 224
KidsMeds, 224
National Childhood Cancer
  Foundation, 224
Pediatric Leukemia, 224
Virtual Children's Hospital, 225
perfume, 312-313
pet care
  American Animal Hospital
    Association (AAHA), 227
  American Pet Association, 228
  AMVA (American Veterinary
    Medical Association), 228
  Animal Health Information, 228
  I Love My Pet, 228
  NetPets, 228
  OncoLink: Veterinary Oncology, 228
  Online Animal Catalog, 228
  PedEducation.com, 229
  Pet Columns from University of
    Illinois College of Veterinary
    Medicine (CVM), 229
  Pet Experts, 230
  PetCat, 225
  PetEducation.com, 229
  Pets Need Dental Care, Too, 229
  Professor Hunt's Dog Page, 229
  Purina Pet Care Center, 229
  Waltham World of Pet Care, 229
pet supplies, 229-230
pets. *See also* animals
  4Vets.com, 394
  AAHA HealthPet.com, 394
  American College of Veterinary
    Surgeons, 394
  American Veterinary Medical
    Association, 395
  AVA Online, 395
  Care for Pets, 395

A
B
C
D
E
F
G
H
I
J
K
L
M
N
O
P
Q
R
S
T
U
V
W
X
Y
Z

Careers in Veterinary Medicine, 395
cats, 225-226
Cats (and People) Who Quilt, 250
Department of Animal Science:
  Oklahoma State University, 395
dogs, 226-227, 230
pet care, 227-229
pet supplies, 229-230
Pets Welcome, 368
ProVet, 396
TalkToTheVet.com, 396
Veterinary Medicine, 396
Veterinary Pet Insurance, 396
Philadelphia, Pennsylvania
Philadelphia Eagles (NFL), 79-80
Philadelphia Zoo Online, 443
philosophy, 283-284. *See also* **religion
  and philosophy**
Phoenix, Arizona
Phoenix Suns (NBA), 23
Phoenix Zoo, 444
phone numbers, 270-273
photography
cameras, 231-233
History of Photography, 96
museums, 153-154
Photo.net, 233
Rapid Shooters, 408
Scuba Diving and Snorkeling
  Worldwide, 406
techniques, 233-234
Wedding Photography—Advice for
  the Bride and Groom, 421
plants, 84-85
plays. *See* **theater and musicals**
political campaigns, 236-238
political parties, 239-240
politics
California Voter Foundation, 237
CIA World Factbook, 268
Congressional Quarterly, 187
Contacting the Congress, 235
Council on Foreign Relations, 235
Forbes Digital Tool, 29
HotWired, 246

Human Rights Campaign, 87
Intellectual Capital, 187
National Journal, 187
National Political Index, 235
National Review Magazine, 187
Office of the Clerk On-line
  Information Center, 235
opensecrets.org, 235
political campaigns, 236-238
Political Money Line, 236
political parties, 239-240
Politics1.com, 236
Salon.com, 188
Sierra Club, 180
Slate.com, 188
UnderWire, 430
United States House of
  Representatives, 391
United States Senate, 391
WashingtonPost.com/OnPolitics, 236
Women and Politics Home Page, 431
pop music, 169-171
population statistics, 273
Portuguese language sites
Dictionary.com, 263
Foreign Languages for Travelers, 124
poverty, 196-197
prayer, 285, 288
pregnancy/birth, 208, 240-243, 341
preschool education, 63
prescription drugs. *See* **drugs; drug-
  stores**
presidents (U.S.)
National Archives and Records
  Administration, 265
Welcome to the White House, 391
price search engines, 310-311
programming languages, 46
psychology, 145
publications
journals and e-zines, 244-245
magazines, 245-249
publishers
AuthorLink!, 434
Bartleby.com, 434
Editors Eye, 435

Harcourt School Publishing, 339

Logos Research Systems, 279

McGraw-Hill School Division, 340

Pearson Technology Group, 27

Puffin House Publishers, 340

storybay, 435

Waterside Productions, 435

Write News, 436

puzzles. *See* games and puzzles

Q - R

quilting, 250-253. *See also* sewing

quotations, 253-254

radio

Art Bell, 385

Earth & Sky Radio Series, 177

KPIG Radio Online, 178

NPR (National Public Radio), 178

Personal Success Radio Network, 146

Radio Shack, 65

Savvy Traveler, 369

Scour.com, 400

Scuba Radio, 406

Welcome to KAOS!, 177

World Radio Network, 192

rafting, 407-409

railroads, 256-258

rap/hip-hop music, 171-172

reading

AdvanceAbility Speech Therapist, 212

Internet Public Library, 270

real estate. *See also* homes

Ads4Homes, 258

America Mortgage Online, 286

Americas Virtual Real Estate Store, 258

Apartments for Rent Online, 259

Buying a Home in Arizona, 259

buying/selling, 258-262

Century 21, 259

Coldwell Banker, 259

Commercial Network, 259

Consumer Information Center, 259

Domainia.com, 259

HomeBuilder.com, 260

HomeFair.com, 260

HomeGain, 260

Homeseekers.com, 260

HUD – Department of Housing and Urban Development, 260

International Real Estate Digest, 260

Land.Net, 260

LoopNet, 261

MSN HomeAdvisor, 261

NewHomeNetwork.com, 261

Nolo.com-Real Estate, 261

Owners.com, 261

Real Estate Center Online, 261

realtor.com, 261

relocation services, 286-287

REMAX Real Estate Network, 261

San Diego County Real Estate Library, 261

SchoolMatch, 262

timeshares, 273, 287-288

Wine Country Weekly Real Estate Reader, 262

RealAudio

Planet Earth Music, 186

RealPlayer, 175

Real.com, 400

Vintage Vaudeville and Ragtime Show, 351

World Radio Network, 192

recipes

alcoholic drinks, 77

CyberDiet, 422

Thriveonline: Nutrition, 423

reference resources

dictionaries and thesauri, 262-264

Dictionary.com, 62

infoplease.com, 63

libraries, 264-267

quotations, 253-255

Reference Tools, 272

research help, 263, 267-273, 285

Web of On-Line Dictionaries, 64

A
B
C
D
E
F
G
H
I
J
K
L
M
N
O
P
Q
R
S
T
U
V
W
X
Y
Z

WhoWhere? People in U.S.
Government, 391

religion and philosophy
Academic Info
Antiquity Online, 275
Philosophy, 274
Religion, 274
Adherents—Religion Statistics and
Geography, 274
ancient, 275
atheism, 275
BBC World Service—Religions of
the World, 274
beliefnet, 274
Buddhism, 275-276
Catholic Charities USA, 326
Christianity, 276-280
cults, 280
Deism, 280
gay/lesbian interests, Unitarian
Universalist Association, 88
Glide Memorial Church, 278
GraceCathedral.org, 278
Hinduism, 280-281
Islam, 281-282
Judaism, 282-283
Machon Chana, 428
philosophy, 283-284
prayer, 285, 288
Religion and Philosophy, 274
Religion News Service, 279
Religious Society of Friends WWW
site, 279
Women in Islam, 431

relocation services, 286-287

rentals (real estate)
Apartments for Rent Online, 259
Nolo.com-Real Estate, 261
Rent.net, 287

research help
555-1212.com, 267
Academic Info, 267
Academy of Achievement, 267
American Sign Language Browser,
267
AnyWho Toll Free Directory, 268

Ask Jeeves, 268
AskERIC, 268
Biography.com, 268
Britannica.com, 268
Car Talk, 268
Central Notice, 268
CIA World Factbook, 268
Consumer Information Center, 268
Cook's Thesaurus, 268
Dismal Scientist, 269
eHow, 269
eLibrary, 269
Encarta Online, 269
FedWorld.gov, 269
FinAid: The Financial Aid
Information Page, 269
Flag of the United States of America,
269
Geographic Nameserver, 269
How Stuff Works, 270
infoplease.com, 270
InfoSpace.com, 270
Internet 800 Directory, 270
Internet Public Library, 270
iTools.com, 270
Library of Congress, 270
MegaConverter, 270
ModemHelp, 270
Morse Code and the Phonetic
Alphabets, 271
National Address and ZIP+4
Browser, 271
National First Ladies' Library, 271
Nobel Foundation, 271
Old Farmer's Almanac, 271
Period.Com Airlines, 271
PhoNETic, 271
refdesk.com, 272
reference tools, 272
Researchpaper.com, 62, 272
Retire Early Home Page, 272
RxList: The Internet Drug Index,
272
Smithsonian Institution Research
Information System, 272
SuperPages.com, 272

Switchboard, 273

THOR: The Virtual Reference Desk, 273

U.S. Census Bureau, 273

United States Postal Service, 273

Virtual Reference Desk, 273

Vital Records Information (United States), 273

World Population, 273

WWW Virtual Library, 285

resorts

All-Inclusives Resort and Cruise Vacation Source, 374

Balsam Shade Resort, 382

Boston Mills-Brandywine Ski Resort, 320

Colorado Resort Net (CRN), 321

Cool Works' Ski Resorts and Ski/Snowboard Country Jobs, 321

GoSki.com, 321

Holiday Junction, 376

Sandals Resorts, 383

SkiCentral, 322

SkiNet, 322

TimeLinx, 288

TimeSharing Today, 273

retirement

401k Center for Employers, 288

401Kafe.com, 288

AARP WebPlace, 288

American Association of Homes and Services for the Aging, 288

communities

American Association of Homes and Services for the Aging, 299

Assisted Living Described, 299

HomeStore.com Senior Living, 299

HUD for Senior Citizens, 300

Maple Knoll Village Retirement Home, 289

seniorresource.com, 301

ElderNet, 289

Kiplinger Online, 335

Maple Knoll Village Retirement Home, 289

Quicken.com Retirement, 289

Retire Early Home Page, 272

Retire.net, 289

Retirement Calculators, 289

Retirement Research Foundation, 289

Seniors-Site.com, 289

SeniorsSearch, 289

Social Security Online, 289

Third Age, 289

rock and roll music, 172-174

rock climbing, 290-291

rodeo, 292-293

Roth IRAs

Fairmark Press—Tax Guide for Investors, 335

Quicken.com Retirement, 289

Quicken.com Taxes, 335

routers

Cisco Connection Online, 181

KarlNet, 182

rowing, 409-411

running

New York City Marathon, 68

Runners World, 248, 358

Running on Full, 68

Terry Fox Foundation, 68

S

San Antonio, Texas

San Antonio Spurs (NBA), 23

San Antonio Zoo, 444

San Diego, California

San Diego Chargers (NFL), 79-80

San Diego County Real Estate Library, 261

San Diego Zoo, 444

San Francisco, California

San Francisco 49ers (NFL), 79-80

San Francisco Museum of Modern Art, 152

San Francisco Zoo, 444

schools

Education Place, 338

Education.com, 338

A
B
C
D
E
F
G
H
I
J
K
L
M
N
O
P
Q
R
S
T
U
V
W
X
Y
Z

Family Education Network: A Parenting and Education Resource, 211

Religious Society of Friends, 279

Researchpaper.com, 272

Scholastic.com, 61, 340

School Psychology, 145

School Report, 287

SchoolMatch, 262

StudyWeb, 266

sci-fi (science fiction)

Analog Science Fiction and Fact, 293

Asimov's Science Fiction, 293

Broadsword, 294

Buffy the Vampire Slayer, 294

Caroline's Hercules Page, 294

The Centre, 294

Dark Planet Science Fiction Webzine, 294

Dark Shadows, 294

FANDOM—*Star Trek* Central, 294

FanGrok, 294

Klingon Language Institute, 123

Lord of the Rings Movie Site, 295

Matrix Reloaded, 295

Netpicker's Guide to the X-Files, 295

Poltergeist: The Legacy, 295

Sci-Fi Experience, 295

Sci-Fi.Net, 295

Science Fiction and Fantasy Writers of America (SFWA), 296

Science Fiction Resource Guide, 296

Science Fiction Weekly, 296

SciFan, 296

SCIFI.COM, 296

SF Site, 296

Smallville Ledger, 296

Songs of the Blue Bird, 297

Star Trek, 297

Star Wars Official, 297

Starship Store, 297

TV Sci-Fi and Fantasy Database, 297

Ultimate Science Fiction Web Guide, 297

Virus The Movie, 297

science

BugBios.com, 107

California State Science Fair, 62

Climate/Weather/Earth Hotlist, 416

Dictionary of Cell and Molecular Biology, 263

Discover Magazine, 246

eNature.com, 107

ENC Online—Eisenhower National Clearinghouse, 339

Expect the Best from a Girl, 427

Insecta, 107

Intel Innovation in Education, 339

Journal of Scientific Exploration, 386

MegaConverter, 270

Popular Science, 188, 248

Science Magazine, 248

ScienceDaily Magazine, 248

Scientific American Editors' Selections, 248

Scientific Computing and Instrumentation Online, 249

Stephen Hawking's Universe, 62

technology museums, 154-155

THOR: The Virtual Reference Desk, 273

Wild World of Wonka, 119

WWW Virtual Library, 285

scuba resources, 406-407

seafood, 76

search engines, 111

Ask Jeeves, 268

Best Book Buys, 27

BuyVideos.com, 400

Centers for Disease Control and Prevention Home Page, 141

child-safe search engines, 111

Christian Missions Home Page, 277

Dog.com, 227

Education World, 338

FragranceNet, 312

The Knot: Weddings for the Real World, 419

LawGuru.com, 126

MavenSearch, 282

The MoJo Wire, 238

A
B
C
D
E
F
G
H
I
J
K
L
M
N
O
P
Q
R
S
T
U
V
W
X
Y
Z

multimedia, 400
OCLC Online Computer Library Center, Inc., 266
products, 313
Real.com, 400
Reel.com, 400
Scour.com, 400
Scuba Source, 406
Search Engine Colossus, 400
SeniorsSearch.com, 301
Shopnow.com, 313
SignWritingSite, 316
U.S. Census Bureau, 273
Videomaker's Camcorder and Desktop Video Site, 249
Votenet, 238
Wall Street City, 73
Yahoo! Shopping, 313

Seattle, Washington
Seattle City Guide, 381
Seattle Seahawks (NFL), 79-80
Seattle SuperSonics (NBA), 23

security/virus hoaxes
Digital Tool Group, 181
McAfee Antivirus, 111
Symantec AntiVirus Research Center, 112

seniors. *See also* **retirement**
AARP, 298
Administration on Aging (AOA), 298
Age of Reason Recommended Senior Living Facilities, 298
AgeNet, 298
Alliance for Retired Americans, 298
Alzheimer's Association, 298
Alzheimer's Disease Education & Referral Center, 298
American Association of Homes and Services for the Aging, 299
Assisted Living Described, 299
Caregiver Network Inc., 299
CareGuide, 211
Choosing an Assisted Living Facility, 299
Elderhostel, 299
ElderWeb, 127

Friendly4Seniors, 299
Health and Age.com, 9
HomeStore.com Senior Living, 299
HUD for Senior Citizens, 300
Masters Track and Field, 357
National Senior Citizens Law Center, 300
New LifeStyles, 300
Over the Hill Gang, 321
Rent.net, 287
Senior Center, 300
Senior Cyborgs, 300
Senior Information Network, 301
Senior Sites, 301
Senior Softball, 329
Senior.com, 301
SeniorJournal.com, 301
SeniorNet, 301
seniorresource.com, 301
Seniors Page—FirstGov For Seniors, 301
SeniorsSearch, 289, 301
Social Security Online, 302
Third Age, 302
Transitions, Inc. Elder Care Consulting, 302
Wired Seniors, 302

sewing. *See also* **quilting**
A Sewing Web, 303
Cranston Village, 302
Fabri-Centers, 50
Fabric Club, 302
Fabrics.net, 302
Fashion Fabrics Club, 302
Fashion Supplies, 303
Fiskars, 303
Home Sewing Association, 303
Jo-Ann etc., 303
Lily Abello's Sewing Links, 303
machines, 304-305
Nancy's Notions, 303
patterns, 305
Patternshowcase.com, 303
QuiltWear.com, 253
Sew News, 303

A B C D E F G H I J K L M N O P Q R S T U V W X Y Z

Sewing.com, 304
Threads Magazine, 304
Vy's Sewing Site, 304
Wild Ginger Software, 304
sexuality
   AltSex, 306
   Australian Love & Sexuality, 306
   Coalition for Positive Sexuality, 306
   Dr. Ruth Online!, 306
   Gender and Sexuality, 306
   Go Ask Alice!: Sexuality, 306
   Good Vibrations, 428
   Guide to Love and Sex, 306
   HisandHerhealth.com, 306
   Impotence Specialists, 306
   intimategifts.com, 306
   Nerve.com, 307
   Oxygen's Relationships & Sex, 307
   Planned Parenthood Federation of America, Inc., 1
   SexualHealth.com, 307
   Sexuality Database, 307
   Sexuality Forum, 307
   Sexuality Information and Education Council of the U.S., 307
   Sexuality.org, 307
   Web by Women for Women, 431
Shakespeare, William, 348-350
shopping
   4Nurses.com, 201
   ABC's of Parenting, 208
   Abe's of Maine, 231
   AdvanceRx.com, 139
   Amazon.com, 308
   Baby Catalog of America, 210
   babyGap, 211
   BabyZone, 242
   BargainDog, 308
   Barnes & Noble.com, 27
   Biography.com, 268
   BizRate, 310
   Bloomingdale's, 309
   Boardgames.com, 352
   Borders.com, 27
   Buy.com, 308

   Buyer's Index, 313
   Cabela's, 105
   Cafe Maison Coffee Roasters, 77
   Cameras Etcetera, 232
   Cartoon Network, 117
   CatalogLink, 308
   Chat: Stay-at-Home Parents, 218
   Christianbook.com, 277
   comparison bots, 310-311
   Consumer Information Center, 268
   Crayola Home Page, 118
   D&J Sports, 412
   DealTime.com, 310
   Death Valley National Park, 220
   DELiAs.com, 309
   Designer Outlet.com, 309
   Digital Camera Imaging Resource Page, 232
   discount stores, 311
   Disney Online Store, 353
   drugstore.com, 139
   Eddie Bauer, 309
   eders.com, 76
   EducationalToys.com, 353
   ePregnancy.com, 243
   eToys: The Internet's Biggest Toy Store!, 211, 353
   FAO Schwarz, 353
   Fashionmall.com, 310
   Feminist Majority Foundation Online, 427
   Firebox.com, 354
   First Aid Products Online, 140
   Focus Camera & Video, 232
   Frugal Knitting Haus, 121
   gifts, 91
   Girls Life Magazine, 341
   Good Vibrations, 428
   GoTennis, 346
   Grand Theatre, 348
   Half.com, 308
   HerRoom.com, 310
   Home School World, 103
   InfoSpace.com, 270
   Inshop.com, 308

A B C D E F G H I J K L M N O P Q R S T U V W X Y Z

iQVC, 308

jewelry, 312

K&L Wine Merchants, 78

KBKids, 354

Kelly's Running Warehouse, 357

The Knot: Weddings for the Real World, 419

L.L. Bean, 310

Land's End, 310

Lycos Shopping Network, 308

Magictricks.com, 132

Martial Arts Equipment, 135

MartialArtsMart.com, 135

Mattel, 355

Medicine Shoppe, 139

Military Links, 393

more.com, 140

MovieTunes, 349

music, 155-156

MyBackStore.com, 8

mySimon, 310

National Women's Hall of Fame, 429

Netmarket.com, 309

New Age Web Works, 186

NexTag, 310

Noah's Pet Supplies, 230

NYStyle, 310

Outlets Online, 309

Oxygen.com, 430

Parenthood, 212

Peet's Coffee & Tea, 77

perfume, 312-313

PetFoodDirect.com, 230

PhotoWorks.com, 234

Pickles, Peppers, Pots & Pans, 77

Ping Pong Mania & Sporting Goods Co., 332

PriceGrabber.com, 311

PriceScan, 311

Productopia, 311

React, 342

Rite Aid, 140

Road Runner Sports Shoe Store, 357

RoboShopper.com, 311

RockClimbing.com, 291

Rower's World, 410

Sam's Club, 311

SavOn.com, 140

Schylling, 356

Scrolls from the Dead Sea, 279

Sega, 356

Sexuality Forum, 307

ShopGuide, 313

Shopnow.com, 65, 313

Shopping The World, 309

Simply OarSome, 410

Skin Diver Online, 407

SmarterKids.com, 356

Smithsonian Institution Libraries, 266

Snowmobiling.net, 324

specialty goods, 313-314

Star Wars Official, 297

Starship Store, 297

SwimNews Online, 414

Tennis Server, 346

TennisONE, 346

Third Age, 302

TigerStrike.com, 135

USRowing, 410

Wal-Mart Online, 311

Walgreen's, 140

Water Skier's Web, 415

Wild Birds Unlimited, 25

Wine.com, 79

Wines on the Internet, 79

Wolf Camera, 233

World of Magic, 132

Yahoo! Shopping, 313

Zipple.com, 283

sign language/deaf resources, 315-316

single parenting, 215

skating, 69, 316-317

skin care/cosmetics, 318-320

skydiving, 69

small business resources, 32

Smithsonian Institution, 152

Libraries, 266

Research Information System, 272

National Museum of American History, 97

A
B
C
D
E
F
G
H
I
J
K
L
M
N
O
P
Q
R
S
T
U
V
W
X
Y
Z

National Museum of Natural History, 97, 153

snow skiing

snowboarding, 320-322

Altrec.com, 320

Boardz.com, 69

SkiCentral, 322

snowmobiling, 323-324

soccer, 325-326

social work/services

AAMFT, 326

The Carter Center, 326

Catholic Charities USA, 326

Centers for Disease Control and Prevention, 326

National Association of Alcoholism and Drug Abuse Counselors (NAADAC), 326

National Center for Missing and Exploited Children, 327

National Children's Coalition (NCC), 327

National Civic League, 327

Native American Culture and Social System, 327

New York State Department of Family Assistance, 327

Social Security Online, 289, 302

Social Work and Social Services, 327

SocialService.com, 327

U.S. Department of Health and Human Services, 327

UnderWire, 430

VISTA, 328

softball, 328-329

software

antivirus

Dr. Solomon, 46

McAfee.com, 46

Symantec, 46

Buy.com, 308

downloads

Download Warehouse, 46

Software Unboxed, 46

egghead, 44

Emulex Network Systems, 181

Scholastic.com, 340

SlaughterHouse, 47

upgrades, Linksys Online, 182

South Africa

South African Broadcasting Corporation Welcome Page, 192

Surfing in South Africa, 412

space

Air Force Association, 392

Climate/Weather/Earth Hotlist, 416

EarthWatch Weather on Demand, 416

NASA, 18

Spanish language sites

Alcoholics Anonymous, 4

Astronomy Thesaurus, 262

Dictionary.com, 263

Foreign Languages for Travelers, 124

Hieros Gamos, 127

Planned Parenthood Federation of America, Inc., 1

Web Spanish Lessons, 124

special needs children, 215-217

special occasion gifts, 90-91

specialty shopping, 313-314

spirituality

beliefnet, 274

Full Circle New Age Book Shop, 185

WWW Virtual Library, 285

sports

ab257's Whitewater Page, 407

About.com Table Tennis, 333

Altrec.com, 320

Amateur Rowing Association, 409

Amateur Softball Association, 328

American Barefoot Club, 414

American Snowmobiler Magazine, 323

American Tennis Professionals, 345

American Volleyball Coaches Association, 402

American Wallyball Association, 402

American Whitewater Resources Online, 408

Arctic Cat, 323

Athens 2004 Olympic Games, 357

Athletics Canada, 357

Athletics Home Page, 357

A B C D E F G H I J K L M N O P Q R S T U V W X Y Z

ATL World Soccer News, 324

Austria Ski Vacation Packages, 320

baseball, 21-22

   Little League Baseball Online,
   440

basketball, 22-23

Beneath the Sea, 404

Board Building, 411

Boston Mills-Brandywine Ski
Resort, 320

Closely Guarded Secrets of the UK
Surfing World, 411

Coastal British Columbia, 411

Collegiate Volleyball Update, 402

Cool Works' Ski Resorts and
Ski/Snowboard Country Jobs, 321

CRN (Colorado Resort Net), 321

D&J Sports, 412

Daily Soccer, 324

Deep Sea Divers Den, 405

Dive Connections, 405

DiverLink, 405

DiversDiscount.com, 405

DiveWeb, 405

Doc's Diving Medicine, 405

English Table Tennis Association
Limited, 332

ESPN.com, 193, 324

FIFA Online, 324

FINA, 412

Find-a-Guide Rafting Guides and
Trips, 408

FIVB WWW Home Page, 403

Fogdog, 313

football, NFL.com, 79

Get Rolling, 317

golf, 92

GORP: Paddlesports, 408

GoSki.com, 321

GoTennis, 346

Grand Canyon River Running, 408

Greg's Comparison Page, 323

hockey, 98-99

Hyperski, 321

International Figure Skating
Magazine (IFS), 317

International Inline Skating
Association, 317

International Snowmobile
Manufacturers Association, 323

International Softball Federation
(ISF), 328

International Surfing Museum, 411

International Swimming Hall of
Fame, 413

International Table Tennis
Committee for the Disabled, 332

International Tennis Federation
Online, 346

International Water Ski Federation,
414

InternetSoccer.com, 325

iROW.com, 409

K2 Skis, 321

Kangaroo's Triple Jump Online, 357

Kelly's Running Warehouse, 357

Las Lenas Ski Packages, 321

Luis Cabanas Scuba Diving and
Instruction, 406

Maine Snowmobile Connection, 323

Major League Soccer (MLS), 325

Masters Track and Field, 357

National Show Ski Association, 414

National Water Ski Racing
Association, 415

NCAA

   Men's and Women's Volleyball,
   403

   Men's Swimming and Diving,
   413

   Softball Championships, 328

   Women's Rowing, 409

   Women's Swimming and Diving,
   413

No Frontiers: A Year in the Life of
Fermoy Rowing, 409

North American Sport Library
Network, 266

North American Table Tennis, Inc.,
332

Northern Michigan Snowmobiling,
323

Northwest River Supplies, 408

NZ Softball - New Zealand, 329

A
B
C
D
E
F
G
H
I
J
K
L
M
N
O
P
Q
R
S
T
U
V
W
X
Y
Z

OceanBlue, 412

Outdoor REVIEW, 321

Over the Hill Gang, 321

Paddling@about.com, 409

PADI (Professional Association of Diving Instructors), 406

Ping Pong Mania & Sporting Goods Co., 332

Planet Waterski, 415

Polaris Industries, 323

ProWrestling.com, 432

Rapid Shooters, 408

Regatta Sport, 409

Riedell Skates, 316

River Wild, 408

Riversearch, 408

Road Runner Sports Shoe Store, 357

Rodale's Scuba Diving - The Magazine Divers Trust, 406

Row Works, 410

Row2K.com, 410

Rower's World, 410

Rowing FAQ, 410

Rowing from an Oarsman's Perspective, 410

Rowing Service, 410

RowingLinks - The Internet's Definitive Source for Rowing Links, 410

Runner's, 357

Runner's World Online, 358

Running Network, 358

Salomon Sports, 321

Schneid's Volleyball Page, 403

Scuba Diving and Snorkeling Worldwide, 406

Scuba Radio, 406

Scuba Source, 406

Scuba Yellow Pages, 406

ScubaDuba, 407

Senior Softball, 329

Simply OarSome, 410

Skatepile.com, 317

SkatesAway.com, 316

Skating.com, 317

Ski-Doo, 323

SkiCentral, 322

Skin Diver Online, 407

SkiNet, 322

Slow Pitch Softball History Page, 329

Snowmobile Online, 323

Snowmobiling.net, 324

Soccer Camps, 325

Soccer Home Page, 325

Soccer Information Systems, 325

Soccer Yellow Pages, 325

SoccerLynx, 325

Softball on the Internet, 329

Softball.net, 329

SoftballSearch.com, 329

Sport Diver, 407

Sport of Table Tennis, 333

SPORTS Authority, 314

Sports Illustrated for Women, 430

St. Moritz Ski Page, 322

Stars On Ice, 317

Steve G's ATP Tour Rankings, 346

Stowe Mountain Resort, 322

Sub-Aqua Association, 407

Surf and Sun Beach Vacation Guide, 412

Surfermag.com, 412

Surfing in South Africa, 412

Surfrider Foundation USA, 412

SwimInfo, 413

Swimmers Guide Online, 413

Swimming Science Journal, 413

Swimming Teachers' Association, 413

SwimNews Online, 414

Table Tennis Coaching Advice, 332

Table Tennis Links, 333

Table Tennis World Championships Videos, 333

Table-Tennis.com, 333

Tennis Canada, 346

Tennis Research Guide, 346

Tennis Server, 346

Tennis.com, 346

TennisONE, 346

Todd's Volleyball Page, 403

A
B
C
D
E
F
G
H
I
J
K
L
M
N
O
P
Q
R
S
T
U
V
W
X
Y
Z

Track and Field News, 358

Training for 400m/800m: An Alternative Plan, 358

U.S. Ski Home Team Page, 322

U.S. Youth Soccer, 325

United States Divers Aqua-Lung, 407

United States Diving Online, 407

United States Masters Swimming, 414

United States Professional Tennis Association (USPTA), 347

United States Soccer Federation, 326

United States Softball Official, 329

United States Specialty Sports Association, 329

United States Tennis Association, 347

USA Swimming, 414

USA Table Tennis, 333

USA Track and Field, 358

USA Volleyball, 403

USA Water Ski/American Water Ski Association, 415

USRowing, 410

Vault World (Pole Vault Paradise), 358

Vball.com, 403

Vespoli USA, 411

Vince's Idaho Whitewater Page, 409

Volleyball Hall of Fame, 403

Volleyball Magazine, 403

Volleyball One, 404

Volleyball Sites on the WWW, 404

Volleyball World Wide, 404

Volleyball.com, 404

Water Skier's Web, 415

WaterSki Online, 415

WebSwim, 414

Wild and Scenic Rivers, 409

Windfall Rafting, 409

Windsurfer.com, 412

Women's Sports Network, 431

World Soccer Page, 326

World Traveler Luggage and Travel Goods, 314

World Wide Ping Pong, 333

World Wrestling Entertainment (WWE), 432

WorldRowing.com, 411

WPSL – Women's Pro Softball League, 329

WTA Tour, 347

WWW Virtual Library, 285

Yamaha Motor Corporation, 324

YMCA Scuba Program, 407

Zephyr Inline Skate Tours, 317

St. Louis, Missouri

St. Louis Rams (NFL), 79-80

St. Louis Zoo, 444

stage. *See* theater and musicals

stamps

American Philatelic Society, 41

United States Postal Service, 273

statistics

Adherents—Religion Statistics and Geography, 274

FedStats, 390

Health Statistics, 390

Infonation, 31, 63

stay-at-home parents, 218-219

stepparenting, 219-220

storms. *See also* weather and meteorology

National Severe Storms Laboratory, 417

National Weather Service, 417

Silver Lining Tours, 359

Storm Chaser Home Page, 418

Storm Chasing Adventure Tours, 359

Weather Channel, 418

stress management, 330-331

students. *See also* K-12 education; schools

C-SPAN Networks, 236

Education World, 338

Educators Net, 338

High School Central, 342

Intel Innovation in Education, 339

Junior Achievement, 197

Leadership U, 278

Library Spot, 265

StudyWeb, 266

A
B
C
D
E
F
G
H
I
J
K
L
M
N
O
P
Q
R
S
T
U
V
W
X
Y
Z

substance abuse and recovery, 4
suicide prevention, 55
surfing
  Board Building, 411
  Boardz.com, 69
  Closely Guarded Secrets of the UK Surfing World, 411
  Coastal British Columbia, 411
  International Surfing Museum, 411
  OceanBlue, 412
  Surf and Sun Beach Vacation Guide, 412
  Surfermag.com, 412
  Surfing in South Africa, 412
  Surfrider Foundation USA, 412
  Windsurfer.com, 412
swimming, 412-414
Sydney, Australia
  Sydney International Travel Centre, 373
  Sydney Opera House, 169

T

table tennis, 332-333
tai chi, 136
taxes
  The Advisor, 288
  Bankrate.com, 334
  Citizens for an Alternative Tax System (CATS), 334
  Citizens for Tax Justice, 334
  eSmartForms, 334
  Essential Links to Taxes, 334
  Fairmark Press—Tax Guide for Investors, 335
  H&R Block, 335
  IRS (Internal Revenue Service), 334-335
  Kiplinger Online, 335
  MoneyCentral on Taxes, 335
  Quicken.com Taxes, 335
  SmartPros Accounting, 335
  State and Local Taxes, 335
  Tax and Accounting Sites Directory, 336
  Tax Exemption Information, 198

Tax Foundation, 336
Tax History Project, 336
Tax Links, 336
Tax Prophet, 336
Tax Resources on the Web, 336
Tax.org, 336
TaxHelp Online.com, 336
TaxPlanet.com, 337
TaxSites.com, 336
United States Tax Code Online, 337
teachers. *See also* K-12 education; schools; students
  Activity Search, 337
  American Federation of Teachers, 337
  Archive.edu, 337
  ArtsEdge, 337
  AskERIC (Educational Resources Information Center), 337
  C-SPAN Networks, 236
  Classroom CONNECT, 338
  Collaborative Lesson Archive, 338
  Early Childhood Educators' and Family Web Corner, 211
  EdLinks, 338
  Education Place, 338
  Education Week on the Web, 338
  Education World, 338
  Education.com, 338
  Educator's Toolkit, 338
  Educators Net, 338
  ENC Online—Eisenhower National Clearinghouse, 339
  Federal Resources for Educational Excellence (FREE), 339
  Figure This!, 339
  Gateway to Educational Materials, 339
  Global SchoolHouse, 339
  Harcourt School Publishing, 339
  History/Social Studies for K-12 Teachers, 339
  How Stuff Works, 339
  ICONnect, 339
  Intel Innovation in Education, 339
  Leadership U, 278
  Lesson Plans Page, 340

Library Spot, 265
McGraw-Hill School Division, 340
National Education Association, 340
New York Times Learning Network, 340
Pitsco's Ask an Expert, 340
Puffin House Publishers, 340
Scholastic.com, 340
Swimming Teachers' Association, 413
Teachers.net, 340
TeacherServe, 340
U.S. Department of Education—Funding Opportunities, 341
Virtual Reference Desk, 273

teens
20 Ways for Teenagers to Help Other People by Volunteering, 199
About Teen Pregnancy, 341
Alloy Online, 341
Bolt.com, 341
Child.net, 208
Consumer Education for Teens, 341
CyberTeens, 341
Dear Lucie, 208
Facts for Families, 209
Girls Life Magazine, 341
Health Ink & Vitality Communications, 423
High School Central, 342
Internet Public Library, 265
IPL Teen Division, 342
The Junction, 342
KidsHealth.org: For Teens, 209
LIQUIDGENERATION.com, 342
MyFuture, 342
National Children's Coalition (NCC), 327
React, 342
SafeTeens.com, 111
Talking with Kids About Tough Issues, 210
TechnoTeen, 342
Teen Advice Online, 342
Teen Chat, 342
Teen Hoopla, 210

TeenLink, 343
Teenmag.com, 343
TeenPeople.com, 343
Teens Today, 210
TeenTalk, 343
Young Investor, 343

television
ABC, 192, 345
Antiques Roadshow (PBS), 11
BBCi, 343
Buffy the Vampire Slayer, 294
Caroline's Hercules Page, 294
Cartoon Network, 117
CBS, 192, 345
Children's Television Workshop, 118
CNN Weather, 416
CSI, 343
Dark Shadows, 294
Discovery Channel, 61
Disney, 118
E! Online, 344
FANDOM—*Star Trek* Central, 294
Food TV Network, 49
FOX, 345
FoxNews.com, 193
HBO, 344
History Channel, 96
Home and Garden Television (HGTV), 101
Learning Channel, 61
Lifetime Online, 428
MSNBC.com, 193
MTV, 157
Mystery Science Theater 3000, 295
National Museum of Photography, Film, and Television, 154
NBC, 345
Netpicker's Guide to the X-Files, 295
The Osbournes, 344
PBS
    Kids, 119
    Nova Online – Lost on Everest, 291
    Online NewsHour, 191
QVC Shopping, 308

A
B
C
D
E
F
G
H
I
J
K
L
M
N
O
P
Q
R
S
T
U
V
W
X
Y
Z

Schoolhouse Rock, 62
SCIFI.COM, 296
Screen Actor's Guild, 350
Sewing with Nancy, 303
The Simpsons, 43
SITCOM Home Page, 350
Smallville Ledger, 296
Star Trek, 297
  Klingon Language Institute, 123
TV Guide Online, 344
TV Land, 344
TV Party, 345
TV Sci-Fi and Fantasy Database, 297
Ultimate TV, 345
VH1.COM, 157
Voices of Women Online, 430
Weather Channel, 418
Who Wants to Be a Millionaire?, 345
Tennessee
  Memphis Zoo Home Page, 443
  Mountain Villas, 383
  Nashville Scene, 380
  Only Toys, 356
  Tennessee Titans (NFL), 79-80
tennis, 345-347
Texas
  Fort Worth Zoo, 442
  Galveston Island Official Tourism
    site, 374
  Houston Museum of Fine Arts, 151
  San Antonio Zoo, 444
theater and musicals, 347-351
theme parks. *See* amusement and
  theme parks
timeshares and vacations, 273, 287
toys
  ALEX, 352
  Archie McPhee, 352
  AreYouGame.com, 352
  Boardgames.com, 352
  BRIO, 352
  CatToys.com, 226
  Copernicus Home Page, 352
  Creativity for Kids, 353
  Discovery Toys, 353

Disney Online Store, 353
Dr. Toy, 353
Dummy Doctor, 353
EducationalToys.com, 353
eToys, 353
FAO Schwarz, 353
Firebox.com, 354
Fisher-Price, 354
Gallery of Monster Toys, 354
Genius Babies.com, 354
Hasbro World, 354
Into The Wind, 354
KBKids, 354
Latoys.com, 355
Learning Curve International, 355
Little Tikes, 355
Mattel, 355
Official Lego World Wide, 355
Only Toys, 356
Rokenbok, 356
Schylling, 356
Sega, 356
SmarterKids.com, 356
Toys for Tots, 356
Virtual Toy Store, 356
Zany Brainy, 356
track and field
  Athens 2004 Olympic Games, 357
  Athletics Canada, 357
  Athletics Home Page, 357
  Kangaroo's Triple Jump Online, 357
  Kelly's Running Warehouse, 357
  Masters Track and Field, 357
  Road Runner Sports Shoe Store, 357
  Runner's World Online, 358
  Running Network, 358
  Track and Field News, 358
  Training for 400m/800m: An
    Alternative Plan, 358
  USA Track and Field, 358
  Vault World (Pole Vault Paradise),
    358
train travel, 377-378

transportation

U.S. Department of Transportation, 389

WWW Virtual Library, 285

travel

adventure travel, 359-360

After I Do, 419

air travel, 360-361

airlines, 361-362

American Snowmobiler Magazine, 323

Amtrak, 377

Amtrak Schedules, 256

bargain travel, 362-363

budget travel, 363-364

Buy.com, 308

car rental, 364-365

cruises, 365-367, 371

Federal Railroad Administration, 256

Foreign Languages for Travelers, 124

Gimponthego.com, 95

Intellicast, 417

international travel, 370-374

island travel, 374-375

lodging, 375-377

Luis Cabanas Scuba Diving and Instruction, 406

Period.Com Airlines, 271

RailServe, 257

Scuba Diving and Snorkeling Worldwide, 406

Scuba Yellow Pages, 406

SeniorsSearch, 289

SkiCentral, 322

Surfing in South Africa, 412

THOR: The Virtual Reference Desk, 273

Time Out City Guides, 420

tips and information

A&E Traveler, 367

Away.com, 367

biztravel.com, 367

Compleat Carry-On Traveler, 367

Culture Finder.com, 367

Ecotourism Explorer, 367

Excite Travel, 367

Fodor's Travel Online, 367

Gimponthego.com, 368

Journeywoman, 368

Lonely Planet Online, 368

North American Virtual Tourist, 368

Parentsoup Family Travel, 368

Pets Welcome, 368

Rough Guides, 368

Round-the-World Travel Guide, 369

Savvy Traveler, 369

The Travel Page, 369

timeout.com, 369

Tourism Offices Worldwide Directory, 369

Travel Channel Online, 369

Travel Facts, 369

Travel Medicine, 369

Travel.com, 369

Travelite FAQ, 369

Travelon, 370

TravelSource, 370

TravelWeb, 370

Uniglobe.com, 370

Virtual Tourist, 370

Zagat.com, 370

train travel, 377-378

Trains.com, 258

Travel Channel Online, 369

Travel Discounts, 363

Travel Facts, 369

Travel Medicine, 369

Travel Source, 360

TravelASSIST Magazine, 249

Travel.com, 369

Travelairline.com, 363

Traveling in the USA, 365

Travelite FAQ, 369

Travelocity, 363

travlang's Translating Dictionaries, 263

vaccinations, 371

Weather Channel, 418

Weather Site, 418

weekend getaways, 382-384

Windfall Rafting, 409

Windsurfer.com, 412

World Traveler Luggage and Travel Goods, 314

U

U. S. government agencies and departments

Census Bureau, 273

Central Intelligence Agency, 388

Department of Agriculture, 388

Department of Commerce, 388

Department of Defense, 388

Department of Education, 267, 341, 388

Department of Energy, 388

Department of Health and Human Services, 327, 389

Department of Housing and Urban Development, 393

Department of the Interior, 389

Department of Justice, 389

Department of Labor, 389

Department of State, 389

Department of Transportation, 389

Department of the Treasury, 389

Department of Veterans Affairs, 389

Environmental Protection Agency, 389

Fish and Wildlife Service, 106

Federal Bureau of Investigation, 389

Federal Trade Commission, 390

FedWorld Information Network, 390

Fish and Wildlife Service, 106

Index to Government, 390

MarineLINK, 390

Peace Corps, 390

U.S. Army, 391

U.S. Navy, 391

United States House of Representatives, 391

United States Senate, 391

White House.gov, 391

WhoWhere? People in U.S. Government, 391

U.S. travel

Access New Hampshire, 378

Alabama Travel, 378

Alaskan Travel Guide, 378

America's Land of Enchantment: New Mexico, 378

Arizona Guide, 378

Arkansas – The Natural State, 379

Blue Ridge Country, 379

Boston.com Travel Page, 379

California Smart Traveler, 379

Cambridge, Massachusetts, 379

Cincinnati Vacation Gateways, 379

Colorado.com, 379

George Washington's Mount Vernon Estate, 380

GrandCanyon.com, 380

Idaho Home Page, 380

Iowa Virtual Tourist, 380

Las Vegas.com, 380

Louisiana Travel Guide, 380

Minneapolis.org, 380

Nashville Scene, 380

Nebraska Travel and Tourism, 380

New Jersey and You, 380

New York State, 381

Oregon Online, 381

RING: Online Michigan's Electronic Magazine, 381

Santa Fe Station, 381

Seattle City Guide, 381

South Dakota World Wide, 381

USA CityLink, 381

Utah! Travel and Adventure Online, 381

Virginia Is for Lovers, 381

Vista Alaska, 382

Washington D.C., 382

Yankee Traveler, 382

UFOs (unidentified flying objects), 385-387

United Kingdom
Abercrombie & Kent, 377
BBC News, 189
Campground Directory, 375
Closely Guarded Secrets of the UK Surfing World, 411
English Actors at the Turn of the Century, 348
FanGrok, 294
Fast Track Index, 1
ForeignWire, 191
International Bed-and-Breakfast Guide, 376
Isles of Scilly Travel Centre, 375
Jesus Army, 278
London Theatre Guide Online, 349
Portico: The British Library, 266
Rowing Service, 410
Sub-Aqua Association, 407
Telindous, 184
UK Fundraising, 198
United Kingdom Pages, 373

V

vacations. *See also* travel
Age of Reason Recommended Senior Living Facilities, 298
Austria Ski Vacation Packages, 320
Century 21 TRI-Timeshares, 287
GoSki.com, 321
Las Lenas Ski Packages, 321
RCI vacationNET, 287
Rent.net, 287
RentCheck, 287
Surf and Sun Beach Vacation Guide, 412
Zephyr Inline Skate Tours, 317
veteran and military organizations, 392-394
veterinary medicine. *See also* animals; pets
4Vets.com, 394
AAHA HealthyPet.com, 394
American College of Veterinary Surgeons, 394
American Veterinary Medical Association, 395

AVA Online, 395
Care for Pets, 395
Careers in Veterinary Medicine, 395
Center for Animal Health and Productivity, 395
Department of Animal Science: Oklahoma State University, 395
Murdoch University: Division of Veterinary and Biomedical Sciences, 395
National Board Exam (NBE), 395
OncoLink: Veterinary Oncology, 396
ProVet, 396
TalktoTheVet.com, 396
Veterinary Medicine, 396
Veterinary Medicine Libraries, 396
Veterinary Pet Insurance, 396
Vetscape, 396
Washington State University College of Veterinary Medicine, 396
World Equine Health Network, 397
World Organization for Animal Health, 397
video
Blockbuster, 400
BuyVideos.com, 400
DVDs, 397-398
FINA, 412
movies, 398-399
multimedia
bThere, 397
IFILM, 399
Metacritic, 399
Oddcast, 398
Waking Life, 399
Real.com, 400
Reel.com, 400
Scour.com, 400
Videomaker's Camcorder and Desktop Video Site, 249
Virgin Islands, 374
Virginia, 380-381
virtual sites
Virtual Children's Hospital, 225
Virtual Jerusalem, 283
Virtual Nutrition Center, 57
Virtual Reference Desk, 273

Virtual Tourist, 370

Virtual Toy Store, 356

Virtual Volunteering Project, 200

viruses

AVP Virus Encyclopedia, 263

McAfee Antivirus, 111

Symantec AntiVirus Research Center, 112

vitamins and supplements

anti-oxidant.com—Quick Reference Guide, 401

Ask Dr. Weil, 423

Champion Nutrition, 401

eNutrition.com, 401

HealthCentral, 424

healthshop.com, 401

MotherNature.com, 401

Pharmaton, 401

Puritan's Pride, 401

Thriveonline.com, 402

Vita-Web, 402

VitaminShoppe.com, 402

volleyball, 402-404

volunteering

20 Ways for Teenagers to Help Other People by Volunteering, 199

Advice for Volunteers, 199

America's Charities, 199

Child Net Volunteers, 199

Corporation for National and Community Service, 199

FIU Volunteer Action Center, 196

Global Volunteers, 196

Idealist, 199

Peace Corps, 200, 390

SeniorsSearch, 289

SERVEnet, 200

Virtual Volunteering Project, 200

Vista—Volunteers in Service to America, 200

Volunteer Today, 200

Volunteering and Service Learning, 200

VolunteerLink, 200

VolunteerMatch, 200-201

Volunteers of America, 201

Wilderness Volunteers, 201

W

Washington (state)

Mount Rainier National Park, 221

North Cascades National Park, 222

Seattle City Guide, 381

Woodland Park Zoo (Seattle, WA), 445

Washington D.C., 382

Shakespeare Theatre, 350

Smithsonian Institution, 152, 266

Washington Post, 194, 384

Washington Redskins (NFL), 79-80

water sports

diving/scuba diving, 404-407

rafting, 407-409

rowing, 409-411

surfing, 411-412

Surfline, 412

swimming, 412-414

waterskiing, 414-415

waterskiing, 414-415

weather and meteorology, 415-418. *See also* storms

wedding planning, 419-421

weekend getaways, 382-384

weight loss, 421-423

wellness, 423-424. *See also* health; nutrition

wildlife

American Zoo and Aquarium Association, 441

BBC Nature Site, 179

Good Zoo Guide Online, 442

Nature Journal, 179

Wilderness Volunteers, 201

Wildlife Conservation Society, 444

windsurfing, 412

wines

Food and Wine Magazine, 78

Gruppo Italiano Vini, 78

Into Wine, 78

K&L Wine Merchants, 78

Robin Garr's Wine Lovers Page, 78

Wine Country Weekly Real Estate Reader, 262

Wine Searcher, 78

A B C D E F G H I J K L M N O P Q R S T U V W X Y Z

Wine Spectator, 78

Wine.com, 79

Wines on the Internet, 79

women/women's issues

Ada Project, 425

AFL-CIO: Working Women Working Together, 425

American Association of University Women (AAUW), 425

Amnesty International USA Women's Human Rights, 425

Artemis Search for Women's Studies Programs, 425

AWARE, 425

BizWomen, 425

Business Women's Network Interactive, 426

CatalystWomen.org, 426

Center for Reproductive Law and Policy, 426

Centre for Women's Studies in Education (CWSE), 426

Christian+Feminist, 426

Cybergrrl, 426

Daremore Quotes, 254

Diotima: Women and Gender in the Ancient World, 426

Expect the Best from a Girl, 427

Feminist Arts-Music, 427

Feminist Majority Foundation Online, 427

Forum for Women's Health, 427

Girl Power!, 427

Girl Scouts of the USA, 427

Girls Incorporated, 427

Global Fund for Women, 427

Go Ask Alice!: Sexuality, 306

Good Vibrations, 428

Herspace.com, 428

HisandHerhealth.com, 306

International Softball Federation (ISF), 328

Inventors Museum, 428

iVillage.com: The Women's Network, 54, 428

Journeywoman, 368

Kotex Guide to Menstruation for Girls and Women, 214

Library Resources for Women's Studies, 428

Lifetime Online, 428

Machon Chana, 428

MotherLinC: Mothers Without Custody, 215

National Association for Female Executives, 428

National First Ladies' Library, 428

National Museum of Women in the Arts, 428

National Organization for Women (NOW), 429

National Partnership for Women & Families (NPWF), 429

National Women's Hall of Fame, 429

National Women's History Project, 429

NBCC—National Breast Cancer Coalition, 429

NCAA Softball Championships, 328

NCAA Women's Rowing, 409

NCAA Women's Swimming and Diving, 413

NCAA Women's Volleyball, 403

NWSA—National Women's Studies Association, 429

Office of Women's Business Ownership, 430

OWBO Online Women's Business Center, 430

Oxygen.com, 430

Perfume Center, 312

Perfumes Direct, 312

Shescape Online, 430

Sports Illustrated for Women, 430

UnderWire, 430

United Nations and the Status of Women, 430

USA Bride, 420

Voices of Women Online, 430

Web by Women, for Women, 431

WomanOwned.com—Business Information for Women Entrepreneurs, 431

Women and Politics Home Page, 431

Women in Islam, 431

Women Leaders Online (WLO), 431

A
B
C
D
E
F
G
H
I
J
K
L
M
N
O
P
Q
R
S
T
U
V
W
X
Y
Z

Women's History Month, 431
Women's Human Rights Net, 431
Women's Human Rights Resources, 431
Women's Sports Network, 431
Working Moms Refuge, 432
WWWomen!, 432
Yale Journal of Law and Feminism, 432
words, 263-264
wrestling, 432-433
writing, 433-436

X - Z

Yahoo!, 111
Yahoo! Groups, 109
Yahoo! Shopping, 313
Yahooligans, 111
yoga, 437-438
youth organizations, 439-440

ZIP Codes
Geographic Nameserver, 269
National Address and ZIP+4 Browser, 271
THOR: The Virtual Reference Desk, 273
United States Postal Service, 273
zoos, 441-445

A
B
C
D
E
F
G
H
I
J
K
L
M
N
O
P
Q
R
S
T
U
V
W
X
Y
Z